Chas. D. Clawson(?)
c/o Dunfey Hotel Corp.
500 Lafayette
Hampton, N.H.
03842

603-926-8911

Nov 82

Menu design, merchandising and marketing

MENU DESIGN, MERCHANDISING AND MARKETING

THIRD EDITION

Albin G. Seaberg

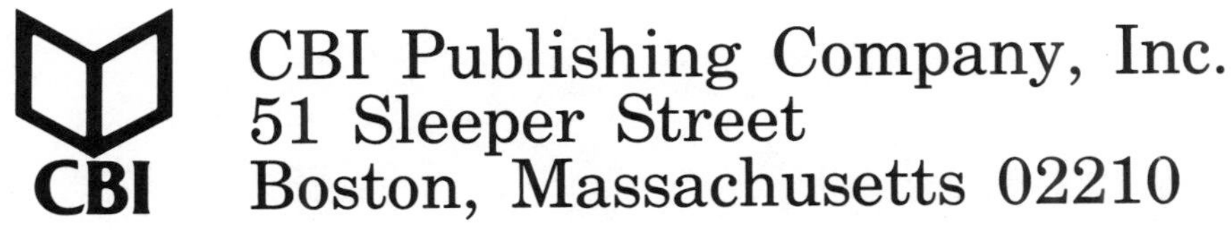

CBI Publishing Company, Inc.
51 Sleeper Street
Boston, Massachusetts 02210

Library of Congress Cataloging in Publication Data

Seaberg, Albin G.
Menu design, merchandising and marketing.

Rev. ed. of: Menu design. 2nd ed. 1973.
Includes index.
1. Menus. I. Title.
TX911.3.M45S4 1982 642'.5 82-1128
ISBN 0-8436-2222-9

Printed in the United States of America

Printing (last digit): 9 8 7 6 5 4 3 2 1

Table of contents

Introduction

In terms of food service systems engineering, the menu is probably the key focal point of the entire operation, and in terms of selling it is very often the number one food service salesman. It should be examined, changed, analyzed, and improved constantly from the viewpoint of design, merchandising and marketing.

As a printed communication, the menu should be looked at in terms of a piece of paper on which words, drawings, designs, colors, illustrations, etc., are printed. It should look attractive, that is colorful, clean, and reflective of the quality, style, and general appearance of the establishment.

A dirty, soiled, poorly printed, hard to read menu creates a first impression that can be disastrous. An attractive, colorful, clean and sparkling appearing menu which, in addition, is easy and entertaining to read, sets up the proper mood for the customer who is inclined to like your operation and its cuisine before he or she even orders.

And, the mere appearance of your menu can condition the customer to order more, building the check higher than he or she probably intended. Selection of the proper paper, type selection, printing, design, and illustration are fields that may seem "afar" to the average food service operator who is, in addition, required to know how to cook like a chef, promote like a showman, balance a set of books, deal with personnel and the public, and finally, perform the ultimate miracle of showing a profit at the end of each month.

But, as in all phases of the food service business, there are experts to help and actually produce and print the menu. The purpose of this menu book is to help you in all of the problems of the menu. With this book, plus the use of the professional expert, writer, artist, and printer, you should produce a better, more effective menu.

THE MENU THAT SELLS

As a merchandising tool, the menu should be written and produced to sell. It should sell what you want it to sell the most of, in terms of specific items—entrees, appetizers, drinks, desserts—no matter what the category of your food and drink offering. Considering popular tastes, what the public will actually "go for," order and reorder, plus what is a high profit item for you, your menu should be written, organized and designed to sell what you want it to sell. There are some basic rules developed in advertising, propaganda, and publicity that will help you sell more and more of what you want to sell. But, in addition, experimentation is necessary to merchandise effectively. Tastes change, prices vary, and what was popular today, may be less so tomorrow.

The menu is not just a selling tool for food and drink. It can sell many other things—catering, take-outs, party-banquet facilities, etc. One of the most common faults of many menus is the blank page. These are pages that have been paid for, but not used.

You should consider every page or panel of the menu in terms of a magazine advertisement; you would not buy two pages of magazine advertising (at an enormous cost) and leave one blank. Yet, your menu is just like an ad. It is read by a considerable number of people every day. If you add up the number of readers for a period of a month or more, you can see that your menu has considerable advertising space value. This space value should be exploited to the fullest and used for every profitable communication purpose possible.

In addition to a well designed, well printed and effective selling tool, the menu is a marketing print-out of your particular food and drink service operation. It is the end result, whether carefully planned and checked out or haphazardly assembled, of your selection of (1) what items of food and drink to serve, (2) how many food and drink items to serve, and finally, (3) how much to charge or the price of everything you serve. A study, therefore, of what other restaurants serve, how many of each category of items they serve, and what they charge cannot help but be of value in making these vital marketing decisions in your own particular operation.

HELP IN MENU PRODUCTION

The plan of this menu book is to give as many different food service operators as possible "help" in a practical, realistic sense. In the case of the big operator in a major metropolitan center who can afford top professional talent—writers, artists, printers, etc.—help is less needed, although sometimes an excellent artist-designer, as well as a creative writer may violate some of the basic rules of menu design and production due to lack of knowledge of the special problems of menu communication. In the case of the restaurateur who operates in a small town or away from the main centers of the graphic arts and advertising skills, the need for help can be much greater.

For this group of food service people, the menu book is designed to give the most complete help. Charts, diagrams, and examples are given in profusion.

Printing and producing the menu can be an expensive item in the over-all budget of a restaurant. As a result, you want to get as much "bang from your buck" as possible. The thing to keep in mind is that you are communicating first and producing a work of art second. This consideration can reduce cost while improving sales.

But the menu should not be the place where you are "penny wise and dollar foolish." Failure to change a menu, both in content (items and prices) and in design and layout, when it is not effectively merchandising, because you have a stack of menus that you want to "use up," can be a most disastrous economy.

What this means in the final analysis is that you are in charge. The printer, artist, designer and writer can help you, but the success or failure of your menu as well as of your operation is up to you. Your general knowledge of the food service business must be translated through the above people into the proper sales tool.

No printer can tell you what to list, what to charge, what to feature, etc., and no artist or writer is qualified to write or list a selection of "high profit, fast moving" food and drink items. But working together with the help of the information in this menu book, you should be able to solve every menu problem in every area—design, merchandising, and marketing.

Menu design, merchandising and marketing

1

Producing a menu

To begin a menu, you have to start somewhere, and you need help from qualified people to design, write, and print your menu. Before you call in help, however, you should have an idea of what you want to serve and what you want to charge.

In the case of a new menu, starting from scratch, you should make a written or typewritten list. Depending on your type of operation, a chart like the one shown in Figure 1 can help you list what you want on your menu.

FOOD

Appetizers

Description	Price

Soups

Description	Price

Salads

Description	Price

Sandwiches

Description	Price

Entrees

Description	Price

Side Orders

Description	Price

Desserts

Description	Price

Beverages

Description	Price

FIGURE 1

DRINKS
Cocktails

Description	Price

Beers

Description	Price

Wines

Description	Price
Red	
White	

Wines

Description	Price
Rosé	
Champagne	

After Dinner Drinks

Description	Price

FIGURE 1 (continued)

After you have listed what you want to serve, to help clarify your menu in your own mind and to help your designer and printer, make up a list of "Specials." These are items you want to feature, sell more of, and in general use to create "menu excitement." Your designer or printer must know what you want to feature before beginning on your menu. Some typical Specials are:

1. "For Two" combinations—dinner, drinks, or desserts.
2. Continental Type Specials—French, German, Italian, etc.
3. Family Specials—this can be almost any entree item that you can offer, usually on an "all you can eat" basis, to the whole family.
4. Daily or Weekly Specials—these can be special nights, Friday Fish Fry, Captain's Table, Sunday Buffet.
5. Special Drinks—a new *in* drink—usually *white* today, that is with a vodka or gin base.

The subject of Specials is covered in more detail in a separate chapter. Mainly, think in terms of some Specials. You may even want to illustrate them as well as feature them in bolder type, more complete copy, and inside a box, circle, or some other graphic device, and this also should be discussed with your printer-designer.

RATE ITEMS FOR POPULARITY AND PROFIT

Next, take your list as indicated above and rate each category in numerical order. For example, under Appetizers, if you are listing six of them, rate them in order of priority 1, 2, 3, 4, 5, 6 as to what you consider (1) popularity with the customer from your experience or from your menu surveys, (2) profit, that is, the appetizer from which you make the biggest profit.

Now, you are ready to call in the artist-designer, writer, printer, or menu company to begin to create a menu for you. If you do not build your menu in this fashion, your outside help cannot intelligently design a menu that does what you want it to do.

The selection of a designer, writer, printer, and producer of a menu can be a problem for you depending on the size and location of your restaurant. Your possibilities are as follows:

1. *An Advertising Agency.* If you are big enough to have an ad agency at present that

handles advertising, publicity, and promotion for you, people at the agency can design and write a menu for you. Agencies usually have competent artists, writers, and merchandising people who can put together a menu, and they have printing production experience that they can apply to your menu problem.

2. *A "Specialist" Menu Printer.* These are printing companies that over the years have come to specialize in the printing of menus. There is a wide selection of these specialists across the country. The best of them will have a complete staff to serve you—artists, designers, writers, etc. The range of competence varies, however, from company to company. To insure a good job, ask about their services and capabilities and also ask to see samples of menus they have produced in various stages from start to finish.

The advantages of a "menu house" are several. First, they have the printing equipment—presses and typesetting—to produce your menu. Not every printing plant is set up to print menus. And secondly, they usually have had a great deal of experience in the problems of producing a menu.

3. *The Artist-Designer.* Any commercial artist or graphic designer can give you help in creating an attractive looking menu and probably will give you a functional layout. He or she cannot, however, write your menu. This you must do yourself under this type of menu production arrangement or get a writer to work with the artist or designer.

4. *A Writer.* A competent advertising copywriter can help you write your menu. He or she can usually add sparkle to your descriptive wording, and may have "ideas" for a different, creative menu. But a writer will have to work with an artist or designer.

5. *A Printer.* Practically any printer can produce a menu for you, but many printing plants do not print menus because printers are specialists. They vary considerably in the types of printing equipment they have—one-color, two-color, and four-color presses, the size of the piece of paper the press can print on, and the various kinds of presses. Also, there are two basic kinds of printing—letterpress and offset. The printer who produces your menu should generally be geared for smaller job, short-run printing, except for large chain or franchise operations where an order of 100,000 menus may be common.

Your menu printer should also have typesetting facilities since most of your menu is words and figures. Check with the printer to see what selection and variety of type faces are available to set up a readable and attractive listing. Also, remember that your menu is a changing list—the prices change and the items change; so you should have a very close arrangement with your printer for constant quick service.

Menus can be designed to fit printing equipment, but this is putting the cart before the horse. If at all possible, design your menu to sell your cuisine, select the paper (from samples furnished by a printer or by a paper merchant), and then have the printer adapt the equipment with possibly some variation in size, fold, and cut to accommodate the plant and produce the menu economically.

2

The menu cover

Your menu cover is a symbol of your identity as well as part of your restaurant decor. Give it all the attention that it deserves to make it effective. A well-designed, colorful, attractive and serviceable menu cover is usually one of the visible signs of a good restaurant, but it should not be the first consideration in creating your menu. A good menu should be designed from the inside out. This means that you should start with an actual list of what you want to sell. This list, plus prices and descriptive copy, is the heart of your menu.

Have a layout, or make a layout yourself, of the internal listing of your menu. This will tell you how many pages and what size your menu should be—2 pages, 3 pages, 4 pages or more. Then have this listing set up in type and see what it looks like. If there is any evidence of crowding or if the type is too small or hard to read, increase the size of your menu. Most menus are too small for the number of items listed.

Then after you have decided on the size and number of pages in your menu, design your cover. Do not start with a preprinted or stock menu cover and try to make your food and beverage listing fit. This is false economy in most cases.

SELECTING ART AND DESIGN

In considering your cover art and design, several things should be taken into account—cost, number of colors, paper, selection of an artist or designer, and the suitability of the cover design to the decor and style of your restaurant.

The more colors you print on your cover, the more expensive it will be. The most economical cover design will be one color on colored paper (black or blue or red, for example, on white or light colored paper, or gold, yellow, or orange on black paper). Next come two, three, and four colors. A four-color printed cover gives all the colors in the spectrum. Usually, two colors on white or colored paper will give you all the color you need on a well-designed menu.

Paper is also very important for a good menu cover. It should be a heavy, durable, grease-resistant paper unless you are printing a daily, throw-away menu. In fact, the paper can be selected first and your designer's layouts made right on the paper you are going to use.

The selection of an artist-designer is no problem in a large metropolitan area. If one is not known, a selection can be made from the yellow pages of your phone book. But, if your restaurant operation is off the beaten path, you will have more difficulty. For your operation, contacting a city artist or using preprinted menu covers from stock are possibilities. There are other possibilities, however, such as using a photograph for your menu cover art. Local photographers (professional or amateur) may have photos or can take photos suitable for menu covers. A good photo of a local scene, a food still-life, or some other eye-catching subject, if printed in black and white with the name of the restaurant in a second bright color, can make an attractive menu cover.

Another inexpensive source of art for menu covers is old prints, woodcuts, engravings, or drawings. They are usually in "line" and, therefore, easy and inexpensive to reproduce. A little research in old bookstores or at the public library can very often turn up interesting and unusual art that is suited to certain types of restaurants. Woodcuts or engravings that are in black on white can be reproduced in other colors and increased or decreased in size.

In addition, going to art fairs and exhibitions can result in finding a print, drawing, watercolor, or oil painting that would be suitable.

DESIGN MUST FIT OPERATION

Your cover design, however, should be suitable to your type of operation. If yours is a Colonial Inn restaurant, your menu art and cover should reflect this, and, with the large amount of Colonial and Early American art available, this should be no problem. Likewise, if yours is a sophisticated Supper Club restaurant, your cover art should reflect this to the extent of going Abstract, Op or even Pop!

Then, too, your menu cover should be considered as part of the decor. Circulated among your customers, the color of your menu should either blend or contrast pleasantly with the color scheme of your restaurant. In a well-designed restaurant operation, the menu cover design is usually planned to harmonize with the theme and color of the decor as well as to illustrate the name appropriately.

There are certain basic items of copy that can be on the front cover such as address, phone number, hours of service, and credit cards honored. But rather than clutter the cover with too much copy, just the name of the restaurant on the front cover is adequate for copy on the cover, with the rest of the copy on the back cover. In addition, the back cover is an ideal place to feature such sales points as party, banquet, meeting facilities, take-out service, history of your restaurant, or a map of your location.

HERB TRAUB'S Nationally Famous
Pirates' House
"...what foods these morsels be!"

The name of your establishment may dictate the artwork and design on your cover. For Herb Traub's Pirates' House, *it had to be pirates. The combination of high quality artwork plus humor make this an especially good cover. It is in full color which also adds to its charm and appeal.*

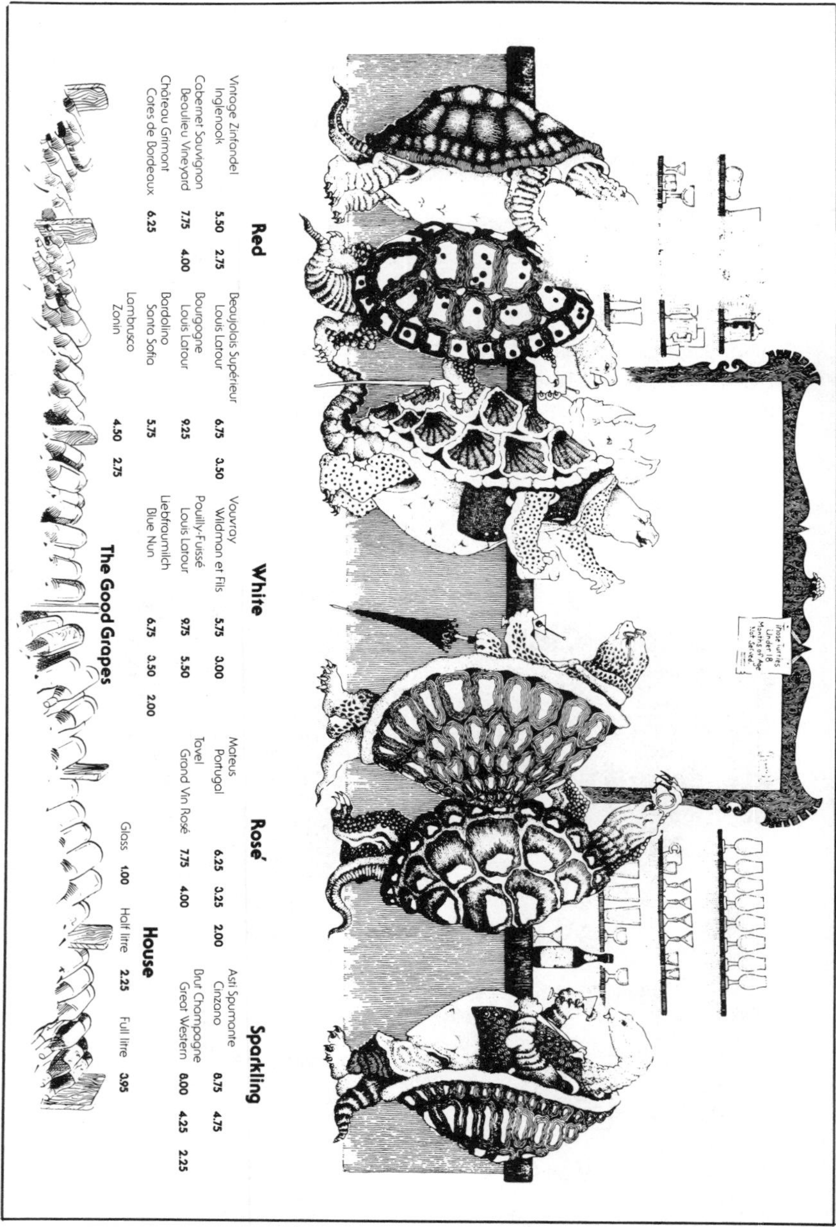

The cover of the Gutherie's Digs *menu is unusual in several ways. A die-cut flap folds down to present the wine list. The cover then opens to show the entire listing. Done in black and white, the clever art and design does the job—well.*

Pork Chop High Rise

Here's the view from the chop. This one-pound two-story is definitely a top level selection. It's decorated by an original cider sauce with a snap of ginger. After this move, you may never go back to beef.

6.75

Lamb Chops Mary

We start with two thick 8-ounce chops. Add a little rosemary. Add a little wine. Grille. Drink a little wine. Add a little herb jelly on the side. This dish is sometimes remembered as Mary's Add-a-Little Lamb. Definitely gourmet. And not baaaaad.

8.95

Rock Cornish Game Chick

Fully boned except for its meaty little thighs, this sporty hen is brushed with cognac by our sporty chef. We wouldn't think of serving it with anything less than wild rice and a mushroom-vegetable cream sauce. It's Gutherie's favorite bird.

6.45

Lasagna Classico

Close your eyes as you taste this, and you may hear Roman chariots and legions of golden trumpets. It's served with slightly less fanfare, spicy with anise, under a Mozzarella blanket. Some authentic words to describe it to your friends: magnifico, sensazionale, bravissima. And economico. For sure.

5.75

The Porterhouse

Sometimes it takes two hands just to turn one of these jumbos over on the grille. It's more than a pound. Save room for a masterpiece.

8.95

Top Sirloin

We call it "top" because it's really better than regular sirloin. Actually it's better than most top sirloin, but who ever heard of Top Lordloin?

198-gram common cut

4.95

284-gram Royal portion

5.95

The Prime

Ah. What Gutherie does to a prime rib is enough to make you rent an apartment, so you can always be nearby. Comes in one irresistible taste and two mouth watering sizes.

Regular 10-ounce slice

6.45

Prime lover's portion, a full pound

8.45

PLEASE NOTE Cash and creditable credit cards are accepted with unaccustomed speed by Gutherie. No checks, please.

Attend the Souper Bowl

Your choice from our bar of homemade soups is included with every entree, along with a basket of buns.

Salad instead of soup? Just ask.
Salad and soup? Yes, but extra.

Ground Half Pound

Here's the biggest burger we can build without calling in an architect. Constructed from aged ground sirloin served on an onion roll. You get a choice of mushrooms or cheese & bacon.

3.50

Soup & Salad, a la carte

Some people remember us warmly for our hearty home-style soups. You take a trip to the Souper Bowl, and we'll bring on the salad & crusty rolls.

3.35

Beverage

The Soft Stuff: Coffee/Tea/Milk

.35

A Happy Ending

The final scene of your role at Gutherie's features you in front of an ice cream mountain under a sunset of fruit or hot fudge. Music. Action. You're a star.

1.50

Very Teriyaki Steak

Once again we prove it's possible to improve a favorite. The difference is our own oriental marinade of pineapple, soy, herbs & vermouth. Wonder if we should move the liquor cabinet farther from the kitchen?

6.45

Sirloin & Teriyaki Chicken

Double team your taster with aged steak and boneless breast of chicken. Rates a double banzai. If you'd rather have only chicken teriyaki, OK. We're flexible.

6.35

Sirloin & Scampi

Another combo which features top sirloin paired with jumbo shrimp. Broiled in butter with a touch of garlic, these biggies come with a dipping sauce that we're keeping a secret. Scampi only is all right on this one, too.

8.25

Sirloin & Lobster

A final classic duo starring our aged steak and young Danish lobster tails. If your taste leans toward the sea, so will we. With a platter of all lobster.

8.95

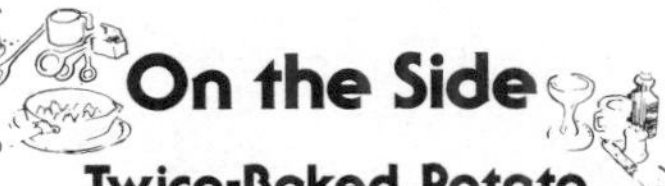

On the Side

Twice-Baked Potato

Not once but twice in the oven. First time, potato only. Second time, blended with chives and seasonings and a topping of our own creamy cheddar sauce. Some things are better with a little imagination.

.95

Country Cottage Fries

Hearty slices of Idaho potatoes, golden fried in their jackets. Better than French. More than American.

.95

Sauteed Mushrooms

Or how to become an instant gourmet. Whole mushroom morsels buttered & seasoned & served in their own hot skillet.

1.25

Red

Vintage Zinfandel Inglenook	5.50	2.75
Cabernet Sauvignon Beaulieu Vineyard	7.75	4.00
Château Grimont Cotes de Bordeaux	6.25	
Beaujolais Supérieur Louis Latour	6.75	3.50
Bourgogne Louis Latour	9.25	
Bardolino Santa Sofia	5.75	
Lambrusco Zonin	4.50	2.75

White

Vouvray Wildman et Fils	5.75	3.00	
Pouilly-Fuissé Louis Latour	9.75	5.50	
Liebfraumilch Blue Nun	6.75	3.50	2.00

Rosé

Mateus Portugal	6.25	3.25	2.00
Tavel Grand Vin Rosé	7.75	4.00	

Sparkling

Asti Spumante Cinzano	8.75	4.75	
Brut Champagne Great Western	8.00	4.25	2.25

House

Glass 1.00 Half litre 2.25 Full litre 3.95

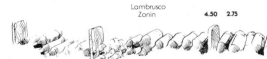

The Good Grapes

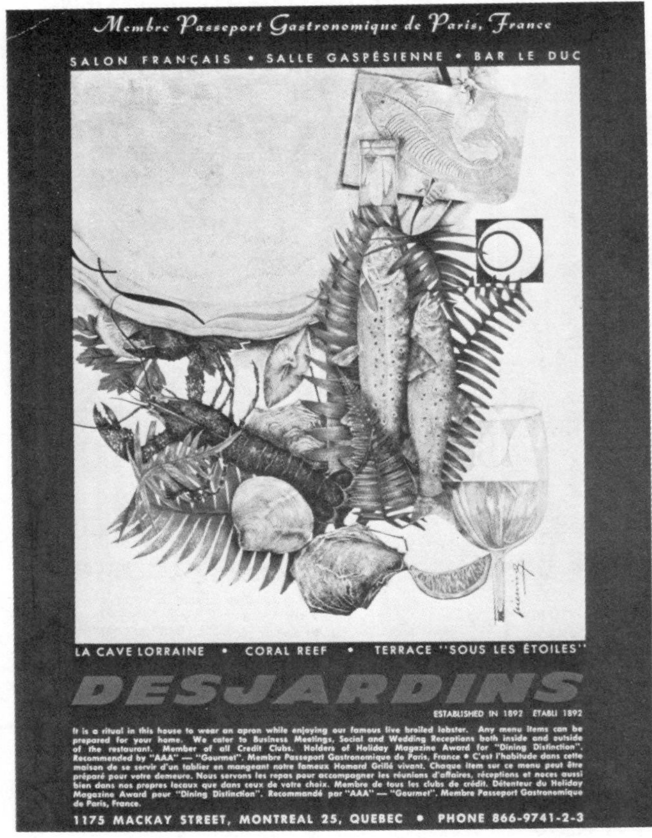

(Above) *This is an unusual cover. The artwork, a drawing in full color, is of very high quality. But, in addition, this cover has a great deal of copy, in both English and French. In most cases, too much copy on the cover spoils the design and makes for a cluttered appearance, but this cover "works" despite type in two languages.*

(Below) *The* Meson Madrid *restaurant uses a "gate" design on the cover in two colors, black and brown, on cream colored paper. The "gate" folds open in a gate fold with the top part die cut so that name of restaurant is not cut in half when the menu is opened.*

The Yankee Drummer *restaurant achieves an interesting and different menu cover that reflects the "flavor" of the operation as well as advertising its "Tavern Tap." The colors are green, brown, and orange with a golden ribbon.*

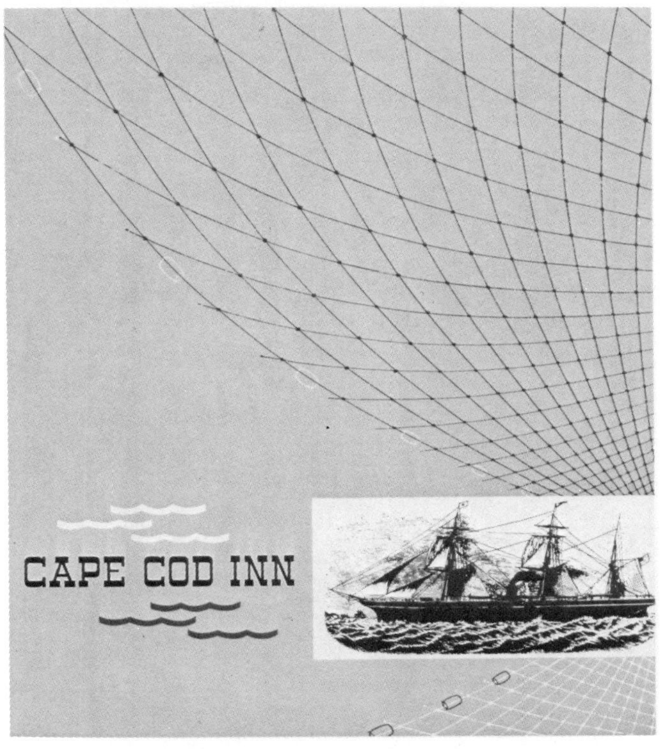

An old print can be used for menu cover art. This line cut of an old sailing vessel is a "natural" for a seafood restaurant—the Cape Cod Inn. *This cover is in two colors, blue-green and black on white.*

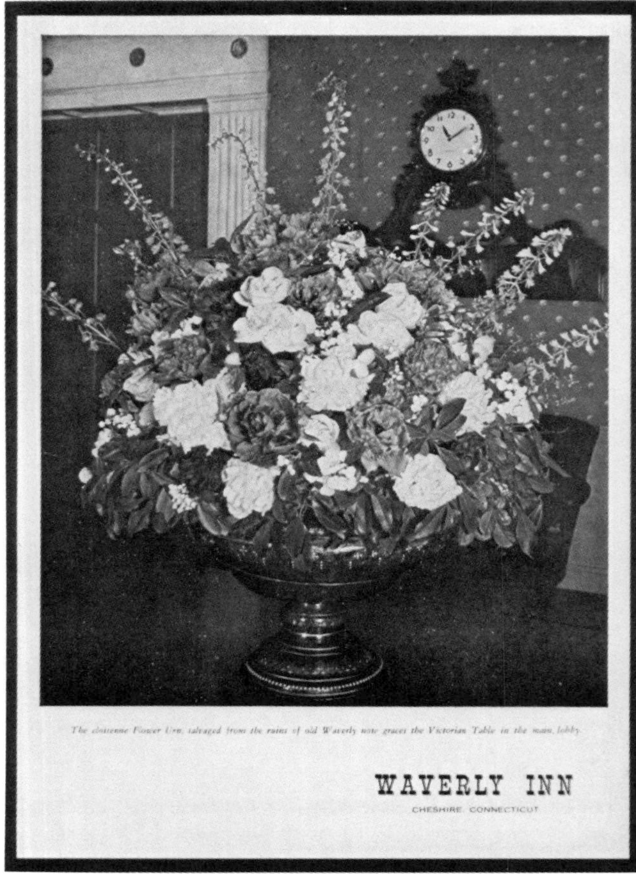

(Above) *The* Waverly Inn *uses a full color photo on the cover of its menu. This happens to be a cloisonne flower urn within the restaurant (part of the decor) with flowers in it. Stock photos in color or in black and white can be used in a similar manner.*

(Below) *An attractive, interesting treatment of just the name of the establishment can make a good cover. This cover of* Alioto's *with its big fancy "A" and the rest of the word in script in white on a dark red background has impact.*

(Above) Rosoff's Restaurant *specializes in before and after theater dinners. They, therefore, use this motif plus an historical approach on their menu cover. The main illustration is a photo of Times Square in 1899, the year* Rosoff's *was established. Below this are individual photos of famous actors and actresses in their most famous roles. Historical photos and photos that associate with the style and atmosphere of the restaurant make good menu cover art. This cover is in two colors, black and blue, on white.*

(Below) *A clever, humorous drawing, the name of the restaurant big and bold and the restaurant's specialty (steak by weight) are all combined in this effective menu cover. It is done in only one color (black) on white stock, but it shows the impact a one-color cover can have if the idea is creative.*

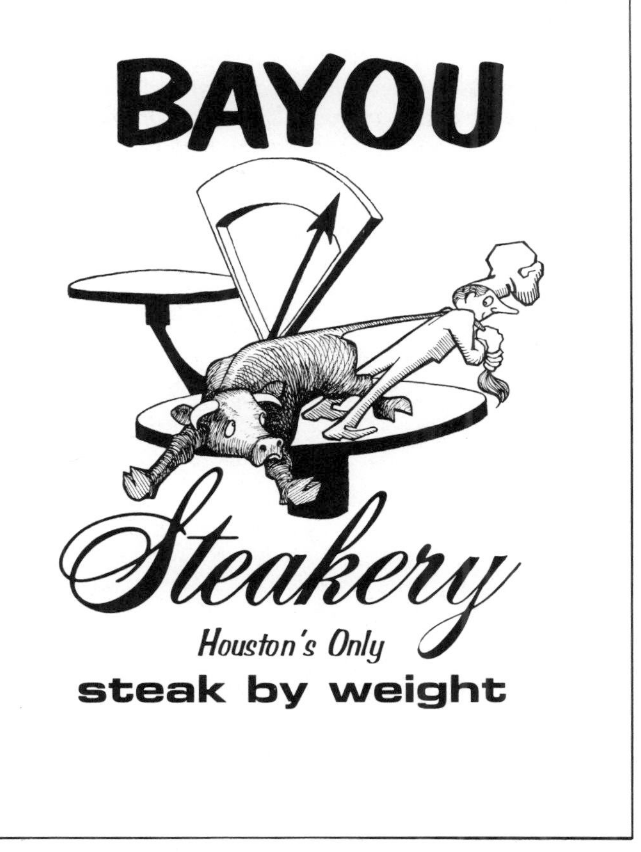

(Above) *This menu cover for a pancake specialty restaurant uses a geometric design approach. The name of the restaurant,* Pancake Corner, *is large and dominant, and the address is easy to read as placed in the lower right-hand corner. The colors are three shades of green and two shades of yellow on white. The paper stock is heavily laminated.*

THE

INTERNATIONALLY KNOWN

COACHMAN'S

INN

10350 MAIN STREET (Route 5)

CLARENCE, NEW YORK 14031

•

PHONE: 759-6852

(Above) *In two colors, red and black, on tan paper stock, this menu cover is attractive while containing considerable information. The coach design is good, the name is large and bold and the address and phone number are included. The tan paper stock is attractive and is also serviceable and grease-resistant.*

This menu cover in two colors, black and brown on white, has an unusual feature since it features five "special" rooms —Black Angus Room, Circle C Bar, Round Up Room, Sirloin Room, and Frontier Room—with appropriate art for each listing. And yet, through good design, the cover works well.

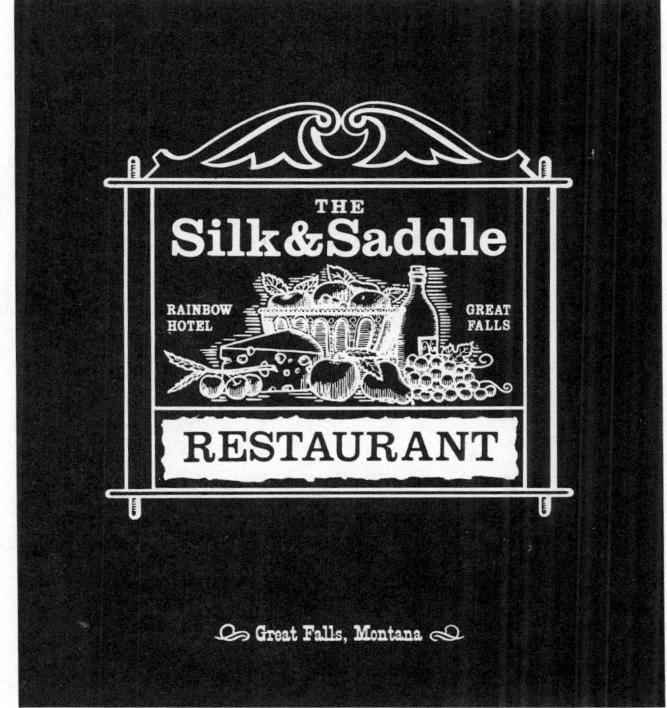

This menu cover is very rich and elegant looking. It is in gold on black. The cover material is a plastic, imitation leather which adds to the quality appearance of this menu.

An old weathered building on the Thames River houses a now legendary restaurant and inn. Called the Barley Mow, it started life as a storage place for barley — that vital element of beer, ale and whiskey.

After its transformation into a delightful inn, the Barley Mow became a watering spot for gentleman farmers, statesmen and boatmen who were drawn to this congenial hostelry by the fine foods and spirits, songs of the best musicians of the kingdom, crackling fireplace and lively conversation. The Barley Mow became a favorite retreat for many authors and poets — among them Kipling, Burns, Jerome K. Jerome and Swift — who would tie their boats on the embankment and stride up for a little liquid refreshment or a hearty meal.

How fitting that a great English tradition should be brought from the Thames to the shores of the Potomac in this Bicentennial year when we are celebrating the best in both cultures.

Dinner Bill of fare

fore dishes
The Barley Mow Pottage
or
The Chef's Whims of the Seasons Salad.

the Main Courses
Roast Prime Ribs of Beef
Barley Mow Cut ...a generous thick slice
Olde English Cut ...thinly sliced in the English Manner
Jerome's Cut ...the outside slice, brown and crusty (when available)
Escorts for the above
Yorkshire Pudding - cream of corn - and yet another vegetable of the Season 8.95

Land and Sea
A royal combination of Roast Prime Ribs of Beef and Cold Water Lobster Tail 9.95
Escorted by Yorkshire Pudding - cream of corn

Lobster Tails
Two cold water lobster tails accompanied by Elizabethan Potato, Drawn Butter Spinach Souffle 10.95

Sweets 1.50
Trifle Pudding
Olde English Chocolate Cake
Fresh Cheesecake

Libations 2.50
Coffee .50

The Lord Fischer
A combination of layers of fruits ice cream and the Barley Mow special sauce topped with chocolate shavings 1.95

Lunch Bill of Fare

fore dishes
The Barley Mow Pottage... 1.25
The Chef's Whims of the Seasons Salad... 1.75

Atlantic Bay Shrimp Salad
...Bay shrimp with our cocktail sauce; served on a shell surrounded by many fresh delights 4.25

The Barley Burger
...½ lb. of choice ground sirloin topped with avocado and bacon and covered with melted cheese 3.50

The Prime Dipper
...slices of choice Roast Beef on a toasted sour dough bun, with our vegetable of the day, au jus 4.25

Fish & Chips
...fingers of fresh fillets, batter dipped and deep fried 3.95

Our Combination
...Ham, Turkey and swiss cheese served open face and covered with our special dressing 3.50

Shepard's Pie
....a combination of beef and kidney in sauce and topped with potato rosetts 3.50

Yorkshire Tidbits
...strips of prime beef together with an array of fresh vegetables, served in a rich brown sauce surrounded by Yorkshire Pudding ... 4.35

The Concoction
Shrimp and crab together with avocado surrounded by fresh fruit escorted by nectar...... 4.50

Brunch

The Barley Mow Brunch includes Blueberry Muffins and your choice of fruit or juice as listed below.
(Champagne Special - $1.50 for all you desire)

The Churchill.. 5.25
Two poached eggs atop Roast Beef Hash covered with Hollandaise Sauce

Barley Mow Omelettes

The Queen.. 4.50
Bacon, Ham Potatoes, & Cheese

The Lord Nelson.................................. 4.75
A combination of shrimp crabmeat, and cheese

The Victorian.................................... 4.50
A sophisticated mushroom omelette combined with cheese

The Townsend (Eggs Benedict — Seafood Style) 5.25
Two Poached eggs atop a base of English muffins with a mixture of crabmeat, shrimp & mushrooms topped with a rich coating of Hollandaise Sauce

French Toast.............................. 3.50
Two slices of cake bread, batter-dipped with strawberries and bananas

Pecan Waffle.............................. 3.95
A crisp waffle with toasted pecans baked right in and served with butter

Fruit and Cheese Platter.............. 3.95
Seasonal fruit and an array of cheeses served with an English Muffin

The Trimmings:
Fresh juices — Orange or Grapefruit
Bananas, with cashew nuts & cream
Strawberries, with cream
Pineapple Slices w/marshmallow sauce

The Barley Mow *menu has an attractive four-color illustration on the front* (above) *with copy describing the restaurant. On the other side, three menus* (right)*—dinner, lunch, and brunch—are painted in black, a simple but effective set of menus.*

(Above) Marrell's *restaurant uses simple but effective graphics. They have taken ads from an old newspaper and reproduced them leaving a panel for printing the restaurant's name. The old ads provide "human interest" and make for conversation. This cover is in black and white.*

(Below) The Waterfront Restaurant *has an interesting and unusual logotype. It has worked its name into the drawing of the fish. Since this is a restaurant specializing in seafood, the trademark is very appropriate. The cover is in one color (blue) on white stock and illustrates how much can be done with only one color.*

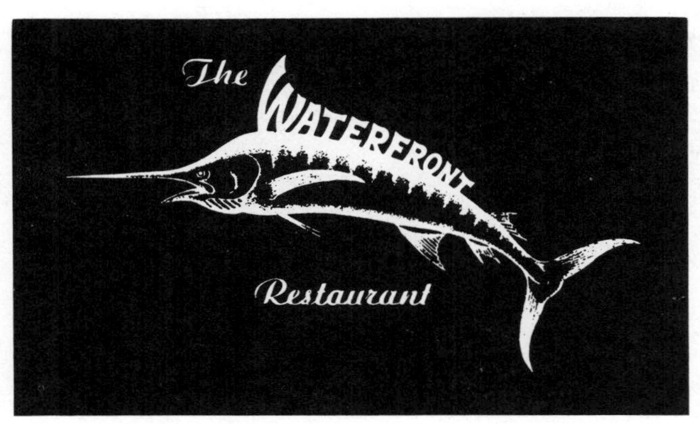

(Above) *The cover of* Zim's *restaurant wastes no time. It starts to work* selling *immediately. First, it tells the story of "The Zimburger and how it grew." Then it presents six "Drink Specialties," including the "CABLE BELLE—A foamy delight made with champagne, sparkling water, powdered sugar, triple sec, and brandy served over fresh strawberries."*

This attractive menu shows how a menu, since it is a piece of paper, can be die-cut into unusual shapes and folded as many times as needed.

Piping hot
SALAMI
SAUSAGE
LINGUISA
CHEESE
BEEF
GREEN PEPPER
MUSHROOM
ONION
ANCHOVY
PEPPERONI 2.05
BACON 2.05
CONFUSION 2.45

Pizza on French Bread

CHEESE	1.55	SALAMI	1.55
SAUSAGE	1.45	MUSHROOM	1.35
ANCHOVY	1.35	BEEF	1.35
PEPPERONI	1.45	CONFUSION	1.95

RAVIOLI with meat ball 2.20
RIGATONI 1.55
RIGATONI with meat ball 1.90
A delicious wide flat noodle in our own meat sauce.
Spaghetti, Ravioli or Rigatoni .... ½ order 1.10
Mushrooms with Pasta .... .80
All above served with French Bread and Butter.

On the Side

French Bread and Butter .... .35
Oven Hot Garlic Bread .... .45
Polpette (Two meat balls) .... .70
Grilled Mushrooms with Butter .... .80
Italian Sausage .... .90

SANDWICHES

Steak Sandwich
2.15

French Dip Sandwich
1.85

American Cheese (Grilled) .... .70
Roast Beef, Italian Style 1.10
Polpette (Meatballs on French bread) .... .95
Italian Sausage, Mama Savaria Style .... .95

IL HAMBURGO

Hamburger .... .95
Cheese Burger 1.05
Mushroom Burger 1.45
Mozzarella Burger 1.15
Onion Burger 1.15
Pizza Burger 1.35

MAMA SAVARIA'S SPECIALTY
Homemade Minestrone Soup — .45
A Specialty of the House, rich, hot and filling!

SALADS

Please Pay Cashier

LUNCHEON

Served daily from 11:00 a.m. to 4:30 p.m.

LINGUISA SANDWICH 1.55
A smoked sausage smothered in green peppers and melted cheese. Served with fresh green salad.

POLPETTE SPECIAL 1.15
Meatballs perfectly seasoned and sauced for a man with French bread and butter.
Served with fresh green salad.

ITALIAN SAUSAGE SANDWICH 1.35
Served open-face—Mama Savaria Style in Giovanni's special sauce. Served with fresh green salad.

GROUND ROUND STEAK 1.95
Covered with our Special Sauce, sauteed mushrooms, and served with spaghetti, garnish, bread and butter.

RIB EYE STEAK 2.35
Served with spaghetti, garnish, bread and butter.

VEAL ALLA POMADORO 2.95
Thinly sliced veal sauteed with cherry tomatoes, mushrooms and green peppers. Served on a bed of Rigatoni with bread and butter.

SLIMLINE 1.35
Broiled ground beef served with cottage cheese and fruit.

ARROSTO FREDDO 1.15
Cold roast beef sandwich served with hot, hot soup or crisp salad.

POOR BOY SANDWICH .... (For One) .95
(For Two) 1.65
Made with cappacola, salami, cheese, tomato, shredded lettuce, and our Italian dressing on French bread — garnished with cherry tomato, black olive and tangy pepperoncini.

All Luncheon items above served until 4:30 p.m. daily.

GIOVANNI'S CHAMPAGNE BRUNCH
Giovanni invites you to a complimentary glass of champagne served with any food on our menu for your enjoyment during a Sunday Brunch — Italian Style.
Sunday Brunch Special
THREE EGG OMELETTE

3

Sequence—the secret of menu arrangement

Like a novel or a symphony, a meal has a beginning, a middle, and an end, and this is the key to the way a menu should be designed. The size of the menu, the fold of the pages, and the number of pages will, of course, create a different problem in each case, but if the menu layout follows the meal sequence, you will usually be doing the right thing. The order of reading on the menu is from outside pages to inside pages, from top to bottom, and from left to right. On a rectangular piece of paper, for example, the starting point is the upper left hand corner where you would usually start a letter.

The meal sequence is as follows, or some portion of the following depending on how large or extensive your menu is: Appetizers, Soups, Entrees, and Desserts. Within this sequence there are items such as Side Orders, Salads, Sandwiches, Beverages, and Children's Menu. The position of salads and sandwiches can present a problem depending on how the establishment wants to treat or sell them. When salads and sandwiches are considered as entrees, they should be given entree treatment. The problem of the children's menu is best solved by a separate menu. Figure 1 shows a one-panel menu.

On this menu, the time sequence is followed by placing the before items, appetizers and soups, at the top; the middle items, entrees, at the center, and the after items, desserts, at the bottom. Salads and side orders are placed in a list to the right. Even the sequence or order that you list your entrees in is important. The top item on any entree listing has the best chance of being ordered and the top group, steaks, seafood, etc., also has the best chance of being ordered. So select and list in the number one position what you want to sell best.

FIGURE 1

Another example of the time sequence layout for a somewhat larger menu is shown in Figure 2, a four-page insert in a four-page cover:

On page 1 of the four-page insert, the appetizers, soups, and salads are listed. This gives room for a large listing with good descriptive

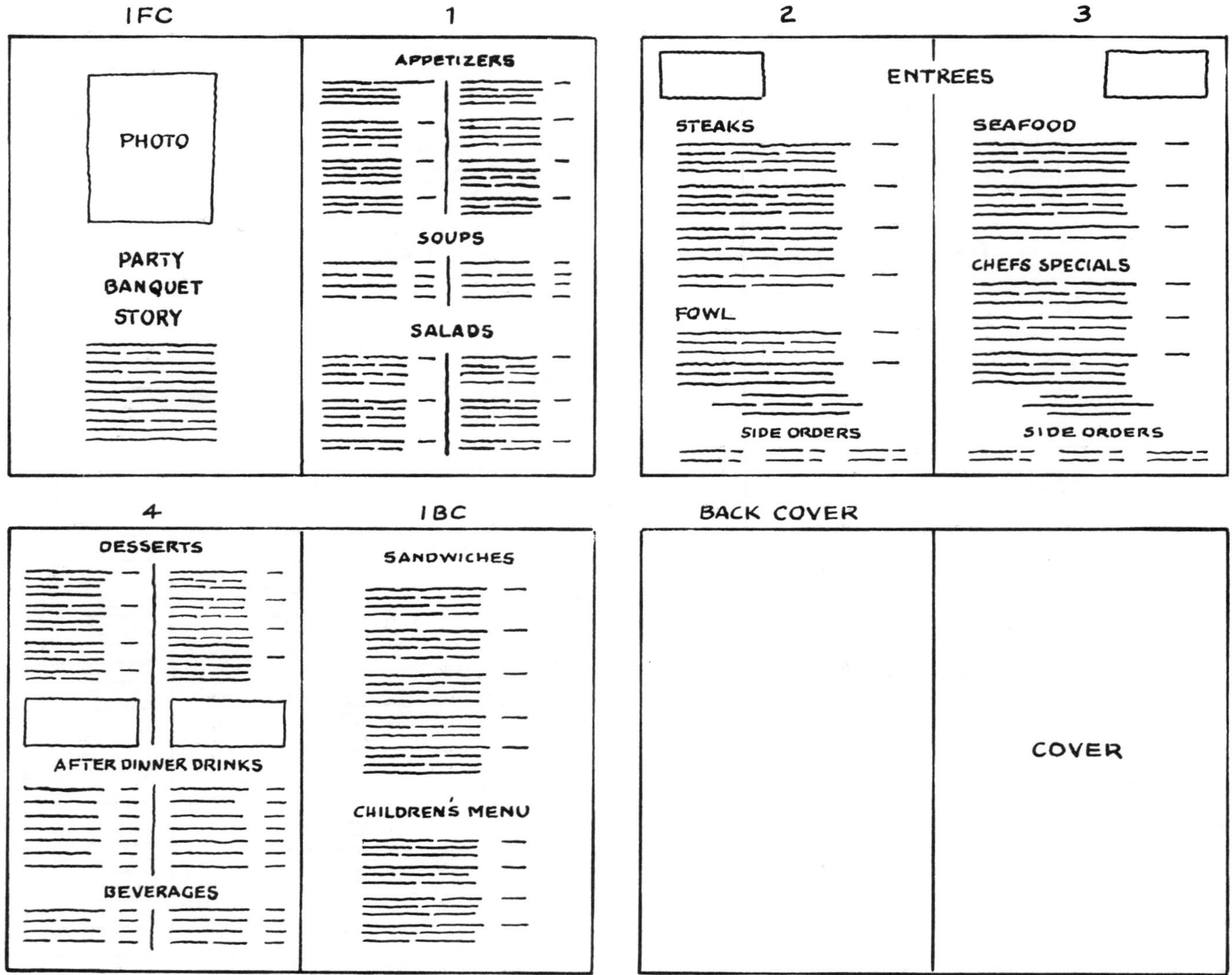

FIGURE 2

copy, especially if they are big, expensive items. The entrees are listed on pages 2 and 3 using the headings—Steak, Fowl, Seafood, and Chef's Specials. In all cases, entrees should be given top billing—best position, largest, boldest type, and most descriptive copy. Desserts and Beverages are listed on page 4. Side orders are listed at the bottom of pages 2 and 3 under the entree listing. A separate page or even better a dessert menu enables the waitress to present this after part of the menu listing to the customer without asking if he or she wants a dessert—positive instead of negative selling.

The four-page cover (Figure 2) is used for the items and services outside of the time sequence. Sandwiches and the children's menu can be listed on the inside back cover. The inside front cover can be used to tell and sell your party-banquet-meeting facilities, illustrated with a photo.

If you list and sell your entrees both as a la carte and complete dinners, another element is added to the entree listing problem. It can be solved in two ways, as shown in Figures 3 and 4. Figure 3 shows two separate listings, one a la carte and one dinner. These can be two identical listings with different prices or the dinner listing can include some of the a la carte items and some "daily" items not offered a la carte. For this type of separate listing, the dinner items can be printed on a tip-on for daily changes.

The layout in Figure 4 shows a la carte and

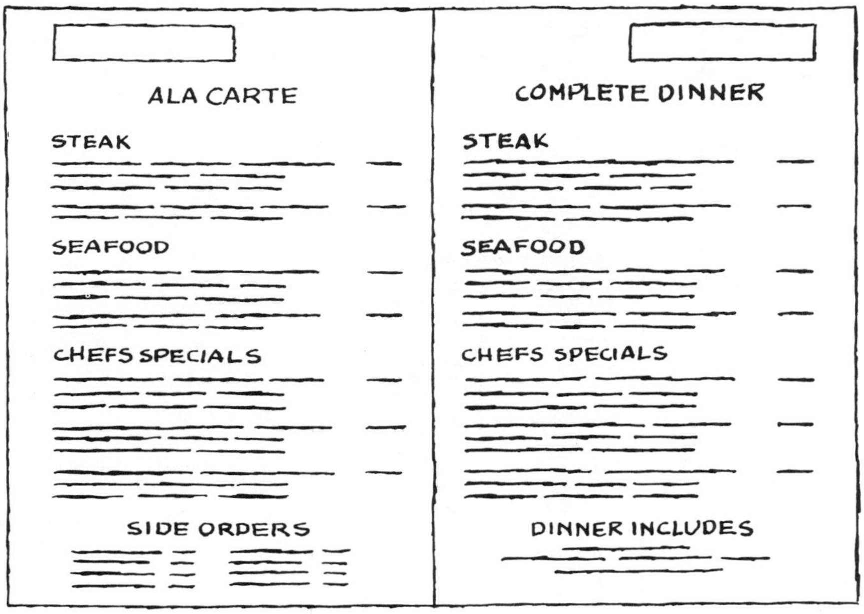

FIGURE 3

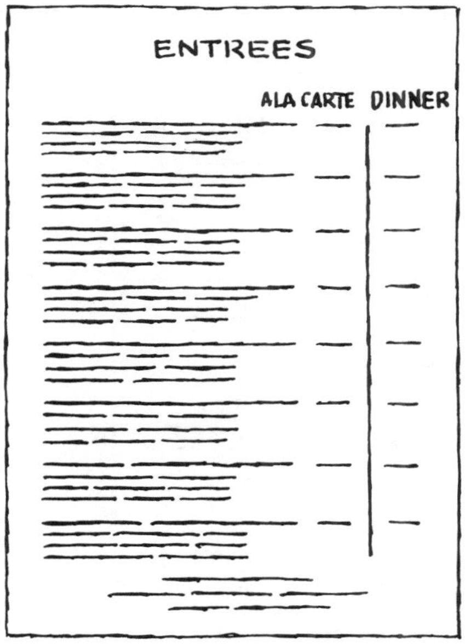

FIGURE 4

complete dinner entrees listed once with two prices. When listing this way, be sure the difference between the two prices is the same in all cases since the "extras" on the complete dinner are always the same.

In both methods of listing, Figures 3 and 4, be sure to list clearly and boldly what is included a la carte and what is included in the complete dinner so that the customer can choose intelligently from either one or the other.

The food service operation that serves alcoholic beverages—cocktails, wines, beers, etc.—has

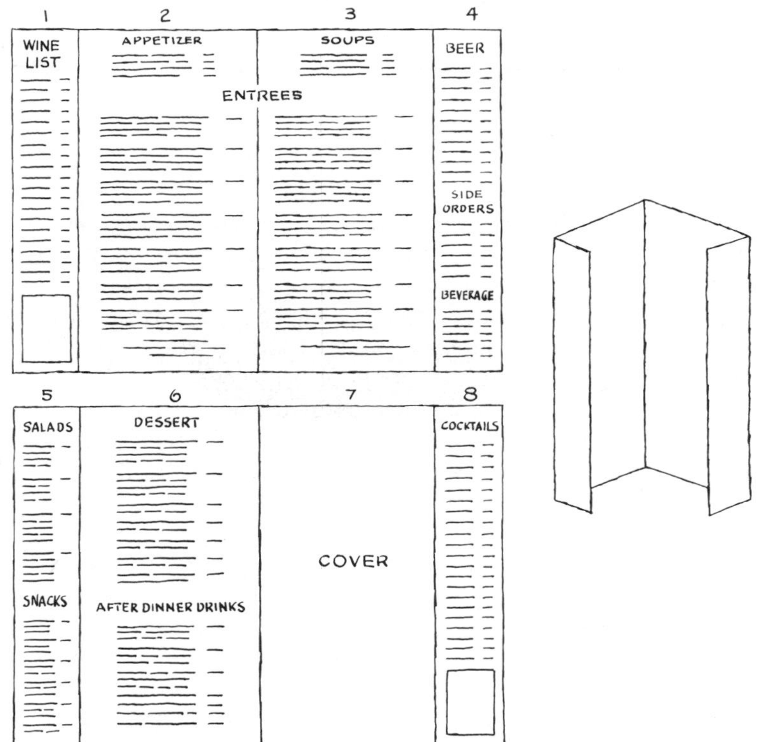

FIGURE 5

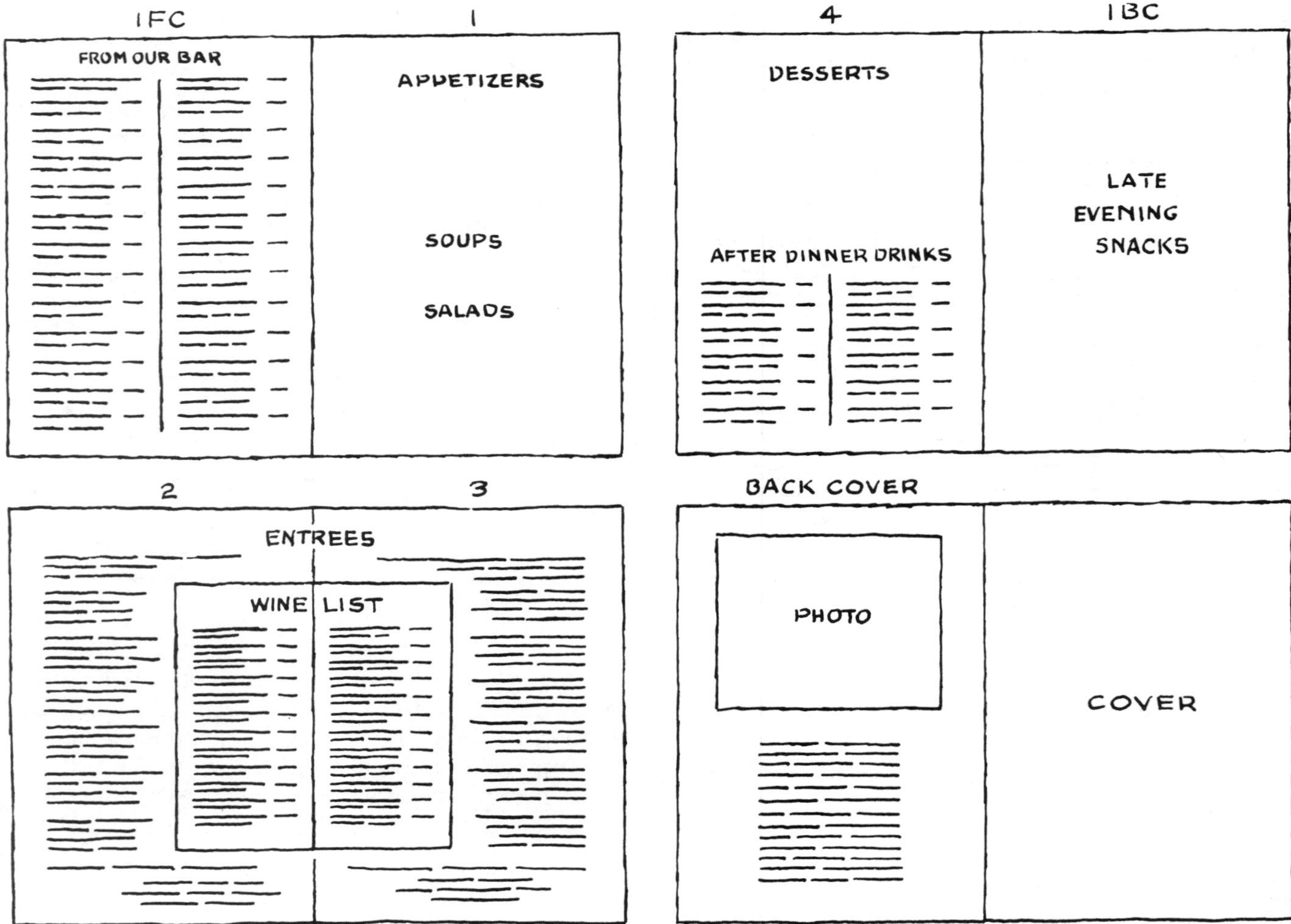

FIGURE 6

an additional menu layout problem, but the sequence formula works again here. Some drinks are before dinner drinks (cocktails), some drinks are with-dinner beverages (wines, beers), and some are for after dinner (brandies, cordials, dessert wines, some cocktails). The idea is to list the beverage item in its proper order so that it will sell itself at the proper time. The cocktail, bourbon, scotch, gin, vodka, etc., list should be what the customer sees first when he or she picks up the menu since this is what you want the customer to order first. The beer and wine list should be next to the entree list since the customer will order these items to have with his or her meal. The after dinner list should be with the dessert listing which presents the other after dinner items of the menu. Figure 5a shows one solution to the drink sequence listing.

This menu folds as shown in Figure 5b. Therefore, the first panel the customer sees after the cover is panel 8 which is the cocktail plus other "before" drinks listing. The wine list is printed on panel 1 next to the entree listing, and beer is listed on panel 4 also next to the food selection. Finally, the after dinner drink selection is printed on panel 6 with the dessert selection. Another way to list your bar selections on the menu, following the sequence pattern, is shown in Figure 6.

This menu is a four-page insert bound into a four-page cover with a smaller wine list bound into the center. A complete before dinner, *From Our Bar* listing is printed on the inside front cover. This includes cocktails, bourbons, scotches, vodkas, gins, rums, etc. The wine list is a smaller four-page insert bound into the center of the menu between pages 2 and 3. Notice that it is right in the middle of the entree listing.

A separate wine list that is not made an integral part of the menu will not work for you. The customer will not ask for it and the waiter or waitress cannot be depended on to present it to the customer. Finally, on Figure 6 the after dinner drinks are listed on page 4 with the desserts.

The After Dinner or Dessert menu shown in Figure 7 is another excellent method of making the menu follow the eating sequence of the customer.

The desserts are listed on page 2, the after dinner drinks on page 3 and the dessert wines on page 4.

Every food service operation has its own menu problem and no two are alike. But if the sequence plan is kept in mind while planning the menu layout, the placement of the various categories of food and drink will be correct, and a correct, working layout will help merchandise and sell your product.

FIGURE 7

★ **Traditional Southern Favorites** ★

★ *Appetizers*

Chincoteague Oysters on Half Shell .90
Jumbo Gulf Shrimp Cocktail, Sauce Louisa 1.10
Select Backfin Crabmeat Cocktail 1.00
Cherrystone Clams, Cocktail Sauce .85
Supreme of Fruit with Port .40
Chilled Fruit Juices .30
Melon in Season with Smithfield Ham 1.25
Cream of Sussex Peanut Soup .30
Chicken Broth with Caroline Rice .30

★ *Seafoods*

Centennial Seafood Platter, Pittsylvania Butter, Sauce Louisa 2.90
Pan Fried Botetourt Trout, Princess Anne Potatoes, Garden Vegetables 2.40
Golden Fried Jumbo Shrimp filled with Crabmeat Madison 2.65
Richmond Imperial Crab on Smithfieid Ham, Crisp Potatoes and Cole Slaw 2.35

★ *Entrees*

(Choice of Vegetables from the Du Jour Menu)

Broiled Bedford Sirloin Steak, Country Butter 4.95
Breast of Capon Chimborazo, Julienne Potatoes 3.25
Filet of Albemarle Beef, Churned Butter 4.60
Grilled Augusta Lamb Chops on Toast, Green Salad 3.50
Smithfield Ham Steak, Red-Eye Gravy, Hot Grits 3.40

★ *Salads*

Fresh Fruit Salad Plate 1.25
Gulf Shrimp and Crabmeat 2.65
Jumbo Shrimp and Garden Tomatoes 2.40
Hearts of Lettuce and Tomatoes. .75
Waldorf Salad .80
Tossed Salad .60

CENTENNIAL COLD SEAFOOD PLATTER 2.90

(Crabmeat, Shrimp, Lobster, Clams, Cole Slaw, Cocktail Sauce, Lettuce and Tomatoes)

★ *Sandwiches*

Smithfield Ham and Turkey, Cole Slaw, Mixed Pickles 1.35
Albemarle Chopped Steak on Toasted Bun, French Fries, Lettuce and Tomatoes 1.05
King George French Toasted Ham and Cheese, Potato Salad, Pickles 1.25
Sliced Rockingham Turkey .80
Smithfield Ham 1.10
Richmond Club Sandwich 1.10 . . . . . . Jr. .90

★ *Desserts*

Richmond Cream Pie .35
Peach Melba .40
Chilled Ripe Albemarle Peaches .35
Nesselrode Parfait .40
Pie du Jour .30
Fresh Berries in Season
Specially Prepared Ice Cream and Sherbet ..30

★ *Beverages*

Centennial Room Coffee .25 Milk .20 Tea .25 Sanka .25

(Above) *A one-page menu listing in a logical sequence with attractive headings.*

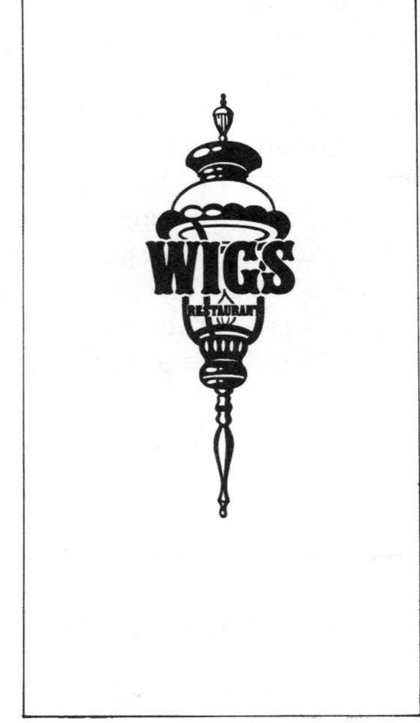

FIGURE A

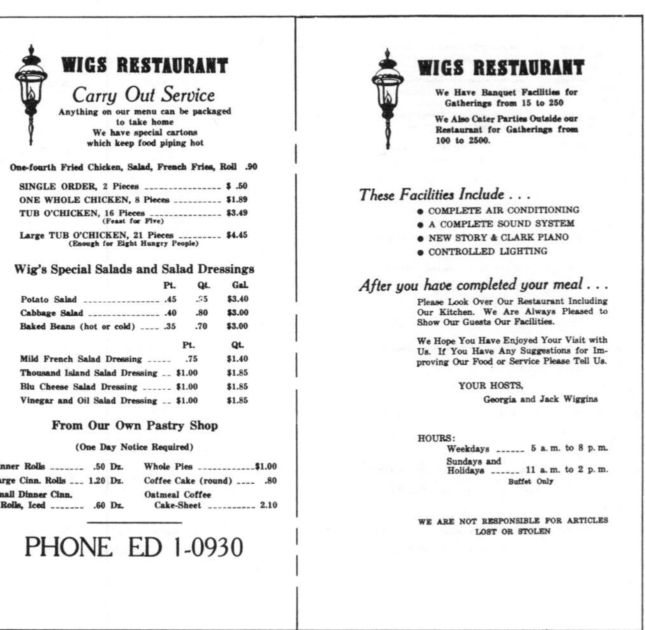

WIGS RESTAURANT

Carry Out Service

Anything on our menu can be packaged to take home
We have special cartons which keep food piping hot

One-fourth Fried Chicken, Salad, French Fries, Roll .90

SINGLE ORDER, 2 Pieces	$ .50
ONE WHOLE CHICKEN, 8 Pieces	$1.89
TUB O'CHICKEN, 16 Pieces (Feast for Five)	$3.49
Large TUB O'CHICKEN, 21 Pieces (Enough for Eight Hungry People)	$4.45

Wig's Special Salads and Salad Dressings

	Pt.	Qt.	Gal.
Potato Salad	.45	.[illegible]5	$3.40
Cabbage Salad	.40	.80	$3.00
Baked Beans (hot or cold)	.35	.70	$3.00

	Pt.	Qt.
Mild French Salad Dressing	.75	$1.40
Thousand Island Salad Dressing	$1.00	$1.85
Blu Cheese Salad Dressing	$1.00	$1.85
Vinegar and Oil Salad Dressing	$1.00	$1.85

From Our Own Pastry Shop

(One Day Notice Required)

Dinner Rolls	.50 Dz.	Whole Pies	$1.00
Large Cinn. Rolls	1.20 Dz.	Coffee Cake (round)	.80
Small Dinner Cinn. Rolls, Iced	.60 Dz.	Oatmeal Coffee Cake-Sheet	2.10

PHONE ED 1-0930

WIGS RESTAURANT

We Have Banquet Facilities for Gatherings from 15 to 250

We Also Cater Parties Outside our Restaurant for Gatherings from 100 to 2500.

These Facilities Include . . .

- COMPLETE AIR CONDITIONING
- A COMPLETE SOUND SYSTEM
- NEW STORY & CLARK PIANO
- CONTROLLED LIGHTING

After you have completed your meal . . .

Please Look Over Our Restaurant Including Our Kitchen. We Are Always Pleased to Show Our Guests Our Facilities.

We Hope You Have Enjoyed Your Visit with Us. If You Have Any Suggestions for Improving Our Food or Service Please Tell Us.

YOUR HOSTS,
Georgia and Jack Wiggins

HOURS:
Weekdays ...... 5 a. m. to 8 p. m.
Sundays and Holidays ...... 11 a. m. to 2 p. m.
Buffet Only

WE ARE NOT RESPONSIBLE FOR ARTICLES LOST OR STOLEN

FIGURE B

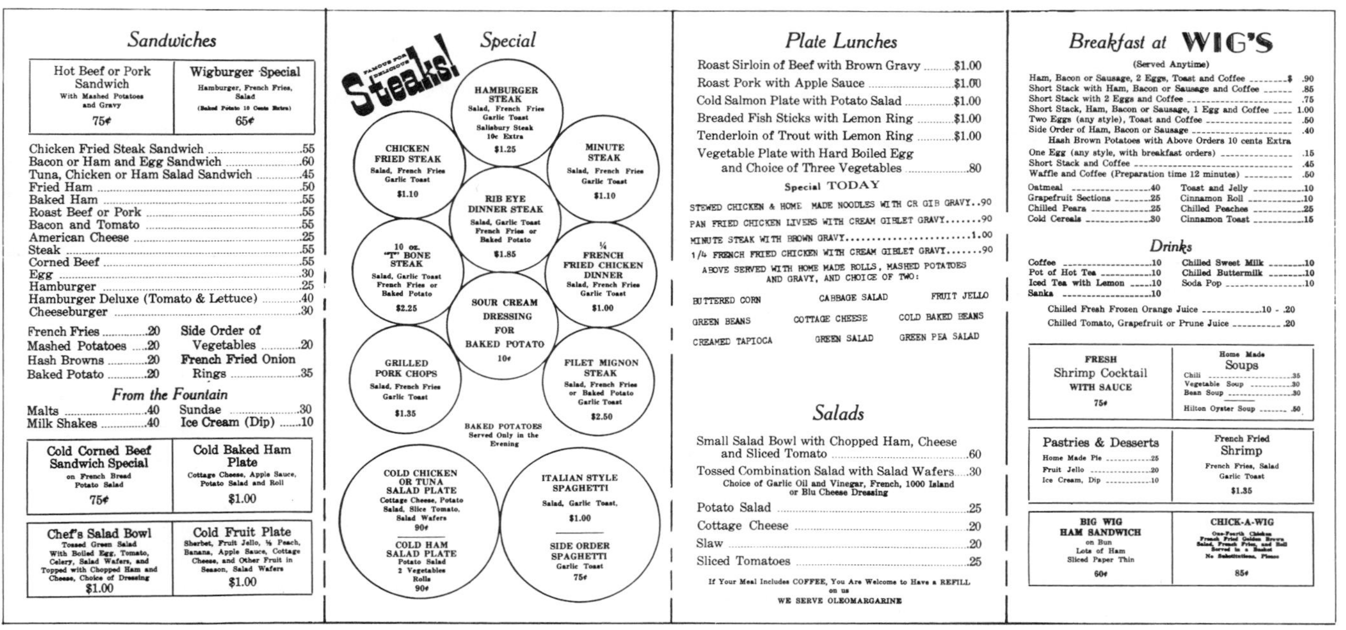

Sandwiches

Hot Beef or Pork Sandwich
With Mashed Potatoes and Gravy
75¢

Wigburger Special
Hamburger, French Fries, Salad
(Baked Potato 10 Cents Extra)
65¢

Chicken Fried Steak Sandwich .55
Bacon or Ham and Egg Sandwich .60
Tuna, Chicken or Ham Salad Sandwich .45
Fried Ham .50
Baked Ham .55
Roast Beef or Pork .55
Bacon and Tomato .55
American Cheese .25
Steak .55
Corned Beef .55
Egg .30
Hamburger .25
Hamburger Deluxe (Tomato & Lettuce) .40
Cheeseburger .30

French Fries .20
Mashed Potatoes .20
Hash Browns .20
Baked Potato .20
Side Order of Vegetables .20
French Fried Onion Rings .35

From the Fountain

Malts .40
Milk Shakes .40
Sundae .30
Ice Cream (Dip) .10

Cold Corned Beef Sandwich Special
on French Bread
Potato Salad
75¢

Cold Baked Ham Plate
Cottage Cheese, Apple Sauce, Potato Salad and Roll
$1.00

Chef's Salad Bowl
Tossed Green Salad With Boiled Egg, Tomato, Celery, Salad Wafers, and Topped with Chopped Ham and Cheese, Choice of Dressing
$1.00

Cold Fruit Plate
Sherbet, Fruit Jello, ½ Peach, Banana, Apple Sauce, Cottage Cheese, and Other Fruit in Season, Salad Wafers
$1.00

Special

Famous for Delicious Steaks!

HAMBURGER STEAK
Salad, French Fries
Garlic Toast
Salisbury Steak 10¢ Extra
$1.25

CHICKEN FRIED STEAK
Salad, French Fries
Garlic Toast
$1.10

MINUTE STEAK
Salad, French Fries
Garlic Toast
$1.10

RIB EYE DINNER STEAK
Salad, Garlic Toast
French Fries or Baked Potato
$1.85

10 oz. "T" BONE STEAK
Salad, Garlic Toast
French Fries or Baked Potato
$2.25

¼ FRENCH FRIED CHICKEN DINNER
Salad, French Fries
Garlic Toast
$1.00

SOUR CREAM DRESSING FOR BAKED POTATO
10¢

GRILLED PORK CHOPS
Salad, French Fries
Garlic Toast
$1.35

FILET MIGNON STEAK
Salad, French Fries or Baked Potato
Garlic Toast
$2.50

BAKED POTATOES Served Only in the Evening

COLD CHICKEN OR TUNA SALAD PLATE
Cottage Cheese, Potato Salad, Slice Tomato, Salad Wafers
90¢

COLD HAM SALAD PLATE
Potato Salad
2 Vegetables
Rolls
90¢

ITALIAN STYLE SPAGHETTI
Salad, Garlic Toast,
$1.00

SIDE ORDER SPAGHETTI
Garlic Toast
75¢

Plate Lunches

Roast Sirloin of Beef with Brown Gravy $1.00
Roast Pork with Apple Sauce $1.0Ɔ
Cold Salmon Plate with Potato Salad $1.00
Breaded Fish Sticks with Lemon Ring $1.00
Tenderloin of Trout with Lemon Ring $1.00
Vegetable Plate with Hard Boiled Egg and Choice of Three Vegetables .80

Special TODAY

STEWED CHICKEN & HOME MADE NOODLES WITH CR GIB GRAVY..90
PAN FRIED CHICKEN LIVERS WITH CREAM GIBLET GRAVY.......90
MINUTE STEAK WITH BROWN GRAVY........................1.00
1/4 FRENCH FRIED CHICKEN WITH CREAM GIBLET GRAVY.......90
ABOVE SERVED WITH HOME MADE ROLLS, MASHED POTATOES AND GRAVY, AND CHOICE OF TWO:

BUTTERED CORN — CABBAGE SALAD — FRUIT JELLO
GREEN BEANS — COTTAGE CHEESE — COLD BAKED BEANS
CREAMED TAPIOCA — GREEN SALAD — GREEN PEA SALAD

Salads

Small Salad Bowl with Chopped Ham, Cheese and Sliced Tomato .60
Tossed Combination Salad with Salad Wafers .30
Choice of Garlic Oil and Vinegar, French, 1000 Island or Blu Cheese Dressing
Potato Salad .25
Cottage Cheese .20
Slaw .20
Sliced Tomatoes .25

If Your Meal Includes COFFEE, You Are Welcome to Have a REFILL on us
WE SERVE OLEOMARGARINE

Breakfast at **WIG'S**

(Served Anytime)

Ham, Bacon or Sausage, 2 Eggs, Toast and Coffee $ .90
Short Stack with Ham, Bacon or Sausage and Coffee .85
Short Stack with 2 Eggs and Coffee .75
Short Stack, Ham, Bacon or Sausage, 1 Egg and Coffee 1.00
Two Eggs (any style), Toast and Coffee .50
Side Order of Ham, Bacon or Sausage .40
Hash Brown Potatoes with Above Orders 10 cents Extra
One Egg (any style, with breakfast orders) .15
Short Stack and Coffee .45
Waffle and Coffee (Preparation time 12 minutes) .50

Oatmeal .40
Grapefruit Sections .25
Chilled Pears .25
Cold Cereals .30
Toast and Jelly .10
Cinnamon Roll .10
Chilled Peaches .25
Cinnamon Toast .15

Drinks

Coffee .10
Pot of Hot Tea .10
Iced Tea with Lemon .10
Sanka .10
Chilled Sweet Milk .10
Chilled Buttermilk .10
Soda Pop .10
Chilled Fresh Frozen Orange Juice .10 - .20
Chilled Tomato, Grapefruit or Prune Juice .20

FRESH Shrimp Cocktail WITH SAUCE
75¢

Home Made Soups
Chili .35
Vegetable Soup .30
Bean Soup .30
Hilton Oyster Soup .50

Pastries & Desserts
Home Made Pie .25
Fruit Jello .20
Ice Cream, Dip .10

French Fried Shrimp
French Fries, Salad
Garlic Toast
$1.35

BIG WIG HAM SANDWICH
on Bun
Lots of Ham
Sliced Paper Thin
60¢

CHICK-A-WIG
One-Fourth Chicken
French Fried Golden Brown
Salad, French Fries, and Roll
Served in a Basket
No Substitutions, Please
85¢

FIGURE C

This menu covers a lot of subjects in a small space through the full use of all panels plus the clever fold. (Left) *Fig. A shows the cover. Figure B shows the first fold when the menu is opened. The Carry Out and general information about the operation—hours, days open, and so on are listed here.* (Above) *In Fig. C, panels 3, 4, 5, and 6 are shown with sandwiches on panel 3 (plus fountain items). Steaks and specials are listed on panel 4. On panel 5 lunches, salads, and specials of the day are listed. On panel 6, the breakfast menu plus drinks and assorted specials are listed. Putting specials on the back page gives them maximum exposure.*

App

Escargots 1.95
Imported snails in the shell
sauteed to a gourmets delight

California Fruit Cocktail Supreme
with Wedge of Fresh Lime 1.40

Iced Tangy Tomato Juice with Lemon Wedge .45

French onion soup au croutons ....

Gourmet

— PREPARED AT

Caesar Salad 1.50
Crisp hearts of romaine, golden brown croutons, anchovies and parmesan cheese, tossed at your table with a dressing of fresh lemon juices olive oil, coddled egg and finished with freshly ground pepper

Marine

BROILED AUSTRALIAN ROCK L
A large juicy lobster tail prepared in the sh
enchanting seafood treat served with golde
drawn butter and lemon wedge

FOR THE UNDECIDED ....
An exotic treat of a moderately sized sirloi
plus one-half rock lobster tail. Truly a uniqu

ROCKY MOUNTAIN RAINBOW T
From the streams and lakes of Montana hig
Three-quarters of a pound of fighting Bow
sauteed in butter and served with a rasher c

FRESH JUMBO PRAWNS ....
Dipped in our own oriental batter and fried
golden brown. Served with Rainbow cole s
tangy cocktail sauce and lemon wedges

GRILLED FILET OF HALIBUT ...
Served with lemon wedge and tartar sauce

Flamed at

BUTTERFLY NEW YORK STEAK
A large choice New York steak superbly pre
in a skillfully blended sauce, laced in flami
and served with a large baked potato

BEEF STROGANOFF ....
Thin strips of beef tenderloin and mushroom
sauteed in butter and wine and a dollop of
sour cream—added at just the right momen
served with homemade noodles with sesame

MALAYAN TENDERLOIN TIPS
Choice beef tenderloin tips, skillfully braised
Flamed with brandy and served on a bed of

Above entrees served with soup du jour, relish trays, dinner sala

Desserts

CHERRIES JUBILEE 1.25
Prepared at your table in a chafing dish, with large pitted cherries flamed in select liqueurs and brandy. Served over large mounds of vanilla ice cream in supreme bowl.

CREME DE MENTHE PARFAIT .... .75
Creamy rich ice cream mingled with green Creme de Menthe, topped with fresh whipped cream.

OLD FASHIONED STRAWBERRY PIE ... .50

HOT APPLE PIE .... .50
An old Dutch treat, served with your choice of cheddar cheese or mounds of whipped cream.

ICE CREAM OR SHERBET .... .40

COCONUT SNOWBALL with
CHOCOLATE SAUCE SUPREME .... .50

After Dinner Drinks

Creme de Menthe	.90	Black Russian	1.30
King Alphonse	1.00	Stinger	1.10
Cognac	1.00	B & B	1.10
Brandy Alexander	1.10	Galliano	1.00
Drambuie	1.00	Grasshopper	1.10
Creme de Cocao	.90	Pink Squirrel	1.10

Steaks and Chops

BIG SKY T-BONE STEAK 6.50
A favorite cut from our specially aged beef loins.

FILET MIGNON 6.25
The queens choice, the most tender of all red meats.

NEW YORK STRIP STEAK 6.00
The finest cut of beef, selected for tenderness from our best strip loins.

FRENCH CUT LAMB CHOPS 4.50
These extra thick chops are selected from the choicest Montana spring lamb.

CLUB SIRLOIN STEAK 4.25
Always a favorite, cut from the finest Montana beef.

CENTER CUT PORK CHOPS 3.75
Grilled until well done, served with fresh apple sauce.

Best in Montana

ROAST PRIME RIB OF BEEF
Aged prime roasted slowly
to retain all natural juices.
Our most popular entree.
4.00

CATTLEMAN'S CUT
Sliced extra heavy
for the hearty appetite.
5.00

All Entrees served with soup du jour, large fresh crisp tossed salad and relish trays, fluffy baked potato, hot rolls and butter choice of beverage

6-69—100

FIGURE A

FIGURE B

App

Escargots 1.95
Imported snails in the shell
sauteed to a gourmets delight

California Fruit Cocktail Supreme
with Wedge of Fresh Lime 1.40

Iced Tangy Tomato Juice with Lemon Wedge .45

French onion soup au croutons ....

Gourmet

— PREPARED AT

Caesar Salad 1.50
Crisp hearts of romaine, golden brown croutons, anchovies and parmesan cheese, tossed at your table with a dressing of fresh lemon juices olive oil, coddled egg and finished with freshly ground pepper

Marine

BROILED AUSTRALIAN ROCK L
A large juicy lobster tail prepared in the sh
enchanting seafood treat served with golde
drawn butter and lemon wedge

FOR THE UNDECIDED ....
An exotic treat of a moderately sized sirloi
plus one-half rock lobster tail. Truly a uniqu

ROCKY MOUNTAIN RAINBOW T
From the streams and lakes of Montana hig
Three-quarters of a pound of fighting Bow
sauteed in butter and served with a rasher c

FRESH JUMBO PRAWNS ....
Dipped in our own oriental batter and fried
golden brown. Served with Rainbow cole s
tangy cocktail sauce and lemon wedges

GRILLED FILET OF HALIBUT ...
Served with lemon wedge and tartar sauce

Flamed at

BUTTERFLY NEW YORK STEAK
A large choice New York steak superbly pre
in a skillfully blended sauce, laced in flami
and served with a large baked potato

BEEF STROGANOFF ....
Thin strips of beef tenderloin and mushroom
sauteed in butter and wine and a dollop of
sour cream—added at just the right momen
served with homemade noodles with sesame

MALAYAN TENDERLOIN TIPS
Choice beef tenderloin tips, skillfully braised
Flamed with brandy and served on a bed of

Above entrees served with soup du jour, relish trays, dinner sala

Complete Dinners

which include

Soup of the day | **Tossed Salad with choice of dressing**

BREAST OF CAPON CORDON BLEU 4.50
Savory breast of capon filled with lightly smoked ham and swiss cheese. Served with fluffy white rice, spiced peach and supreme sauce

BEEF AND BACON 3.25
Choice ground sirloin of beef, topped with crisp bacon and encircled with onion rings

FILLET OF DOVER SOLE 3.25
Dipped in egg batter and grilled to a golden brown, served with Rainbow tartar sauce

FRIED CHICKEN 3.25
Country style, golden brown and done to a turn

GRILLED BABY BEEF LIVER with BACON or ONIONS 2.95

Above items served with
Large baked potato or fluffy white rice.
Fresh dinner rolls with butter.
Choice of beverage.
Ice cream or Sherbet

House Specialty

NEOPOLITAN SPAGHETTI DINNER
Real Italienne Spaghetti with a delightfully rich meat sauce. Served with ravioli, and shredded parmesan cheese.
3.25
Served complete with tossed salad and choice of dressing.
Dinner rolls with butter. Choice of beverage.

nd Chops

.... 6.50
.... 6.25
.... 6.00
tenderness
.... 4.50
from
.... 4.25
.... 3.75

Montana

RIB OF BEEF
asted slowly
atural juices.
ular entree.
0
AN'S CUT
ra heavy
ty appetite.
0

, large fresh crisp tossed salad and
otato, hot rolls and butter
beverage

Appetizers

Escargots 1.95
Imported snails in the shell sauteed to a gourmets delight

California Fruit Cocktail Supreme with Wedge of Fresh Lime 1.40

Iced Tangy Tomato Juice with Lemon Wedge .45

Alaskan King Crab Legs on Ice 1.95

Gulf Prawn Cocktail Supreme 1.50

Seafood Cocktail Supreme 1.50

Marinated Herring 1.50

French onion soup au croutons .... .40

Gourmets Delight

— PREPARED AT YOUR TABLE —

Caesar Salad 1.50
Crisp hearts of romaine, golden brown croutons, anchovies and parmesan cheese, tossed at your table with a dressing of fresh lemon juices, olive oil, coddled egg and finished with freshly ground pepper.

Innkeeper's Salad 1.60
Originally created in our kitchens, prepared at your table with fresh hearts of lettuce and romaine. Served with a hot sweet and sour dressing and crisp bacon chips.

Mariners Choice

BROILED AUSTRALIAN ROCK LOBSTER TAIL 7.25
A large juicy lobster tail prepared in the shell. An enchanting seafood treat served with golden drawn butter and lemon wedge.

FOR THE UNDECIDED 7.25
An exotic treat of a moderately sized sirloin steak plus one-half rock lobster tail. Truly a unique taste treat.

ROCKY MOUNTAIN RAINBOW TROUT 3.50
From the streams and lakes of Montana high country. Three quarters of a pound of fighting "Bow," sauteed in butter, and served with a rasher of bacon

FRESH JUMBO PRAWNS 3.25
Dipped in our own oriental batter and fried to a golden brown. Served with Rainbow cole slaw, tangy cocktail sauce and lemon wedges.

GRILLED FILET OF HALIBUT 2.95
Served with lemon wedge and tartar sauce

Flamed at Your Table

BUTTERFLY NEW YORK STEAK 6.25
A large choice New York steak superbly prepared in a skillfully blended sauce, laced in flaming brandy and served with a large baked potato

BEEF STROGANOFF 5.25
Thin strips of beef tenderloin and mushrooms, sauteed in butter and wine and a dollop of sour cream—added at just the right moment—served with homemade noodles with sesame seed.

MALAYAN TENDERLOIN TIPS 5.25
Choice beef tenderloin tips, skillfully braised in a mild curry sauce. Flamed with brandy and served on a bed of fluffy white rice.

Above entrees served with soup du jour, relish trays, dinner salad, large baked potato or rice, rolls, butter and choice of beverage.

Wine

"A meal without wine is like a day without sunshine"

Champagnes

	Bottle	½ Bottle
Mumm's Extra Dry	10.50	6.65
Taylors New York	6.50	4.50

Sparkling Burgundy

Taylors New York	6.50	4.50
Christian Brothers	6.00	4.50

Red Wines

Paul Masson Burgundy	3.50	2.90
Martini Pinot Noir	4.40	3.30
Charles Krug Cabernet Sauvignon	4.35	3.25
B and G Prince Noir	4.30	3.40
B and G Beaujolais	4.85	

Chablis

Wente Pinot Blanc	3.85	
Chenin Blanc Krug	3.90	
Paul Masson	3.65	

Rhine

Paul Masson Rhine Castle	3.90	3.00
J. Kayser, Glockenspiel	5.00	3.65
Charles Krug, Gray Riesling	4.00	3.00

Rose

Lancers Crackling Rose	6.10	4.25
Nectarose, Vin Rose d' Antou	4.50	
Masson Rose	3.65	2.95

Italian

Italian Swiss Tipo Red	3.45	2.85

nd Chops

.... 6.50

.... 6.25

.... 6.00
tenderness

.... 4.50
from

.... 4.25

.... 3.75

Montana

RIB OF BEEF
oasted slowly
atural juices.
oular entree.

AN'S CUT
ra heavy
ty appetite.

, large fresh crisp tossed salad and
otato, hot rolls and butter
beverage

The full use of a center insert is demonstrated with this menu. Fig. A shows the main panel at left and the wine list. Fig. B shows the insert—complete dinner and house specialty, and Fig. C shows the dessert menu and the right hand main panel. Note that the narrower center panel never completely covers the two large main panels so the patron is always aware of the variety of choices available.

FIGURE C

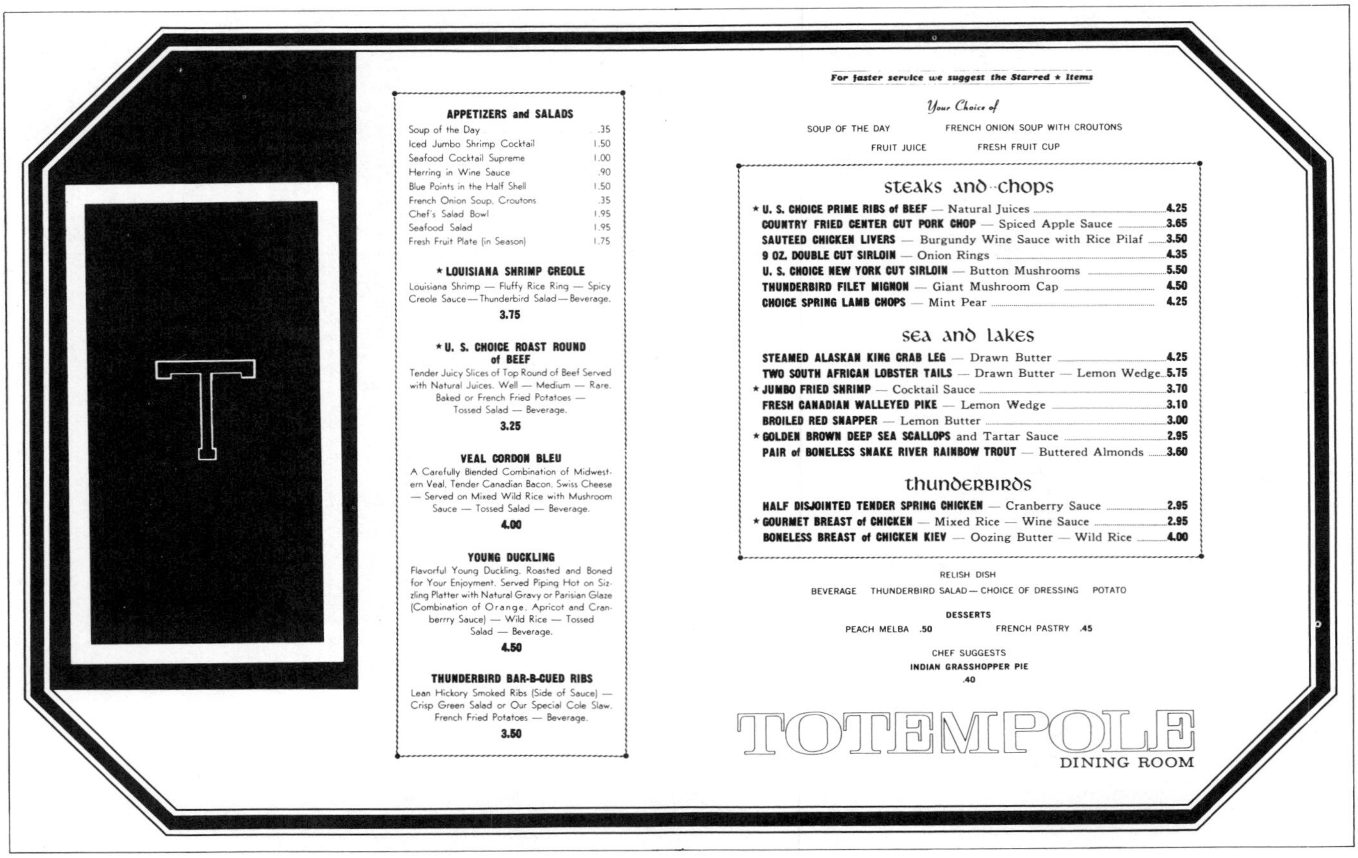

T

APPETIZERS and SALADS

Soup of the Day	.35
Iced Jumbo Shrimp Cocktail	1.50
Seafood Cocktail Supreme	1.00
Herring in Wine Sauce	.90
Blue Points in the Half Shell	1.50
French Onion Soup, Croutons	.35
Chef's Salad Bowl	1.95
Seafood Salad	1.95
Fresh Fruit Plate (in Season)	1.75

★ LOUISIANA SHRIMP CREOLE
Louisiana Shrimp — Fluffy Rice Ring — Spicy Creole Sauce — Thunderbird Salad — Beverage.
3.75

★ U. S. CHOICE ROAST ROUND of BEEF
Tender Juicy Slices of Top Round of Beef Served with Natural Juices. Well — Medium — Rare. Baked or French Fried Potatoes — Tossed Salad — Beverage.
3.25

VEAL CORDON BLEU
A Carefully Blended Combination of Midwestern Veal, Tender Canadian Bacon, Swiss Cheese — Served on Mixed Wild Rice with Mushroom Sauce — Tossed Salad — Beverage.
4.00

YOUNG DUCKLING
Flavorful Young Duckling, Roasted and Boned for Your Enjoyment. Served Piping Hot on Sizzling Platter with Natural Gravy or Parisian Glaze (Combination of Orange, Apricot and Cranberrry Sauce) — Wild Rice — Tossed Salad — Beverage.
4.50

THUNDERBIRD BAR-B-CUED RIBS
Lean Hickory Smoked Ribs (Side of Sauce) — Crisp Green Salad or Our Special Cole Slaw, French Fried Potatoes — Beverage.
3.50

For faster service we suggest the Starred ★ Items

Your Choice of

SOUP OF THE DAY — FRENCH ONION SOUP WITH CROUTONS
FRUIT JUICE — FRESH FRUIT CUP

steaks and chops

★ **U. S. CHOICE PRIME RIBS of BEEF** — Natural Juices	4.25
COUNTRY FRIED CENTER CUT PORK CHOP — Spiced Apple Sauce	3.65
SAUTEED CHICKEN LIVERS — Burgundy Wine Sauce with Rice Pilaf	3.50
9 OZ. DOUBLE CUT SIRLOIN — Onion Rings	4.35
U. S. CHOICE NEW YORK CUT SIRLOIN — Button Mushrooms	5.50
THUNDERBIRD FILET MIGNON — Giant Mushroom Cap	4.50
CHOICE SPRING LAMB CHOPS — Mint Pear	4.25

sea and lakes

STEAMED ALASKAN KING CRAB LEG — Drawn Butter	4.25
TWO SOUTH AFRICAN LOBSTER TAILS — Drawn Butter — Lemon Wedge	5.75
★ **JUMBO FRIED SHRIMP** — Cocktail Sauce	3.70
FRESH CANADIAN WALLEYED PIKE — Lemon Wedge	3.10
BROILED RED SNAPPER — Lemon Butter	3.00
★ **GOLDEN BROWN DEEP SEA SCALLOPS** and Tartar Sauce	2.95
PAIR of BONELESS SNAKE RIVER RAINBOW TROUT — Buttered Almonds	3.60

thunderbirds

HALF DISJOINTED TENDER SPRING CHICKEN — Cranberry Sauce	2.95
★ **GOURMET BREAST of CHICKEN** — Mixed Rice — Wine Sauce	2.95
BONELESS BREAST of CHICKEN KIEV — Oozing Butter — Wild Rice	4.00

RELISH DISH
BEVERAGE — THUNDERBIRD SALAD — CHOICE OF DRESSING — POTATO

DESSERTS
PEACH MELBA .50 — FRENCH PASTRY .45

CHEF SUGGESTS
INDIAN GRASSHOPPER PIE
.40

TOTEMPOLE
DINING ROOM

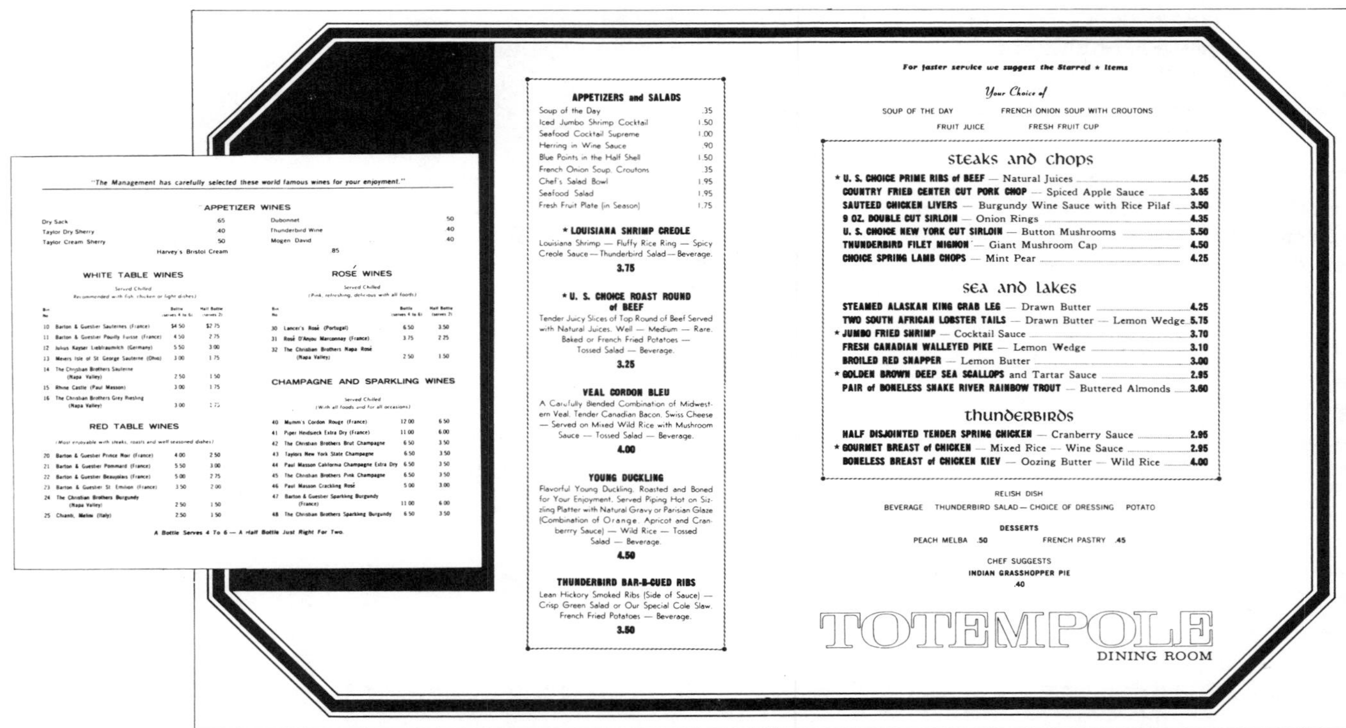

"The Management has carefully selected these world famous wines for your enjoyment."

APPETIZER WINES

Dry Sack	.65	Dubonnet	.50
Taylor Dry Sherry	.40	Thunderbird Wine	.40
Taylor Cream Sherry	.50	Mogen David	.40
Harvey's Bristol Cream	.85		

WHITE TABLE WINES
Served Chilled
(Recommended with fish, chicken or light dishes)

Bin No.		Bottle (serves 4 to 6)	Half Bottle (serves 2)
10	Barton & Guestier Sauternes (France)	$4.50	$2.75
11	Barton & Guestier Pouilly Fuisse (France)	4.50	2.75
12	Julius Kayser Liebfraumilch (Germany)	5.50	3.00
13	Meiers Isle of St. George Sauterne (Ohio)	3.00	1.75
14	The Christian Brothers Sauterne (Napa Valley)	2.50	1.50
15	Rhine Castle (Paul Masson)	3.00	1.75
16	The Christian Brothers Grey Riesling (Napa Valley)	3.00	1.75

RED TABLE WINES
(Most enjoyable with steaks, roasts and well seasoned dishes)

20	Barton & Guestier Prince Noir (France)	4.00	2.50
21	Barton & Guestier Pommard (France)	5.50	3.00
22	Barton & Guestier Beaujolais (France)	5.00	2.75
23	Barton & Guestier St. Emilion (France)	3.50	2.00
24	The Christian Brothers Burgundy (Napa Valley)	2.50	1.50
25	Chianti, Melini (Italy)	2.50	1.50

ROSÉ WINES
Served Chilled
(Pink, refreshing, delicious with all foods)

Bin No.		Bottle (serves 4 to 6)	Half Bottle (serves 2)
30	Lancer's Rosé (Portugal)	6.50	3.50
31	Rosé D'Anjou Marconnay (France)	3.75	2.25
32	The Christian Brothers Napa Rosé (Napa Valley)	2.50	1.50

CHAMPAGNE AND SPARKLING WINES
Served Chilled
(With all foods and for all occasions)

40	Mumm's Cordon Rouge (France)	12.00	6.50
41	Piper Heidsieck Extra Dry (France)	11.00	6.00
42	The Christian Brothers Brut Champagne	6.50	3.50
43	Taylors New York State Champagne	6.50	3.50
44	Paul Masson California Champagne Extra Dry	6.50	3.50
45	The Christian Brothers Pink Champagne	6.50	3.50
46	Paul Masson Crackling Rosé	5.00	3.00
47	Barton & Guestier Sparkling Burgundy (France)	11.00	6.00
48	The Christian Brothers Sparkling Burgundy	6.50	3.50

A Bottle Serves 4 To 6 — A Half Bottle Just Right For Two.

This menu has three tip-on panels. One is a wine list, one includes appetizers, salads, and specials, and the third is the main dinner menu. This is a highly flexible menu.

4

Menu copy

Every menu is a written communication. Some are just a list—a bill of fare; some list the items for sale with haphazard description. The best menus describe, romance, and sell what is being served. A menu should be compared with an advertisement in a national magazine, and as much time and effort should go into the writing of a menu as a four-color ad. In addition, the menu is an ideal place to sell your operation, its unique character and cuisine, and through this institutional sell help to create atmosphere and good publicity—the sort of publicity that makes for repeat business.

The copy in a menu can be broken down into three main categories: (1) listing of food items; (2) description and sell of food listing; and (3) institutional copy about the restaurant, its service, and cuisine.

To begin with, just the listing of food is not the simple matter it would seem at first. For example, let's consider a common item such as potatoes. Is a potato a potato or a potato per Gertrude Stein? The following is a sample listing of potatoes taken from many menus:

Hashed Brown Potatoes
Brabant Potatoes
French Fried Potatoes
Lyonnaise Potatoes
Parsley Potatoes
Baked Idaho Potatoes
Au Gratin Potatoes
Whipped and Creamed Potatoes
Parisienne Potatoes
Escalloped Potatoes
Country Fried Potatoes
Potato du Jour
Boiled Potatoes
Mashed Potatoes
Cottage Fried Potatoes
Potato Salad

There are several observations to be made from the above list. First, the name of the food item is important. A rose by any other name may smell the same, but the name rose conjures up a definite mental picture; the same is true of the name of a food item. Every item on the bill of fare, therefore, must be named with care and exactness. Second, the name of a food item is not an exact scientific label. From the above list of potatoes, for example, how many people could describe exactly what they would get if they ordered Brabant Potatoes or Parisienne Potatoes? A short survey in your own dining room could show more than one word on your menu that the general public does not understand. How many customers know that au jus means served in gravy or juice of the meat? Or how many people know that lyonnaise means cooked with flaked or sliced fried onions?

For a chef, or an experienced restaurateur, all the above terms are well known, but unless the customer has been educated to all the foreign, uncommon words, he or she needs help. The alternative is a Berlitz blitz course in all foreign words used in menus as part of the American language!

The next consideration, therefore, is the descriptive copy covering the individual menu item. This can be simple or elaborate, but, in any case, it usually adds interest and sales value to a menu. For example, bread and butter can be described better as "Oven Fresh Rolls and Creamery Butter." This is a short but mouth watering description. Some other descriptions that add to the menu mental picture are as follows:

"TENDER THICK PORK CHOPS . . . cut from the loins of finest native pork and broiled to perfection. A unique experience that will long be remembered."

"DANISH BROOK TROUT . . . from cold Scandinavian waters by way of the gentle savory heat of the hearth coals . . . to you . . . truly the perfect fish. Served with lemon butter."

"OYSTERS AND BACON EN BROCHETTE . . . ten of the most delicious, salty, fresh Gulf Oysters we can find, skewed with bacon, brushed with butter and broiled. Served with crisp Brabant potatoes, baked tomato and mushroom."

"BONELESS FRIED CHICKEN . . . TRANSOCEAN AIRLINES. Something to remember Hawaii by. Tender halves of chicken in which all the bones have been carefully replaced with pineapple sticks, then dipped in fresh coconut cream and rolled in grated coconut. Baked to a golden crunchy brown and sauced with coconut cream giblet gravy. Served with baked banana."

From the above appetizing adjectives, dripping with flavor and taste, it's easy to see that a few extra, well chosen words are in order.

The meal does not have to be described in a list-description manner, however, as shown by the following description (on the menu, not in a travel brochure) of a breakfast (served until midnight) at *Brennan's French Restaurant* in New Orleans.

"A TRADITIONAL BRENNAN BREAKFAST . . . This is the way it was done in leisured antebellum days; first an absinthe Suissesse to get the eyes open, then a fresh Creole cream cheese. Now an egg Benedict, followed by a hearty sirloin with fresh mushrooms. Hot French bread and marmalade, and a chilled Rose wine. For the finale, crepes Suzette, cafe au lait, and a Cognac snifter. Important: DON'T HURRY!"

If the above doesn't start a "Better Breakfast" trend in America, words have lost their power to fire the imagination.

It's not just food, though, that warrants a good word. If you have a wine cellar worth a wine list, a bit of descriptive copy as the following from *The Old Mill* Wine List is appropriate:

"Wine is wholesome food which stimulates digestion, makes fine foods taste better, and lends an air of festivity and congeniality at the dinner table; it's natural, therefore, that the enjoyment of a bottle of wine with dinner is fast becoming an American tradition."

And here is a listing from *Canlis' Charcoal Broiler Restaurant:*

"FRESH SALMON STEAK . . . Volumes and volumes of words have been written about salmon. You've had it a la this and a la that. All we can say is praise be to Allah for bringing this fish to us. We just charcoal broil it."

The third broad copy category covering menu writing is institutional copy. Just as a company has a "corporate image," which is the total picture the public has about it, so a food service operation has a public image, and the menu is one of the best places to build the image. The approach varies with every establishment because each has its special feature, character, service, or history which makes for interesting copy material.

For example, the *El Rancho* restaurant builds its institutional approach around a local industry, a glassware company. The glassware is used in the restaurant and sold to the public. This copy, therefore, serves two purposes. It adds local color to the restaurant and it merchandises and sells the glassware. Tie-ins with local industries are a natural for a certain type of restaurant.

Henrici's restaurant in Chicago uses, for their point of departure on institutional copy, the historical approach. The restaurant was established in 1868, so in copy and illustration they sketch some of the great historical events of the last 100 years, such as the Chicago Fire of 1871 and the Columbian Exposition. The history of a great city adds to the fame of *Henrici's* restaurant.

The decor of a restaurant can have publicity value. The Pontchartrain Hotel, New Orleans, for instance, has a series of Murals (The Marfield Murals), that they describe in the first page of their menu. Special decorations, paintings, sculpture, and other objets d'art can very appropriately be referred to in a menu.

The Ranch Kitchen in Gallup, New Mexico, features a short history of Gallup and the surrounding country. Then they give a thumbnail sketch of the Navajo, Zuni, and Hopi Indian tribes of New Mexico. They describe the silver work, turquoise jewelry, and rugs of the Navajo weavers, which they just happen to have for sale!

Kolb's restaurant in New Orleans has a new approach in restaurant merchandising through the menu. They have taken a magazine article from Down South Magazine and reprinted the entire article (with photos) on the inside front and back covers of the menu. On the cover of the menu they describe the four dining rooms of the restaurant. This makes the menu a complete merchandising piece which can be used as a give-away or mailing brochure.

A more common copy approach which can be used by almost every restaurant is to feature and romance the speciality of the house. *Al Farber's* restaurant in Chicago, for example, calls their introductory copy "MUCH ADO ABOUT STEAK" with such phrases as "discriminating epicureans—prepared to delight the palate of all—the eye of the beef is an 'eye opener' and a taste sensation." Any specialty of the house worth its salt is worth some special "hard sell" copy to establish authentic character for the operation.

A location which is out of the way can be used as an asset to hang your sales message to. *The White Turkey* and the *Red Barn* restaurants in Connecticut use their country location to advantage in their menu institutional promotion. The copy begins . . . "If You Love the Country . . . But Live in the City . . ." and leads into the pleasures of a trip into the New England countryside which ends at one of these restaurants for a relaxing, pleasant, and gracious meal, with appetites keener and more appreciative because of the ride. This approach is really creative meal merchandising.

Another institutional approach is the "Our Philosophy—Our Creed—The Tradition of This Restaurant" approach. This type of "Cafe Editorial" is a good general method of presenting the restaurateur as a serious student of the customer's gastronomic needs. *Vic's Tally Ho* restaurant in Des Moines, Iowa, begins their story along this line with . . . "You're on the board of directors . . ." From this they lead into a description of the goals and ideals of the restaurant.

From the above mentioned and the reprinted examples of institutional copy, it can be seen that there is a great variety in points of departure for merchandising and publicizing the particular quality, flavor, or specialty of almost any restaurant.

As for the actual writing of menu copy, the putting together of words, phrases, and apt expressions, the best advice for a food service operator (unless he or she is a writer) is to secure the use of professional talent, usually through an advertising agency, or the services of a freelance writer. The writing of a menu is too important to be left to an amateur.

downing square
500 Lexington Avenue, New York, New York

This is original, creative copy all the way through from beginning to end—from appetizers to desserts.

Inside front cover.

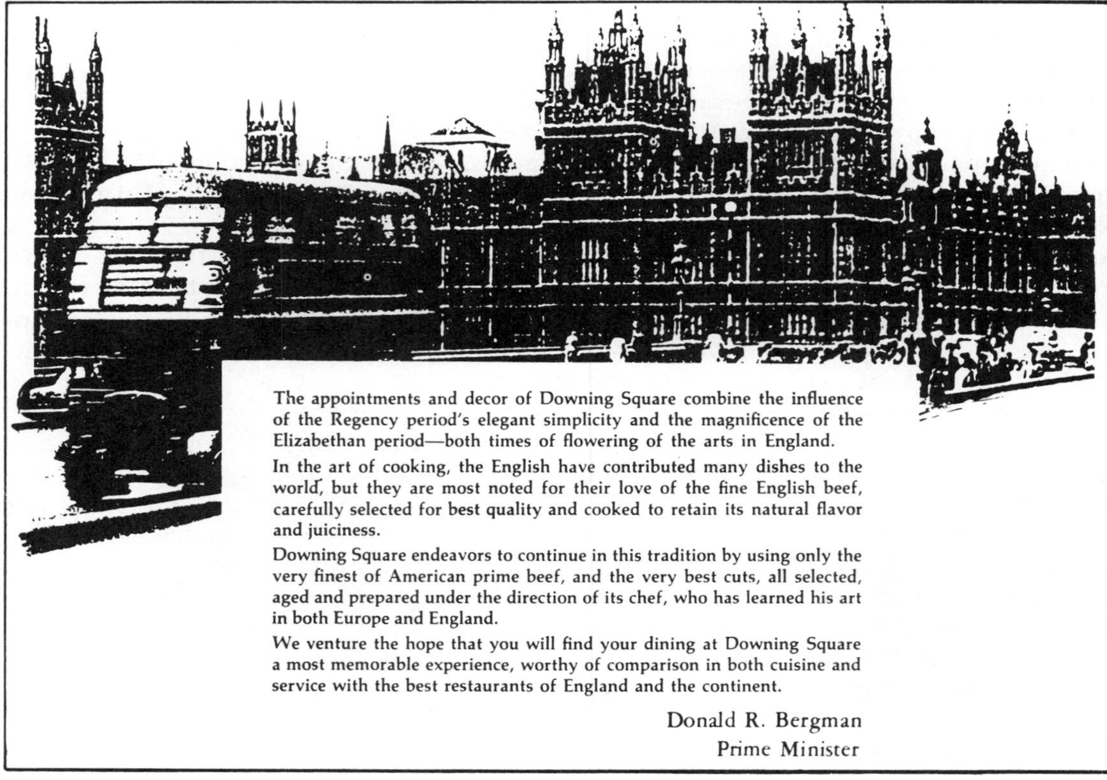

The appointments and decor of Downing Square combine the influence of the Regency period's elegant simplicity and the magnificence of the Elizabethan period—both times of flowering of the arts in England.

In the art of cooking, the English have contributed many dishes to the world, but they are most noted for their love of the fine English beef, carefully selected for best quality and cooked to retain its natural flavor and juiciness.

Downing Square endeavors to continue in this tradition by using only the very finest of American prime beef, and the very best cuts, all selected, aged and prepared under the direction of its chef, who has learned his art in both Europe and England.

We venture the hope that you will find your dining at Downing Square a most memorable experience, worthy of comparison in both cuisine and service with the best restaurants of England and the continent.

Donald R. Bergman
Prime Minister

Center spread, Downing Square *menu.*

Main or Principle Motions

DOWNING SQUARE PRIME BONELESS SIRLOIN STEAK 7.95

The usually unflappable British can get very excited about their beef. Portly Henry VIII, who knew a good piece of beef when he tasted it, was so delighted with a particularly appetizing one that he drew his sword and knighted it on the spot. Ever since, that cut has been known as Sir Loin. Our Boneless Sirloin Steak is true heir to the title. Just the very best prime quality beef, aged to develop the flavor fully in our own aging box.

Jr. Prime Sirloin Minute Steak 6.95
Filet Mignon, with Mushroom Cap 7.95
Double Prime Sirloin Steak (for two) 15.75
planked and surrounded with Dutchesse Potatoes and Bouquet of Fresh Garden Vegetables, Broiled Mushrooms Cresson 16.95
Chopped Sirloin Steak 4.95
Chateaubriand, Sauce Béarnaise, Mushroom Caps (for two) 15.75
with a Bouquet of Fresh Vegetables & Duchesse Potatoes 16.95
DOWNING SQUARE ENGLISH MIXED GRILL 6.95
(Lamb Chop, Calf's Liver, Chopped Steak, Bacon Strip, Filet Mignon & Grilled Tomato)
Jersey Pork Chops, Apple Sauce 5.50
Calf's Liver, Saute or Broiled, Bacon or Onions 5.95
Two (2) Broiled Triple Rib Lamb Chops (25 minutes) 6.95

DOWNING SQUARE THICK MUTTON CHOP WITH KIDNEY 7.00

The English are pretty particular about their mutton too. Charles II earned the epithet "The Mutton Eating King," and Shakespeare's Falstaff gorged upon a succulent joint of mutton. Downing Square's magnificent mutton chop is skewered around a kidney and broiled just to perfection.

DOWNING SQUARE FILET MIGNON EN BROCHETTE, Wild Rice 6.75
Broiled Half Spring Chicken, Grilled Tomato, Spiced Apple Ring 4.75
Steak Tartar, Garni 6.95

Putting the Q

HEAVY CUT ROAST PRI
OF BEEF, AU JUS . . . . . .

DOWNING SQUARE
ENGLISH CUT . . . .
both with Yorkshire Pudd
Baked Potato, Caesar or M
Green Salad

The English are colloquially
eaters" . . . with good reas
rather stuffy about insisting
quality beef, such as our Ro
The name Beefeaters origin
the beruffled Yeomen of th
still stand watch at the Tow
Way back in the 17th centu
obstinately insisted on their
stone of beef a day" prefera
here, in its own succulent jui

BONELESS CHICKEN PAI
Potato, and Caesar or Mi
Green Salad . . . .

Braised Brisket of Beef, Pot
Pancake, Apple Sauce & V
Caesar or Mixed Green Sa

Opening menu page.

The shadow of Big Ben falls on the heart of royal and aristocratic London — Westminster Abbey, Charing Cross, Parliament Square and Downing Street.

Introduction of Business

Marinated Herring in Cream w. Onion . . 1.25
Shrimp, Scampi, ... 2.75
Blue Point Oyster Cocktail (in season) . . 1.95
Jumbo Shrimp Cocktail 2.50
Lobster Cocktail 2.75
Littleneck or Cherrystone Clams 1.50
Crablump Cocktail 2.95
English Potted Shrimp, Maison. 1.95
Seafood Cocktail Supreme 2.95
Smoked Nova Scotia Salmon 1.95
Portuguese Boneless Sardines 1.50
Baked Clams Casino or
Oysters Casino (in season) 2.75
Hot Shrimp Balls, Sauce Remoulade 1.75
Chopped Chicken Livers,
w. Bermuda Onion 95
Grapefruit Supreme 85
Melon in Season 1.00
Chilled Tomato, Clam or V-8 Juice 60
Fresh Fruit Cocktail 1.00

Downing Square was inspired by the traditions and atmosphere of this part of London, as well as the recollection of an era when the great Escoffier reigned supreme as maitre chef at the Savoy and British chefs were the best in the world.

What Precedes Debate

Onion Soup au Gratin 85
Chicken Consomme w. Fine Noodles
and Matzoh Ball .75
Soup du Jour 75

Rules of Order

All entrees served with Downing Square Caesar Salad or Tossed green salad, (Choice of dressing) and choice of either baked potato, baked stuffed potato, or french fried Idaho potato.

ıestion

ΛE RIB
. . . . 6.95

. . . . 5.75
ing,
lixed

called "Beef-
ɔn. They are
on the highest
ıst Prime Rib.
ılly applied to
e Guard who
er of London.
ːry the guards
ration of "six
ıbly served, as
ces.

ꝛMIGIANA
ːed
. . . . 5.25

aꝛo
'egetable,
lad 5.50

Subsiding Motions

ENGLISH DOVER SOLE, Broiled or
Saute Meuniere or Amandines 5.95
Incomparable Dover Sole has been called the wonder of the fish world. The sole served at Downing Square is snatched from British waters and cooked à la meunière– or broiled or Amandines, seasoned, and served with a delicate butter sauce—to reveal the natural flavor at its best.

Broiled Swordfish Steak, Lemon Butter . . 4.95
Broiled Scampi, Downing Square Sauce. . 5.50
Broiled Digby Bay Scallops 5.50
King Crabmeat Saute, Rice and Peas 5.25

BROOK TROUT SAUTE,
AMANDINES or BROILED 5.75

Broiled Salmon Steak, Maitre D'Hotel . . 4.95
Broiled Filet of Sole 4.75
Lobster a la Newburgh 6.25
Shrimp a la Newburgh 5.95
BROILED STUFFED LOBSTER TAILS,
WILD RICE, PEA PODS 6.95
BROILED LIVE LARGE MAINE
LOBSTER 7.95
Stuffed with Shrimp or Crabmeat 1.75 extra

Announcing the Vote

MEDALLION OF VEAL CORDON
BLEU 6.25
The Medallion is the very finest cut of veal, taken from the fillet. Our chef, a very fussy fellow, insists on this sort of thing. . . . He prepares it a la cordon bleu with cheese and a spicy Italian ham called prosciutto sealed between two slices of veal. Samuel Pepys, 17th century English diarist, was equally vain about his veal, noting in his diary that he served it to his guests along with "a dozen larks" at "a pretty dinner, most neatly dressed by our own, only maybe."

Boiled Beef, in Pot with Noodles,
Matzoh Ball & Vegetables 5.50
Boiled Spring Chicken in Pot with
Noodles, Matzoh Ball & Vegetables . . 5.25
Veal Cutlet Parmigiana 5.50
Schnitzel Holstein, Garni 5.50

ROAST STUFFED ROCK CORNISH HEN
Wild Rice & Montmorency Sauce 5.95

Miscellaneous

Fresh Seafood Downing Square with
Lobster, Shrimp, Crabmeat 5.50
Special Chef's Salad Bowl 4.75
Shrimp or Lobster or Crabmeat Salad . . . 4.75
Assorted Cold Cuts, Potato Salad,
Sliced Tomatoes 4.75

Final pages.

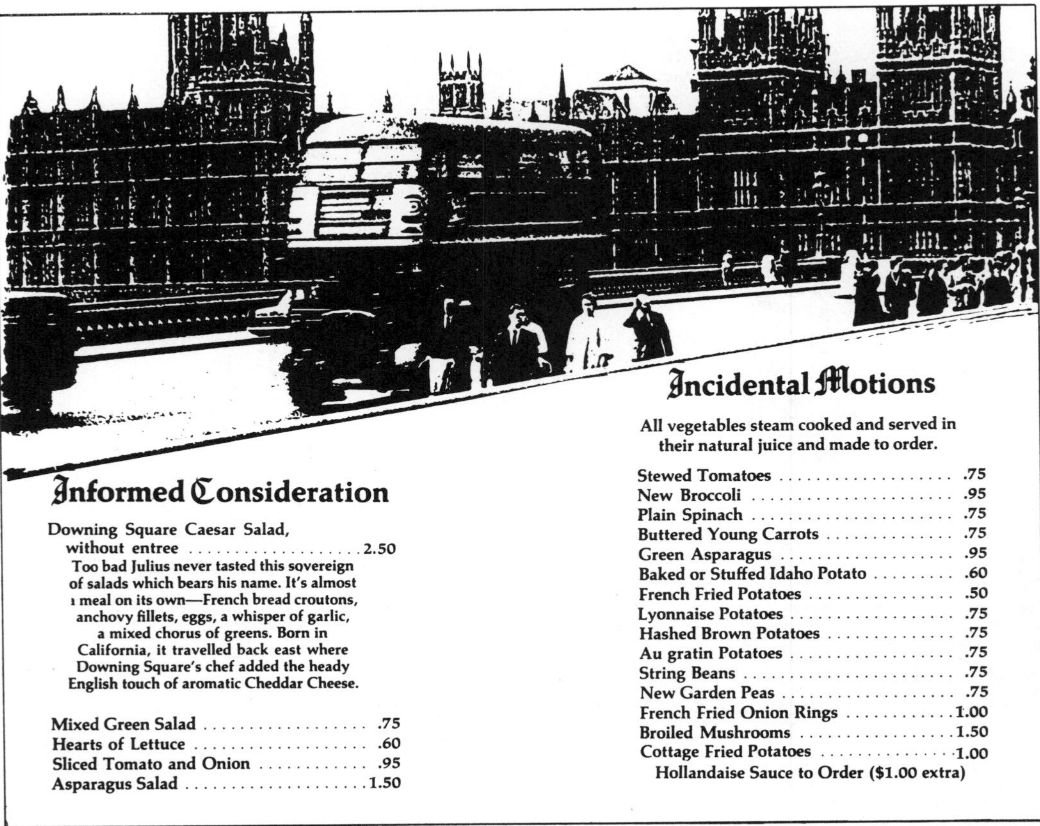

Informed Consideration

Downing Square Caesar Salad, without entree 2.50

Too bad Julius never tasted this sovereign of salads which bears his name. It's almost a meal on its own—French bread croutons, anchovy fillets, eggs, a whisper of garlic, a mixed chorus of greens. Born in California, it travelled back east where Downing Square's chef added the heady English touch of aromatic Cheddar Cheese.

Mixed Green Salad 75
Hearts of Lettuce .60
Sliced Tomato and Onion 95
Asparagus Salad .1.50

Incidental Motions

All vegetables steam cooked and served in their natural juice and made to order.

Stewed Tomatoes .75
New Broccoli 95
Plain Spinach 75
Buttered Young Carrots 75
Green Asparagus .95
Baked or Stuffed Idaho Potato 60
French Fried Potatoes 50
Lyonnaise Potatoes 75
Hashed Brown Potatoes 75
Au gratin Potatoes 75
String Beans 75
New Garden Peas .75
French Fried Onion Rings 1.00
Broiled Mushrooms 1.50
Cottage Fried Potatoes 1.00
Hollandaise Sauce to Order ($1.00 extra)

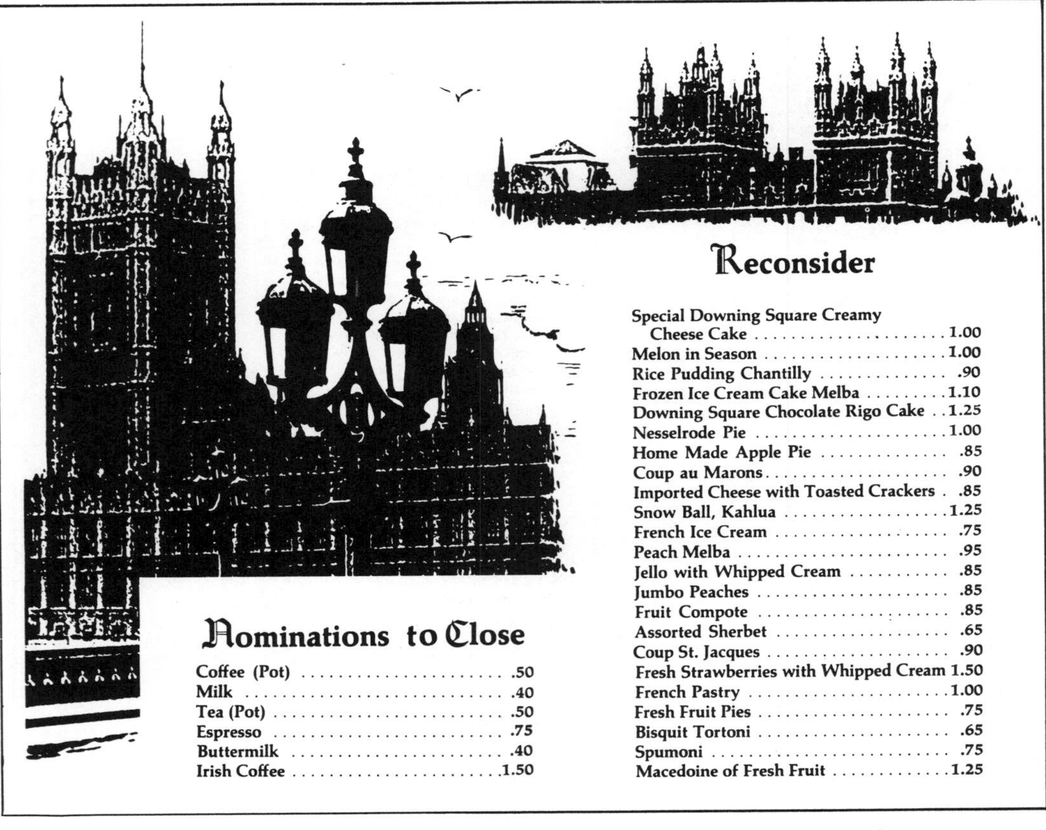

Reconsider

Special Downing Square Creamy Cheese Cake 1.00
Melon in Season .1.00
Rice Pudding Chantilly 90
Frozen Ice Cream Cake Melba 1.10
Downing Square Chocolate Rigo Cake . .1.25
Nesselrode Pie 1.00
Home Made Apple Pie 85
Coup au Marons 90
Imported Cheese with Toasted Crackers . .85
Snow Ball, Kahlua 1.25
French Ice Cream .75
Peach Melba 95
Jello with Whipped Cream 85
Jumbo Peaches 85
Fruit Compote 85
Assorted Sherbet .65
Coup St. Jacques .90
Fresh Strawberries with Whipped Cream 1.50
French Pastry 1.00
Fresh Fruit Pies 75
Bisquit Tortoni 65
Spumoni 75
Macedoine of Fresh Fruit 1.25

Nominations to Close

Coffee (Pot) 50
Milk 40
Tea (Pot) 50
Espresso 75
Buttermilk 40
Irish Coffee 1.50

Theme is carried through to flap on inside of back cover of Downing's *menu.*

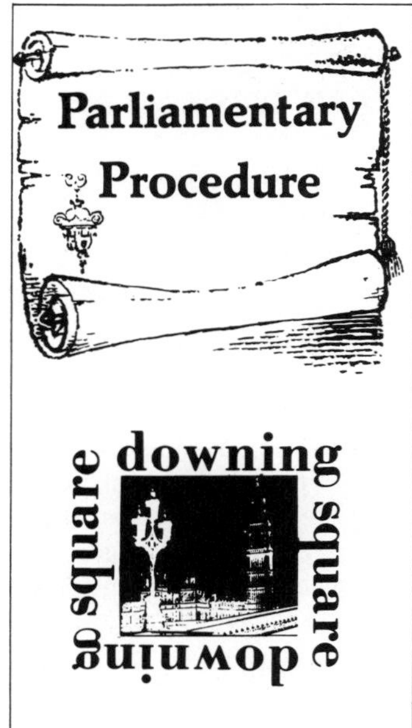

★

MAMMY'S FAMOUS FRIED CHICKEN
Half Fried Disjointed, Delicious, Delectable Milk Fed Chicken, cooked a golden brown with oodles of French Fried Potatoes, Vegetable Salad and Home Made Rolls—ummm
$2.30

★

FRIED JUMBO SHRIMP IN SHORT PANTS
From the clear, blue Atlantic, come our especially Selected Jumbo Shrimp, Batter Dipped and Fried in deep fat, Cocktail Sauce, Cole Slaw, and never-to-be-forgotten Mammy's Hush Puppie
Coffee or Tea
$2.35

★

FRIED OCEAN-FRESH OYSTERS
Rolled in cracker crumbs and fried all succulent and brown created for hungry landlubbers with a sea going air, Cole Slaw, Cocktail Sauce, French Fried Potatoes, and Hush Puppie!
Coffee or Tea
$2.35

★

FRIED FRESH DEEP SEA SCALLOPS
A treat to the palate that sends taste buds soaring! Cole Slaw, Cocktail Sauce, French Fried Potatoes, and Hush Puppie
Coffee or Tea
$2.25

★

FRIED RED SNAPPER STEAK a la MAMMY'S
Caught not too many miles off Daytona at the World's Famous Snapper Banks in the deep Atlantic, served with Cole Slaw, Cocktail Sauce, French Fried Potatoes and Hush Puppie as only we serve them!
Coffee or Tea
$2.95

★

MAMMY'S SEA FOOD PLATTER
For all those who can't make up their minds about our Famous Sea Foods, Fried Jumbo Shrimp, Fried Oysters, Fried Sea Trout, Fried Scallops, French Fried Potatoes and add a Hush Puppie for a true fisherman
Coffee or Tea
$2.60

★

STUFFED TOMATO WITH SHRIMP SALAD
Stuffed Tomato with Shrimp Salad, Hard Boiled Eggs, Potato Chips, Pickles, Saltines
Coffee or Tea
$1.60

★

ICED SHRIMP
Truly a Shrimp Connoisseur's Delight, Tomatoes, Lettuce, Pickles and Sea Food Sauce, Saltines
Coffee or Tea
$1.60

Mammy knows how to cook and write.

OLE!

You'll shout "Ole!" when you first taste this treasure of Early California. Tender chunks of Choice Lamb, Tiny Onions, fresh California Peppers, red Garden Tomatoes and broiled Mountain Mushrooms—all skewered on a sword. Charbroiled to your taste, served over Rice Pilaf with a Crisp Green Salad.

4.25

EL PESCADOR

Large succulent Gulf Shrimp deep fried to a Golden Brown served with TIA MARIA special Sauce. French Fries and a Crisp Green Salad.

2.95

EL TORITO

Chopped Tenderloin of Beef. Served with French Fries and a Crisp Green Salad.

3.25

SENOR TORO

Originally known in Early California as the "Trail-steak" and now famous as the "New York Cut." Subtly seasoned with Spicy Black Peppercorns and lightly brushed with Golden Butter. Charbroiled to your taste over the TIA MARIA hearth. Served with French Fries and a Crisp Green Salad.

5.95

Featuring Spanish or English cuisine, the right words help to sell.

Literary Delights $1.35

freshly ground beef with a variety of trimmings and potatoes — choose your favorite

CHARLES DICKENS—*bacon, tomato and onion make this our favorite; served on an English muffin*

WILLIAM WORDSWORTH—*melted tangy cheese and mushrooms top this specialty*

OLIVER GOLDSMITH—*a plain and juicy burger cooked to perfection; served on a homemade bun—your choice of a bleu or Swiss cheese topping if you desire.*

ROBERT BURNS—*a delightful caper for those young at heart; green pepper, onion and a special sauce with capers*

THE FOLLOWING QUOTES ARE PRESENTED FOR USE ON YOUR MENU TO ADD THE SPICE OF WORDS TO YOUR FOOD & DRINK LISTING

"Oh, herbaceous treat!
'Twould tempt the dying anchorite to eat;
Back to the world he'd turn his fleeting soul;
And plunge his fingers in the salad bowl." *Sidney Smith*

"Beautiful Soup! Who cares for fish,
Game or any other dish?" *Lewis Carroll*

"Of all the things I ever swallow,
Good well-dressed turtle beats them hollow,
It almost makes me wish, I vow,
To have two stomachs, like a cow!" *Thomas Hood*

"Taking food and drink is a great enjoyment for healthy people, and those who do not enjoy eating seldom have much capacity for enjoyment or usefulness of any sort." *Charles W. Eliot*

"Socrates said that the best sauce in the world for meat is to be hungry." *Erasmus*

"Better is a dinner of herbs where love is" than a fatted ox and hatred with it." *Proverbs 15:17*

"When mighty roast beef was the Englishman's food,
It enobled our hearts and enriched our blood,
Our soldiers were brave and our courtiers good.
Oh! The roast beef of old England!"
Richard Leveridge (1670-1758)

"Cookery is the most ancient of the arts, for Adam was born hungry; and the infant, scarcely come into the world, utters cries which the breast of the nurse can only still. It is of all the arts the one that has rendered the most important service to social life; for the necessities of preparing food have taught us how to use fire, and it is by fire that man has subdued nature." *Brillat-Savarin*

"An animal swallows its food; a man eats it, but only a man of intellect knows how to dine."
Brillat-Savarin

"A man who is indifferent to what he swallows, who says that one food is like another is bragging of a defect in himself, not of a virtue. It is like boasting that one has no ear for music, or no eye for color. All of a man's senses are the arts. Remember that every man who has been worth a fig in this world—as poet, painter or musician—has had a good appetite and a good taste." *Thackeray*

"The discovery of a new dish does more for the happiness of mankind than the discovery of a new star." *Brillat- Savarin*

"Dessert without cheese, is like a pretty girl with only one eye." *Brillat- Savarin*

BEN FRANKLIN'S ODE TO WINE (1745)

The Antediluvians were all very sober
For they had no Wine, and they brew'd no October;
All wicked, bad Livers, on Mischief still thinking,
For there can't be good living where there is no good Drinking.

Derry down

'Twas honest old Noah first planted the Vine,
And mended his Morals by drinkings its Wine;
He justly the drinking of Water decry'd;

Derry down

From this Piece of History plainly we find
That Water's good neither for Body or Mind;
That Virtue and Safety in Wine-bibbing's found
While all that drink Water deserve to be drown'd.

Derry down

So for Safety and Honesty put the Glass round.

5

Type selection for a more readable, attractive menu

A study of the correct type face to use is vital to creating a more readable and more attractive restaurant menu. The obvious purpose of a restaurant menu is to communicate the food items served and their prices to the customer; this must be done in words that must be typeset, if not lettered by hand.

It may seem to some that a study of typefaces is a small detail in the operation of a restaurant, but since there is very little verbal communication between the server and the served, as well as a general reluctance to ask questions, written communication becomes very important. Also, a study of thousands of menus has shown many on which the type was too small for easy reading, set too close together (which creates confusion and obstructs readability) and where listings of dinners, appetizers, salads, sandwiches, desserts, and beverages were jammed together in such an illogical manner as to make selection a chore instead of a pleasure.

There are many typefaces to choose from. Your printer will have a type book from which a selection can and should be made. The basic varieties that we will discuss here are Roman, Modern, and Script.

The Roman typefaces are older and are patterned after Roman inscriptions carved on statues. They are a thick-and-thin type with much grace and beauty and are extremely readable. Most books, magazines, and newspapers are set in some version of a Roman style typeface such as Bodoni, Garamond, Caslon, Century Schoolbook, and other variations.

Modern typefaces are newer faces which do not have the thick-thin character of Roman faces. They are cleaner looking without serifs, more regular in shape and, therefore, more Modern looking. Examples of Modern typefaces are Futura, 20th Century, Spartan, and Venus.

Script typefaces are generally an imitation of handwriting or lettering. The free flow of the hand is achieved to a certain extent in these typefaces. Generally speaking, script typefaces should be used for headings and subheads. A continued use of script type becomes hard to read, but an occasional use adds variety and beauty to a menu. Some script faces are Commercial Script, Lydian Cursive, and Brush.

Within the many type faces there are two subdivisions. Almost all type comes in upper and lower case. Upper case are the capitals (A, B, C, D, E). Lower case are lower-case letters (a, b, c, d,

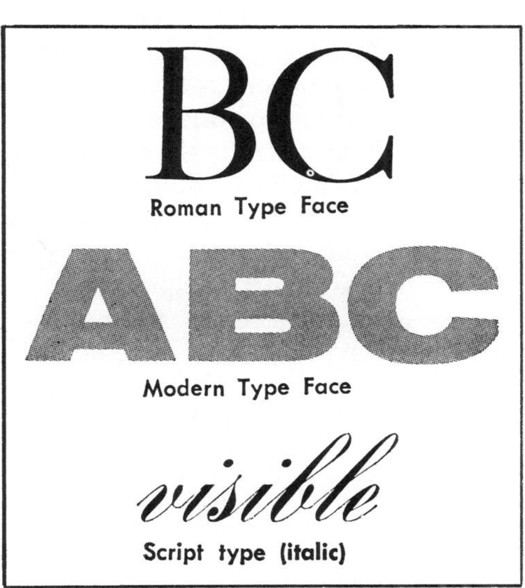

e, f). The important rule for the menu builder to remember is that it is easier to read lower-case type than upper-case. The reason is the irregular appearance that the line of lower-case type presents. This catches the eye as it moves swiftly along in the process of reading.

BODONI REGULAR

36 POINT

ABCDEFGHI
abcdefghijklm

Caps and Lower case

BODONI REGULAR ITALIC

36 POINT

ABCDEFGHI
abcdefghijklm

Caps and Lower case

Evidence of the easier readability of lower case type is the fact that the body copy of books, magazines, and newspapers is always set in lower-case type. This does not mean that upper-case capitals do not have their use. For headings, subheads, and special emphasis, upper-case letters are most effective. They provide a change of pace from the lower-case type and establish categories and breaks in the menu listing which should generally be in lower-case type face. In addition to lower- and upper-case letters, most typefaces have an italic variation. The italic typeface should be used only for accent or special emphasis. It should never be used in large doses because it becomes tiring to the eye and hard to read.

Next, we must consider type sizes. Type is measured by points. Starting usually with 6-pt. type, the size of a particular face will increase in size from 6-pt. on through 8-, 10-, 12-, 14-, 16-, 18-, 24-, 48-, and 72-pt. type. The important consideration for the restaurateur building a menu is never to set any part of the menu smaller than 12-pt. type. Remember that your menu is going to be read by members of the general public who have a great variation in their seeing ability. Generally, older people have trouble reading small type. Also, the person who wears glasses for reading only is reluctant to take out his or her glasses when in a public place such as a restaurant. So, if you want to be considerate of all of your customers, set your menu in large, easy to read type.

The next consideration in the typesetting of your menu is the space between lines or, as it is called in the printing trade, leading. Leading, like type, is measured in points. Type set without any leading between lines is set solid. As a rule of thumb for menu typesetting, 3 points of leading should be the minimum between lines. This gives air or white space around the type so that it is readable and easy on the eye.

SOLID

The main purpose of letters is the practical one
of making thoughts visible. RUSKIN says that "al
l letters are frightful things, and to be endured o
nly upon occasion, that is to say, in places wher
The main purpose of letters is the practical one
of making thoughts visible. Ruskin says that "all
THE MAIN PURPOSE OF LETTERS IS THE PRACTICAL O
THE MAIN PURPOSE OF LETTERS IS TH

Type set solid—no leading.

3 PT. LEADED

The main purpose of letters is the practical one
of making thoughts visible. RUSKIN says that "al
l letters are frightful things, and to be endured o
nly upon occasion, that is to say, in places wher
e the sense of the inscription is of more importa
The main purpose of letters is the practical one
of making thoughts visible. Ruskin says that "all

Same type set with 3 points of leading.

In the discussion so far of type for menus, the emphasis has been on readability, as it should be. Communication is the primary purpose of a menu and any other considerations, such as design, character, or color, while they are important, are secondary to the basic consideration of smooth, easy communication of the message.

Of secondary consideration, however, when selecting type for a menu, should be the style or character of the type. To begin with, you have to consider the character of your restaurant. This should determine the character and appearance of your menu and the styles of type you use. If your restaurant is of modern design—concrete, lots of glass, clean simple lines and decor—then the type for your menu should be modern, set in a clean simple manner to compliment your decor.

If your restaurant has a different character—Old English, Rathskeller, Chinese, Italian, Greek—a typeface should then be considered that will match the character and cuisine. As a rule, with the wide selection of types available, one can be found that will enhance your bill of fare. A word of warning, however—strange, exotic, and unusual types are usually more difficult to read, and, therefore, should be used sparingly. Just as seasoning is used to add flavor to food, unusual type is used to add flavor to a menu. But, as you well know, seasoning must be used with care.

Typesetters, when discussing typefaces, will refer to "color" even when they are talking about black type on white paper. What they are referring to is the weight, lightness, grayness, or open or closed character of the type. Some type is heavy, thick, or very black due to a bold design, while other type is open, light, and airy in character. Selecting type for its character is important for your restaurant menu. If your type is all bold and heavy (shouting in a loud voice) while your restaurant is a quiet, elegant place that caters to the "carriage trade," the result will be a sour note!

Type should usually be printed black on white or light tinted paper (cream, tan, ivory, gray, etc.), but type may be printed in colored ink on white or colored paper. If your type is printed in green, blue, or brown, for example, be sure it is a very dark green, blue, or brown. The rule, again, is readability. Copy printed in a light color on a grey or dark paper will be hard to read. Section headings such as "Sandwiches, Salads, Appetizers, Beverages, Complete Dinners," can very often be printed in a second color from the general black or dark-colored type. As a rule, reverse type (white type on black background) should be avoided.

This discussion on type is, of course, elementary. It is not intended to make the reader a type expert, but it is intended to make the restaurateur aware of the type problems in menu design. For functional, effective menu type design, the services of an expert designer and printer should be employed, especially a printer with an adequate type selection.

To recapitulate, the following are some general rules to follow in selecting type for an effective menu:

*Petit Tenderloin Steak . . . 6.75 6.00

A smaller cut of Filet Mignon broiled and served with mushroom cap.

#22 St. Emilion—$3.50 Paul Masson Gamay Beaujolais—$2.75

*Heavy Steer Sirloin Steak . . 7.75 7.00

Beautifully grained heavy cut sirloin trimmed to perfection broiled with buttered herb sauce.

#27 Pommard-Épenots—$7.00 Almaden Pinot Noir—$3.00

*Delmonico Steak 6.75 6.00

An excellent cut of eye of the rib with its own distinct flavor.

#23 Haut Medoc—$3.25 Paul Masson Burgundy—$2.50

*Chopped Sirloin Steak . . . 4.50 3.75

A large patty of beef ground from our choice cuts, served with butter.

#26 Beaujolais—$3.00 Paul Masson Gamay Beaujolais—$2.75

*Broiled Spring Chicken . . . 4.00 3.40

One half young broiler rubbed with butter and broiled to a golden brown served with currant jelly.

#12 Soave Bolla—$3.00 Paul Mnsson Emerald Dry—$2.50

Breaded Veal Cutlet, Parmesan . 4.75 4.00

A delightfully breaded cutlet fried in butter covered with rich tomato sauce, Parmesan cheese and served in an au gratin dish.

#30 Valpolicella Bolla—$3.00 Almaden Chianti—$2.25

*Broiled Double Lamb Chops . 6.95 6.25

Two thick chops cut from young lamb and served with mint jelly.

#24 St. Julien—$3.75 Almaden Cabernet Sauvignon—$2.75

The old-looking antique type in a nice variation of light and bold fits in with the style, decor, and cuisine of this Colonial style eatery.

1. Do not use a typeface in less than 12-pt. type.
2. Use lower-case type for most of the menu listing for readability.
3. Use upper-case type for heads and subheads.
4. Have at least 3 pts. of leading between lines.
5. Select typefaces that match the character of your restaurant.
6. Use strange, exotic faces sparingly.
7. If the type is in color, be sure it is a dark color.
8. Avoid reverse type.

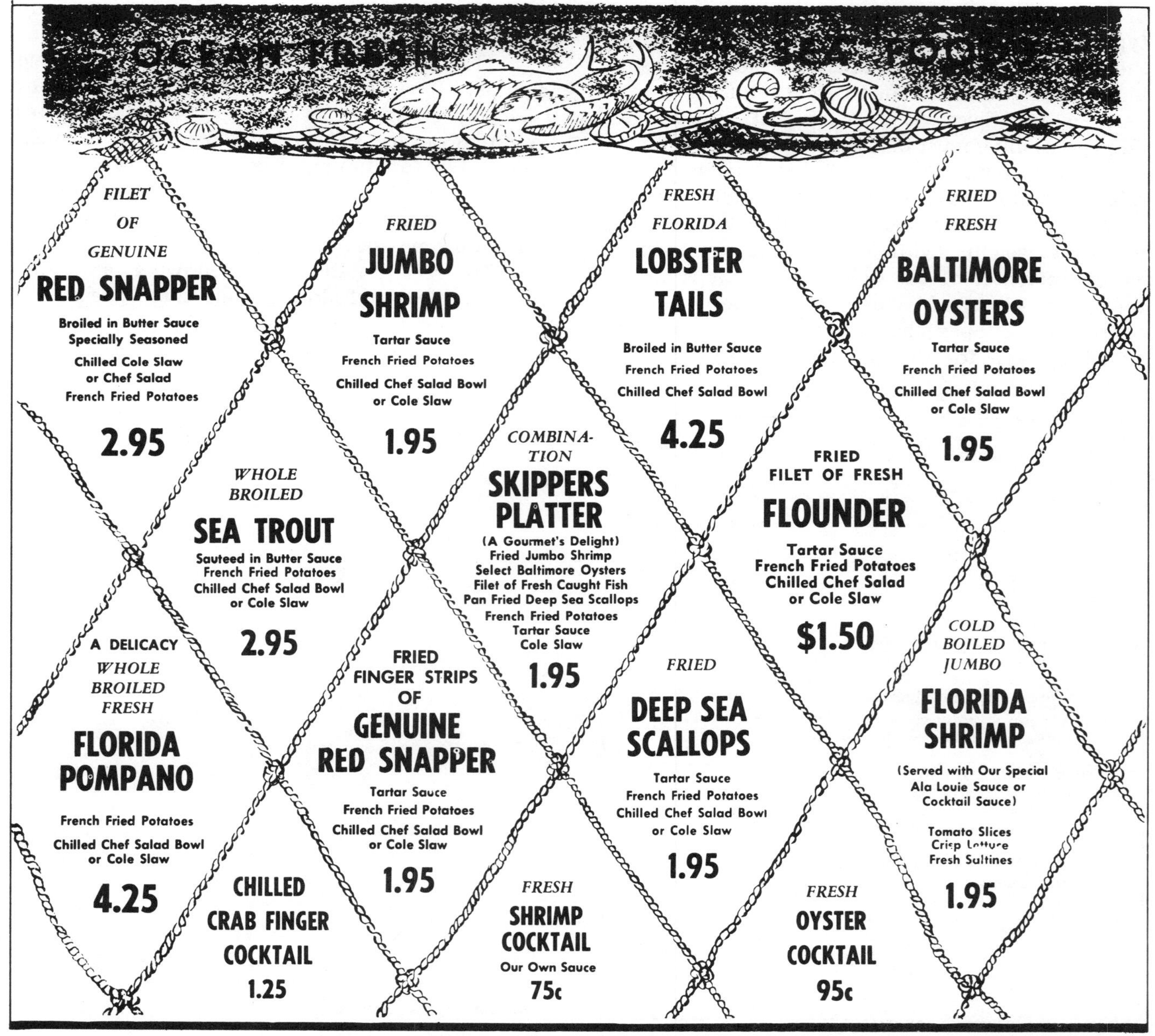

Unusual "special" type listing with appropriate graphics lift the seafood selection out of the ordinary and make it a faster moving entree.

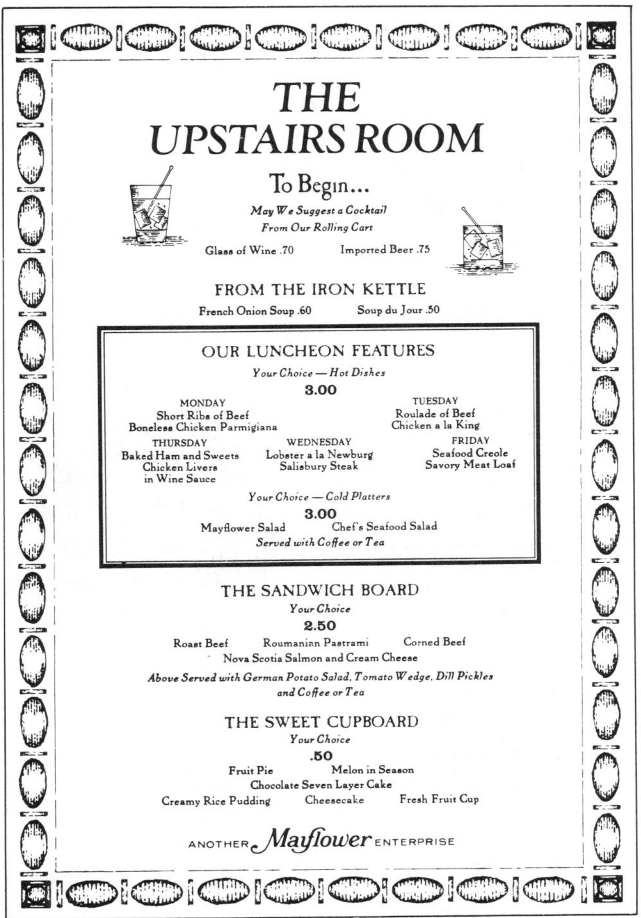

THE UPSTAIRS ROOM

To Begin...

May We Suggest a Cocktail
From Our Rolling Cart

Glass of Wine .70 Imported Beer .75

FROM THE IRON KETTLE

French Onion Soup .60 Soup du Jour .50

OUR LUNCHEON FEATURES

Your Choice — Hot Dishes

3.00

MONDAY
Short Ribs of Beef
Boneless Chicken Parmigiana

TUESDAY
Roulade of Beef
Chicken a la King

THURSDAY
Baked Ham and Sweets
Chicken Livers in Wine Sauce

WEDNESDAY
Lobster a la Newburg
Salisbury Steak

FRIDAY
Seafood Creole
Savory Meat Loaf

Your Choice — Cold Platters

3.00

Mayflower Salad Chef's Seafood Salad

Served with Coffee or Tea

THE SANDWICH BOARD

Your Choice

2.50

Roast Beef Roumanian Pastrami Corned Beef
Nova Scotia Salmon and Cream Cheese

Above Served with German Potato Salad, Tomato Wedge, Dill Pickles and Coffee or Tea

THE SWEET CUPBOARD

Your Choice

.50

Fruit Pie Melon in Season
Chocolate Seven Layer Cake
Creamy Rice Pudding Cheesecake Fresh Fruit Cup

ANOTHER *Mayflower* ENTERPRISE

Type selection and decorative border compliment each other.

The type selection indicated a German menu.

FIVE COURSE DINNERS INCLUDE - Relish plate, soup or juice, salad and choice of dressing, bread and butter, coffee or tea, dessert:

1. **Sauerbraten** - Tender Cut of Beef - marinated at least 48 hours - roasted and served with a deliciously different sauce and potato dumplings. $3.50

2. **Wienerschnitzel** - Choice Veal breaded with farm fresh eggs and cracker meal, sauteed to a rich golden brown. $3.55

3. **Knackwurst** - Spicy Beef Sausage - country style served with our special German style sauerkraut and choice of potatoes. $3.35

4. **Bratwurst** - A Delicious Sausage served hot off the grill (one part pork two parts veal) served with our special German style sauerkraut and choice of potatoes. $3.35

5. **Kasseler Rippchen** - Truly different Smoked Pork Chops served with our special German sauerkraut & choice of potatoes $3.45

6. **Pilsner Huhn** - Half of a Golden-brown Caponette dipped in our unique batter served with spicy beets & choice of potatoes. $3.25

7. **Shrimp** - Large Dinner Shrimp - golden brown in special batter with cocktail sauce and choice of potatoes. $3.25

8. **Steak** - Filet Mignon 8 ounce - bacon wrapped - garnished with onion rings and served with choice of potatoes. $4.50

9. **Rind Rouladen** - FRIDAY & SATURDAY ONLY - Rolled and Stuffed Top Round braised in its own gravy Bavarian style - served with choice of potatoes and sweet-sour red cabbage. $3.45

CHILDRENS PORTIONS (under 12 years) - $2.00

APPETIZERS • SIDE ORDERS • ALA CARTE

1. Shrimp Cocktail - 85¢
2. Onion Rings - 45¢
3. Herring-Creamed (marinated) - 85¢
4. Clam Chowder Friday Only - 90¢

SANDWICHES

BARB BURGER 1.65
An original Barb Creation . . . a grilled double deck sandwich on rye, choice ground beef with sauted onions and sharp Cheddar cheese, French fries, tossed green salad.

SPECIAL DELUXE HAMBURGER 1.30
Served on toasted bun with relish, tomato, lettuce, French fries and tossed green salad.

CHEESEBURGER 1.05
Served open-faced with relish, tomato and lettuce. Onion if desired.

HAMBURGER .95
Served open-faced with relish, tomato and lettuce. Onion if desired.

CHEESE 'N FRUIT 1.25
Grilled cheese sandwich, a nest of chilled fruits, honey lime dressing.

GRILLED CHEESE .80

HOT ROAST BEEF SANDWICH 1.95
Open-face sandwich served with potato; Barb-Q sauce or brown gravy and tossed green salad.

HOT TURKEY SANDWICH 1.95
Open-face sandwich served with turkey dressing, potato, cranberry sauce, giblet gravy and tossed green salad.

RUEBEN SANDWICH 1.85
Grilled double-deck sandwich on rye with Swiss cheese, corned beef and sauerkraut, tossed salad.

KOSHER CORNED BEEF SANDWICH ON RYE 1.75
Served with tossed green salad and French fries.

CLUB HOUSE SANDWICH 1.95
Served with potato salad.

DUNGENESS CRAB SANDWICH 1.95
Fresh crab meat with melted cheese, served on toasted English muffin with tossed green salad or cole slaw.

SPECIAL TREAT HAMBURGER 1.65
Our own choice chopped sirloin, fresh daily, served on crusty French bread with Barb-Q dip or au jus, French fries and tossed green salad.

OUR FAMOUS

FISH'N CHIPS

Dipped in our special batter, French fries, tartar sauce, cole slaw or tossed salad.
1.50

LOW CALORIE PLATE 1.55
Broiled chopped sirloin patty with cottage cheese, peach slices and Melba toast.

SPAGHETTI ITALIANE 1.75
Featuring the Barb's popular meat sauce, combination green salad with garlic bread.

HAM or BACON & EGGS 1.85
Served with hash brown potatoes, toast and jelly.

OUR POPULAR

DIP SANDWICHES

BEEF DIP 1.45

BREAST OF TURKEY 1.45

PREMIUM HAM 1.45

The above sandwiches are served on hot French bread with Barb-Q dip or au jus. Choice of tossed green salad, cole slaw or French fries.

SALADS

CRAB OR SHRIMP LOUIE 2.85
Small Order 2.50
Choice Dungeness crab or Alaskan shrimp on crisp shredded lettuce, tastefully garnished with sliced tomato, hard-boiled egg and ripe olives, Thousand Island dressing.

CHEF'S SALAD 1.85
Julienne of ham, turkey and cheese, served on crisp tossed salad, garnished with egg, tomato, olives and your favorite dressing.

BARB'S MIXED GREEN SALAD 1.35
Small Order 1.05
Special chef's dressing topped with bacon and Parmesan cheese.

BROILED STEAKS

Includes tossed green salad, choice of dressings, choice of potato or spahetti, hot French bread.

U.S.D.A. CHOICE TOP SIRLOIN STEAK 2.95
"Tender and Juicy"

U.S.D.A. CHOICE NEW YORK STEAK 3.95
"Cattlemen's Favorite"

CHOPPED SIRLOIN STEAK 2.45
Choice lean ground beef—excellent RARE.

U.S.D.A. CHOICE TOP SIRLOIN STEAK SANDWICH 2.45
Served on toast, tossed green salad, choice of dressing and French fries.

When ordering please indicate your preference:
RARE — Dark red inside
MEDIUM RARE — Light red inside
MEDIUM — Pink inside
WELL DONE — Brown inside
(It breaks our heart to do it!)

CHILDREN'S MENU

UNDER 12

SPAGHETTI 1.15
Includes Salad and Hot French Bread.

FISH and CHIPS 1.15
With Salad.

COMPLETE DINNERS
Includes French Fries, Tossed Green Salad, Choice of Beverage and Dessert.

TURKEY 1.75

GROUND SIRLOIN 1.55

SIRLOIN OF BEEF 1.85

APPETIZERS

Crab or Shrimp Cocktail Supreme 1.85

Dinner Size Crab or Shrimp Cocktail .95

SOUP OF THE DAY
BOWL .35 CUP .25

POPULAR DINNERS

Our dinners are served with chef-made soup or tossed green salad with choice of dressing, choice of potato or spahetti Italiane, hot French bread.

SPARERIBS 3.75
Western style Barb-Q spareribs with our delicious tangy Barb-Q sauce.

ROAST SIRLOIN OF BEEF 2.95
The heart of roast, expertly seasoned, served with natural juices.

ROAST BREAST OF TURKEY 2.95
A traditional holiday feast that is a year-round favorite.

GULF PRAWNS 2.95
Dipped in our special batter, deep fried to the peak of their natural flavor.

QUILCENE OYSTERS 2.95
Direct from the cool waters of Quilcene Bay, prepared to a delicious golden brown.

DEEP FRIED EASTERN SCALLOPS 2.95
Dipped in our special batter, deep fried to a golden brown.

CAPTAIN'S PLATE 3.75
Combination of shrimp, scallops, halibut and oysters. A perfect assortment for seafood lovers.

Type and graphics go together exceptionally well on this menu. Notice that items are listed in large, bold caps while descriptive copy is in lower-case type.

A La Carte Dining

Continued

FRIAR TUCK'S CORNISH HEN
WILD RICE, BLACK CHERRY SAUCE
3.25

BROILED PORK CHOPS
Two center cut chops chosen from tender young stock. Applesauce.
3.75

LAMB CHOPS
(TWO EXTRA THICK CENTER CUT)
Tender young spring lamb chops done to just the right turn; garnished with mint jelly and all dressed-up in the latest of French "panties"
4.25

VEAL SCALLOPINI, MARSALA
Cutlet of milk fed veal and fresh mushrooms with our own special sauce
3.50

BROILED FLORIDA LOBSTER
Large "Select" Lobster, stuffed with our special dressing, and served with hot drawn butter.
4.50

BROILED
FILET OF RED SNAPPER
Freshly caught in the Gulf of Mexico, with Almandine or Lemon Butter
3.95

MEDIEVAL
MORSELS OF THE SEA
A creation of Fresh Florida Seafood, including Scallops, Oysters, Shrimp, Deviled Crab Patties, plus Half Broiled Lobster. Your choice of Cocktail or Romoulade Sauce.
4.95

BOUNTIFUL RELISH TRAY, SALAD, VEGETABLE, POTATO, HOT ROLLS, BUTTER AND BEVERAGE ARE SERVED WITH ENTREE.

Specialties of Our Master Chef

A La Carte Dining

Headings should be bolder and in a different typeface (or hand lettering) from the descriptive or listing copy.

Roast Long Island Duckling a la Orange (½ Duck) **$4.25**
Always crisp. Our duck is considered by many to be the finest available, served either with a flavorful orange sauce or a tasty brown gravy.
Recommended wine: #12 Neumagener "Moselle" or #42 Beaujolais

Baby Beef Liver **$3.25**
(Served either with fried onions or crisp bacon slices) Long famous here at the Inn due to the extra care we take in the selection and preparation of this delicacy.
Recommended wines: #43 Fleurie or #33 Tavel Rose

Sauerbraten and Spatztles **$3.50**
A German pot roast of beef marinated in wine and spices for several days. The marinade, our own recipe, adds a deliciously different flavor to the roast. Served only on Wednesdays and Saturdays, this savory treat is delightfully complimented by the Spatzles and Red Cabbage.
Recommended wine: #12 Neumagener "Moselle" or #42 Beaujolais

The Couplet **$6.75**
Filet Mignon coupled with South African Lobster Tail provide a new taste sensation.
Recommended wine: #13 Schloss Vollards or #43 Fleurie

Crabmeat Au Gratin **$5.00**
Fresh backfin crabmeat is embraced by our own cheese sauce. A delectable treat you will enjoy.
Recommended wine: #27 Pouilly Fuisse or #33 Tavel Rose

Broiled Seafood Combination **$6.00**
Lobster Tail, Trout, Jumbo Shrimp, Scallops and Haddock, broiled to perfection.
Recommended wine: #26 Montrachet

Benetz Inn Stuffed Shrimp **$3.75**
Jumbo shrimp stuffed with our famous deviled crab stuffing.
Recommended wine: #32 Mateus or #23 Chablis

This is clean, simple sans-serif type, but the heavy, bold type of the name and price of the entree stand out well from the descriptive copy which is still large enough to be read with ease.

6

The menu is a piece of paper

Your menu will last longer and look better if you take the time to select a good, suitable paper. The design of a menu should begin with the selection of the paper on which it will be printed because paper is as integral to creating good design and, thereby, an effective menu as copy, typography, and art. Also, since paper represents about one-third of the printing cost of a menu (exclusive of art and copy), the selection of the paper (or papers) on which a menu is printed is well worth the consideration of all parties concerned in menu design—the designer, typographer, printer, and food service operator.

What is paper? One answer may be that paper is the ideal printing surface, and, of course, nearly all menus are printed on some kind of paper. Papers (up until the modern industrial revolution) were made almost completely by hand from rags. With the invention of machinery and with the development of chemistry, modern papermaking processes were developed. Most modern papers used at present for printing purposes are machine-made from wood pulp.

For the restaurateur, there are two basic approaches to the selection of paper for the menu. This paper selection depends upon how the menu is used or whether immediate obsolescence or maximum permanence is desired.

For a menu that changes every day, it is obvious that immediate obsolescence is the criterion. This menu can be printed on a lighter weight, noncoated stock since it is going to be printed, used only one day, and then thrown away. A light, inexpensive paper stock, however, can still have color, texture, and good tactile qualities that will enhance the design of the menu. No concern, however, need be given on this type of menu for resistance to stain, handling, and rough usage since it is practically a throw-away item comparable to the daily newspaper. In fact, some menus of this type have been printed on newsprint.

The second basic paper approach to the menu is the one designed for maximum permanence. This type of menu is usually printed on a heavy, durable, coated paper that will last a long time despite much handling by the customer. It should probably be on a water-resistant paper that can be wiped clean with a damp cloth. This type of paper is usually a heavy Cover, Bristol, or Tag stock that is coated or treated with clay, pigment, varnish, or plastic. This coating makes the paper water- and grease-resistant and gives it a longer life, even with constant customer handling.

Compromise Solutions That Work

There are variations or combinations, of course, to these two approaches. A menu does not have to be printed entirely on the same kind of paper. A common solution to the immediate versus the permanent menu problem is to design the cover of the menu on heavy, coated stock while the inside pages are of lighter, less permanent (and less expensive) paper. This type of paper selection can be tailored to fit the permanent and the daily items on the menu.

The permanent items on the menu—usually beverages, sandwiches, salads, specials of the house, etc., will be on the heavy-paper part of the menu, while the special daily menu will be on an insert or insert pages which will be on lighter paper.

The use of different kinds of paper in the same menu can serve a design and functional purpose, also. Papers of different texture, thickness, and color can emphasize a particular part of the bill of fare that the restaurateur wishes to give an extra sales push.

Selecting the right paper for the menu is a no

less complicated problem than selecting the right silverware, dishwasher, or china to be used in a restaurant. First, there are the physical and esthetic qualities of paper such as strength, dimensional stability, opacity, ink receptivity, smoothness, and whiteness. Then, there is texture. Paper comes in textures varying from very coarse to the most smooth. Considering that the menu is held in the customer's hand, as well as read, the texture or "feel" of a menu can be important.

Color can be added to the menu through the use of paper that comes in the purest white, through the softest pastels, to the richest solids. It can, too often, become the habit to think of color as something added to white paper via printing when color can be in the paper as well as in the ink.

Some of the printing and design techniques that can be used in connection with paper and menu design are listed here:

1. Opaque and transparent inks on colored and white paper
2. Embossing
3. Light inks on dark paper
4. Tints and metallics on tinted paper
5. Three-dimensional use of paper
6. Printing on transparent (cellophane) or semi-transparent stock
7. Textural, tactile, and other sensorial effects
8. Varieties of paper within the same menu

Printing Process Determines Paper

The printing process also dictates the kind of paper to be used in successful menu design, although the quality of the paper itself will largely determine the success of the finished product. Most menus are printed by letterpress or offset lithography methods of printing or by a combination of the two. Menu covers are usually printed by the offset lithography method, while the inside listings are usually printed letterpress since the type can be left standing, and day-to-day changes can be made in prices and the bill of fare without making new plates.

For the selection of paper for these two printing processes, the following characteristics should be taken into consideration:

LETTERPRESS—

1. Type and line cuts bite into paper.
2. Almost any paper is suitable for type and line printing surfaces.
3. Hairlines will increase in weight materially.
4. Halftones require smooth, plate-finished, or coated papers.

OFFSET LITHOGRAPHY—

1. The process allows for greater latitude in paper selection and printing.
2. There is no impression or bite into the paper.
3. There is enough flexibility or give to compensate for textured surfaces.

In addition, paper can be folded in many different ways to create interesting configurations, and paper can be die-cut into unusual shapes other than the conventional square or rectangular form most used. These two characteristics of paper—foldability and the fact that it can be cut into almost any shape—should be used to advantage to create interesting menu design.

In conclusion, it must be repeated again that paper is important to the success of a good menu. For the restaurateur, it is vital to have the printer or designer show a variety of papers for selection. The right paper will do a better job and do it for less money. Make paper part of the operation's menu picture.

BASIC PAPER DEFINITIONS

Antique paper — paper with a rough, textured surface.

Bond — paper for letterheads, forms, and business uses.

Book paper — papers having characteristics suitable for books, magazines, brochures, etc.

Bristol — cardboard of .006 of an inch or more in thickness (index, mill, and wedding are types of bristol)

Coated — paper and paperboard whose surface has been treated with clay or some other pigment.

Cover stock — a variety of papers used for outside covers of menus, catalogs, booklets, magazines, etc.

Deckle edge — a rough-edge paper formed by pulp flowing against the frame (deckle) providing a feathered, uneven edge when paper is left untrimmed.

Dull-coated — paper with a low gloss coated surface.

Eggshell — a semi-rough surface paper similar to the surface texture of an egg.

Enameled — any coated paper.

English finish — book paper with a machine finish and uniform surface.

Grain — a weakness along one dimension of the paper—folding of papers should be with the grain.

Machine finish — book paper with a medium finish—rougher than English finish but smoother than eggshell.

Offset paper — coated or uncoated paper suitable for offset lithography printing.

Vellum finish — similar to eggshell but from harder stock with a finer grained surface.

A great deal can be done with paper. This unusual fold treatment uses paper of different size for each page of the menu. Folded over, it allows the customer to lift up and look at each panel or page. Also, each page is identified with a heading at the bottom—appetizers, supreme soups, gourmet salads—for easy identification when the menu is closed.

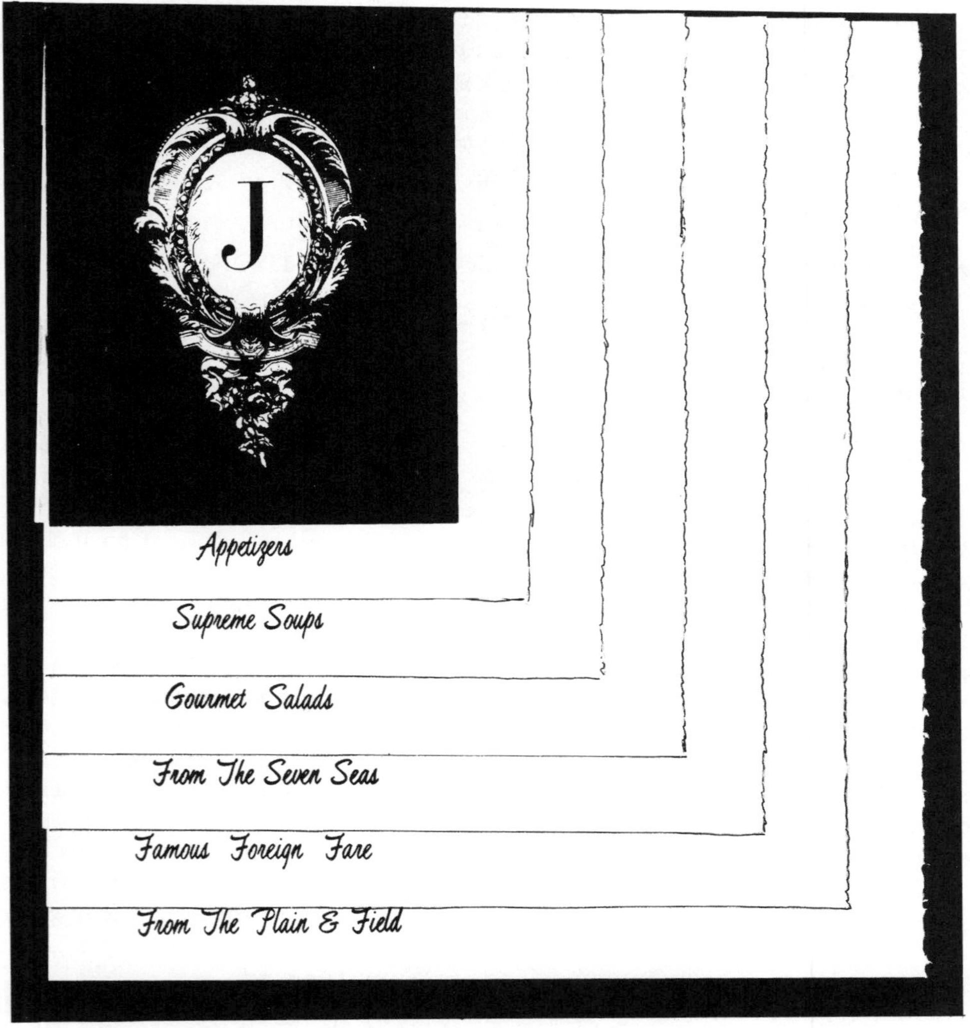

7

For a more creative menu

Most food service operators will admit the importance of creativity in the success of a food service business, that is, creativity in the selection, preparation, and serving of foods and drinks, and in the decor, general appearance, and operation of the establishment. Equal in importance, the menu itself, in appearance, design, and style, can be more creative to attract attention, create comment, and increase business. Following are some creative suggestions to help stimulate your imagination. Some of the ideas are taken from interesting, creative menus, and some are just "top of the head" ideas.

First, let's consider what your menu is printed on. Most often it is paper of varying kinds and quality. Menus do not have to be printed on paper, however; they have successfully been printed on cloth, plastic, and even wood. For example, some restaurants print (silk screen) their menu on a wooden board shaped like a bread board with a hole for hanging on the wall. This is expensive, of course, but the restaurant usually sells the menu as a souvenir. In fact, one restaurant operator with this type of menu is supposed to have made more money out of selling his menu than selling food and drink!

One type of printing surface that would seem to me a "natural" for a Steak House or a restaurant featuring wild game would be a menu printed on real or imitation leather so that it looked like animal skin. This could be die-cut as shown in Figure 1.

Paper itself, of course, comes in many varieties, sizes, textures, colors, etc. Most menus do not take advantage of the many kinds and colors of papers available. For example, a menu consisting of a four-page cover, a four-page insert and an additional four-page smaller insert as shown in Figure 2, can be put together from three different papers of three different colors and textures to create an interesting, "creative" effect.

An interesting combination of menu and decor is to use wallpaper for the cover of your menu if you have an interesting paper on the walls of your establishment.

Since most menus are printed on paper, consideration should be given to the ways paper can be used. First, paper can be folded, and second, paper can be die-cut into various shapes and configura-

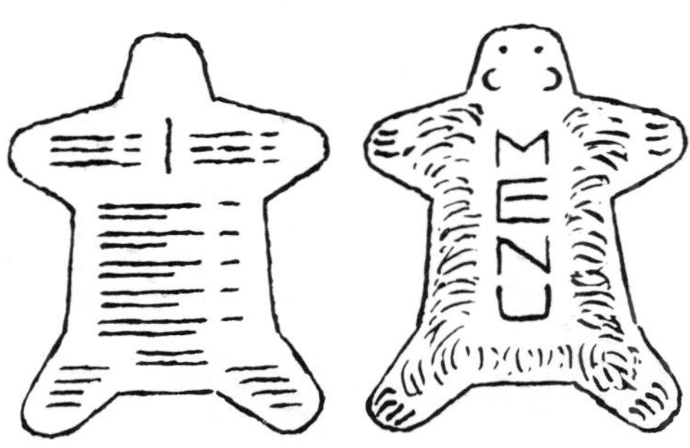

FIGURE 1

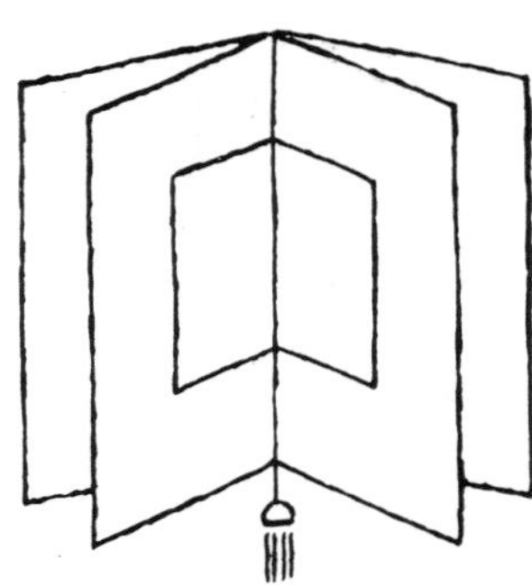

FIGURE 2

tions. First, let us consider folding, because too many food service operators, printers, and designers take the easy way out and just take a piece of paper, fold it in half, and there is their menu. But there are other ways.

A piece of paper can be folded to look like a napkin. A very simple way is to take a square piece of paper, fold it twice from corner to corner, and you have a menu that looks like a napkin (see Figure 3).

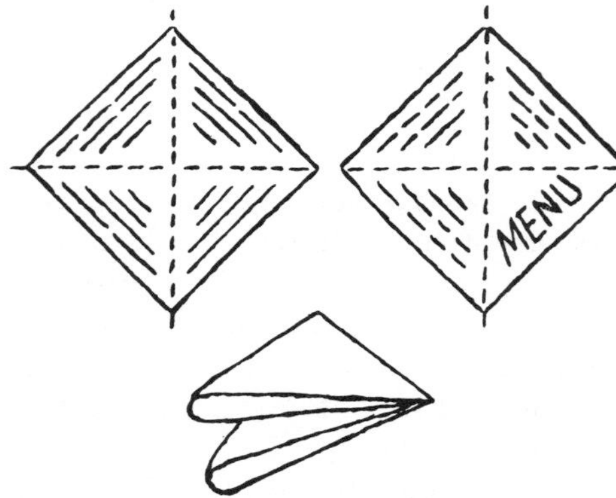

FIGURE 3

Another simple fold that can be used with a menu is shown in Figure 4.

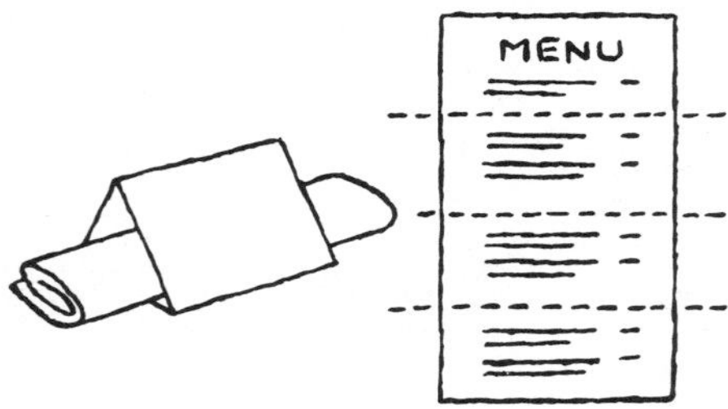

FIGURE 4

This menu is just a long piece of paper folded three times into the shape of a triangular tent and then the napkin is placed inside to hold it down securely. Another interesting way to fold a piece of paper for a menu is to fold it unevenly into different sized panels as shown in Figure 5.

This menu has five panels and four folds. Panel 3 is the largest, panels 2 and 4 are smaller and of the same size, and panels 1 and 5 are the smallest and also of the same size. The menu folds up "accordion" style.

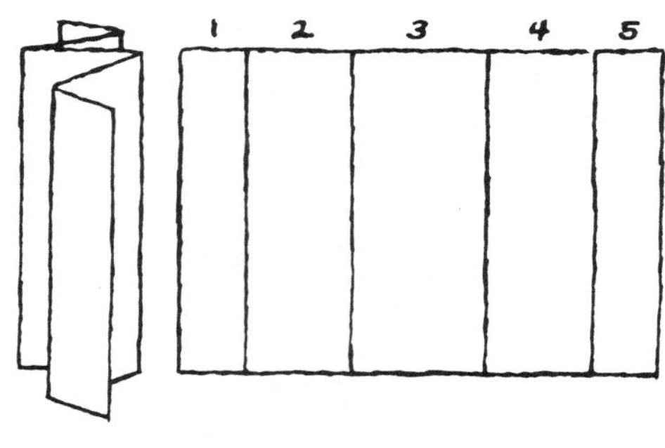

FIGURE 5

A simple irregular fold used by some restaurants is a good method for visualizing the index for a large menu, by folding each insert in the menu a little off center as shown in Figure 6.

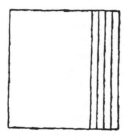

FIGURE 6

A word of caution is in order on the subject of folding paper for a menu. All paper does not fold well, even when scored. Certain papers crack when folded, leaving a ragged, unsightly edge and one that will soon wear out and cut down on the life of a menu. Check the "foldability" of your paper before the printer prints up 10,000 menus!

The second characteristic of paper is that it can be cut into various shapes—geometric, squares, circles, triangles, octagons, as well as irregular shapes. Among examples of varied shapes used successfully are Pancake House menus which are printed on a round sheet that corresponds to the

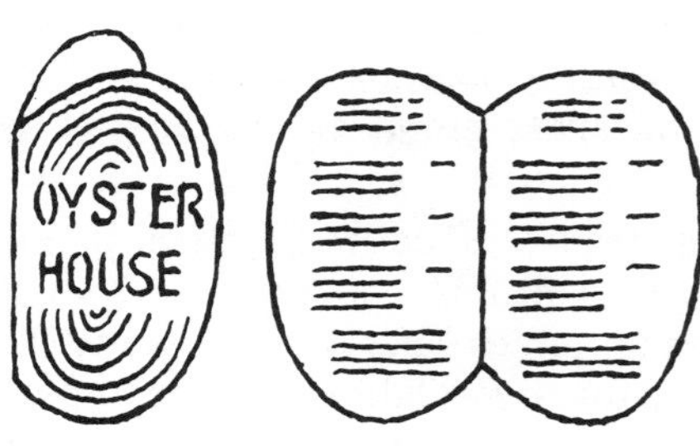

FIGURE 7

shape of a pancake. Steak Houses have printed menus in the shape of steaks and an Oyster House has printed a menu in the shape of an oyster (see Figure 7).

A die-cut menu is, of course, more expensive, but once you have paid for the original die, it is yours and at a one-time cost only.

A few dining rooms print their menu in the form of a newspaper. This is an idea that can be expanded. In addition to a newspaper format, why not a magazine format? The idea is to give more information than just the listing of the food and drink served. The menu becomes a merchandising-advertising vehicle. If your restaurant is in a theater district, theater news printed in a newspaper-magazine format menu is a good idea. Or, if your operation is in a financial district, financial or stock-market news makes good editorial copy.

The problem with this kind of menu is that it usually takes professional journalistic personnel to write it and keep it current, and if it contains changing up-to-date information, the menu must be printed anew fairly often—daily, weekly, or monthly. But many food service operations do have a daily or weekly menu anyhow, so this is not an unusual problem.

Another menu possibility is the three-dimensional menu. A menu need not be a flat, two-dimensional piece of paper. It can be in the form of a cube, pyramid, etc., as shown in Figure 8.

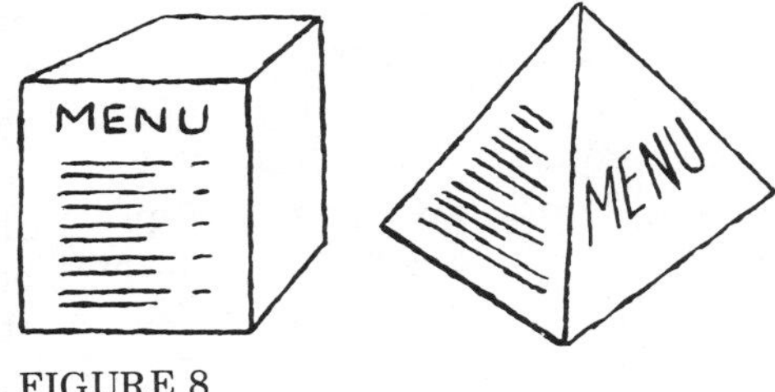

FIGURE 8

This kind of menu would sit in the center of the table. An especially appropriate use of a three-dimensional menu is a three-dimensional Wine List using the actual bottle of wine as shown in Figure 9.

Finally, let's look at some really "way-out" menu ideas. How about a "Gambler's Menu," not really encouraging gambling for money or profit, however. This type of gambling would just be taking a chance on which menu entree to order. This menu could have a dial that could be spun around until it stopped at a number which would correspond to a numbered entree (Figure 10).

Another unusual kind of menu would be a "Dial an Entree" type of menu. This menu would be printed on a circular dial which could be rotated from a central pivot and menu items "selected" one at a time. Figure 11 shows how this menu would be designed. Menu items, entrees, appetizers, desserts, etc., would be printed on both sides of the circular dial.

FIGURE 9

FIGURE 10

FIGURE 11

From just ideas for menus let's turn to some actual creative menus. First, let's look at the *Paparazzi* crepe menu. It is creative in several ways. To begin with, it has an unusual fold and shape. It begins as a rectangle. Then when four

1

2

3

4

folds are "unfolded," we have a round menu—just like a crepe.

This menu is an "extra" menu, in addition to *Paparazzi*'s regular menu, and, of course, it gives extra *sell* to these items. A total of 39 entree crepes are listed (also numbered) plus six dessert crepes. They sell their crepes with the following copy:

> "We hate to blow our own horn BUT . . . It's probably safe to say we have the best crepes, fillings, and crepemaker in New York. No wait! Why not go all the way? Yes, *Paparazzi* has the best crepes in the whole country! The secret is in our special buckwheat batter cooked lovingly by our own Crepetiere on oval griddles especially designed for this type of crepe. Try them and you'll agree!"

Houligans is a wild, different, and creative menu. It is a large menu—measuring 17″ × 22″ when open. The cover is done in four colors and in a clever, cartoon style. Inside the cartoon, hand-lettering style is continued. The menu folds in the middle, and on one side is the luncheon listing, on the other is the dinner listing.

This menu looks disorganized, but it isn't. Ordering is easy. The copy is also clever and interesting including: Garbage Salad, Antifatso Salad, Houligan Stew, and Teetotalers—soft drinks, coffee, milk, tea, and chocolate.

Skoby's World has a menu that is creative in several ways—a creativity that reflects the restaurant itself. To begin with, as the menu says, *Skoby's World* truly is more than a restaurant! Affectionately called "A Department Store of Dining Rooms," you are invited to browse through and sample its authentically imaginative decor and atmosphere. The "department stores" are: The General Store, The Orient, The Butcher Shop, The Galley, and The Mid-Day Muncherie.

The food offerings are also different. Under the entrees for example, there are "Platemates," which the diner can combine such as: Lobster Tail, Fillet of Red Snapper, Ham Steakette, Deep Fried Jumbo Shrimp, and Filet Mignon Steak. Any two of these, served for one person, is priced at $9.95; and any three of these, served for one person, is priced at $10.95.

The *Skoby's World* menu also sells steak in the following manner:

Cover

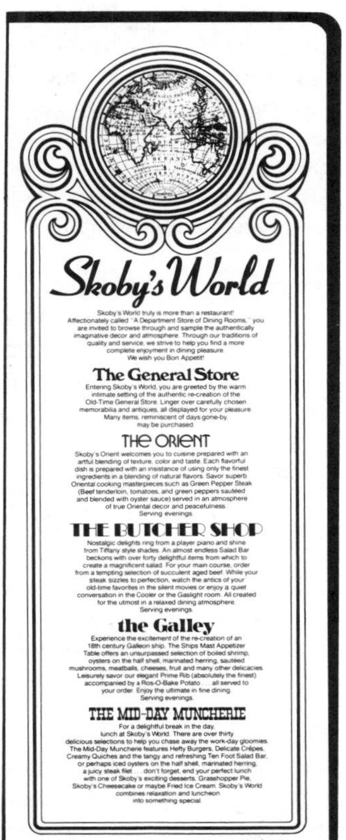

Skoby's World

Skoby's World truly is more than a restaurant! Affectionately called "A Department Store of Dining Rooms," you are invited to browse through and sample the authentically imaginative decor and atmosphere. Through our traditions of quality and service, we strive to help you find a more complete enjoyment in dining pleasure.
We wish you Bon Appetit!

The General Store

Entering Skoby's World, you are greeted by the warm intimate setting of the authentic re-creation of the Old-Time General Store. Linger over carefully chosen memorabilia and antiques, all displayed for your pleasure. Many items, reminiscent of days gone-by, may be purchased.

THE ORIENT

Skoby's Orient welcomes you to cuisine prepared with an artful blending of texture, color and taste. Each flavorful dish is prepared with an insistance of using only the finest ingredients in a blending of natural flavors. Savor superb Oriental cooking masterpieces such as Green Pepper Steak (Beef tenderloin, tomatoes, and green peppers sauteed and blended with oyster sauce) served in an atmosphere of true Oriental decor and peacefulness.
Serving evenings.

THE BUTCHER SHOP

Nostalgic delights ring from a player piano and shine from Tiffany style shades. An almost endless Salad Bar beckons with over forty delightful items from which to create a magnificent salad. For your main course, order from a tempting selection of succulent aged beef. While your steak sizzles to perfection, watch the antics of your old-time favorites in the silent movies or enjoy a quiet conversation in the Cooler or the Gaslight room. All created for the utmost in a relaxed dining atmosphere.
Serving evenings.

the Galley

Experience the excitement of the re-creation of an 18th century Galleon ship. The Ships Mast Appetizer Table offers an unsurpassed selection of boiled shrimp, oysters on the half shell, marinated herring, sauteed mushrooms, meatballs, cheeses, fruit and many other delicacies. Leisurely savor our elegant Prime Rib (absolutely the finest) accompanied by a Ros-O-Bake Potato . . . all served to your order. Enjoy the ultimate in fine dining.
Serving evenings.

THE MID-DAY MUNCHERIE

For a delightful break in the day, lunch at Skoby's World. There are over thirty delicious selections to help you chase away the work-day gloomies. The Mid-Day Muncherie features Hefty Burgers, Delicate Crêpes, Creamy Quiches and the tangy and refreshing Ten Foot Salad Bar, or perhaps iced oysters on the half shell, marinated herring, a juicy steak filet . . . don't forget, end your perfect lunch with one of Skoby's exciting desserts, Grasshopper Pie, Skoby's Cheesecake or maybe Fried Ice Cream. Skoby's World combines relaxation and luncheon into something special.

From steak by the ounce to fried ice cream. Skoby's World *presents an imaginative bill-of-fare.*

Inside spread

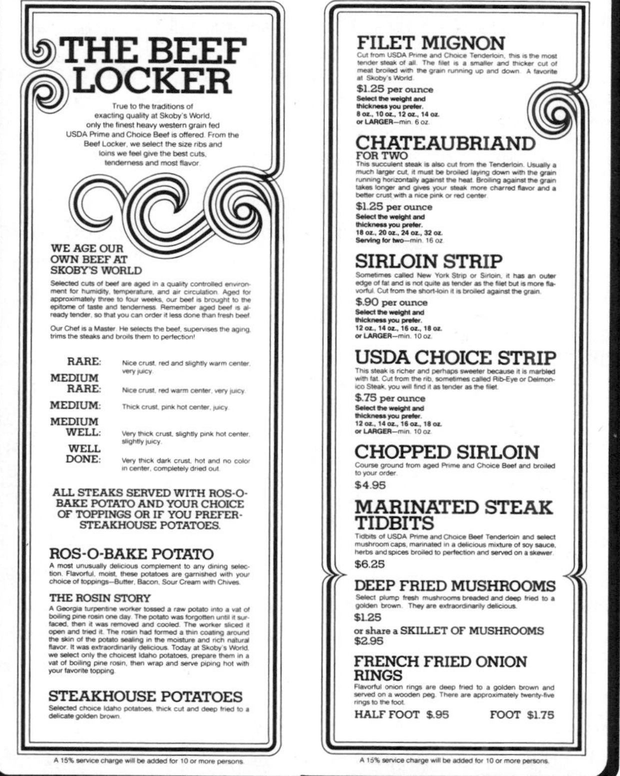

THE BEEF LOCKER

True to the traditions of exacting quality at Skoby's World, only the finest heavy western grain fed USDA Prime and Choice Beef is offered. From the Beef Locker, we select the size ribs and loins we feel give the best cuts, tenderness and most flavor.

WE AGE OUR OWN BEEF AT SKOBY'S WORLD

Selected cuts of beef are aged in a quality controlled environment for humidity, temperature, and air circulation. Aged for approximately three to four weeks, our beef is brought to the epitome of taste and tenderness. Remember aged beef is already tender, so that you can order it less done than fresh beef.

Our Chef is a Master. He selects the beef, supervises the aging, trims the steaks and broils them to perfection!

RARE:	Nice crust, red and slightly warm center, very juicy.
MEDIUM RARE:	Nice crust, red warm center, very juicy.
MEDIUM:	Thick crust, pink hot center, juicy.
MEDIUM WELL:	Very thick crust, slightly pink hot center, slightly juicy.
WELL DONE:	Very thick dark crust, hot and no color in center, completely dried out.

ALL STEAKS SERVED WITH ROS-O-BAKE POTATO AND YOUR CHOICE OF TOPPINGS OR IF YOU PREFER-STEAKHOUSE POTATOES.

ROS-O-BAKE POTATO

A most unusually delicious complement to any dining selection. Flavorful, moist, these potatoes are garnished with your choice of toppings—Butter, Bacon, Sour Cream with Chives.

THE ROSIN STORY

A Georgia turpentine worker tossed a raw potato into a vat of boiling pine rosin one day. The potato was forgotten until it surfaced, then it was removed and cooled. The worker sliced it open and tried it. The rosin had formed a thin coating around the skin of the potato sealing in the moisture and rich natural flavor. It was extraordinarily delicious. Today at Skoby's World, we select only the choicest Idaho potatoes, prepare them in a vat of boiling pine rosin, then wrap and serve piping hot with your favorite topping.

STEAKHOUSE POTATOES

Selected choice Idaho potatoes, thick cut and deep fried to a delicate golden brown.

A 15% service charge will be added for 10 or more persons.

FILET MIGNON

Cut from USDA Prime and Choice Tenderloin, this is the most tender steak of all. The filet is a smaller and thicker cut of meat broiled with the grain running up and down. A favorite at Skoby's World.

$1.25 per ounce
Select the weight and thickness you prefer.
8 oz., 10 oz., 12 oz., 14 oz. or LARGER—min. 6 oz.

CHATEAUBRIAND FOR TWO

This succulent steak is also cut from the Tenderloin. Usually a much larger cut, it must be broiled laying down with the grain running horizontally against the heat. Broiling against the grain takes longer and gives your steak more charred flavor and a better crust with a nice pink or red center.

$1.25 per ounce
Select the weight and thickness you prefer.
18 oz., 20 oz., 24 oz., 32 oz.
Serving for two—min. 16 oz.

SIRLOIN STRIP

Sometimes called New York Strip or Sirloin, it has an outer edge of fat and is not quite as tender as the filet but is more flavorful. Cut from the short-loin it is broiled against the grain.

$.90 per ounce
Select the weight and thickness you prefer.
12 oz., 14 oz., 16 oz., 18 oz. or LARGER—min. 10 oz.

USDA CHOICE STRIP

This steak is richer and perhaps sweeter because it is marbled with fat. Cut from the rib, sometimes called Rib-Eye or Delmonico Steak, you will find it as tender as the filet.

$.75 per ounce
Select the weight and thickness you prefer.
12 oz., 14 oz., 16 oz., 18 oz. or LARGER—min. 10 oz.

CHOPPED SIRLOIN

Course ground from aged Prime and Choice Beef and broiled to your order.

$4.95

MARINATED STEAK TIDBITS

Tidbits of USDA Prime and Choice Beef Tenderloin and select mushroom caps, marinated in a delicious mixture of soy sauce, herbs and spices broiled to perfection and served on a skewer.

$6.25

DEEP FRIED MUSHROOMS

Select plump fresh mushrooms breaded and deep fried to a golden brown. They are extraordinarily delicious.

$1.25

or share a SKILLET OF MUSHROOMS
$2.95

FRENCH FRIED ONION RINGS

Flavorful onion rings are deep fried to a golden brown and served on a wooden peg. There are approximately twenty-five rings to the foot.

HALF FOOT $.95 FOOT $1.75

A 15% service charge will be added for 10 or more persons.

"USDA Choice Strip. This steak is richer and perhaps sweeter because it is marbled with fat. Cut from the rib, sometimes called Rib-Eye or Delmonico Steak, you will find it as tender as the filet. This strip steak is offered at 75¢ per ounce. The customer selects the weight and thickness he prefers from 12 oz., 14 oz., 16 oz., 18 oz., or LARGER—minimum 10 oz. Filet Mignon is offered the same way at $1.25 per ounce."

The most unusual item offered on this menu is the Ros-O-Bake Potato. This is "A most unusually, delicious complement to any dining selection. Flavorful, moist, these potatoes are garnished with your choice of toppings—Butter, Bacon, Sour Cream with Chives."

This "different" potato is described in the Rosin Story as follows:

"A Georgia turpentine worker tossed a raw potato into a vat of boiling pine rosin one day. The potato was forgotten until it surfaced, then it was removed and cooled. The worker sliced it open and tried it. The rosin had formed a thin coating around the skin of the potato sealing in the moisture and rich natural flavor. It was extraordinarily delicious. Today at Skoby's World, we select only the choicest Idaho potatoes, prepare them in a vat of boiling pine rosin, then wrap and serve piping hot with your favorite topping."

Finally, this menu lists some creative dessert items. They are Grasshopper Pie and Fried Ice Cream. Grasshopper Pie is described as follows:

"At *Skoby's World*, we use creme-de-menthe, creme-de-cacao, whipped cream, marshmallows and an oreo cookie crumb crust to make this delightfully refreshing dessert. Light and flavorful, a perfect finish to a perfect meal."

Fried Ice Cream is vanilla ice cream, dipped in egg yolk, rolled in coconut macaroom cookie crumbs and frozen. Before being served it is deep fried for a few seconds. Crispy on the outside, cold on the inside . . . an exciting dessert not soon forgotten.

The *Cajun Kitchen* and *Oyster Bar* menu is printed on one side of a large brown paper bag. Still, it's a very complete and interesting listing including entrees, salads, sandwiches (including Po-Boys and Hungry Cajun Burgers), afterthoughts and meal toppers (desserts and beverages). In addition, at the bottom, there is a "Breakfast with the General" listing—grits and all.

An interesting seafood item (creative) in this Cajun restaurant is Oysters on a Nail. It is a Louisiana oyster wrapped in bacon, then dipped in the restaurant's own batter and lightly deep fried. It is served over Louisiana dirty rice and a French loaf.

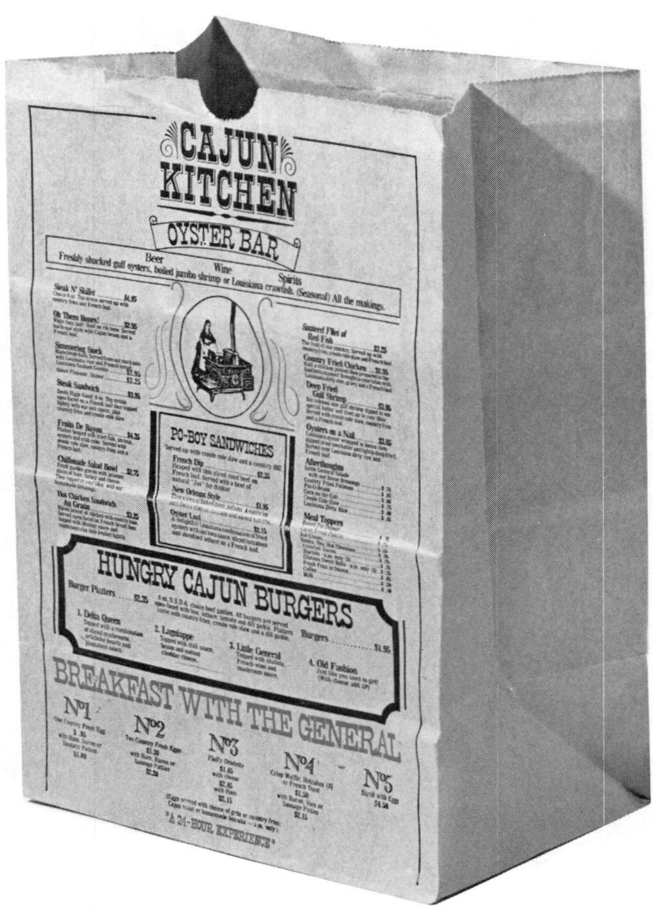

Cajun Kitchen *menu is printed on a brown paper bag. This is not only clever and original but also provides the customer with a "take-home bag."*

The table tent can also be a menu as this wine and appetizer offering of the Elliot Bay Fish and Oyster Co. *illustrates.*

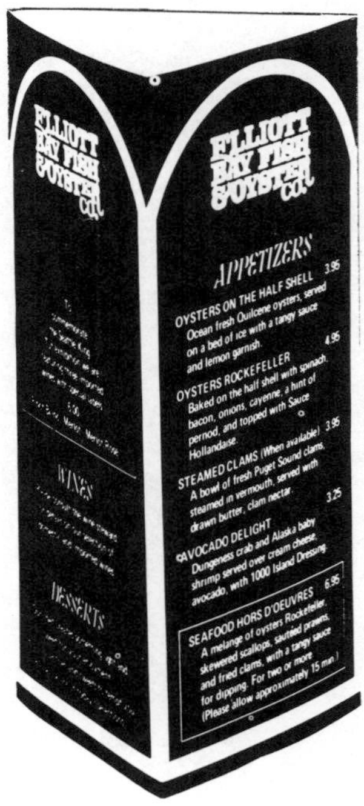

Howard Johnson's *has a three-dimensional approach — in the motel room and on the restaurant table — to selling their menu items.*

On the Common–Sturbridge, Mass. 1771 01566-Telephone (617) 347-3313

Publick House

Vol. XXIII No.7–1771

What was happening in 1771

Martha Dandridge Custis and George Washington celebrated their 12th anniversary of their marriage.

Yale was 70 years old.

Napoleon Bonaparte was 2 years old.

Ben Franklin was 65. He began his autobiography in this year. At which time, his "Poor Richard's Almanac" was famous throughout this country and Europe.

Paul Revere advertised his new process for false teeth.

The Newport Mercury hired the first woman editor for their newspaper. American Magazine, the first magazine published in this country, founded in Philadelphia, was 30 years old.

Daniel Boone was cutting roads through the wild wooded hills of Kentucky.

Spanish priests and settlers were settling out in Monterey, California.

The Mason Dixon line was two years old.

Tom Paine was to write and publish his "Common Sense" book 5 years later.

Patrick Henry was chief orator in Virginia lawmakers' House of Burgesses. Years later, he said, "If this be treason, make the most of it."

James Watt had invented the Steam Engine and began producing a working model in 1771.

A. A. MKETHAN, CARRIAGE MAKER, FAYETTEVILLE, N.C.

"Love blows the Trumpet of Fame!" THAT'S SO: AND THUS THE BLAST! OLD IRON, PEWTER, Lead, COPPER, ROPES AND RAGS, GUNNYBAGS.

Voltaire Writes in 1771:

"One should regard all human beings as one's brothers, a Turk, a Chinaman, and a Siamese. We are all children of the same father, and creatures of the same God, who did not give us hearts to hate one another, nor hands to slay one another. Do not let trifling differences in language, religious customs, imperfect laws be signals for hatred, and persecution among the puny atoms called mankind."

BEN FRANKLIN'S INFALLIBLE REMEDY FOR TOOTHACHE

Wash the root of an aching tooth in Elder Vinegar, and let it dry half an hour in the sun; after which it will never ache more.

General Lafayette and his son, George Washington Lafayette, visit Publick House in 1824:

Over 3,000 people assembled on the village green in Sturbridge village, to greet the Revolutionary hero, General Lafayette and his son George Washington Lafayette. Great preparations had been made for his visit. One good lady of our town carried her best china in a cart all the way to Publick House for his use. Not one piece of this china was broken, although it underwent considerable jogging.

Unfortunately, the General was way behind in his schedule, and although the taproom of the Publick House was to his liking, he could venture no further into the Inn.

PUFF'S FRAGRANT WEEDS. Cheroots! Meerschaums! Brier Roots! PIPES OF PEACE FOR FAMILY USE. CONGRESS SNUFF FOR TAX PAYERS. Politicians' Stumps constantly on hand.

Colonel Ebenezer Crafts drills cavalry on Sturbridge Common.

During revolutionary times, Colonel Ebenezer Crafts equipped and drilled a cavalry company on the Sturbridge Common in front of the Publick House.

The **Publick House** *menu is designed in early colonial New England style to match the food served.*

The Publick House Celebrates Winter and Spring

Sometimes we think we can sit back and rest on the laurels of our good Yankee cooking. But we always reconsider: It wouldn't be the Publick House if we didn't acknowledge the coming and going of the seasons and holidays with our little celebrations and special events.

Now at Christmas, we have a special menu that lasts throughout the 12 days of Christmas.

It's a good time to be at the Publick House, where there's a real holiday spirit and plenty of traditional ceremonies are on the agenda:

Our Boar's Head Ceremony is performed several times over the course of two days of celebrating. This includes the traditional Yule Log Celebration, toasting with Wassail, lots of beefeaters, spirits, wenches, minstrels and a mischievous jester.

New Year's Eve is informal. You can have dinner with us. Or just pop in on us before or after your party. We'll keep the musicians playing all evening long.

This season, our main social event is our Yankee Winter Weekend: 2 days and nights of real old New England fun. Visits to Old Sturbridge Village and the Sturbridge Yankee Workshop, sleigh rides, square dancing, sugaring off. And of course plenty of that good Yankee cooking at the Publick House: a candlelight buffet, a game dinner, and our special Open Hearth Breakfast.

Yankee Winter Weekend is a lot of fun for a lot of people, and if you're interested, why don't you ask for a brochure.

Every March, we like to share a little of the luck of the Irish. That means our An Tostal Celebration. We cook up some real Irish specialties, and we bring out the good Irish whiskey we've been saving.

On Easter Sunday, our good Yankee cooking includes some unusual things. Jelly beans and chocolate bunnies. The Easter Bunny is here giving them out to all the children. We serve a hearty Open Hearth Brunch in the morning, and then we put out our special Easter menu.

BEN FRANKLIN
On employing a maid:
Let thy maid-servant be faithful, strong and homely.

King George the Third and his Coronation 1760.

As King George the Third entered Westminster Abbey for his coronation, the largest diamond in his crown fell out. This was later taken as a symbol for his losing the American Colonies.

The Menu

Appetizers

Chilled Tomato Juice .... .60
Fresh Fruit Cup with Cranberry Sherbet 1.50
Chopped Chicken Livers, Red Onions 1.60
Cherrystone Clams 2.95
Iced Shrimp, a half dozen with Cocktail Sauce 3.50
Cranberry Orange Shrub .. .75

Cold Larder

*The Cooks Salad Bowl of Meat, Fowl and Cheese ... 6.95
*Twin Tomatoes Stuffed with Crabmeat Salad 8.50
Served with Publick House Bakery Basket

Native Fowl

*Boneless Country Fried Breast of Chicken, Supreme Sauce 6.50
*Sauteed Chicken Livers, Wild Rice Blend and Mushroom Sauce 5.95
Baked Chicken Breast, Country Stuffing, White Wine Sauce with Mushrooms ... 7.50

Soups

New England Clam Chowder Cup .... 1.35 Bowl 1.95
French Onion Soup Cup .... .95 Crock ... 1.75

From the Sea

Baked Lemon Sole with Crabmeat Stuffing 8.50
*Fried Native Scallops, 6.95 Broiled if you like 8.50
*Baked Stuffed Shrimps, Publick House 9.95
*Individual Baked Lobster Pie, our Specialty 9.95
Broiled Boston Schrod, Lemon Butter 6.75

Sturdy Viands

*Freshly Chopped Sirloin Steak, Smothered in Mushroom Sauce 6.50
Filet Mignon, Bordelaise Sauce 11.95
A hearty New York Cut Sirloin Steak, Full Pound 11.95
*Double Thick Lamb Chops, Apple Mint Conserve 10.95
All Hot Entrees served with Potato, Vegetable, Salad & Bakery Basket

Coffee .60 Pot of Tea .60 Milk .60

Desserts

Ice Cream Sundae with Butterscotch, Chocolate or Strawberry Sauce 1.50
Grasshopper Pie 1.60
Baked Indian Pudding, Vanilla Ice Cream 1.35
Coffee Jelly with Whipped Cream .... .75
Joe Froggers .... .60
Irish Coffee 2.25
Hot Deep Dish Apple Pie a la Mode or with Cheddar Cheese 1.50
Pecan Pie with Chilled Cream 1.75
Cheese Cake, Publick House .. 1.60
Angel Food Cake with Strawberry Sauce and Vanilla Ice Cream 1.50
Ice Cream Pie, Strawberry Sauce 1.60
Peppermint Stick Ice Cream with Chocolate Sauce 1.35
Ice Cream or Sherbet ..... .95

Joe Froggers .60
These large, flat molasses cookies take their name from an old Marblehead gent called Uncle Joe, who loved his rum so, he would bake his wonderful cookies, big as the bullfrogs in his pond, in return for a jug of it. Fishermen who made the barter discovered Uncle Joe's cookies kept fresh so long, they would sail off to sea with enormous batches of them.

Wine List

White Burgundy

Bin No.		Bottle	Half Bottle
10	Chablis, Beringer	5.95	3.50
11	Chablis, Vintage	14.50	7.75
12	Pouilly-Fuisse, Vintage	16.50	6.75
14	Puligny-Montrachet, Vintage	17.95	
15	Blanc DeBlancs, Wente		6.75

Rhine and Moselle

Bin No.		Bottle	Half Bottle
20	Liebfraumilch, Vintage	7.50	4.25
21	Grey Riesling, Wente	6.75	3.75
23	Piesporter Treppchen Vintage	8.95	—
24	Bernkastle Riesling, The Bishop of Riesling	7.50	—

White Bordeaux

Bin No.		Bottle	Half Bottle
30	Chateau Graville LaCoste, Vintage	7.95	4.50
31	Sauternes, Vintage	8.95	4.95
32	Chateau Sonoma, Vintage	6.50	—

Red Burgundy and Rhone

Bin No.		Bottle	Half Bottle
60	Pinot Noir, Burgundy Almaden	7.95	4.50
61	Beaujolais, Vintage	9.75	4.95
62	Pommard, Vintage	15.00	8.00
63	Gevrey-Chambertin, Vintage	17.50	—
64	Chateauneuf-du-Pape, Vintage	13.95	7.50
65	Gamay Beaujolais, Wente	6.95	3.95

Red Bordeaux

Bin No.		Bottle	Half Bottle
50	St. Emilion, Vintage	9.50	5.25
	Chateau Batailley, Pauillac, Vintage	14.95	—
52	Chateau Giscours, Vintage	14.95	8.00
53	Cabernet Sauvignon	9.50	5.25
54	Chateau-Margaux, Vintage	35.00	
55	Chateau Haut-Brion, Vintage	49.50	
56	Chateau Lafite Rothschild, Vintage	45.00	—

Rose

Bin No.		Bottle	Half Bottle
40	Grenache Rose, Almaden	5.95	3.50
41	Mateus (Portugal)	7.95	4.25
42	Cabernet Rose d'Anjou, Vintage	6.50	
43	Lancers Crackling	8.75	4.75

Champagne and Sparkling Wine

Bin No.		Bottle	Half Bottle
70	Gold Seal, Brut	9.95	5.50
71	Lambruscos, Ruffino Contessa	7.50	—
72	Piper Heidsieck, Vintage	27.50	14.50
73	Mumm's Cordon Rouge, Brut	21.00	—
74	Asti Spumante	12.95	6.95

The Bake Shoppe

People have always asked us where they could buy our homemade breads and relishes. Now we have an answer: Around back of the Publick House is our Bake Shoppe, a wonderful 18th Century bakery where you'll find our famous Publick House muffins, cakes, pies, cookies, jams, jellies, relishes and candies. We hope you'll visit us at The Bake Shoppe, even if it's only to say hello and breathe in all that fresh-from-our-Yankee-oven aroma.

Sturbridge Gristmill Grinds Meal for Publick House

In Old Sturbridge Village, there's a mill where corn meal is ground and sold daily. All the Publick House's Indian pudding and johnny cake and corn bread sticks are made from this meal. And the corn bread sticks are baked in authentic 18th Century molds.

BEN FRANKLIN
on doctors:
God heals and the doctor takes the fee.

BEN FRANKLIN
on marriage:
He that has not got a wife, is not yet a complete man. Keep your eyes wide open before marriage, half shut afterwards.

In 1884, Madame Carlotta of New York Ascends in a Balloon at Sturbridge Fair

This is the first time this has happened in this part of New England. It took place right on Sturbridge Common, right in front of the Publick House. And the performance increased the gatekeeper's profits by $700.00.

*Child's portion available for children under 10

Publick House is Included in the National Register of Historic Places

Mass. Meals Tax

This "brown bag" menu lists some unusual burgers besides the regular "old fashioned" burger or cheeseburger. They are: Delta Queen—a burger topped with a combination of sliced mushrooms, artichoke hearts, and plantation sauce; Lagniappe—a burger topped with chili sauce, beans, and melted cheddar cheese; and Little General—a burger topped with shallots, French wine, and mushroom sauce.

The *Publick House* restaurant, located on the common in Sturbridge, Massachusetts, has a combination of creative touches in design, copy, and interesting/different food offerings. This is a "newspaper"-style menu printed in dark brown ink on newsprint. It uses old cuts, ads, and copy.

Since the *Publick House* was established in 1771, a front-page story is about "What was happening in 1771." To begin with, Martha Dandridge Custis and George Washington celebrated the twelfth anniversary of their marriage; Yale University was seventy years old; and Napoleon Bonaparte was two years old. Another front page story on this menu is headlined "General Lafayette and His Son George Lafayette, Visit Publick House in 1824." Then there are the quotes from Ben Franklin's *Poor Richard's Almanac* (Franklin was age 65 in 1771). For example, his Infallible Remedy for Toothache—"Wash the root of an aching tooth in Elder Vinegar, and let it dry half an hour in the sun; after which it will never ache more." Or, on marriage—"Keep your eyes wide open before marriage, half shut afterwards." Or, on doctors—"God heals and the doctor takes the fee."

The copy is not all historical, however. Under the heading of *The Publick House* Celebrates Winter and Spring, a series of special events are advertised. These events include the twelve days of Christmas with a Boar's Head Ceremony and a Yule Log Celebration.

Since the *Publick House* is also an inn, they feature a Yankee Winter Weekend:

> 2 days and nights of real old New England fun. Visits to Old Sturbridge Village and the Sturbridge Yankee Workshop, sleigh rides, square dancing, sugaring off. And of course plenty of that good Yankee cooking at the Publick House: a candlelight buffet, a game dinner, and our special Open Hearth Breakfast.
>
> Yankee Winter Weekend is a lot of fun for a lot of people, and if you're interested, why don't you ask for a brochure.

And in March, the *Publick House* has its An Tostal Celebration with Irish specialties and Irish whiskey!

Creative entrees and desserts are also part of this menu. An Individual Baked Lobster Pie is a specialty. The unusual desserts include Baked Indian Pudding with Vanilla Ice Cream, Coffee Jelly with Whipped Cream, and Joe Froggers. What are Joe Froggers? Well, it just so happens that the menu tells you:

> "These large, flat molasses cookies take their name from an old Marblehead gent called Uncle Joe, who loved his rum so, he would bake his wonderful cookies, big as the bull frog in his pond, in return for a jug of it. Fishermen who made the barter discovered Uncle Joe's cookies kept fresh so long, they would sail off to sea with enormous batches of them."

Another creative "extra" on this menu is the meal ground at the Sturbridge Gristmill. The descriptive copy reads: "In Old Sturbridge Village, there's a mill where cornmeal is ground and sold daily. All the *Publick House's* Indian pudding and johnny cake and corn bread sticks are made from this meal. And the corn bread sticks are baked in authentic 18th Century molds."

And finally, the menu also folds into a mailer. Thus, when it is given to customers, they can spread the word.

8

Most common menu mistakes

A careful study of over a thousand menus over a period of two years shows a certain pattern of mistakes in menu design, listing, and merchandising that repeat themselves. A list of these cardinal mistakes and what should be done to correct them follows. This list should be of interest to the menu conscious food service operator and if any of these mistakes appear on your menu, you should take a second, critical look at it.

However, before listing the common errors, a general observation can be made that it is obvious in too many cases important design and merchandising decisions are being made by the printer of the menu, not the food service operator. Matters such as layout (which items should be given the most importance and where they should be listed), type size and style, size of the menu, and kind of paper used are too often determined by the limitations of the printer's presses and type selections and the stock of paper available in the storeroom. The food service operator should be in charge of the menu, not the printer.

The first, most common mistake is a menu that is too small (physically) to accommodate the listing of items. The results are crowding, type too small to read, no descriptive copy, and no "specials" in larger, bolder type. This kind of menu is hard to read and harder to order from. Very often it will include a large listing of excellent (and expensive) entrees that do not get the treatment they deserve simply because the menu is not big enough.

The next most common mistake is listing items in type that is too small. What is too small type? It is type your customers cannot read easily (preferably without glasses if they are far sighted) in the lighting conditions of your restaurant. Too many menu planners assume that everybody has the eyesight of a jet fighter pilot (20/20 vision under twilight conditions). Actually, only a minority of people have perfect vision (without glasses) and many don't always bring their glasses with them when they eat out. The answer to this menu problem is simple, too—set your menu in larger type.

Another common menu problem is a lack of descriptive copy. Strangely enough, if you were to ask a restaurant owner about the food being served, he or she could probably speak fluently about it. The restaurateur is proud of the food served, can describe it, and tell you how it is prepared, the originality of the recipe, the quality of the ingredients, etc., etc. But when it comes to listing these same items in cold type on the menu, often the restaurateur is at a loss for words.

This does not mean that a menu should be a literary creation. "Just the facts, ma'am" are enough; but too often just the facts (which can usually be contained in one average length sentence) are left out.

A professional writer, of course, will give you the best menu copy (if properly informed about what you serve), but any restaurant menu builder can write copy. Answer the following questions (some or all) about the entrees that are your specialties, and also about expensive and unusual drinks, appetizers, salads, sandwiches, and desserts:

1. What is it?
2. How is it prepared?
3. How is it served?
4. Does it have unusual taste and quality properties?

Foreign menu items—French, German, Italian, Chinese, etc.—especially need descriptive copy or translations so that the customer can order intelligently.

Do you treat every item on your menu the same? That is, do you list everything in the same size type and give no "special position" to any item? If so, you are committing another menu mistake. It's just common sense that a $15.00 steak and a 50¢ cup of coffee should not be given the same importance on the menu, but in a surprising number of cases, this is so.

The answer to this problem is easy, too. List your "big" items, usually your entrees, either dinners or a la carte, in bigger, bolder type than the other "smaller" items on the menu. Give them better position (usually center) and give them the most descriptive merchandising, sell copy. The situation is simple. You decide which items of those listed on your menu you would like to sell the most of (big profit, most popular, etc.) and treat them accordingly.

Another strange but common menu mistake is that of omission. It usually involves liquor, a big profit, easy to serve and store item. Many a menu will sell this big item with the line, "Ask for your favorite cocktail." This philosophy, carried to its ultimate conclusion, could result in a menu that consisted of a piece of paper on which the following informative message was printed, "Ask for your favorite food and drink, we may have it."

If you serve liquor, list it, all of it, cocktails, tall drinks, mixed drinks, coolers, bourbons, scotches, gins, vodkas, rums, beers, wines, etc., etc. Then list the price per drink (or bottle, split, etc.) because you wouldn't list a T-bone steak without listing the price. And, finally, list brand names when possible. Brand names mean quality, plus, they represent millions of dollars of advertising that the food service operator ignores at his or her own expense.

Another menu mistake area involves the sequence of items. This means that food and drink is consumed in a time sequence and should be listed in that order on the menu. Cocktails, soups, and appetizers are before items; entrees (dinners or a la carte) and most wines are middle items; and desserts, after dinner drinks (brandies, cordials, etc.), cigars, coffees, etc., etc. are after items. The menu should be organized in this time sequence (for the above items) and side items, such as sandwiches, salads, side dishes, etc., should literally be listed on the side or in some less important place, unless you specialize in sandwiches or salads, in which case, they become entree items.

A common menu mistake for which there is no excuse is tip-ons, clip-ons, or daily menus that, when attached to the menu, cover some printed portion of the menu. If you use tip-ons or have a changing daily menu that is attached to the regular menu, design your menu to allow for these tip-ons. Customers, in most cases, will not lift up a tip-on to read under it.

And while on the subject of the changing "daily special" portion of the menu, we have arrived at another common menu mistake or more often catastrophe. Many a menu, which otherwise is well designed and printed, will have a daily menu, luncheon or dinner, done on a typewriter, poorly organized, poorly printed (mimeographed) on poor paper. Very often these "daily" items are repetitions of regular items on the permanent menu which makes them a double menu mistake. The solution to this menu problem can be achieved in three steps as follows:

1. Cut down on the number of your daily specials.
2. Do not repeat "regular" items already listed on the menu.
3. Print in regular type on good quality paper.

Finally, to wrap up this list of most common menu mistakes (not all of the menu mistakes could be covered at this time), here is a common group of errors of omission. This is the failure of too many restaurants to list somewhere on the menu the following basic information: address, phone number, days open, hours of business, and credit cards honored.

9

How many menus should you have?

Every food service operation has a different menu problem depending on the number of meals it serves and the type of operation it has. The basic separation of menu types is into the breakfast, lunch, and dinner menu, but there are many more. A list of possible different, separate, and distinct menus is as follows:

1. Breakfast menu
2. Luncheon menu
3. Dinner menu
4. Late Evening Snack menu
5. Sunday Brunch menu
6. Children's menu
7. Dessert or After Dinner menu
8. Room Service menu
9. Poolside menu
10. Banquet menu
11. Take-Out menu
12. Wine List

No restaurant and hardly any hotel or motel would create and print twelve menus, but the fact that it is possible to print and use twelve different menus for twelve different purposes shows the scope and importance of how you use the menu. The other possibility is to have only one menu and cover all twelve subjects on that one menu. There are problems, however, in combining too many subjects in one menu, and there are times when a separate menu will do a better job. Let's examine the problem.

First, there is the Breakfast, Luncheon, and Dinner problem. An establishment that serves all three meals can either print three separate menus or one menu that combines all three or some combination such as a separate Breakfast menu and the Luncheon and Dinner menu together. Visually, the three combinations work out as shown in Figure 1.

Figure 1 illustrates three separate menus.

FIGURE 1

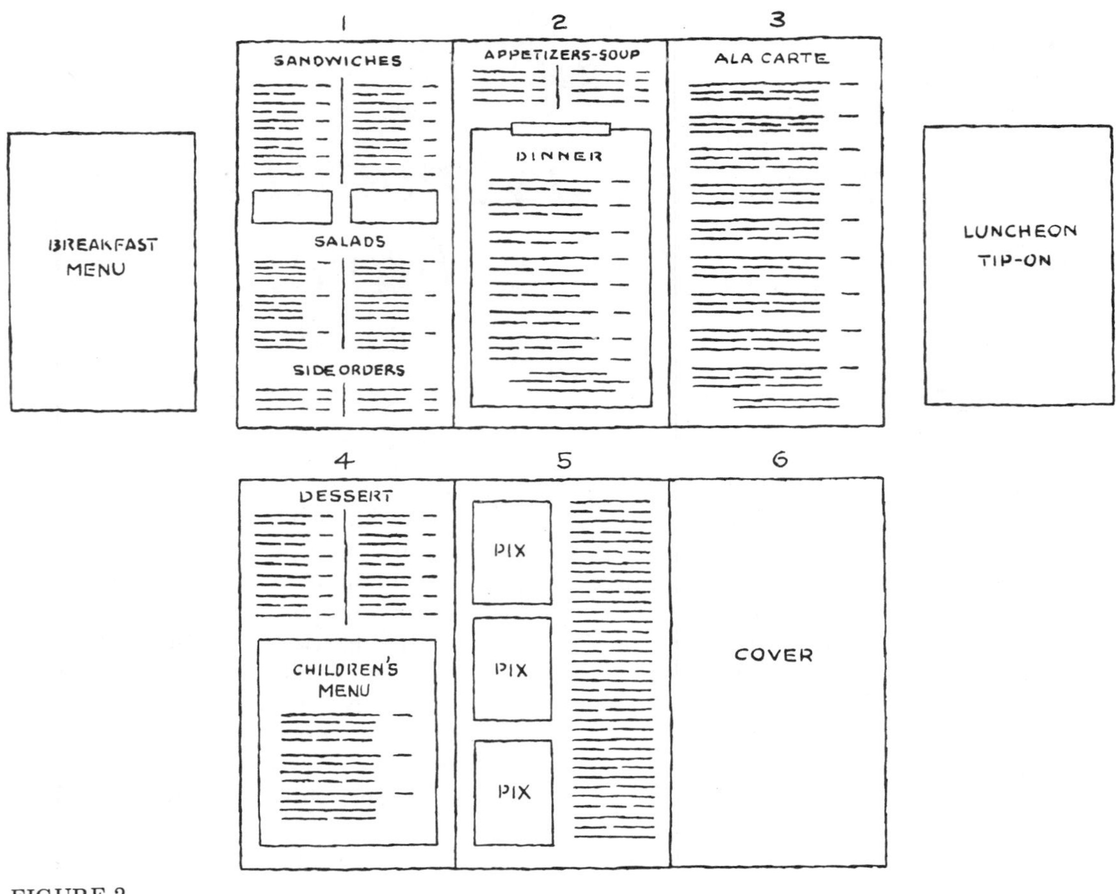

FIGURE 2

Figure 2 shows a separate Breakfast menu and the Luncheon and Dinner menu combined on one menu. If you have a cut-off time for serving breakfast, it is almost mandatory that you have a separate breakfast menu since the customers will continue to order the breakfast items after you have stopped serving them. On the other hand, it is always good communications to list the hours the Breakfast menu is served, even if it is served 24 hours a day.

The key to listing both the Luncheon and Dinner menu on one menu is the tip-on. This means that the Luncheon menu can be removed and the Dinner menu placed in the same space. The Luncheon and Dinner (complete Dinner or Dinner Specials for the Day) listing, however, must be small enough to fit into the space allowed. If you have a big, varied and complicated Luncheon or Dinner listing, a separate menu for each is recommended. The menu should fit what you serve, not the other way around. Also, since the tip-ons is the key to the functioning of this type of menu, care should go into its preparation and printing. The typesetting should be as good as the rest of the menu, and the printing and paper should be of the same good quality.

Figure 3 illustrates one possible combination of all three meals—Breakfast, Luncheon, and Dinner on one menu. The Dinner-Luncheon combination is the same as in Figure 2, but, in addition, the Breakfast menu is printed on panel 5 (back) of this 2-fold, 3-panel menu. This allows the breakfast part of the menu to be presented to the customer without exposing the rest of the menu when folded up. Combining all three meal listings on one menu and using tip-ons can save you money in printing, but the menu must be designed with care so that each part functions separately.

Consideration should be given to future changes in the menu. When all three menus are combined in one, the only change that can be made without changing or reprinting the entire menu is on the tip-ons, and there is a limit to the

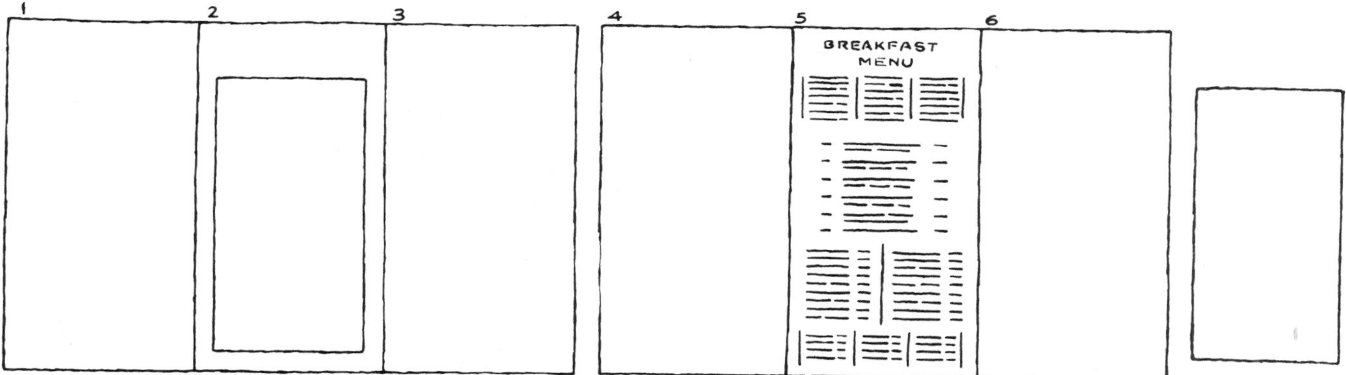

FIGURE 3

number of tip-ons that can be put on a menu. Another menu possibility that works for the three-meal problem is shown in Figure 4.

Figure 4 is the type of menu that has a permanent cover into which you bind listings as needed—luncheon, dinner, or even breakfast. In Figure 4, insert A could be one of the three menus, and Figure 2 could be the Luncheon or Breakfast menu. The main advantage of this type of menu, besides its flexibility, is that the cover (4 pages) can be of heavier, more expensive, coated paper while the inserts which change more often can be of lighter, less expensive paper. Also, your expensive 2-, 3-, or 4-color printing can be on the cover and the run can be larger to bring the unit cost down.

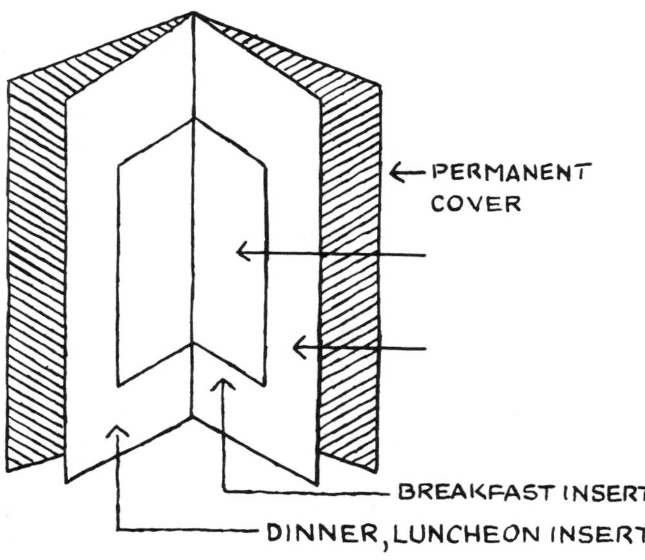

FIGURE 4

One factor to keep in mind when using a semi-permanent cover is to use all four pages (front cover, back cover, inside front cover, and inside back cover). In too many cases, only the front cover is used and the other three pages are left blank. This is a waste of valuable advertising, selling space. Some of the possible uses for these three pages are:

1. From Our Bar Listing
2. Wine List
3. Party-Banquet Story
4. Late Evening Snacks
5. Weekly Menu
6. Take-Outs
7. History of Establishment

If you are worried about price changes on this semi-permanent part of the menu (Liquor Listing, Wine List, Take-Outs, Late Evening Snacks) you can utilize a tip-on here also as shown in Figure 5. However, since they will not be changed very often, these tip-ons can be pasted right on the menu. Then when a change is required, the new listing can be pasted right over the old one and the cover can continue to be used.

Children's menus are very often separate menus. There are a great variety of these entertainment-type menus on the market. Any menu house or printer can show you samples of this type of menu. If you have a large, or desire a larger, "family" business, a separate Children's menu that entertains as well as lists the food for children is a good idea. If your service to children is not sizable, a small listing on the menu is enough, or in some cases merely the statement, "children's portions available at half price." The emphasis you put on this part of the menu depends on your market and type of restaurant.

FIGURE 5

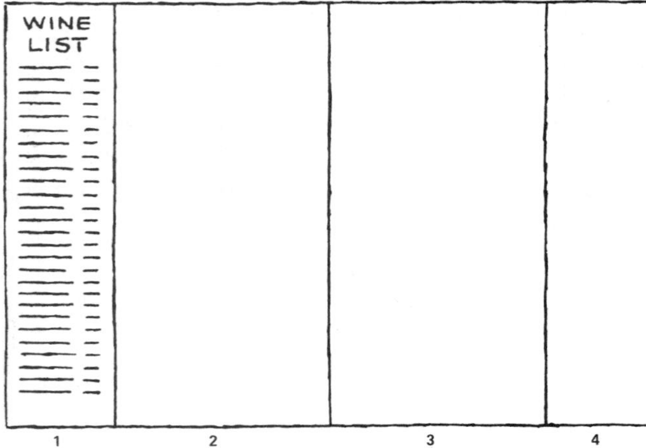

FIGURE 6

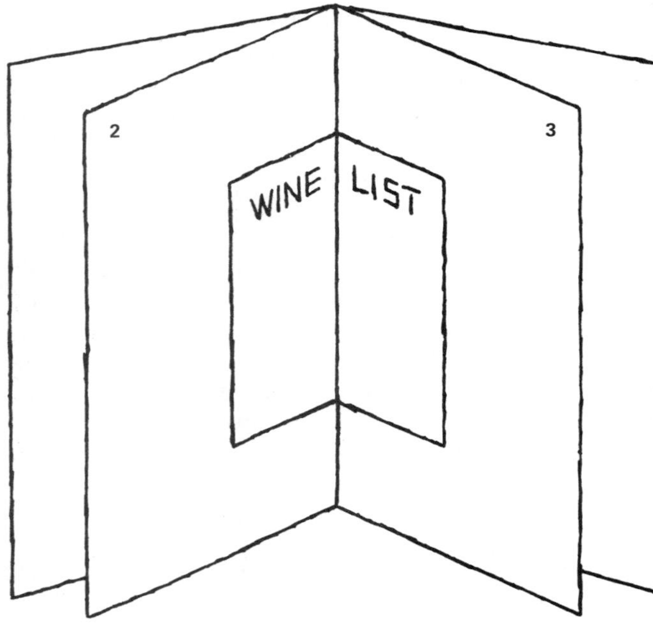

FIGURE 7

A separate Wine List is often printed by restaurants, but this is one case where there should not be a separate menu. The problem is to get the list to the customer at the right time. A separate Wine List, unless it is asked for or is on the table and used, will not sell anybody except the customer who orders wine regularly. Even a Wine List on the table can get overlooked; unless the customer opens it, and looks at it, he or she is not exposed to wine merchandising. The Wine List as an integral part of the menu and located next to the entree listing is a selling part of the menu. The idea is to make it impossible to ignore the wine listing. Figures 6 and 7 below show two possible methods of making the Wine List part of the menu by placing it next to the entree listing: In Figure 6 the Wine List is a panel or separate fold of the menu next to the entree listing, and in Figure 7 the Wine List is bound into the center of the entree listing.

In the case of Desserts and After Dinner Drinks, a separate menu is an exception, and in this case, a separate menu can do a better job. The effectiveness of an After Dinner menu is in how it is used. The menu must be presented to the customer after he or she has finished the meal or entree without asking if the customer wants dessert or an after dinner drink. Only after the customer has had time to look at the menu and be exposed to the sell on it should the question be asked.

The Dessert and After Dinner Drinks listing can be part of the total integrated menu as well as a separate menu, but when this is the case, it should get separate treatment. Figures 8, 9, and 10 show three possibilities for listing the "after" portion of the menu.

Figure 8 is the separate After Dinner menu with Desserts listed on page 2, After Dinner Drinks on page 3 and Dessert Wines on page 4. Figure 9 is a 3-panel, 2-fold menu with the Dessert and After Dinner Drink listing printed on panel 4. Figure 10 is a 4-page insert bound into a 4-page cover with the Dessert and After Dinner Drink

4 1 2 3
DESSERT WINES
AFTER DINNER MENU
DESSERT
DRINKS

FIGURE 8

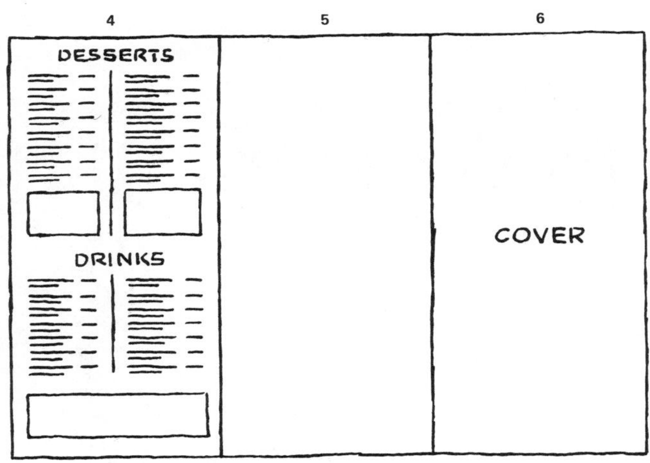

FIGURE 9

FIGURE 10

listing on page 4. The two menus illustrated in Figures 9 and 10 should be used the same way the separate After Dinner menu is used, that is, presented to the customer after he or she has finished the entree. Another advantage of the separate Dessert and After Dinner menu is that changes in price and item selection (and experimentation) can be made without changing the rest of the menu.

Specialty menus, such as Banquet, Room Service, Poolside, Take-Out, Sunday Brunch, and Late Evening Snack menus, are used depending on the type of specialized services you offer. In most cases, if you want to increase any one of these specialized parts of your menu, a separate menu or separate treatment on your regular menu is the answer. This means presenting information, items, prices, etc., selling with good copy, good art (illustrations), and good printing. In other words, any list of items or services that you sell as part of your food service should be sold somewhere on the menu or on a separate menu.

10

Creating atmosphere on the menu

The success of many food service establishments is based on a friendly atmosphere as well as the good food served. The decor and the attitudes of the owner and employees will, to a large extent, determine the atmosphere of the operation. Most operators are friendly, outgoing, extroverted people or they would not be in the food service business, but, in addition to people, decor, and general atmosphere, the menu, too, can reflect a friendly environment. A few, well-chosen words on the menu can help create a welcome and hospitable atmosphere. The following examples are chosen from actual "in use" menus to show how the imaginative use of words can create a happy menu.

In Atlanta, Georgia, the people who run *Mammy's Shanty* like to pose as simple, country folk, not like their smart city friends, but the following shows that they are a lot smarter than most:

"GEORGIA CRACKER"
Sampler Plate
$3.25

(an assortment of foods us natives like)
Us crackers always got a chicken, and a pig or two.
Nearly any place there's water,
You can find some crabs. (How true. How true.)
And shrimp! we have as many as taxes.
Apples grow in most backyards (as well as 5 or 6 brats).
Add 'em all together, and they really spell eating.
(Everything except the brats.)

So we decided, for our perspicacious Northern cousins, to let them try all our good easy eating at one sitting, by arranging in our best Georgia Manner a selected piece of Fried North Georgia Chicken, one South Georgia Pork Chop, one deviled Crab, and a Florida Avocado, stuffed with Fresh Texas Shrimp Salad, French Fried Idaho Potatoes, rolls and butter, coffee, and

THE WORLD'S BEST PECAN PIE

Michel's Restaurant in Harlan, Iowa, is happy that the customer came, and says so:

Yes, We're Glad You Came
Thanks for visiting us! We're happy,
gratified and complimented.
Happy to prepare for you the finest
food in town.
Gratified for this opportunity to demonstrate
our service and hospitality.
Complimented that you chose us to satisfy
your appetite. We appreciate your confidence
and will always do our utmost to deserve your
friendship and patronage.

Copy need not be long or involved to brighten up a menu. The *Gay Nineties Restaurant* in Rock Island, Illinois, for example, heads its fountain listing—Ice Cream Saloon, a bit of imaginative menu copy.

A few words about steak—other than the actual listing and description of the steak—is possible, as *The Look-Out Below Restaurant* menu shows:

Like a timeless work of art, steaks demand the perfection that only European trained chefs, working with the finest beef and years of experience, can create.

The result? A true masterpiece as prepared by our chefs that you'll savor and remember until your next visit . . .

One of the best pieces of menu copy of a general nature is the Ode to Dining as it appears on *Saska's* menu:

We may live without poetry, music and art
We may live without conscience and live without heart

We may live without friends, we may live without books
But where is the man who can live without cooks?
We may live without books, what is knowledge but grieving?
We may live without hope, what is hope but deceiving?
We may live without love, what is passion but pining?
But where lives the man who can do without dining?

Many establishments have names that are of historical or topical interest. It makes good advertising sense to take advantage of the situation, and *The Epicurean Restaurant* does just this, as shown below:

EPICURUS (341-270 B.C.)
The Greek philosopher to whom the phrase "Eat, drink, and be merry for tomorrow we die" has been ascribed. Though his philosophy taught that pleasure or happiness is the goal of all morality, it made a distinction between pleasures, advising the cultivation of the most enduring ones. Stressing the pleasures of the intellect and particularly those of friendship, it was held that genuine pleasure is derived from a life of prudence, honor and justice.

The word "epicure" has become the term used for one who displays fastidiousness in his tastes or enjoyments.

A topical reference, in an election year, appears on the dessert menu of *Latz's Knife and Fork Inn.* It says, "Where Hungry and Thirsty Democrats and Republicans Are Always Welcome."

A few words about your restaurant, its cuisine, history, etc., is always good on the menu. The following example from the *Smith Farm Restaurant* in Maine, is good, friendly, hospitality copy:

Years ago . . . having a surplus of vegetables and fruits, the Smiths erected a simple highway vegetable stand. It prospered. Home-made ice cream was added . . . it too became popular . . . and more popular. Then home grown turkeys were added in the form of luscious home-made sandwiches. The demand was so great that real farm style turkey dinners were added to the growing business. More room was needed and the barn was "fixed up" so that customers could "set 'n eat."

The Smith Farm reputation for good food grew and grew. More dining space was made available . . . more additions made and the menu increased . . . until today . . . Smith Farm customers come from all over the nation for our now famous "New England Cookin'."

From East, South, West and North, thousands who have been guests here have discovered a certain character at the Smith Farm, and a certain excellence in the service that they like.

In every city of any distinction there are hotels and eating places that stand out and give it a memorable character. Pity the town, no matter how large and important, that has no restaurant that people tell each other about and plan to revisit.

It has been said that Smith Farm is such a restaurant, and it is our intention to deserve that reputation . . . and preserve it. It's a two-way street, of course. So long as we bring credit to Maine, our friends in Maine will make Smith Farm Restaurant a frequent rendezvous. You who are reading these lines are the final judge and arbiter, and we invite your judgment in presenting this menu of the dishes we are prepared to serve—many of them are old family recipes—all of them tested by discerning people.

Even such pedestrian copy as what credit cards you honor and what the various food and travel guides think of you can be said in a better way, as shown by the following from *Poor Richard's Restaurant:*

To all our esteemed customers
At this point we urge you to use your Carte Blanche or American Express credit cards whenever you like. Further, we beg you not to leave hats, coats, and other stuff behind. We can't be responsible for them. And finally, to toot our horn a little, we remind you that Poor Richard's is approved by the A.A.A., is listed in Mobil's "Northwest Travel Guide," and has been given the full-page treatment from "Ford Times." However, we do not sell gasoline or autos, just superb food.

For the hotel-motel restaurant, this copy about "The Innkeeper" from the *Surf and Surrey* menu is good, friendly, and informative copy:

Arriving by stagecoach, bareback or mule, hungry and thirsty they came in from the harsh, hot, dusty roads in summer and the cold, soggy and wet trails of winter. Often they had been traveling difficult distances at great personal peril. Bandits and highwaymen waited around almost every crook in the road to harm them and steal their money.

The Inn was a refuge. It was a place of cheer, warmth and generous hospitality. The Innkeeper was ready with a quick greeting, a friendly smile, a haunch of mutton and a gill of kill-devil. The fireplace was large and warm. The pub was a cacophony of laughter and good conversation. The kitchen sent out its magical odors and culinary masterpieces, while the resting wayfarer was safe, happy and well fed as well as being protected from the storm and the dangers of the highwayman.

A hearty Appetite . . English
Bon Appetit . . . . . French
Buon Appetito . . . . . Italian
Guten Appetit . . . . German
Buen Apetito . . . . Spanish
Bkychot Kywahgr . . Russian
B'et E-Avon . . . . Hebrew
Smaeznego . . . . . . Polish
Smak-lig-Målted . . Swedish

Gourmet information creates atmosphere on the menu.

A Warning

Since the "Les Amis d'Escoffier" Society is dedicated to the art of good living only, it is forbidden, under threat of expulsion, to speak of personal affairs, of one's own work or specialty, and more particularly to attempt to use the Society as a means of making business contacts. It is unnecessary to elucidate further upon this delicate subject which everyone understands. Furthermore, at these dinner-meetings reference will never be made on the subjects of: politics, religious beliefs, personal opinions of either members or guests irrespective of their profession or social status.

La Serviette Au Cou

Too often we find, as we come to the table,
an elegant "rag" no larger than a hand,
That futilely and pretentiously means to supplant
That napkin of old, so ample and comfortable.
The dining room lacks the grandeur of yore:
Varnished floors, mirrors clear and of tinted glass
Give the illusion of hospital, clinic, or bath.
Bring back the large tablecloth, we humbly implore.
So flattering to gleaming arms, softening to the sounds,
A background sublime for the flowers and fruits,
Whose whiteness enchants the guests sitting 'round.
If a toast to your health you would enjoy,
Madame, bring out that entrancing linen
For then indeed would we abound in joy!

Dinner Rules

The napkin must be tucked under the collar. There will be no reserved seats. Persons under the influence of liquor will not be permitted to sit at the table. Members and guests will attend the dinner-meetings in informal dress.

The wines, carefully selected to accompany and enhance the delicacy of each course, must be drunk during the course for which they are intended. To enforce this ruling, the glasses—even if full—will be removed at the end of each course.

Smoking is absolutely forbidden up to the time dessert is served. A person who smokes while eating does not deserve the title of "Gourmet."

The Wine Does It...

Liberal amounts of fine California wines add extra flavor and excitement to these savory dishes

ENTREES:

Stroganoff of Beef Tenderloin Burgundy 3.90
tenderloin tips in our own rich and delightfully tasty sauce—with buttered noodles and a splash of BURGUNDY

Veal Scaloppini Burgundy 3.95
tender veal steak sauteed with parmesan cheese and served in a tomato-mushroom-BURGUNDY wine sauce with rice pilau

Veal Scaloppini Marsala 3.95
prepared the same as the scaloppini above, however, the MARSALA wine makes it a sweeter and richer combination

Tournedos of Beef Tenderloin Burgundy 5.60
fine broiled tenderloin tournedos, broiled tomato, mushroom caps and our own elegant BURGUNDY wine sauce

Broiled Sweetbreads in Sherry 3.85
an unusual dinner of sweetbreads broiled in SHERRY and served with crisp bacon

Chicken Livers, Sauteed 3.95
fresh chicken livers sauteed with mushrooms and SHERRY wine on toast points

SEAFOOD SPECIALTIES WITH WINE:

Roulades of Sole Bordeaux 4.25
Filet of Red Snapper Chardonnay 4.50
Alaskan King Crab Newberg 3.90

"The Wine Does It . . ." food cooked in wine creates its own atmosphere.

The OPEN HEARTH INTELLIGENCER

Philadelphia, Penna. - Summer 1876 One Cent

PHILADELPHIA, "The Centennial City"

The luxurious new *Transcontinental Hotel* has been built especially for *the Centennial*, it has accommodations for a thousand guest at five dollars per day. To right of picture is a corner of the sprawling *Hotel Globe* with room for two thousand guest. The crowded intersection shown is at Elm (Parkside) and Belmont, close by *the Centennial* and the route of the official parades.

Philadelphia is host to travelers from throughout the world during Centennial

The *Great Exhibition* opened on May 10th and thousands continue to converge on city. The fair is a challenge to the hardy visitor who wishes to see it all on foot. There are 25 miles of outdoor walks which cover the entire 236 acres and eleven miles of indoor walking.
The main attraction, the great Corliss engine, which was started on opening day by *President Grant* continues to be the star attraction. Its fourteen hundred horsepower engine could, if necessary, drive the entire shafting machinery required to operate the exhibits.

ULYSSES S. GRANT

Elegant New DINING SALOON Open...

Upon returning from the Centennial, *Harper's* warned that at *the Open Hearth's Dining Saloon . . .*" you shall find the mere fragments from a roast brisket of beef or the segment of a lobster so bedecked and so dressed with piquant sauces, and so flanked with savory vegetables that you shall come to a new knowledge of the triumphs of cookery." At an official dinner held at this fine dining saloon, Philadelphia's Mayor Wm. S. Stokley warned . . . "if any of the attractions which have made this Exhibition so great is to survive for future generations enjoyment, let's hope it is the *Original Open Hearth*. If a century from now there be a *Bi-Centennial*, let us hope that our offsprings dine as well as we do tonight. I propose toast to Mr. Segal and his Excellent staff."

Original Open Hearth

Mr. Segal recalls playing host to James Buchanan Brady, better known as Diamond Jim. In the days of the fifteen-course dinner, he was recognized as Number One eater, the man whom restaurateur Al Segal admiringly designated "the best twenty-five customers the Open Hearth has." After a recent party held in the Wedgewood Room, Mr. Segal recalled, "When Diamond Jim pointed at a platter of French pastry, he didn't mean any special piece of pastry. He meant the whole platter of pastry."

PRESIDENT GRANT IN PHILA, PA.

On May 10, President U. S. Grant led a procession officially opening the *"Centennial."* Flags of all nations whipped in the breeze and all buildings in Philadelphia were gaily decorated. The many bands played a march written for the occasion by Richard Wagner and the poet Whittier and a chorus of six hundred voices singing Handel's "Hallelujah Chorus."
A reception followed honoring *President U. S. Grant* and other officials at the *Original Open Hearth Restaurant*, which is located at nearby Belmont and City Line Avenues. The elegant banquet menu featured Saddle of Mutton, Potted Pigeon with Mushrooms, Gallinteen of Quail with Truffles and Mr. Segal's own . Romanian Garlic Rib Steak.

LABRADOR
French Steamship arrives.

The French Motor Steamship "LABRADOR," which docked in Philadelphia on March 24th was the largest vessel to ever navigate the Delaware River. Most of its cargo was goods for *the Centennial Exhibition*, however there were 200 cases of J. Goerg & Co., La Perie de la Cuvee Champagne aboard and destined for the *Open Hearth's* wine cellar.

CONTINENTAL RAILWAY

Philadelphia, May 1 — A new era has begun in the field of modern transportation with the opening of the Continental Railway. Eight beautiful enclosed four-wheeled carriages have been put into use and eleven more are to follow. A stable of twenty healthy, vigorous horses will be used on the Continental Railway line, which extends from Front and Market Streets to the Centennial grounds. The ride from Belmont and Elm (Main entrance to the fair) to City Hall can be made in only one hour and fifteen minutes. The fee for a round-trip being 7¢.

This unusual menu cover designed from newspaper stories and illustrations of 100 years ago creates an old time atmosphere.

11
Color on the menu

Advertising in America vividly illustrates the effectiveness of color as a sales and merchandising tool for products of all kinds. Because people are known to respond to it, color fills our magazines, books, newspapers, and even TV.

Color photography plus modern methods of color reproduction have made color illustration commonplace in printed media. Today there is an accelerating trend to colorful menus.

Color on the menu can function in many ways. First, it can act as decoration, making the menu more attractive and interesting. Second, it can be used through color photography reproduction to *illustrate* your food and drink, and third, color can set the mood and style for your restaurant.

Using color as decoration or design on your menu can be done simply, with the use of one additional color plus black, or all of the colors of the rainbow can be used. Color can also be added to the menu through the use of colored paper.

The *amount* of color used on a menu for design purposes will depend on two factors—cost and the effect desired. The more colors used on a menu, the more expensive it is to print. One color on colored paper is the least expensive. Next comes two colors down, then three and finally four, which gives you all the colors of the spectrum. Four colors are necessary to reproduce illustrations developed from food photography.

Color will also produce an *effect* on your menu. If you use many bright colors in panels, headings and illustrations, you will create a menu that characterizes a certain type of restaurant, usually a sandwich shop, pancake house, short order, fast service type of restaurant. If, on the other hand you use pastel shades or tans, buffs, ivory, gray or blue plus black with gold, etc., and use any bright colors sparingly, you will create a more sophisticated mood. This use of color is typical of the supper club, the continental, more expensive type of restaurant.

The simplest and easiest way to use a second color in the design of your menu is to print your headings, Seafood, Steak, Appetizers, Desserts, etc., in color—red, blue, brown, green, or gold—while printing the rest of the food listing in black.

As a rule, however, only a limited amount of type should be in a second color since any large amount of type in color becomes hard and tiresome to read. The human eye seems to *read* black and white best of all.

The selection of colored paper can enhance the appearance of your menu without adding to the printing cost. There is an almost unlimited selection of papers available in every color imaginable, including metallic gold, silver and copper.

In selecting colored paper, however, be careful of two things. First, if you are going to print a considerable amount of readable copy, be sure that the color is not too dark. Some reds and blues are too dark to allow for black type to be read when printed over these dark colors.

In addition, some papers are chosen for cover stock use that are the same color, red, black and blue for example, on both sides. This usually means that the inside front cover, inside back cover and back cover cannot be used for merchandising either in the form of a printed message or illustrations. Paper can be obtained that is colored on one side and white on the other. This is more practical for menu use.

Another simple and inexpensive method of

Reprinted from *Institutions* magazine.

adding color and elegance to a menu is to use wide, colorful ribbons as part of the design. A wide red or blue ribbon, for example, glued to the front cover or "wrapped around" from the front to the inside front cover, adds color and texture to the menu and creates a rich-appearing menu.

Full color food illustrations with menu listings are a natural merchandising combination. Color photography means that your food and drink can be presented exactly the way it looks when served in your restaurant. And food illustration needs *color*.

No food advertiser would think of picturing his product in black and white or with line drawings. If a picture is worth a thousand words, a color reproduction is the closest thing there is to the actual food entree, appetizer or dessert itself.

The main objection to color halftones on the menu, of course, is cost. First, there is the cost of color photography. Unless the restaurant operator can use stock photographs of food set-ups similar to what he serves, he will have to buy the services of a photographer. The cost of a good (professionally competent) color photograph can vary from $50 to $250 or more.

Then there is the cost of positives, color separations and plates (the process of making the color photograph ready for printing). An 8½ by 11 four-color positive costs around $250 in Chicago. Smaller color positives cost somewhat less, but the cost of 4 or 6 color illustrations on a menu will not be small.

Finally, the printing of a four-color menu will be more expensive. A restaurant operator can figure on his printing costs alone to be 35 per cent more for color than for his present one or two-color menu. So, if color reproduction is so much more expensive, why consider it at all?

In the first place, color is in. From color TV to decor and even to the way men and women dress, color is being used more and more in our society. Therefore, the dull and drab gray of yesterday is just not good enough for today.

In the second place, nothing illustrates and thereby sells food as well as a good color illustration. You can describe your steak, roast beef, chicken or shrimp with the best copy in the world, and it will never do the communication job that a color illustration will do.

Color illustration is especially effective as a selling tool in the restaurant that wants to make the customer decide quickly what he wants, order it, eat it, pay his check and leave so that a new customer can take his place. The agonizing slowness that some customers exhibit when ordering, which can cost the restaurant operator money, can be partly eliminated by color photography.

Of course, not every item on the menu can be illustrated in color. First, there are too many items, and, second, the cost is prohibitive. The most commonly color illustrated items on the menu are:

1. Appetizers
    a. Shrimp cocktail
    b. Antipasto
2. Salads
    a. Tossed or Chef
    b. Fruit
    c. Caesar
3. Sandwiches
    a. Hamburger
    b. Cheeseburger
    c. Club
4. Entrees
    a. Steaks
    b. Shrimp
    c. Chicken
5. Desserts
    a. Pie
    b. Cake
    c. Sundaes

The selection of what you illustrate in color on your menu, of course, should be based on what you want to sell most. The items you illustrate in color will get the most attention and probably the fastest action.

This brings up another aspect of the use of color illustrations. Because of the high cost of color, your selection of items to be illustrated should be made with care. You will have to live with your selection for some time unless you want to go to the considerable expense of new photography, positives and color printing. Items that are proven sellers and profitable should be the ones selected for color illustration.

Color food illustrations are used in two basic ways on the menu—a square or rectangular picture including some background and the vignette picture, or only the food on the plate.

The vignette illustration will be more expensive since the engraver has to eliminate the background from the color photo, but it does concentrate the viewer's attention on the food. The square or rectangular illustration, however, can be just as effective if the background is simple and does not interfere with the main subject, the food being served and sold.

Another important factor relative to color illustration is the quality of the illustration and the quality of the printing reproduction. The entire effort and cost of color illustration on the menu can be defeated by poor reproduction.

The appetite appeal of food illustration depends upon accurate color reproduction. A greenish steak, salad with brown lettuce or a gray apple pie is worse than no illustration at all. Many menu items, especially French-fried shrimp or fried chicken, tend to look more like brown lumps of nothing rather than appetizing entrees.

Care and competence in color reproduction are essential requirements. Your printer and your photographer should be professionals who know what they are doing, or else you could be wasting a good deal of money.

A common error in the use of color illustrations is failure to list the items sold and price next to the color illustration. Just an illustration of a steak at the top of your steak listing is not good enough. You cannot illustrate a steak without it being some specific steak—tenderloin, filet mignon, butt, N.Y. strip, etc. For this reason, the relevant copy—name of entree, what "goes with it" and the price should be next to the illustration.

The easiest way to make sure that the illustration and copy go together is to put them in a box or a panel. This can be a simple black line around the picture and type, a more complicated design border or a color panel.

At present, color illustrations on the menu are used mostly by chain operations that can spread the cost of color over a large run of menu printing to be used in a large number of outlets. But independent operators are using color more often, especially those restaurants that emphasize customer turnover. With the improvement of new color printing techniques and the accompanying reduction in cost, more and more color will be used on the menu.

The Dessert Menu of the *Keyaki Grill* in the Tokyo Hilton is the ultimate use of beautiful color photography. The page size is relatively small—7" × 10", but this only makes it easy to handle. The hard cover is buff velour with gold embossing. The inside twelve pages are a delight to the gourmet's eye. Each has one, two, or a selection of desserts.

The photos are not just views of isolated food items. Instead, they are carefully composed still-lifes with flowers, fruits, and other props in the background. Various wines, liqueurs, and after dinner drinks are also part of each set up. The desserts featured are not your garden variety of pie and ice cream. The following elegant selection shows how different they are and how their gastronomic appeal matches the eye appeal of the illustrations:

A selection of cheeses
Sherry trifle
A selection of stewed fruits and cakes
Vacherin Glace aux Cassis
Kaiserschmarrn
Salzburger Nockerln
Crepes "Suzette" or Normandy
Baked Alaska
Fresh Strawberry "Poivre"
Cafe Diable

An absolutely "tops in color" menu is *Lum's* 8-page, all color photography food and drink listing. It is a large menu, 10" × 13", with correspondingly large illustrations. The hamburgers, for example, are even bigger than life size. Besides the Beautiful Batch of Burgers, and Ollie's Greatest Creations (10 hamburgers and cheeseburgers) there is a page of Deep Sea Delights, Steak Dinners, Lumberjack Sandwiches, and Desserts, Beverages, and Side Orders.

There is also a complimentary *Lum's* Breakfast Menu also using large, colorful life-size photos.

Another clever use of color plus good design is the menu cover of *The Pavilion* restaurant in the Shamrock Hilton, Houston, Texas. The illustration is flowers made from torn paper. The flat, bright areas of color make this menu vibrate with attractiveness.

(Opposite page, top) *This menu shows an effective use of color panels—squares, circles, rectangles, plus other color design uses. Notice how breakfast "specials" are given the color panel treatment.*

(Opposite page, bottom) *Color food illustrations do not have to be photographs. These three color drawings of chicken, steak, and fish are very effective and attractive.*

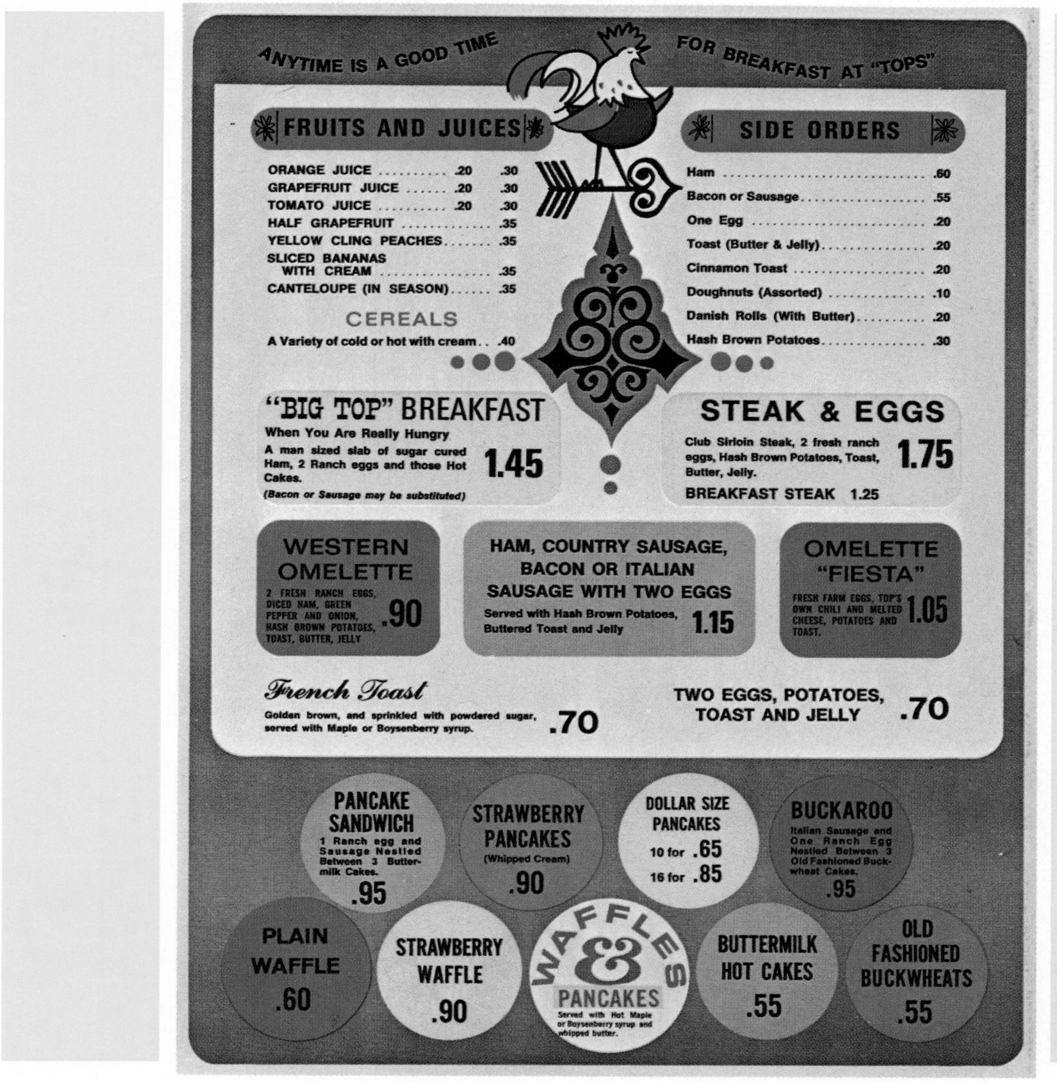

ANYTIME IS A GOOD TIME FOR BREAKFAST AT "TOPS"

FRUITS AND JUICES

ORANGE JUICE	.20	.30
GRAPEFRUIT JUICE	.20	.30
TOMATO JUICE	.20	.30
HALF GRAPEFRUIT		.35
YELLOW CLING PEACHES		.35
SLICED BANANAS WITH CREAM		.35
CANTELOUPE (IN SEASON)		.35

CEREALS

A Variety of cold or hot with cream . . .40

SIDE ORDERS

Ham	.60
Bacon or Sausage	.55
One Egg	.20
Toast (Butter & Jelly)	.20
Cinnamon Toast	.20
Doughnuts (Assorted)	.10
Danish Rolls (With Butter)	.20
Hash Brown Potatoes	.30

"BIG TOP" BREAKFAST

When You Are Really Hungry

A man sized slab of sugar cured Ham, 2 Ranch eggs and those Hot Cakes. **1.45**

(Bacon or Sausage may be substituted)

STEAK & EGGS

Club Sirloin Steak, 2 fresh ranch eggs, Hash Brown Potatoes, Toast, Butter, Jelly. **1.75**

BREAKFAST STEAK 1.25

WESTERN OMELETTE

2 FRESH RANCH EGGS, DICED HAM, GREEN PEPPER AND ONION, HASH BROWN POTATOES, TOAST, BUTTER, JELLY **.90**

HAM, COUNTRY SAUSAGE, BACON OR ITALIAN SAUSAGE WITH TWO EGGS

Served with Hash Brown Potatoes, Buttered Toast and Jelly **1.15**

OMELETTE "FIESTA"

FRESH FARM EGGS, TOP'S OWN CHILI AND MELTED CHEESE, POTATOES AND TOAST. **1.05**

French Toast

Golden brown, and sprinkled with powdered sugar, served with Maple or Boysenberry syrup. **.70**

TWO EGGS, POTATOES, TOAST AND JELLY .70

PANCAKE SANDWICH
1 Ranch egg and Sausage Nestled Between 3 Buttermilk Cakes.
.95

STRAWBERRY PANCAKES
(Whipped Cream)
.90

DOLLAR SIZE PANCAKES
10 for .65
16 for .85

BUCKAROO
Italian Sausage and One Ranch Egg Nestled Between 3 Old Fashioned Buckwheat Cakes.
.95

PLAIN WAFFLE
.60

STRAWBERRY WAFFLE
.90

WAFFLES & PANCAKES
Served with Hot Maple or Boysenberry syrup and whipped butter.

BUTTERMILK HOT CAKES
.55

OLD FASHIONED BUCKWHEATS
.55

CHICKEN COUNTRY FRIED
Three generous pieces of tender, juicy chicken cooked to our own formula, rich gravy, fluffy whipped potatoes, creamy cole slaw, cranberry-orange relish, served with warm roll and butter.
1.89

STEAK "SIZZLER" SANDWICH
7 ounces of U.S. choice butt sirloin broiled and on buttered toast makes this a real bargain with tossed salad and choice of dressing.
2.19

FISH 'N FRIES
Golden brown Lake Perch fillets from icy waters, firm and sweet with crisp French fries, creamy cole slaw and lots of tartar sauce, warm roll and butter.
1.49

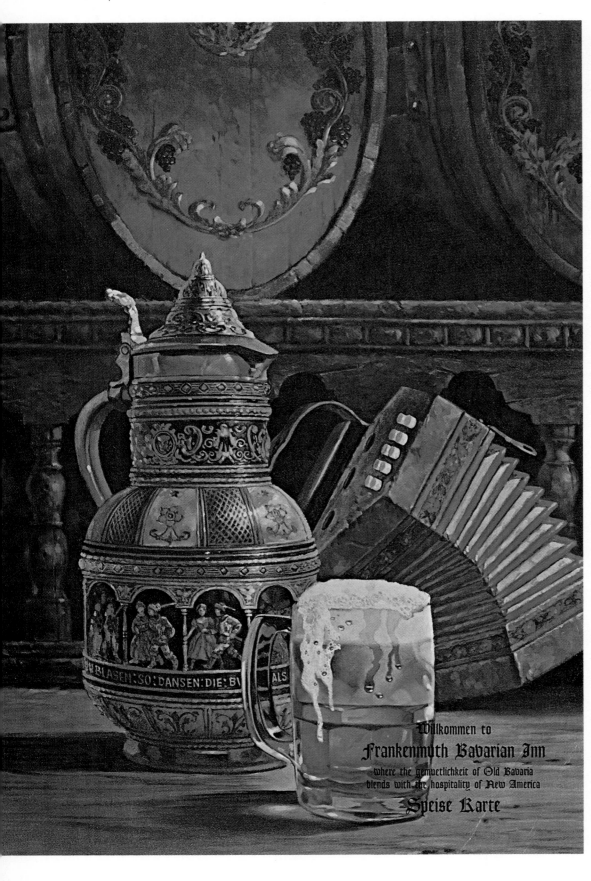

Willkommen to
Frankenmuth Bavarian Inn
where the gemuetlichkeit of Old Bavaria
blends with the hospitality of New America
Speise Karte

MARTINI

MANHATTAN

WHISKEY SOUR

CREME DE MENTHE

(Extreme Left) *This beautiful as well as colorful cover illustration sets the mood for this restaurant specializing in German food. The glass of beer looks real and appetizing enough to drink!*

(Near left) *Cocktails, wines, beers, and after dinner drinks can also be illustrated in color. Considering their "high profit" value, perhaps more drinks should be illustrated, and in color!*

(Right) *This attractive menu cover is in full color on white stock. In addition to the name shown prominently, it has a drawing of the restaurant plus color photos of four* feature *items—shrimp, chicken, fruit salad, and steak. This cover illustrates that many merchandising factors can function on a menu cover if it is well organized.*

(Right) *Ozzie's restaurant uses a four-color illustration nearly actual size of a steak with French fried onion rings and a baked potato on its cover. This gives "number one" position to this entree item and should sell a lot of steaks.*

The Casa Conti *uses color photography on the back cover of its menu to illustrate its eight different dining rooms plus the lobby and lounge.*

Casa Conti

Glenside, Penna.

Virginia Room

Dining Room

Ballroom

Lorraine Room

This menu shows the use of both outline and square color photos.

MAY WE SUGGEST
THESE BEFORE DINNER
COCKTAILS . . .

* Martini
* Manhattan
* Old Fashioned
* Daiquiri
* Bacardi

Appetizers

SHRIMP COCKTAIL	.75
MARINATED HERRING	.50
ASSORTED RELISH TRAY, Per Person	.25
HOMEMADE SOUP, du Jour	.35
CHILLE' 'RUIT COCKT	
GRAF 'UICE	

Steaks & Chops

CHOICE T-BONE STEAK	4.50
BROILED CHOICE FILET MIGNON, with Mushroom Caps	4.85
BROILED CHOICE BABY FILET MIGNON, with Mushroom Caps	3.75
BROILED CHOICE NEW YORK CUT SIRLOIN STEAK	4.50
ED CHO'CE TOP SIRLOIN B' 'STEAK	4
'D SIR' 'N S'	

Cregar's Famous Club
A Giant Triple Decker
Sliced Turkey, Crisp Bacon,
Lettuce, Tomato and Dressing
1.30

Jumbo Hamburger Deluxe
An extra large Hamburger Patty
Served on a Toasted Bun
French Fried Onion Rings
French Fried Potatoes
Cole Slaw, Lettuce, and Tomato
1.40
Topped with Melted Cheese 1.50

Homemade Apple Pie
a la Mode
.45

From Our Sandwich Board

Kosher Style Corned Beef on Rye with Dill Pickle and Cole Slaw .80
Bacon, Lettuce, and Tomato on Toast .75
Combination Ham, Cheese, Lettuce, and Tomato on a Bun .80
Cream Cheese and Chopped Olives on Raisin Toast .55
Egg, Ham, Tuna, or Chicken Salad .60
Imported Boneless and Skinless Portuguese Sardines on Rye Bread with Hard Boiled Egg, Onion, and Tomato Slice 1.15

Hot Sandwiches

Delicious All Beef Hamburger with Lettuce, Tomato, and Onion .60 Cheeseburger .65
Grilled Open Faced Tenderloin Steak Sandwich with French Fries and a Salad 1.55
Pickwick Delight: Open Faced Broiled Cheese, Bacon, and Tomato with French Fries 1.15
Hot Roast Vermont Turkey, Gravy and Potatoes 1.25
Hot Roast Sirloin of Beef, Gravy and Potatoes 1.35
Swankie Frankie: A Frankfurter Stuffed with Cheese wrapped in Bacon, and served on a Toasted Bun with Pickle .55
Grilled Cheese .50 Fried Egg .45 Western Sandwich .70

On The Light Side

Two Country Fresh Eggs with Toast and Jelly .60
Poached or Boiled Eggs .65
Light Fluffy Egg Omelette .70
Choice of: Western, Cheese, Jelly, Chopped Ham, Bacon, or Mushroom Omelette .90
Golden Brown Waffle, Maple Syrup .55
Delicious Silver Dollar Pancakes, Maple Syrup .75

Side Orders

Ham, Bacon, or Sausage .50 Canadian Bacon .60
American or French Fried Potatoes .30 Hashed Brown .40
Golden Deep Fried Onion Rings .50 For Two .95

Desserts and Beverages

All the Pies, Cakes, and Pastries Served are Baked Fresh Daily in Our Own Bake Shop
Homemade Pies and Cakes .35 a la Mode .45
Strawberry Shortcake, Whipped Cream .50
Cheese Cake .35 with Strawberries .55
Fresh Fruit Cocktail .40 Jello .25
Sodas .40 Sundaes .45 Banana Split .70
Ice Cream or Sherbet .25 and .40 Malted Milk .45
Coffee, Tea, Sanka, or Postum .15 Iced Tea .15
White or Chocolate Milk .15 Hot Chocolate .15
Soft Drinks .10 and .20

Quality color illustration plus the copy that "goes with" the picture right next to it, makes this use of color function effectively. Note the unusual layout of the other, not illustrated, items on this menu—a simple, balanced yet functional organization.

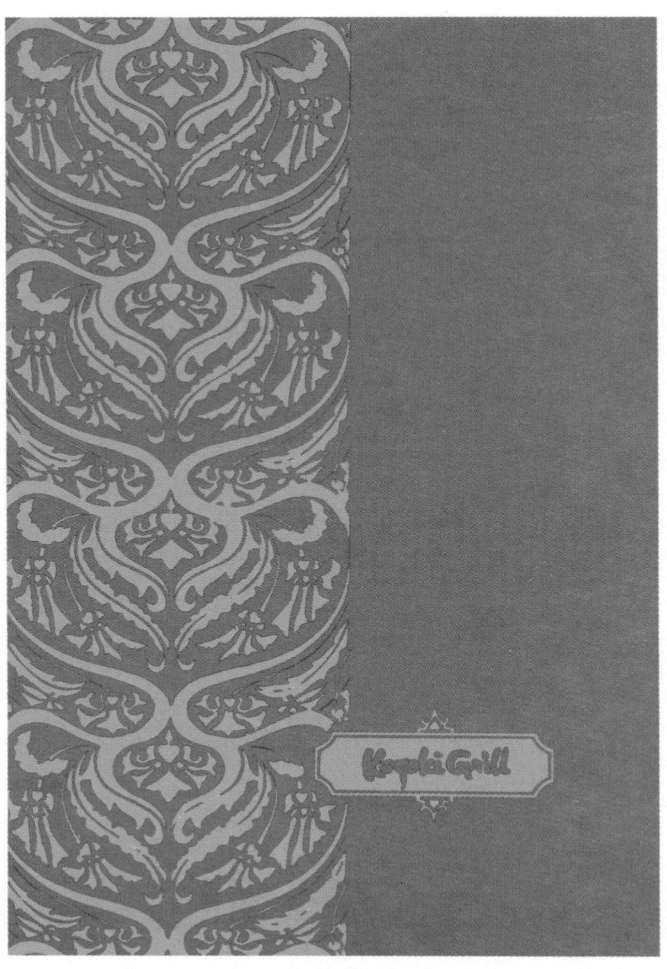

The beautiful color photography of food and drink makes the Keyaki Grill *menu exceptional.*

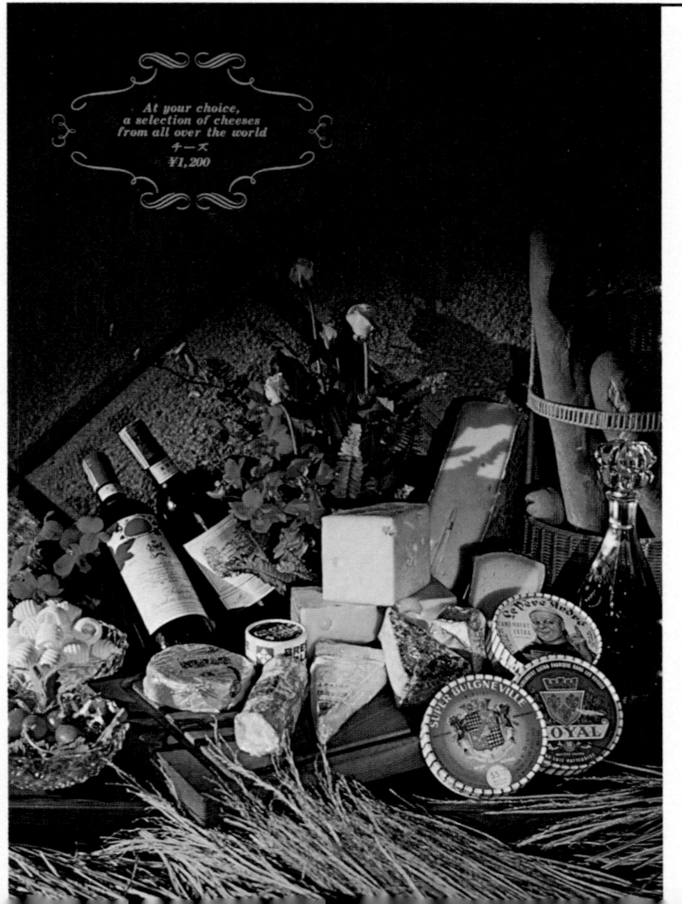

At your choice,
a selection of cheeses
from all over the world
チーズ
¥1,200

*If our selection of desserts does not include your favorite one,
please let us know and we will be delighted
to take care of your special request.*

もしメニューにございます以外のデザートをご希望でしたら、
どうぞご遠慮なくそのむねお申し付け下さいませ。
お食事を最後まで楽しく
お過ごしいただきたく思っております。

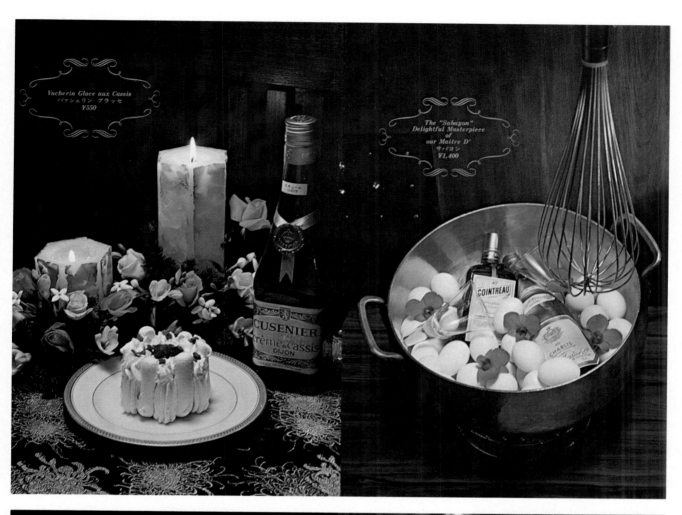

Vacherin Glace aux Cassis
バァシェリン グラッセ
¥550
CUSENIER
Crème de Cassis
DIJON

The "Sabayon"
Delightful Masterpiece
of
our Maitre D'
サバヨン
¥1,400
COINTREAU
CHABLIS

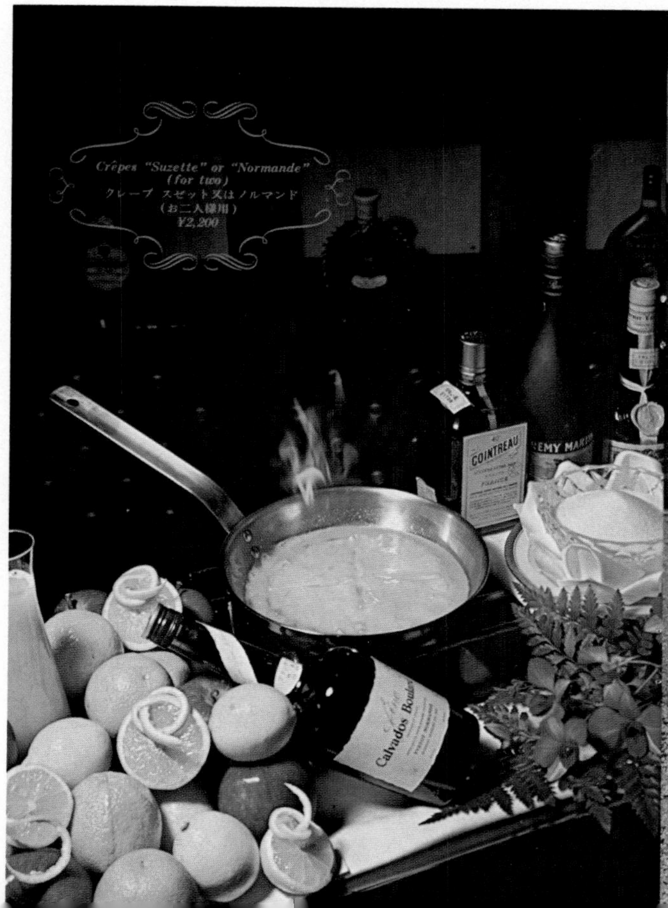

Crêpes "Suzette" or "Normande"
(for two)
クレープ スゼット又はノルマンド
(お二人様用)
¥2,200
COINTREAU
REMY MARTIN
Calvados Boulard

Baked Alaska
ベイク アラスカ
¥1,000
REMY MARTIN
V.S.O.P.
COGNAC

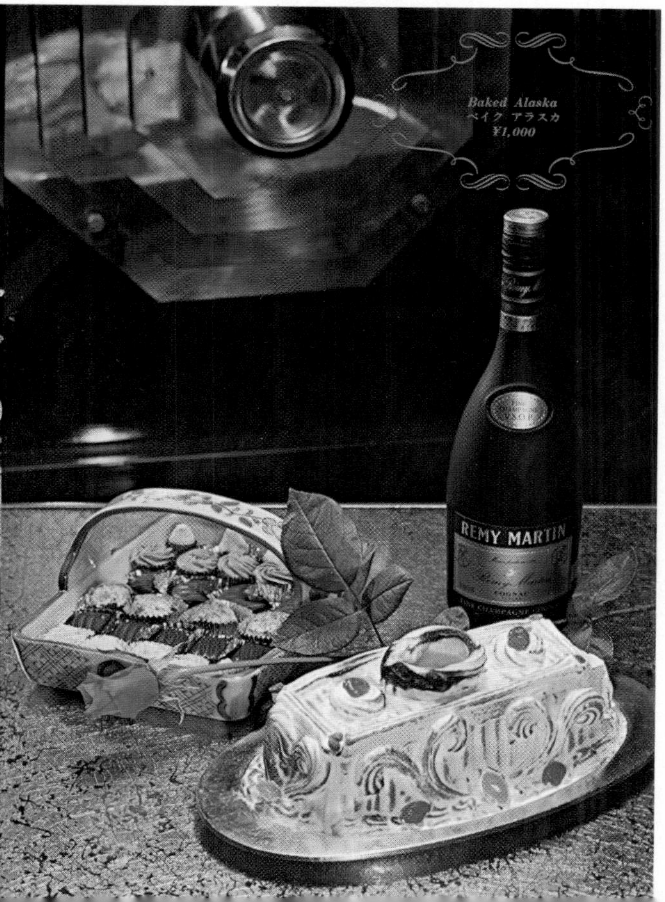

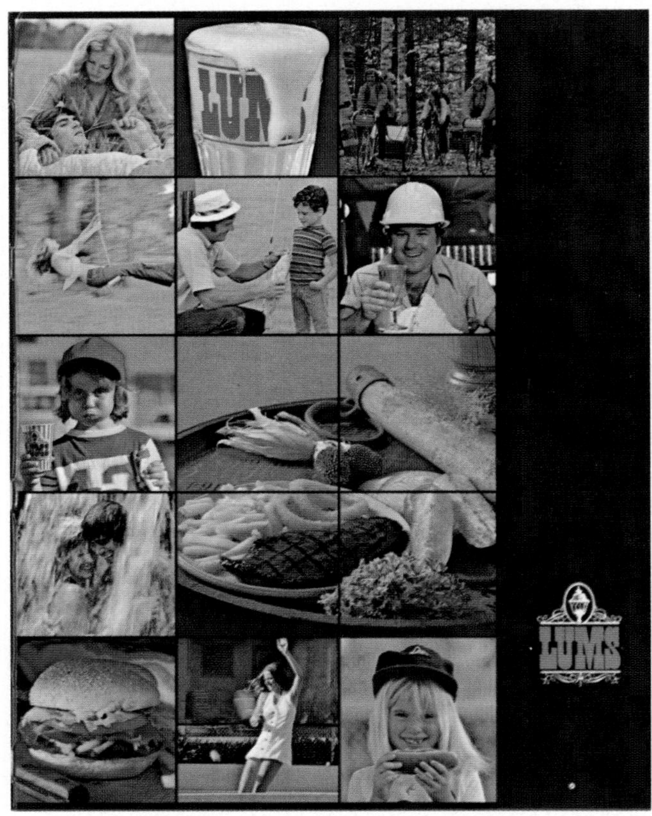

The Lums *menu is picture oriented. Color photographs tell the customer what he will get—in advance. This facilitates ordering in a fast food restaurant.*

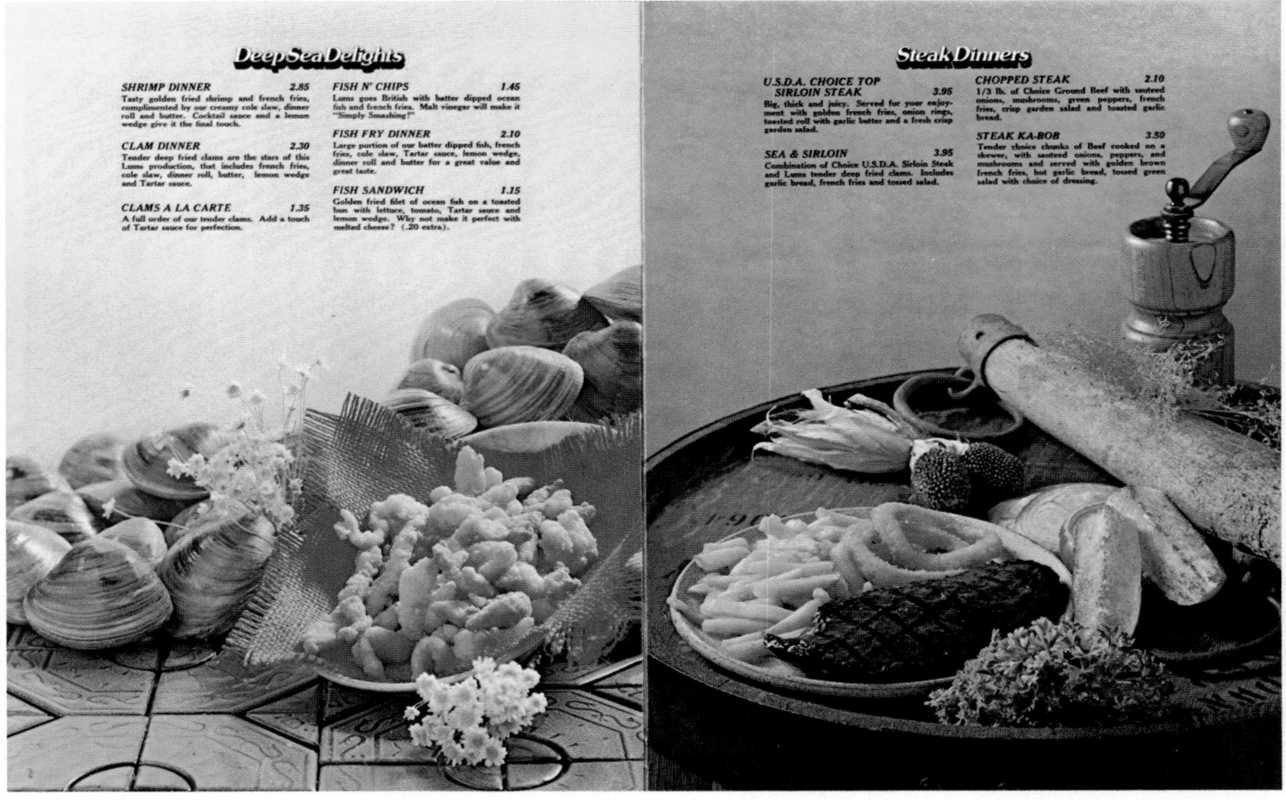

DeepSeaDelights

SHRIMP DINNER 2.85
Tasty golden fried shrimp and french fries, complimented by our creamy cole slaw, dinner roll and butter. Cocktail sauce and a lemon wedge give it the final touch.

CLAM DINNER 2.30
Tender deep fried clams are the stars of this Lums production, that includes french fries, cole slaw, dinner roll, butter, lemon wedge and Tartar sauce.

CLAMS A LA CARTE 1.35
A full order of our tender clams. Add a touch of Tartar sauce for perfection.

FISH N' CHIPS 1.45
Lums goes British with batter dipped ocean fish and french fries. Malt vinegar will make it "Simply Smashing!"

FISH FRY DINNER 2.10
Large portion of our batter dipped fish, french fries, cole slaw, Tartar sauce, lemon wedge, dinner roll and butter for a great value and great taste.

FISH SANDWICH 1.15
Golden fried filet of ocean fish on a toasted bun with lettuce, tomato, Tartar sauce and lemon wedge. Why not make it perfect with melted cheese? (.20 extra).

Steak Dinners

U.S.D.A. CHOICE TOP SIRLOIN STEAK 3.95
Big, thick and juicy. Served for your enjoyment with golden french fries, onion rings, toasted roll with garlic butter and a fresh crisp garden salad.

SEA & SIRLOIN 3.95
Combination of Choice U.S.D.A. Sirloin Steak and Lums tender deep fried clams. Includes garlic bread, french fries and tossed salad.

CHOPPED STEAK 2.10
1/3 lb. of Choice Ground Beef with sauteed onions, mushrooms, green peppers, french fries, crisp garden salad and toasted garlic bread.

STEAK KA-BOB 3.50
Tender choice chunks of Beef cooked on a skewer, with sauteed onions, peppers, and mushrooms and served with golden brown french fries, hot garlic bread, tossed green salad with choice of dressing.

12

Selling other things on the menu

While food and drink are obviously the two primary items to be sold on the menu, "other" items, services, information, and general promotion will vary from operation to operation. Not every establishment has decor, location, or history to sell. Not every food service sells take-outs or has catering or banquet-party meeting facilities. But even the operation with nothing special to sell can create some extras to add to its reputation, and often these extras can add extra income.

A list of "extra" or "other" items that appear most often on the menu may include:

History of food service operation
Story about management
Take-out or take-home service
Catering
Party-banquet meeting facilities
Gift shop
Museum connected with establishment
Tourist attractions in the neighborhood, city or nearby area
City, state and national association affiliations
AAA, Mobile, and other guide book recommendations
Credit cards honored
Map showing location

These are the more or less normal extras, but a surprising number of food service operations do not sell any of these merchandising possibilities on their menu. In fact, the average menu has a surprising number of blank pages—back cover, inside back, and front cover, etc.—that could be used for some of this merchandising.

The following examples of extra or other merchandising on the menu are from restaurants across the country.

Rosoff's Restaurant at Times Square in New York City makes a big thing out of its proximity to the theater, movies, and other places of entertainment. It has a map on the back cover of its menu showing the location of *Rosoff's*, 35 theaters, 18 movie theaters, and 6 other auditoriums and meeting places. In addition, on the inside of the menu, the restaurant lists what is currently playing at the 35 theaters listed. This makes an excellent tie-in with people who eat out before going to the theater. Where do they eat out? *Rosoff's*, of course.

The *Russ' Restaurants* in Holland and Muskegon, Michigan, get a lot of merchandising extras on a small menu. First, they feature a gift certificate as follows: "Give your friends a Russ Gift Certificate. Everyone likes to eat out. Certificate prices begin at 50¢. Inquire from our cashier."

Next, *Russ'* features copy on the preparation of their foods and take-home service:

> We prepare all the foods we serve right here on the premises. We make our own soups from plump tender chickens or juicy fresh beef and garden fresh vegetables. Try a bowl—pipin' hot! We grind our own steer beef daily, roast our own meats and turkeys. That's why our hamburgers and bar-b-que sandwiches are so tasty. We prepare our own salads and make our own dressings—to assure you a fresh crisp salad every time. We bake our own pastries—right here in our bake shop—M-m-m-m they're good! Try them here or take home some of those fresh strawberry tarts or a whole pie. We thank you for visiting us. We are happy to prepare for you the finest food in town and are gratified for this opportunity to demonstrate our service and hospitality. If you prefer, you can order by phone and take 'em home. Every item on our menu is available for carry-out service. For 31 years Russ' have taken every step possible to give you The Best of Foods, Cleanliness and Service.

THE ORIGINAL WAVERLY INN

The Twentieth Century was four years distant when Waverly Inn first opened in 1896.

Walter Scott, a gentleman-scholar from Waterbury, purchased the white house with the square roof and cupola in the center from Judge Joel Hinman, chief justice of the Connecticut Supreme Court.

Chandelier estimated to be worth $70,000.

Scott converted what had been a historical homestead into an Inn he called Waverly, named from the epochal novels of his illustrious namesake, famed author Sir Walter Scott.

Located on the historically-significant College Highway, Waverly soon became a rendezvous for discriminating diners. Among its early and frequent visitors was William Taft, at the time a member of the Yale Law School faculty and, of course, later to become president.

In 1905, Scott purchased additional land and erected a building adjoining the Inn which became known as the Casino. No dinners were served here. Scott placed antiques in the Casino and diners browsed among them. Notable in the collection was a two-wheel shay which George Washington had imported from England and later used to tour New England. Scott established the tradition of providing attractive and artistic antiques at Waverly, a custom continued to the present.

At the turn of the century and in the decade that followed under Scott's ownership, the Inn specialized in serving fish and game dinners. The Waverly soon acquired a reputation for serving the finest "hot birds and cold bottles" in New England.

Piano - at which Victor Herbert composed many of his famous scores, including "Kiss Me Again", from Mmle. Modiste.

In 1952, the original Inn was destroyed by fire. The only object salvaged from the ashes was a black, cloisonne tole urn that still embellishes the Victorian table in the main lobby. Under the guiding genius of then owners, Rocco Diorio and Louis Ricciuti, a new Waverly rose on the same site, capturing in every detail the antiquity of the past and the charm of the present.

Many Nineteenth Century hallmarks lend an air of nostalgic enchantment to Waverly, most acquired from the famous Grand Union Hotel at Saratoga Springs, N. Y. Included are the Waterford cut glass chandelier hanging in the main dining room, subject of a Life magazine story several years ago; a Rosewood grand piano, upon which composer Victor Herbert created many of his musical scores, and an exquisite rolltop desk used by President U. S. Grant to write his memoirs.

In the lobby is a complete set of Waverly Novels which were purchased in London. Descending to the sumptuous Saratoga Room, one views 18 treasured old English wall prints.

Unique mahogany clock, which houses one of the oldest self-winding mechanisms in the country.

Each of the facilities at Waverly has a blend of the old and the new to make dining more delightful. Present facilities, including the Crystal Room, Colonial Room, Saratoga Room, Tea Room, Directors Room, Blue Boy Room, Continental Room and the attractive cocktail lounge, can comfortably hold more than 1,000 diners.

Present Waverly proprietor Frank J. Nastri pledges to preserve the Inn's glorious traditions and enhance its future, not for a thousand persons, but only one . . . . you.

History, tradition, and decor can all be sold on the menu.

Then they have a couple of paragraphs on Holland, Michigan, and their growth since their founding.

> Holland is truly a 'favored city'! Dune-shored Lake Michigan and beautiful Lake Macatawa, rich fields, thriving industry, a most moving beginning with hardy Dutch pioneers seeking a haven for religious freedom . . . all have made Holland the wonderful community it is today. It's Tulip Time in Holland Every Year in May. Holland is famous for its internationally known Tulip Time Festival, held every year in mid-May; and for Windmill Island—an authentic bit of old Holland complete with working windmill, gardens and recreational attractions. As you travel through our town on the well-kept streets and through the rolling countryside and farmlands, you, too, will feel that indefinable something about the thrifty, clean, deeply religious and progressive Dutchman . . . still carried on in the first and second generation.
>
> We here at Russ' Drive-In feel gratefully favored also. It is difficult to put into words our appreciation for your loyalty and friendship . . . guaranteeing our success since our humble beginning in July of 1934. We, the management and personnel, are just as interested now, as we were in the growing up process, to merit your continued patronage through giving you the best food and service in the most pleasant and congenial surroundings . . . and, we invite your constructive suggestions and criticisms at any time.

And finally, they have two good maps showing their locations.

McGarvey's Restaurant sells some unusual other merchandising extras. To begin with, in the summer they serve the following Sip-Sup and Sail special:

> Every Wednesday, Sip-Sup-Sail. Enjoy a choice of Manhattan, Martini or Sip & Sail Cocktail, Dinner from the Captain's Table which includes:
>
> Juicy Roast Sirloin of Beef
> Fresh Lake Erie Perch
> ½ Tender Milk Fed Chicken
> Fried Deep Sea Scallops
>
> And then—Relax on Lake Erie for an Hour's Moonlite Cruise—$4.85."

General copy helps sell your total restaurant and a map tells them where it is.

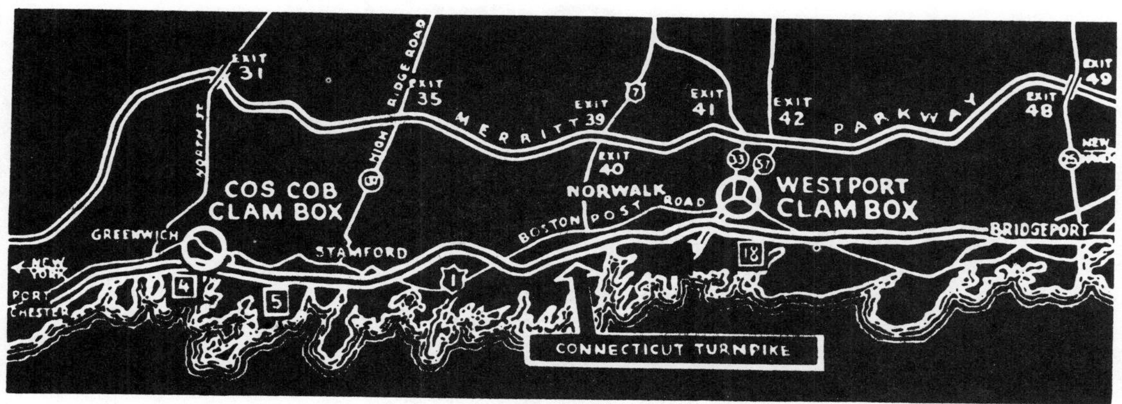

THE EIGHT WONDERS OF THE GREAT CARUSO!

The Great Caruso beholds one of the largest and most important assemblages of fine European antiquities ever to be found in one restaurant. It also displays one of the greatest and most valuable collections of operatic memorabilia in the world (e.g., the two large framed opera posters on the stage wall are priceless). Some of the more imposing antiquities – The Eight Wonders of The Great Caruso – are described below.

The grand circular brass chandelier hanging aloft the entrance level once hung in the ballroom of the Luxemburg Theatre des Arts.

The two arched handpainted and stained jeweled windows to the right of the marble pulpit are museum-quality pieces. They were removed from the chapel of the famous Earl of Whitby Castle in England.

The spectacular marble staircase pulpit, looming two stories high, was created by master marble craftsmen in Italy during the past century. Built of an incredible twelve tons of the world's finest marbles – deep-etched and chiseled in the tradition of its day – it cannot be reproduced today at any price! It was shipped to the U.S. in the late 1880's, where it graced a Buffalo, N.Y. cathedral for many decades. When the cathedral was razed recently, we purchased the grand pulpit at auction, bidding against 130 individuals and firms. It was transported here in a convoy of trucks, together with the marble railings. It took several nationally-recognized marble masons two months to reconstruct and clean it.

The ornate balcony fronts and supporting columns were once part of the famous J. Crow & Sons traveling vaudeville theatre of Ireland. The exquisite lettering on the balcony fronts is an exact duplication of the Irish company's logotype which existed on the balcony fronts previously.

A piece de resistance is the priceless handpainted and stained window in the lobby. This one-of-a-kind art masterpiece was sought after by nearly every major bidder in the now-famous 1972 Golden Movement Emporium Auction.

The backbar, perhaps the longest of its type, was built in New York in 1894 and stood in an old turn-of-the-century apothecary house in lower Manhattan. An identical twin stands in an historic chemist shop in the old section of downtown Savannah, Ga.

The astounding, ornate brass railing under the opera balconies may be the most intricate of its type in the world. A local brass craftsman who helped restore it said, in his forty years' experience, he has seen nothing like it. It was removed from The Bank of India in London.

Other points of interest:

The seven-foot statue of Hermes at the entrance-way was originally commissioned for the grand opening of the old Majestic Theatre on Main Street in 1921 when it opened as a vaudeville theatre. Incidentally, the caryatids also were retrieved from the same theatre.
The teak and pearl inlaid fire mantle onstage, circa 1870's, came from a razed library house in England, then reappeared in the Beverly Hills home of a Hollywood screenwriter...the imposing large, grand brass-bracket dome lamps outside and within the restaurant once hung in an old Chicago hotel...the twin stained and handpainted lute player windows onstage once formed part of a window wall of a centuries-old music conservatory in Holland...the heavy and luxurious wood-carved railing at the bar level came from a now-demolished New Hampshire court house...the massive stained glass rectangular section hanging aloft the lower pit area is a stunning example of rococo handfired art glass, circa 1880's...the handcarved mahogany pulpit centering the front bar came from a century-old ministry house in Australia...the opera theatre seats were removed from the old Kansas City Opera House...the sculptured relief angel sections at the entrance-way once formed part of the opera loges of the extinct Shreveport Opera House...we regret there is insufficient space to tell of the scores of other items herein displayed.

THE GREAT CARUSO
A FINE EUROPEAN STEAK HOUSE
VAUDEVILLE THEATRE & OPERA BAR

The Great Caruso, circa 1977, is owned by the Criezis Group. It was designed by Ms. Toni Renee. 10001 Westheimer at Carillon West in Houston, Texas

(Left) *The back cover of* The Great Caruso *menu features the unusual, historical, antique decor of the restaurant.*

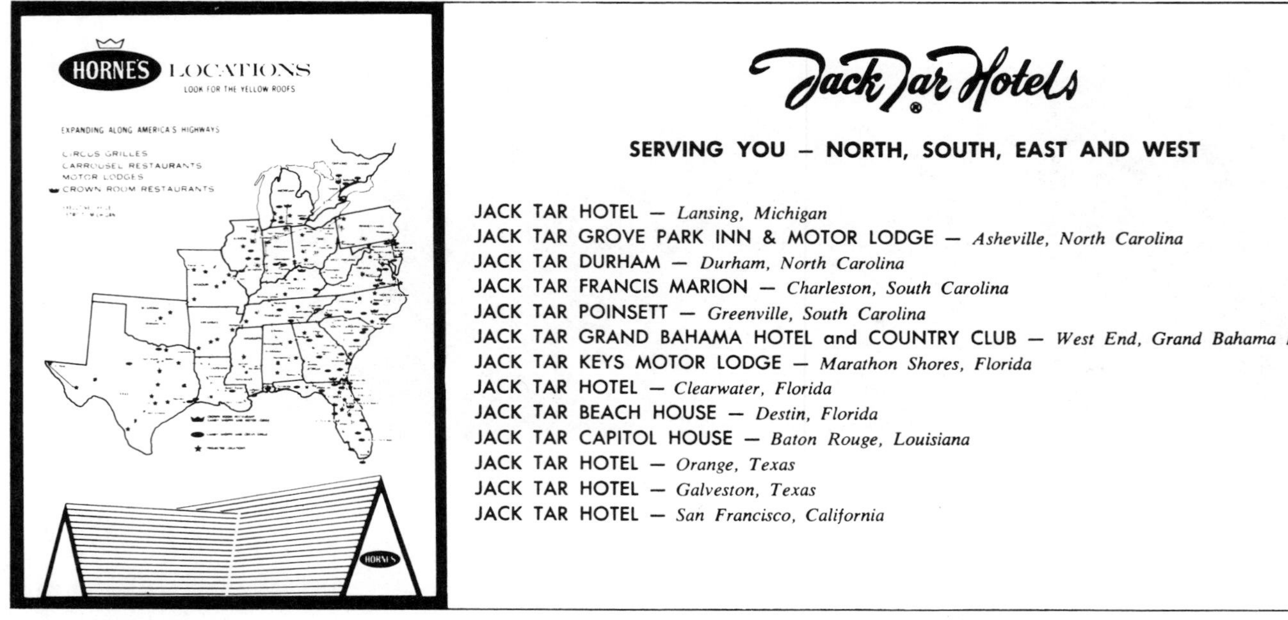

Jack Tar Hotels

SERVING YOU – NORTH, SOUTH, EAST AND WEST

JACK TAR HOTEL — *Lansing, Michigan*
JACK TAR GROVE PARK INN & MOTOR LODGE — *Asheville, North Carolina*
JACK TAR DURHAM — *Durham, North Carolina*
JACK TAR FRANCIS MARION — *Charleston, South Carolina*
JACK TAR POINSETT — *Greenville, South Carolina*
JACK TAR GRAND BAHAMA HOTEL and COUNTRY CLUB — *West End, Grand Bahama Island*
JACK TAR KEYS MOTOR LODGE — *Marathon Shores, Florida*
JACK TAR HOTEL — *Clearwater, Florida*
JACK TAR BEACH HOUSE — *Destin, Florida*
JACK TAR CAPITOL HOUSE — *Baton Rouge, Louisiana*
JACK TAR HOTEL — *Orange, Texas*
JACK TAR HOTEL — *Galveston, Texas*
JACK TAR HOTEL — *San Francisco, California*

A multiple operation should list its other locations on the menu.

Kolb's Famous Rooms

Smartest Meeting Place for Clubs, Civic Groups, Luncheons, Parties

Four fine rooms for banquets, dinners, luncheons. Varying in size from the immense to the intimately private.

- ★ ROSE ROOM. The Old European charm of crystal chandeliers and elegant carpeting make this room a favorite for the discriminating host. From 20 to 75 guests.
- ★ TYROLEAN ROOM. Banquet size, which will accommodate over 175 guests, also available in conjunction with the Rose Room for cocktail parties for larger groups.
- ★ DRESDEN ROOM. This exquisite room takes its name from the priceless collection of Dresden figurines on display therein. With its tapestry walls it is ideal for dignified dining for the small, select group, up to 12.
- ★ BAVARIAN ROOM. Lunch or dine in the atmosphere of an Old Bavarian Inn. Enjoy the ease of the roomy captain's chairs. Ideal for from 12 to 25.

(Left) *The customer can eat in only one room at a time, so if you have a multiple facility, sell the rest of the establishment on the menu.*

(Below) *Besides being a self-mailer, this memo sells a special drink, party-banquet facilities, special rooms, and a gift certificate.*

TRY OUR FAMOUS SPECIALTY
THE COACHMAN'S INN WHISKEY SOUR
SERVED IN A LARGE GOBLET WITH ICE
80¢

Party and Banquet Facilities

For your next party, banquet or business conference . . . we offer

- **THE PUMP ROOM . . .** Elegant and Pleasant.
- **THE TALLY-HO ROOM . . .** Very charming with book shelves flanking the fireplace and a picture window overlooking the fountain in our formal garden.
- For larger groups or weddings . . . during the day . . . all rooms and lounges are at your disposal.
- For more details, call between 9:00 A.M. and 4:00 P.M. and ask for our Banquet Manager . . . 759-6852.

We Honor AMERICAN EXPRESS, DINERS CLUB,
CARTE BLANCHE and MARINE MIDLAND Credit Cards.

GIFT CERTIFICATE
Gift certificates, made out in any amount, good towards the purchase of dinners and cocktails of your choice.
Ask The Host For Further Information.

THE COACHMAN'S INN IS OPEN EVERY DAY

RECOMMENDED BY THE MOBILE TRAVEL GUIDE

THE COACHMAN'S INN
10350 MAIN STREET (Route 5)
4 Miles East of Transit Road (Route 78)
CLARENCE, NEW YORK 14031

A gracious welcome awaits you at the COACHMAN'S INN. After a stretch of daily routine, one appreciates its peacefulness and quietude. One also likes the INN for its attractive, cozy lounges and cheerful atmosphere of its three huge woodburning fireplaces. Forget the mad rush of the world outside while you partake of the leisurely atmosphere this friendly INN offers. The rich panelled walls of pecky cypress have mellowed and taken on a distinguished appearance, and as a result, are a feature of the dining-rooms. The lounges grouped around the merrily burning fireplaces are just the place to relax and visit with friends while sipping your favorite cocktail. The cuisine will impress you. The food is unusually good because quality is of the very best. You always dine by candlelight at the COACHMAN'S INN with soft soothing music lingering in the background. The Innkeepers courteous, congenial and efficient staff is always at hand ready to serve you. The COACHMAN'S INN represents a nostalgic era of the past where charm and old fashioned hospitality lingers again.

Write your message here

Address

PLACE 6¢ STAMP HERE

The *Honey Bear Farm* Luncheon Menu sells a great number of things besides a very adequate selection of entrees, sandwiches, cocktails, and selected wines. First, since the Farm is located in the Wisconsin countryside, there is a map showing how to get there. Then there is a second map showing all the shops, gardens, barns, and other facilities at the Farm.

Next, there is a schedule for Spring, Summer, Fall, and Winter telling when the restaurant—and the entire Farm—is open, daily and for the year. Relative to dining, this menu-sales promotion piece advertises the following:

> *HONEY BEAR FARM RESTAURANT & LOUNGE*
> Country-style cooking. Specialties Chicken & Ham. Home made desserts, freshly baked pies and cakes. Luncheon—Dinner—Cocktails.
>
> *BRAT ROOM*
> Casual dining. Tender, juicy bratwurst and thick burgers grilled to order.
>
> *PRIVATE PARTY ROOM*
> A special place just for you and yours. Group functions, large family gatherings—relax and dine in private.

The shops which include the Country Kitchen, Smoke House & Bakery, the Gift Barn, the Yum Yum Tree, and Sugar 'n Spice are also described. The merchandising part of this promotion piece is printed in four colors. The Luncheon Menu part is printed in one color—dark brown.

The *Chart House* group of restaurants features, along with its steaks, seafood, and prime rib on the menu, its *Chart House* Mud Pie as a special dessert and its *Chart House* Bleu Cheese Dressing. Then, a special tip-on and handout gives the recipes for these two items, and on the back side of the recipe card there is a listing of the 28 cities where all of the *Chart House* restaurants are located.

Arnie's North restaurant in Highland Park, Illinois, likes to sell its food and beverages in a *big* way. To do this they have a special party or group menu. For Dinner they offer Sliced Filet Mignon or Prime Rib for 400 guests for $8,500; or Baked Chicken or Breast of Chicken, also for 400 people at $7,500. This includes unlimited cocktails, wine, disco balcony and dancing to Jim Burke's band. These dinners start with the Grand Buffet featuring Poached Trout and Steak Tartare.

For Lunch, *Arnie's* offers Saturday—Noon to 4:00 P.M.—$14.95 per person—served with unlimited cocktails, wine, and a lavish lunch. Tuesday

THE CHART HOUSE
STEAKS • SEAFOOD • PRIME RIB

CHART HOUSE MUD PIE

½ Package Nabisco chocolate wafers
½ cube Butter, melted
1 qt. Coffee ice cream
1½ c. Fudge sauce

CRUSH WAFERS AND ADD BUTTER, MIX WELL. PRESS INTO 9" PIE PLATE. COVER WITH SOFT COFFEE ICE CREAM. PUT INTO FREEZER UNTIL ICE CREAM IS FIRM. TOP WITH COLD FUDGE SAUCE (IT HELPS TO PLACE IN FREEZER FOR A TIME TO MAKE SPREADING EASIER). STORE IN FREEZER APPROXIMATELY 10 HOURS.

PRESENTATION:
SLICE MUD PIE INTO EIGHT PORTIONS AND SERVE ON A CHILLED DESSERT PLATE WITH A CHILLED FORK. TOP WITH WHIPPED CREAM AND SLIVERED ALMONDS.

The Chart House guarantees the quality of everything it serves.

CHART HOUSE LOCATIONS

CALIFORNIA
CARDIFF
CORONADO
IDYLLWILD
LA JOLLA
LONG BEACH
LOS GATOS
LOS OLIVOS
MALIBU BEACH
MARINA DEL REY
NEWPORT BEACH
OCEANSIDE
REDONDO BEACH
SAN DIEGO
SANTA BARBARA
WESTWOOD

HAWAII
LAHAINA
KAHULUI

COLORADO
ASPEN

VIRGINIA
VIRGINIA BEACH

IDAHO
SUN VALLEY
BOISE

MASSACHUSETTS
BOSTON
DUXBURY

NEW HAMPSHIRE
NASHUA

CONNECTICUT
CHESTER
SIMSBURY
NEW HAVEN

NEW YORK
DOBBS FERRY

RHODE ISLAND
NEWPORT

NEVADA
STATELINE

LOUISIANA
NEW ORLEANS

through Friday, the same is offered from $6.95 to $9.95, and . . . the entire restaurant goes with these party/banquet occasions, but the minimum is 200 to 350 guests.

The *Cabaret* has a Sunday Brunch offering—10:30 A.M. to 3:30 P.M. for $7.95 plus two drink minimum for 150 to 200 people.

(Opposite page and below) The Chart House *restaurant gives out recipes along with its menu.*

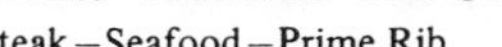

THE CHART HOUSE

Steak—Seafood—Prime Rib

DID YOU KNOW THAT THE CHART HOUSE MAKES ITS OWN DRESSINGS FROM *SCRATCH?*

CHART HOUSE BLEU CHEESE DRESSING

PLACE IN MIXING BOWL:
¾ cup sour cream
½ tsp. dry mustard
½ tsp. black pepper
scant ½ tsp. salt
scant ⅓ tsp. garlic powder
1 tsp. Worchestershire sauce
BLEND 2 MINUTES AT LOW SPEED.
ADD:
1⅓ cups mayonnaise
BLEND ½ MINUTE AT LOW SPEED, THEN BLEND 2 MINUTES AT MEDIUM SPEED.
CRUMBLE:
4 ozs. imported Danish bleu cheese by hand into very small pieces and add.
BLEND AT LOW SPEED NO LONGER THAN 4 MINUTES.
Must sit 24 hours before using. Makes approximately 2½ cups.

If you don't find a party plan that fits your needs on the enclosed outline: Call Jill at 432-1200 and she will custom-design a menu perfectly suited for your next occasion.

DINNER

1. $8,500 - 400 guests - Sliced Filet Mignon, or Prime Rib
2. $7,500 - 400 guests - Baked Chicken, or Breast of Chicken

$7,000 - 300 guests - Same choice as in 1.
$6,000 - 300 guests - Same choice as in 2.

Sumptuous dinner, served with unlimited Cocktails, Wine, Disco Balcony, Dancing to Jim Burke's Band

Start with the Grand Buffet, featuring Poached Trout to Steak Tartare
entree and dessert will be served at your table

LUNCH

Saturday Noon to 4:00 p.m. - $14.95 per person
Served with unlimited Cocktails, Wine and a lavish lunch

Tuesday thru Friday
from $6.95 to $9.95

Entire restaurant is yours in the above
Minimum 200 - 350

CABARET

Sunday Brunch
(10:30 - 3:30 p.m.)
150 — 200
$7.95 plus two drink minimum

Dinner
(6:30 to midnight)
60 — 200
$16.50 per person — Same choices as in 2.
$18.50 per person — Same choices as in 1.
Lavish Dinner served with unlimited Cocktails, Wine

Add 5% Tax and 15% Gratuity to the above

— Prices subject to change —
For party information call Jill 432-1200

The Arnie's North *banquet menu sells meals on a large scale.*

13
Specials

Few, if any, food service operators consider every item on the menu—whether appetizers, soups, salads, entrees, or desserts—as equal to every other item in the same category. There are always some items that deserve or should get "special" treatment. From the operator's point of view, there are two basic types of specials. They are the items that the establishment is famous for (if it is famous at all) and, therefore, they deserve (and usually get) special treatment.

The second basic kind of "special" is the item that the operator would like to sell more of—high profit, easy to prepare items—entree, appetizer, salad, dessert, or even side order items. The special, therefore, serves two purposes. It advertises the top selling items and it is a selling tool for making slow-moving items into faster-moving, profit items.

The important thing for the menu planner to do is to decide which items to give special treatment to, and then be sure that they are getting special treatment. The methods for giving "special" items special treatment are:

1. List specials in larger, bolder type than the rest of the menu.
2. Give specials more descriptive, merchandising "sell" copy.
3. Place specials in boxes, panels, or some kind of graphic device to make them stand out from the rest of the layout.
4. Use more color and illustrations for specials.

Like all other segments of the menu, some appetizers can be "specials" as listed here: hot saute shrimp; oysters Bienville covered with a spicy sauce of chopped mixed seafood; baked, baby western ribs; and, of course, the antipasto tray or relish tray (for two or more) is often a natural appetizer special.

The following are some "specials" that show imaginative and better than average treatment in the various menu categories from appetizer to dessert. The list of entree "specials," luncheon or dinner, could be endless, but those listed here are some unusual ones:

SPECIAL LUNCHEON—clam chowder, tossed green salad, grilled fillet of turbot, french fried potatoes, sour dough french bread, ice cream, coffee—$3.50.

DINNER SPECIAL—Relish platter, salami, mortadella, clam chowder, ravioli, tossed green salad, veal scaloppine, lobster thermidor, filet of turbot, garden vegetables, sour dough french bread, ice cream, coffee.

DANISH DINNER—consomme a la Mermaid, flounder filet, roast Long Island duck, red cabbage (Danish style), cucumber salad, lingonberries, petite browned potatoes, Ris-a-l'Allemande with Cherry Heering sauce, coffee—$5.50.

SAINT AND SINNER—a combination of lobster and choice tenderloin of beef—a delightful treat—$4.95. This is a popular "special" combination of beef and seafood sometimes called SURF AND TURF. It is popular enough on many menus to indicate considerable public acceptance.

CONTINENTAL SPECIAL—steak Diane Flambee with wild rice—mignonettes of beef cooked at your table, sauted in sweet butter, bathed in their own sauce. Served with fresh mushrooms on a bed of wild rice and flavored with brandy. This is typical of flaming dish specials.

PLANKED STEAKS BOUQUETIERRE—sirloin planked steak for two—only U.S. prime steaks are used—"broiled to a turn," and planked with a generous selection of fresh garden vegetables and mushrooms. This is just one of the many "for two" specials which are becoming very popular on the menu.

EGGS BENEDICT on toasted English muffins. Specially selected broiled ham, poached fresh eggs covered with sauce hollandaise and topped with a truffle, a mark of distinction—$3.00. This entree shows that a "special" does not have to be beef or seafood.

CARPETBAG STEAK—tenderloin steak stuffed with Sydney rock oysters, served with french fries, field mushroom sauce and hearts of lettuce. This is certainly a different steak special.

OLD FASHIONED SHORE DINNER—the works, choice of Maine chowder or lobster stew, crackers and pickles, steamed clams, bouillon and drawn butter. Then, fried clams, hot boiled lobster, chef salad, french fried potatoes, rolls, old fashioned Indian pudding with whipped cream and coffee. An adventure in good eating (Amen).

CHATEAUBRIAND—the ultimate in superior steaks. Thick and generous, this rich U.S. choice steak is recognized the world over as an epicurean masterpiece. Served for two or more, the chateaubriand is a king-sized cut of tenderloin broiled with the grain running horizontal, against the heat. This gives a succulent, crisp, tender crust with a pink warm center. This is an "occasion" steak which should be sliced cross-grain and served with a good wine and enjoyed by good company.

FROM THE BAR

The Hearthini, a masterful blend of imported gin, vodka and French vermouth. This is a change from the run of the mill martini; it was created by the *Hearth* restaurant and featured in a box at the top of its liquor listing. Another unusual way to sell and "specialize" manhattans and martinis is to sell them by the bucket. *Patterson's Supper Club*, for example, sells a bucket of Martinis and Manhattans (more than half a pint) for $2.15.

BREAKFAST

The breakfast menu can have "specials" just like any other part of the menu. Steak and eggs are a common breakfast special, but *Norm's Restaurant* goes one (or two) better. It lists and features three breakfast steak and egg combinations. They are: 1. Large porterhouse steak and eggs, $1.95; 2. Large New York cut steak and eggs, $1.95; 3. Large top sirloin steak and eggs, $1.85—served with hashed brown potatoes, toast and jelly.

SIDE DISHES

Even the lowly side dish or extra, a la carte, can be a "special" if you decide you want to give it special treatment. Some more common side dishes that have been given "special" treatment on the menu are: garlic rolls, cheese rolls, charcoal broiled mushrooms, charcoal broiled Bermuda onions.

DESSERTS

Some of the most popular "special" desserts, as noted on menus with big dessert listings are: cherries jubilee, crepes suzette (for two, usually), peaches flambeau kirsch, and baked Alaska. But a simple dessert such as ice cream can get a "special" treatment. One restaurant, for example, sells an 8-inch high, super sundae for 75¢, a "haystack" (5 scoops high) for 69¢ and a super soda (4 scoops of ice cream—2 vanilla, 2 your choice) for 60¢. The number of specials on a menu, of course, is important. If everything is made a special, then nothing becomes special. The rule should be to keep specials down to 20 to 30 percent of the items listed on the menu. This means that, if you list ten entrees or appetizers, desserts, etc., two or three of them should or can be specials. To alternate and create variety in specials, they can be printed on tip-ons and changed daily, weekly or rotated in any other way you wish to experiment.

Specials Hot

Please ask your server for the Carved Meat Feature and Prepared Dishes of the day which includes potatoes, vegetable of the day, hot rolls and butter

OR

The carved Weight Watcher of the day consisting of the same Specials served with cottage cheese, freshly sliced tomatoes, ry-krisp, polyunsaturated margarine.

$1.60

Buffet

We invite you to serve yourself from Verdugo Oaks fine Luncheon Buffet . . . a wondrous variety of enticing salads, meats, cheeses, fruits and a choice of delicious hot dishes

(Includes coffee, tea or milk and oven-hot rolls)

$2.10

SOUP DU JOUR ....35 SMALL DINNER SALAD ..50

Weight Watchers

The following entrees can also be served as Weight Watcher dishes, priced as below. We are proud to feature at your request, low fat milk, polyunsaturated margarine, ry-krisp, sanka and sucaryl.

Broiled and Grilled

CHOICE PETITE FILET MIGNON 3.25
BROILED LAMB CHOPS 2.75
BROILED GROUND SIRLOIN 1.65
LIVER AND ONIONS 1.65
GRILLED HALIBUT STEAK, Lemon and Tartar Sauce 1.60
FILET OF SOLE, Saute Meuniere 1.75
Served with Potatoes and Vegetable, Hot Rolls and Butter

THE GOLD MEDAL SANDWICH 2.35
(A Blue-Ribbon Open-Faced Sandwich on Thin Pumpernickel Bread, Paired with Choice Medallions of Beef Tenderloin and Paté de Maison. French Fries and Sliced Sweet Bermuda Onion Garni, Make this a Real Winner!)

NEW YORK STEAK SANDWICH, Garlic Bread, French Fries, Garni 2.65
VERDUGO SPECIAL HAMBURGER 1.35
(Choice Ground Sirloin, Accented with a Slice of Cheese, on one of Our Famous Onion Rolls)
LONDON RAREBIT au Maison, Garnished with Crisp Bacon 1.50
TURKEY, HAM AND AVOCADO SUPREME en Casserole . 1.85

Eggs and Omelettes

EGGS BENEDICT 2.25
(Ham and Poached Eggs on Toasted English Muffin, topped with Hollandaise Sauce)
HAM OR BACON AND (3) EGGS 1.90
(Potatoes, Toast and Butter)
CREAM SCRAMBLED EGGS 1.50
(Tomatoes and Chives, Potatoes, Toast and Butter)
SPANISH OR MUSHROOM OR CHEESE OMELETTE 1.75
(Potatoes, Toast and Butter)
GAMBLER'S EGGS 1.75
(Cream Scrambled Eggs (3) and French Toast)
CORNED BEEF HASH AND POACHED EGGS 1.75
(with Toasted English Muffin)

We reserve the right to refuse service to anyone.
Not responsible for loss of personal property.
5% Sales Tax will be Added to the Price of All Food and Beverage Items Served at Tables in this Room

MICHELOB BEER 50c

Salads

VERDUGO OAKS SALAD (Mixed at Your Table) 2.35
(Lobster, Shrimp and Crabmeat)
SHRIMP, CRAB OR LOBSTER LOUIE 2.25
OUR SUPREME FRUIT SALAD, Crowned with a Fluff of Whipped Cream 1.95
SOUTHLAND CHEF'S SALAD 1.85
STUFFED RIPE TOMATO WITH SHRIMP 1.95
TRI-SALAD (interesting salad assortment) 1.75
HALF AVOCADO STUFFED WITH SHRIMP OR CRABMEAT 2.10
COLD PRIME RIB PLATE 2.60
(Potato Salad and Sliced Tomatoes)

CAESAR SALAD (mixed at your table) .... for one 1.45
Each additional person, $1.00

Specialties and Sandwiches

COLD PRIME RIB SANDWICH on French Bread 1.75
(with French Fries - Garni)
GRILLED HAM OR BACON AND CHEESE on White Bread 1.50
(Cole Slaw and French Fries)
BACON AND TOMATO 1.35
CLUB SANDWICH 1.85
(Towering Layers of Delectable Bacon, Tomato and Sliced Turkey)
SLICED TURKEY on White Bread 1.50
(Cole Slaw and French Fries)
FRIED SHRIMP SANDWICH (3) on Toast 1.50
(Cole Slaw and French Fries)
DODGER SPECIAL (This came from Brooklyn, too) 1.75
(Finely Sliced Turkey, Ham and Cheese on Country Rye Bread, Kosher Dill and Cole Slaw)
BLACK FOREST SANDWICH 1.60
(A Grilled Delicacy on Pumpernickel Bread, Thin-Carved Roast Beef and Swiss Cheese, with Cole Slaw)
THE MONTE CRISTO 1.95
(An Aristocratic French-Toasted Sandwich Combining Ham, Turkey and Cheese)

Sweet Talk

THE FINEST IN FRENCH PASTRIES FROM THE CART 60
FRESH FRUIT AND FRESH CREAM PIES 45
OAK RUM CAKE 65 ICE CREAM OR SHERBET 40
CHEESE CAKE 50 SMALL STRAWBERRY SUNDAE 50

Coffee 25 Tea 25 Sanka 25 Milk 25
Iced Tea or Coffee 25 Low Fat Milk 25

Graphics can help to make specials even more special. These are very good and blend with the type and general appearance of the menu.

Our Special Flaming Dishes

Sword of Beef Tenderloin, Flamed with Cognac —
Served on a Bed of Saffron Rice
Vegetable or Chef's Salad
Rolls & Whipped Butter $3.95

Half Roast Boneless Native Duckling, Sliced Orange,
Sauce Bigarade, Flamed with Triple Sec
Baked Potato
Fresh Vegetable or Chef's Special Salad
Hot Rolls & Whipped Butter $4.25

POP SIZE -- one-half Chicken - $1.95
5 Pieces Tender, Golden Fried Chicken, Crisp Fries or Mashed Potatoes, Country Gravy, Green Salad, Freshly cooked Vegetables, Hot Roll and Honey

MOM SIZE $1.60
3 Pieces Golden Fried Chicken, Crisp Fries or Mashed Potatoes, Country Gravy, Green Salad, Hot Roll and Honey

ALL WHITE -- 3 pcs. -- $1.75

ALL DRUMSTICKS -- 4 pcs. -- $1.75

ALL THIGHS -- 3 pcs. -- $1.80

ALL WINGS -- 6 pcs. -- $1.40

GIZZARDS -- 7 pcs. -- $1.15

Above served with soup or tossed green salad, choice of potatoes, country gravy, freshly cooked vegetables, hot roll and honey

Flaming dishes make a natural special and chicken can be "specialized" as shown on the menu directly above.

OUR SPECIALTY
FOR OVER TEN YEARS
YOUNG DOMESTICATED RING-NECKED PHEASANT
Disjointed, Saute Sec with spiced crabapple. Delivered fresh to us from a Santa Cruz Mountain flock which is raised under the inspection of the California Department of Agriculture.
A COMPLETE DINNER 4.10

Broiled Live Maine Lobster
with Hot Drawn Butter, Vegetable, Fresh Garden Salad

Medium - 1¾ lbs. avg. $6.25
Large - 2½ lbs. avg. $7.25

Prime Sirloin Steak
Our ultimate in fine steaks, served with mushroom caps, baked potato tossed mixed green salad with french dressing
$6.50

Filet Mignon
Well marbled and rich, served with mushroom caps, baked potato tossed mixed green salad with french dressing
$6.50

An unusual item such as pheasant makes a "special," and unusual graphics and type make lobster and steak "special."

MONDAY

No. 1 **MEAT BALL & SPAGHETTI,** Tossed Green Salad, Rolls, Butter, Coffee or Tea 1.00

No. 2 **CHICKEN FRIED STEAK,** Green Garden Peas, Carrot and Raisin Salad, Rolls, Butter, Coffee or Tea 1.00

No. 3 **ITALIAN SAUSAGE & SPAGHETTI,** Tossed Green Salad, Rolls, Butter, Coffee or Tea 1.00

TUESDAY

No. 1 **SPAGHETTI & BRACIOLONI,** Tossed Green Salad, Rolls, Butter, Coffee or Tea 1.00

No. 2 **CHICKEN GIZZARDS,** Rice and Gravy, Leon's Salad, Rolls, Butter, Coffee or Tea 1.00

No. 3 **STUFFED BELL PEPPER** with Tomato Sauce, French Fried Potatoes, Tossed Green Salad, Rolls, Butter, Coffee or Tea 1.25

WEDNESDAY

No. 1 **IRISH STEW,** Cole Slaw, Rolls, Butter, Coffee or Tea 1.00

No. 2 **CHICKEN & SPAGHETTI,** Tossed Green Salad, Rolls, Butter, Coffee or Tea 1.00

No. 3 **POT ROAST OF BEEF,** Jardiniere Sauce, Creamed Potatoes, Peas, Rolls, Butter, Coffee or Tea 1.25

THURSDAY

No. 1 **VEAL MOZZARELLA & SPAGHETTI,** Tossed Green Salad, Rolls, Butter, Coffee or Tea 1.00

No. 2 **LASAGNE,** Tossed Green Salad, Rolls, Butter, Coffee or Tea 1.00

No. 3 **SALISBURY STEAK,** French Fried Potatoes, Leon's Salad, Rolls, Butter, Coffee or Tea 1.00

FRIDAY

No. 1 **FRIED CATFISH,** French Fried Potatoes, Tossed Green Salad, Rolls, Butter, Coffee or Tea 1.00

No. 2 **MEAT LOAF,** Garden Green Peas, Potato Salad, Rolls, Butter, Coffee or Tea 1.00

No. 3 **HALF DOZEN FRIED OYSTERS,** French Fried Potatoes, Pickled Bean Salad, Rolls, Butter, Coffee or Tea 1.00

A weekly menu that offers three specials every day is a special "special." "All You Can Eat" always makes a "special."

Specials in a Basket

CHICKEN-IN-THE-BASKET
Chicken Fried to a Crisp Golden Brown. Served with French Fries, Cole Slaw, Buttered Roll. **1.35**

HAMBURGER BASKET
2 Patties of Freshly Ground Beef.
French Fries and Cole Slaw. **.75**

JUMBO HAMBURGER BASKET
¼ lb. of Freshly Ground Beef.
French Fries, Cole Slaw **1.00**

SHRIMP-IN-THE-BASKET
Ocean Fresh Shrimp Deep Fat Fried and Served with Cocktail Sauce, French Fries, Cole Slaw, Buttered Rolls. **1.55**

FRIED PERCH BASKET
with Tartar Sauce, Grilled Bun.
French Fries and Cole Slaw. **.95**

SWARZBURGER BASKET
with French Fried Onion Rings, French Fries, Cole Slaw. **1.25**

More than one item can be a "Special in a Basket."

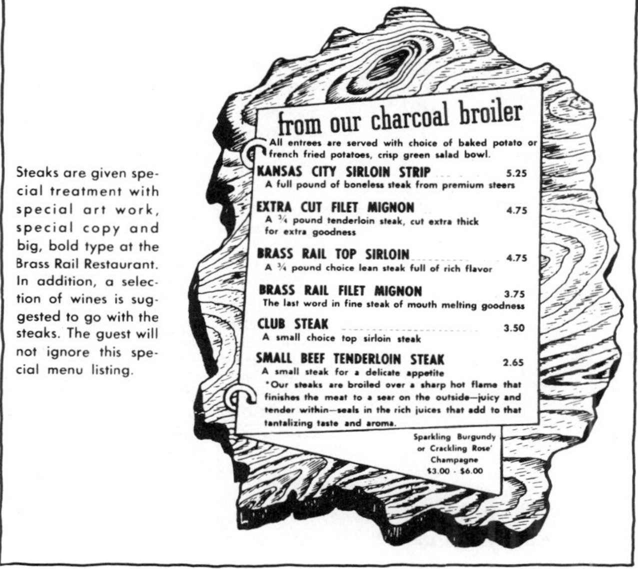

from our charcoal broiler

All entrees are served with choice of baked potato or french fried potatoes, crisp green salad bowl.

KANSAS CITY SIRLOIN STRIP 5.25
A full pound of boneless steak from premium steers

EXTRA CUT FILET MIGNON 4.75
A ¾ pound tenderloin steak, cut extra thick for extra goodness

BRASS RAIL TOP SIRLOIN 4.75
A ¾ pound choice lean steak full of rich flavor

BRASS RAIL FILET MIGNON 3.75
The last word in fine steak of mouth melting goodness

CLUB STEAK 3.50
A small choice top sirloin steak

SMALL BEEF TENDERLOIN STEAK 2.65
A small steak for a delicate appetite

*Our steaks are broiled over a sharp hot flame that finishes the meat to a sear on the outside—juicy and tender within—seals in the rich juices that add to that tantalizing taste and aroma.

Sparkling Burgundy
or Crackling Rose'
Champagne
$3.00 - $6.00

Steaks are given special treatment with special art work, special copy and big, bold type at the Brass Rail Restaurant. In addition, a selection of wines is suggested to go with the steaks. The guest will not ignore this special menu listing.

OUR SPECIALTIES

WILLOW GROVE CRAB CAKE DINNER
French Fries, Cole Slaw
$2.00

CHESAPEAKE BAY ROCK FISH
Tartar Sauce, Lemon Wedge
French Fries, Cole Slaw
$1.75

BROILED TOP SIRLOIN STEAK
Baked Potato, Chef Salad
$4.00

ONE-HALF MARYLAND FRIED CHICKEN
French Fries, Green Peas
$1.75

Illustrations—in this case line drawings—can be used to highlight and feature specials.

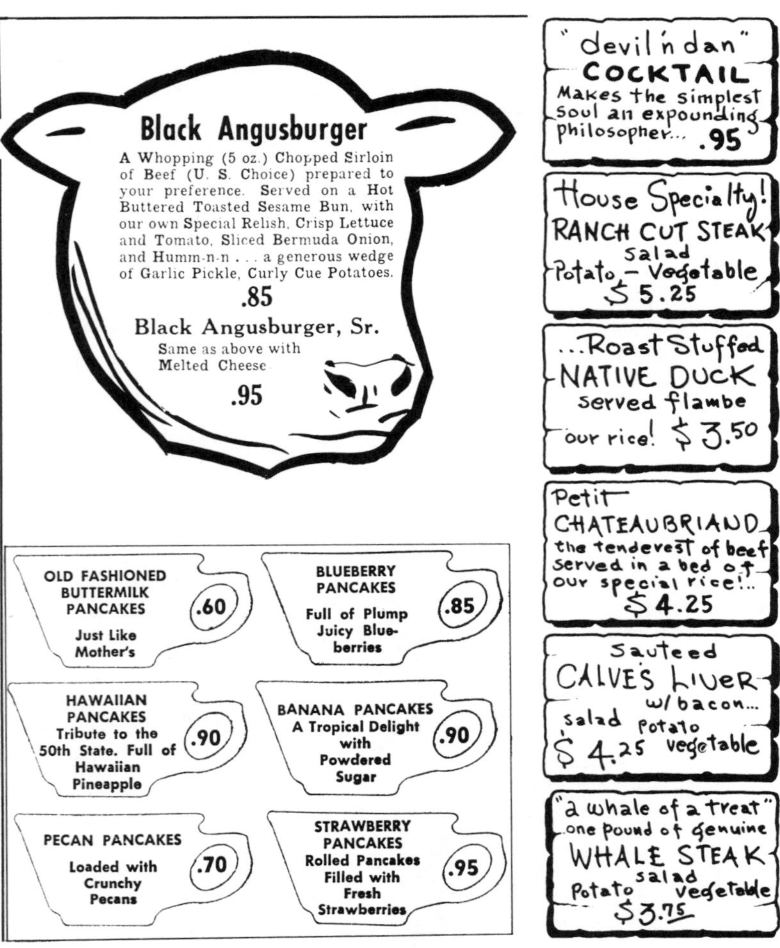

Black Angusburger
A Whopping (5 oz.) Chopped Sirloin of Beef (U. S. Choice) prepared to your preference. Served on a Hot Buttered Toasted Sesame Bun, with our own Special Relish, Crisp Lettuce and Tomato, Sliced Bermuda Onion, and Humm-n-n . . . a generous wedge of Garlic Pickle, Curly Cue Potatoes.
.85
Black Angusburger, Sr.
Same as above with Melted Cheese
.95
OLD FASHIONED BUTTERMILK PANCAKES
Just Like Mother's
.60
BLUEBERRY PANCAKES
Full of Plump Juicy Blueberries
.85
HAWAIIAN PANCAKES
Tribute to the 50th State. Full of Hawaiian Pineapple
.90
BANANA PANCAKES
A Tropical Delight with Powdered Sugar
.90
PECAN PANCAKES
Loaded with Crunchy Pecans
.70
STRAWBERRY PANCAKES
Rolled Pancakes Filled with Fresh Strawberries
.95
"devil n dan"
COCKTAIL
Makes the simplest soul an expounding philosopher... .95
House Specialty!
RANCH CUT STEAK
salad
Potato – Vegetable
$5.25
...Roast Stuffed
NATIVE DUCK
served flambe
our rice! $3.50
Petit
CHATEAUBRIAND
the tenderest of beef served in a bed of our special rice!..
$4.25
Sauteed
CALVES LIVER
w/bacon...
salad potato
$4.25 vegetable
"a whale of a treat"
one pound of genuine
WHALE STEAK
salad
Potato vegetable
$3.75

Specials can fit into a variety of shapes and panels.

Special deals for children on the Family Style Chicken Dinner and two sizes of steak (one for the man, another for the woman) plus WOP salad and Complimentary Cake for that Special Lady—make for extra special specials.

Foote Cafe's Special Dinners

Family Style Chicken Dinner ----$1.75

EVERY WEDNESDAY, 5:00 TO 10:00 P.M.

Pan fried chicken with all the trimmings. Children four to 10 years of age $1.00, under three free. With the chicken you will be served mashed potatoes, creamed chicken gravy, corn, cole slaw, cottage cheese, biscuits, ice cream and drink.

Family Style Dinner -------------$1.75

EVERY FRIDAY NIGHT

We start your dinner with an appetizer of stuffed celery, radishes, onions, pickles, crackers, and a large combination salad with dressing. Next we serve you with all the fried shrimp, chicken, and fillet of deep sea cat fish you can eat. All of the French fried potatoes and hot garlic bread you can eat and you can have second or third helpings of anything on this dinner at no extra cost. The price for children, four to 10 years is $1.00, under four free. **These special dinners are served in the dining room only.**

Please Call FA 4-5674 For Reservations

BEEF N' BOTTLE

MR. & MRS. CHAMPAGNE DINNER

For That Special Festive Occasion

Aperitif—Two Glasses Rose Wine
For Mr. a Planked 12-Oz. New York Cut Sirloin
For Mrs. a Planked 8-Oz. New York Cut Sirloin
10th of Paul Masson Champagne
WOP Salad (a House Specialty) or Dinner Salad and Choice of Dressing
Relish Dish
Rolls and Butter Coffee, Tea or Milk
Baked Alaska for Two
Complimentary Cake for That Special Lady

14.75

14

Variety is the spice of the menu

To get the "same old food," the customer can eat at home. Of course, the standard entree, appetizer, dessert, sandwich and salad items, perennial favorites, are necessary for a successful menu, but the unusual, exotic gourmet treat is the sign of a successful restaurant. Even if these unusual items do not get ordered as often as the old "standbys," since some people are afraid to venture into unknown cuisine territory, the "word of mouth" advertising from those who do try your exotic entrees makes them worthwhile.

The following examples show actual creative menu building. Even if they do not sound like items that would fit into your menu, they should stimulate your creative thinking so that your menu will become more interesting, exciting, and salesworthy.

Gordon's Rainbow Inn, for example, has a clever listing of "Combinations." These are entree items that are half one entree and half another. This is an easy method of extending the menu, without really adding any new entree to it, while creating unusual items. They are:

COMBINATIONS

THE SPECIAL (Patty Ground Sirloin, Half Order Chicken)	$2.95
THE TWIN (Patty Ground Sirloin, Half Order Giant Lobster Tail)	$5.25
THE DUET (Half Order Chicken, Half Order Giant Lobster Tail)	$5.25
THE GOURMET (Half Order Chicken, Half Order Filet Mignon)	$4.95
RAINBOW DELIGHT (Half Order Filet Mignon, Half Order Giant Lobster Tail)	$6.50
THE FAVORITE (Half Order King Crab Legs, Half Order Filet Mignon)	$5.75

Neither soup nor salad need be "ordinary." The two following examples from *Herb Traub's Pirate House* illustrate exciting menu ideas:

SOUL SATISFYING SOUPS

Served with mixed cracker basket or home baked bread and butter, Miss Edna's Seafood Bisque. Something to write home about! Nourishing nuggets of fresh, flavorful crabmeat and plump Savannah shrimp swimming in a skillful blend of cream of tomato and pea soup . . . delicately flavored with sherry. . . . Bowl $1.60 Cup $1.10

GEMS FROM OUR SALAD GALLEY

Served with hot home-baked bread and crisp crackers, Pineapple Dreamboat—so cooling, so delightfully refreshing is this sun-ripened Hawaiian pineapple that's been scooped out and filled with mixed fruit, then topped with coconut and orange ice, orange—cream cheese—pecan dressing; date-nut bread sandwiches too! . . . $2.75.

Nearly everybody serves the ubiquitous hamburger in some shape or form, but *The Governor's Tavern* serves it nine different ways. Here they are:

BEEFBURGERS

A luncheon specialty of the house, available in nine delicious variations, each one man-sized, solidly constructed of at least one-quarter pound of choice ground beef. Broiled over charcoal and served on a fresh roll.

Your choice of Nine Varieties. . . . $.90

1. RELISH BURGER, our regular beefburger topped with old-fashioned red pepper relish.
2. CHEDDAR BURGER, a real favorite served with melted New York State cheddar cheese.
3. PEPPER BURGER, a beefburger served with sauteed Italian green peppers.
4. GOURMET BURGER, our famous beefburger garnished with imported Danish bleu cheese.

5. ONION BURGER, a breath taking beefburger topped with a raw or sauteed Bermuda onion.
6. MUSHROOM BURGER, if you like sauteed mushrooms, you'll enjoy this beefburger, it's smothered with 'em.
7. DIET BURGER, for the calorie conscious—no roll, but accompanied by some cottage cheese.
8. DANDY BURGER, a beefburger, all dressed up with a slice of tomato, lettuce and mayonnaise.
9. BRINY BURGER, breaded whitefish fillet served like a beefburger and garnished with tartar sauce.

If there is unusual wildlife, fish, or other edibles available in the area of your restaurant, consider serving it on your menu. The *Holiday Inn* of Thomasville, Georgia, for example, serves South Georgia Quail in its Orchid Room. It is served southern style with grits, salad, biscuits and honey, coffee or tea. One quail is $3.00, two quails are $5.50.

Many restaurants serve spaghetti and many restaurants serve chili, but few serve them together as *Tops* restaurant does. They call it Pasta Fiesta, and it is spaghetti covered with *Tops'* own piping hot chili, melted cheese, cherry pepper, and toast for $.90.

Many restaurants use imagination in naming their entrees. *The Pickwick Room*, a restaurant in Lancashire, England, shows imagination in the entree listing shown here:

MR. TUPMAN'S TREAT
Half, barbecued English chicken served with old fashioned sage and onion stuffing, small tasty carrots, watercress and potatoes.

SAM WELLER'S CHOICE
Prime sirloin steak, garnished with mushrooms, tomato, tasty small carrots, watercress and your choice of potatoes.

AUGUSTUS SNODGRASS DELIGHT
Sliced Gammon ham with fresh farm egg, tomato, mushrooms, garden peas, watercress and potatoes.

ALFRED JINGLE "PUTTING ON"
Three egg omelette, your choice of cheese, herbs or mushrooms, served with garden peas, tomato, watercress and potatoes.

MRS. BARDELL'S FAVORITE
Choice fillet steak, garnished with mushrooms, tomato, watercress, garden peas and potatoes.

JOE THE FAT BOY'S SNACK
Juicy T-bone steak served with mushrooms, tomato, watercress, tasty carrots and potatoes.

MR. PICKWICK'S SPECIALTY
Half Norfolk duckling, roasted to a crispy tenderness, served with apple and cherry, old fashioned sage and onion stuffing, garden fresh peas, watercress and your choice of potatoes.

MR. WINKLE'S CHOICE
Selected deep fried scampi served with creamy tartar sauce and garnished with lemon, watercress, tomato, garden peas and potatoes.

Occasionally, what the entree is served in can make the difference. The following is an entree item served by the *Chandelier* restaurant at the Queen's Quarter Hotel in the Virgin Islands.

"IN A COCONUT"
Lobster meat, shrimp and langostinos in a rich Newburg sauce, baked in a pastry sealed coconut . . . $6.50

And at the same restaurant, the following flaming dessert is unusual to say the least:

BAKED BANANAS AND ORANGE GRENADA
Bananas and orange slivers baked slowly in brown sugar, lime and other delectables, served flaming at your table in a juice you will not soon forget.

Finally, the answer to "assorted pies" on the menu, which never really sells pies, we have again the *Pirate's House* menu—the dessert menu this time:

Pies: Like Mother wishes she could make!

BLACK BOTTOM PIE
Rich, mouth-melting chocolate fudge custard in a crunchy chocolate wafer crust, topped with a triple-thick layer of tantalizing rum-flavored chiffon filling, whipped cream and bitter-sweet chocolate shavings . . . . Merely Terrific!

GRASSHOPPER PIE
Totally Different! Totally Delightful! Absolutely Delicious! Just imagine . . . A luscious light-as-a-cloud chiffon concoction made with pure cream, pale green creme de menthe and mellow creme de cacao nestled atop a rich bittersweet chocolate fudge base . . . all this in a crunchy chocolate wafer crust . . . then on top, a crown of thick whipped cream and bitter-sweet chocolate shavings! Better save room for a slice or two! . . . . . $.75

FRESH GEORGIA PEACH ICE CREAM SUNDAE PIE
Double-rich peach ice cream piled high in a crunchy almond-flavored crust . . . topped with thick whipped cream, loads of luscious sliced peaches and a cherry impaled on a tiny plastic sword. Wotta way to die!

THE BROTHERS

RESTAURANT NINETEEN SOUTH SEVENTH STREET MINNEAPOLIS

SANDWICHES from our Delicatessen Counter

The Brothers Famous Corned Beef Sandwich	
Hot or Cold	.95
Jumbo Size	1.35
SPECIAL: Hot or Cold Corned Beef Sandwich, With Potato Salad	1.20
THE RUBEN SANDWICH Hot Corned Beef, Sauerkraut and Grilled Swiss Cheese	1.35
THE "PEPE" SANDWICH Hot Pastrami and Grilled Hot Pepper Cheese	1.25
Turkey 1.00 All White Meat	1.15
Hot Roumanian Pastrami	.95
Cold Peppered Beef Sandwich	.95
Grilled Cheese, Bacon and Tomato	1.00
Roast Beef, Hot or Cold Beef	.95
Baked Ham	.95
Kosher Salami	.75
Kosher Bologna	.75
Liverwurst	.70
Swiss Cheese	.60
Chopped Chicken Liver	.90
Chicken Salad	.85
Tuna Salad	.75
Egg Salad	.50
Bacon, Lettuce and Tomato	.85
Grilled Cheese	.65

Sandwiches on Bagel, Onion Roll or Kaiser Rolls 5c Extra

COLD COMBINATION SANDWICHES

Hot or Cold Corned Beef and Swiss Cheese	1.25
Baked Ham and Swiss Cheese	1.25
Turkey, Cole Slaw and Russian Dressing	1.25
Hot Corned Beef, Cole Slaw and Russian Dressing	1.20
Turkey, Swiss Cheese, Cole Slaw and Russian Dressing	1.45

"COLOSSALS" on individual French Bread

1. "Dora's Favorite" Club Turkey, Bacon, Lettuce and Tomato 1.50
2. "Brother Fred" Open Face Sliced Turkey, Corned Beef, Swiss Cheese, Lettuce and Tomato with French or Thousand Island Dressing 1.65
3. "Brother Sam" Turkey, Baked Ham and Swiss Cheese 1.50
4. "Brother Len" Corned Beef, Pastrami and Swiss Cheese 1.50
5. "Little Brother" Corned Beef, Salami and Grilled Cheddar Cheese 1.60
6. "Charlie Boone in the Afternoon" Treat Hot Pastrami, Swiss Cheese, Cole Slaw Combination 1.45
7. Randy Merriman's "Honest To Goodness" Special Turkey, Corned Beef, Cole Slaw, Swiss Cheese and Russian Dressing 1.60
8. Bill Carlson's Late Show Special Turkey, Hot Pastrami, Swiss Cheese, Cole Slaw and Russian Dressing 1.60

HOT SANDWICHES

Roast Turkey, Mashed Potato, Gravy 1.40
All White Meat 1.50
Roast Sirloin of Beef, Mashed Potato and Gravy 1.40
Bar B Q Beef Sandwich, French Fries, Cole Slaw 1.15

KOSHER HOT DOGS

1. Sauerkraut and Mustard .60
2. Mustard, Relish and Onions .60
3. Hickory Smoked Bar-B-Q Sauce .60
4. Chili, Onions and Grated Cheese .70
5. Zesty Cheddar Cheese, Bacon Strips and Bar-B-Q Sauce .80

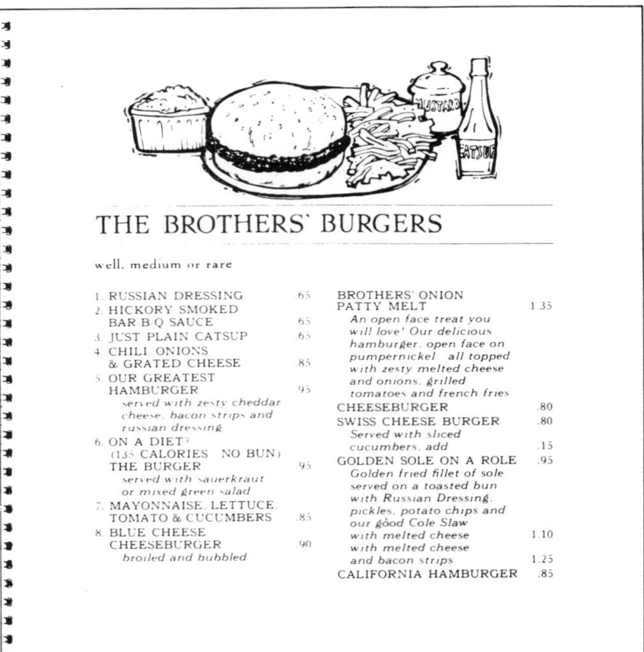

THE BROTHERS' BURGERS

well, medium or rare

1. RUSSIAN DRESSING .65
2. HICKORY SMOKED BAR-B-Q SAUCE .65
3. JUST PLAIN CATSUP .65
4. CHILI, ONIONS & GRATED CHEESE .85
5. OUR GREATEST HAMBURGER .95
served with zesty cheddar cheese, bacon strips and russian dressing
6. ON A DIET? (135 CALORIES NO BUN) THE BURGER .95
served with sauerkraut or mixed green salad
7. MAYONNAISE, LETTUCE, TOMATO & CUCUMBERS .85
8. BLUE CHEESE CHEESEBURGER .90
broiled and bubbled

BROTHERS' ONION PATTY MELT 1.35
An open face treat you will love! Our delicious hamburger, open face on pumpernickel all topped with zesty melted cheese and onions, grilled tomatoes and french fries

CHEESEBURGER .80

SWISS CHEESE BURGER .80
Served with sliced cucumbers, add .15

GOLDEN SOLE ON A ROLE .95
Golden fried fillet of sole served on a toasted bun with Russian Dressing, pickles, potato chips and our good Cole Slaw
with melted cheese 1.10
with melted cheese and bacon strips 1.25

CALIFORNIA HAMBURGER .85

First spread, The Brothers Delicatessen *menu.*

Second spread.

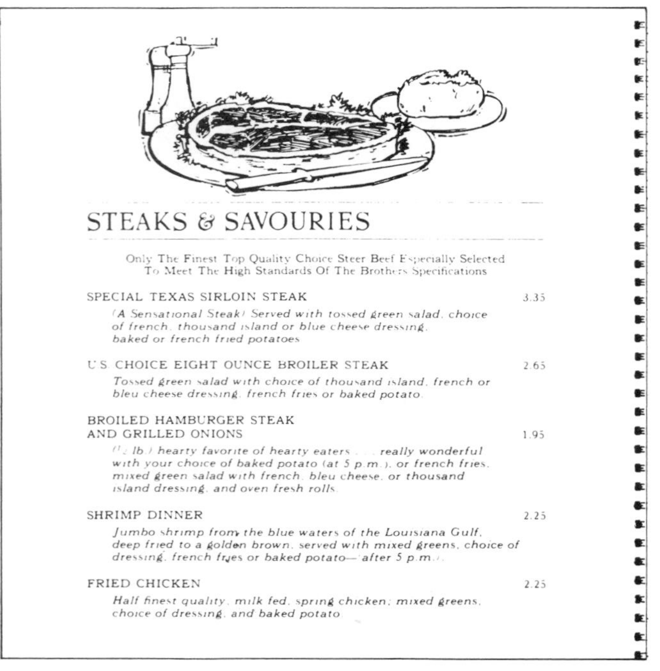

STEAKS & SAVOURIES

Only The Finest Top Quality Choice Steer Beef Especially Selected To Meet The High Standards Of The Brothers Specifications

SPECIAL TEXAS SIRLOIN STEAK 3.35
(A Sensational Steak) Served with tossed green salad, choice of french, thousand island or blue cheese dressing, baked or french fried potatoes

U.S. CHOICE EIGHT OUNCE BROILER STEAK 2.65
Tossed green salad with choice of thousand island, french or bleu cheese dressing, french fries or baked potato

BROILED HAMBURGER STEAK AND GRILLED ONIONS 1.95
(½ lb.) hearty favorite of hearty eaters ... really wonderful with your choice of baked potato (at 5 p.m.), or french fries, mixed green salad with french, bleu cheese, or thousand island dressing, and oven fresh rolls

SHRIMP DINNER 2.25
Jumbo shrimp from the blue waters of the Louisiana Gulf, deep fried to a golden brown, served with mixed greens, choice of dressing, french fries or baked potato— after 5 p.m.)

FRIED CHICKEN 2.25
Half finest quality, milk fed, spring chicken; mixed greens, choice of dressing, and baked potato

THE BROTHERS DELICATESSEN PLATTERS

Corned Beef Platter with Potato Salad and Sliced Tomato 1.65
Combination Corned Beef and Pastrami, Potato Salad and Sliced Tomato 1.65
Sliced Roast Beef Platter, with Potato Salad and Sliced Tomato 1.75
Chopped Chicken Liver Platter, with Potato Salad and Egg Wedges 1.50
Fresh Smoked White Fish with Potato Salad, Sliced Tomato 1.75

The Brothers Special: ASSORTED COLD CUTS PLATTER 1.95
Corned Beef, Pastrami, Roast Beef, Chopped Liver, Salami, Breast of Turkey, and Cheese, Potato Salad, Sliced Tomato
Kosher Knockwurst Platter served with Potato Salad and Baked Beans 1.20
Kosher Frankfurter Platter with Potato Salad and Baked Beans 1.20

Oven Fresh Rolls and Butter Served with Above Orders

BAGELS ON PARADE

Plain or Toasted .20
with Cream Cheese .40
with Cream Cheese and Jelly .50
with Smoked Salmon .85
with Smoked Salmon and Cream Cheese 1.10

COUNTRY MATTERS - Carry Out Only

DRUMS OF FRIED CHICKEN

8 pieces serves 2 or 3 2.50
12 pieces serves 4 or 5 3.75
16 pieces serves 6 to 8 4.95
20 pieces serves 8 to 12 6.25

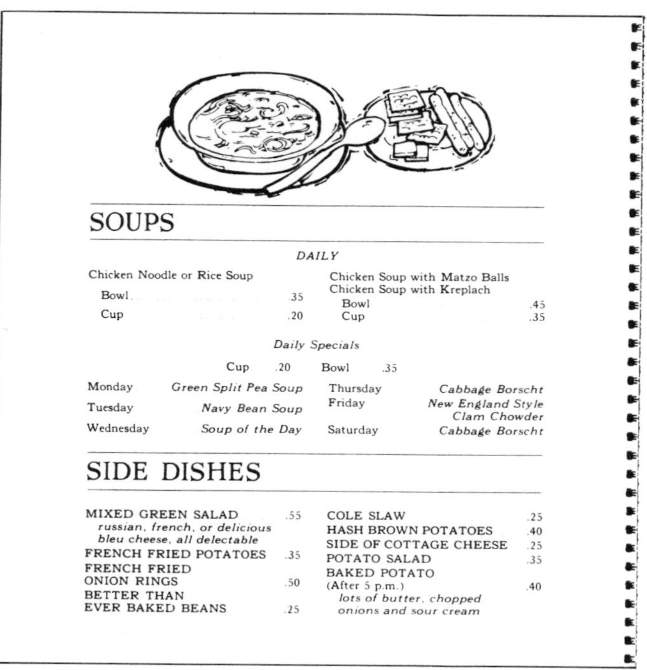

SOUPS

DAILY

Chicken Noodle or Rice Soup
Bowl .35
Cup .20

Chicken Soup with Matzo Balls
Chicken Soup with Kreplach
Bowl .45
Cup .35

Daily Specials

Cup .20 Bowl .35

Monday	*Green Split Pea Soup*	Thursday	*Cabbage Borscht*
Tuesday	*Navy Bean Soup*	Friday	*New England Style Clam Chowder*
Wednesday	*Soup of the Day*	Saturday	*Cabbage Borscht*

SIDE DISHES

MIXED GREEN SALAD .55
russian, french, or delicious bleu cheese, all delectable
FRENCH FRIED POTATOES .35
FRENCH FRIED ONION RINGS .50
BETTER THAN EVER BAKED BEANS .25

COLE SLAW .25
HASH BROWN POTATOES .40
SIDE OF COTTAGE CHEESE .25
POTATO SALAD .35
BAKED POTATO (After 5 p.m.) .40
lots of butter, chopped onions and sour cream

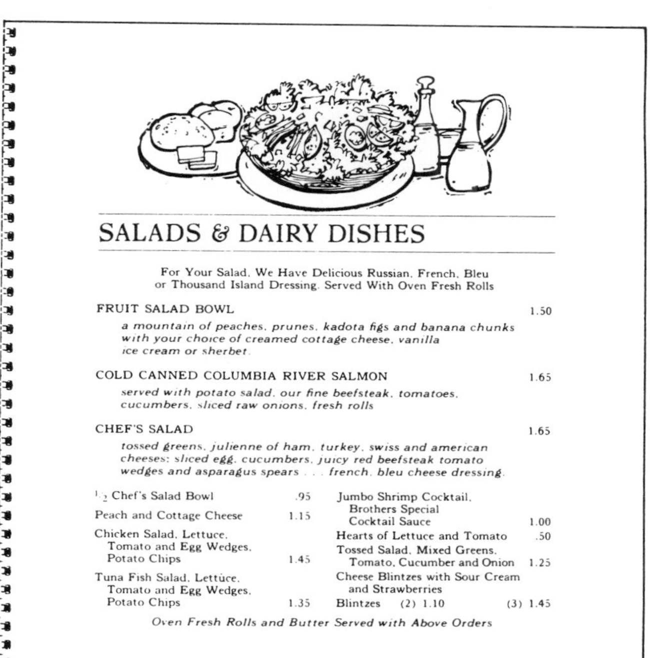

SALADS & DAIRY DISHES

For Your Salad, We Have Delicious Russian, French, Bleu or Thousand Island Dressing. Served With Oven Fresh Rolls

FRUIT SALAD BOWL 1.50
a mountain of peaches, prunes, kadota figs and banana chunks with your choice of creamed cottage cheese, vanilla ice cream or sherbet

COLD CANNED COLUMBIA RIVER SALMON 1.65
served with potato salad, our fine beefsteak, tomatoes, cucumbers, sliced raw onions, fresh rolls

CHEF'S SALAD 1.65
tossed greens, julienne of ham, turkey, swiss and american cheeses: sliced egg, cucumbers, juicy red beefsteak tomato wedges and asparagus spears . . . french, bleu cheese dressing

½ Chef's Salad Bowl .95
Peach and Cottage Cheese 1.15
Chicken Salad, Lettuce, Tomato and Egg Wedges, Potato Chips 1.45
Tuna Fish Salad, Lettuce, Tomato and Egg Wedges, Potato Chips 1.35

Jumbo Shrimp Cocktail, Brothers Special Cocktail Sauce 1.00
Hearts of Lettuce and Tomato .50
Tossed Salad, Mixed Greens, Tomato, Cucumber and Onion 1.25
Cheese Blintzes with Sour Cream and Strawberries
Blintzes (2) 1.10 (3) 1.45

Oven Fresh Rolls and Butter Served with Above Orders

Third spread, The Brothers Delicatessen *menu*.

Final page.

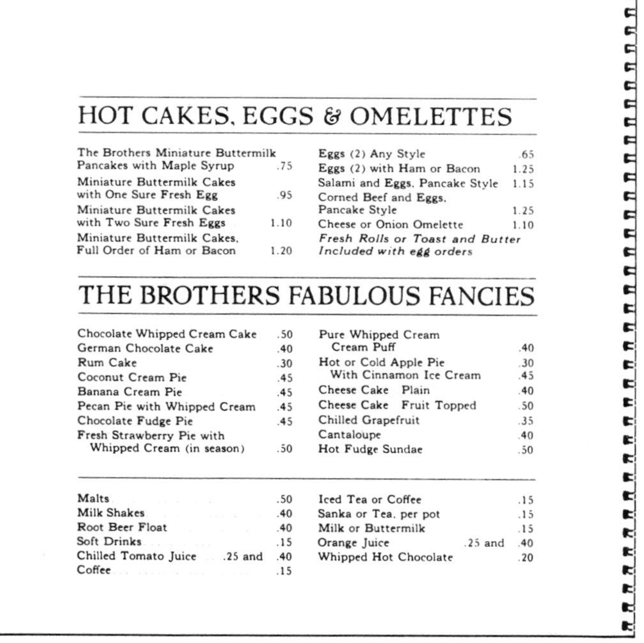

HOT CAKES, EGGS & OMELETTES

The Brothers Miniature Buttermilk Pancakes with Maple Syrup .75
Miniature Buttermilk Cakes with One Sure Fresh Egg .95
Miniature Buttermilk Cakes with Two Sure Fresh Eggs 1.10
Miniature Buttermilk Cakes, Full Order of Ham or Bacon 1.20

Eggs (2) Any Style .65
Eggs (2) with Ham or Bacon 1.25
Salami and Eggs, Pancake Style 1.15
Corned Beef and Eggs, Pancake Style 1.25
Cheese or Onion Omelette 1.10
Fresh Rolls or Toast and Butter Included with egg orders

THE BROTHERS FABULOUS FANCIES

Chocolate Whipped Cream Cake .50
German Chocolate Cake .40
Rum Cake .30
Coconut Cream Pie .45
Banana Cream Pie .45
Pecan Pie with Whipped Cream .45
Chocolate Fudge Pie .45
Fresh Strawberry Pie with Whipped Cream (in season) .50

Pure Whipped Cream Cream Puff .40
Hot or Cold Apple Pie .30
With Cinnamon Ice Cream .45
Cheese Cake Plain .40
Cheese Cake Fruit Topped .50
Chilled Grapefruit .35
Cantaloupe .40
Hot Fudge Sundae .50

Malts .50
Milk Shakes .40
Root Beer Float .40
Soft Drinks .15
Chilled Tomato Juice .25 and .40
Coffee .15

Iced Tea or Coffee .15
Sanka or Tea, per pot .15
Milk or Buttermilk .15
Orange Juice .25 and .40
Whipped Hot Chocolate .20

BEVERAGE PRICE LIST

CHAMPAGNES

gay, bubbly and delicious, the perfect complement to your meal or after

	BOTTLE	½ BOTTLE
Great Western Extra Dry Champagne	6.00	3.50
Great Western Sparkling Burgundy	6.00	3.50

RED DINNER WINES

robust wine . . . a complement to any red meat or game

	BOTTLE	½ BOTTLE
Great Western Burgundy	2.50	1.50
Great Western Rose	2.50	1.50
Chianti (Imp.)	3.50	2.00
Pommard St. Vincent (Imp.)	4.50	2.75
Lancers (Sparkling)	4.95	2.95

WHITE DINNER WINES

Delicate and delicious . . . goes well with seafood or fowl to give added pleasure to dining

	BOTTLE	½ BOTTLE
Great Western Sauternes	2.50	1.50
Great Western Rhine	2.50	1.50
Widmer's Lake Niagara	2.50	1.50
Liebfraumilch (Imp.)	3.75	2.00

COCKTAILS (Per Gallon)

Mahattan 25.00 Daiquiri 25.00
Martini 25.00 Whiskey Sours 25.00
1 Gallon of Wine Punch 15.00
1 Gallon of Fruit Punch 7.00
1 Gallon of Champagne Punch 20.00

WHISKIES (Quarts)

Seagram's 7 Crown 12.50 Jim Beam Bourbon 15.00
Seagram's V.O. 15.00 DeWar's White Label Scotch 15.00
Canadian Club 15.00 J & B Scotch 15.00

Set-Ups Included

Local Beer 8.00 PER CASE
Premium Beer 9.50 PER CASE
Canadian 11.00 PER CASE

PLACE 6¢ STAMP HERE

THE COACHMAN'S INN
10350 MAIN STREET CLARENCE, N. Y. 14031

TO

The Coachman's Inn AN IDEAL SETTING FOR YOUR PARTY
10350 MAIN STREET CLARENCE, N. Y. 14031 Phone 759-6852

THE COACHMAN'S INN  BANQUET MENU

BANQUET DINNER MENU

(FOR 15 OR MORE)

CHOICE OF:
Fruit Cup - Tomato Juice - Onion Soup or Soup du Jour - Shrimp Cocktail .75 Extra

ASSORTED RELISH TRAY

PRIME RIBS OF BEEF au Jus *"Our Specialty"* 4.95

BROILED HALF SPRING CHICKEN *"Excellent for Banquets"* 3.50

Ham Steak, raisin sauce	3.50
Prime Ribs of Beef and Lobster	5.25
Broiled Tenderloin Steak with Garlic Toast	4.50
Filet Mignon	5.95
Lobster Tails Two	5.50
One	4.50
Lobster Newburg	3.95
New York Strip Steak	5.50
Broiled Country Inn Pork Chops	3.95
Roast Turkey, stuffing	3.50
Tavern Style Beef with Gravy	3.50

Choice of Potato: Baked, French Fries or Whipped
Coachman's Chef Salad - Choice of Dressings
Vegetable
Home Made Bread and Butter
Sundae — Chocolate, Mint, Rum
Sherbet
Coffee Tea Milk

(PLEASE LIMIT TO 2 ENTREES)

BUFFET (For 40 or More)

$3.25 Per Person

Assorted Relish Trays
Sliced Ham
Hot Swedish Meat Balls
Sliced Turkey
Cottage Cheese
Potato Salad
Cheese Platter
Macaroni Salad
Jello Mold with Fruit
Chef Salad
Home Made Sliced Bread
Choice of: Coffee, Tea or Milk
Choice of: Ice Cream or Sherbet

BUFFET (For 40 or More)

$4.25 Per Person

Assorted Relish Trays
Macaroni Salad
Chef Salad
Chicken a la King
Cottage Cheese
Sliced Roast Beef
Potato Salad
Sliced Turkey
Jello Mold with Fruit
Sliced Ham
Cheese Platter
Hot Swedish Meat Balls
Baked Beans
Home Made Sliced Bread
Choice of: Coffee Tea Milk
Choice of: Ice Cream Sherbet Sundae

BANQUET LUNCHEON MENU

(FOR 35 OR MORE)

Tomato Juice - Onion Soup - Soup du Jour

Chicken a la King	3.00
Roast Turkey, Dressing	3.00

Potato or Vegetable
Chef Salad
Home Made Rolls - Butter
Sundae or Sherbet
Coffee, Tea or Milk

Also . . .

Coachman's Plate: Slices of roast beef, ham, turkey, cheese, potato salad	3.00
Chicken Salad Plate: Garnish of tomato wedges and egg quarters, cottage cheese	3.00
Fruit Salad Plate: Sherbet, cottage cheese	3.00

Includes rolls, dessert and coffee.

A GRACIOUS WELCOME

awaits your party at the COACHMAN'S INN. Everyone likes the INN for its gaiety and cheerful atmosphere. The huge fireplaces and rich panelled walls provide an attractive setting for your party, just the place to relax and be with friends. The drinks are superb and the food is unusually good because quality is of the very best. You always dine by candlelight at the COACHMAN'S INN. Your party is sure to be a success because the inkeeper's courteous, congenial and efficient staff will be on hand to greet and serve your guests.

FOR MORE INFORMATION AND RESERVATIONS

May we suggest you contact our
Banquet Manager any Monday thru Friday
from 8:30 A.M. to 4:30 P.M.

PHONE 759-6852 And Ask For MRS. WEISSER

GRATUITY AND SALES TAX NOT INCLUDED IN ABOVE PRICES.

This banquet menu is excellent. In addition to an outstanding selection of banquet, buffet, and luncheon items plus a wine and liquor list, this menu is also a mailer. Good merchandising.

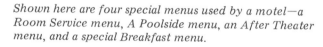

Shown here are four special menus used by a motel—a Room Service menu, A Poolside menu, an After Theater menu, and a special Breakfast menu.

Notice that while there are four different menus, the items served are interchanged—sandwiches, desserts, and even breakfast items can be served at different times and places.

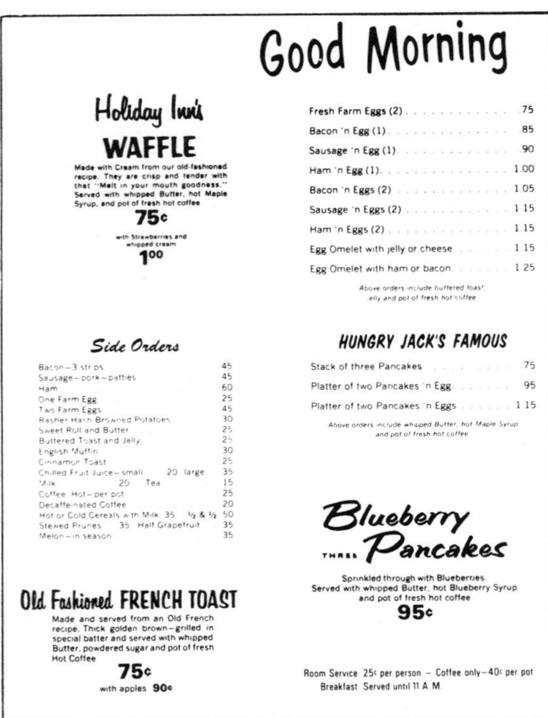

Good Morning

Holiday Inn's
WAFFLE
Made with Cream from our old-fashioned recipe. They are crisp and tender with that "Melt in your mouth goodness." Served with whipped Butter, hot Maple Syrup, and pot of fresh hot coffee
75¢
with Strawberries and whipped cream
1^{00}

Fresh Farm Eggs (2) .75
Bacon 'n Egg (1) .85
Sausage 'n Egg (1) .90
Ham 'n Egg (1) 1.00
Bacon 'n Eggs (2) 1.05
Sausage 'n Eggs (2) 1.15
Ham 'n Eggs (2) 1.15
Egg Omelet with jelly or cheese 1.15
Egg Omelet with ham or bacon 1.25
Above orders include buttered toast, jelly and pot of fresh hot coffee

Side Orders

Bacon—3 strips	45
Sausage—pork—patties	45
Ham	60
One Farm Egg	25
Two Farm Eggs	45
Rasher Hash Browned Potatoes	30
Sweet Roll and Butter	25
Buttered Toast and Jelly	25
English Muffin	30
Cinnamon Toast	25
Chilled Fruit Juice—small 20 large	35
Milk 20 Tea	15
Coffee Hot—per pot	25
Decaffeinated Coffee	20
Hot or Cold Cereals with Milk 35 ½ & ½	50
Stewed Prunes 35 Half Grapefruit	35
Melon—in season	35

HUNGRY JACK'S FAMOUS
Stack of three Pancakes 75
Platter of two Pancakes 'n Egg 95
Platter of two Pancakes 'n Eggs 1.15
Above orders include whipped Butter, hot Maple Syrup and pot of fresh hot coffee

Blueberry
THREE Pancakes
Sprinkled through with Blueberries. Served with whipped Butter, hot Blueberry Syrup and pot of fresh hot coffee
95¢

Old Fashioned FRENCH TOAST
Made and served from an Old French recipe. Thick golden brown—grilled in special batter and served with whipped Butter, powdered sugar and pot of fresh Hot Coffee
75¢
with apples 90¢

Room Service 25¢ per person — Coffee only—40¢ per pot
Breakfast Served until 11 A.M.

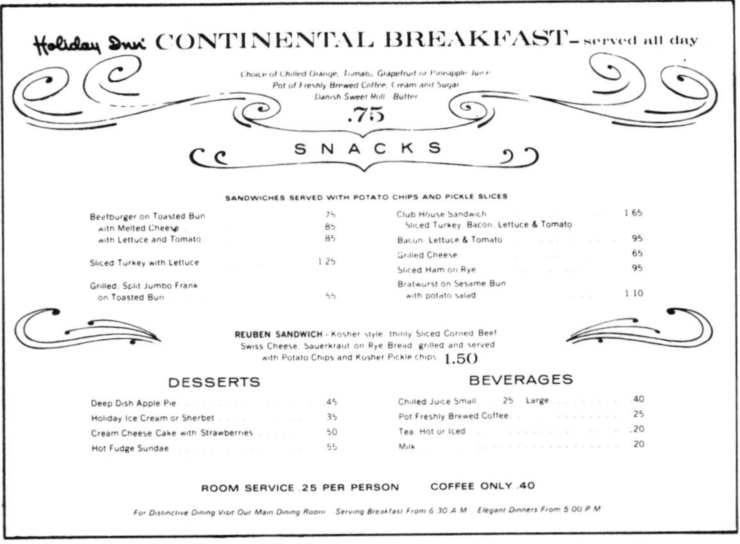

Holiday Inn CONTINENTAL BREAKFAST—served all day

Choice of Chilled Orange, Tomato, Grapefruit or Pineapple Juice
Pot of Freshly Brewed Coffee, Cream and Sugar
Danish Sweet Roll Butter
.75

SNACKS

SANDWICHES SERVED WITH POTATO CHIPS AND PICKLE SLICES

Beefburger on Toasted Bun 75
with Melted Cheese 85
with Lettuce and Tomato 85
Sliced Turkey with Lettuce 1.25
Grilled, Split Jumbo Frank on Toasted Bun 55
Club House Sandwich 1.65
Sliced Turkey, Bacon, Lettuce & Tomato
Bacon, Lettuce & Tomato 95
Grilled Cheese 65
Sliced Ham on Rye 95
Bratwurst on Sesame Bun with potato salad 1.10

REUBEN SANDWICH—Kosher style, thinly Sliced Corned Beef, Swiss Cheese, Sauerkraut on Rye Bread, grilled and served with Potato Chips and Kosher Pickle chips 1.50

DESSERTS
Deep Dish Apple Pie 45
Holiday Ice Cream or Sherbet 35
Cream Cheese Cake with Strawberries 50
Hot Fudge Sundae 55

BEVERAGES
Chilled Juice Small 25 Large .40
Pot Freshly Brewed Coffee .25
Tea, Hot or Iced .20
Milk .20

ROOM SERVICE .25 PER PERSON COFFEE ONLY .40

For Distinctive Dining Visit Our Main Dining Room Serving Breakfast From 6:30 A.M. Elegant Dinners From 5:00 P.M.

Club House
SANDWICH
Sliced Turkey, Bacon, Lettuce, Tomato
$\$1^{65}$
Served with potato chips and garne

SANDWICHES

HAMBURGER with Potato Chips & Garne .75
HOT DOG on Bun with Potato Chips & Garne .35
BRATWURST on Sesame Seed Bun with Sauerkraut & Garne .95
SLICED HAM on Rye with Potato Chips & Garne .95
GRILLED CHEESE with Potato Chips & Garne .55
BACON, LETTUCE & TOMATO on Toast with Potato Chips & Garne .95
CLUB HOUSE SANDWICH, Potato Chips & Garne 1.65
SLICED TURKEY, BACON, LETTUCE & TOMATO with Potato Chips & Garne 1.65
All sandwiches served with potato chips and dill pickle stick

Reuben
SANDWICH
Kosher Style Corn Beef
Swiss Cheese
Sauerkraut on Rye Bread
Grilled and served with Potato Chips and dill pickle stick
$\$1^{50}$

Desserts
Deep Dish Apple Pie 45¢
Holiday Ice Cream or Sherbet 35¢
Creme Cheese Cake with Strawberries 50¢
Hot Fudge Nut Sundae 55¢

PLATE LUNCHES

Golden Broasted Chicken (½ Chicken) 1.75
French Fries & Cole Slaw, Roll & Butter
French Fried Shrimps—6 jumbo 1.75
French Fries and Cole Slaw, Roll and Butter
Fresh Fruit Plate with Cottage Cheese and assorted crackers 1.50
Cold Cuts, Cheese, Potato Salad Plate 1.50
(Sliced Ham, Bologna, Corned Beef, American and Swiss Cheese, assorted crackers)

Ala Carte
French Fries 35¢
French Fried Onion Rings 50¢
Coke 25¢
Root Beer 25¢
Teem 25¢
Diet Soda 25¢
Ice Tea 25¢
Milk 25¢
Coffee 15¢

Holiday Inn® DOWNTOWN

CACKLE BERRIES
SCRAMBLED EGGS, SLICE OF HAM & HASH BROWN POTATOES
TOAST, JELLY, COFFEE
1^{15}

SNACKS

SANDWICHES SERVED WITH FRENCH FRIES AND PICKLE SLICES

Beefburger on Toasted Bun .85
with Melted Cheese .95
with Lettuce and Tomato .95
Sliced Turkey with Lettuce 1.50
LITTLE ABNER 1.65
A combination sandwich with cooked salami, corned beef, bologna, American cheese, Swiss cheese and mozzerolla cheese served on a huge French roll with lettuce and tomato
Club House Sandwich 1.75
Sliced Turkey, Bacon, Lettuce & Tomato
Bacon, Lettuce & Tomato 1.00
Grilled Cheese 65
Sliced Ham on Rye 95
Bratwurst on Sesame Bun with potato salad 1.10

RIVER ROOM SPECIAL—Sliced Turkey with Bacon—creamy cheddar cheese sauce topped with special cheeses and broiled to a golden brown 1^{75}

REUBEN SANDWICH—Kosher style, thinly Sliced Corned Beef, Swiss Cheese, Sauerkraut on Rye Bread, grilled and served with French Fries and Kosher Pickle chips 1^{50}

DESSERTS
Deep Dish Apple Pie 55
Holiday Ice Cream or Sherbet 35
Cream Cheese Cake with Strawberries 50
Hot Fudge Sundae 55

Holiday Inn's WAFFLE
Made with Cream from our old-fashioned recipe. They are crisp and tender with that "Melt in your mouth goodness." Served with whipped Butter, hot Maple Syrup, and pot of fresh hot coffee 75¢
with Strawberries and whipped cream 1^{00}

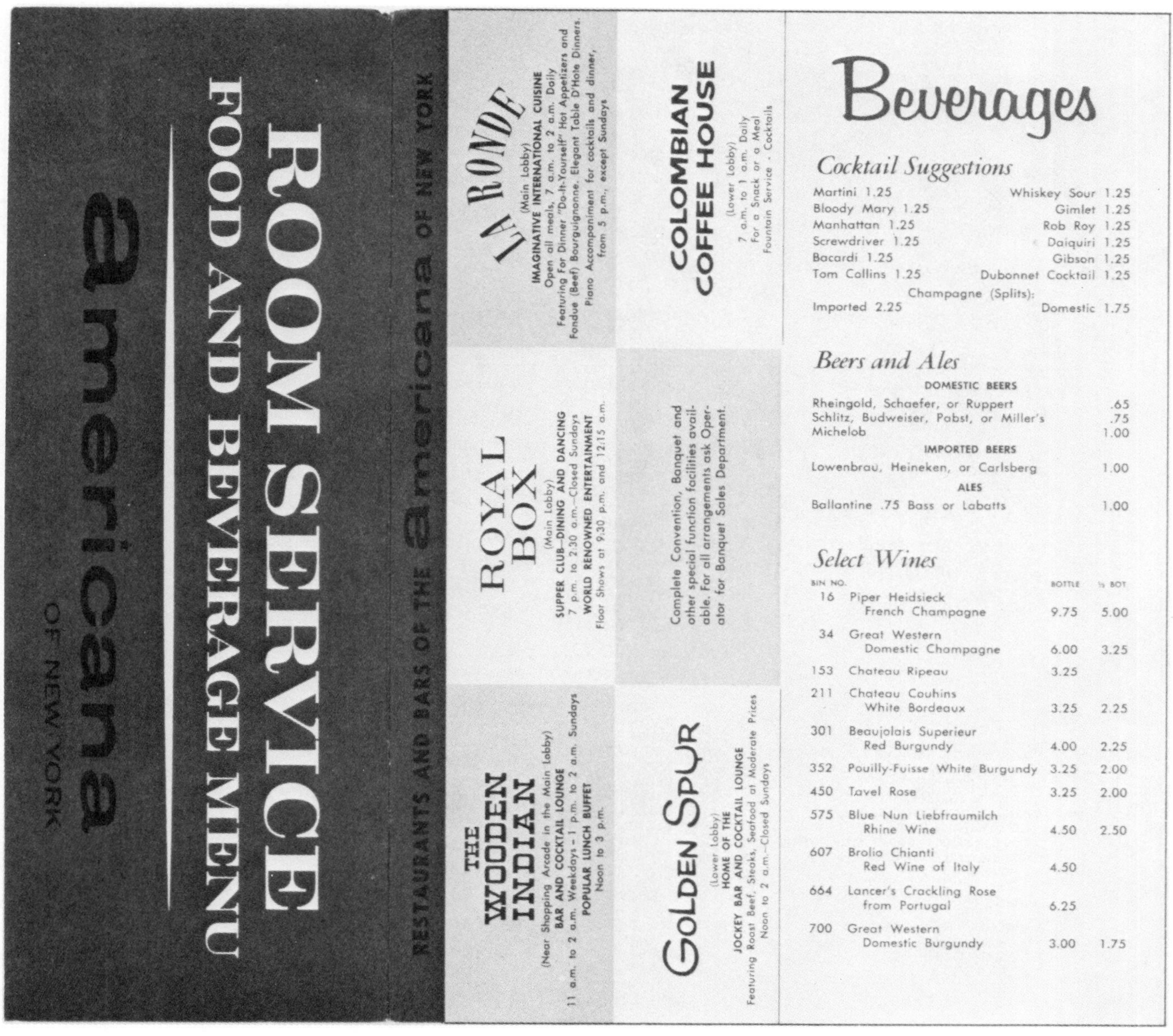

ROOM SERVICE
FOOD AND BEVERAGE MENU
americana
OF NEW YORK

RESTAURANTS AND BARS OF THE americana OF NEW YORK

LA RONDE
(Main Lobby)
IMAGINATIVE INTERNATIONAL CUISINE
Open all meals, 7 a.m. to 2 a.m. Daily
Featuring For Dinner "Do-It-Yourself" Hot Appetizers and Fondue (Beef) Bourguignonne. Elegant Table D'Hote Dinners.
Piano Accompaniment for cocktails and dinner, from 5 p.m., except Sundays

ROYAL BOX
(Main Lobby)
SUPPER CLUB—DINING AND DANCING
7 p.m. to 2:30 a.m.—Closed Sundays
WORLD RENOWNED ENTERTAINMENT
Floor Shows at 9:30 p.m. and 12:15 a.m.

THE WOODEN INDIAN
(Near Shopping Arcade in the Main Lobby)
BAR AND COCKTAIL LOUNGE
11 a.m. to 2 a.m. Weekdays - 1 p.m. to 2 a.m. Sundays
POPULAR LUNCH BUFFET
Noon to 3 p.m.

COLOMBIAN COFFEE HOUSE
(Lower Lobby)
7 a.m. to 1 a.m. Daily
For a Snack or a Meal
Fountain Service - Cocktails

Complete Convention, Banquet and other special function facilities available. For all arrangements ask Operator for Banquet Sales Department.

GOLDEN SPUR
(Lower Lobby)
HOME OF THE
JOCKEY BAR AND COCKTAIL LOUNGE
Featuring Roast Beef, Steaks, Seafood at Moderate Prices
Noon to 2 a.m.—Closed Sundays

Beverages

Cocktail Suggestions

Martini 1.25 — Whiskey Sour 1.25
Bloody Mary 1.25 — Gimlet 1.25
Manhattan 1.25 — Rob Roy 1.25
Screwdriver 1.25 — Daiquiri 1.25
Bacardi 1.25 — Gibson 1.25
Tom Collins 1.25 — Dubonnet Cocktail 1.25

Champagne (Splits):
Imported 2.25 — Domestic 1.75

Beers and Ales

DOMESTIC BEERS

Rheingold, Schaefer, or Ruppert	.65
Schlitz, Budweiser, Pabst, or Miller's	.75
Michelob	1.00

IMPORTED BEERS

Lowenbrau, Heineken, or Carlsberg	1.00

ALES

Ballantine .75 Bass or Labatts	1.00

Select Wines

BIN NO.		BOTTLE	½ BOT
16	Piper Heidsieck French Champagne	9.75	5.00
34	Great Western Domestic Champagne	6.00	3.25
153	Chateau Ripeau	3.25	
211	Chateau Couhins White Bordeaux	3.25	2.25
301	Beaujolais Superieur Red Burgundy	4.00	2.25
352	Pouilly-Fuisse White Burgundy	3.25	2.00
450	Tavel Rose	3.25	2.00
575	Blue Nun Liebfraumilch Rhine Wine	4.50	2.50
607	Brolio Chianti Red Wine of Italy	4.50	
664	Lancer's Crackling Rose from Portugal	6.25	
700	Great Western Domestic Burgundy	3.00	1.75

By advertising all of its restaurants, bars, and coffee shops on its room service menu, this hotel sells more than just room service.

"COMPARE OUR QUALITY AND PRICE"

IVANHOE
GOURMET MASTERS
DINNER SERVICE
P. O. Box 52 - 395
MIAMI, FLORIDA 33127
633 - 0215
FLORIDA'S OLDEST AND FINEST CATERER FOR ANY OCCASION
"NO BOTHER OR FUSS . . . LEAVE THE COOKING TO US"

PRICE SCHEDULE
PAYABLE IN ADVANCE

	3 Day	4 Day	5 Day	6 Day
1 Person	5.00	6.25	7.50	8.50
2 Persons	8.45	10.50	12.35	14.00
3 Persons	11.85	15.00	17.95	20.00
4 Persons	14.65	18.75	22.45	25.75
5 Persons	17.75	22.85	27.35	31.75
6 Persons	20.70	26.80	32.45	37.25

For 7th Day Service (Delivered Sat.) 1.00 per Person. Add sales tax and 1.00 local delivery charges. (Outlying Areas 1.50. Remote Areas 1.75)

DELIVERY TIME BEFORE 6 P.M.

MONDAY, FEBRUARY 13, 1967

SERVINGS ________ ACCT. ________

SELECT ONE (1) PER FAMILY

1 ☐ GOLDEN BROWN FILET OF SOLE, TARTAR SAUCE
2 ☐ SOUTHERN FRIED CHICKEN
3 ☐ BAKED MEAT LOAF, MUSHROOM GRAVY
4 ☐ BREADED MILK-FED VEAL CUTLET, PARMAGAN
5 ☐ VIRGINIA HAM STEAK, RAISIN SAUCE
6 ☐ BROILED BABY BEEF LIVER, ONION SAUCE
7 ☐ POTTED SWISS STEAK, JARDINERE

SELECT THREE (3) PER FAMILY

8 ☐ CHINESE EGG DROP SOUP
9 ☐ OLD FASHIONED VEGETABLE SOUP
10 ☐ CALIFORNIA TOMATO JUICE
11 ☐ HOT GERMAN POTATO SALAD
12 ☐ OVEN BROWNED POTATO
13 ☐ GARDEN GREEN PEAS
14 ☐ CAULIFLOWER BUDS
15 ☐ HEARTS OF LETTUCE, THOUSAND ISLAND DRESSING
16 ☐ CHOCOLATE PUDDING

SUGGESTED HOT DINNER

17 ☐ POTTED SWISS STEAK, JARDINERE
HOT GERMAN POTATO SALAD
HEARTS OF LETTUCE, THOUSAND ISLAND DRESSING
CHOCOLATE PUDDING

(Incomplete Menus Will Receive Above Selections)

SUGGESTED COLD DINNER

18 ☐ TOMATO JUICE
COLD SLICED BAKED HAM
HEARTS OF LETTUCE, THOUSAND ISLAND DRESSING
CHOCOLATE PUDDING

LOW CALORIE DINNERS

	CALORIES
19 ☐ Broiled Baby Beef Liver, Onion Sauce	350
20 ☐ Baked Meat Loaf, Mushroom Gravy	350
Served With	
California Tomato Juice	50
Cauliflower Buds	30
Hearts of Lettuce, Thousand Island Dressing	25
Diet Rolls	55

TUESDAY, FEBRUARY 14, 1967

SERVINGS ________ ACCT. ________

SELECT ONE (1) PER FAMILY

1 ☐ BROILED NATIVE SNAPPER, BUTTER SAUCE
2 ☐ YANKEE POT ROAST OF BEEF, JARDINERE
3 ☐ STUFFED CABBAGE ROLLS, HUNGARIAN STYLE
4 ☐ BRAISED LAMB STEAK, JARDINERE
5 ☐ ROAST LOIN OF PORK, SWEET & SOUR SAUCE
6 ☐ CUBED BEEF, CANTONESE (Tasty Choice Beef with Chinese Vegetables)
7 ☐ HALF BROILED CHICKEN, AU NATURAL

SELECT THREE (3) PER FAMILY

8 ☐ CONSOMME WITH NOODLES
9 ☐ GREEN SPLIT PEA SOUP
10 ☐ SWEET AND SOUR MEAT BALL APPETIZER
11 ☐ CREAMY WHIPPED POTATOES
12 ☐ CHINESE FRIED RICE
13 ☐ BUTTERED BROCCOLI
14 ☐ SLICED CARROTS, BUTTERED
15 ☐ PICKLED GREEN BEANS WITH ONIONS
16 ☐ PINEAPPLE CRUMB PIE

SUGGESTED HOT DINNER

17 ☐ HALF BROILED CHICKEN, AU NATURALE
SWEET AND SOUR MEAT BALL APPETIZER
CHINESE FRIED RICE
PINEAPPLE CRUMB PIE

(Incomplete Menus Will Receive Above Selections)

SUGGESTED COLD DINNER

18 ☐ APPLE SAUCE
ONE HALF COLD BROILED CHICKEN
PICKLED GREEN BEANS WITH ONIONS
PINEAPPLE CRUMB PIE

LOW CALORIE DINNERS

	CALORIES
19 ☐ Broiled Native Snapper, Butter Sauce	150
20 ☐ Half Broiled Chicken, au Naturale	100
Served with	
Buttered Broccoli	40
Sliced Carrots	30
Pickled Green Beans with Onions	25
Diet Rolls	55

WEDNESDAY, FEBRUARY 15, 1967

SERVINGS ________ ACCT. ________

SELECT ONE (1) PER FAMILY

1 ☐ BAKED FILET OF WHITE FISH, CREOLE
2 ☐ CHICKEN A LA KIEV (Chicken Breast stuffed with Chopped Liver, Breaded and Fried)
3 ☐ OUR OWN CORNED BEEF HASH WITH POACHED EGG
4 ☐ VEAL PAPRIKASH, WIDE NOODLES
5 ☐ HAM HAWAIIAN (BONELESS HAM DIPPED IN EGG BATTER, DEEP FRIED)
6 ☐ BRAISED SHORTRIBS OF BEEF, BROWN GRAVY
7 ☐ ROAST YOUNG TURKEY, GIBLET GRAVY, DRESSING, CRANBERRY SAUCE

SELECT THREE (3) PER FAMILY

8 ☐ CREAM OF MUSHROOM SOUP
9 ☐ TURKEY GUMBO SOUP
10 ☐ STEWED PRUNES
11 ☐ CANDIED LOUISIANA YAMS
12 ☐ FLUFFY LONG GRAIN RICE
13 ☐ CUT GREEN BEANS
14 ☐ WHOLE KERNEL CORN
15 ☐ MIXED GREEN SALAD, FRENCH DRESSING
16 ☐ JELLY ROLL

SUGGESTED HOT DINNER

17 ☐ ROAST YOUNG TURKEY, GIBLET GRAVY, DRESSING, CRANBERRY SAUCE
STEWED PRUNES
CANDIED LOUISIANA YAMS
JELLY ROLLS

(Incomplete Menus Will Receive Above Selections)

SUGGESTED COLD DINNER

18 ☐ STEWED PRUNES
COLD TURKEY PLATTER, CRANBERRY SAUCE
MIXED GREEN SALAD, FRENCH DRESSING
JELLY ROLL

LOW CALORIE DINNERS

	CALORIES
19 ☐ Roast Young Turkey, Gravy, Dressing, Cranberry Sauce	225
20 ☐ Braised Brisket of Beef, Gravy	250
Served with	
Fruit Nectar Juice	60
Cut Green Beans	15
Mixed Green Salad, French Dressing	25
Diet Rolls	55

A catering service menu presents a special menu problem but it can be solved as shown on these two pages.

Name ____________________ Acc't No. __________

Address ____________________ Apt. No. __________

No. of People ____________________ No. of Days __________

Phone ____________________

INSURE PROMPT SERVICE—RETURN COMPLETED MENU BY FRIDAY
INCOMPLETE MENUS WILL RECEIVE SELECTION No. 17
Families May Order 2 Different Dishes by Paying a 15¢ Charge per Item

PROFESSIONAL PARTY SERVICE
FOR ANY TYPE FUNCTION AT NO CHARGE
Phone 633-0215
Ask For Our Catering Manager

Cancellation And Change Must Be Received By 11 A.M.

THURSDAY, FEBRUARY 16, 1967

SERVINGS ________ ACCT. ________

SELECT ONE (1) PER FAMILY

1 ☐ FILET OF FLOUNDER, MIRABEAU
2 ☐ CHICKEN SAUTE, CACCIATORE
3 ☐ BROILED CHOPPED STEAK, HOME FRIED ONIONS
4 ☐ IRISH LAMB STEW, DUBLIN STYLE
5 ☐ BRAISED PORK STEAK, SAUCE ROBERT
6 ☐ BREADED MILK-FED VEAL CUTLET, TOMATO SAUCE
7 ☐ SLICED BAR-B-QUE BEEF, IVANHOE SAUCE

SELECT THREE (3) PER FAMILY

8 ☐ FRENCH ONION SOUP, CHEESE CROUTONS
9 ☐ LENTIL SOUP WITH FRANKS
10 ☐ FLORIDA ORANGE JUICE
11 ☐ PARSLEY BOILED POTATO
12 ☐ BUTTERED WIDE NOODLES
13 ☐ LEAF SPINACH, AU BEURRE
14 ☐ STEWED TOMATOES
15 ☐ LETTUCE AND ASPARAGUS CLUB SALAD, MAYONAISE SAUCE
16 ☐ ORANGE LAYER CAKE

SUGGESTED HOT DINNER

17 ☐ SLICED BAR-B-QUE BEEF, IVANHOE SAUCE
FLORIDA ORANGE JUICE
PARSLEY BOILED POTATO
ORANGE LAYER CAKE

(Incomplete Menus Will Receive Above Selections)

SUGGESTED COLD DINNER

18 ☐ CHOPPED LIVER, APPETIZER
ASSORTED COLD CUTS, GARNI
POTATO SALAD
ORANGE LAYER CAKE

LOW CALORIE DINNERS

	CALORIES
19 ☐ Broiled Filet of Flounder	125
20 ☐ Broiled Chop Steak, Fried Onions	35(
Served with	
Buttered Wide Noodles	30
Stewed Tomatoes	4(
Continental Salad (Diced Garden Vegetables, Italian Dressing)	25
Diet Rolls	55

FRIDAY, FEBRUARY 17, 1967

SERVINGS ________ ACCT. ________

SELECT ONE (1) PER FAMILY

1 ☐ JUMBO SHRIMPS, SCAMPI (Baked Shrimp in a Garlic Butter Sauce with Fine Herbs)
2 ☐ CHICKEN-EN-POT (Simmered Chicken with Vegetables in its own broth)
3 ☐ BRAISED BRISKET OF BEEF, BROWN GRAVY
4 ☐ CRABMEAT CAKES IMPERIAL, TARTAR SAUCE
5 ☐ BAKED VIRGINIA HAM, CORN FRITTER
6 ☐ SAUTE CHICKEN LIVERS WITH ONIONS
7 ☐ BROILED FILET OF HADDOCK, PARSLEY BUTTER SAUCE

SELECT THREE (3) PER FAMILY

8 ☐ CHICKEN CONSOMME WITH MATZOH BALL
9 ☐ NEW ENGLAND CLAM CHOWDER
10 ☐ FRUIT COMPOTE
11 ☐ HOME FRIED POTATOES
12 ☐ BAKED MACARONI AND CHEESE
13 ☐ SLICED CARROTS AND PEAS
14 ☐ BABY LIMA BEANS
15 ☐ CREAMY COLE SLAW
16 ☐ BOBKA (Russian Coffee Cake)

SUGGESTED HOT DINNER

17 ☐ BROILED FILET OF HADDOCK, BUTTER SAUCE
BAKED MACARONI AND CHEESE
CARROTS AND PEAS
BOBKA (RUSSIAN COFFEE CAKE)

(Incomplete Menus Will Receive Above Selections)

SUGGESTED COLD DINNER

18 ☐ FRUIT COMPOTE
SALMON SALAD PLATTER
CREAMY COLE SLAW
RUSSIAN COFFEE CAKE

LOW CALORIE DINNERS

	CALORIES
19 ☐ Jumbo Shrimp, Scampi	150
20 ☐ Chicken-en-Pot (Simmered Chicken with Vegetables in its own Broth)	100
Served with	
Fruit Compote	75
Carrots and Peas	40
Creamy Cole Slaw	50
Diet Roll	55

SATURDAY, FEBRUARY 18, 1967

SERVINGS ________ ACCT. ________

SELECT ONE (1) PER FAMILY

1 ☐ FRIED FINGER OF SNAPPER, TARTAR SAUCE
2 ☐ SLICED LONDON BROIL, MUSHROOM SAUCE
3 ☐ SPAGHETTI AND MEAT BALLS, ITALIENNE
4 ☐ BRAISED LAMB SHANK, JARDINERE
5 ☐ GOLDEN BROWN PORK CHOPS
6 ☐ COC AU VIN (Tasty Chicken in a Fine Wine Sauce)
7 ☐ ROAST TURKEY DRUMSTICK, SAGE DRESSING, GRAVY

SELECT THREE (3) PER FAMILY

8 ☐ CONSOMME VERMICELLI
9 ☐ ITALIAN MINESTRONE
10 ☐ GRAPEFRUIT SECTIONS
11 ☐ BAKED STUFFED POTATO
12 ☐ SPAGHETTI WITH TOMATO SAUCE
13 ☐ MIXED VEGETABLES
14 ☐ BOSTON BAKED BEANS
15 ☐ PINEAPPLE WALDORF SALAD
16 ☐ ENGLISH CHOCOLATE BROWNIE

SUGGESTED HOT DINNER

17 ☐ ROAST TURKEY DRUMSTICK, SAGE DRESSING GRAVY
ITALIAN MINESTRONE
MIXED VEGETABLE
ENGLISH CHOCOLATE BROWNIE

SUGGESTED COLD DINNER

18 ☐ GRAPEFRUIT SECTIONS
CHICKEN SALAD PLATTER
PINEAPPLE WALDORF SALAD
ENGLISH CHOCOLATE BROWNIE

LOW CALORIE DINNERS

	CALORIES
19 ☐ Sliced London Broil, Mushroom Sauce	200
20 ☐ Baked White Fish	100
Served With	
Grapefruit Sections	55
Mixed Vegetables	40
Pineapple Waldorf Salad	40
Diet Roll	55

SUNDAY (Delivery Saturday)
SELECT FOUR (4) DISHES
(1 ENTREE - 3 SIDE DISHES)
FROM SATURDAY'S MENU
Write Numbers Here

No. of People ____________

Selection Numbers

______ ______ ______ ______

(1)

15

Little extras make a menu big

Michelangelo is supposed to have said, "Trifles make perfection, and perfection is no trifle." While perfection is probably unattainable in a menu, and trifles certainly will not make a menu perfect, there are ways of imaginatively treating or expanding nearly every department of the menu from appetizers to desserts in a manner that will sell more. Also, any unusual items, drink or food, will advertise your operation by word of mouth which is the best form of advertising there is (and the least expensive).

Furthermore, the public expects something extra when eating out. The ordinary, routine cuisine they can get at home, but when they dine out they prefer unusual gastronomic surprises. This is also good business because, besides attacting more customers, the public is willing to pay more for culinary concoctions that are different as well as delicious.

The following examples are taken from menus of successful restaurants showing creative menuship on a variety of food and drink items, large and small.

The *Beef 'N Bottle* restaurant lists the following special dinner that is a gourmet and a merchandising combination designed to build business as well as make happy, come-again customers:

> MR. & MRS. CHAMPAGNE DINNER, For That Special Festive Occasion, Aperitif—Two Glasses Rose Wine, For Mr., a Planked 12 oz. New York Cut Sirloin, for Mrs., a Planked 8 oz. New York Cut Sirloin. 10th of Paul Masson Champagne, WOP Salad (a House Specialty) or Dinner Salad and Choice of Dressing, Relish Dish, Rolls and Butter, Coffee, Tea or Milk, Baked Alaska for Two, Complementary Cake for That Special Lady, $14.75.

The specialty restaurant can also feature a "special" dinner. The following menu from the *Venetian Inn* is a special dinner for parties of four or more that shows gourmet imagination and sales imagination, too:

> Dinner a Siciliano, served to parties of four or more, PESCHE AL-VINO COCKTAIL, ANTIPASTO, Four Assortments of Spaghetti, TAGLIATELLE A LA SICILIANO, RIGATONI, RAVIOLI, MOSTACCIOLA, SIX VARIETIES OF MEAT, prepared exclusively a Siciliano, VEGETABLE TOSSED SALAD, ITALIAN BREAD AND BUTTER, and for the finale, A PIATO OF SPUMONI, $6.00 per person.

The southern restaurant with a homey, country menu style may seem to have a country bumpkin approach, but the folksy style usually contains clever, solid, creative merchandising that makes the biggest "city slicker" restaurant look slow by comparison. The following example from *Creighton's Restaurant* is a good example of "Confederate" merchandising:

> "Florida Cracker" Sampler Plate, $4.75. (an assortment of foods us natives like). Us Crackers always got a Chicken, and a pig or two. Nearly any place there's water, you can find some crabs. (How true!) And shrimp! We have as many as taxes. Avocados grow in most backyards (as well as 5 or 6 brats). So we decided, for our perspicacious Northern Cousins to let them try all our good easy eating at one sitting, by arranging in our best Florida Manner a selected piece of Fried Florida Chicken, One Florida Pork Chop, One Deviled Crab, and a Florida Avocado stuffed with Fresh Florida Shrimp Salad, French Fried Potatoes, Assorted Breads and Butter, Coffee.

The drink portion of your menu need not be dull. The usual Martini and Manhattan (and all their cousins) are necessary, of course, but drinks can be exotic, imaginative and exciting, too. The following examples from Paul Shank's Restaurant should point the way to better drink merchandising:

CHI-CHI, An intriguing, superbly smooth concoction of pineapple juice, coconut milk and vodka, mixed on the Waring blender and served in a tall cool glass, $1.25. MAI-TAI, this favorite of the South Seas Isles consists of blended tropical fruit juices generously spiked with both light and dark rum . . . sheer delight! $1.50. ORGIE D' AMOUR, a 60-oz. loving cup of mellow, festive wonderment. Enough to gladden the hearts of four lucky people and guaranteed to send you spiraling into the misty blue yonder frivolous —but happy. $6.00 PER FOURSOME.

Sandwiches can be exciting and different, too. In addition to the standards—Hamburger, Steak, Ham, etc.—which most operations serve, the following unusual sandwiches served by *Tally*'s, the *Prairie Room* and the *Town House*, respectively, show sandwich selling at its best:

"DIP AND EAT" PRIME BEEF DIP, $1.00. Delicious Tender Prime Beef Sandwich made on an Individual Loaf of French Bread and a cup of Tasty Au Jus for your Dippin' Pleasure. French Fries.

AN OLD FASHIONED SOUTHERN KENTUCKY HOT BROWN. An open-faced sandwich with chicken, cheese, mushroom sauce, broiled with sliced tomatoes and bacon strips, served on a sizzling platter.

SUBMARINE SANDWICHES. Served in a quarter-pound freshly baked French Loaf with Sauerkraut and Dill. YOUR CHOICE . . . $1.10. (1) Barbecued Turkey or Beef, with dip of our Special Sauce, (2) Sliced Ham, Canadian Cheese, Breast of Turkey with Russian Dressing.

The lowly vegetable need not take a back seat, either, on any menu. The following a la carte vegetable listing by the *Buon Gusto Restaurant* (at buon gusto prices) shows how to give your vegetables that "extra" merchandising treatment:

Special Baked Eggplant Parmigiana, $1.50; Andy Boy Broccoli Saute in Garlic and Olive Oil, $1.00; Boiled Escarole, Olive Oil and Clove of Fresh Garlic, $1.00; Escarole Saute in Garlic, Olive Oil, $1.00; Fresh Mushroom Saute, $1.25; Stuffed Artichoke, $1.00.

The same restaurant (*Buon Gusto*) has an a la carte listing of sauces that is unusual—just another "extra" to make an extraordinary menu. The following is the sauce list, a la *Buon Gusto*: White or Red Clam Sauce, 75¢; Mushroom Sauce, 75¢; Garlic & Oil Sauce, 50¢; Marinara Sauce, 65¢.

If you think you have served and sold every part of the chicken in every way possible, consider the following item served both as an entree and an appetizer by the *Ozark Barbeque Restaurant:* Hickory Smoked Gizzards (Tender as Livers), Mashed Potatoes & Gravy, Hot Rolls and Butter, $1.50.

Even Take-Outs can get special treatment for "sellability." The following example from *Crowe's Dinner House* is not a fancy listing, but it wraps up the two items neatly and makes them salable:

Fisherman's Box Lunch, 2 Pieces Fried Chicken, Home-made Bread, Potato Chips, Piece of Fruit, Apple Sauce Cake, $1.15; Sack Lunch, Roast Beef Sandwich, Baked Ham Sandwich, Potato Chips, Piece of Fruit, Apple Sauce Cake, 2 sandwiches $1.35, 1 sandwich $1.00.

The fountain menu does not have to be a dull listing of ice cream flavors. It can have all the imagination and flair of the biggest gourmet items. The following examples, from the *2-K Restaurant* in Houston, show real fountain flair:

DUSTY ROAD, 2 Scoops Vanilla Ice Cream, Hot Caramel Topping, Sprinkled with Malted Milk Powder, Sliced Peaches, Whipped Cream, Cherry, 65¢, Half Size 45¢. OLD TIMER, An Old Fashioned Treat Made with Peppermint Stick and Coffee Ice Cream, Fresh Frozen Strawberries, Pineapple, Whipped Cream, Cherry, 65¢. TOUCHDOWN, Chocolate Covered Brazil Nut, Toasted Almond and Coffee Ice Cream, Coffee Syrup, Whipped Cream, Cherry. When you find the football, Touchdown! 65¢.

To add a twist to the after dinner menu, *Garzanelli's Restaurant* adds ice cream to brandy (combining dessert and an after dinner drink) and lists it as follows:

DELICADO—after dinner you'll love this delicious dessert-drink; brandy or your favorite liqueur multi-mixed with ice cream, 85¢.

As a final, super example of what can be done with the ordinary, common, every day cup of coffee, we list the coffee menu from *The Cloister Restaurant* which should show how a little item can make a menu big:

ESPRESSO (lungo), finely roasted, dark Italian coffee, 50¢; ESPRESSO ROMANO, dark Italian coffee, with lemon peel, 55¢; CAFFELATTE, half caffe espresso, half foaming steamed milk, 75¢; GRANITA, caffe espresso, ice, with whipped cream, 75¢; AUTHENTIC CAPPUCCINO, caffe espresso with steamed milk, chocolate, 75¢.

Specialties: CIOCCOLATA, hot chocolate with foaming steamed milk, 65¢; CIOCCOLATA CON PANNA, hot chocolate with whipped cream, 80¢; BOGOTA COFFEE, highland Colombian coffee, 80¢; INDIAN COFFEE, coffee, sugar, fragrant spices, topped with floating cream, 80¢; MOCHA COFFEE, combination of Viennese coffee and hot chocolate, 50¢.

Mit etwas Besonderem (with "something special"): CAPPUCCINO, caffe espresso, steamed milk, Italian chocolate, brandy, 95¢; MISCHIEVOUS CHOCOLATE, chocolate, steamed milk, gold label rum, 95¢; IRISH COFFEE, coffee, Irish whiskey, cream float, $1.25; CAFE DIABLO, coffee with flaming brandy, kirsch, $1.25; CAFE ROYAL, coffee with brandy, 95¢; CAFE AU RHUM, coffee with rum, 95¢; CAFE PONCINO, caffe espresso with whiskey or brandy, 95¢; CAFE CACAO, caffe espresso, creme de cacao, whipped cream, $1.00; CAFE COINTREAU, caffe espresso, Cointreau, lemon peel, $1.00; CAFE VENEZIA, caffe espresso, dark chocolate, milk, brandy, $1.00; COFFEE GROG, large coffee, buttered rum, spices, cinnamon stick, $1.25; "SANKY-PANKY," any of the above may be made with Sanka, $1.00; KAHLUA COFFEE, Mexican Kahlua refreshingly iced, $1.25.

Other good menu copy describing "extras" comes from the *Yardarm* menu:

Riverside Villas. A unique recreational complex. Riverside Villas offers relaxation and an outdoor pleasure potential unmatched on Florida's West Coast. Here you will find pleasure boating and cruising of every description. Offshore Gulf fishing where every species abound . . . combined salt and fresh water fishing in the springfed headwaters—preserve hunting for quail, chukkar and pheasant.

Air-conditioned motel and efficiency units . . . all with TV and telephone . . . swimming pool . . . marina . . . boat ramps . . . bait store . . . tackle shop. Complete convention and meeting facilities. Convention hall with capacity of 150. Facilities for private parties and banquets for 25 to 125 people. Three bars and lounges.

Homosassa Springs. Nature's Fish Bowl. A visit to this popular tourist attraction is truly one of Florida's most unusual recreational adventures. Thousands of fresh and salt water fish intermingle in giant fishbowl spring. Wild life in profusion along nature trail. Alligators and crocodiles. Feed the deer and squirrels. Walk among water-fowl from worldwide collection. Scenic ride on sightseeing boats along spectacular wilderness canal. On U.S. Highway 19-98, 75 miles north of Tampa-St. Petersburg.

In addition, the *Yardarm* menu reproduces the complete flag alphabet for the information of nautical buffs.

Mammy's Shanty Restaurant has a gift shop where it sells special Civil War glasses, but to help sell the glasses and to help sell a special cocktail called the "Surrender" (1½ oz. rum, pineapple juice, crushed ice, dash of grenadine, chunk of pineapple, and red cherry), "You can keep the glass to remember the battle. Additional glasses available in our gift shop."

Think you're selling everything possible on your menu? Then consider this. *Rod's Shadowbrook Restaurant* in Shrewsbury, N.J., offers the following list of cigars along with its desserts and after dinner drinks listing:

Coronas No. 3 - 50¢
Coronas Coronas - 40¢
Coronas Belvederes - 25¢
Coronas Chicas - 35¢
Cambridge Monarch - $1.00
Oxford Romeo - 50¢
Command Performances - 3/50¢
Medalist Naturals No. 7 - 3/50¢

Manners Big Boy Restaurant chain offers a special selection of take-outs, not just the common "Everything on the menu available for take-out." They list the following:

You Can Take it with You! Enjoy these specialities in your home.

Manners Famous Big Boy Sauce . . . . 50¢
Manners Sweet Red Pepper Relish . . . 50¢
Big Boy's Seasoning Salt . . . . . 39¢

The Idlewild Cafe in Buffalo, Wyoming, gives the traveling customer a little extra help. Instead of a map, they give distances in miles from Buffalo to 17 cities and towns (from 17 to 406 miles away) on the four main highways going north, south, east, and west. A welcome bit of information along with good food, we're sure.

Another big chain of restaurants and motels—*Horne's* has an excellent map on the back cover of its menu. It is keyed to show Candy Shoppe and Circus Grill restaurants, Crown Room Restaurants, Candy Shoppes, and Motor Lodges with another symbol for projected locations.

These examples of other selling, promotion, and merchandising uses of the menu do not begin to exhaust the possibilities in use by many creative and selling-wise food service operations, but perhaps these examples will stimulate you to add a few extras to your menu.

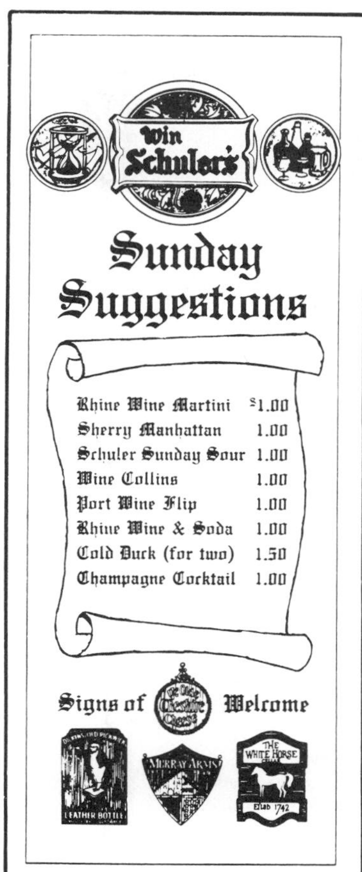

Win Schuler's
Sunday Suggestions
Rhine Wine Martini $1.00
Sherry Manhattan 1.00
Schuler Sunday Sour 1.00
Wine Collins 1.00
Port Wine Flip 1.00
Rhine Wine & Soda 1.00
Cold Duck (for two) 1.50
Champagne Cocktail 1.00
Signs of Welcome
Murray Arms
The White Horse
Leather Bottle

Try our International Cheese Plate,

served with a special Rye Bread

for $ .90 —

JUST THE RIGHT EVENING SNACK

****

A La Carte

Cheeses

Camembert (France) 30
Cream Cheese (USA) 30
Swiss Cheese (Switzerland) 30
Gouda (Holland) 30
Blue Cheese (Denmark) 35
Served with Bread & Butter

A WORD ABOUT OUR DRESSINGS FOR OUR GARDEN SALAD

All our dressings are made with 100% Safflower oil, the highest Poly-unsaturated oil known! Many Doctors feel that Poly-unsaturated Oil such as Safflower Oil, has a tendency to reduce Cholesterol in the Blood Stream. Not all Doctors agree to this. But to be safe we have added 100% SAFFLOWER OIL to all our Dressings.

LAZIO'S
RECOMMENDS THE FOLLOWING LOCAL
FISH AS A PERSONAL SUGGESTION:
Filet of Petrale Sole
Grilled California Rex Sole
Filet of Sea Bass
Broiled Fresh Caught Salmon—In Season

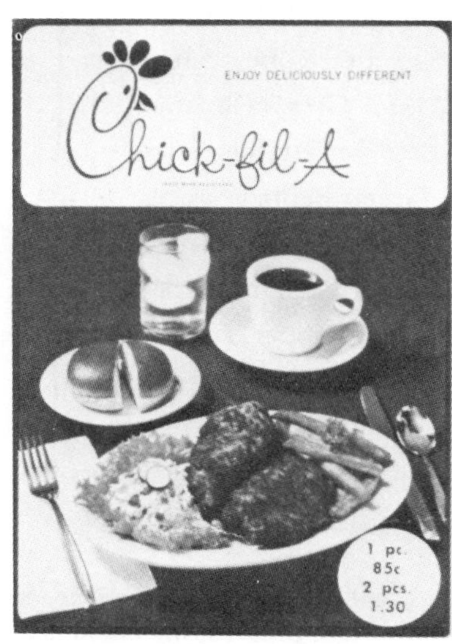

Special Sunday drinks, an unusual cheese listing, a listing of local fish, a colorful tip-on, and a well described salad dressing are unusual menu extras.

Hours of Service

Breakfast Daily
7:00 a.m. to 11:30 a.m.

Luncheon—Tue. thru Sat.
11:30 a.m. to 4:00 p.m.

Dinner—Tue. thru Sat.
11:30 a.m. to 10:00 p.m.

Sundays 12:00 noon to 8:00 p.m.

Holidays 12:00 noon to 7:00 p.m.

Late Snacks in Parlour Car Bar
Daily except Sundays
9:00 p.m. to 12:00 midnight.

Closed Mondays and Christmas

Private Parties

For those festive occasions or business meetings the Silversmith can provide private dining rooms to take care of a few or as many as 250.

SAUCES AND CONDIMENTS

Brand's A-1 Sauce
Escoffier Robert Sauce
Major Grey's Chutney
Escoffier Diable Sauce
Green Pepper Sauce
Bahamian Mustard
House of Parliament Sauce
Red Pepper Sauce
Epicure Steak Sauce
Harvey's Sauce
Dijon French Mustard

5 TREATS CREATED WITH BONELESS CHICKEN

Each one is created with 4 oz. of Boneless Breast of Spring Chicken.

FRENCH

Breast of Chicken Cordon Bleu. Saut'eed boneless chicken with juicy grilled imported ham topped with thick melted cheese and mushroom cap, green garden peas. $1.55

SPANISH

Breast of Fresh Chicken cubes on Skewer. Broiled boneless chicken, diced onion, green pepper, saut'eed in tangy barbecued sauce, whipped potatoes. $1.50

AMERICAN

Breast of Chicken Rancher. Fried boneless farm chicken on open toasted bun with crisp bacon strips, cranberry sauce, French Fried potatoes. $1.35

SWEDISH

Breast of Chicken Low Calorie. Boiled boneless chicken, creamy cottage cheese, sliced egg and tomato on crisp lettuce leaves, Melba toast. $1.25

BAMBERGER'S

Breast of Chicken Ideal. Boneless chicken, fried to golden perfection, on toasted bun, served with delicious cranberry sauce and crisp cole slaw ....$.95

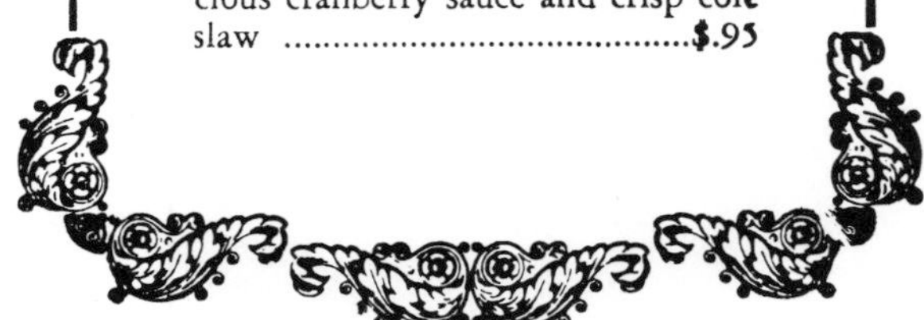

Whether basic information like hours and days open, special sauces and condiments, or a special chicken offering, extras like these on the menu add to sales.

Hear Ye! Hear Ye!

All Items are complemented with the Hospitality Plate . . . yours without asking.

SALAD a la IVANHOE
A delectable combination of crisp, fresh greens, thoroughly chilled.
Served with your choice of Salad Dressings,
French, Thousand Island, Roquefort, Oil and Wine Vinegar, Garlic and Ivanhoe's Dressing
We'll be flattered if you take extra helpings.
Your salad and choice of dressing will be served from the salad cart.

(CHOICE OF ONE)

IDAHO BAKED POTATO
Wrapped in foil, served with butter, or sour cream and chives.

RICE PILAFF
Cooked in beef stock with tomatoes served in casserole.
Cup yogurt on the side.

IVANHOE'S OVEN BROWN POTATOES
(A Dish from The Crusade)

GOLDEN FRENCH FRIED POTATOES
(A King's Portion)

Basket of Bread, Crackers and Butter

A lot of "extras" with the meal, or an extra, unusual nationality dish deserve extra copy attention.

Introduccion A Las Tortillas

The tortilla is one of the earliest Mexican foods. It has passed through the centuries unchanged. Long before the Spanish conquistadors embarked for the American continent, the Aztecs were not only using the tortilla (Spanish for "little cake") as the staple food of their diet, they were also using it as an eating implement!

TIA MARIA proudly continues this long Mexican tradition. We think you will enjoy watching the tortillas being pounded from the unleavened cornmeal in the manner that has been the age-old custom.

Today many people are at first confused about handling a tortilla. We suggest you attack it in the traditional Mexican fashion. Hold it flat in one hand, butter it, add the red sauce—sparingly at first—roll and eat! Your basket of hot tortillas will be delivered as soon as your order has been taken. We particularly recommend you enjoy them with an imported Mexican beer.

From the tortilla come many other traditional Mexican dishes. An Enchilada is a soft-rolled tortilla filled with meat or cheese and covered with a special sauce. A crisp fried tortilla containing meat and shredded lettuce is a Taco.

The Tamale is made of tortilla dough spread on corn-husks, then wrapped around a meat filling. Even chips are deep fried tortillas. As a matter of fact, the only Mexican dish on the TIA MARIA Menu which does not start with the tortilla is a Chile Relleno, a mild chile pepper filled with cheese and fried in egg batter.

GRANSON'S SWIRLERS
SWIRL YOUR OWN
Extra Size - Extra Kick
Smooth and Deeply Satisfying

1—Martini Swirler 1.25

2—Vodka Swirler 1.35

3—Whiskie Sour Swirler ..1.25

IF WE KNOW YOU'RE COMING WE'LL BAKE A CAKE

Given 24 hours notice we will be happy to furnish FREE of charge a cake for your birthday or anniversary party — for groups of 6 or more.

FOR RESERVATIONS

PRIVATE PARTIES AND BANQUETS CALL BA 3-7534

GARLIC BREAD . . . Sprinkled with Parmesan Cheese, Made to order, and served Oven Hot! Per Slice....... 25

CREDIT CARD HOLDERS:

New York State liquor law does not permit us to charge alcoholic beverages to your account. BEFORE YOU ORDER, kindly inform your waitress that you will be charging your meal to your credit card. This will facilitate your billing.

Thank you!

WE HONOR AMERICAN EXPRESS,
DINER'S CLUB AND
CARTE BLANCHE CREDIT CARDS

A varied selection of little extras in information and food and drink offerings.

(Below) The front and back cover art and design of this wine list (as well as the menu itself) includes a flag and signal alphabet that complements and underlines the nautical or seafood type of cuisine as well as supplying information and table conversation.

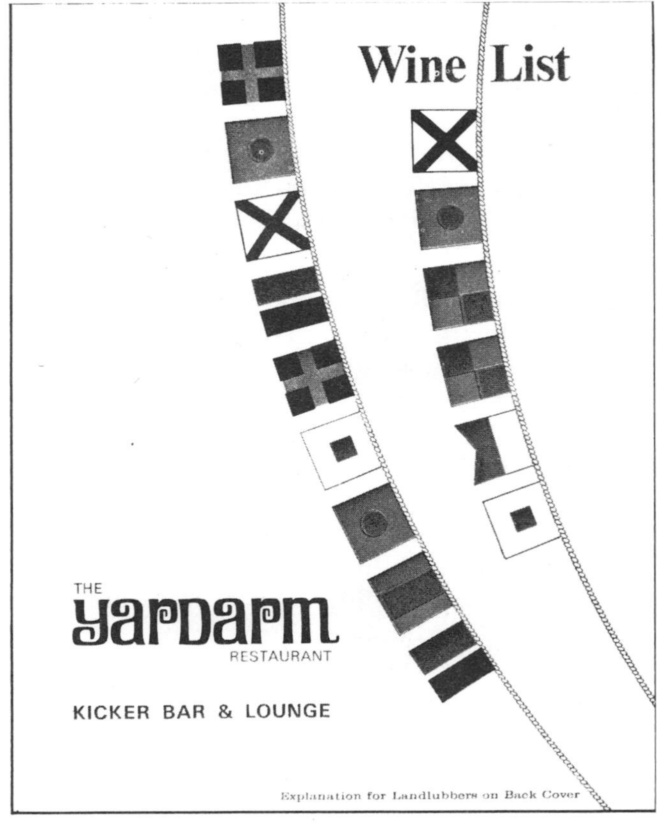

Wine List
THE
yardarm
RESTAURANT
KICKER BAR & LOUNGE
Explanation for Landlubbers on Back Cover

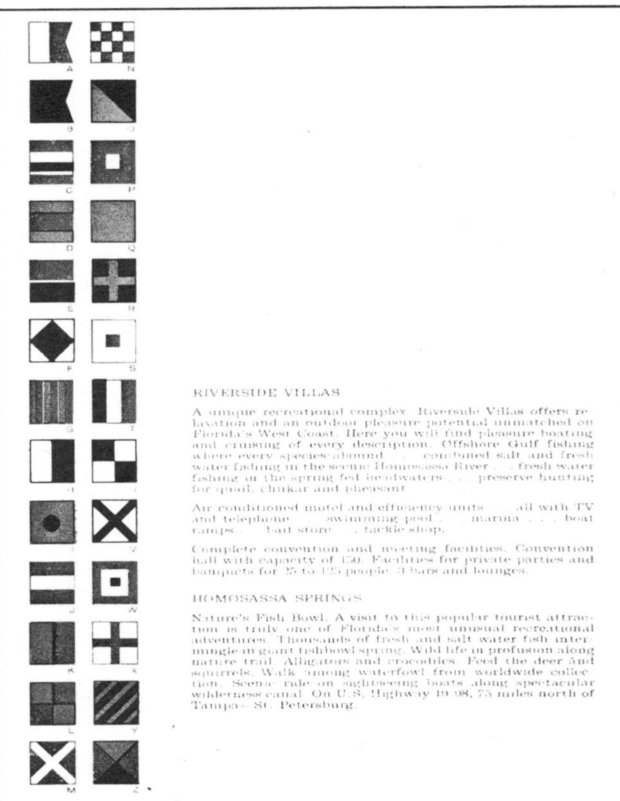

RIVERSIDE VILLAS
A unique recreational complex. Riverside Villas offers relaxation and an outdoor pleasure potential unmatched on Florida's West Coast. Here you will find pleasure boating and cruising of every description. Offshore Gulf fishing where every species abound . . . combined salt and fresh water fishing in the scenic Homosassa River . . . fresh water fishing in the spring fed headwaters . . . preserve hunting for quail, chukar and pheasant.
Air conditioned motel and efficiency units . . . all with TV and telephone . . . swimming pool . . . marina . . . boat ramps . . . bait store . . . tackle shop.
Complete convention and meeting facilities. Convention hall with capacity of 150. Facilities for private parties and banquets for 25 to 125 people. 3 bars and lounges.
HOMOSASSA SPRINGS
Nature's Fish Bowl. A visit to this popular tourist attraction is truly one of Florida's most unusual recreational adventures. Thousands of fresh and salt water fish intermingle in giant fishbowl spring. Wild life in profusion along nature trail. Alligators and crocodiles. Feed the deer and squirrels. Walk among waterfowl from worldwide collection. Scenic ride on sightseeing boats along spectacular wilderness canal. On U.S. Highway 19-98, 75 miles north of Tampa—St. Petersburg.

16

Take-outs on the menu

There is no convenience food as convenient as take-out food; therefore, this part of the food service business is sure to continue to grow. The kinds of cuisine being sold in take-out packaging are increasing daily. The take-out business is a relatively easy way to increase food service business without increasing table and counter space, but this kind of new business will not sell itself. It must be advertised and promoted, and one of the most logical as well as inexpensive places to advertise take-out business is on the menu.

Point of sale displays and signs will sell take-out service, but they tend to spoil the decor and appearance of a fine dining room. The take-out story can be told more completely, effectively, and in good taste right on the menu. Many operators do mention take-out service on their menus, but in a very inadequate manner. A line will very often appear at the bottom of a large menu listing that says, "Ask about our take-out service," or, "All items listed on this menu are available for take-out." This is not good merchandising.

A more effective, creative advertising approach is to give the entire take-out story careful and complete treatment on the menu. The most logical place for this story is on the back cover. At present, over 50 percent of all the back covers of menus are blank—a complete waste of good advertising space. Considering the number of customers who look at a menu every day, month in and month out, the "advertising space" on the average menu is probably worth more than a large ad in most local newspapers. The food service operator who does not use this space is missing another promotional and merchandising opportunity.

Using the back cover, however, means using it effectively. Sell your take-out foods the way other advertisers sell in their space advertising. Start with a good heading—"Take-Outs, Tops in Convenience." Use a subhead—"Enjoy Gourmet Foods at Home—Pick Up or Delivery Service." Then use illustrations. The easiest way to illustrate take-outs is to photograph your most popular items (or the items you would like to make popular) in their take-out containers, or in the process of being packaged in the containers. This is important, because, while customers may be sold on your good cooking, quality ingredients, and varied and interesting cuisine, they do not know (if they are new customers, and these are the ones you are looking for) how the take-out items are packed. By using packaging photographs, you overcome any consumer resistance concerning strength of packages, flavor loss, heat loss, and carrying inconvenience.

Then, as in any good ad, use plenty of good copy. Describe each take-out item, list its price, tell how it is packed (paper box, tub, bucket—aluminum foil or returnable metal container). Also, list how many people each portion sold serves. Regardless of whether or not these same items are listed in the regular menu, it is good advertising to list them again. Even if the prices are the same as your regular menu, price repetition will not hurt.

If you have delivery service, sell this service also, and be sure to list your phone number prominently. If you treat your menu back cover as you would paid space, write good copy, use good illustrations, and tell all the facts—you will have a "menu ad" that pulls. In addition, refer to your take-out story inside the menu so that the customer will not fail to read it on the back cover.

Obviously, your menu take-out story will sell only the customer who already patronizes your operation in a regular table or counter service capacity. To sell the public outside of your operation, you must use other advertising media, but for this, you can still use the menu. Print your back cover menu ad story on light paper suitable for mailing, either in an envelope or as a self-mailer. This will save you money, since all of the preparation costs (copy, art, photos, typesetting) have been done for your menu. All you have to pay for is printing and paper.

In fact, if you want to use the entire menu—regular listing plus take-out story—as a promotion piece, you can use the same method and print it on lightweight paper to be used as a direct-mail piece. Do not print "miniature" menus. In nearly all cases, the type becomes so small it is impossible to read, and the entire cost of printing becomes a total waste.

An almost separate category of take-outs is the party-banquet take-out or catering service. If you have room on your menu, tell this story there, also. Use photos to illustrate your party settings, center pieces, etc., and tell a detailed story in your copy. Some food service operations use a separate party-banquet catering menu to sell this feature of their food service which is good, but for the customer who will not ask (the average customer) about these services, the regular menu is still the place where this story can be told to the "mostest for the leastest."

Take Home Our Specialties

Oil Salad Dressing with Cheese, ½ Pint . . . . **1.50** Full Pint **2.50**
Creamed Roquefort, ½ Pint . . . . **1.50** Full Pint **2.50**
Our Own Cheese Crocks, 11 oz. . . . **2.00** 20 oz. . . . **3.75** 40 oz. . . . **4.95**
Chopped Chicken Liver Pate, ½ Pint . . . . **1.50** Full Pint **2.50**

We Will Deliver Any Entree On Our Menu, Complete With Relishes, Soup, Salad and Potato To Your Home or Motel. Another of the Charcoal Inn's Unique Services.

We Use Imported Roquefort In Our Dressing

Verdile's

TAKE HOME CORNER

1 quart of Spaghetti Sauce 1.75
1 quart of Marinara Sauce 1.50
Meat Balls . . . . 2 for .30
Fresh Sausage Links . . . . 4 for .75

All Our Menu Items Are Available For Take Home Consumption.

Just Call 235-9848
We Would Be Happy To Cook For You.

Take-outs should be specialties of the house or unusual items not readily available at the supermarket.

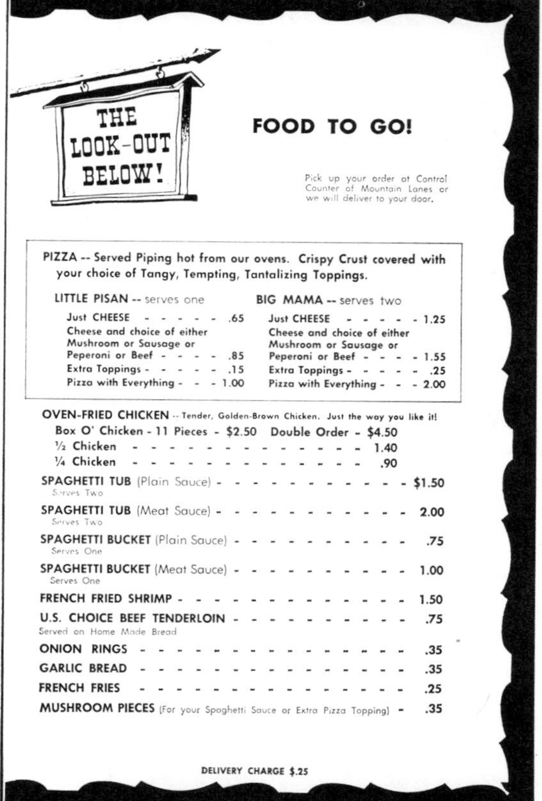
THE LOOK-OUT BELOW!

FOOD TO GO!

Pick up your order at Control Counter of Mountain Lanes or we will deliver to your door.

PIZZA -- Served Piping hot from our ovens. Crispy Crust covered with your choice of Tangy, Tempting, Tantalizing Toppings.

LITTLE PISAN -- serves one		BIG MAMA -- serves two	
Just CHEESE	.65	Just CHEESE	1.25
Cheese and choice of either Mushroom or Sausage or Peperoni or Beef	.85	Cheese and choice of either Mushroom or Sausage or Peperoni or Beef	1.55
Extra Toppings	.15	Extra Toppings	.25
Pizza with Everything	1.00	Pizza with Everything	2.00

OVEN-FRIED CHICKEN -- Tender, Golden-Brown Chicken. Just the way you like it!
Box O' Chicken - 11 Pieces - $2.50 Double Order - $4.50
½ Chicken - - - - - - - - - - - - - 1.40
¼ Chicken - - - - - - - - - - - - - .90

SPAGHETTI TUB (Plain Sauce) - - - - - - - - - - - - $1.50
Serves Two
SPAGHETTI TUB (Meat Sauce) - - - - - - - - - - - - 2.00
Serves Two
SPAGHETTI BUCKET (Plain Sauce) - - - - - - - - - - .75
Serves One
SPAGHETTI BUCKET (Meat Sauce) - - - - - - - - - - 1.00
Serves One
FRENCH FRIED SHRIMP - - - - - - - - - - - - - 1.50
U.S. CHOICE BEEF TENDERLOIN - - - - - - - - - - .75
Served on Home Made Bread
ONION RINGS - - - - - - - - - - - - - - - .35
GARLIC BREAD - - - - - - - - - - - - - - - .35
FRENCH FRIES - - - - - - - - - - - - - - - .25
MUSHROOM PIECES (For your Spaghetti Sauce or Extra Pizza Topping) - .35

DELIVERY CHARGE $.25

An example of good take-out merchandising that does an effective selling job.

17

Continentalize your menu

Continental cuisine is becoming more popular on the menu. With the advent of new convenience food techniques, special continental-type entrees are becoming easier to prepare and serve than they ever were before. Your chef need not be French or German to serve French and German foods, but the presentation on the menu of these foreign foods does present a menu problem. The two elements that seem to continentalize a menu are the sauce, either added or cooked in, and wine, either added or cooked in.

Here we are not concerned with the actual recipes for Continental cuisine, but rather about how these entrees are listed on the menu. As usual, we go to the source for menu information—menus of successful food service operators who are serving and merchandising continental cuisine on the menu.

To begin with, headings for types of entrees, appetizers, desserts, etc., can be in a foreign language, with an English translation, of course. The *Trattoria Gatti*, a restaurant specializing in Italian cuisine, does it like this:

ANTIPASTI
Hors D'Oeuvres
ZUPPE
Soups
FARINACEI
Noodles
FARINACEI DELLA CASA
Home Made Pasta
SPECIALITA DELLA CASA
Specialties of the House
PESCE
Fish

GRIGLIA
Grill
LEGUMI
Vegetables
INSALATE
Salads
DOLCI
Desserts
FORMAGGI
Cheeses
BEVANDE
Beverages

As you can see, before even beginning to list the menu selections, this restaurant operator has raised the Italian food selection out of the ordinary, and out of the ordinary price category, too.

As one would expect, the *Mews Dining Room*, home of the Provincetown Mews Wine & Food Tasting Society, Inc., has a very Continental cuisine. To begin with, the Dinner is not just listed in plain fashion, but DINER TABLE D'HOTE (Full Course Dinners) and the Appetizers (Hors D'Oeuvres on the Menu) are out of the ordinary, as listed here:

Eggplant Maison
Demi Pamplemousse
Coquille Cape Cod
Les Escargots de Bourgognes
Sardines Portugaise
Assiette de Crudites

The following four entrees from the same restaurant give you an idea of the French approach with sauces and wines:

Sole Dieppoise
  Sole poached with mushrooms, shrimps, and mussels in a light cream sauce.
Shrimp per Bacco!
  Shrimp prepared with lobster sauce served with rice pilaf
Poulet Chasseur
  Chicken in the French style with tomatoes, mushrooms, and spices.
Escallope de Veau au Madre
  Veal with Portuguese wine sauce

You will note that in each case while a French name is given to the entree, the item is explained in English.

Your entire menu need not be continental. In fact, most restaurants will have a mainly American cuisine with a few continental items added. *Hasenour's Restaurant*, for example, has the two following German entrees included with its otherwise American menu:

Wienerschnitzel ala Holstein
  A tender cutlet of choice veal steak topped with a fried country egg
Sauerbraten mit Kartoffel Pfannekuchen
  U.S. choice beef roast marinated for seven days in vinegar and spice brine, roasted to a juicy goodness with spicy sweet-sour wine gravy
  Served with potato pancakes and wilted lettuce salad, typifying Old World eating at its best

For the ultimate in continental listing on the menu, the *Old Swiss Village Restaurant* in Tampa, Florida lists its appetizers, soups, entrees, desserts, and beverages in three languages—French, German and English, as shown here:

Hors D'Oeuvres
  Pate de foie gras a la gelee
  Gaensleberpastete mit gelee
  The French goose liver classic with aspic
Escargots "Swiss House"
  Schnecken "Swiss House"
  Snails "Swiss House style"
Cocktail des crevettes frais
  Frischer krevetten cocktail
  Fresh shrimp cocktail
Filets de hereng Chantilly
  Hering mit schlagsahne
  Herring in sour cream
Huitres ou moules
  Austern oder muscheln
  Oysters or cherrystone clams
Potage-Suppen-Soups
  Consomme au sherry
  Klare fleischbruehe mit sherry
  Clear beef broth with sherry wine
Soupe de jour, chaude ou froide
  Heisse oder kalte tasgesuppe
  Today's hot or cold soup specialty
Soupe a l'oignon au gratin
  Zwiebelsuppe au gratin, cup
  French onion soup gratine, marmite
Filet de sabre fraise
  Frischer schwertfisch
  Fresh Block Island swordfish tenderloin charcoal broiled
Pompano en court bouillon
  Pompano in kraftbruehe
  Fresh Florida pompano in herb broth with wine

SPECIALTIES DE LA MAISON-
HAUSSPEZIALITAETEN-
HOUSE SPECIALTIES

Escalopes de veau a la "Marsala," flambes
  Kleine kalbsschnitzel a la "Marsala," flambiert
  Veal cutlets coated in Romano cheese and sauteed with shallots, mushrooms and wine
Tournedoes Henri IV
  Thin slices of filet mignon on artichoke hearts with Bearnaise sauce
Roti de boeuf au jus
  Feinstes roastbeef in eignen saft
  A generous slice of prime beef rib in natural juices
Poulet tropical
  Brathendl tropical
  Pineapple filled with chicken breast in white wine sauce

DESSERTS

Peche Melba
  Pfirsich Melba
  Peach half on vanilla ice cream topped with red raspberry puree
Une selection de patisserie fine du wagon
  Auswahl von feinem gebaech von dem wagon
  Selection of fine pastries from the wagon
Glaces ou sorbets siverses
  Auswahl von verschiedenen eissorten
  Choice of ice cream or sherbet
Coupes: fraises, chocolat ou ananas
  Sundaes: erdbeer, schokolade oder ananas
  Sundaes: strawberry, chocolate, or pineapple

BOISSONS-GETRANKE-BEVERAGES

Creme cafe cognac
  Eis kaffee mit kognac
  Chilled coffee, chocolate, cream and brandy
The, chaud ou froid
  Tee, heiss oder kalt
  Tea, hot or cold
Cafe irlandais
  Irischer kaffee
  Irish coffee
Cafe a la maison
  Haus kaffee
  Swiss House blend coffee

Along with this continental selection, the *Swiss House* menu lists an excellent selection of wines as part of the menu. In fact, it is hard to visualize a real continental menu without a good wine selection. So if you plan to continentalize your menu, you'd better take a look at your wine cellar, or if you don't have one, call your wine merchant at once!

It's not often that a military installation menu, Officer's or N.C.O. Club has anything special to offer, but the menu of the *International Grill* at the Garmisch Recreation Area in Germany has an interesting feature. They list Grill Specialties from around the world. These are twelve entrees each from a different country—France, Yugoslavia, Russia, England, Germany, Austria, Hungary, Italy, Spain, Turkey, Hawaii and the United States. The entrees for Yugoslavia, Hungary, and Spain are listed here:

From Yogoslavia:

Rasnici

This specialty of a Balkan country features small pieces of tenderloin of beef, on a skewer, topped with fried onions and served on toast, salad.

From Hungary:

Fleica

From the smoky campfires of gypsies comes this exciting delicacy of two grilled pork chops topped with a tangy paprika sauce, and surrounded by French fries and cole slaw. Still wonderfully flavored even though there isn't a campfire.

From Spain:

Albondiguillas Creole

Talked about from Barcelona to Madrid and now in Garmisch, we bring you especially prepared meat balls grilled on a skewer, and served over rice with a spicy tomato-paprika sauce, salad.

The ultimate reason for adding French, German, Italian, Spanish, or any other foreign names to the menu is, of course, not to make it harder to read. It is, let's face it, adding a certain snob appeal to your otherwise pedestrian listing, and thereby enabling you to charge more. Just adding foreign names, however, to a menu will not make the food, service, and decor of a restaurant any better. But, if you are upgrading your food, service and decor, then adding foreign terminology is telling your customer that your entire restaurant package is getting better. So get yourself a French, German, or Italian dictionary and start up-grading your menu.

Chicken or beef—dressed up and served in continental style, it becomes dining instead of just eating, with the price set accordingly.

Continental Dishes

STEAK DIANE FLAMBÉE, Wild Rice **7.25**
Mignonettes of Beef cooked at your Table, Sautéed in Sweet Butter, Bathed in our own Sauce. Served with Fresh Mushrooms on a Bed of Wild Rice and Flamed in Brandy

STEAK AU POIVRE, FLAMBE A L'ARMAGNAC, Wild Rice .. **8.00**

TOURNEDOS, ROSSINI, Wild Rice **7.50**

COQ AU VIN, Wild Rice **4.75**

Chicken Curry Calcutta
Plump Cubes of Breast of Chicken cooked in an Exciting Sauce of Apples, Fresh Ginger and Specially Blended Spices. Served with Saffron Rice and Assorted Condiments 4.55

Escalope de Veau Provencale
Veal Cutlet stuffed with Ham and Gruyere Cheese, Sautéed in Butter, then Topped with Mushrooms in Provencale Sauce. Served with Artichoke Florentine and Buttered Noodles 4.65

Emincé of Tenderloin Stroganoff
A Delightful Combination of Choice Beef Strips, gently braised, then simmered with Tomatoes and Seasonings, served with Rice Pilaff and Tomato Parmesan 4.65

Breast of Chicken Romana
Stuffed with Mushrooms, rolled in Parmesan Cheese, sautéed in foaming butter, served with Rice Pilaff and Artichoke Bottoms Florentine 4.55

Dining in the Grand Manner

CHATEAUBRIAND **9.75**
The ultimate in superior Steaks! Thick and generous, this rich U. S. Choice Steak is recognized the world over as an epicurean masterpiece. A cup of delicious French Onion Soup is served while this full cut Steak is being prepared. When ready, it is brought piping hot to your table. (Cooking time 25 min.) Serves two.

ROAST PRIME RIB OF BEEF AU JUS **3.95**
A standing Rib Roast of the finest aged Beef, roasted as succulently rare or tenderly well done as may please the most discriminate palate. Medium rare at its best.

Specialita Della Casa

Grenadins of Beef Chasseur Beef Tenderloin, Marsala Wine, Mushrooms, Tomato, Tarragon, Risolé Potatoes	7.00
Breast of Chicken Jerusalem Suprème Sauce, Madiera Wine, Artichoke, Mushrooms, Turnips, Rice Pilaf	5.00
Fritto Piccato Medaillons of Veal, Zucchini Doré, Mushrooms, Tomato, Gnocchi Romani	5.50
Escalope de Veau, Cordon Bleu Imported Swiss Cheese, Ham, Mushrooms, Asparagus, Broiled Tomato	6.00
Medaillon of Veal Normande Tenderloin of Veal, Fresh Mushrooms, Xères Wine, Sauce Normande, Dauphine Potatoes, Cream of Spinach	7.00
Scampi Catalonia Langostinas imported from Spain, Sautéed in Olive Oil, Shallots, Garlic, Wine, Spices, Rice	6.00
Tournedos Henry IV Beef Tenderloin, Artichoke, Bearnaise, French String Beans, Rissolées Potatoes	7.95
Steak Diane Dauphine Potatoes, French String Beans	7.95
Steak Armagnac New York Steak Sauté, Black Cracked Pepper, Armagnac, Poivrade Sauce, Dauphine Potatoes, French String Beans	8.50

Italian, Spanish, and French entrees with unusual vegetables make this a true continental listing.

Exotic Specialties from Far Off Lands!

•

Mexican Iquana, Mole Sauce	4.95
French Fried Grasshoppers (Japan)	1.25
French Fried Butterflies (Japan)	1.95
Chocolate Covered Giant Ants (The genuine ants from South America which have been eaten there many years as the finest delicacy)	3.50
French Fried Ants	3.50
Quail Eggs	1.75
Sliced Smoked Octopus (Japan)	1.50
Baby Bees in Soya Sauce (Japan)	2.95
Chocolate Covered Baby Bees	3.50
Roasted Caterpillars (Japan)	1.50
Chocolate Covered Caterpillars	3.50
Fried Agave Worms (Mexico)	3.50
Diamondback Rattlesnake in Supreme Sauce	3.75
Romanoff Beluga Caviar	3.00
Rooster Comb in Jelly (France)	2.95
Smoked Baby Clams (Japan)	1.25
Kangaroo Steaks in Wine Sauce (Australia)	10.00
Kangaroo Tail Soup (Australia)	2.50
Smoked Quails (Japan)	1.95
Alligator Soup	3.50
Birds Nest Soup (England)	2.25
Sharks Fin Soup (England)	2.50
Cream of Snails Soup (Germany)	2.25
Norwegian Reindeer Steak in Madeira Wine Gravy	3.95
Smoked Petite Oysters (Japan)	1.50
Smoked Frog Legs (Japan)	1.50
Smoked Filet of Swordfish (Japan)	1.75

Exotic and then some.

Les Poissons

WALLEYED PIKE SAUTEE 4.75
Wisconsin's favorite lake treasure sauteed in the traditional country manner

COLORADO MOUNTAIN TROUT "VERONIQUE" 4.95
From the crisp, clear creeks of Colorado, sauteed in butter and served with California grapes and toasted almonds

* SOUTH AFRICAN LOBSTER TAILS 7.50
Broiled to perfection and served with sizzling Wisconsin butter

FROG LEGS SAUTEE PROVENCALE 5.25
Sauteed in oil and garlic butter, served with grilled tomato

IMPORTED DOVER SOLE "MEUNIERE" 6.25
The delicacy of the North Sea sauteed in lemon butter sauce with a cover of finely chopped parsley

SCAMPI DANIELLE 5.50
This Danish Lobster Tail delicacy is a delicious addition for the friends of all sea foods. This shellfish is sauteed in butter and au gratin a la Cafe de Paris, with the famous special seasoned butter

Specialité de Pioneer

VEAL SCHNITZEL CORDON BLEU 4.95
The European specialty stuffed with Swiss Cheese and ham, breaded and sauteed, served with buttered noodles and broiled tomato

WISCONSIN SELECTED CALVES LIVER 4.75
Sauteed young liver, delicately prepared with smothered onions and apple rings

TENDERLOIN and SWEETBREADS "PARISIENNE" En Casserole . . . 5.50
Filets of beef and tender slices of sweetbreads, sauteed and served with white asparagus, peppers, and tomatoes

ORIGINAL RUSSIAN BEEF "STROGANOFF" 4.50
Prepared after the unique old St. Petersburg recipe that was a delicacy of the late Czar Nicholas

LONG ISLAND DUCKLING "NATURELLE" 6.25
This succulent Eastern bird is baked crisp in its own juice and served with fresh vegetables and croquette potatoes

SOFT OMELETTE WITH PFIFFERLINGE 3.50
For the gourmet with á light diet this fluffy egg dish is served with imported pfifferlinge, a special European mushroom. An interesting and excellent addition to our menu

PAN FRIED PORK CHOPS 4.50
Two Iowa cornfed pork chops pan fried in butter in the Early American manner, served with fresh apple sauce

DOUBLE CUT LAMB CHOPS DIABLO 5.95
Sauteed to perfection and glazed with English mustard and finished with fine herbs, garlic and bread crumbs

Les Legumes

SWISS PATTIE 50
SAUTEED MUSHROOMS 1.25
FRESH VEGETABLE du jour . . .50
WHITE ASPARAGUS 1.25
With sauce Hollandaise

Dining in high style.

This is a "Dutch Treat" that is completely out of the ordinary, with pea or potato soup, beef, fish, chicken, and ham. And for dessert, Dutch Tarts, Mint Ice Cream, and Hague Bluff.

The twelve-page menu that is reproduced in its entirety on the next three pages lists all information and items in three languages—French, German, and English. See inside front cover and pages 1, 2, and 3 of menu on the facing page.

les Antiques d'Art

The priceless collection of rare antiques in the Old Swiss House was gathered for your enjoyment by Mrs. August A. Busch, Jr. and her brother, Willy J. Buholzer. Mr. Buholzer operates the original Old Swiss House in Lucerne.

Intricately hand-carved in oak, this German Baroque hutch was built in 1601. Grille Room, 2nd floor.

The KACHELOFEN, one of the oldest pieces in the collection (right) was used for heating and ornamentation in the 18th century. Delft blue and white tiles are of Swiss Baroque styling. 1st floor.

Bronze, brass and wood polished crystal Louis XV chandelier. "Views of Switzerland" wall murals, done from wood blocks carved a century ago, was the first wallpaper scenic ever printed. Only one other set exists. Banquet Room.

Swiss motto between antique French hand-carved grape columns, reads: "Time passes swiftly. Enjoy the hours as they come. If they're not good, let them pass. If they are good, enjoy them." Lounge, 2nd floor.

Hand-carved figures in polychrome and gold leaf, from a dismantled 18th century church. St. Catherina and St. Loedegar (far right), a Bishop born in 616, later beheaded. Foyer, 1st floor.

LEUCHTERWEIBCHEN or Light Lady, chandelier from the original Swiss House in Lucerne, has a woman's body and dolphin's tail, in the 17th century mermaid legend. Foyer, 1st floor.

Hors-d'oeuvres

Pâté de foie gras à la gelée
Gaensleberpastete mit Gelee
The French goose liver classic with aspic 1.50

Escargots "Swiss House"
Schnecken "Swiss House"
Snails "Swiss House" style 1.50

Cocktail de crevettes frais
Frischer Krevetten Cocktail
Fresh shrimp cocktail 1.50

Filets de hareng Chantilly
Hering mit Schlagsahne
Herring in sour cream 1.00

Huitres ou moules
Austern oder Muscheln
Oysters or cherrystone clams 1.50

Carte Des Vins

Bin No.

Swiss:

Fine Selections from Cantons, Neuchatel, Valais and Vaud—in the best vintages.

1 NEUCHÂTEL
Bouteille 4.25
Demi-Bouteille 2.50

2 OEIL DE PERDRIX
(Neuchatel Rose) Bouteille 6.00
Demi-Bouteille 3.25

3 FENDANT DE SION
Bouteille 5.50
Demi-Bouteille 3.00

4 JOHANNISBERGER du VALAIS
Bouteille 5.50
Demi-Bouteille 3.00

5 DÔLE DE SION ROUGE
Bouteille 5.50
Demi-Bouteille 3.00

6 DEZALEY DE LAVAUX
Bouteille 4.75
Demi-Bouteille 2.50

7 AIGLE
Bouteille 5.50
Demi-Bouteille 3.00

8 LA COTE
Bouteille 3.75

Moselle:

19 BERNKASTELER
Bouteille 5.25
Demi-Bouteille 2.75

20 PIESPORTER GOLDTROEPFCHEN
Bouteille 6.00
Demi-Bouteille 3.25

21 ZELLER SCHWARZE KATZ
Bouteille 5.25
Demi-Bouteille 2.75

Bin No.

Rhine:

10 LIEBFRAUMILCH: MADONNA OR BLUE NUN
light, fruity and fresh, fleeting sweetness.
Bouteille 5.00
Demi-Bouteille 2.75

11 RUDESHEIMER ROSENGARTEN,
fragrant, tangy.
Bouteille 5.00
Demi-Bouteille 2.75

12 RUDESHEIMER BISCHOFSBERG SPATLESE,
Exceptional tastiness.
Bouteille 5.75
Demi-Bouteille 3.00

14 SPARKLING LIEBFRAUMILCH,
Sumptuous liveliness.
Bouteille 7.00
Demi-Bouteille 3.75

15 NIERSTEINER
Bouteille 4.50
Demi-Bouteille 2.75

ANHEUSER FEHR
16 LAUBENHEIMER
Bouteille 4.50
Demi-Bouteille 2.75

17 LIEBFRAUMILCH
Bouteille 4.50
Demi-Bouteille 2.75

18 JOHANNISBERGER
Bouteille 4.75
Demi-Bouteille 3.00

Bin No.

White Bordeaux:

22 SAUTERNES GRANDE TERRASSE,
moderately sweet.
Bouteille 5.00
Demi-Bouteille 2.75

23 CHATEAU d'YQUEM,
definitely the finest sweet full-bodied sauterne.
Bouteille 10.00
Demi-Bouteille 5.50

24 GRAVES, CHATEAU DE LA BREDE,
more to dryness, full-bodied.
Bouteille 5.00
Demi-Bouteille 2.75

Red Bordeaux:

25 CHATEAU LAFITE ROTHSCHILD,
tangy and light, having pronounced flavor.
Bouteille 7.50
Demi-Bouteille 4.00

26 SAINT JULIEN
Bouteille 5.00
Demi-Bouteille 2.75

27 MEDOC
Bouteille 5.25
Demi-Bouteille 3.00

28 PONTET CANET
Bouteille 6.00
Demi-Bouteille 3.25

BUDWEISER .60 BUSCH BAVARIAN .50

Carte Des Vins

Bin No.

White Burgundy:

29 CORTON CHARLEMAGNE,
Outstanding, medium full-bodied.
Bouteille 10.00
Demi-Bouteille 5.25

30 CHABLIS,
Very dry and flinty.
Bouteille 5.00
Demi-Bouteille 2.75

31 POUILLY FUISSE,
Pale, Light, Dry and "Clean" on the palate.
Bouteille 5.00
Demi-Bouteille 2.75

32 MEURSAULT,
Soft and full.
Bouteille 6.00
Demi-Bouteille 3.25

Rhone Valley:

33. CHATEAUNEUF DU PAPE
Bouteille 5.00
Demi-Bouteille 2.75

Rose:

34 ANJOU ROSE
Bouteille 4.00
Demi-Bouteille 2.25

Red Burgundy:

35 CLOS DE VOUGEOT,
full and rich, excellent bouquet.
Bouteille 10.50
Demi-Bouteille 6.50

Bin No.

36 POMMARD,
Well known, light and soft.
Bouteille 6.50
Demi-Bouteille 3.50

37 BEAUJOLAIS SUPERIOR,
light, gusty and fresh.
Bouteille 4.75
Demi-Bouteille 2.50

38 GEVREY CHAMBERTIN,
deep red, full-bodied.
Bouteille 6.50
Demi-Bouteille 3.50

39 CRUSE SPARKLING BURGUNDY,
very popular and festive.
Bouteille 7.75
Demi-Bouteille 4.00

Champagnes:

Need no introduction, only an occasion.

40 DOM PERIGNON,
Distinct Masterpiece, absolutely the finest. Vintage
Bouteille 15.00

41 BOLLINGER, brut,
extra quality. Vintage
Bouteille 12.00

42 MUMM'S CORDON ROUGE,
brut.
Bouteille 12.00

43 PIPER HEIDSIECK,
extra dry.
Bouteille 11.00
Demi-Bouteille 6.00

Italian Wines:

44 BARDOLINO,
red, vivacious.
Bouteille 4.00
Demi-Bouteille 2.25

45 SOAVE BOLLA,
White, dry.
Bouteille 4.00
Demi-Bouteille 2.25

Bin No.

Spanish:

46 CEPA DE'ORO,
Dry, White, fine table wine.
Bouteille 3.50
Demi-Bouteille 2.00

47 MARQUES DE RISCAL,
Deep red, robust, rich and nutty on the palate.
Bouteille 4.50
Demi-Bouteille 2.50

Portuguese:

48 LANCER'S CRACKLING ROSE
Bouteille 6.50
Demi-Bouteille 3.50

America's Fine Wines:
from California

	Bottle	Half	Glass
49 Pinot Noir	2.75		.50
50 Pinot Chardonnay	3.00		.50
51 Champagne Brut	6.25	3.25	.85
52 Sparkling Burgundy	7.00	3.75	
53 Dubonnet	4.50		.50

Other Imports:

	Bottle	Half	Glass
54 Dry Sack	7.00		.85
55 La Ina	6.50		.65
56 Harvey's Bristol Cream	9.00		1.00
57 Double Century	5.00		.50
58 Harvey's Hunting Port	6.50		.65

MICHELOB - Bottle or Stein .85

Potages · Suppen · Soups

Consomme au sherry
Klare Fleischbruehe mit sherry
Clear beef broth with sherry wine .40

Soupe du jour, chaude ou froide
Heisse oder kalte Taggessuppe
Today's hot or cold soup specialty .40

Soupe à l'oignon au gratin
Zwiebelsuppe au Gratin
French onion soup gratine *cup* .40 *marmite* .75

Les Fruits de la Me · Fische · Seafood

Homards du Maine
Gedaempfter Hummer von Maine
Steamed Maine lobsters 6.25

Filet de sabre fraise
Frischer Schwertfisch
Fresh Block Island swordfish tenderloin charcoal broiled 3.80

Sole meunière
Gebratene Dover Schollen
Imported Dover sole saute in lemon butter 3.90

Pompano en court bouillion
Pompano in Kraftbruehe
Fresh Florida pompano in herb broth with wine 4.25

Spécialités de la Maison · Hausspezialitaeten · House Specialities

Escalopes de veau à la "Marsala," flambés
Kleine Kalbsschnitzel à la "Marsala" flambiert
Veal cutlets coated in Romano cheese and sauteed with shallots, mushrooms and wine 4.40

Rôti de boeuf Au Jus
Feinstes Roastbeef im eigenen Saft
A generous slice of prime beef rib in natural juices 4.75

Tournedoes Henrie IV
Tournedoes Henri IV
Thin slices of filet mignon on artichoke hearts with Bearnaise sauce 5.90

Poulet Tropical
Brathendl Tropical
Pineapple filled with chicken breast in white wine sauce 3.75

From the Charcoal Broiler

Choice sixteen-ounce sirloin 5.50
Planked Chateaubriand (2 persons) 12.00
Choice tenderloin steak (ten ounces) 5.20
Double rib French lamb chops 4.50
Small six-ounce tenderloin 3.70

All entrees served with fresh French rolls, butter,
tossed Swiss House green salad, and Alpine potatoes or saffron risotto.

Desserts

Pêche Melba
Pfirsich Melba
Peach half on vanilla ice cream topped with red raspberry puree .60

Une Séléction de Patisserie Fine du wagon
Auswahl von feinem Gebaech von dem wagen
Selection of fine pastries from the wagon .50

Glaces ou sorbets diverses
Auswahl von verschiedenen Eissorten
Choice of ice cream or sherbet .40

Coupes: fraises, chocolat ou ananas
Sundaes: Erdbeer, Schokolade oder Ananas
Sundaes: strawberry, chocolate or pineapple .50

Banana Flambé 1.40

Crêpes suzette 1.40

Boissons · Getranke · Beverages

Crème café cognac
Eis Kaffee mit Kognac
Chilled coffee-chocolate, cream and brandy 1.25

Café Irlandais
Irischer Kaffee
Irish coffee 1.15

Thé, chaud ou froid
Tee, heiss oder kalt
Tea, hot or cold .30

Café à la maison
Haus Kaffee
Swiss House blend coffee .30

Liqueurs Importes

1.00

Williams Pear Brandy . . . Swiss Kirschwasser . . . Goldwasser
Crème de Cacao (Blanche ou Brune) . . . Cherry Heering . . . Crème de Menthe (Verte ou Blanche)
Curacao . . . Benedictine . . . Drambuie . . . Benedictine und Brandy
Chartreuse (Verte ou Jaune) . . . Grand Marnier . . . Cognacs
Galliano . . . Tia Maria

Fondue

THE NATIONAL DISH OF SWITZERLAND

The one whose morsel of Swissbread falls off the spear into the bubbling kirschwassered cheese, by custom, buys the wine. (A round of drinks will do.)

1.75 per person
(Not less than two, please)

Lass' uns das gute Mahl geniessen und mit einem Glase Wein begiessen.

History of the Old Swiss House

The Old Swiss House is an enlarged replica of the famous restaurant of the same name in Lucerne, Switzerland, built in the early 18th century. The original Swiss House, one of Switzerland's outstanding restaurants, is operated by Willy and Kurt Buholzer, who took over its management from their late father. The Old Swiss House, like the original restaurant, contains an antique collection of rare beauty.

Colorful flags outside the Swiss House represent the 22 cantons, or provinces, of Switzerland. The wood-carved doors are massive replicas of those on the Swiss House in Lucerne. Notice the 17th century walnut hutch in the Grille Room and the magnificent 18th century walnut chest in the second floor Powder Room. The signed oil-on-wood still life by Swiss master Petrus Schotanus (Grille Room), and the solid copper holy water reservoir with its original hinged lid, are collectors' items. The original Jean Holbein hand-colored engravings are dated 1751.

Many of the smaller items have fascinating histories. The sand urns are solid copper cooking utensils used over 200 years ago. The canton shields, Buholzer crests, game trophies and the grape masher are hand-carved. In the Cocktail Lounge, the Chemine' Fence, the wine bottles, solid copper foot and bed warmers all were used in the 17th century, as were the Alpine cattle yokes and ancient Swiss weapons. Notice the tole coal scuttle at the fireplace, the warrior's shield above it and the ceramic beer stein from the year 1508.

All items of construction, decorating and furnishing are either an exact replica or an antique import. From this exacting completeness, plus the perfection of superb cuisine deftly served in an atmosphere of continental luxury, comes the Old World charm of the Old Swiss House.

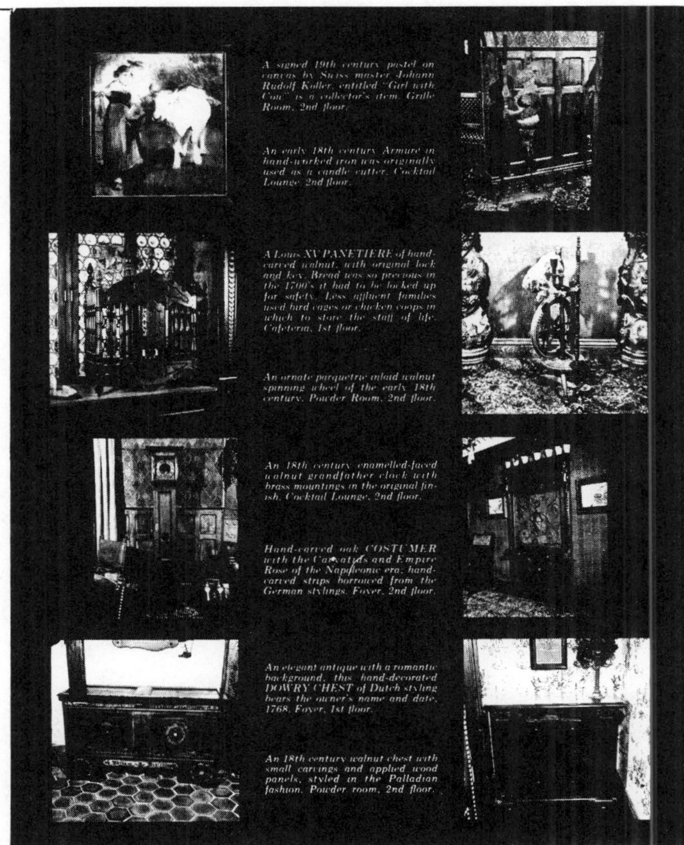

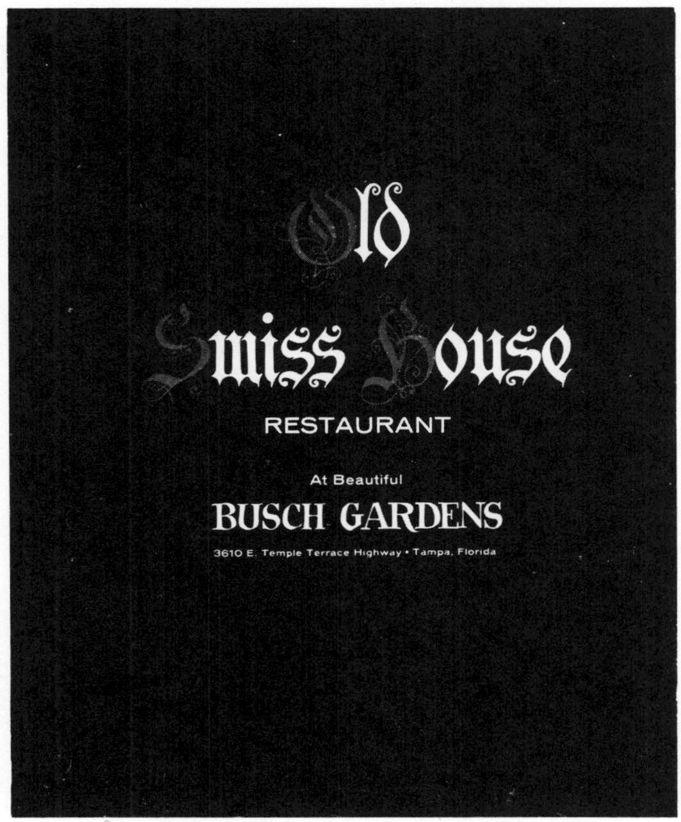

Foreign menus can be studied for ideas usable by American food service operations.

SPÉCIALITÉS DU CHEF	OUR CHEF'S SPECIALITIES	SPEZIALITAETEN UNSERES CHEFS	
Brochette Stördebecker	Roasted meat on spit Stördebecker	Gebratenes Fleisch nach Stördebeckerart	12.—
Mignons de veau Sans Gêne	Small veal-fillets Sans Gene	Kleine Kalbsfilets Sans Gene	12.—
Caneton de Nantes vigneronne**** (4 personnes)	Duckling Nantes-style with raisins**** (4 persons)	Ente nach Nanteserart mit Trauben**** (4 Personen)	44.—
Poulet sauté Belle Othéro** (2 personnes)	Sauted chicken Belle Othero** (2 persons)	Sautiertes Hähnchen Schöne Othero** (2 Personen)	28.—
Emincé de volaille Idaho (2 personnes)	Flakes of chicken Idaho (2 persons)	Geschnetzeltes Geflügelfleisch Idaho (2 Personen)	20.—

GRILLADES ET BROCHE	GRILLADES AND BARBECUES	GRILLADEN UND SPIESS	
Casserole vieux Berne	Mixed grill on Rösti	Mixed-Grill auf Rösti	12.—
Tranche de foie de veau	Sliced calf's liver	Kalbsleber	10.—
Rosette de Charollais Rachel	Tournedos Rachel	Tournedos Rachel	13.—
Rognon de veau aux herbettes de la Provence	Veal kidneys with spices	Kalbsniere mit Kräutern aus der Provence	10.—
Carré d'agneau de lait chatillonnaise* (2 personnes)	Lambchops Chatillonnaise* (2 persons)	Lammkarree Chatillonerart* (2 Personen)	26.—
Jeune coq grillé aux trois moutardes** (2 personnes)	Grilled young cock with mustards** (2 persons)	Junges grilliertes Hähnchen mit Senf** (2 Personen)	19.—
Châteaubriand périgourdine* (2 personnes)	Châteaubriand perigourdine* (2 persons)	Châteaubriand Perigordinerart* (2 Personen)	26.—
T-Bonesteak grillé Montfort** (4 personnes)	T-Bonesteak grilled Montfort** (4 persons)	Grilliertes T-Bonesteak Montfort** (2 Personen)	50.—

This excellent menu lists everything in three languages—French, German, and English.

18

What Americans can learn from foreign menus

Generally, American menus are the best in the world, but there still are menus from around the world that have some ideas of interest to restaurateurs in the United States. Following are some examples. Besides the specific ideas, they give the words and entrees that can be added to American menus to give a continental or cosmopolitan flavor or style.

MUHLE (THE MILL)

The *Muhle* restaurant in the Sheraton-Munich Hotel has an attractive, well-designed menu with several features that can give ideas to American menu creators. Each page plus the cover has an original drawing of a landscape from some European country, usually featuring a windmill. The color scheme is brown and orange. The cover is of heavy, coated paper, and the inside eight pages are of light tan, 80 lb. text stock. The food listings and headings are large and legible while being printed in dark brown. The menu is 13″ × 11″ in size and organized in the following categories:

Vorspeisen	Appetizers
Suppen	Soups
Sandwiches	Sandwiches
Fisch	Fish
Vom Grill	From our Grill
Wild	Game
Spezialitalen	Specialties
Nachspiesen	Desserts

This adds up to 21 entrees, 9 appetizers, 5 soups, 5 sandwiches and 12 desserts—a generous listing. The obvious "different" categories are From Our Grill and Game. The Grill listing, similar to the American From the Broiler, is common in European menus, but it usually contains some different items. The Mixed Grill, for example, is often included, and this item could be added to American menus. It is a combination of meats with—in this menu—hash browned potatoes and morel sauce.

The Filet Steak, also under Grills, is prepared, served, and listed on the menu with style and panache, i.e., merchandising flair. It is listed as Filet Mignon "Henry IV" with artichoke bottom, 7 oz., filled with Sauce Bernaise. Sauces are important to continental cooking so they are listed on the menu. This one lists beside the Sauce Bernaise, Mint Sauce, Cream Sauce, Redwine Sauce, Sauce Hollandaise, Curry Sauce, and Sauce Grand Veneur.

In the Wild Game listing, of special interest is the Half Pheasant "Souvaroff" in Copper Casserole with Sauce Grand Veneur, goose liver, truffles, cranberries, and salad. Everything about this entree listing is elegant, sophisticated, and very continental. Copy—if you can procure a pheasant . . . and truffles!

The Specialties listing includes four veal entrees—a typical continental touch—plus Breast of Chicken (in champagne—that makes it different), Calf's Liver, Pork Medallions, and Wiener Schnitzel. Notice also that the items that "go with" these entrees—salads, vegetables, sauces, etc.—are different for each entree.

The Dessert offering continues the "creme de la creme" merchandising approach. Besides the cheeses, there are fruits and a variety of ice cream dishes. But to add real flair and style, in the evening three flaming desserts are presented to tantalize the diner. Two are basically ice cream and fruit, in sauce or fresh, with an alcoholic beverage poured over it . . . lit, and allowed to burn for a few seconds. The ingredients are simple and available in most restaurants; so these fancy desserts, with a little practice, could be added to many American menus. The other flaming dessert on the *Muhle* menu is Crepes Suzette.

As is to be expected with a continental menu, everything is listed a la carte which could bring the tab up to 40 marks (about $22.00) for one soup, entree and dessert order, without the drinks. This includes a 15 percent service charge and an 11 percent value added tax.

LE SOUFFLE

Both the dinner and dessert menus of the Hotel Inter-Continental, London, are attractive, interesting, and worthy of study. The cover is of metallic silver with the design and copy printed in red and black. The graphics and type selection are in Art Deco style from the 1920s and 1930s. It is a large and expensive menu with many appetizers, entrees, and desserts plus some unusual extras.

Although this is a menu for a restaurant in an English hotel, everything is listed in French. This adds a certain "gourmet class" and helps to justify the high prices, but every item is described in English.

MENU PROFILE

Hors d'oeuvres	13
Souffles	6
Entrees	6
Seafood	9
Grilles	5
For Two	3
Cold Buffet	3
Vegetables	14
Desserts	14

Typical of an expensive menu, everything is listed a la carte. In keeping with the restaurant's name, six souffles are offered in the Dessert menu. This immediately makes for a different listing since a variety of souffles are seldom seen on American menus. There is also a large number of appetizers and desserts. The *before* and *after* gets a big play.

Les Grillades—From the Grill—here again we see this typically European menu category. The items included are steaks, veal, and lamb. Under a Les Legumes listing is a large a la carte selection of vegetables. Here also there are souffles—souffle potatoes, spinach and souffle with wild mushrooms, bacon, and onions. Unusual vegetable items and combinations are a way of adding gastronomic variety at low cost to a menu.

Elegance and style are also built into this food presentation by having a large number of items flamed or cooked at the table. This includes Lobster Souffle, flamed at your table; and Lobster flamed with Cognac and Pernod in tarragon cream sauce. In the dessert listing there is: Strawberries flamed with green pepper, Grand Marnier, and Kirsch served with vanilla ice and whipped cream.

All of these "action" items add *show biz* and excitement to this menu making customers feel they are getting their money's worth. As an added touch, the Chef des Cuisines and the Maitre d' Hotel are listed by name.

The entree menu is 10″ × 15″ with a heavy duplex—silver on one side—cover, and four pages inside. It is held together by a red tasseled silk cord. The dessert menu is 6½″ × 9″ with the cover and the four inside pages of the same paper with the same type and design. It also has a clip-on for adding variety to the dessert listing without reprinting the whole inside of the menu.

The *Alt Bayern Stube* has a special listing that illustrates creative menu planning. It is called "Sheraton International." The introduction says: "Our chef brought for you the best recipes from the following Sheraton Hotels." Then eight entree items are listed, from Frankfurt, Brussels, London, Stockholm, Paris, Madeira, Lisbon, and Copenhagen. This is an idea that could be copied by both American hotels—entrees from Chicago, New Orleans, San Francisco, etc., and by restaurants by offering an international menu.

From the Caribbean, the *La Boucan* restaurant of the Trinidad Hilton offers an interesting selection of foods and presents them with a colorful, attractively illustrated menu. Organized in three panels—which means that the customer sees every thing offered except the desserts at once—the number of items is large, but the way they are presented and described gives the customer a chance to pick exactly what he wants from a variety of exotic items. It also solves the problem of the hotel guest who may look at the same menu over a period of days or weeks. With this menu the guest will not get bored.

Of special interest is "Old Port of Spain Cookery" which includes such items as East Indian Lamb Curry "Rajah" and Caribbean Jambalaya (for two). The latter is described as "An

Exciting Blend of Seafood Including Shrimps, Lobster and Crabmeat, Sauteed with Onion and a Touch of Garlic, Flamed with Brandy and Served with Spanish Rice".

Another interesting and different category on this menu is called From the Smoke Oven. The explanation reads: "These Dishes are Smoke Roasted and Delicately Scented by the Tropical Guava Wood Used to Fire the Smoke Oven." One of these smoke oven entrees is Pirate Lamb Roast which is a rack of young lamb marinated in pure native honey, seasoned with Chinese spices, then smoke prepared and served with cashew nut rice and Chinese vegetables.

The illustrations on this menu are in four colors. The headings are in red and blue and the individual listings are in black. Each of the three panels measures 7″ × 14″ and there is space at the top of the center panel for a tip-on for listing daily specials.

Just when you think you have seen every kind of menu, along comes a new one. It's the Snack Menu of the *Lipo Bar* of the Tokyo Hilton. A square menu 7″ × 7″, it has a red and black cover and twelve inside pages with full color photographs of the snacks. They include: Smoked Hokkaido Salmon, Coppa Meat, Yakitori, Croque Monsieur Old Fashion, Cheese Boreks, Filet of Kobe Beef Skewer, Fried Shrimp "Kalamaki," Chicken Wings "Oriental," Foie Gras Strasbourg, and Smoked Ham and Salami.

The pictures do the selling. The "snacks" are shown as served with some liquor—scotch, brandy, bourbon—in the background. These items are obviously of an *impulse* nature. That is, the customer comes usually to a bar to drink, not eat; but when he sees the colorful illustrations on the menu, he gets the idea . . . the impulse, and orders. Good merchandising. If you have a bar . . . copy!

The Taipei Hilton has a beautiful Room Service Menu. It used traditional Chinese illustrations in full color. It is 12″ × 7¼″ in overall size, and each section of pages—Breakfast, All Day Dining, Snacks, Beverages—overlaps the previous one so that items are easy to find. Also, all items are listed in three languages—English, Chinese, and Japanese. The layout and style of this menu could be copied by a hotel stateside, and it may be a friendly gesture to list some items in a foreign language. Los Angeles, for example, has many Japanese visitors, so why not a hotel menu that's bilingual?

19

Merchandising low calorie items

It's hard to open a newspaper, read a magazine, or watch TV these days without being aware of weight problems, diets, and calorie counting, and the related foods, pills, and doctor's recommendations. Even for people without a weight problem, there is an awareness of the problem. As a result, there is evidence that the public is changing its eating habits. Certain types of foods, usually the high protein, low carbohydrate items, are favored. Also, the amount of food eaten at each meal is a subject for concern.

For the food service operator this may seem to be a problem. After all, if guests don't eat a lot, the operation will not sell as much and, therefore will not make as much money. But a problem can be turned into an opportunity. The food service establishment can change its menu in many ways to meet this challenge and, in effect, serve less food for the same price.

The first way to adjust the menu to the changing, selective, and calorie-aware public is to list more items a la carte. This gives the customer more choice. A customer may want an appetizer, but no potatoes, just a salad to go with a steak, or an after dinner drink instead of a dessert. There is a definite trend toward more a la carte listing on the menu, and the menu that is more a la carte is usually a more expensive menu which means more profit to the restaurant.

The second way to adjust to the calorie-conscious customer is to deliberately list low-calorie specials. There is a limited amount of this kind of listing on the menu at present. The following are some examples:

LOW CALORIE HI PROTEINS

Waist Watcher. $1.15
For the diet conscious, broiled ground sirloin with melted nippy cheese, Melba peach, cottage cheese, and Ry-krisp. Try a low cal Tab—1 calorie per 8 oz. serving.

Tiger-High Protein $1.35
½ lb. of ground sirloin, cottage cheese and tomato wedges, roll and butter.

Lou Jones $1.45
Slices of rare roast beef—cottage cheese and fruit or cole slaw, roll and butter.

LOW CALORIE SPECIALS

Broiled Chopped Sirloin Patty $1.15
with creamy cottage cheese, peach half, sliced tomatoes and melba toast.

Cold Sliced Turkey $1.25
with creamy cottage cheese, peach half, sliced tomatoes and melba toast.

DIET SPECIALS

½ Lb. GROUND ROUND STEAK $1.40
(with cottage cheese, choice of two peach halves or two pineapple rings).

THE BOYS' STEAK SANDWICH. $2.45
(½ lb. choice beef served on French roll with cottage cheese and fruit. Choice of two peach halves or two pineapple rings).

FILET OF SOLE. $1.25
(cottage cheese and choice of two peach halves or two pineapple rings).

NIK'S LOW CALORIE SPECIAL

Choice of tomato or orange juice, freshly ground hamburger patty, cottage cheese or garden fresh lettuce, sliced tomato, melba peach. $1.10

CALORIE SPECIALS

New York Steak $1.40

Jumbo Sirloin Patty. $1.20
Sirloin Patty. . . . .$ .95
above served with mound of cottage cheese, hard boiled egg and Ry-krisp.

THE SKINNY VIRGINNY BURGER
Minus the bun for weight-watchers, and served with a bowl of sliced egg, a mountain of cottage cheese and juicy tomato wedges on lettuce. Melba toast, of course $1.25

DIET BURGER for the calorie conscious—no roll, but accompanied by some cottage cheese.

The low-calorie item par excellence on the menu, of course, is the salad. Therefore, the menu that lists no entree salads is taking a chance of losing customers. Salads do not have to be listed as low-calorie items. The public generally is convinced of the diet value of salads, but some restaurants do list salads as low-calorie, diet entrees as shown in examples here.

DIET PLATES
LOW CALORIE DIET PLATE
(approximately 224 calories)
Choice of chilled shrimp, chopped beef or sliced chicken, sliced tomato, half peach, cottage cheese, melba toast and coffee or tea. $1.55

CHICKEN SALAD BOWL
(approximately 320 calories)
A salad of tossed greens and vegetables. Your favorite dressing. Rolls, butter and coffee or tear $1.45

SHRIMP SALAD BOWL
(approximately 285 calories)
A salad of tossed greens and vegetables. Rolls, butter and coffee or tea. $1.45

FRUIT SALAD PLATE
(approximately 305 calories)
Cottage cheese, fruit cocktail, peach half, orange and pineapple slice. Rolls, butter and coffee or tea..$1.45

Even the salad dressing can be sold from a diet angle as shown in the example below:

ON A DIET?
ASK YOUR WAITRESS FOR
"SAFFLOWER"
French dressing
Garlic dressing
Oil
Mayonnaise
with the highest ratio of polyunsaturated fats of all edible oils
WONDERFUL FOR SALADS

Finally, a real calorie opportunity presents itself when the subject is desserts. The "Decline of the Desserts," if it is real, is probably due to the common comment, "Oh, I shouldn't, it's fattening." The easiest way to get around this dessert obstacle and still build the check is to sell after-dinner drinks—brandies, cordials, dessert wines, after-dinner cocktails, coffee royal, etc. They are easy to serve, come prepared to a large extent and present no storage problem. They may still have calories, but to the customer they "seem" to be less fattening.

So, from beginning to end, the menu that presents more gourmet excitement and less "bulk" may be the menu of tomorrow.

The Red Roof Restaurant *lists a selection of diet plates in a prominent place on the menu plus a selection of sandwich, salad, and cold cuts.*

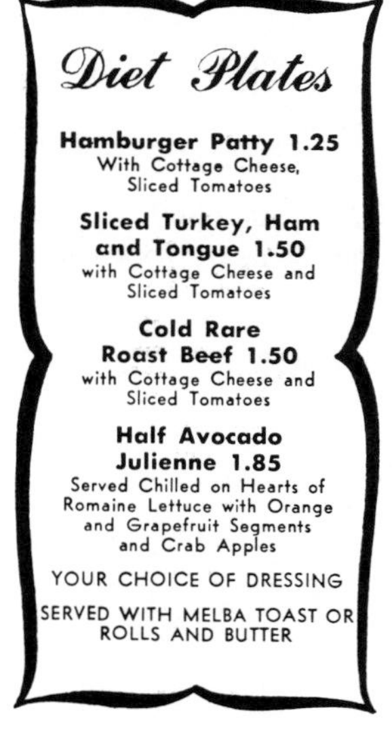

Diet Plates
Hamburger Patty 1.25
With Cottage Cheese, Sliced Tomatoes
Sliced Turkey, Ham and Tongue 1.50
with Cottage Cheese and Sliced Tomatoes
Cold Rare Roast Beef 1.50
with Cottage Cheese and Sliced Tomatoes
Half Avocado Julienne 1.85
Served Chilled on Hearts of Romaine Lettuce with Orange and Grapefruit Segments and Crab Apples
YOUR CHOICE OF DRESSING
SERVED WITH MELBA TOAST OR ROLLS AND BUTTER

The breakfast menu can also feature a low-calorie, high protein special, as shown here.

Low Calorie—High Protein Breakfast

(LESS THAN 400 CALORIES!)
ORANGE JUICE
SPECIAL K
(PROTEIN CEREAL) WITH MILK
ONE POACHED EGG
WHITE TOAST (1 SLICE)
BLACK COFFEE
$1.00

Shuller's Wigwam "Slim Jim" Diet Menu

Please Order Combinations By Total Calorie Numbers

Fresh Jumbo Shrimp Cocktail with Lemon Wedge .... 95 (85 calories)

The following appetizers included with Lo-Calorie Specials:

Beef Bouillon .... 25 calories — Tomato Juice .... 25 calories
Grapefruit Juice ..... 45 calories — Sea Food Cocktail ... 65 calories

"328" (CALORIES)

Fresh Fruit Plate 150
(Artificially Sweetened)
With Cottage Cheese Center .. 100
1 Slice of Boston Brown Bread 78
Black Coffee or Tea - No Sugar 0
328

1.65

"334"

Broiled Yearling Liver
with onion 172
1 slice of Whole Wheat
or Rye Bread 60
1 Pat of Butter 45
Creamed Cole Slaw 42
Fresh Green Beans 15
Black Coffee or Tea - No Sugar 0
334

1.45

"341"

Broiled Center Cut
Halibut Steak 150
With Lo Cal Tartar Sauce 12
Small Baked Potato (no butter) 95
Lo-Cal Creamed Cole Slaw 24
1 slice of Whole Wheat Toast 60
Black Coffee or Tea - No Sugar 0
341

1.60

"352"

Broiled Small Lobster Tail 100
With Melted Butter 125
Tossed Green Salad 16
Small Baked Potato (no butter) 95
1 slice of Melba Toast 16
Black Coffee or Tea No Sugar 0
352

2.15

"362"

Roast Turkey, no dressing, 3 oz 230
Cranberry Relish 50
Tossed Green Salad 16
1 slice of Melba Toast 16
1 small Whole Sweet Potato 50
Black Coffee or Tea - No Sugar 0
362

1.65

"363" (CALORIES)

Gulfport Salad Bowl
4 Fresh Shrimp 50
Crab Meat, ½ cup 85
1 Hard Cooked Egg 75
Tossed Green Salad 24
3 Tablespoons Lo-Cal Dressing 24
1 slice of Whole Wheat Toast 60
1 pat of Butter 45
Black Coffee or Tea - No Sugar 0
363

2.00

"367"

Lean Roast Beef
with mushrooms 240
Medium Baked Potato, no butter 95
Tossed Green Salad 16
1 slice of Melba Toast 16
Black Coffee or Tea - No Sugar 0
367

1.75

"377"

Broiled Lean Hamburger 300
On 1 slice Whole Wheat Toast 60
Sliced Tomato, slice raw onion 12
Lo-Cal Pickle Chips 5
Black Coffee or Tea - No Sugar 0
377

1.10

"391"

Sliced Ham & Turkey
Combination (4 oz) with
Lo-Cal Cream Sauce 300
On Slice of Whole Wheat Toast 60
Fresh Green Beans 15
Tossed Green Salad 16
Black Coffee or Tea No Sugar 0
391

1.95

"416"

Broiled Pork Chop 335
with Apple Sauce 50
Fresh Green Beans 15
1 Slice of Melba Toast 16
Black Coffee or Tea - No Sugar 0
416

1.65

Choice of French, 1000 Island, Italian or Bleu Cheese Lo-Calorie Dressing

SPECIAL DESSERTS (For Those Who Still Have a Few Calories Coming!)

Dietetic Vanilla Ice Cream .... 66 cal 20
Artificially Sweetened Grapefruit Segments 40 cal 30
Sliced Yellow Cling Peaches .... 28 cal 30
Sugar Free Puddings .... 40 cal 30

Skimmed Milk .... 66 cal 15
Relish Dish of Celery, Carrot Sticks, Green Peppers, Green Onion
Lo Cal Pickle Chips & Radishes .... 25 cal .... 50 (for 1)
50 cal .... 55 (for 2)

Please tell your waitress if any foods are to be prepared without salt
She will furnish you with a salt substitute if you so desire

No Substitutions

Made with Vodka (95 calories) or Gin (85 calories) 75c
Try a refreshing "Slim Jim Cooler"

Here is a complete "Slim Jim" diet menu that lists the total calorie count for each entree as well as the price.

Salads and cold plates can be converted to "Diet Plates" by listing calories for each item.

Diet Plates

CHICKEN SALAD BOWL
(APPROXIMATELY 320 CALORIES)
A Salad of Tossed Greens and Vegetables, Your Favorite Dressing. Rolls, Butter and Coffee or Tea. **1.45**

SHRIMP SALAD BOWL
(APPROXIMATELY 285 CALORIES)
A Salad of Tossed Greens and Vegetables, Your Favorite Dressing. Rolls, Butter and Coffee or Tea. **1.55**

LOW CALORIE DIET PLATE
(APPROXIMATELY 225 CALORIES)
Choice of Chilled Shrimp, Chopped Beef or Sliced Chicken Sliced Tomato, Half Peach, Cottage Cheese, Melba Toast and Coffee or Tea. **1.55**

FRUIT SALAD PLATE
(APPROXIMATELY 305 CALORIES)
Cottage Cheese, Fruit Cocktail, Peach Half, Orange and Pineapple Slice. Rolls, Butter and Coffee or Tea. **1.45**

20

Where you list it on the menu makes a difference

Without changing any of the items on the menu or their prices, you can improve your menu and your profit picture just by rearranging your listing. The secret is in knowing how does the customer's eye travel as he or she first looks at your menu. What is seen first? What catches the eye, holds the attention and make the customer order one item over the other? The answer is not complete. There is no science of eye or mind attention; advertising has been studying the problem for years. There are some rules, though, that you can follow that are the result of research and trial and error methods, especially involving menus.

The first two rules to remember are that in the Western world we read from left to right and from top to bottom, just the opposite of the Chinese. The reader's eye, to a large extent therefore, will follow this route, but not entirely. To begin with, let us take a simple one-page menu as shown in Figure 1.

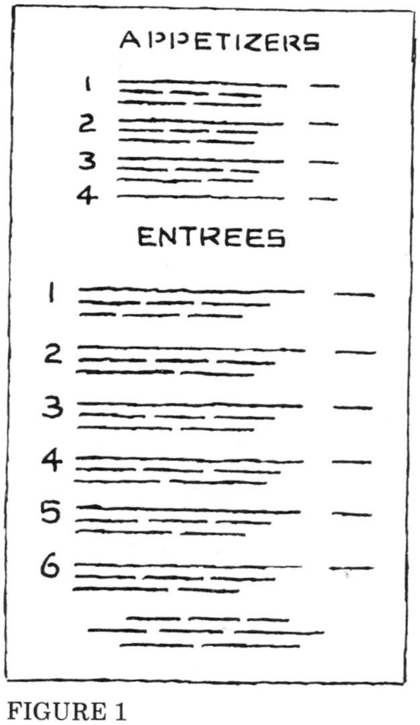

FIGURE 1

The one-page menu is arranged with the appetizers at the top, numbered 1, 2, 3, and 4. The entrees are next, numbered 1, 2, 3, 4, 5, and 6. Through the method of trial and error of many food service operations and menu printers and designers, it has been found that the general rule is that appetizer number one, entree number one, and dessert number one will be your best sellers simply because they are number one on this list. There are probably two reasons for this. First, the fact referred to before, that we read from top to bottom, makes the top number one item the one that hits the eye first and makes the first and probably most lasting impression. Second, we are psychologically conditioned to assume that number one is really "number 1," that is, it is the best, the tops, the winner in the category, no matter what kind of a list it is—food, beverage, class standing, athletes, etc.

The important thing for a menu planner to remember when arranging the items from top to bottom in any category—appetizers, salads, sandwiches, entrees, desserts, etc.—is to select item number one carefully and consciously. It should be the item restaurant wants to sell the most of. This does not mean that it should necessarily be the most expensive item on the menu. In the case of steak and lobster versus chicken, for example, steak and lobster are big ticket items, while chicken is a lower priced item, but the profit to the food service operator from a chicken entree may be higher. The important thing is to list first what you want to sell the most. The

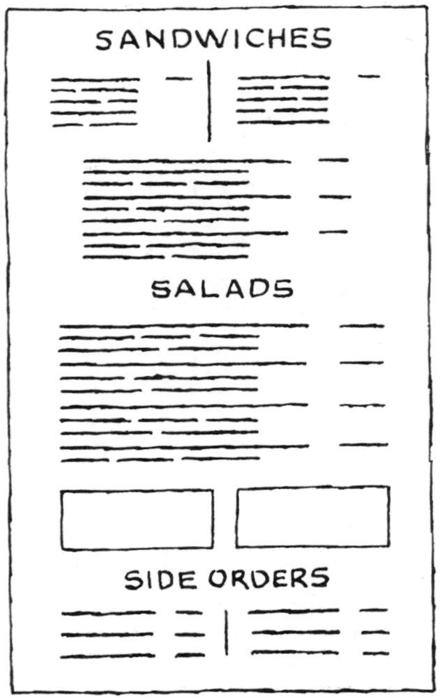

FIGURE 2

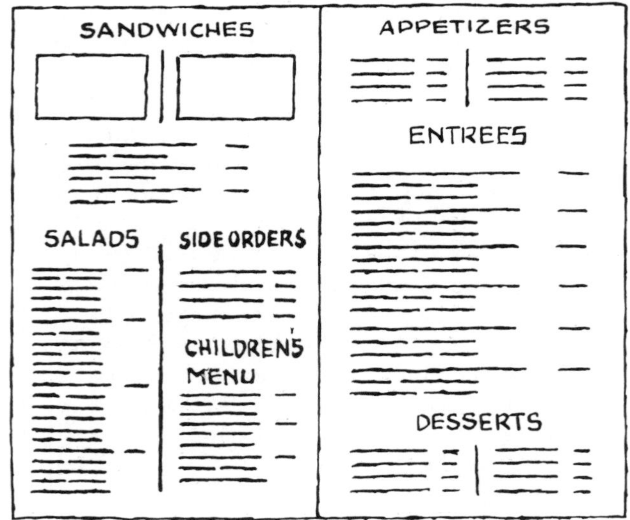

FIGURE 3

number 2, 3, 4, 5, etc. order of listing is also important, but number one is the most important.

In addition to the order of item listing, there is the order of category of items. An example is shown in Figure 2.

Figure 2 could be a page or panel of a menu, but here again there is an order of importance. In this particular case, sandwiches are number 1, salads number 2, and side orders number 3. The important thing is that this is a conscious, deliberate selection. The desire in this particular case would be to sell more sandwiches than salads, more salads than side orders.

The next menu layout to consider is a two-page menu design as shown in Figure 3.

Contrary to the reading rule of left to right, in this particular case, the eye of the reader-customer goes first to page 2, item number 1. The reason for this is not clear, but trial and error experiments have shown that this is the case. The answer probably is that this type of menu (in fact, most menus except the one-page card type) is held in a three dimensional fashion and should be considered three dimensional rather than just two

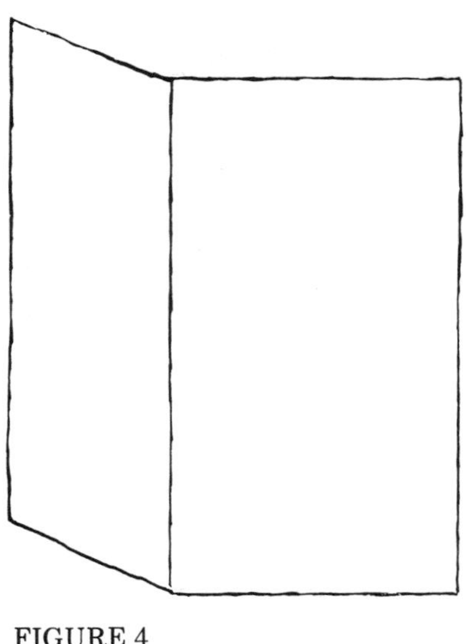

FIGURE 4

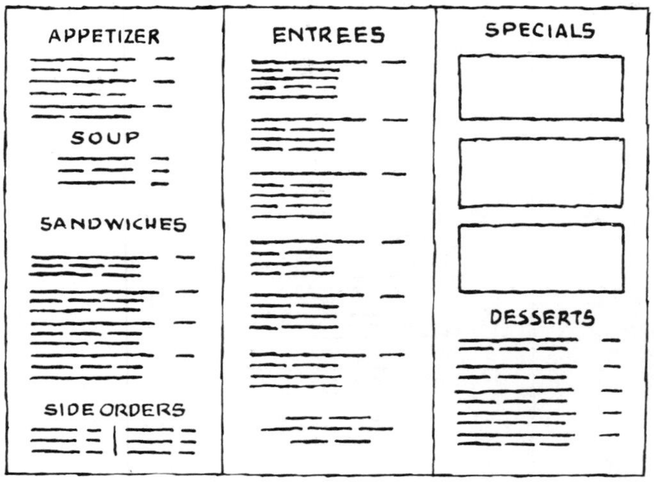

FIGURE 5

dimensional. The drawing in Figure 4 shows what happens: panel or page one is held at an angle (usually) so that panel or page two gets number one attention. Carrying this analysis further and considering the three dimensional aspect of a folded piece of paper, let us look at a three-panel, two-fold layout, as shown in Figure 5.

In the case of this type of menu layout, panel number two is the number one panel for attention. Therefore, those items that the food service operator wants to sell most of should be listed on panel two. The reason for panel two being number one in attention is again probably the three dimensional factor as shown in Figure 6.

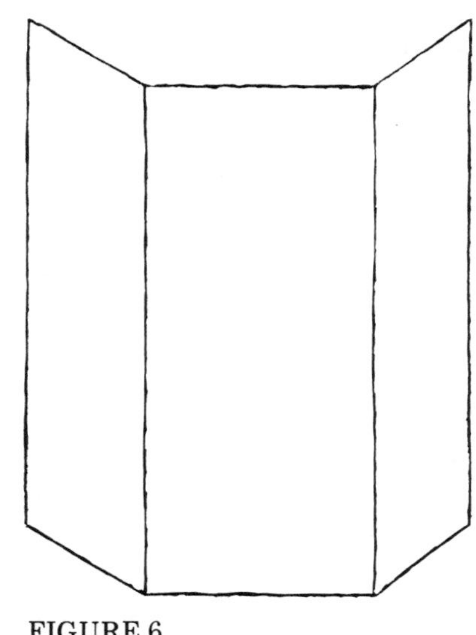

FIGURE 6

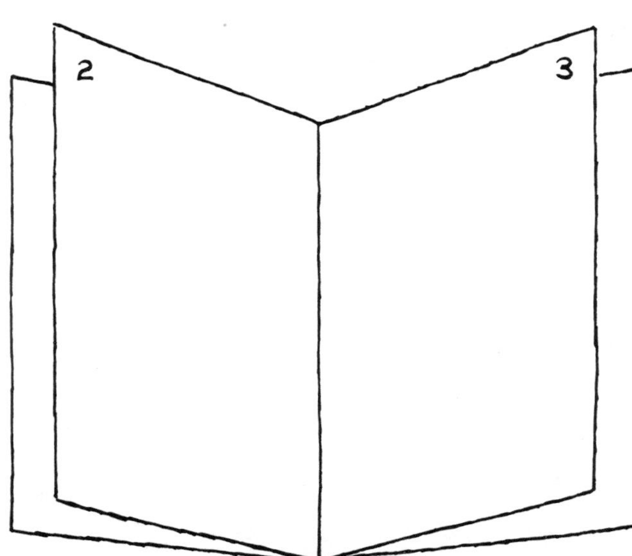

FIGURE 7

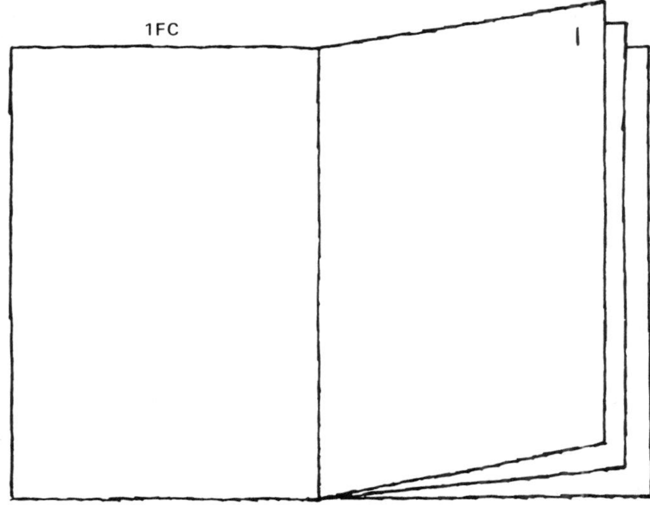

FIGURE 8

As shown in Figure 6, the eye goes to panel two naturally when the menu is held in Figure 6 position. When the menu is laid out flat, of course, this factor is less important, but when the customers pick up the menu, they tend to hold it first in the manner as shown in Figure 6. A larger menu, the four page insert in a four page cover, for example, presents a particular problem. Figure 7 shows what can happen.

The problem here is that while all eight pages of this kind of menu—cover, back cover, and inside front cover and back cover, plus pages 1, 2, 3, and 4 of the insert, should be used, the result may be that if the menu opens up sort of naturally, as shown in Figure 7, only pages 2 and 3 will get the customer's attention. This can be overcome in several ways. First, have the waiter or waitress present the menu with page one and the inside front cover open, as shown in Figure 8.

The result will then be that the customer is exposed to the copy on the inside front cover and page one (in this case the liquor listing and the appetizer-soup listing). The customer after looking at these two pages is going naturally to turn to the next two pages to look at the entree listing. The customer may not, however, look at page four and the inside back cover. But if the desserts are listed on page four and the after dinner drinks on the inside back cover, this presents no problem since the menu will be presented a second time to the customer and should be presented as shown in Figure 9.

As you can see, if the waiter or waitress presents the menu a second time to the customer

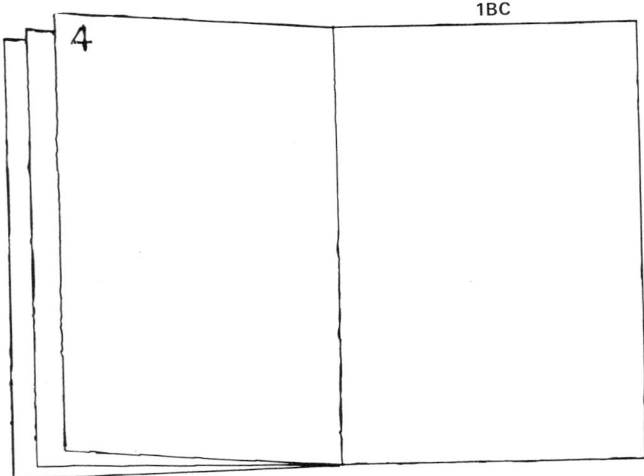

FIGURE 9

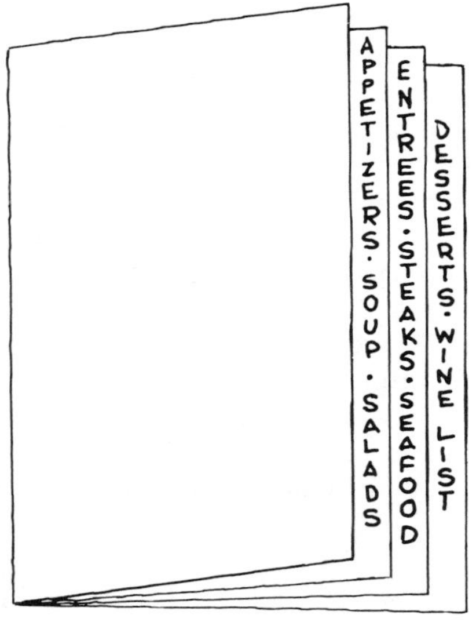

FIGURE 10

as shown in Figure 9, page four and the inside back cover will be read. A separate after dinner dessert and drink menu will, of course, function in the same manner. Another way of making sure that all eight pages of an eight-page menu get attention and readership is to provide an index. This can easily be done as shown in Figure 10 by folding each piece of paper off center.

The off center folds provide space for printing an index for the pages, listing particular items. The words Appetizers, Soups, and Drinks can be printed on the page showing what is on page one and the inside front cover. The words Steaks, Seafoods, Chef's Specials, etc., can be listed on page three showing what is listed on pages two and three, and the projecting part of the inside back cover can be used to list the words Dessert, After Dinner Drinks, etc., to show what is listed on page 4 and the inside back cover.

It should be repeated that where you list items on the menu is important. It has been proven by experience that changing the order and the page where you list the menu items can improve the profit picture for any food service operation.

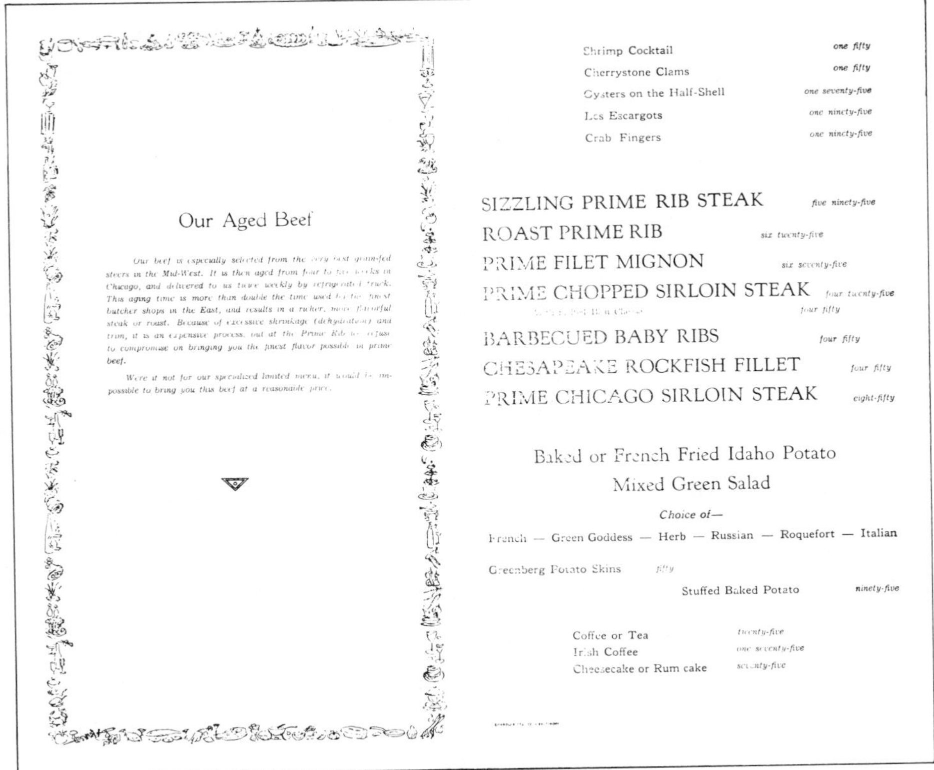

Our Aged Beef

Our beef is especially selected from the very best grain-fed steers in the Mid-West. It is then aged from four to five weeks in Chicago, and delivered to us twice weekly by refrigerated truck. This aging time is more than double the time used by the finest butcher shops in the East, and results in a richer, more flavorful steak or roast. Because of excessive shrinkage (dehydration) and trim, it is an expensive process, but at the Prime Rib we refuse to compromise on bringing you the finest flavor possible in prime beef.

Were it not for our specialized limited menu, it would be impossible to bring you this beef at a reasonable price.

Shrimp Cocktail — *one fifty*
Cherrystone Clams — *one fifty*
Oysters on the Half-Shell — *one seventy-five*
Les Escargots — *one ninety-five*
Crab Fingers — *one ninety-five*

SIZZLING PRIME RIB STEAK — *five ninety-five*
ROAST PRIME RIB — *six twenty-five*
PRIME FILET MIGNON — *six seventy-five*
PRIME CHOPPED SIRLOIN STEAK — *four twenty-five*
four fifty
BARBECUED BABY RIBS — *four fifty*
CHESAPEAKE ROCKFISH FILLET — *four fifty*
PRIME CHICAGO SIRLOIN STEAK — *eight-fifty*

Baked or French Fried Idaho Potato
Mixed Green Salad
Choice of—
French — Green Goddess — Herb — Russian — Roquefort — Italian

Greenberg Potato Skins — *fifty*
Stuffed Baked Potato — *ninety-five*

Coffee or Tea — *twenty-five*
Irish Coffee — *one seventy-five*
Cheesecake or Rum cake — *seventy-five*

This limited, all a la carte menu puts its entire listing on page 2. Less important general copy describing their "Our Aged Beef" is on page 1. The menu also explains that . . . "Were it not for our specialized, limited menu, it would be impossible to bring you this beef at a reasonable price." Notice that each a la carte item (including coffee and tea) is listed with the price in words rather than figures—one fifty instead of $1.50.

WINE LIST

SATISFYING SELECTIONS FROM THE BAR TO SHARPEN YOUR APPETITE AND MAKE YOUR DINNER EVEN MORE ENJOYABLE

APPETIZERS
Dubonnet .65 Martini & Rossi Vermouths .65
Harvey's Bristol Cream Sherry .80 Victoria Sherry .65
Findlater's Dry Fly Sherry .65 Bright's "74" Sherry .55

COCKTAILS
Daiquiri (light rum base) .90 Martini (gin base) .90
Manhattan (rye base) .90 Rob Roy (scotch base) .90
Old Fashioned (rye base) .90

HIGHBALLS
Scotch .85 Rye .80 Bourbon .85
Light Rum .85 Dark Rum .80
Gin .80 Vodka .80
including your choice of mix

BEERS & ALES
Newfoundland and Canadian Beers & Ales
Tuborg Danish Beer .60 Heineken's Dutch Lager .60
McEwan's Strong Scotch Ale .60 Guinness' Irish Stout .60

DINNER & SPARKLING WINES
Red Dinner Wines — Usually served with dark meats
St. Emilion – Bottle 3.80 St. Julien – Bottle 3.80
Chianti Bosca – Bottle 3.80 ½ Bottle 2.30
Beaujolais Red Burgundy – Bottle 4.80 ½ Bottle 2.30
Sorgrape Mateus, Rose – Bottle 4.20

White Dinner Wines — with light coloured meats, sea foods,
Guntrum's Liebfraumilch – bottle 4.70, Niersteiner – bottle 4.70
Bosca Orvieto – bottle 4.30, ½ bottle 2.30,
Chateau-Gai (Canadian) Sauternes 3.40

Dessert Wines — to conclude the meal
Newman's "A" Port .65, Chateau-Gai Port .50

Champagne — a highlight for any festive meal
Mumm's Cordon Rouge – bottle 10.50, ½ bottle 5.50
Chateau-Gai (Canadian) – bottle 6.30

LIQUEURS & BRANDIES
Drambuie .80 Cointreau .80 Creme de Menthe .80
Brandy & Benedictine .80 Hennessey's XXX Brandy .80
Bols Apricot Brandy .80 Bols Cherry Brandy .80

A Simple Guide to the Selection of Drinks
Appetizers – Before meals (sherries may also be taken with soup course or after meals)
Cocktails – Before meals **Highballs** – Before or after meals
Beers, Ales or **Champagne** – Before, during or after meals
Red or White Wines – During dinner **Liqueurs, Brandies** – After meals

BILL OF FARE

All of our luncheons and dinners include soup or juice, Woodstock dinner rolls and melba toast, potatoes, peas, carrots (or side salad), your choice of dessert and beverage. You will find both luncheon and dinner size orders in most selections, to suit your mood and appetite. Toward providing maximum dinner pleasure, we shall be offering special features every day. These will include seasonal delicacies such as salmon, lobster, flippers, strawberries and the like, when they are available.

WOODSTOCK SPECIALTIES

1 Country-style
GOLDEN CRISP CHICKEN PIECES
with glazed peaches
light luncheon size $2.00 dinner size $2.50 children's orders $1.50

2 Woodstock
TENDER YOUNG ROAST TURKEY
with stuffing, partridgeberry jelly
light luncheon size $2.25 dinner size $2.75 children's orders $1.75

3 Old English
ROAST PRIME RIBS OF BEEF
with Yorkshire pudding, horseradish sauce
light luncheon size $2.75 dinner size $3.25 children's orders $2.25

4 Prime Western
FILET MIGNON STEAK
with mushroom gravy boat
light luncheon size $4.00 dinner size $4.50 children's orders $3.25

5 Newfoundland
SEAFOOD SAMPLER
cod tongues, scallops, smoked salmon or cod, baked smoked herring, salt codfish, boiled potatoes, drawn butter, tartar sauce
order per person $2.50 minimum of two orders except on Fridays

6 Woodstock
COLD PLATE SPECIAL
two meats, two salads, lettuce, tomatoes
order per person $2.50 children's orders $1.50

ADDITIONAL TODAY

YOUR CHOICES WITH THE SPECIALTIES
Juices — tomato, apple, orange
Soups — homemade turkey or split pea
Desserts — homemade pie, steamed pudding, trifle, ice cream and cookies, cheese and crackers
Beverages — coffee, tea, milk

A LA CARTE — A side salad may be ordered in place of a regular vegetable at no charge. Side salad as an extra .30, mushrooms .30, onion rings .30, broccoli .30, cauliflower .30

Lighter luncheon selections are shown on the next page, subject to 25c additional per person ordering, for dining room service.

SPECIAL ORDERS

Given four hours' notice, we are delighted to prepare your special choice of dinners such as roast duck, squab, steak and kidney pie, rabbit stew and so on — for parties of two or more.

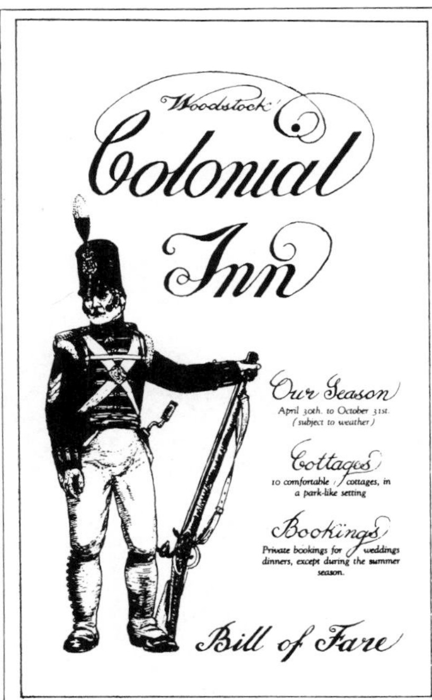

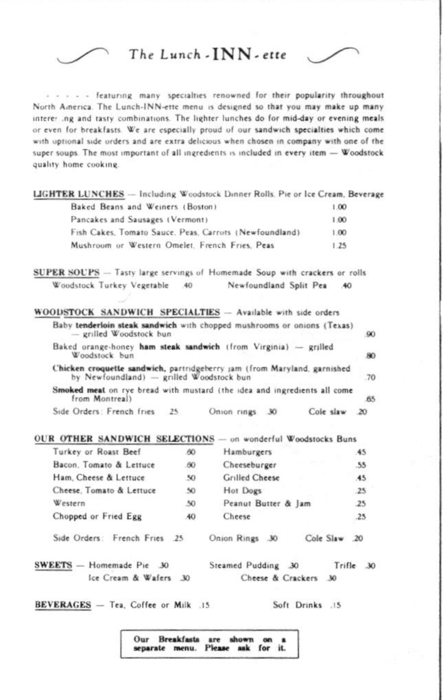

The Lunch-INN-ette

- - - - - featuring many specialties renowned for their popularity throughout North America. The Lunch-INN-ette menu is designed so that you may make up many interesting and tasty combinations. The lighter lunches do for mid-day or evening meals or even for breakfasts. We are especially proud of our sandwich specialties which come with optional side orders and are extra delicious when chosen in company with one of the super soups. The most important of all ingredients is included in every item — Woodstock quality home cooking.

LIGHTER LUNCHES — Including Woodstock Dinner Rolls, Pie or Ice Cream, Beverage
Baked Beans and Weiners (Boston) 1.00
Pancakes and Sausages (Vermont) 1.00
Fish Cakes, Tomato Sauce, Peas, Carrots (Newfoundland) 1.00
Mushroom or Western Omelet, French Fries, Peas 1.25

SUPER SOUPS — Tasty large servings of Homemade Soup with crackers or rolls
Woodstock Turkey Vegetable .40 Newfoundland Split Pea .40

WOODSTOCK SANDWICH SPECIALTIES — Available with side orders
Baby **tenderloin steak sandwich** with chopped mushrooms or onions (Texas) — grilled Woodstock bun .90
Baked orange-honey **ham steak sandwich** (from Virginia) — grilled Woodstock bun .80
Chicken croquette sandwich, partridgeberry jam (from Maryland, garnished by Newfoundland) — grilled Woodstock bun .70
Smoked meat on rye bread with mustard (the idea and ingredients all come from Montreal) .65
Side Orders: French fries .25 Onion rings .30 Cole slaw .20

OUR OTHER SANDWICH SELECTIONS — on wonderful Woodstocks Buns

Turkey or Roast Beef	.60	Hamburgers	.45
Bacon, Tomato & Lettuce	.60	Cheeseburger	.55
Ham, Cheese & Lettuce	.50	Grilled Cheese	.45
Cheese, Tomato & Lettuce	.50	Hot Dogs	.25
Western	.50	Peanut Butter & Jam	.25
Chopped or Fried Egg	.40	Cheese	.25

Side Orders: French Fries .25 Onion Rings .30 Cole Slaw .20

SWEETS — Homemade Pie .30 Steamed Pudding .30 Trifle .30
Ice Cream & Wafers .30 Cheese & Crackers .30

BEVERAGES — Tea, Coffee or Milk .15 Soft Drinks .15

Our Breakfasts are shown on a separate menu. Please ask for it.

Here also the important Bill of Fare items are listed on page 2—where the eye hits first—and the wine list is on page 1. Notice the numbering —1, 2, 3, 4, 5, 6 of the entrees for easy ordering. Also notice space for tip-on—Additional Today. This menu solves the problem of where to put the luncheon menu by putting it on the back cover. A Simple Guide to the Selection of Drinks is included with the wine list.

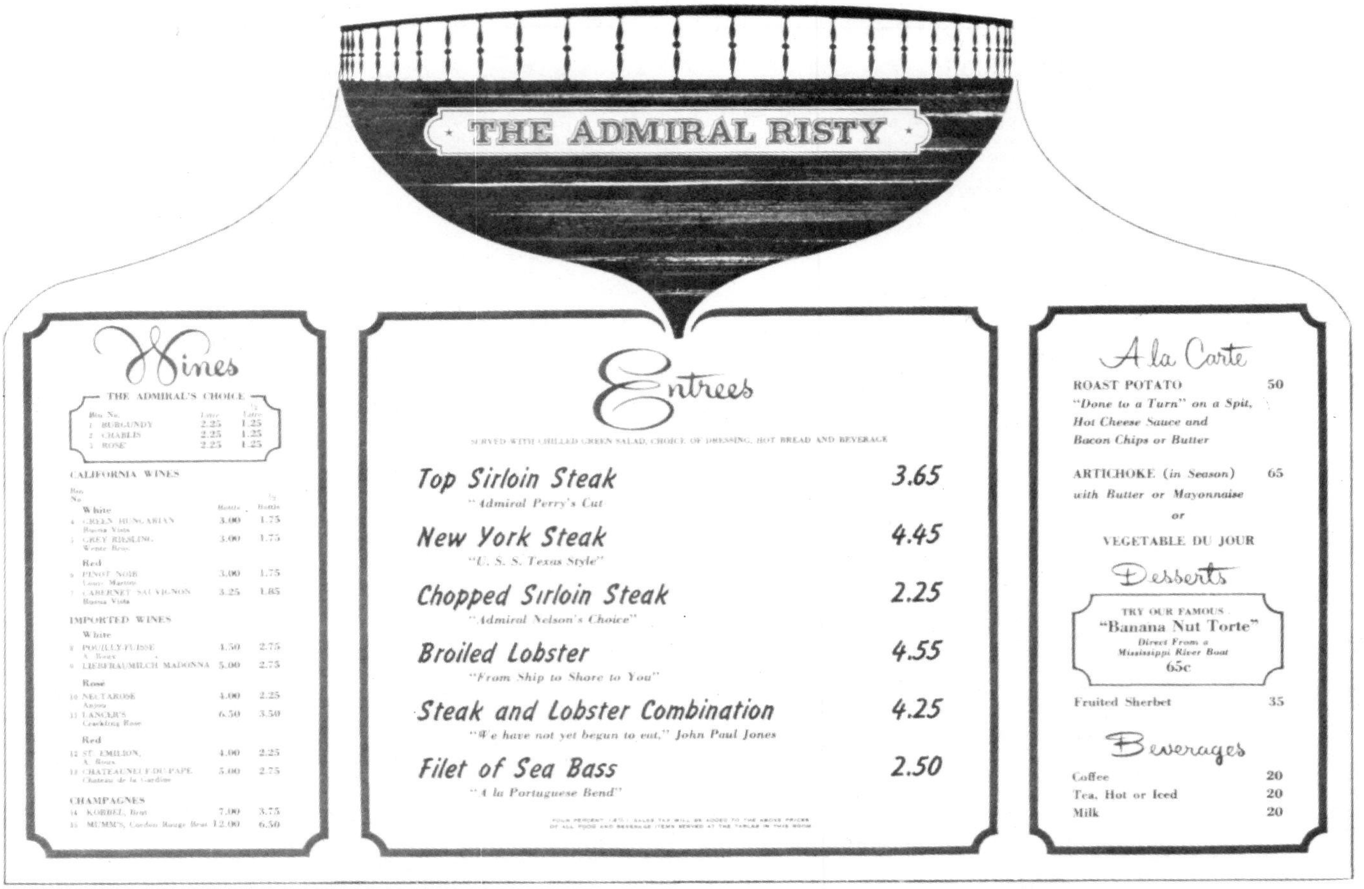

THE ADMIRAL RISTY

Wines

THE ADMIRAL'S CHOICE

Bin No.		Litre	½ Litre
1	BURGUNDY	2.25	1.25
2	CHABLIS	2.25	1.25
3	ROSE	2.25	1.25

CALIFORNIA WINES

Bin No.		Bottle	½ Bottle
	White		
4	GREEN HUNGARIAN Buena Vista	3.00	1.75
5	GREY RIESLING Wente Bros.	3.00	1.75
	Red		
6	PINOT NOIR Louis Martini	3.00	1.75
7	CABERNET SAUVIGNON Buena Vista	3.25	1.85

IMPORTED WINES

Bin No.		Bottle	½ Bottle
	White		
8	POUILLY-FUISSE A. Roux	4.50	2.75
9	LIEBFRAUMILCH MADONNA	5.00	2.75
	Rose		
10	NECTAROSE Anjou	4.00	2.25
11	LANCER'S Crackling Rose	6.50	3.50
	Red		
12	ST. EMILION, A. Roux	4.00	2.25
13	CHATEAUNEUF-DU-PAPE Chateau de la Gardine	5.00	2.75

CHAMPAGNES

Bin No.		Bottle	½ Bottle
14	KORBEL, Brut	7.00	3.75
15	MUMM'S, Cordon Rouge Brut	12.00	6.50

Entrees

SERVED WITH CHILLED GREEN SALAD, CHOICE OF DRESSING, HOT BREAD AND BEVERAGE

Top Sirloin Steak *"Admiral Perry's Cut*	3.65
New York Steak *"U. S. S. Texas Style"*	4.45
Chopped Sirloin Steak *"Admiral Nelson's Choice"*	2.25
Broiled Lobster *"From Ship to Shore to You"*	4.55
Steak and Lobster Combination *"We have not yet begun to eat," John Paul Jones*	4.25
Filet of Sea Bass *"A la Portuguese Bend"*	2.50

A la Carte

ROAST POTATO 50
"Done to a Turn" on a Spit, Hot Cheese Sauce and Bacon Chips or Butter

ARTICHOKE (*in Season*) 65
with Butter or Mayonnaise

or

VEGETABLE DU JOUR

Desserts

TRY OUR FAMOUS
"Banana Nut Torte"
Direct From a Mississippi River Boat
65c

Fruited Sherbet 35

Beverages

Coffee	20
Tea, Hot or Iced	20
Milk	20

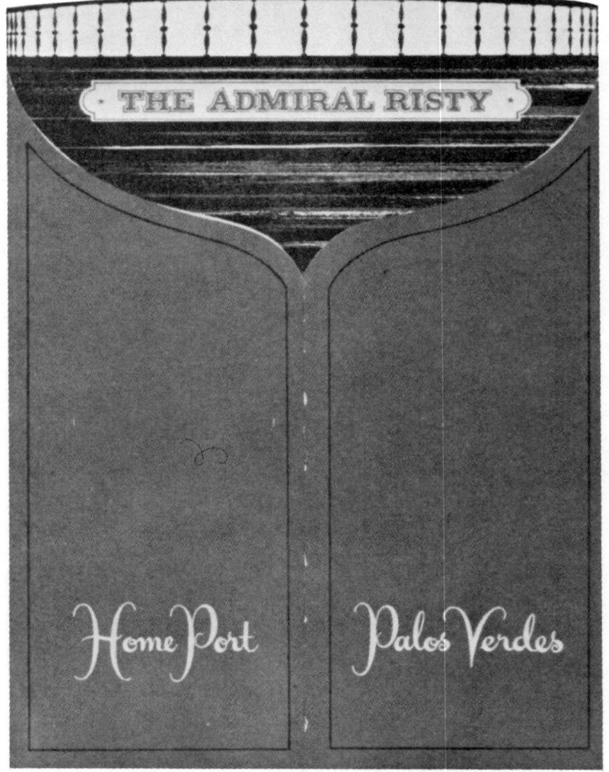

This interesting gate-fold menu is also die cut showing how paper can be cut into unusual shapes. The important big entree items—steaks and seafood—are listed in the center which is where the eye goes first. On the left hand small panel, a Wine List is printed. Since wine is a "with dinner" drink, this is a good place to list it. On the right hand small panel, a la carte vegetables, desserts, and beverages are listed. Notice that when the side panels are closed, the name of the restaurant The Admiral Risty, *at the top of the menu, is still in evidence.*

On an ideal menu, of course, if you can make it interesting and informative enough, the customer will read every page. The customer will let his or her eye peruse every page and read all of the words. *The General Store* restaurant in the Hiliday Inn of Lumberton, North Carolina, is one of these menus.

It is an eight-page menu. On the cover it has a "Real Table of Contents" with a Page Fowl-Poultry Items and a Page Ate-Desserts 'n Beverages. Cover copy also informs the customer that Bank Americard, Master Charge, American Express, Diners Club, and Cash are accepted.

All of the foods and beverages listed have an item number. Page 2, for example, has items 11 through 32. This page headed "Rise and Shine" is the breakfast menu. Page 3 is "The Pickle Barrel" which is an assortment of appetizers, soups, and salads. Page 4 is "Pa's Fishing Tips" seafood, and Page Fowl, "Henhouse Favorites" says, "We got a powerful big hen house so you hep' us out by orderin' some of this chicken!"

Page 6 is "Hearty Meats from the Smokehouse" which includes the beef and pork entrees. Page 7 is "the Soda Shoppe" which lists a sandwich listing. Page Ate—and the back cover—is the "Old Time Cupboard Desserts." Altogether 91 items are listed. For a motel that usually has a bigger menu or several menus so that the guest who stays several days does not get tired of its food or the "same" menu, this is a clever, creative, and well-organized menu.

Printed in dark brown ink on heavy tan paper, this menu is only 8½″ × 11″ yet it does a better selling job than many bigger, full-color, much more expensive menus.

FOUNDED IN 1975
THE OFFICIAL FOOD ORDER CATALOGUE
THE
GENERAL STORE
AN EATING ESTABLISHMENT
1ST EDITION
REFERENCES
BY SPECIAL PERMISSION
Bank Americard
Mastercharge
American Express
Diners Club
Cash
PAGE TWO Breakfast Items: 11 thru 32
PAGE THREE The Pickle Barrel (Soups and Appetizers). Items: 33 thru 44
PAGE FOUR Pa's Fishing Tips (Seafood served for Lunch and Supper). Items: 45 thru 52
PAGE FOWL Poultry Items (Served for Lunch and Supper). Items: 53 thru 56
PAGE SIX Smokehouse Favorites (Choice beef and pork served for Lunch and Supper). Items: 57 thru 67
PAGE SEVEN Soda Shoppe (Your favorite sandwiches are prepared for you at Lunch and Supper). Items: 68 thru 79
PAGE ATE Desserts 'n Beverages Items: 80 thru 91
THIS IS WHAT'S CALLED A "REAL TABLE OF CONTENTS"
HOLIDAY INN, PROP.
50¢
or
MAKE US AN OFFER!
In addition to all the fine foods for sale, the General Store also has available a wide variety of goodies that are on display in the Lobby. These items are pretty souvenirs and gifts found in the General Store so you can take 'em home without havin' to snitch them. The cashier also sells cigaritts by the carton (not to young'uns though)
COPYRIGHT: 1975
Interstate 95 & North Carolina 211, Lumberton, North Carolina 28358 · (919) 378-4261

The General Store *menu* (reproduced in full on pages 131 to 133) *is printed in black ink on tan paper. It is well-designed, well-written, and well-organized.*

ORCHARD SPECIALS

ITEM NO. 11
One-Half Grapefruit or Melon ..... $.60

ITEM NO. 12
Stewed Prunes
(Ma eats these rite regular) .... .60

ITEM NO. 13
Chilled Fruit Juice .... .45

FARMLAND CEREALS

ITEM NO. 14
Assorted Cereals with Sweet Milk .. $.65

ITEM NO. 15
Cream of Wheat .... .65

ITEM NO. 16
Oat Meal .... .65

FRESH FROM THE HEN HOUSE

ITEM NO. 17	One Egg and Ham	$1.80
ITEM NO. 18	One Egg and Bacon or Sausage	1.80
ITEM NO. 19	Two Eggs and Ham	2.10
ITEM NO. 20	Two Eggs and Bacon or Sausage	2.10
ITEM NO. 21	Cheese or Bacon Omelette	2.10
ITEM NO. 22	One Egg (no fresh eggs allowed—only friendly ones)	.45
ITEM NO. 23	Two Eggs	.75

Served with choice of biscuits or toast.

FROM THE WOOD STOVE

ITEM NO. 24
Stack of Three Pancakes (the one in the middle is best) .... $.95

ITEM NO. 25
Short Stack (short, but powerful) .... .65

ITEM NO. 26
Waffle .... .95

ITEM NO. 27
Country Toast (thick and yummy—also known as French Toast, but better) .... .95

EARLY IN THE DAY SPECIALTIES

THE ROOSTER

Freshly Baked English Muffin Topped with Two Poached Eggs Served with Jelly ....

ITEM NO. 28 $1.50

THE SMOKE HOUSE

Country Ham from our own Smoke House (don't ask to see the smoke house, 'cause we keep it hid' in from the revenooers) with two eggs, toast, and coffee ....

ITEM NO. 29 $2.60

THE POT BELLY

(Named after our stove and not our cook).
Danish Pastry, Coffee, Choice of Juice, served with Jelly and Butter.........

ITEM NO. 30 $1.50

GRIT & CHEESE OMELETTE

This treat is an original General Store specialty. ....

ITEM NO. 31 $2.15

BISCUITS & CREAM GRAVY

Three biscuits smothered in white gravy (just right for a quick pick up) ..

ITEM NO. 32 $.60

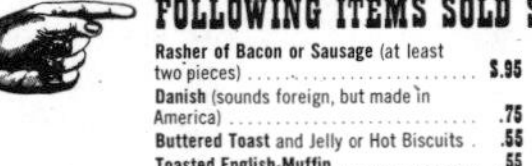

FOLLOWING ITEMS SOLD SEPARATELY ON A CLEAN PLATE

Rasher of Bacon or Sausage (at least two pieces)	$.95
Danish (sounds foreign, but made in America)	.75
Buttered Toast and Jelly or Hot Biscuits	.55
Toasted English Muffin	.55
Ham (a fair to middlin' slice)	.95
Homefries	.50
Grits (this is no lie—a real true grit)	.30
Country Ham (completely covers a small plate)	1.45

Page TWO

THE PICKLE BARREL

AN ASSORTMENT OF APPETIZERS, SOUPS, AND SALADS SERVED FOR LUNCH AND SUPPER.

ITEM NO. 33

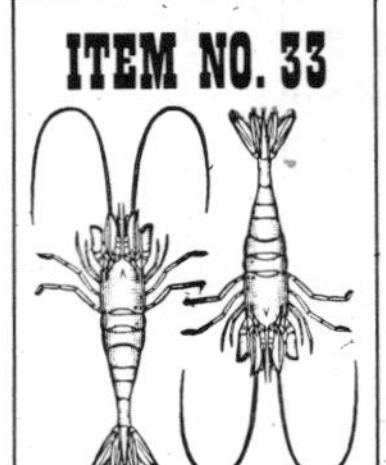

BOILED COASTAL SHRIMP
Already Peeled
Large shrimp served with our own cocktail sauce (a city slicker from New Orleans taught us this recipe).
$2.15

ITEM NO. 34

HOMEMADE VEGETABLE SOUP
A hearty serving of hot, rich beef broth chock full of delicious vegetables (during the summer we pick our own).
$.45

ITEM NO. 36

STUFFED PASTRY
A homemade vegetable pot pie served in a stuffing shell—a good meal for you light eaters.
$1.15

ITEM NO. 35

ASSORTED PICKLE PLATTER
Cherry peppers, pickles, cheese, and bean salad (you can ask for seconds on the bean salad 'cause it's cheap).
$.50

ITEM NO. 37

CITRUS SECTION FRUIT CUP
Assorted orchard fruit sections in their own sweet juices.

$.65

ITEMS 38 THRU 44 ARE A VARIETY OF SMALL AND LARGE SALADS

(you can tell by the price which ones are the large ones).

ITEM NO. 38	Peach or pear halves with cottage cheese	$ .55
ITEM NO. 39	Mixed garden salad	.75
ITEM NO. 40	Chef salad	2.50
ITEM NO. 41	Assorted fruit plate	2.75
ITEM NO. 42	Sliced tomatoes	.55
ITEM NO. 43	Chicken salad plate	1.95
ITEM NO. 44	Tuna salad plate	1.95

Page THREE

PA'S FISHING TIPS

PA HAS CAUGHT A LOT OF FISH IN HIS DAY, BUT, I BELIEVE THAT MA HOOKED THE BIGGEST ONE OF THEM ALL!

ITEM NO. 45

GOLDEN BROWN FRIED SHRIMP
(these are caught with a big net).
$4.25

ITEM NO. 46

STUFFED FLOUNDER
(you'll be stuffed after eating this dish).
$5.95

ITEM NO. 47

SEAFOOD PLATTER
Just a little bit of everything from the creek.
$4.75

ITEM NO. 48

RAINBOW TROUT
(this is a real colorful treat).
$4.25

ITEM NO. 49

FRIED FILLET OF PERCH
Lots of flaky white goodness under that golden brown skin.
$2.25

ITEM NO. 50

FRIED CATFISH
(Pa has been catchin' these since he was a boy).
$2.50

ITEM NO. 51

DEVILED CRABS
(my mother-in-law likes this one).
$2.95

ITEM NO. 52

BAKED WHOLE FLOUNDER
(you folks ought t' try this local favorite).
$4.25

All of our fish items are served for Lunch and Supper and come with your choice of two vegetables, hot breads, and butter.

Page FOUR

HENHOUSE FAVORITES

WE GOT A POWERFUL BIG HENHOUSE SO YOU CAN HEP'US OUT BY ORDERIN' SOME OF THIS CHICKEN!

ITEM NO. 53

FRIED OR BROILED CHICKEN We fix this Southern style, either fried or broiled. (We prefer to serve it fried 'cause it takes less time to fix).

¼ Chicken (that's two Pieces). $2.50

½ Chicken (that's four Pieces, providin' we don't lose one in the kitchen). $3.95

ITEM NO. 54

SAUTEED CHICKEN INNERS (LIVERS)
these are so good that even the chicken hated to part with them.
$2.95

ITEM NO. 55

ROAST TURKEY & DRESSING
This big yard bird is good all year 'round.
$4.25

ITEM NO. 56

HAM & CHEESE OMELETTE
This is especially for you late sleepin' city slickers.
$2.50

All of our Henhouse favorites are served for Lunch and Supper and come with your choice of two vegetables, hot breads, and butter.

Page FOWL

ITEMS FOUND ON THIS PAGE ALL COME FROM OUR SMOKEHOUSE OUT BACK. WE HOPE YOU LIKE OUR SELECTION OF BEEF AND PORK DISHES 'CAUSE WE FIXED THEM ESPECIALLY FOR YOU.

SUGGESTED RETAIL PRICE GUIDE:

ITEM NO. 57	London Broil	$4.00
ITEM NO. 58	Rib-Eye Steak	7.25
ITEM NO. 59	Pot Roast	3.95
ITEM NO. 60	Beef Tips	4.25
ITEM NO. 61	Meat Loaf	2.95
ITEM NO. 62	Chopped Sirloin	3.95
ITEM NO. 63	Pork Chops (2)	$5.95
ITEM NO. 64	Pork Chop (1)	3.95
ITEM NO. 65	Baked Ham	4.25
ITEM NO. 66	Barbeque Platter	3.75
ITEM NO. 67	Country Ham and Redeye Gravy	4.75

Served with garden salad, choice of potato or vegetable, hot bread, and butter.

Page SIX

THESE SANDWICHES ARE PREPARED IN OUR SODA SHOPPE & SERVED FOR LUNCH AND SUPPER.

ITEM NO. 68	Beefburger—a big quarter of a pound	$1.20
ITEM NO. 69	Cheeseburger	1.30
ITEM NO. 70	Sliced Turkey	1.45
ITEM NO. 71	Garden Club—a big triple decker	1.95
ITEM NO. 72	Reuben	1.95
ITEM NO. 73	Bacon, Lettuce, Tomato	1.75
ITEM NO. 74	Chicken Salad Sandwich	1.60
ITEM NO. 75	Barbeque Pork Sandwich	1.95
ITEM NO. 76	Grilled Cheese	.85
ITEM NO. 77	Peanut Butter and Jelly Sandwich	.75
ITEM NO. 78	Meat Loaf Sandwich	1.50
ITEM NO. 79	Tuna Fish Sandwich	1.60

All of our sandwiches are served with a small handful of potato chips ('cause we have a young'un fixin' these).

Page SEVEN

OLD TIME CUPBOARD DESSERTS

THESE SWEET THINGS ARE KEPT IN THE PIE SAFE 'CAUSE PA'S GOT A SWEET TOOTH!

ITEM NO. 80	ICE CREAM	$.45
ITEM NO. 81	CHEESE CAKE OR TORTE	$.85
ITEM NO. 82	HOMEMADE COBBLERS	$.50
ITEM NO. 83	SUNDAES	$.65
ITEM NO. 84	APPLE PIE	$.60
ITEM NO. 85	HOMEMADE PINEAPPLE CAKE	$.70

BEVERAGES

ITEM NO. 86	MILK	$.45
ITEM NO. 87	ICED TEA	$.35
ITEM NO. 88	SOFT DRINKS	$.35
ITEM NO. 89	COFFEE	$.35
ITEM NO. 90	LEMONADE	$.35
ITEM NO.91	HOT CHOCOLATE	$.35

Page ATE

21

List in French but explain in English

The twentieth century is supposed to be the century of the "common man," but homage, fame, and money still go to the uncommon man—and to the uncommon restaurant. Few outstanding restaurants try to serve an ordinary cuisine. In fact, the hallmark of a restaurant meal is usually its unusualness (best recipes often come from restaurants). To accent this different character of your menu, French words and phrases add a gourmet, continental flavor to menu copy. This is admittedly snob appeal, but, if it is good business, if it adds character and class to your cuisine, and if it enables you to charge a little more—why not use it? It's the little "extras" in any restaurant operation that add up to the big profit. You don't need a French cuisine to use French terminology. For example, if you serve any kind of entree (American, Italian, or any other nationality) and serve or prepare it with almonds, the French word "Amandine" is appropriate.

Just using the word "Amandine," though, is not enough. In the descriptive copy, include a translation. To this, the restaurateur may say, "Why bother? Why not list it in English in the first place?" The answer again is snob appeal. *Joe's Diner* may serve just as good, nutritious and appetizing food as the *Cafe d'Josephe*, but the odds are that Joe gets less for his time and effort than Josephe! There is also the reputation (well-deserved) that French cooking has. Good restaurants take pride in engaging a French chef and serving French food, which has influenced both the language of the menu and the kitchen. Listed here is a glossary of basic French menu items for use on your menu:

Agneau	Lamb
Aigre	Sour
Ail	Garlic
Aileron	Wingbone
Allumette	Match stick potatoes
Alsacienne	Alsatian style; usually served with saurkraut
Amandine	With almonds
Americaine	American style
Ananas	Pineapple
Anchois	Anchovy
Andalouse	With tomatoes & peppers
Auguille	Eel
Argenteuil	With asparagus
Artichaut	Artichoke
Asperges	Asparagus
Aspic	Decorated jellied piece
Aubergines	Eggplant
Bearnaise	In America, a sauce similar to hollandaise, fortified with meat glaze, and with tarragon flavor predominating
Becasse	Woodcock
Bechamel	Cream sauce
Beignet	Fritter
Beurre	Butter
Bifteck	Beefsteak
Bisque	Thick, rich soup
Blanc	White
Blanquette	Stew with white wine
Boeuf	Beef
Boisson	Drink, Beverage
Bouillabaisse	Fish stew
Bouillon	Broth
Bouquetiere	With mixed vegetables
Bourguignonne	With onions and red Burgundy wine
Bouteille	Bottle
Cafe	Coffee
Canard	Duck

Caneton	Duckling
Carre	Rack
Cervelle	Brain
Champignon	Mushroom
Chapon	Capon
Chateaubriand	Thick Filet Mignon
Chaud	Warm, Hot
Chevreuil	Venison
Chou-Fleur	Cauliflower
Choux de Bruxelles	Brussels sprouts
Cochon	Suckling pig
Coeur	Heart
Compote	Stewed fruit
Concombre	Cucumber
Confiture	Jam, Preserve
Consomme	Clear soup
Coquille	Shell for baking
Cote	Rib, Chop
Creme	Cream
Creme Fouettee	Whipped cream
Crepe	Pancake
Crevette	Shrimp
Croquette	Patty of meat
Dejeuner	Breakfast, Lunch
Diable	Deviled
Dinde	Turkey
Du Barry	With cauliflower
Eau	Water
Ecrevisse	Crayfish
Entrecote	Sirloin steak
Entremets	Sweet, Desserts
Epinard	Spinach
Escargots	Snails
Faisan	Pheasant
Farce	Ground meat
Farci	Stuffed
Filet	Boneless ribbon
Flambe	Flamed
Foie	Liver
Foie Gras	Goose liver
Fondue	Melted cheese
Forestiere	With mushroom
Four	Oven baked
Fricandeau	Braised veal morsels
Fricassee	Chicken or veal stew
Frit	Deep fat fried
Froid	Cold
Fromage	Cheese
Fume	Smoked
Gateau	Cake
Gelee	Jelly
Gibier	Game
Gigot	Leg
Glace	Ice, Ice cream
Gratin	Brown, baked with cheese
Grenouille	Frog
Grille	Broiled
Hereng	Herring
Haricot Vert	String beans
Hollandaise	Sauce made with egg yolk, melted butter, and lemon
Homard	Lobster
Hors d'Oeuvres	Pre-dinner tid-bits
Huitre	Oyster
Jambon	Ham
Jardiniere	With vegetable
Julienne	Thin strips
Jus	Juice, Gravy
Lait	Milk
Langouste	Sea crayfish or rock lobster
Lapin	Rabbit
Legume	Vegetable
Macedoine	Mixed fruits
Maitre D'Hotel	With spiced butter
Marmite	Beef consomme
Meringue	Beaten egg white
Meuniere	Pan fried and served with brown butter
Mignon	Dainty
Mornay	Cheese sauce
Mousse	Whipped foam
Mouton	Mutton
Nantua	Lobster sauce
Naturel	Plain
Noir	Black
Noisette	Hazelnut
Nouille	Noodle
Oeuf	Egg
Oeufs Poches	Poached eggs
Oie	Goose
Oignon	Onion
Pain	Bread
Pate	Meat pie
Patisserie	Pastry
Peche	Peach
Petit	Small
Poire	Pear
Pois	Peas
Poisson	Fish
Poitrine	Breast
Pomme	Apple
Pomme de Terre	Potato
Potage	Soup
Pot Au Feu	Boiled beef with a variety of vegetables and broth served as a meal
Poulet	Chicken
Puree	Sieved food

Quenelle	Dumpling
Ragout	Stew
Ris	Sweetbread
Riz	Rice
Rognon	Kidney
Roti	Roasted
Roulade	Rolled meat
Saumon	Salmon
Saute	Pan fried in butter
Sel	Salt
Selle	saddle
Sorbet	Sherbet
Souffle	Whipped pudding
Tasse	Cup
Tete	Head
Tournedos	Two small tenderloin steaks
Tranche	Slice
Truite	Trout
Veau	Veal
Veloute	White sauce made from fish, chicken, or veal stock
Vichyssoise	Hot or cold potato and leek soup
Viennoise	Vienna style, breaded
Vinaigrette	Dressing with oil, vinegar and herbs
Volaille	Poultry
Vol Au Vent	Patty shell

Filet de Truite, Amandine 2.95

A generous Filet of Rainbow trout, delicately seasoned and covered with a browned butter sauce, fresh Lemon juice and toasted almond slices.

Suprême de Volaille, Le Ruth 3.50

A whole boneless chicken breast, stuffed with a real butter ball and lightly coated with toasted crumbs. Browned in butter and served over a mild wine sauce.

Emincé de Veau, René 3.75

Thin slices of milk-fed veal sauteed in butter and covered with a subtle wine sauce made with pure cream, chantrelle mushrooms and fresh seasonings.

Filet de Boeuf Aux Champignons 3.25

A petit tenderloin steak, selected for its rich, delicate flavor and pan broiled to your exact pleasure. Topped with sliced mushrooms in a natural sauce.

Entrecôte de Boeuf Au Poivre 4.50

A thick sirloin strip of choice beef, seasoned freely with fresh, coarse-ground peppercorns, broiled and served in a pungent sauce of burgundy and special herbs.

The descriptive copy tells what each of the French entrees is.

This interesting type and layout arrangement (on pages 137 and 138) *lists everything on the left in French with the same item listed on the right in English.*

Diner

Hors-d'Oeuvres

Hors-d'Oeuvres Variées	2.50	Assorted Hors-d'Oeuvres
Pâté Strasbourg	2.00	Pâté Strasbourg
Caviar Malossol — Blinis	5.00	Malossol Caviar — Blinis
Escargots à la Bourguignonne	2.00	Vineyard Snails Bourguignonne
Crevettes a l'Ail au Four	2.00	Baked Shrimp with Garlic Sauce
Cocktail de Crevettes ou Crabe	1.50	Shrimp or King Crabmeat
Artichauts aux Sauces Diverses	1.25	Artichoke — Various Dressings
Champignons Farcis	1.25	Stuffed Mushrooms
Huitres Rockefeller	2.25	Oysters Rockefeller
Huitres	1.50	Oysters on the Half Shell
Coquille St. Jacques à la Parisienne	2.00	Scallops à la Parisienne

Potages

Soupe a l'Oignon Française	.50	French Onion Soup
Vichyssoise	.75	Vichyssoise
Soupe du Jour	.50	Soup of the Day
Avocado	.75	Avocado

Oeufs

Oeufs Pochés à la Benedict	2.50	Poached Eggs à la Benedict
Omelette au Gout	2.00	Omelette as Desired

Poissons

Sole à la Meunière, Pommes, Salade	4.95	Dover Sole à la Meunière, Potato, Salad
Cuisse de Grenouille à la Meunière, Garni	4.00	Frog Legs Meunière, Garni
Queue de Homard Danois, Salade	4.75	Danish Lobster Tails, Saffron Rice, Salad
Carrelet Farci, Brocolis, Tomate Grillée	4.75	Flounder Stuffed with Crab Meat, Broccoli, Grilled Tomato
Filet de Turbot Forestiere, Pommes, Salade	4.95	Filet of Turbot, Forestiere, Potatoes, Salad

Entrees

Poulet Sauté Trois Fontaines, Garni	3.95	Chicken à La Three Fountains, Garni
Escalope de Veau, Garni	4.00	Veal Scallopini, Garni
Coq à la Mode de Bourgogne	3.95	Chicken in Red Wine Sauce
Tournedos — Vieux Marché,	4.95	Beef Tenderloin — Old French Market Style
Filet de Boeuf à la Stroganoff	4.75	Beef Stroganoff
Riz de Veau Eugène	4.00	Sweetbreads Eugène
Foie de Veau au Bacon	4.00	Calf's Liver with Bacon
Daube de Boeuf à la Provençale	4.25	Braised Beef à La Provençale

Rotis

Caneton Rôti au Zeste d'Orange ou Cerise	4.75	Roast Long Island Duckling, Orange or Cherry Sauce
Côte de Boeuf Rôti, Garni	5.25	Prime Rib of Beef au Jus Idaho Baked Potato, Salad

Grillades

Châteaubriand (Pour Deux), Bouquetière, Salade	12.95	Chateaubriand (For Two), Bouquetière, Salad
Aloyau de Boeuf, Pomme au Four, Salade	5.95	Prime Sirloin Steak, Baked Potato, Salad
Côte d'Agneau, Pomme au Four, Salade	5.00	Double French Lamb Chops, Baked Potato, Salad
Filet Mignon, Pommes, Salade	5.95	Filet Mignon, Potatoes, Salad
Petit Filet Mignon, Pommes, Salade	4.95	Petit Filet Mignon, Potatoes, Salad

Pommes de Terre

Pont-Neuf	.50	French Fried
Pommes au Gratin	.50	Au Gratin
Pommes Fondante	.50	Oven Browned
Pomme au Four	.50	Idaho Baked Potato
Pommes Noisette	.50	Hazel Nut Potatoes

Légumes

Brocolis	.75	Broccoli
Aubergines Meunière	.75	Egg Plant Meunière
Asperges	.75	Asparagus
Oignons Glacés	.75	Glazed Onions
Chou-Fleur	.75	Cauliflower
Champignons Sautés	.75	Sautéd Mushrooms

Salades

Salade à La Russe	1.80	Russian Salad Bowl
Poire Avocado	1.00	Avocado Pear with Fresh Fruit Slices
Endive Belge (En Saison)	1.00	Belgian Endive (In Season)
Salade Les Trois Fountaines	.75	The Three Fountains Salad
Salade César (Pour Deux)	3.00	Caesar Salad (For Two)

Sauces — Roquefort, Française, à la Russe, de la Maison, Vinaigrette, à l'Aille

Entremets

Patisserie Varíees	.65	Assorted Pastries
Cerise Jubilée (Pour Deux)	3.50	Cherries Jubiiee (For Two)
Gateaux au Fromage	1.00	Lemon Cheese Pie
Parfait Cognac	1.25	Cognac Parfait
Boule Noix de Coco au Rum	1.00	Coconut Snowball — Rum Sauce
Crêpes Suzette (Pour Deux)	4.00	Crêpes Suzette (For Two)
Pêche Flambée ou Pêche Melba	1.50	Peach Flambé or Peach Melba
Mousse au Chocolat	1.00	Chocolate Mousse

Fromages

Gruyère - Port Salut - Roquefort - Brie - Camembert 1.00

Café et Thé

American Coffee	.35	Café Diable	2.00
Café à la Turque	.50	Café Espresso	.75
Tea	.35	Imported Tea	.75

22

Listing liquor on the menu

The first rule for your cocktail and wine menu list should be: "If you have it in your bar, service bar, or wine cellar, list it on your menu." This sounds extremely elementary, but it is amazing how many establishments will have a wide bar and cellar selection and list only a few items on the menu. The result is "money in bottles" giving no return on the investment. No food service operation would prepare food items in the kitchen and not list them on the menu, but with liquor, wine, and beer, the operator often seems to think that the customer knows what he wants. Yet a great number of liquor sales are of the impulse variety; so the sensible approach is to list it if you have it.

Next, where you list your beverages on the menu is important. Continuing the time sequence in the menu listing, let us examine the liquor time sequence. Which drinks are consumed when by most restaurant guests?

1. Before Dinner
   a. Cocktails
      (Martinis, Manhattans)
   b. Mixed Drinks
      (Scotch, Bourbon, etc.)
   c. Beer
   d. Wines
2. During Dinner
   a. Wines
   b. Beer
3. After Dinner
   a. Wines
   b. Cordials
   c. Brandies
   d. Liqueurs

To take advantage of this, the ideal would be three separate lists that are presented at the three appropriate times during the meal (a procedure, incidentally, which I think would pay the operator who trained the employees to use such lists). In lieu of three lists, the location and order on the single menu is very important. If your menu has several pages, the beverage listing should be on the first page. If your menu is the standard two-page, self-cover type, the list should be on the left hand side.

The purpose is to expose customers to the drink list first so that they will order a cocktail before ordering the meal. The standard question, "Do you care for a cocktail?" voiced by the waiter or waitress may do a partial job (if the question is asked), but a complete list, in large readable type with prices and brand names, if brought to the customer's attention at the right time, will do the complete merchandising job. Prices should be included with the beverage list. You would not think of listing your entrees or your a la carte appetizers, salads, and desserts without prices; therefore, the customer expects to see prices on the liquor list. An elementary observation, yet many menus still list drinks without prices.

Also, list brand names on your liquor menu. The reasons are many. First, by listing brand names you are telling your customers that you serve quality liquor not just "bar liquor," and quality liquor is as important to a food service reputation as quality food. Next, your customer is used to brand names in scotch, bourbon, gin, wines, and beer. The customer has preferences and buys by the bottle at the store by brand name, and so is conditioned to buy the same way when in your establishment.

Listing brand names is also just good dollar sense for the food service operator. The public has been sold on brand name quality by million dollar ad campaigns. The public, therefore, knows that quality scotch and quality bourbon cost more and the public expects to pay more for a nationally advertised brand when they are drinking in your establishment. You, therefore, can charge more, and your percentage of profit or mark-up will be higher.

The two popular cocktails are Martinis and Manhattans although in recent years the "white" drinks with gin, vodka, rum, and tequila have become more popular. Many menus, therefore, feature these drinks in a box or panel, in larger type and with extra copy. They describe the size and quality of their Martini and often refer to it as the "World's Finest Martini." This is good merchandising, but it does not have to be confined to Martinis and Manhattans. Just as you have many unusual and creative specials in the food portion of your menu, so you should create cocktails special to your operation. Give them a special name and feature them on your menu. Just a simple twist in serving or naming a cocktail will do the trick. Serving a "French 75" with an American flag transforms it into an "American 76."

If you have a large enough wine cellar, you will probably want a separate wine list, but, if you have just a few wines, list them with your other beverages. It is also good merchandising to recommend wines with entrees (in smaller type under the entree name and as part of the descriptive copy).

Finally, the customer has had a cocktail before dinner, a bottle of wine or beer with dinner, and now is ready for dessert. To continue your menu liquor merchandising, list your desserts and after dinner drinks together. You will probably make a greater profit on an after dinner drink and you may even sell both the drink and dessert.

The ideal way to list the after dinner drinks is in a separate dessert and after-dinner drink menu. The advantage of the separate menu is that the waiter or waitress (without asking) just presents to the customer this menu which has only after dinner items on it. The chances of ordering with this kind of merchandising are much better than the standard, "Would you care for dessert?" and the very seldom heard, "Would you care for an after dinner drink?" In lieu of a separate list of after dinner drinks (brandy, cordial, liqueur, B & B, etc.), the next best method is to list them with your dessert listing on a separate page or at the bottom of the page after your entree listing.

MENU BEVERAGE CHECK LIST

1. If you serve a beverage, list it on your menu.
2. List beverages according to whether they are served before, with, or after the meal.
3. List all prices on all beverages.
4. List brand names.
5. List some "special" drinks.
6. List after dinner drinks with desserts.
7. List cocktails first so customer orders before meal.

Carry Nation Cocktails

SHIRLEY TEMPLE 25
ALFIE 25
TWIGGY 25
SPANKY 25

For the kiddies!

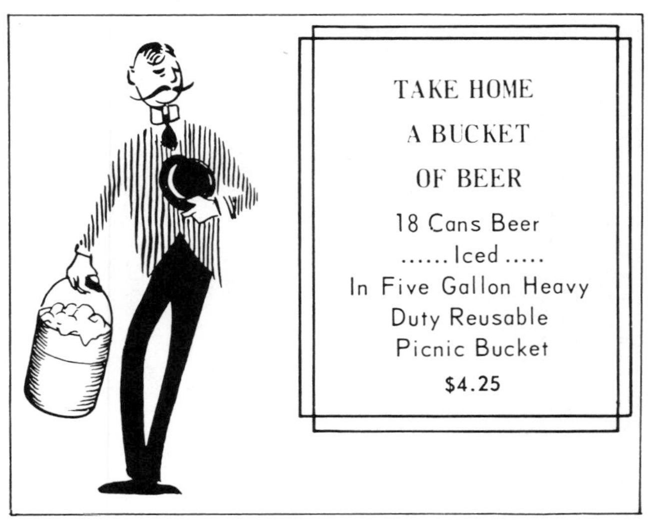

TAKE HOME
A BUCKET
OF BEER
18 Cans Beer
......Iced.....
In Five Gallon Heavy
Duty Reusable
Picnic Bucket
$4.25

Liquor can be a "Take-Home" too.

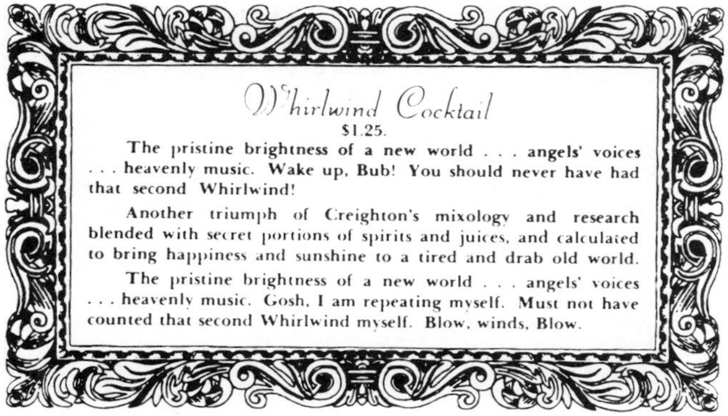

Whirlwind Cocktail
$1.25

The pristine brightness of a new world . . . angels' voices . . . heavenly music. Wake up, Bub! You should never have had that second Whirlwind!

Another triumph of Creighton's mixology and research blended with secret portions of spirits and juices, and calculated to bring happiness and sunshine to a tired and drab old world.

The pristine brightness of a new world . . . angels' voices . . . heavenly music. Gosh, I am repeating myself. Must not have counted that second Whirlwind myself. Blow, winds, Blow.

Really "way-out" copy.

Before Dinner Drinks

.60 MARTINI
Dry Vermouth or Taylor's Pale Dry Cocktail Sherry, Dry Gin with Olive

.60 MANHATTAN
Sweet Vermouth, Blended Whiskey, Angostura Bitters with Maraschino Cherry

.60 GIBSON
Martini with Pickled Onion, Lemon Peel

.65 OLD FASHIONED
Blended Whiskey, Angostura Bitters, Sugar, Orange and Cherry

.60 DAIQUIRI
Light Puerto Rican Rum, Lime Juice and Sugar

.65 WHISKEY SOUR
Blended Whiskey, Lemon, Sugar, Cherry, Orange

.85 PINK LADY
Dry Gin, Grenadine, Egg White and Cream

1.25 CHAMPAGNE COCKTAIL
One Cubette Green Creme de Menthe, One Cubette Grenadine, Bitters, Champagne

.60 TOM COLLINS
Dry Gin, Lemon Juice, Sugar, Club Soda and Fruit

.60 CHERRY FIZZ
Cherry Liqueur, Lemon Juice

.60 BACARDI
Light Puerto Rican Rum, Lime Juice and Grenadine

.85 SIDE CAR
Imported Brandy, Cointreau and Lemon Juice

.85 ALEXANDER
Dry Gin or Brandy, Creme de Cacao Cream and Nutmeg

.65 ORANGE BLOSSOM
Gin, Orange Juice, Sugar

.75 DUBONNET
Dry Gin, Dubonnet Wine and Fruit

.75 ROB ROY
Scotch Whiskey, Vermouth and Angostura Bitters, Lemon Peel

.80 WARD VIII
Bourbon, Lemon and Orange Juice and Grenadine

.75 HORSE'S NECK
Brandy, Angostura Bitters, Ginger Ale and Fruit

.60 SCREWDRIVER
Vodka and Orange Juice

.60 GIN AND TONIC
Dry Gin, Schweppes Quinine Water with A Slice of Lime

.75 GIN RICKEY
Dry Gin, Lime Juice and Club Soda

.60 SLOE GIN FIZZ
Sloe Gin, Lemon Juice and Club Soda

All Above Drinks Using Scotch, Bourbon, Canadian Whiskies, Imported Gins and Brandies — 15c Extra

All Above Drinks on the Rocks or Extra Dry (Extra Portion) 15c Above Listed Price.

A short descriptive listing of their ingredients helps to sell these mixed drinks.

Three drinks really merchandised like this are better than a hundred just listed.

THE THREE HOUSE DRINKS...

BEST...BAR NONE

Shoyer's Gay Nineties Cocktail .90

It's Velvety, Exciting and Refreshing. Tell us, Mr. Bartender, tell us the secret of your Shoyer's Gay Nineties Special. The bartender smiles proudly. Why should he reveal the secret that is his fortune . . . the secret of the finest drink this side of heaven. Truly, this is no ordinary cocktail. Men and women who know its taste, proclaim it Shoyer's premier concoction. We warn you in advance . . . neither kind words nor harsh, fair means nor foul, will pry loose the recipe. You will not be able to duplicate it at home. Once you taste it we have you . . . you must become a regular visitor at Shoyer's. It's a scurvy trick, but you'll bless us for it.

1874 OLD FASHIONED

Like nowhere else is the distinctively original Shoyer Old Fashioned. You'll positively flip when this smoothie is deftly delivered for your pleasure. It comes in a beautiful and unique glass that is a museum piece.
A true masterpiece priced at .90

THE SOUVENIR GLASS $1.25

The Gaslight .95

A sprightly refresher in Scotch, complemented by vermouth and orange curacao, is a replenisher in the true spirit of the fabulous gaslight era. This fabulous drink is called Gaslight and is an inimitable Shoyer creation. We prefer to call it a gasser. The recipe: Scotch, Italian Vermouth, a dash of orange Curacao; shake well and let glisten down the rocks in a thin glass; garnished with a twist of orange skin; and pour a thimbleful of Drambuie over THE GASLIGHT.

IF THE "*Scotch*" DISTILL IT,
WE SERVE IT!

Ambassador 8 - 12 - 20 yrs.
B & L (Bulloch & Lades)
Ballantine's
Bell's Royal Vat 8 - 12 yrs.
Black & White, Extra Light
Buchanan's Deluxe
Catto's G. L. DeLuxe 12 yrs.
Chequers
Chivas Regal
Chivas Salute 21 yrs.
Clan McGregor
Cluny's 8 yrs.
Cutty Sark
Dewar's White Label
Gilbey's Spey-Royal
Glen Rossie
Grand Macnish
Grant's 8 - 12 yrs.
Haig & Haig 5 Star – Pinch
Highland Mist
House of Lords
House of Stuart
Hudson's Bay "Best Procurable"
Inver House
J & B Rare
John Begg "Blue Cap"
Johnnie Walker, Black Label & Red Label
J. W. Dant
King George IV
King William IV
Lauder's Royal Northern Cream
Long John
Macnish V.L.
Martin's V.V.O.
McCullough's
McMaster's
Muirhead
Old Mr. Boston
Old Rarity
Old Smuggler
Park & Tilford Special
Peter Dawson
Prince of Scots
Queen Anne
Robertson's Yellow Label
Robbie Burns
Royal Scott
Sandy McDonald
Scottish Majesty
Sir Malcolm
Something Special
Teacher's Highland Cream
Usher's "Green Stripe"
Vat 69
Wee Burn
White Heather DeLuxe
White Horse

Pride of the Bar

HAVE YOU TRIED . . .

KING SIZE ROB ROYS
MANHATTANS
MARTINIS

Served to you in swirlers.

Five unusual drinks listed big and bold with good copy make this a good "before" drink listing.

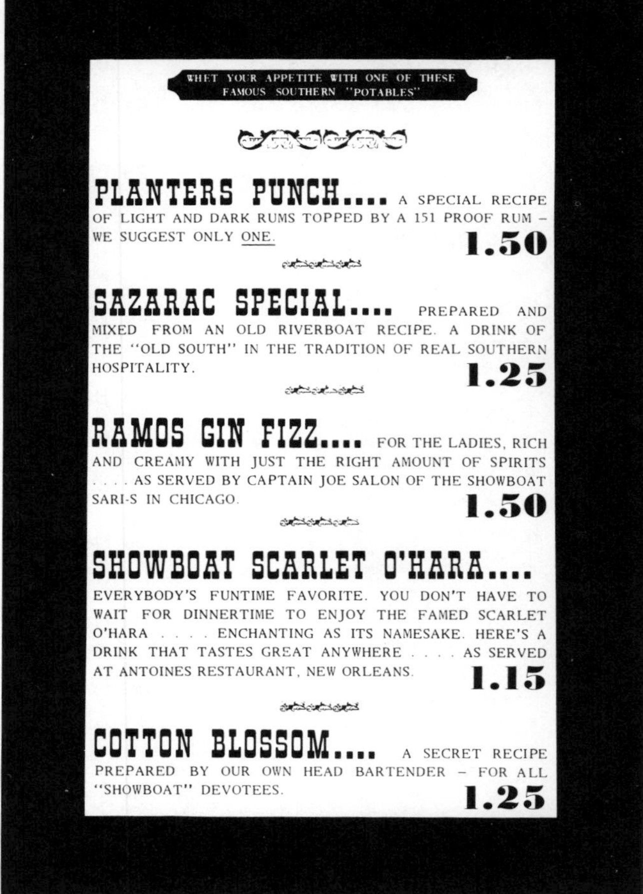

WHET YOUR APPETITE WITH ONE OF THESE FAMOUS SOUTHERN "POTABLES"

PLANTERS PUNCH.... A SPECIAL RECIPE OF LIGHT AND DARK RUMS TOPPED BY A 151 PROOF RUM – WE SUGGEST ONLY ONE. **1.50**

SAZARAC SPECIAL.... PREPARED AND MIXED FROM AN OLD RIVERBOAT RECIPE. A DRINK OF THE "OLD SOUTH" IN THE TRADITION OF REAL SOUTHERN HOSPITALITY. **1.25**

RAMOS GIN FIZZ.... FOR THE LADIES, RICH AND CREAMY WITH JUST THE RIGHT AMOUNT OF SPIRITS . . . . AS SERVED BY CAPTAIN JOE SALON OF THE SHOWBOAT SARI-S IN CHICAGO. **1.50**

SHOWBOAT SCARLET O'HARA.... EVERYBODY'S FUNTIME FAVORITE. YOU DON'T HAVE TO WAIT FOR DINNERTIME TO ENJOY THE FAMED SCARLET O'HARA . . . . ENCHANTING AS ITS NAMESAKE. HERE'S A DRINK THAT TASTES GREAT ANYWHERE . . . . AS SERVED AT ANTOINES RESTAURANT, NEW ORLEANS. **1.15**

COTTON BLOSSOM.... A SECRET RECIPE PREPARED BY OUR OWN HEAD BARTENDER – FOR ALL "SHOWBOAT" DEVOTEES. **1.25**

An unusual liquor listing like this will make your bar selection "special."

COCKTAILS

MANHATTAN
Calvert Reserve, imported sweet vermouth, maraschino cherry

DRY MARTINI
Dry gin, imported dry vermouth, olive

VODKA MARTINI
Vodka, imported dry vermouth, olive

ROB ROY
Scotch, imported sweet vermouth, maraschino cherry

ALEXANDER No. 1
Dry gin, creme de cacao, sweet cream

ALEXANDER No. 2
Brandy, creme de cacao, sweet cream

GRASSHOPPER
Creme de menthe, creme de cacao, sweet cream

GIMLET
Gin, lime juice, fine sugar

BACARDI
Bacardi Silver rum, lemon juice, sugar, grenadine

DAIQUIRI
Light rum, lemon juice, sugar

JACK ROSE
Applejack brandy, lemon juice, grenadine

OLD FASHIONED
Calvert Reserve, lump sugar, soda water, angostura bitters, fruit

PINK LADY
Dry gin, apple brandy, cream, grenadine

SIDE CAR
Cointreau, brandy, lemon juice

STINGER
Brandy, white creme de menthe

SCREW DRIVER
Vodka, orange juice

BLOODY MARY
Vodka, tomato juice

DUBONNET
Dubonnet wine, dry gin

WHISKEY SOUR
Calvert Reserve, lemon juice, sugar

LONG, TALL AND COOLING

TOM COLLINS
Dry gin, lemon juice, sugar, soda water

BRANDY COLLINS
Brandy, lemon juice, sugar, soda water

JOHN COLLINS
Calvert Reserve, lemon juice, sugar, soda water

RUM COLLINS
Bacardi Gold rum, lemon juice, sugar, soda water

SINGAPORE SLING
Dry gin, cherry brandy, bitters, sugar, lemon juice, soda water

BRANDY PUNCH
Brandy, Benedictine, lemon juice, sugar, soda water

McKINLEY PUNCH
Calvert Reserve, grenadine, lemon juice, soda water

PLANTERS PUNCH
Rum, lime juice, sugar, orange juice

RE-FRESHERS

WARD 8
Calvert Reserve, lemon juice, grenadine, slice of orange, maraschino cherry

BRANDY FLIP
Cognac, sugar, whole egg

CUBA LIBRE
Bacardi Gold rum, fresh lime, cola

GIN BUCK
Dry gin, ginger ale

GIN RICKEY
Dry gin, lime juice, soda water

SLOE GIN FIZZ
Sloe gin, lemon juice, sugar, soda water

IMPORTED GIN and TONIC
Imported gin, fresh lime, tonic

DOMESTIC GIN and TONIC
Domestic gin, fresh lime, tonic

VODKA and TONIC
Vodka, fresh lime, tonic

WINE, BEER AND ALE

PLEASE ASK YOUR SERVICE HOSTESS FOR THE SELECTION

Illustrations, good copy, and a large listing make this a selling drink menu.

Beer is the most popular of all alcoholic beverages, yet it probably gets the least attention on the menu, wine, or drink list. Not so at the *Black Sheep Tavern* in Manchester, Michigan. There they have a special Beer List that lists 75 different beers from 23 countries. This is a small restaurant in a small town, but this Beer List idea is something that the "big city" boys might copy. Naturally, it makes for an inventory problem (but beer in a bottle doesn't spoil quickly), but it also adds a distinctive touch to the menu.

Mexican restaurants and the Mexican menu are becoming more and more popular. Along with this ethnic food acceptance is the growth in popularity of Mexican/Spanish drinks. The *Su Casa* restaurant in La Jolla, California, does a good job of merchandising their Mexican drinks on the cover page of the Dinner Menu. The copy reads as follows:

> CON MUCHO GUSTO. Let's start with one of our famous *Margaritas* (they are great). *Su Casa Margarita*—Tequila, triple sec liqueur, piece of fresh lime in a cocktail glass frosted with rock salt. Four sizes: small, regular, grande, pitchers. *Su Casa Fruit Margaritas*—Banana, Strawberry, Rosa (cranberry).
>
> OTHER TEQUILA ESPECIALIDADES. *Tequila Sangrita*—Tequila, lime and salt, with the devil's own chaser. *TNT*—(Tequila and Tonic). *Tequila Sunrise*—Tequila, grenadine, creme de cassis, sweet and sour, orange juice, and sparkling water in a tall glass with cherry, lime and orange. *Tequila Sour; Tequila Martini; Tequila Collins; Tequila Mockingbird—Tequila, creme de menthe*, and a piece of lime in a cocktail glass. *Brave Bull*—Kahlua, tequila, with a lemon twist served over the rocks.

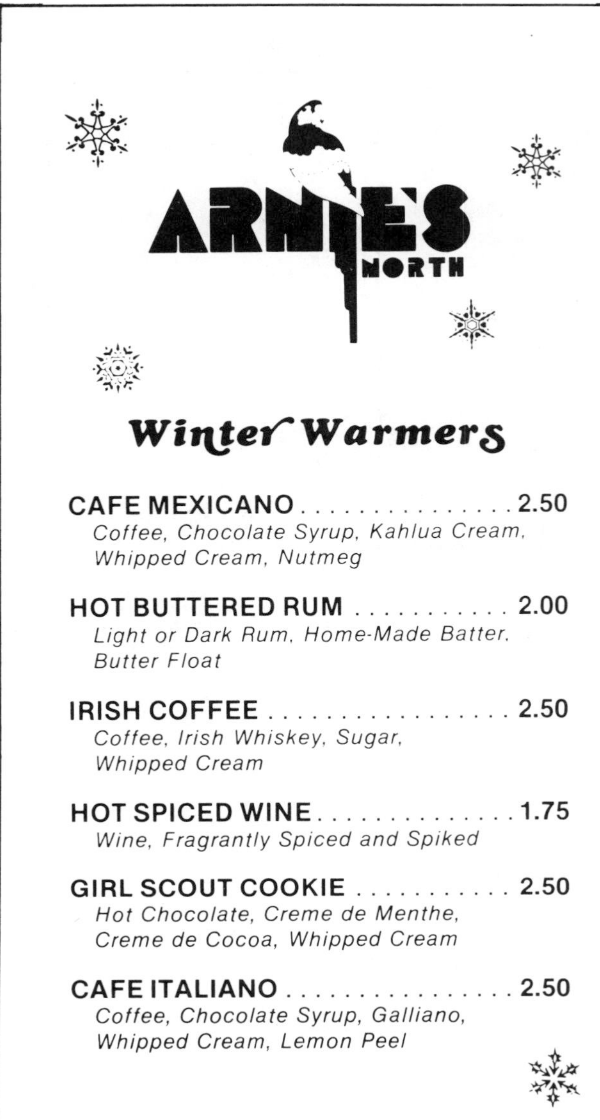

ARNIE'S NORTH

Winter Warmers

CAFE MEXICANO 2.50
Coffee, Chocolate Syrup, Kahlua Cream, Whipped Cream, Nutmeg

HOT BUTTERED RUM 2.00
Light or Dark Rum, Home-Made Batter, Butter Float

IRISH COFFEE 2.50
Coffee, Irish Whiskey, Sugar, Whipped Cream

HOT SPICED WINE 1.75
Wine, Fragrantly Spiced and Spiked

GIRL SCOUT COOKIE 2.50
Hot Chocolate, Creme de Menthe, Creme de Cocoa, Whipped Cream

CAFE ITALIANO 2.50
Coffee, Chocolate Syrup, Galliano, Whipped Cream, Lemon Peel

House Drinks

BANANAS FROSTER 2.50
Fresh Banana, Dark Rum, Creme de Banana, Brown Sugar, Ice Cream

ARNIES PET PARROT 2.50
Rum, Pineapple Juice, Grapefruit Juice, Grenadine, Fresh Pineapple

MARGARITA 2.50
Tequila, Triple Sec, Lime Juice and Plenty of Salt on the Rim

PINA COLADA 2.50
Pineapple Juice, Creme of Coconut, Rum, Fresh Pineapple

(Try it Strawberry!)

Ask Your Waiter
About Our Excellent Wine Selection

Arnie's North *has a small but very creative drink list.*

After dinner, among six other after dinner drinks *Su Casa* serves: *Mexican Keoki Coffee*—Kahlua, brandy and fresh whipped cream.

Arnie's North restaurant has two small (4″ × 7″) handout type drink suggestion menus with interesting offerings. One is "House Drinks" which includes: *Bananas Foster*—Fresh banana, dark rum, creme de banana, brown sugar and ice cream. Another special house drink is *Arnie's Pet Parrot*—Rum, pineapple juice, grapefruit juice, grenadine, and fresh pineapple.

On *Arnie's* "Winter Warmers" list of drinks is: *Cafe Mexicano*—Coffee, chocolate syrup, kahlua cream, whipped cream, and nutmeg; *Hot Buttered Rum; Irish Coffee; Hot Spiced Wine; Girl Scout Cookie*—Hot chocolate, creme de menthe, creme de cocoa, and whipped cream, plus *Cafe Italiano*—Coffee, chocolate syrup, galliano, whipped cream, and lemon peel.

The *Ivy Barn* in San Diego, California, and West Palm Beach, Florida, presents a most creative drink list and is not afraid of a little *tell and sell* to get the customer interested. Called "Country Sippin'" it tells you first that All Popular

The Ivy Barn *drink menu tempts the customer with unusual before-, with-, and after-dinner drinks.*

COUNTRY SIPPIN'

WHISKY RUN

CIDER PRESS 1.85
The essence of the hills on a crisp autumn evening. A stout blend of vodka and apple jack.

MOUNTAIN DEW 2.45
A tale of country roads, revenuers and free spirited souls. A fortified brew of sour mash corn whiskey.

SIP-A-DEE-DOO-DAH 2.45
Southern Comfort at its best, mingling with the bitter sweetness of the refreshing cranberry and accented with lemon and lime.

ALL POPULAR DRINKS ARE DOUBLES

THE GOOD OLD BOYS

CUCUMBER FIELDS 2.45
A definitive statement on the boys resourcefulness and love of drink. Who'd ever think that a cucumber could taste like this!

SASSAFRAS TEA 1.85
If only, the good ol' boys knew what the women folk had concocted for those Sunday afternoon gatherings! A banana brandy base

FRESH FRUIT DRINKS

STRAWBERRY HILL DAIQUIRI 1.85
Let us take you down to Strawberry Fields, Forever.

BIG ROCK CANDY MOUNTAIN 1.85
As he roamed along he sang a song, of the land of coconut milk and honey, and the buzzing of the bees in the sycamore trees, at the lemonade springs, where the blue bird sings, on the big rock candy mountain.

A GEORGIA PEACH DAIQUIRI 1.85
Remember your first taste of a Georgia Peach?

FOR TWO OR MORE FRIENDS

MELON PATCH BREW 4.90
This refreshing rum based concoction is a blend of canteloupe, lemon, lime, served in a whole canteloupe. Serves two when in season.

WATERMELON SUGAR
Trout fishing in America has never been the same since the country boys started packing a melon instead of the rod. Served in half a watermelon to four rascals.
Our melon 9.25
Your melon no questions asked 8.25

RAG DOLL 7.35
A potent yet wonderful creation of pineapples, oranges, grapefruit juice and two rums. Serves four in a manner only Granny would think of.

WINE DRINKS & JUGS

FERMENTED FRUIT FANTASY 1.25
Our delightfully refreshing blend of wines with fresh fruits, accented with lime.

WINE COOLER 1.25
A refreshingly light mixture of wine and ginger ale with a hint of lime.

JUG OF WINE: 1.75

BIG JUG OF WINE: 3.00

GLASS OF WINE: .80

HORS D'OEUVRE PLATES

SHRIMP COCKTAIL 1.75

DIP-IT PLATE 2.25
A tangy dip with chips and vegetable dip-its.

AFTER DINNER DRINKS

CREAM DRINKS

MOON BEAM 1.85
As gentle as a porch swing on a warm summer's night with fresh cream and other delights.

PEACH FUZZ 1.85
The sweetness of fresh cream mingled with fresh honey and tingled with peach brandy.

COFFEE DRINKS

IRISH COFFEE 1.55
A dark coffee blend, Irish Whiskey and whipping cream.

KIOKE COFFEE 1.55
If the country kitchen served coffee like this, we'd all be country boys. A blend of brandy, Kahlua and heavy whipping cream.

FUN DRINKS

BED WARMER 2.45
First we tempt the ladies with red licorice and follow that with a delightful nectar of Annisette and vodka. Zam . . . penny candy was never like this!

SNUGGLE UP TO A NAVEL Orange, that is 2.45
Fresh cream, vodka and erotic bedtime stories. Made with bourbon, Galliano and fruit juices.

SQUEEZE 2.45
That's what mountain men call it. Story has it that they used to fill a handkerchief with fresh grapes, bananas, and coconuts and then squeeze it over a glass of white lightning.

FEATHER DUSTER 1.85
This is not recommended for those who are ticklish, combining peach brandy and lemon in a collins base.

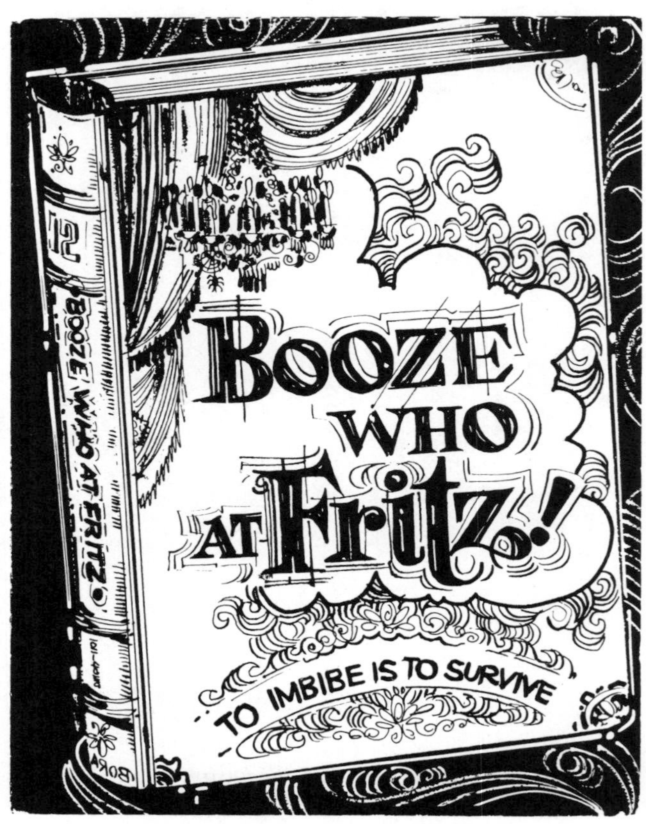

This "way-out" drink listing fits the ambience and clientele of the Fritz That's It *restaurant.*

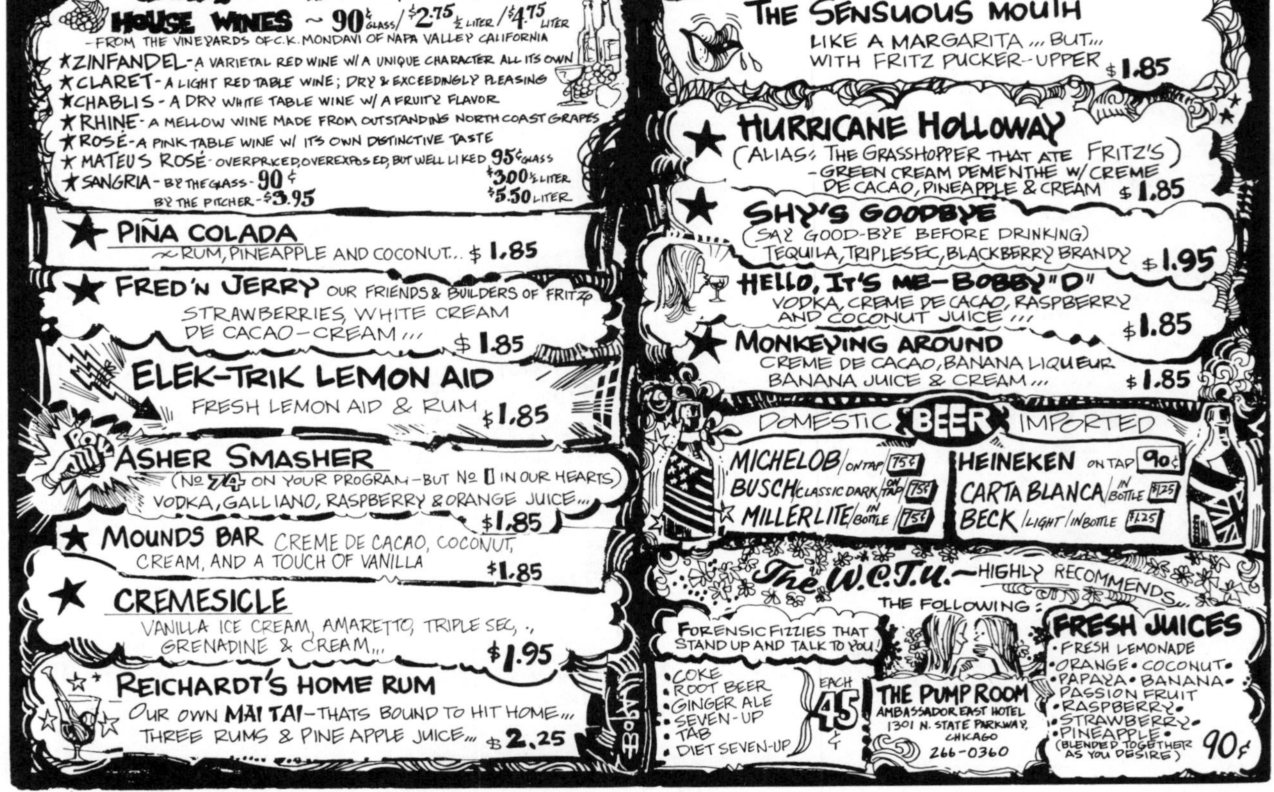

Drinks are Doubles. Then under the heading of Whisky Run is listed: *Cider Press*—A stout blend of vodka and apple jack; *Mountain Dew*—A fortified brew of sour mash corn whiskey; and *Sip-A-Dee-Doo-Dah*—Southern comfort at its best, mingling with the bitter sweetness of the refreshing cranberry and accented with lemon and lime.

Then, under the headings of "Fresh Fruit Drinks" and "For Two or More Friends" there are more interesting drinks. One is called *Watermelon Sugar*—Trout fishing in America has never been the same since the country boys started packing a melon instead of the rod. Served in half a watermelon to four rascals. (Our melon—$9.25, Your melon—no questions asked—$8.25).

The *Ivy Barn* drink menu also lists Wine Drinks & Jugs, After Dinner Cream and Coffee Drinks, and Fun Drinks. These include:

Bed Warmer—First we tempt the ladies with red licorice and follow that with a delightful nectar of anisette and vodka. Zam . . . penny candy was never like this!

Snuggle Up to a Navel—Orange, that is. Fresh cream, vodka and bed time stories. Made with bourbon, galliano and fruit juices.

Squeeze—That's what mountain men call it. Story has it that they used to fill a handkerchief with fresh grapes, bananas, and coconuts and then squeeze it over a glass of white lightning.

Feather Duster—This is not recommended for those who are ticklish, combining peach brandy and lemon in a collins base.

This drink menu is die cut in the shape of a basketful of vegetables carrying on the *Ivy Barn* motif, is printed in only one color (dark brown), and it has a small pocket for holding a special insert.

A drink menu, as well as the regular food menu, should reflect the character of a restaurant. The *Booze Who at Fritz* drink menu does reflect a young, swinging, casual type of atmosphere. It is all hand lettered in a free-and-easy manner with creative, fun copy. Such drinks as Elek-Trik Lemon Aid, Asher Smasher, Mounds Bar, Cremesicle, The Sensuous Mouth, Hurricane Holloway, and Monkeying Around. Three domestic and three imported beers are also listed.

The South Seas type of food and drink establishment such as the *Mai-Kai* in Fort Lauderdale, Florida, features special tropical drinks in a comprehensive list. First, there are 14 Strong Tropical Drinks such as *Mai-Tai*, *Planters Punch*, and *Sidewinder's Fang*. The center spread features After Dinner Tropical Drinks (6), Standard Drinks and Mild Tropical Drinks (15). On the back page, 13 Medium Tropical Drinks are listed. To top the entire listing is the Mystery Drink for four which sells for $13.50.

All of the tropical drinks are illustrated in color and described with colorful copy. It is a large menu—17″ × 10″—with a heavy, imitation leather cover with illustration in white and copy in embossed gold.

23
Wine lists

"A beer is a beer" . . . goes part of a recent TV commercial, but nobody ever said "a wine is a wine," and this is part of both the problem and the opportunity of serving wine in your dining room. Though the subject of wine is complex, however, every food service operation can serve some wine, even if it is only a glass of rose, or a selection of one red and one white wine served by the glass. Some simple rules for listing and serving on the menu are in order.

The first rule is to list the wines you serve on the menu. A separate Wine List means the customer must ask for it and most people do not ask. As for where on the menu to print the Wine List, the answer is next to the entrees. Wine is a beverage to drink with the meal more than before (cocktails) or after (cordials). There are, of course, aperitif (appetizer) wines and dessert wines, but most wines are consumed with the entree.

Another good wine menu merchandising rule is to suggest food to go with types of wines—red, white, rose, champagne, etc. This affinity of certain wines with certain foods can be merchandised on the menu by listing with the entree descriptive copy in a second color, red, for example.

Wine can also be merchandised on the menu by selling "packages," individual or for two. This means such combinations as a complete dinner with a glass of rose wine thrown in or a Champagne Dinner—all the champagne you can drink for a fixed price or a combination special, Beef, Bay, and Burgundy. The combinations are unlimited, and many are offered by wine-aware food service operators.

The wines available for your menu are numerous and they can be either inexpensive, moderately priced, or expensive. American wines, for example, include New York, Ohio, and Michigan; eastern wines from the native American grape (Vitis Labrusca), and the wines of California from the vines transplanted from Europe (Vitis Vinifera).

From Europe there are the great wines of France and Germany plus those from Spain, Portugal, and Italy, and there are good wines from South America, Chile, and Argentina, for example. It is obvious, therefore, that you can tailor your wine selection to fit your menu. If you serve Italian food, you can match it with good Italian wines, and if you have a German cuisine, the delightful wines of Germany (as well as German beer) can make a good menu great.

A concern voiced by some operators is "If I offer wine they will not order cocktails." This need not be so because cocktails are a before dinner drink while wine is a with dinner beverage. The trick is to sell both—cocktails and wine. Also, unless you are a very exclusive, very expensive restaurant where only gourmets eat who order wine as a matter of routine, you should have a price range that allows the customer with a smaller budget to order a glass or bottle of wine. This usually means some American wines (often just as good or better than imported wine) that are less expensive. This also means offering wine by the glass.

Every distinctive atmosphere restaurant should have a Wine List, preferably a separate list, but if not this, at least a separate section of the menu for wines. Some of the best cooking is French. Some of the best wines come from France. Therefore, if a restaurant has a wine list (no matter how small), there is an automatic "association" by the customer. The wine list becomes an inferred testimonial that the cuisine is better than average . . . and it usually is.

Wine is actually the drink par excellence to

go with food. This fact has been testified to by gourmets for thousands of years. Cocktails may be good before the meal, and brandy, cordials and liqueurs may be good after the meal; but the right wine is good before, with, and after the meal. Thousands of years ago the Greeks appreciated this chemical affinity of wine to food so highly that they named one of the gods on Mt. Olympus Bacchus, in honor of the juice of the grape. Ancient custom and modern usage have continued this happy association, and every Gourmet Dinner worthy of the name serves a different, appropriate wine with each course. Besides, if you are a practical American food service operator, there is profit in wine.

Before you can create a wine list, of course, you must have a wine cellar. We do not propose to suggest any such grave undertaking, but would suggest the following to any operator who is not a wine "expert" at present or cannot afford an expensive advisory service. First, collect the wine lists of some of the better restaurants and clubs in this country, and there are many. Next, consult a reputable wine merchant. The thing to avoid with wine merchants, however, is their propensity to recommend only the wines they sell. Also, the wine list should include both imported and American wines. For additional help, the Wine Advisory Board in San Francisco gives valuable service to the wine-interested food service operator.

As to the size of the wine list (and the cellar), from eight to ten good wines are enough to make an excellent wine list. And, a list with twenty good wines is a real gourmet selection which will enhance the reputation of any quality establishment. The wine list can be printed in the following forms:

1. Separate wine list—wines only.
2. Separate wine list with other drinks (cocktails, beer, etc.).
3. Separate section of the menu—wines only.
4. Separate section of menu—wines and other drinks (cocktails, beers, etc.).

We will consider the separate wine list first. The listing of wines in a wine list is usually broken down under the following categories:

1. Place of origin
   a. Imported—France, Germany, Italy, Portugal, etc.
   b. American—California, eastern.
2. Type of wine
   a. Sparkling—champagne, sparkling burgundy.
   b. Still wines—all others.
3. Style of wine
   a. Dry
   b. Medium
   c. Sweet
4. Color of wine
   a. Red
   b. White
   c. Rose
5. Vintage (or Non-vintage)

In America especially, it is the custom to separate the imported and American wines, and it is generally considered better form to refer to American wines as American and not "Domestic." The reason for separating California from eastern (New York, Michigan, etc.) wines is that each is made from a different grape—the eastern from the Concord grape, and the California from the vines transplanted from Europe.

The imported section of the wine list usually (and rightly so) begins with the great wines of France—Bordeaux, Burgundy, Champagne. This can be followed by the fine wines of Germany—Rhine, Moselle, Rhinegau, Rhinehesse. A listing of the "special" wines of Alsace, Rhone, Loire, Italy, Portugal, Spain, and South America can follow if a really "big" list is in the making.

The best California wines, which will stand comparison with most of the wines of Europe, are produced from an area of famous valleys around San Francisco Bay. These valleys and counties are Napa, Sonoma, Livermore, and Santa Cruz. The best wines from these areas are the varietals—wines that take their name and their characteristic flavor and bouquet from the grape variety from which they were produced. Care must be used in selecting California wines for the wine list. For example, any red California wine can be labeled "Burgundy," but a varietal red wine such as Pinot Noir must be made from a minimum of 51% of Pinot Noir grapes, the same grape used exclusively to make the finest French red Burgundies.

In listing the wines on the wine list, each wine should be identified by a bin number. The bin number should be written on the label of each bottle in the bin for further identification. The names of wines are usually French or German, and are hard to pronounce, identify, and remember, The average waiter or waitress who is not a trained sommelier needs the bin number system for easy identification and efficient service. The bin number system also provides for quick, easy inventory.

Prices for wine are usually broken down into three categories—per bottle, half-bottle, and glass. A word of caution is offered here. Don't charge too much. The retail wine store is restricted by law to a 50 percent mark-up. Therefore, a wine which a retailer buys for $1.00, he usually sells for $1.49. If the restaurant charges $3.00 for this same bottle, the customer is going to resent the difference. A 100 percent mark-up is a good rule for restaurants.

The names of most wines are French, and, therefore, unless the customer is French or has studied French, the pronunciation presents a challenge if not an insurmountable obstacle. To overcome this problem on the wine list, a pronouncing glossary or phonetic spelling under the wine name is recommended. The following are some phonetic pronunciations for wines:

Beaujolais— BOW-ZHOW-LAY	Graves— GRAH-VE
Chablis— CHAH-BLEE	Haut Brion— O-BREE-ON
Chateau d'Yquem— SHAT-O-DEEKEM	St. Emilion— SANT-EH-MEE-YON

The rule for the wine list intended for the average customer, who knows little about wine, is to make it easy for the customer to order wine without showing his or her lack of wine knowledge.

The next question to be considered is which wines to order with which foods. For the guest who has sampled many wines and knows the wine-food combinations that he or she prefers, rules are not necessary (and besides it's a free country). But, there is a consensus among gourmets as to what wines are best with certain foods. For the nonexpert, also, it is reassuring when the wine list recommends certain wines to go with certain entrees.

First, Champagne is the most versatile of all wines. It may be served with any food, or by itself, and it is an elegent aperitif, an ideal dinner, and a perfect after dinner wine. Pink wines (Rose) are also intermediate and go with almost any food.

If more than one wine is being served, the rule is to start with the lighter (usually white) and proceed to the heavier, more pungent (usually red) and finish with a sweet dessert wine (Sauternes-Rhine or California).

The following simplified Wine-Food Chart is offered for reference:

CANAPES Cheese, crackers Olives, etc.	 *SHERRY* *CHAMPAGNE*
SOUP	*SHERRY*
SEAFOOD	*CHABLIS* *DRY SAUTERNE* *RHINE* *WHITE BURGUNDY*
FOWL Cold chicken, turkey, roast chicken, duck, turkey, pheasant	 *CHAMPAGNE* *DRY SAUTERNE* *RHINE* *WHITE OR RED BURGUNDY*
MEATS Steak, veal, lamb, roast beef, stew	*CLARET* *BURGUNDY* *ROSE*
ITALIAN DISHES	*CHIANTI* *ZINFANDEL* *BARBERA*
DESSERTS	*SWEET SAUTERNE* *CHAMPAGNE*

The next consideration on the wine list is vintage. Vintage means "gathering of the grapes," and vintage wine is one produced from grapes of a specified year. Weather plays an important part in the quality of French and German wines. In bright, sunny weather the grapes grow to full maturity, size, and flavor while bad weather will result in a hard, green, small-sized grape. A high rated vintage year indicates that the weather was so favorable that it resulted in top quality grapes from which the extra high quality wine was made. Because the weather and growing conditions in California are so constant from year to year, it is not customary to give vintage year labels to California wine.

On the wine list, vintage can be listed several ways. The best and biggest wine lists give the vintage year for each wine. Other equally good but less detailed wine lists just add the word vintage after the vintage wines on the list with no year. For a wine that is non-vintage, it is better usage not to list the fact that it is a non-vintage wine or even use the abbreviation N.V. One problem with listing vintage years is that the wine in a vintage year does get used up and cannot be replaced. The wine list then has to be reprinted, or "paste-ons" must be used to show the replacement.

Concerning descriptive copy on each wine served, it is not absolutely necessary, but it helps the guest who has had limited acquaintance with the many wines available. The following descriptions from the *Standard Club* wine list do the job very well with a few well chosen words:

CHATEAU LA DAME BLANCHE 1955
A very good vintage, medium dry with a pleasant bouquet.

CHATEAU LA GUARDE, ESCHENAUER
A fine dry Chateau bottle Claret, light and full flavored.

Copy describing the main categories of wine (Bordeaux, Burgundy, Rhine, etc.) is most helpful on any wine list. It indicates that the operator knows wines and has stocked the cellar with skill and loving care.

As for listing other beverages on the wine list, it is the custom on Continental wine lists to list the other drinks at the end of the wine list after all the wines have been listed. The Central Hotel in Glasgow, Scotland, for example, lists the following beverages on the wine list after the wines, as follows: Cognac, Armagnac, Liqueurs, Aperitifs, Gin, Rum, Scotch Whiskey, Irish Whiskey, Canadian Whiskey, Beer, Stout and Lager, Cider and Mineral Waters. It's obvious that nobody leaves Scotland thirsty!

When the wine list is a section, page, or panel of the food menu, be sure that it gets the proper billing and attention. If the wines get lost in the printed scramble of the menu, they will age forever in the wine cellar and never get sold. And it's not always true that the older the wine the better!

An effective method of selling wine is to list it right with the food it complements. For example, the following entree and wine could be listed together:

Rack and Loin of Spring Lamb served with
Baby Carrots, Pearl Onions, Garnished with Watercress
For a wine to accompany this entree, we recommend
Red Bordeaux
La Chateau Margaux
1953

In short, wine helps to sell the food, and the food helps to sell the wine, and both help to keep the operation solvent.

The wine list of Jacques French Restaurant *features French wines and a wine map.*

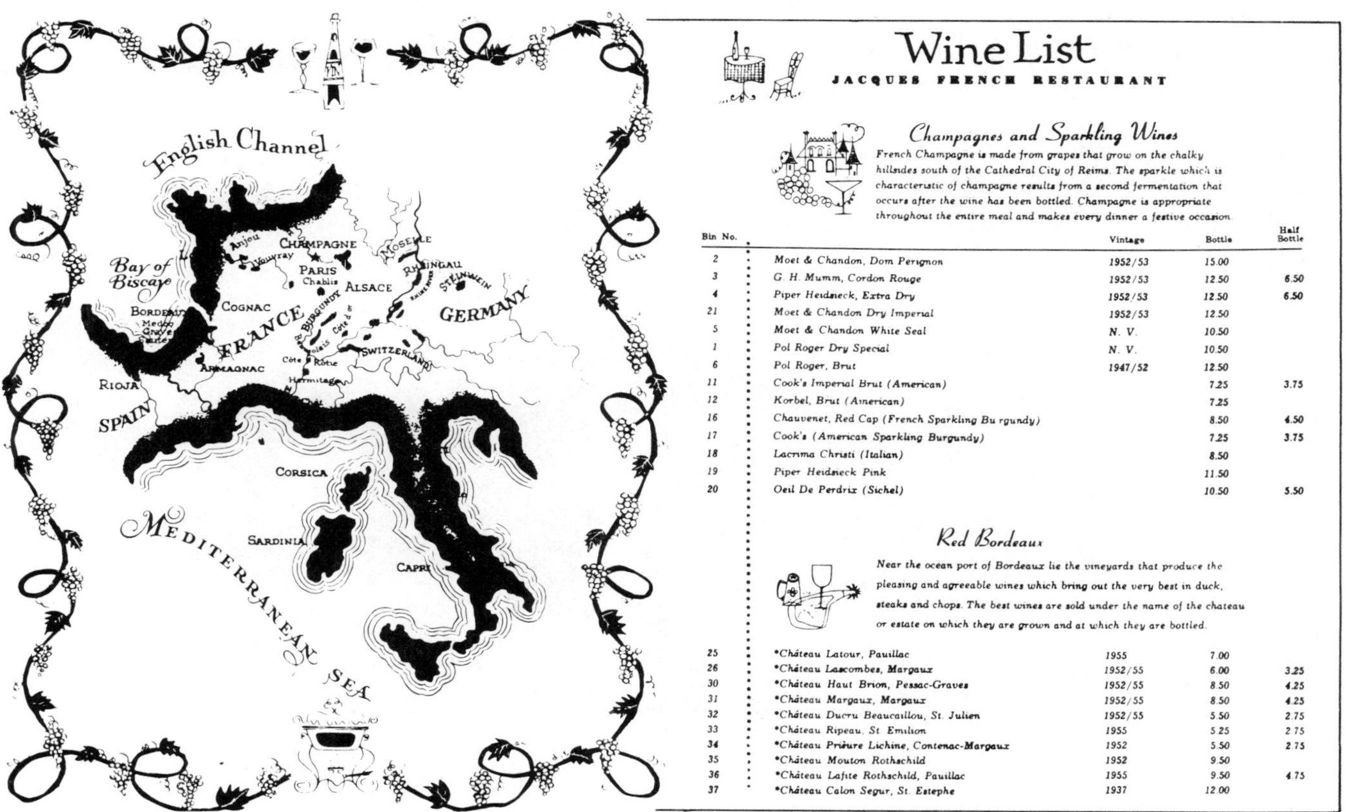

Wine List
JACQUES FRENCH RESTAURANT

Champagnes and Sparkling Wines

French Champagne is made from grapes that grow on the chalky hillsides south of the Cathedral City of Reims. The sparkle which is characteristic of champagne results from a second fermentation that occurs after the wine has been bottled. Champagne is appropriate throughout the entire meal and makes every dinner a festive occasion.

Bin No.		Vintage	Bottle	Half Bottle
2	*Moet & Chandon, Dom Perignon*	*1952/53*	*15.00*	
3	*G. H. Mumm, Cordon Rouge*	*1952/53*	*12.50*	*6.50*
4	*Piper Heidsieck, Extra Dry*	*1952/53*	*12.50*	*6.50*
21	*Moet & Chandon Dry Imperial*	*1952/53*	*12.50*	
5	*Moet & Chandon White Seal*	*N. V.*	*10.50*	
1	*Pol Roger Dry Special*	*N. V.*	*10.50*	
6	*Pol Roger, Brut*	*1947/52*	*12.50*	
11	*Cook's Imperial Brut (American)*		*7.25*	*3.75*
12	*Korbel, Brut (American)*		*7.25*	
16	*Chauvenet, Red Cap (French Sparkling Burgundy)*		*8.50*	*4.50*
17	*Cook's (American Sparkling Burgundy)*		*7.25*	*3.75*
18	*Lacrima Christi (Italian)*		*8.50*	
19	*Piper Heidsieck Pink*		*11.50*	
20	*Oeil De Perdrix (Sichel)*		*10.50*	*5.50*

Red Bordeaux

Near the ocean port of Bordeaux lie the vineyards that produce the pleasing and agreeable wines which bring out the very best in duck, steaks and chops. The best wines are sold under the name of the chateau or estate on which they are grown and at which they are bottled.

Bin No.		Vintage	Bottle	Half Bottle
25	*•Château Latour, Pauillac*	*1955*	*7.00*	
26	*•Château Lascombes, Margaux*	*1952/55*	*6.00*	*3.25*
30	*•Château Haut Brion, Pessac-Graves*	*1952/55*	*8.50*	*4.25*
31	*•Château Margaux, Margaux*	*1952/55*	*8.50*	*4.25*
32	*•Château Ducru Beaucaillou, St. Julien*	*1952/55*	*5.50*	*2.75*
33	*•Château Ripeau, St. Emilion*	*1955*	*5.25*	*2.75*
34	*•Château Prieure Lichine, Contenac-Margaux*	*1952*	*5.50*	*2.75*
35	*•Château Mouton Rothschild*	*1952*	*9.50*	
36	*•Château Lafite Rothschild, Pauillac*	*1955*	*9.50*	*4.75*
37	*•Château Calon Segur, St. Estephe*	*1937*	*12.00*	

DEUTSCHE ROTWEINE

60er Walporzheimer Steinkaul Spätburgunder	8.50
64er Affenthaler Rotwein Spätburgunder *Affenflasche Beerwein*	10.—
64er Ihringer Winklerberg Spätburgunder natur *Kaiserstühler Winzergenossenschaft*	12.50

SÜSS- UND DESSERTWEINE

Insel Samos		7.—
Malaga Hellgold Lagrimas Christi		7.50
Mavrodaphne		9.—
Original TERRY-Sherry pale, trocken *Reidemeister & Ulrichs, Bremen*		10.—
Portwein, Old Tawny *Butler, Nephew & Co.*	½ 6.50	12.—
Fine Old Madeira Boal, Portugal *Reidemeister & Ulrichs, Bremen*		12.—
Sandeman's Portwein, rot		13.50
Sandeman's Portwein, weiß		15.50
Sandeman's Sherry „Apitiv"		15.50

SCHAUMWEIN UND CHAMPAGNER

54	KUPFERBERG Gold, Zwerg Dry		4.—
55	Schloß Wachenheim Grün		9.—
56	HENKELL TROCKEN		14.—
57	KUPFERBERG Gold	½ 7.50	14.—
58	Matheus Müller extra Auslese		14.—
59	BURGEFF Grün		14.—
60	Deinhard CABINET -TROCKEN-		14.—
61	Deinhard LILA -EXTRA DRY-	½ 9.—	17.—
62	SÖHNLEIN Fürst v. Metternichscher Schloß Johannisberg Sekt		17.—
63	SÖHNLEIN Assmannshäuser Spätburgunder		18.—
64	Mumm ELTVILLE, Dry		18.—
65	KUPFERBERG Schwarz-Gold Fürst von Bismarck, Extra Dry		20.—
66	Heidsieck Monopole, Red Top	½ 17.—	32.—
67	Champagner Heidsieck Monopole Dry		40.—

Brand names are important for wine listing. Also, if yours is a "national" restaurant—French, German, Italian, etc., feature the wines of that country plus American wines.

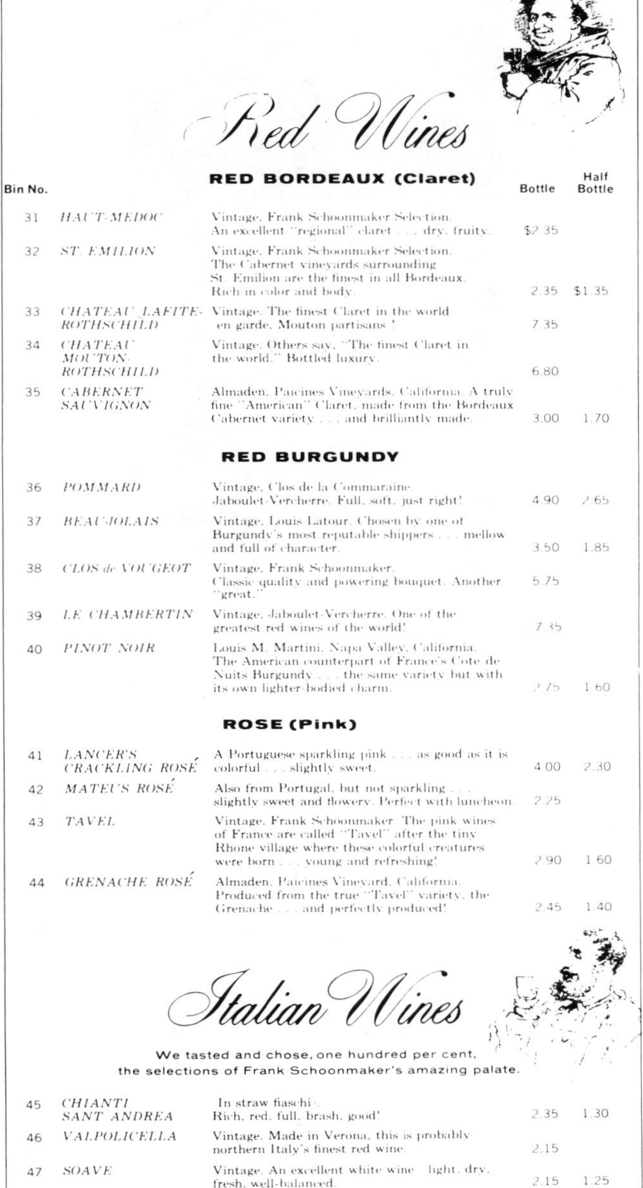

Red Wines

Bin No.		RED BORDEAUX (Claret)	Bottle	Half Bottle
31	*HAUT-MEDOC*	Vintage, Frank Schoonmaker Selection. An excellent "regional" claret . . . dry, fruity.	$2.35	
32	*ST. EMILION*	Vintage, Frank Schoonmaker Selection. The Cabernet vineyards surrounding St. Emilion are the finest in all Bordeaux. Rich in color and body.	2.35	$1.35
33	*CHATEAU LAFITE-ROTHSCHILD*	Vintage. The finest Claret in the world en garde. Mouton partisans !	7.35	
34	*CHATEAU MOUTON-ROTHSCHILD*	Vintage. Others say, "The finest Claret in the world." Bottled luxury.	6.80	
35	*CABERNET SAUVIGNON*	Almaden, Paicines Vineyards, California. A truly fine "American" Claret, made from the Bordeaux Cabernet variety . . . and brilliantly made.	3.00	1.70
		RED BURGUNDY		
36	*POMMARD*	Vintage, Clos de la Commaraine. Jaboulet-Vercherre. Full, soft, just right!	4.90	2.65
37	*BEAUJOLAIS*	Vintage, Louis Latour. Chosen by one of Burgundy's most reputable shippers . . . mellow and full of character.	3.50	1.85
38	*CLOS de VOUGEOT*	Vintage, Frank Schoonmaker. Classic quality and powering bouquet. Another "great."	5.75	
39	*LE CHAMBERTIN*	Vintage, Jaboulet-Vercherre. One of the greatest red wines of the world!	7.35	
40	*PINOT NOIR*	Louis M. Martini, Napa Valley, California. The American counterpart of France's Cote de Nuits Burgundy . . . the same variety but with its own lighter-bodied charm.	2.75	1.60
		ROSE (Pink)		
41	*LANCER'S CRACKLING ROSÉ*	A Portuguese sparkling pink . . . as good as it is colorful . . . slightly sweet.	4.00	2.30
42	*MATEUS ROSÉ*	Also from Portugal, but not sparkling . . . slightly sweet and flowery. Perfect with luncheon.	2.25	
43	*TAVEL*	Vintage, Frank Schoonmaker. The pink wines of France are called "Tavel" after the tiny Rhone village where these colorful creatures were born . . . young and refreshing!	2.90	1.60
44	*GRENACHE ROSÉ*	Almaden, Paicines Vineyard, California. Produced from the true "Tavel" variety, the Grenache . . . and perfectly produced!	2.45	1.40

Italian Wines

We tasted and chose, one hundred per cent, the selections of Frank Schoonmaker's amazing palate.

Bin No.			Bottle	Half Bottle
45	*CHIANTI SANT ANDREA*	In straw fiaschi. Rich, red, full, brash, good!	2.35	1.30
46	*VALPOLICELLA*	Vintage. Made in Verona, this is probably northern Italy's finest red wine.	2.15	
47	*SOAVE*	Vintage. An excellent white wine light, dry, fresh, well-balanced.	2.15	1.25

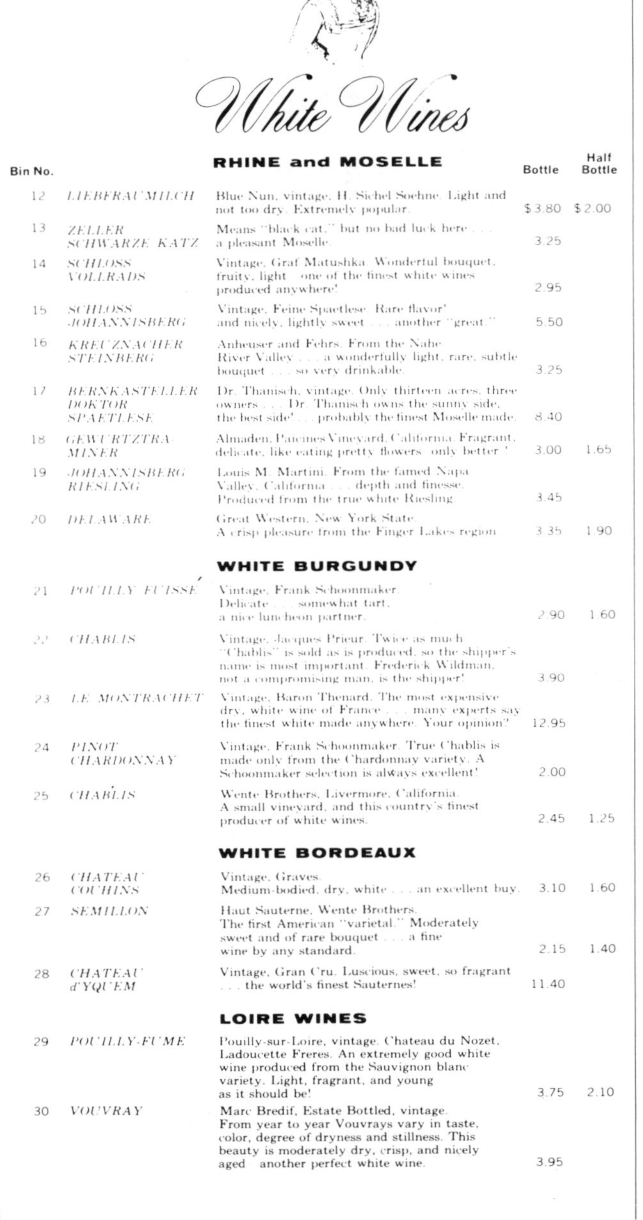

White Wines

Bin No.		RHINE and MOSELLE	Bottle	Half Bottle
12	*LIEBFRAUMILCH*	Blue Nun, vintage, H. Sichel Soehne. Light and not too dry. Extremely popular.	$3.80	$2.00
13	*ZELLER SCHWARZE KATZ*	Means "black cat," but no bad luck here . . . a pleasant Moselle.	3.25	
14	*SCHLOSS VOLLRADS*	Vintage, Graf Matushka. Wonderful bouquet, fruity, light one of the finest white wines produced anywhere!	2.95	
15	*SCHLOSS JOHANNISBERG*	Vintage, Feine Spaetlese. Rare flavor! and nicely, lightly sweet . . . another "great."	5.50	
16	*KREUZNACHER STEINBERG*	Anheuser and Fehrs. From the Nahe River Valley . . . a wonderfully light, rare, subtle bouquet . . . so very drinkable.	3.25	
17	*BERNKASTELLER DOKTOR SPAETLESE*	Dr. Thanisch, vintage. Only thirteen acres, three owners . . . Dr. Thanisch owns the sunny side, the best side! . . . probably the finest Moselle made.	8.40	
18	*GEWURTZTRAMINER*	Almaden, Paicines Vineyard, California. Fragrant, delicate, like eating pretty flowers only better !	3.00	1.65
19	*JOHANNISBERG RIESLING*	Louis M. Martini. From the famed Napa Valley, California . . . depth and finesse. Produced from the true white Riesling.	3.45	
20	*DELAWARE*	Great Western, New York State. A crisp pleasure from the Finger Lakes region	3.35	1.90
		WHITE BURGUNDY		
21	*POUILLY FUISSÉ*	Vintage, Frank Schoonmaker. Delicate . . . somewhat tart, a nice luncheon partner.	2.90	1.60
22	*CHABLIS*	Vintage, Jacques Prieur. Twice as much "Chablis" is sold as is produced, so the shipper's name is most important. Frederick Wildman, not a compromising man, is the shipper!	3.90	
23	*LE MONTRACHET*	Vintage, Baron Thenard. The most expensive dry, white wine of France . . . many experts say the finest white made anywhere. Your opinion?	12.95	
24	*PINOT CHARDONNAY*	Vintage, Frank Schoonmaker. True Chablis is made only from the Chardonnay variety. A Schoonmaker selection is always excellent!	2.00	
25	*CHABLIS*	Wente Brothers, Livermore, California. A small vineyard, and this country's finest producer of white wines.	2.45	1.25
		WHITE BORDEAUX		
26	*CHATEAU COUHINS*	Vintage, Graves. Medium-bodied, dry, white . . . an excellent buy.	3.10	1.60
27	*SEMILLON*	Haut Sauterne, Wente Brothers. The first American "varietal." Moderately sweet and of rare bouquet . . . a fine wine by any standard.	2.15	1.40
28	*CHATEAU d'YQUEM*	Vintage, Gran Cru. Luscious, sweet, so fragrant . . . the world's finest Sauternes!	11.40	
		LOIRE WINES		
29	*POUILLY-FUME*	Pouilly-sur-Loire, vintage. Chateau du Nozet, Ladoucette Freres. An extremely good white wine produced from the Sauvignon blanc variety. Light, fragrant, and young as it should be!	3.75	2.10
30	*VOUVRAY*	Marc Bredif, Estate Bottled, vintage. From year to year Vouvrays vary in taste, color, degree of dryness and stillness. This beauty is moderately dry, crisp, and nicely aged another perfect white wine.	3.95	

The wine list (reproduced on pages 153 and 154) *is designed to reflect the care which this food service operator used in assembling his wine offerings.*

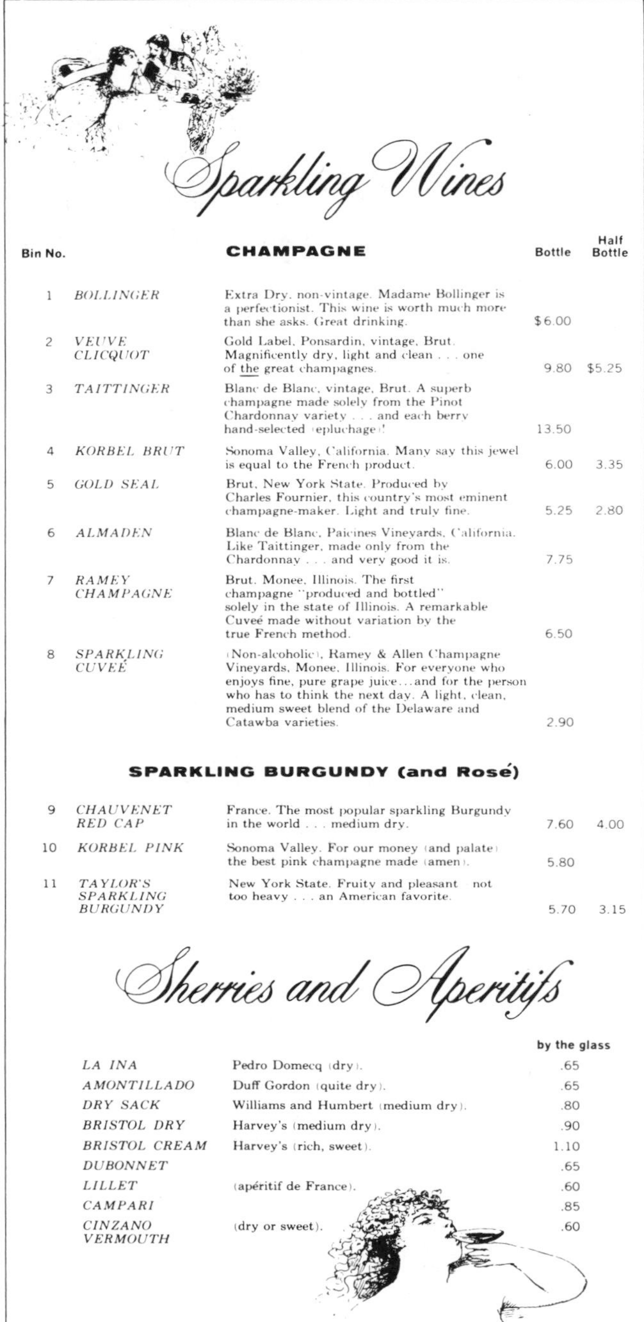

Sparkling Wines

Bin No.	CHAMPAGNE		Bottle	Half Bottle
1	*BOLLINGER*	Extra Dry, non-vintage. Madame Bollinger is a perfectionist. This wine is worth much more than she asks. Great drinking.	$6.00	
2	*VEUVE CLICQUOT*	Gold Label, Ponsardin, vintage, Brut. Magnificently dry, light and clean . . . one of the great champagnes.	9.80	$5.25
3	*TAITTINGER*	Blanc de Blanc, vintage, Brut. A superb champagne made solely from the Pinot Chardonnay variety . . . and each berry hand-selected (epluchage)!	13.50	
4	*KORBEL BRUT*	Sonoma Valley, California. Many say this jewel is equal to the French product.	6.00	3.35
5	*GOLD SEAL*	Brut, New York State. Produced by Charles Fournier, this country's most eminent champagne-maker. Light and truly fine.	5.25	2.80
6	*ALMADEN*	Blanc de Blanc, Paicines Vineyards, California. Like Taittinger, made only from the Chardonnay . . . and very good it is.	7.75	
7	*RAMEY CHAMPAGNE*	Brut. Monee, Illinois. The first champagne "produced and bottled" solely in the state of Illinois. A remarkable Cuveé made without variation by the true French method.	6.50	
8	*SPARKLING CUVEÉ*	(Non-alcoholic), Ramey & Allen Champagne Vineyards, Monee, Illinois. For everyone who enjoys fine, pure grape juice...and for the person who has to think the next day. A light, clean, medium sweet blend of the Delaware and Catawba varieties.	2.90	

SPARKLING BURGUNDY (and Rosé)

Bin No.			Bottle	Half Bottle
9	*CHAUVENET RED CAP*	France. The most popular sparkling Burgundy in the world . . . medium dry.	7.60	4.00
10	*KORBEL PINK*	Sonoma Valley. For our money (and palate) the best pink champagne made (amen).	5.80	
11	*TAYLOR'S SPARKLING BURGUNDY*	New York State. Fruity and pleasant not too heavy . . . an American favorite.	5.70	3.15

Sherries and Aperitifs

		by the glass
LA INA	Pedro Domecq (dry).	.65
AMONTILLADO	Duff Gordon (quite dry).	.65
DRY SACK	Williams and Humbert (medium dry).	.80
BRISTOL DRY	Harvey's (medium dry).	.90
BRISTOL CREAM	Harvey's (rich, sweet).	1.10
DUBONNET		.65
LILLET	(apéritif de France).	.60
CAMPARI		.85
CINZANO VERMOUTH	(dry or sweet).	.60

In both selection and listing this is an excellent wine list, and it can be followed by any food service operator who wants to create a fine wine list. (See page 153 for rest of list.)

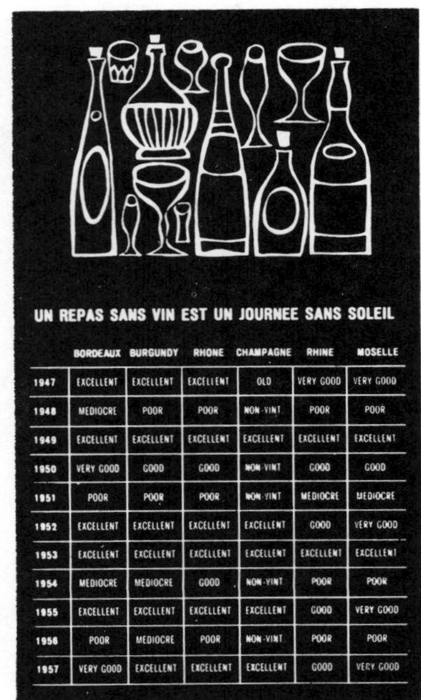

UN REPAS SANS VIN EST UN JOURNEE SANS SOLEIL

	BORDEAUX	BURGUNDY	RHONE	CHAMPAGNE	RHINE	MOSELLE
1947	EXCELLENT	EXCELLENT	EXCELLENT	OLD	VERY GOOD	VERY GOOD
1948	MEDIOCRE	POOR	POOR	NON-VINT	POOR	POOR
1949	EXCELLENT	EXCELLENT	EXCELLENT	EXCELLENT	EXCELLENT	EXCELLENT
1950	VERY GOOD	GOOD	GOOD	NON-VINT	GOOD	GOOD
1951	POOR	POOR	POOR	NON-VINT	MEDIOCRE	MEDIOCRE
1952	EXCELLENT	EXCELLENT	EXCELLENT	EXCELLENT	GOOD	VERY GOOD
1953	EXCELLENT	EXCELLENT	EXCELLENT	EXCELLENT	EXCELLENT	EXCELLENT
1954	MEDIOCRE	MEDIOCRE	GOOD	NON-VINT	POOR	POOR
1955	EXCELLENT	EXCELLENT	EXCELLENT	EXCELLENT	GOOD	VERY GOOD
1956	POOR	MEDIOCRE	POOR	NON-VINT	POOR	POOR
1957	VERY GOOD	EXCELLENT	EXCELLENT	EXCELLENT	GOOD	VERY GOOD

A vintage rating chart is a good guide for the wine ordering customer.

NO.	BORDEAUX, RED	VINT.	BOT.	½ BOT.
185	CHÂTEAU LA TOUR CANON *Fronsac*	1950	27/6	
140	CHÂTEAU MARTINET *Grand Cru Saint-Emilion*	1950	27/6	
195	CHÂTEAU MEYNEY *Saint-Estèphe*	1950	29/–	
	CHÂTEAU COS D'ESTOURNEL *2me Cru Saint-Estèphe*	1953	29/–	15/–
194	CHÂTEAU CHEVAL-BLANC *1er Grand Cru Saint-Emilion*	1953	30/–	16/–
188	CHÂTEAU SMITH-HAUT-LAFITTE *Graves. Château Bottled*	1952	32/6	
114	CHÂTEAU LÉOVILLE-POYFERRÉ *2me Cru Saint-Julien*	1953	29/–	
183	CHÂTEAU RAUSAN-SÉGLA *2me Cru Margaux. Château Bottled*	1937	45/–	
138	CHÂTEAU MOUTON-ROTHSCHILD *2me Cru Pauillac. Château Bottled*	1952		
134	CHÂTEAU HAUT-BRION *1er Cru Pessac. Château Bottled*	1950	52/6	
122	CHÂTEAU LATOUR *1er Cru Pauillac. Château Bottled*	1950	52/6	
95	CHÂTEAU LAFITE-ROTHSCHILD *1er Cru Pauillac. Château Bottled*	1950	52/6	
86	CHÂTEAU MARGAUX *1er Cru Margaux. Château Bottled*	1934		

This wine list shows vintage years of wine served.

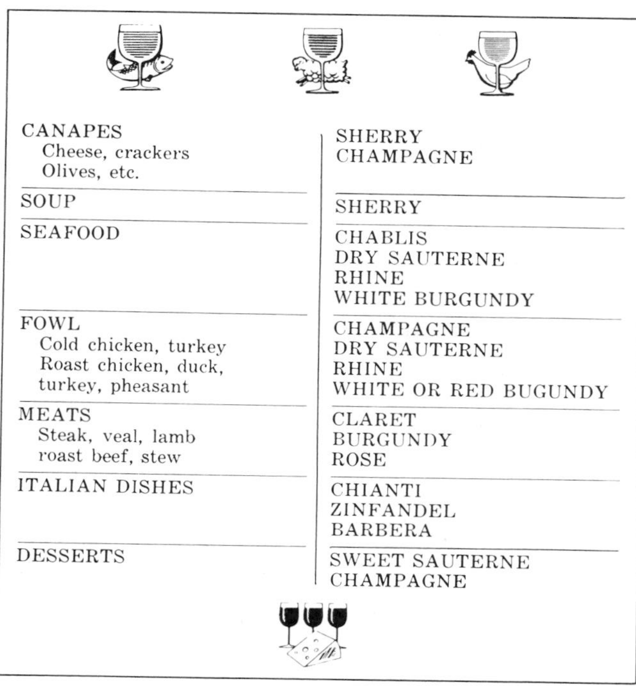

CANAPES Cheese, crackers Olives, etc.	SHERRY CHAMPAGNE
SOUP	SHERRY
SEAFOOD	CHABLIS DRY SAUTERNE RHINE WHITE BURGUNDY
FOWL Cold chicken, turkey Roast chicken, duck, turkey, pheasant	CHAMPAGNE DRY SAUTERNE RHINE WHITE OR RED BUGUNDY
MEATS Steak, veal, lamb roast beef, stew	CLARET BURGUNDY ROSE
ITALIAN DISHES	CHIANTI ZINFANDEL BARBERA
DESSERTS	SWEET SAUTERNE CHAMPAGNE

A wine and food affinity chart helps the customer select the wine most suitable to the food being eaten.

Bohemian Grove Wine List

1960

WHITES

*1.	Bohemian Club White, Inglenook Vineyard	$1.20
2.	Grey Riesling, Wente Bros.	1.60
3.	Johannisberger Riesling, Souverain	2.00
4.	Traminer, Charles Krug	1.90
5.	Pinot Chardonnay, 1958, Wente Bros.	2.20
6.	Gewüerztraminer, 1957, Gaschy	2.60
7.	Schloss Vollards, 1955, Originalabfülling	3.30

PINKS

*10.	Bohemian Club Vin Rosé, Charles Krug	1.20
11.	Grenache Rosé, Almadén Vineyard	1.60

REDS

21.	Bohemian Club Red, Zinfandel, Martini	1.20
22.	Pinot Noir, 1956, P. R. Beaulieu Vineyard	2.10
*23.	Cabernet Sauvignon, 1954, P.R. Beaulieu Vineyard	2.20
24.	Cabernet Sauvignon, 1949, Hallcrest Vineyard	1.80
25.	Château Belair, 1954, St. Émilion	3.90
26.	Les Grands Eschezaus, 1953, Drouhin	5.30
27.	Aloxe-Corton, Les Chaillots, 1952, Latour	4.00
28.	Châteauneuf-du-Pape, 1955, Chapoutier	3.80

SPARKLING

*30.	Bohemian Club N. V. (California)	4.50
31.	Korbel, Brut	5.15
32.	Deutz, Brut, N. V.	6.30
33.	Roederer "Cristal," 1953, Brut	11.00

*Also available at the Bohemian Grove Grill.

The Bohemian Grove *wine list is a centerpiece for the table. It fits into a wooden holder and is printed on both sides.*

"Wine is one of the most civilized things in the world, and one of the natural things that has been brought to greatest perfection. It offers a greater range for enjoyment and appreciation than possibly any other purely sensory thing that may be purchased."

ERNEST HEMINGWAY

FINE AMERICAN AND IMPORTED WINES

Fine foods deserve fine wines. The management has endeavored to offer our patrons a selection of excellent wines, appropriate to every occasion and menu, and suited to every individual taste. Particular care, too, is taken to serve the wine of your choice at precisely the correct temperature to produce its finest flavor and bouquet.

SPARKLING WINES

Before, During and After Meals	Bottle	½ Bottle	Glass
Great Western Extra Dry Champagne	6.50	3.50	
Great Western Sparkling Red Burgundy (sweet)	6.50	3.50	
Mumm's Cordon Rouge Brut (very dry)	10.75		
Lancers Vin Rosé (Portugal)	6.25	3.50	

APÉRITIF WINES

Before Dinner Wines	
Dubonnet	.75
Duff Gordon Amontillado Sherry (dry and pale)	.75
Martini & Rossi Sweet Italian Vermouth	.60
Noilly Prat French Dry Vermouth	.60
Taylor's Sherry (not sweet or dry)	.60

WHITE DINNER WINES

With Fish, Shellfish, Fowl and Lighter Meats			
Barsac — A. deLuze & Fils Bordeaux (sweet, full-bodied)	4.50	2.50	
Almadén Rhine (semi dry, fruity)	3.25	2.25	.60
Almadén Sauterne (dry, fruity Bordeaux)	3.25	2.25	.60
Almadén Chablis (light, delicate, dry)	3.25	2.25	.60
Liebfraumilch Guilden Krone (medium dry Rhine)	4.75	3.00	
Tavel Rosé (Rosé Rhone wine, delightful with any dish)	3.75	2.50	

RED DINNER WINES

With Steaks, Roasts, Chops, Ham and Heartier Foods			
Beaujolais — A. deLuze & Fils (light Burgundy)	4.50	2.50	
Almadén Claret (fresh, soft, delightful)	3.25	2.25	.60
Almadén Burgundy (full bodied)	3.25	2.25	.60
Melini Chianti Imported	4.50		
Tavel Rosé (Rosé Rhone wine, delightful with any dish)	3.75	2.50	
Tipo California Chianti	2.25		
Mogen David Concord	2.25		.60

DESSERT WINES

To Enhance the Flavor of Every Dessert	Glass
Harvey's Bristol Cream Sherry (full pale)	.95
Molinet Ruby Port (Portugal)	.70
Sandeman Tawny Port (Portugal)	.75
Taylor's Port (sweet)	.60
Taylor's Muscatel	.60
Great Western White Port	.60
Mogen David Concord	.60

A good selection of before-, with-, and after-dinner wines in bottle, half bottle, and glass.

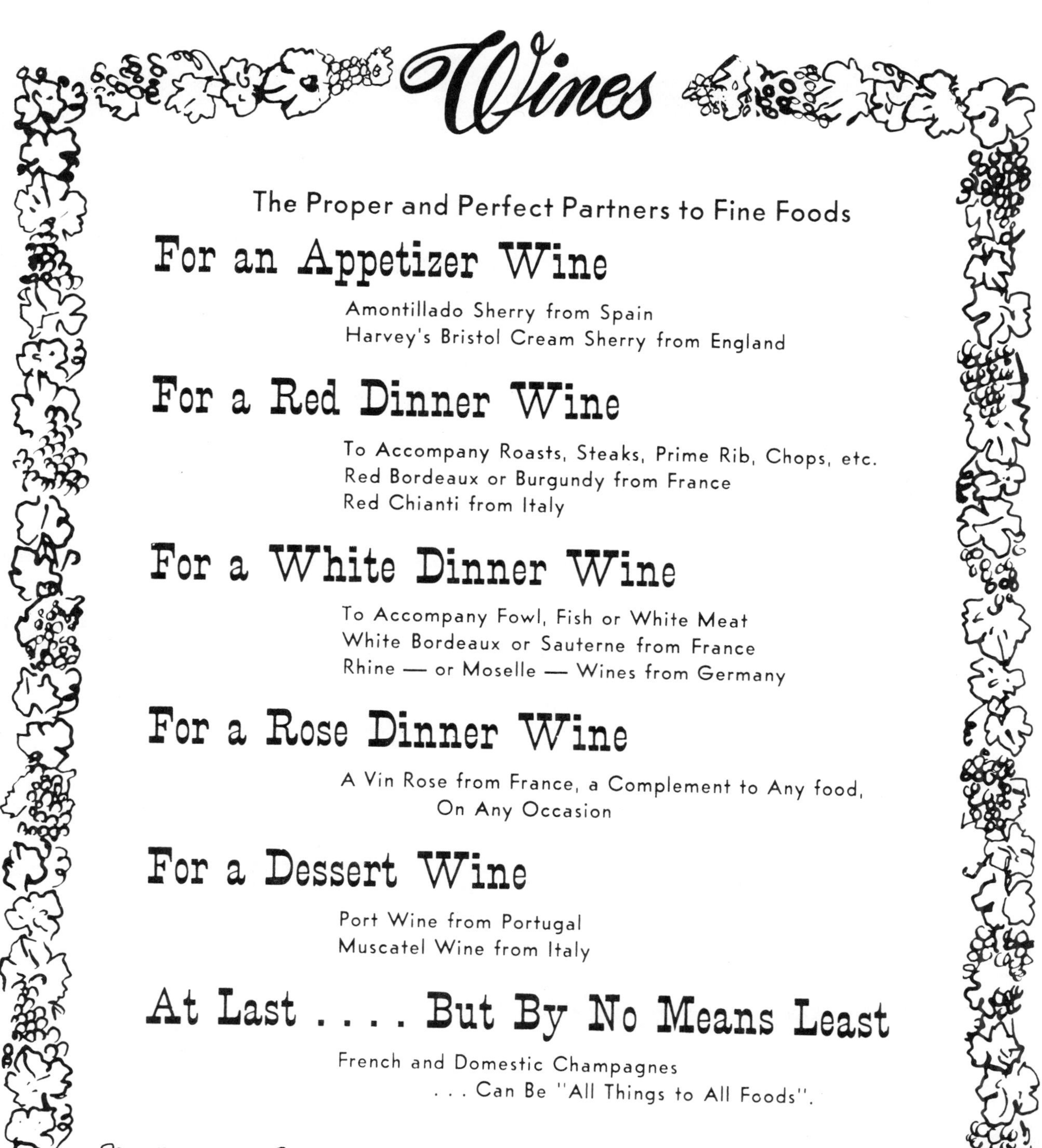

Wines

The Proper and Perfect Partners to Fine Foods

For an Appetizer Wine

Amontillado Sherry from Spain
Harvey's Bristol Cream Sherry from England

For a Red Dinner Wine

To Accompany Roasts, Steaks, Prime Rib, Chops, etc.
Red Bordeaux or Burgundy from France
Red Chianti from Italy

For a White Dinner Wine

To Accompany Fowl, Fish or White Meat
White Bordeaux or Sauterne from France
Rhine — or Moselle — Wines from Germany

For a Rose Dinner Wine

A Vin Rose from France, a Complement to Any food,
On Any Occasion

For a Dessert Wine

Port Wine from Portugal
Muscatel Wine from Italy

At Last . . . . But By No Means Least

French and Domestic Champagnes
. . . Can Be "All Things to All Foods".

Good information, attractively presented with good type selection and a decorative border, adds to the wine story.

BORDEAUX CLASSIFICATIONS

MEDOC

Premiers Crus
(FIRST GROWTHS)

CHATEAU LAFITE
CHATEAU LATOUR
CHATEAU MARGAUX
CHATEAU HAUT-BRION (Graves)

Deuxiemes Crus
(SECOND GROWTHS)

Chateau Mouton-Rothschild
Chateau Rausan-Segla
Chateau Rauzan-Gassies
CHATEAU LEOVILLE-LAS CASES
Chateau Leoville-Poyferre
Chateau Leoville-Barton
Chateau Dufort-Vivens
CHATEAU LASCOMBES
Chateau Gruaud-Larose
Chateau Brane-Cantenac
Chateau Pichon-Longueville
Chateau Pichon-Longueville-(Lalande)
Chateau Ducru-Beaucaillou
CHATEAU COS-D'ESTOURNEL
Chateau Montrose

Troisiemes Crus
(THIRD GROWTHS)

Chateau Giscours
Chateau Kirwan
Chateau d'Issan
Chateau Lagrange
Chateau Langoa
Chateau Malescot-Saint-Exupery
Chateau Cantenac-Brown
Chateau Palmer
Chateau la Lagune
Chateau Desmirail
Chateau Calon-Segur
Chateau Ferriere
Chateau Marquis-d'Alesme-Becker
Chateau Boyd-Cantenac

Quatriemes Crus
(FOURTH GROWTHS)

Chateau Saint-Pierre-Bontemps
Chateau Saint-Pierre-Sevaistre
Chateau Branaire-Ducru
Chateau Talbot
Chateau Duhart-Milon
Chateau Poujet
Chateau la-Tour-Carnet
Chateau Rochet
Chateau Beychevelle
Chateau le Prieure
Chateau Marquis de Terme

Cinquiemes Crus
(FIFTH GROWTHS)

Chateau Pontet-Canet
Chateau Batailley
Chateau Haut-Batailley
Chateau Grand-Puy-Lacoste
Chateau Grand-Puy-Ducasse
Chateau Lynch-Bages
Chateau Lynch-Moussas
Chateau Dauzac
Chateau Mouton-d'Armailhacq
Chateau le Tertre
Chateau Haut-Bages
Chateau Pedesclaux
Chateau Belgrave
Chateau Camensac
Chateau Cos-Labory
Chateau Clerc-Milon
Chateau Croizet-Bages
Chateau Cantemerle

ST. EMILION

Premiers Grand Crus
(FIRST GREAT GROWTHS)

CHATEAU AUSONE
Chateau Cheval Blanc
Chateau Beausejour
Chateau Bel-Air
Chateau Canon
Chateau Clos Fourtet
Chateau Figeac
Chateau Magdelaine
CHATEAU PAVIE

POMEROL

Premier Grand Cru
(OUTSTANDING GROWTHS)
(Unofficial)

CHATEAU PETRUS
Chateau l'Evangile
Chateau La Conseillante
Chateau Vieux Certan
Chateau Trotanoy

SAUTERNES

Grand Premier Cru
(GREAT FIRST GROWTH)

CHATEAU D'YQUEM

Premiers Crus
(FIRST GROWTHS)

Chateau La Tour-Blanche
Chateau Peyraguey
Chateau Rayne Vigneau
Chateau Suduiraut
CHATEAU COUTET
Chateau Climens
Chateau Bayle (Guiraud)
Chateau Rieussec
Chateau Rabaud

GRAVES (Red)

(OUTSTANDING VINEYARDS)
(Unofficial)

CHATEAU HAUT BRION
Chateau La Mission Haut Brion
Chateau Pape Clement
Chateau Haut Bailly
Chateau Carbonnieux

GRAVES (White)

(OUTSTANDING GROWTHS)
(Unofficial)

CHATEAU HAUT BRION BLANC
Chateau Carbonnieux
Chateau La Ville Haut Brion
CHATEAU OLIVIER
Domaine de Chevalier

OUTSTANDING WINES of RHINE and MOSELLE

RHINEGAU

(From west to east)

RUDESHEIM–Rudesheimer Berg, Schlossberg, Roseneck

GEISENHEIM–Rotherberg, Katzenloch, Lickerstein

JOHANNISBERG–SCHLOSS JOHANNISBERG, Erntebringer, Holle, Klaus

WINKLER–SCHLOSS VOLLRADS, Hasensprung, Jesuitengarten, Steinacker

MITTELHEIM–Bangert

OESTRICH–Lechnchen, Eiserweg, Doosberg

HALLGARTEN–Schonhelt, Deitelsberg

HATTENHEIM–Engelmannsberg, Willborn, Nussbrunnen

ERBACH-ELTVILLE–Schloss Reinhartshausen, MARKOBRUNN, Bruhl

KLOSTER EBERBACH–Steinberg

KIEDRICH–Grafenberg, Sandgrube

RAUENTHAL–Steinacher, Burggraben

HOCHHEIM–Domdechaney, Daubhaus

RHINEHESSE

(North to south)

LAUBENHEIM–Burg, Edelmann, Kalkofen

BODENHEIM–Kahlenberg, Silberbergt, Burgweg

MACKENHEIM–Rotenberg

NIERSTEIN–Domtal, Glock, Hipping, Rehbach

OPPENHEIM–Sacktreger, Zuckerberg, Schlossberg

WORMS–Liebfrauenkirche (its wine is labeled Liebfrauen Stiftstein or Kirchensteuck, but not Liebfraumilch).

BENSHEIM–Streichling

MIDDLE MOSELLE

(Trier to Traben, south to north)

NEUMANN–Lasenberg

HRON–Hofberg

PIESPORT–Goldtropfchen, Falkenberg, Lay, GRAFENBERG

WINTERICH–Geierslay

BRAUNENBERG–Juffer, Falkenberg

LIESER–Niederberg, Schlossberg

BERNCASTEL-CUES–DOCTOR, Badstube

GRAACH–Domprobst, Himmelrich, Abtei

JOSEPHSHOFER–Josephshofer

WEHLEN–Sonnenuhr, Nonnenlay, Rothlay

ZELTINGER–Himmelrich, Rotlay, Schlossberg

UERZIG–Wurzgarten, Kranklay

ERDEN–Treppchen, Pralat, Herrenberg

CROV–Crover-Steffenberg

OUTSTANDING WINES OF BURGUNDY

GEVREY-CHAMBERTIN

Tetes de Cuvees
(OUTSTANDING VINEYARDS)

Le Chambertin
CHAMBERTIN CLOS DE BEZE

Premiers Crus
(FIRST GROWTHS)

Latricieres
Mazoyeres
Charmes
MAZIS
Ruchottes
Griotte
Chapelle

MOREY-SAINT-DENIS

Tetes de Cuvees
(OUTSTANDING VINEYARDS)

Clos de Tart
Clos des Lambrays
Bonnes-Mares

CHAMBOLLE-MUSIGNY

Tetes de Cuvees
(OUTSTANDING VINEYARDS)

LES MUSIGNY
Les Bonnes-Mares

Premiers Crus
(FIRST GROWTHS)

Les Amoureuses

VOUGEOT

Tete de Cuvee
(OUTSTANDING VINEYARD)

CLOS DE VOUGEOT

FLAGEY-ECHEZEAUX

Tetes de Cuvees
(OUTSTANDING VINEYARDS)

Les Grands-Echezeaux
Les Echezeaux

VOSNE-ROMANEE

Tetes de Cuvees
(OUTSTANDING VINEYARDS)

Romanee-Conti
La Romanee
La Tache
Les Gaudichots
LES RICHEBOURG

Premiers Crus
(FIRST GROWTHS)

La Romanee Saint-Vivant
Les Malconsorts
Les Beaux-Monts
Les Suchots

NUITS-SAINT-GEORGES

Tetes de Cuvees
(OUTSTANDING VINEYARDS)

Les Saint Georges
Les Boudots
Les Cailles
Les Porrets
Les Pruliers
LES VAUCRAINS

ALOXE-CORTON

Tetes de Cuvees
(OUTSTANDING VINEYARDS)

Le Corton
LE CLOS DU ROI
CHARLEMAGNE
Les Bressandes
Les Renardes

BEAUNE

Tetes de Cuvees
(OUTSTANDING VINEYARDS)

LES FEVES
Les Greves
Les Marconnets
Les Bressandes
Les Clos de Mouches

POMMARD

Tetes de Cuvees
(OUTSTANDING VINEYARDS)

Les Epenots
LES RUGIENS

Premiers Crus
(FIRST GROWTHS)

La Platiere
Les Pezerolles
Les Petite Epenots
Clos de la Cammaraine
Les Jarollieres

VOLNAY

Tetes de Cuvees
(OUTSTANDING VINEYARDS)

Les Caillerets
Les Champans
Les Premiets
Santenots

MEURSAULT

Tetes de Cuvees
(OUTSTANDING VINEYARDS)

Clos de Perrieres
Les Perrieres

Premiers Crus
(FIRST GROWTHS)

LES GENEVRIERES
Les Charmes (Dessus)
Santenots
Sous Blagny

PULIGNY-MONTRACHET

Tetes de Cuvees
(OUTSTANDING VINEYARDS)

LE MONTRACHET

Premiers Crus
(FIRST GROWTHS)

Le Chevalier Montrachet
Le Batard Montrachet
Les Combettes
Blagny-Blanc
Champ-Canet
La Pucelle

CHASSAGNE-MONTRACHET

Tetes de Cuvees
(OUTSTANDING VINEYARDS)

LE MONTRACHET

Premiers Crus
(FIRST GROWTHS)

Le Batard Montrachet
Les Ruchottes
Cailleret

CHABLIS

Grand Crus
(OUTSTANDING GROWTHS)

Vaudesir
LES CLOS
Blanchots
Bougros
Valmur
Grenouilles
Les Preuses
La Moutonne

General information about wine gives your wine list a more authentic aspect.

The *Criterion* Fine Steak Restaurant in Miami and Tampa, Florida, does a very thorough as well as creative job of selling wine through its Wine Book. It is both a big and a little wine list. It is only 5″ × 6½″ in size, but it has 52 pages plus a 4-page cover. Printed in only one color, black, it is perfect-bound like a book.

It begins with a Table of Contents, and then has an easy to read page (not too much copy) on "How to Select Wine" (a good way to start). Sixteen different categories of wine are listed.

Under the heading Champagne, for example, first there is a photo of a bottle—Taittinger—against a map of France with an indication of the area in France where Champagne comes from. Facing the photo is a page of description, short but very adequate. On the following page, eight different champagnes are offered, in bottles and half bottles. Bin numbers are used for easy ordering—for the customer who hesitates over French pronunciation—and for easy serving; the waiter can go right to the bin and pick out the correct wine.

This Wine List Book is very complete. The classifications include: Champagne, Sparkling Wines, Red Burgundy, White Burgundy, Red Wines of the Rhone, White Wines of the Loire Valley, Red Bordeaux, White Bordeaux, Rose Wines, Spanish Wines, Italian Wines, California Wines, Japanese Wines, and Magnums of Wine.

The only criticism is that Japanese Wines are not usually included in a fine wine list. The listing Magnums of Wine is very good. The copy reads, "If you have six or more people in your dinner party, we suggest the following wines, available in Magnum size." A good idea.

While functioning as a selling tool, the Wine Book is also sold for $1.00. To write a book of this size, range, and accuracy takes someone with a knowledge of wine or else a writer who can research the subject thoroughly. To begin with, the wine cellar of the *Criterion* restaurants is very complete and indicates a buyer and/or a wine merchant of very high competence.

One aspect of the *Criterion* Wine Book is that the customer can go back to it time after time, whenever he or she is eating at the restaurant. It would take a long time to "drink through" this list while learning about wine. There are 36 different California Wines, for example, and 18 Chateaux Wines of Bordeaux. Altogether, 152 different wines are served from this cellar.

Old World and New World WINES

Since the dawn of civilization wine has held an important place in man's inventory of delights and necessities. It long ago became a basic medium in the art of dining.

When America was young, slips were cut from the vines of the great vineyards of Europe, tenderly wrapped and brought to these shores as part of the humble treasures of the early settlers. Many were brought by monks to serve the need for sacramental wines in the New World missions.

Here these cuttings found similar combinations of soil, climate, and sunlight on the hills overlooking New York's Finger Lakes and on the foothill slopes along the great valleys of California. From these slips out of century-old vineyards in Europe has developed a great American wine industry, producing today not only the traditional wines but many new varieties. Thus, the Hershey Motor Lodge wine cellar is international, too, providing a colorful assortment of the finest in imported and American wines.

PLANNING YOUR DINNER

To assist you in planning a completely delightful meal, this menu has been designed to offer appropriate wines for each course of your dinner. They appear on the page opposite our food course offerings: aperitif wines with appetizers, dinner wines with entrees. Your preference, however, may be one wine or possibly a champagne to complement your entire meal. We hope your dining adventure in the Hershey Motor Lodge will be complete in enjoyment and truly memorable.

As Ben Johnson once said, "Eat thy bread with joy and drink thy wine with a merry heart."

Copy like this creates a "wine atmosphere" on the menu.

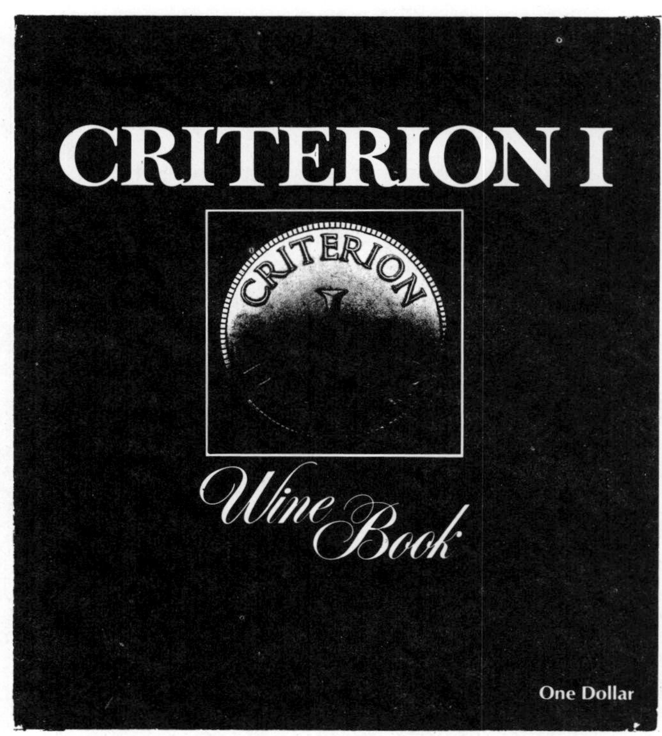

How to select wine.

Selecting the right wine to complement a meal has provided many a diner with vast pleasure. But there are so many wines and so many rules, the choice may indeed seem bewildering.

We suggest you start with the traditional pairings of food and wine and see why so many people have found them rewarding. As you discover your own preferences, you may wish to experiment. After all, wine is meant to be enjoyed. And rules are meant to be broken.

The broad generalization of "white wine with white meat and red wine with red meat" has merit to it. It also has some notable exceptions. Consequently, Criterion I is pleased to offer an expansive selection of rich full bodied reds and a comparably large selection of whites. Seafood almost always causes red wine to taste slightly odd; therefore a chilled white wine is preferable. Yet many people enjoy white wine with steak.

Another point to be considered is how the food is prepared. The heartier the dish, the fuller flavored the wine should be.

Rosé wines and dry champagne are generally considered safe choices for any meal. If you enjoy them, by all means, choose them. But please don't be limited to them simply because they're safe.

We remind you that there are many kinds of wine—all worth your exploration. And what may at first appear to be a bewildering choice can become a delight—and a gastronomic adventure.

5

The Criterion I *wine list is more than just a list. It is a complete, if miniature, wine book.*

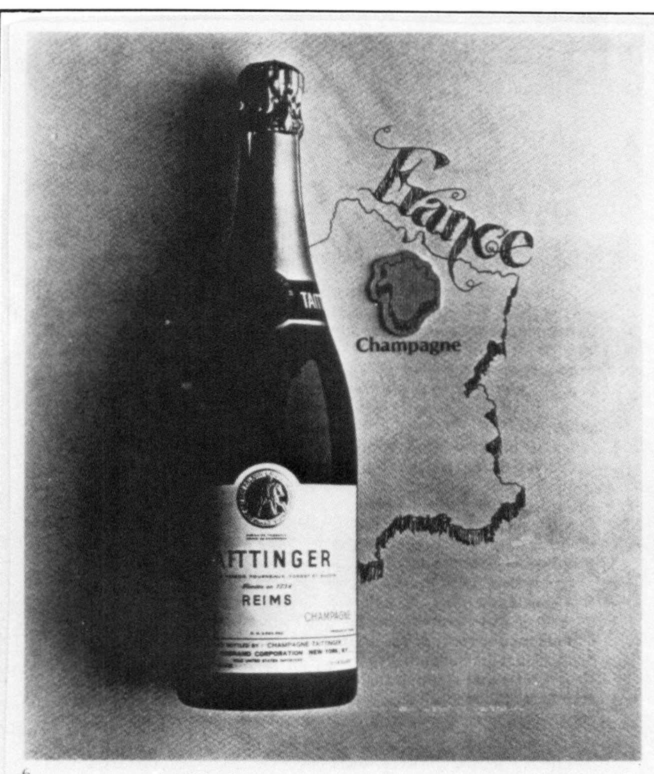

Champagne

If excitement has a taste, it tastes like champagne. On at least two continents, nothing says hooray quite like a bottle of champagne.

And if there's any question as to what goes with champagne, there's an easy answer: Champagne tastes great with everything. Strictly speaking, the only sparkling wines that may legally be classified as champagne come from the tiny region of Champagne, some 90 miles northeast of Paris. The chalky subsoils and short ripening season of the area help give champagne part of its distinctive flavor.

Each bottle of champagne produced requires some six to seven years of tender handling—including racking, blending, disgorging (removing sediment) and storing at a constant temperature until it is matured. This explains some of the costliness of champagne—and why almost all champagnes are made by large companies with the facilities and capital necessary for such grandiose undertakings.

Great vintage champagnes improve with age and keep up to two decades; non-vintage champagnes keep up to seven years under proper storage.

Sec denotes dry champagne; Extra Sec champagne is dryer still, and Brut is the dryest of all. If you prefer a sweeter taste, try one labeled rich, doux or dry.

6 7

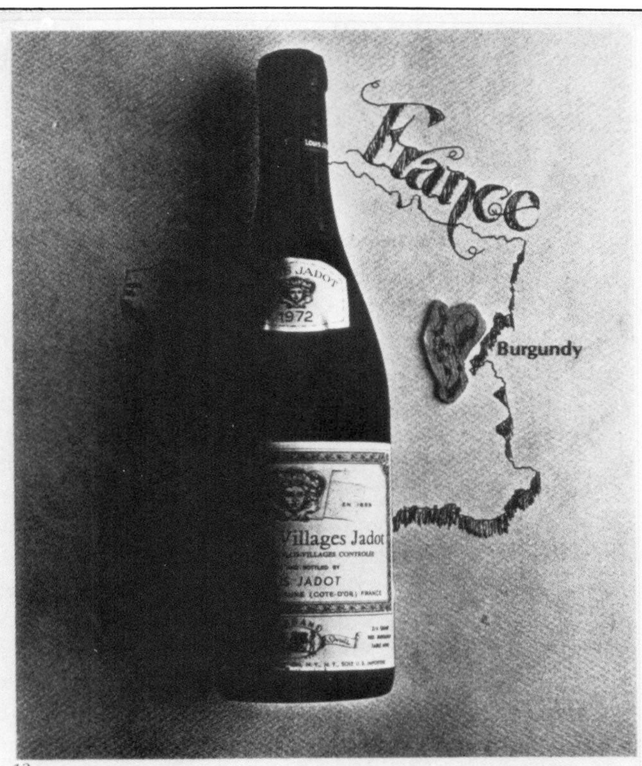

Red Burgundy

The heart of Burgundy, source of those superlative ruby-coloured wines acclaimed throughout the world, is a single slope about thirty-one miles long, known as the Cote d'Or. By law, only one grape varietal, the majestic Pinot, may be grown in the Cote d'Or.

The Cote d'Or is divided in the middle by a quarry. The northern half, or Cote de Nuits, produces full-bodied wines that epitomize everything a great Burgundy should be—at once powerful and delicate, substantial yet exquisite. The southern slope, or Cote de Beaune, produces wines that are soft, slightly dry and lighter in flavor.

Moving south, we find the Beaujolais district home of fruity, lively wines produced from the Gamay grape. Unlike the Cote d'Or wines which develop with age, Beaujolais is best drunk young. Beaujolais also benefits from chilling. A neighboring district, Macon, also produces some very good red wines.

No.	WINES OF THE COTE DE NUITS	Bottle	Half Bottle
5238	Gevrey Chambertin,Sichel, Vintage	11.50	6.25
5264	Nuits St. Georges, Jadot, Vintage	15.00	
5234	Eschezeaux, Vintage	20.00	
5280	Grands Eschezeaux, Vintage	24.00	
5256	Chambolle Musigny, Jadot, Vintage	15.00	
5218	Charmes Chambertin, Sichel, Vintage	13.50	
5250	Richebourg, Sichel, Vintage	13.50	
5214	Bonne Mares, Sichel, Vintage	26.00	

12 13

24
Steak merchandising

Don't just list your steaks, sell them with informative, descriptive, merchandising copy that motivates the guest. Expensive items deserve top billing on any restaurant menu. Most restaurants list steaks on their menu, but in too many cases it is only a listing. The supposition is probably that everybody knows what a steak is, so why talk about it. This, however, is not the case. In the first place, there are many kinds of steaks, and in the second place, there are many grades of steaks. These two factors alone call for copy, and when you combine them with size, weight, and type of preparation, you can see that there is plenty to talk about. The following is "steak copy" which can be used by any restaurant to increase "steak business," which, considering prices, is an important part of any restaurant.

STEAK DESCRIPTIONS

1. Porterhouse—this is considered by some to be the finest, greatest steak cut of all. It is a combination of two steaks in one divided by the bone, a filet and a strip steak. Aged and broiled on the bone to retain more juice, this is a steak to take the appetite by the horns!
2. Filet Mignon—this is the tenderest steak of all, cuts like butter, melts in your mouth! Specially selected from heavy U.S. choice tenderloins; selection, aging, and trimming make this filet fabulously flavorful.
3. T-Bone—the steak that "won the West," practically two steaks in one. You get a U.S. prime center-cut strip plus a small filet. Broiled "bone-in" for extra flavor to make appetites expand.
4. Tenderloin—a large cut of U.S. choice tenderloin with a slight trace of sweet fat for flavor makes this choice cut "tenderful and flavor fabulous," an all-time favorite.
5. Bone-in-Strip—sometimes called Kansas City sirloin, this is the same strip as the sirloin—tender, flavorful, succulent. The bone, however, is not trimmed away. Broiling with the bone helps broil in more flavor and juice. This is a great steak worthy of any gourmet prize.
6. Strip Sirloin—often called New York strip or New York sirloin, this is a tender, but not too tender, filet that is even more flavorful than the regular filet. The sweet, prime fat on the sides of this cut should be eaten with the meat to make it even tastier. A steak worthy of the name Sir Loin!
7. Butterfly Filet—this is the same piece of U.S. choice as Filet Mignon but sliced lengthwise before cooking. The chef suggests this steak for those who order steaks medium well to well done. All the tender, soft, juicy flavor will make you say—"well done!"
8. Tip Butt Sirloin—a solid, generous cut of top U.S. prime beef done to perfection. Easy on the budget, this steak will satisfy the biggest appetite ever. Called Club or Chef's Special some places, this steak has all the taste appeal of prime grade beef, an All American Favorite!
9. Chateaubriand—the royalty of steak, prepared and served for two or more, the chateaubriand is a king size cut of tenderloin broiled, with the grain running horizontal, against the heat. This gives a succulent, crisp, tender crust with a pink, warm center. This is an "occasion" steak which should be sliced cross-grain and served with a good wine and enjoyed by good company.
10. Chopped Steak—a generous tasty serving

using only U.S. choice and prime beef, and lifted out of the ordinary with whipped egg and good burgundy wine, a 'good eatin' item.

While steak descriptions are probably the most important words on your steak menu, the question of how the customer likes his steak is also important in keeping him happy. In order that everyone has the same definitions, it is well to print the descriptions in the adjoining column and also to tell your guests what grade you serve:

HOW DO YOU LIKE STEAK?

1. Rare—brown, seared crust with a cool red center.
2. Medium Rare—brown, seared crust, steak warmed through with a red warm center.
3. Medium—outside of steak well done, dark brown with a pink hot center.
4. Medium Well—outside dark brown, inside done through, steak has little juice left.
5. Well Done—outside black-brown, inside dried out, restaurant not responsible for well done steaks.

What kind of meat (in the form of steak) does your restaurant serve? If you serve good meat, say so. The following is a list of U.S. Beef Grades:

BEEF GRADES

1. Prime—highest possible quality beef, flavorful, juicy, and tender. From young, well-fed beef cattle, this lean meat is well "marbled" with fat.
2. Choice—this is high quality beef with less fat than prime. Highly acceptable and palatable, this is juicy and tender meat.
3. Good—this meat has little fat, therefore lacks juiciness of higher quality beef, but with acceptable quality.
4. Standard—thin fat covering, meat is mild, unflavorful, and lacking in juice.

The final thing to remember about your steak menu listing is that we are talking about important, expensive items on your menu that deserve "Top Billing." This means that they should get the best possible portion on the menu, be set in the largest type that you use for listing and they should get the most descriptive, merchandising, sell copy.

Know Your Steaks

• A steak by any other name is still a steak, but when it's called a Delmonico or a shell steak you may have trouble identifying the exact cut. Here is a list of common steaks, giving, first, the name used by the U.S. Department of Agriculture and the National Live Stock and Meat Board, then other names by which the cut is known in various sections of the country. To make sure of getting the cut you want, check the sketches.

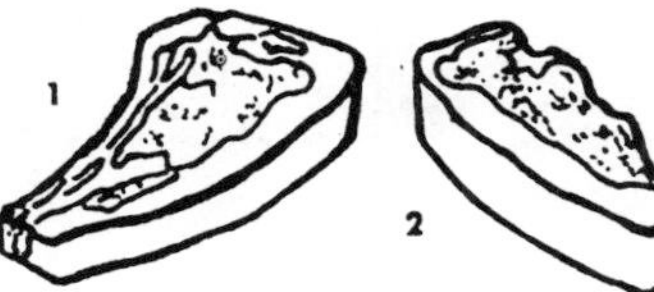

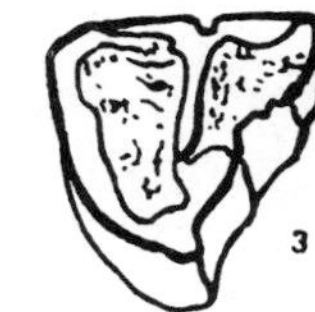

1. Club steak: Delmonico steak, T-bone steak, porterhouse steak, sirloin strip steak.

2. Top loin steak or New York Cut: Kansas City steak, boneless hip steak, shell steak, boneless hotel steak, minute sirloin steak, loin strip steak, Delmonico steak, club steak, boneless sirloin steak.

3. Porterhouse and T-Bone steaks: Tenderloin steak, club steak.

4. Tenderloin or Filet mignon: (Chateaubriand steak), filet.

5. Sirloin steak: Hip steak, short hip steak, sirloin butt steak, rump steak.

The more you tell, the more you sell, applies to steaks as well as the rest of the menu.

Steak House Special . . .

STEAKS

To help stamp out home cooking

THE FIESTA PORTERHOUSE: Best we got, an extra thick so thick you won't want it cooked no more than medium, with salad, taters and coffee.
4.75

THE FLYING T-BONE: A man-sized slab of meat that sprawls all over the platter, so that it don't hardly leave no room for the taters. You get salad and coffee, too.
3.85

RANCHERS STRIP STEAK: A thick hunk of extra fine flavored steak for when you aint hongrey enough to tackle the Fiesta, with all the handsome fringe beneyfits, too.
3.50

THE ROUGH-HOUSE: Also knowed as the poremans T-bone, cut from where the reglar T-bone plays out, with salad, taters, and a heaping glass of ice water.
3.40

DELMONICO STEAK: Enough to please anyone.
3.15

RANCHERS RIB STEAK: Purt 'n' near the same as the rough-house, an you git salad, taters and coffee, too.
2.95

SIRLOIN TIP: Delicious, juicy sirloin smothered with mush-rooms or onions. Salad, taters and coffee.
2.35

LADIES SPECIAL: A tremendous minaturee filly clobbered with mushrooms. And you get salad, taters and coffee, too.
2.60

THE CHARKY: Sirloin, cooked with charcoal seasoning to give it that cooked out-of-doors flavor. For folks who dont have their own Bar-B-Qpit. Salad and taters, too.
1.80

STEERBURGER STEAK: Half a pound of steerburger meat cooked the way you like it, steak style, salad and taters, too.
1.35

FRENCHMAN'S STEAK: Served with Roquefort Salad, Potatoes and Beverage.
2.70

An interesting selection of steaks very well described with creative selling copy. The type is also large and easy to read.

ENTRECOTE DOUBLE (For Two)

An Extra Thick Cut of Charcoal Broiled Blue Ribbon Prime Strip Sirloin Flamed and Carved at Your Table. A Beautiful Array of Fresh Vegetables en Bordure. Your Selection of Salad and Potato. Hot Rolls and Butter.

13.00 (for 2)

We Suggest Champagne or Burgundy

CHATEAUBRIAND BOUQUETIERE (For Two)

A Double Special Center Cut from a Selected Prime Beef Tenderloin. Garden Fresh Vegetables en Bordure. Potato and Salad Selections of Your Choice. Flamed at Table-side for Added Flavor. Hot Rolls and Butter.

13.00 (for 2)

We Recommend Beaujolais or Pommard

TOURNEDOS ROSSINI

Two Delicate Tenderloin Steaks Broiled to a Turn. Served with a Broiled Tomato and an Intriguing Deviled Butter Sauce Prepared and Flamed at Table-side. Tossed Salad and Your Choice of Vegetable or Potato. Hot Rolls and Butter.

5.75

We Suggest Rosé or Burgundy

Dressed-up beef for two or beef prepared in a special manner with wine suggestions add up to steak specials that make dining an occasion and help pay the overhead.

Old Time Western Cattle Ranchers Who Should Know, Prefer Their Steaks 'Charred'. These Are Seared and Charred On The Outside and Remain Rare Or Very Rare On The Inside. Accomplished With Tenderloin Or 'Sir-Loin' Steaks Only.

Treat Yourself To It . . .

No Extra Charge.

A bit of "extra" steak copy.

OMAHA STEAKS FROM OUR AGEING ROOM

CHARCOAL BROILED OMAHA FILET MIGNON (Hi-Protein and Lean) . . . .

Here you will find a tasty, juicy, tender . . . real delicious Steak that is also very **lean.** Those eating just for pleasure or folks on a "Lean Meat" and Hi-Protein Diet, can find great enjoyment with this fine steak. This tender piece of steak is a favorite with many. (With Idaho Baked Potato)

PRIME RIB ROAST OF BEEF, WITH AU JUS (June thru Oct.) . . . .

This beautiful Beef from Steers that have been kept over an extra year on CORN, is well floured and marbled. Roasted under a Blanket of Rock Salt to insure full flavor and juiciness. This is Roast Beef at its BEST (With Idaho Baked Potato) PLEASE DO NOT ASK FOR MEDIUM OR WELL-DONE PRIME RIB. It only comes PINK RARE accomplished by roasting in a slow oven under the heavy cover of Rock Salt. We do have two "outside cuts" on each loin which gives us a very few outside cuts. BUT WE ONLY SERVE THE PRIME RIB . . .PINK RARE: Which Beef lovers demand and we cater to them.

CHARCOAL BROILED "SHORT LOIN" STEAK (11-oz.) . . . .

These delicious and tasty "short loins of beef" are selected especially for us. These Steaks, in the Loin, are carefully "aged" in our modern Beef Ageing Room (Customers are welcome to see). For those who are interested in "cuts" of meat . . . the "Short Loin" is that section of beef, found only between the "hipbone and the rib". This Steak is our favorite recommendation. Tender, full of delicious juice and flavor . . . A REAL HEALTH BUILDER. (With Idaho Baked Potato)

DOUBLE "XX" SHORT LOIN STEAK. (Full 1-lb.) . . . .

Double "XX" Steak is named after a Beef Ranch in Nebraska. This Double "XX" Steak is from steers . . . carried over an extra year on corn. **Our Favorite** when you **are real hungry.** A REAL CELEBRATING MEAL! (With Idaho Baked Potato)

Each year, we have Swift and Co. of Omaha, Neb., buy just over 700 head of **Half White Faced Herefords** and **Half Black Angus.** See if you can tell the difference! (This is Prime Beef) After they have been fattened on CORN. **(Corn is low in unsaturated fat)** This gives us a flowing supply of 1,400 Short-Loins for our Steaks. **Our Steaks** are **babied** and **pampered** ALL THE WAY.
Then into our Special "Ageing Room" and then to the Charcoal Broiler and then to you . . .m . . .m . .mm BUT THEY ARE GOOD!
The **Secret** is in **the Corn** and **The Ageing!**

This very good steak listing not only describes the steak individually, it indicates how it is prepared, size by weight, where the quality beef served comes from, and also describes the aging process.

U. S. PRIME N.Y. STRIP SIRLOIN 5.00
A steak of Royal Flavor! It's cut thick and juicy from the top of a beef short loin, then boned and trimmed. We cook it to the tenderest turn, so the meat just sizzles with juicy flavor. Served with Potatoes and Salad.

U. S. PRIME PORTERHOUSE 5.00
A treat for hearty steak eaters! By cutting the heavy end from the T-Bone cut, we create our tender and tempting Porterhouse steaks. Each one is a beauty that rewards your every bite with delite. Served with Salad and Potatoes.

U. S. PRIME FILET MIGNON (For those who want the best) 6.00
A tenderness unexcelled! Prime tenderloin meat with all surface fat and outside membrane material removed. Served with Potatoes and Salad.

If you serve top grade U.S. prime, say so!

All steaks are U.S.D.A. Graded Choice or Better Western Beef

Carefully Selected and Aged
Grilled, or Broiled
All Steaks are Served with Relish Tray
A Large Scrubbed and Rubbed Baked Idaho or French Fries
Green Salad, Choice of Dressing or Cole Slaw
Bread and Beverage

$1.00 Extra will be Charged Persons Sharing a Steak

Our Varieties of Steaks only Requires You to Pay What Your Appetite Calls for

New York Sirloin Strip

10 oz.	$3.75
12 oz.	4.25
16 oz.	5.50
24 oz. Steak for 2	8.50

Filet Mignon Steak

6 oz.	$3.25
8 oz.	4.25
10 oz.	5.25

T Bone Steaks

16 oz. T Bone	$4.25
20 oz. T Bone	5.25

Boneless Club Steak

6 oz.	$2.75
8 oz.	3.50

Fried Sweet Crispy Bermuda Onion Rings 35c

All he-man appetites can be appeased in grand style if the variety of steaks we have listed on our menu does not suit that big hungry man appetite. We will have our Chef roll out the butcher-block and scales, cut and weigh before your eyes any size boneless sirloin steak that your appetite might suggest. This succulent steak is sized and priced at 40c an ounce and, presto, the noblest prime sirloin anyone could command goes back to our broilers to be cooked just the way the KING OF THE ROAD wants it, and all the goodies listed above go with it.

Listing steaks by size with a different price for each size makes sense for both the customer and the food service operator.

STEAK CLUB DINNERS

You are invited to select and brand your steak at our Steak Throne

THE SIRLOIN SALAD
Crisp Tender Salad Greens Flavored with Chopped Chives, Garnished with Tomato, Anchovy and Grated Egg Yolks Blended with your Choice of Dressing

*HEREFORD SIRLOIN ROOM SPECIAL Our Most Popular Bone-in Sirloin Steak	$5.75
*BLACK ANGUS SADDLE & SIRLOIN A Hefty, Hearty Boneless Sirloin as Served in the Club	$6.75
*SHORTHORN TENDERLOIN STEAK Beautifully Finished Filet Mignon Cut from Heavy Beef	$6.25
SIRLOIN ROOM À LA MINUTE Aged Boneless Sirloin, Branded and Fired as a Saddle & Sirloin Jr.	$5.25
TENDERLOIN STEAK À LA MINUTE A Minute Filet Mignon of Beef for the Smaller Appetite	$5.25

SPECIAL STEAK PREPARATION FOR TWO

SADDLE & SIRLOIN ENTRÉCOTE STEAK Bone-in Double Sirloin Steak Thick and Juicy, Sliced at Your Table	$12.00
POSTILLION DOUBLE TENDERLOIN Beautifully Finished Chateaubriand Style Gourmet's Dream . . . Sliced at Your Table	$13.00

CLASSICAL WINE SAUCE WITH STEAKS IF DESIRED

Above entrees include

French Fried Potatoes or Baked Potato — Crispy and Crunchy French Fried Onion Rings

Sour Dough Bread or French Hard Roll

*NOTE: The names of our steaks do not necessarily reflect the fact that these steak cuts come from the breeds named. It is just our way of paying tribute to our nation's traditional breed lines.

The listing of the former Stockyard's Inn, *with its steak selection from a "Steak Throne," is a good model for any food service operation to use.*

25

Describe your seafood

Seafood is an important entree on most food service menus, and its importance should be enhanced by good descriptive, merchandising copy. Many seafood items and methods of preparation are unknown to many guests, so just plain facts are needed in many cases.

A one- or two-sentence line under the seafood listing is usually enough to set the word picture. Some of the points that should be covered in the copy are: where the fish or seafood comes from, how it is prepared, special sauces, flavoring, etc., with a few adjectives like flavorful, epicurean, enticing, mouth-watering, succulent, tender, etc.

When printing the descriptive copy, be sure it is set in a smaller and different typeface from the entree listing, but not so small that it is hard to read. A good rule is to set the entree listing in caps—bold face, and the descriptive copy in a lighter, lower-case typeface. The descriptive copy for seafood entrees reproduced here can be used as examples and guides for your menu:

LOBSTER THERMIDOR (in shell)
Chunks of lobster meat sauteed in butter, blended in our own sherry 'n egg sauce, placed in the original shell, sprinkled with parmesan cheese and baked to an epicurean turn . . . . .

LOBSTER SALAD
A large epicurean delight. Enticing flavor with just the right spice 'n herb combination. Cole slaw and crisp lettuce served with this gourmet treat . . . . .

BROILED SWORDFISH STEAK
Something to write home about. The tender fillet of this exotic fish—found only in the waters of James Michener's South Pacific, served with drawn butter . . . . .

COLUMBIA RIVER SALMON
Only hours ago flashing silver through the cascading Columbia. Fresh, firm, delicate pink, broiled to your taste. Only in the Pacific Northwest do you find this world-famous fish. Find out why salmon is king . . . . .

SHRIMP
They're pink perfection. Straight out of the "Gourmet's Almanack," smacking of that special shrimp flavor—spice too. In essence, nobody prepares shrimp the way we prepare shrimp . . . let us introduce you herewith . . . . .

DEEP SEA SCALLOPS
These small bivalves we bring in from the coast. They are good enough to import if need be. Tiny, succulent balls of white meat, these scallops are like abalone, only more tender . . . . .

CRAB AU GRATIN
A mystic blend of mushrooms, delicate crab meat and satiny cheddar cheese sauce that becomes ambrosia in the deft hands of our chef. It's simmered 'til there's mouth-watering flavor in every cranny of this bubbling casserole . . . . .

SEAFOOD PLATTER
If you'd like a little of everything listed under seafood, this is it! Shrimp, oysters, scallops and crab legs. A potpourri of succulence meriting the gastronomic Pulitzer Prize! . . . . .

JUMBO CRAB LEGS
All of our crab legs are large, but a select few are even larger than that! These we save. Hoard is a better word—to deep fry for you, sealing-in that distinctive flavor . . . . .

SHRIMP POLYNESIAN
Fresh, succulent shrimp marinated with exotic South Pacific spices and sauces. Broiled on a skewer with pineapple and bacon . . . . . flavors from Paradise . . . . . .

WHOLE ATLANTIC FLOUNDER

We flounder to find the right words to describe this fish feast. Perfectly seasoned and gently pampered and broiled in pure creamery butter . . .

OLD-FASHIONED SHORE DINNER

The works . . . like grandpa used to eat . . . choice of Maine chowder or lobster stew, crackers and pickles, steamed clams, bouillon and drawn butter. Then . . . fried clams, hot boiled lobster, chef salad, french fried potatoes, rolls, old-fashioned Indian Pudding with whipped cream and coffee. An adventure in good eating . . . . .

SWORDFISH STEAK

A flavored, flavorful treat from the sea. A boneless fish steak skillfully broiled to the peak of perfection and served with drawn butter and tartar sauce . . . . .

JUMBO LOBSTER LUMPS

Tender, tasty lumps of lobster meat prepared en casserole with pure creamery butter. A delectable, palate-pleasing treat for those who like lobster but dislike the mess . . . . .

FILLET OF PERCH

From off the shores of New England, from the deep sea. Breaded, broiled and seasoned with tender loving care by our chefs, this is a real fish delicacy . . . . .

FROG LEGS

This delicacy is marinated lightly in Chablis, sauteed in butter (garlic if you want it). This specialty has attracted gourmets to this restaurant from all over the country . . . . .

FRESH CATFISH

From the mighty waters of the Missouri River, fresh catfish fried the Dixie way—smothered with Southern flavor—and served with "taters," cole slaw and hot hush puppies . . . .

RAINBOW TROUT

Shipped to us daily from the cold, clear waters of our nearby Ozark streams and cooked Ozark style. This is the golden taste treat in your pot at the end of the rainbow . . . . .

LOBSTER NEWBURG

Our chef delights in cooking this delicacy to your taste, choice pieces of lobster sauteed in butter with cognac and madeira wine and cream. Served on a bed of rice . . . . .

BOUILLABAISSE

Neptune's harvest in the form of a special fish soup consisting of fresh lobster meat, scallops, filet of sole, shrimp (and any other good seafood that's handy) baked en casserole with brandy (a real gourmet specialty) . . .

Assorted Seafood Platters

SEAFOOD SPECIALTY No. 1, (KING OF THE SEA) **5.00**
Half Maine Lobster, Florida Frog Legs, Louisiana Shrimp, Maryland Crab Cake, French Fried Potatoes, Sliced Tomatoes

SEAFOOD SPECIALTY No. 3 ... **4.50**
Half Broiled Lobster, Jumbo Shrimp, Imperial Crab, Deep Sea Scallops, Creamy Slaw, French Fried Potatoes

SEAFOOD SPECIALTY No. 4, (FRANK ROBERTS) **4.75**
Shrimp Imperial, Crab Lumps Imperial, Sun-Ripe Tomato stuffed with buttered Lobster Chunks, Jumbo Shrimp, Deep Sea Scallops, Creamy Slaw, French Fried Potatoes

COLD SEAFOOD SPECIALTY No. 5 **5.00**
Half Cold Lobster, Crab Lumps, Jumbo Shrimp, Cherrystone Clams on Half Shell, Creamy Slaw, Sliced Tomatoes

Combination seafood plates, whether hot or cold, should be unusual and creative without causing impractical problems for the chef in the kitchen.

FRESH LOBSTER A La Newburg $4.95

Chunks of Fresh Steamed Lobster Meat Blended with Tasty Newburg Sauce, Served in Casserole, Potato, Mixed Green Salad with Choice of Dressing

FRESH LOBSTER THERMIDOR $4.85

Lobster Meat Sauted with Shallots, Sliced Mushrooms, Sherry Wine, then placed in ½ Lobster Shell, Topped with Grated Parmesan Cheese and Browned Under the Broiler, Served with Potato, Mixed Green Salad with Choice of Dressing

FRESH LOBSTER CHUNKS Saute $5.25

Large Chunks of Fresh Steamed Lobster Sauted in Fresh Creamery Butter, Served on Toast, on Hot Skillet, Hot Melted Butter Pan, Potato Mixed Green Salad with Choice of Dressing

FRESH MARYLAND LUMP CRAB MEAT - A La Newburg $3.45

Choice Lumps Selected Fresh Crab Meat (pride of the house), Blended with Newburg Sauce, made with Pure Light Cream, Sherry Wine Seasoned to Perfection, Served in Casserole, Potato, Mixed Green Salad with Choice of Dressing

ALASKAN KING CRAB MEAT Au Gratin $3.35

Chunks of King Crab Meat Sauted in Creamery Butter, Selected Seasoning Herbs

COLD SEA FOOD PLATTER $5.25

Half Cold Boiled Lobster, Shrimp with Mayonnaise, Crab Meat with Russian Dressing, Clams on Half Shell, Cocktail Sauce

COMBINATION FRY $3.50

Clams, Filet of Sole, or Oysters (in season) Scallops, Shrimp, Soft Shell Crab (in season) Breaded and Cooked to Individual Order, served with Potato, Chilled Cole Slaw, Home Made Tartar Sauce, and Lemon Wedge

FRESH SHELLED SEA FOOD Au Gratin $3.50

Freshly Opened Clams, Fresh Deep Sea Scallops, Lobster, Crab Meat, Sauted in Creamery Butter, Selected Seasoning Herbs, Blended with Pure Sweet Cream, Sherry Wine, Served in Casserole, Topped with Grated Parmesan Cheese and Browned Under the Broilers, Potato, Mixed Green Salad with Choice of Dressing.

CLAMS CASINO $2.60

Freshly Opened Cherrystone Clams, Crispy Bacon, Diced Pimentos, Diced Green Peppers

FROM OUR SKILLET

Fresh Catfish and Hushpuppies

From the mighty waters of the Missouri River fresh catfish fried the Little Dixie way and served with fried potatoes, southern cole slaw and hot hush puppies.

2.25

Ozark Mountain Rainbow Trout

Shipped to us daily from the cold clear waters of our nearby Ozark streams, cooked Ozark style and served with a hot baked potato, our famous tossed salad, and plenty of hot corn muffins and fresh butter.

3.00

Whether fresh from the ocean or the local rivers, streams, and lakes, good selling in words moves the product.

CRAB IMPERIAL
Large Lumps of Seasoned Backfin Crabmeat
Baked in a Scallop Shell
Try It — You'll Love It
4.25

FILET OF GULF TROUT ALMONDINE
Fresh Gulf Trout Sauteed in Butter and Covered
with Toasted Almonds
4.25

STUFFED SHRIMP
Fresh Jumbo Shrimp Stuffed with Deviled Crabmeat
Rolled in Fresh Bread Crumbs and Deep Fat Fried
Tartar Sauce
3.50

MAINE LOBSTER TAILS
Three (3) Broiled — Drawn Butter
7.95

GIANT MUSHROOM CAPS
Filled with Seasoned Gulf Shrimp Stuffing and
Fine Herb Sauce — Spiced Crabapple
3.25

CRABMEAT AU GRATIN EN CASSEROLE
Lumps of White Crabmeat Topped with
Toasted Cheese
3.75

CRABMEAT SAUTE ROYALE
No Rich Sauce, No Abundance of Seasoning to
Overpower the Delicate Flavor of the Crabmeat —
We Saute in Butter Only the Backfin Lump and
Added Just Enough Zest to Make This a
Gourmet's Delight — Served with Seafood Pilaff Rice
4.25

FLORIDA LOBSTER
One-half Florida Lobster Broiled in Butter Sauce.
A Real Seafood Delight
4.25

CONTINENTAL SEAFOOD PLATTER
Crab or Oyster Bisque (in season) — Main Lobster
Tail — Stuffed Shrimp — Filet of Trout Almondine
Crab Imperial — Shrimp Rockefeller — Hearts of
Romaine — Susie Q Potatoes
5.50

BONELESS STUFFED FLOUNDER
Stuffed with the Rich Meat of Crab and Shrimp
and Deftly Seasoned by Our Happy Chef
4.25

STUFFED CRAB
Only the Finest Backfin Lump Crabmeat Sauteed in
Sweet Cream Butter and Prepared with
that Special Touch of Our Happy Chef
3.50

FRESH SPRING CHICKEN LIVERS
Sauteed in Sweet Cream Butter — Almond Rice
3.15

FRESH ICED WHITE LUMP CRABMEAT
Red or Remoulade Sauce — This Crabmeat Is
Picked Daily Just 80 Miles from Houston
3.50

RED SNAPPER STEAK PONTCHARTRAIN
One of Our True Seafood Delicacies Is This Fine
Preparation — Filet of Red Snapper Sauteed in
Brown Butter and Topped with Fresh Crabmeat,
Shrimp and Lobster
4.95

CRAB LORENZO
Delicately Seasoned Lump Crabmeat on Holland
Rusk, Tópped wih Sauce Hollandaise
3.50

STUFFED RED SNAPPER STEAK
Stuffed with Delicately Seasoned Crabmeat, Topped
with Boiled Shrimp, Baked in Lemon Butter
4.50

This is not just adequate seafood copy, but complete descriptive explanations.

	DINNER	A LA CARTE
*Baked Filet of Sole	4.25	3.50
Baby filets stuffed and served with Lobster Sauce. #5 Pouilly-Fuissé—$4.50 Almaden Chenin Blanc—$2.25		
*Broiled Swordfish or Halibut Steak	4.75	4.00
Thick center cuts broiled and served with hot butter sauce. #7 Macon Superior—$4.00 Paul Masson Chablis—$2.50		
*Baked Stuffed Jumbo Shrimp .	5.25	4.50
Large chunky shrimps stuffed with scallops and fresh bread crumbs, seasoned with cheddar cheese and laced with sherry wine. #10 Liebfraumilch—$4.00 Paul Masson Emerald Dry—$2.50		
*Broiled or Fried Baby Sea Scallops	4.85	4.10
These scallops come to us from down the Atlantic Coast and are fried or broiled as desired. #9 Traminer—$4.50 Almaden Gewurztraminer—$3.00		
*Broiled Boston Schrod . . .	3.65	2.90
A tender filet of the traditional New England baby Cod served with lemon butter. #5 Pouilly-Fuissé—$4.50 Almaden Chenin Blanc—$2.25		
Crabmeat Remick	5.25	4.50
Alaskan King Crabmeat in casserole topped with a tangy sauce and bacon browned under broiler. #7 Macon Superior—$4.00 Paul Masson Pinot Blanc—$3.00		
Alaskan King Crabmeat . . .	5.50	4.75
Boiled Crabmeat Chunks served in hot creamery butter on toast points. #8 Chablis Vaillon—$6.50 Almaden Pinot Chardonnay—$3.00		
*Baked Stuffed Lobster in Casserole	6.50	5.75
Lobster meat baked with fresh bread dressing, butter and cheddar cheese. #12 Soave Bolla—$3.00 Paul Masson Emerald Dry—$2.50		
Lobster Newburg in Casserole .	6.50	5.75
Chunks of lobster meat served on toast in a sauce of sherry, cream and egg yolks in casserole. #8 Chablis Vaillon—$6.50 Paul Masson Pinot Blanc—$3.00		
*Broiled Large Maine Lobster .	on request	
Ocean fresh lobster from the cold waters of Maine, stuffed with our own dressing and drawn butter, approx. 1½ lb. #8 Chablis Vaillon—$6.50 Almaden Pinot Chardonnay—$3.00		

In addition to good descriptive copy, this seafood listing suggests an imported and an American wine to go with each entree.

Seafood

South African Lobster Tail **$4.25**
Broiled or perhaps for something different "Maine Style", breaded and then fried to the correct doneness

Fresh Fillet of Flounder, Lemon Butter **$3.25**
A delicacy of the sea, broiled or deep fried as you may desire

Sauteed Shrimp in Garlic Butter **$3.50**
The zesty garlic butter brings out the best in this epicurean treat from the sea

Crabmeat Casserole **$3.00**
Fresh lump backfin crabmeat served either hot in brown butter or cold with cocktail sauce

Benetz Inn Stuffed Shrimp **$3.00**
Jumbo shrimp stuffed with our famous deviled crab stuffing

Deviled Crab **$2.50**
Our own recipe prepared with skill and care

Fillet of Haddock **$2.50**
Broiled or fried and served with tartar sauce and lemon wedge

Fried Jumbo Shrimp **$2.50**
Served with tartar or cocktail sauce

Rocky Mountain Brook Trout, Meuniere Butter . . . **$3.75**
Meuniere butter is a delicious mixture of brown butter, lemon juice, and parsley. A worthy complement to the delicious trout

Seafood Combination **$4.00**
For the seafood enthusiast, Lobster Tail, Jumbo Shrimp, Fillet of Haddock, Scallops, and our Deviled Crab

Deep Sea Scallops **$2.75**
Tender scallops broiled or deep fried to suit your fancy

Appropriate graphics help to distinguish this appetizing seafood listing.

When a menu is 99 percent seafood (the two exceptions being a Hamburger Supreme and a Top Sirloin Steak Sandwich), and well written from introduction to desserts, it deserves study. *The Elliot Bay Fish & Oyster Co.* in Seattle, Washington, is one such menu.

Organized in six panels with an accordion fold (each panel 4¾″ × 15″), the first panel has introductory copy. Panel two has ten seafood appetizers. Panel three has chowder, oyster stew, bouillabaisse, and three seafood salads. Panel four has six seafood sandwiches (a neglected sandwich idea), while panel five sells seven seafood entrees plus Today's Catch. The last panel has another surprise—seafood waist-watchers.

This attractive menu (on pages 172 to 174) *is organized, by way of panels, for easy customer ordering.*

ELLIOTT
BAY FISH
& OYSTER
CO.

ELLIOTT BAY FISH & OYSTER CO.

Every seaport city has its own character, shaped by the rivers, lakes, bays, sounds and seas surrounding it. And each has its own style of cuisine, shaped by the seafood of the region.
The Elliott Bay Fish and Oyster Company has netted the best of the abundant seafood of Puget Sound and the Pacific Ocean.
We present it fresh every day, simply prepared to enhance its own unique flavor, paired with fresh, natural accompaniments and carefully selected wines.
As the seasons change, so may our menu, which depends particularly on fresh ingredients. If your favorite dish is not available, it will be soon . . . perhaps at the next tide. Meanwhile, try another from the sea around you.

Chef de Cuisine—Jim Jinhong

APPETIZERS

Oysters on the Half Shell **$2.95**
Ocean fresh Quilcene oysters, served on a bed of ice with a tangy sauce and lemon garnish.

Oysters Rockefeller **$3.95**
Baked on the half shell with spinach, bacon, onions, cayenne, a hint of pernod, and topped with Hollandaise sauce.

Oysters Casino **$3.95**
Freshly shucked oysters baked on the half shell with chopped chives, wine, seasonings, then topped with Mornay sauce and sprinkled with bacon.

Oysters Maitre d' **$2.95**
On the half shell, baked with wine and butter and served with our own cocktail sauce.

Shrimp Cocktail Supreme **$2.95**
Baby Alaska shrimp, served chilled over chopped lettuce with a tangy tomato sauce, lemon garnish.

Crab Cocktail Supreme **$3.75**
Dungeness crabmeat with chopped lettuce, tangy tomato sauce, lemon garnish.

Clams Bordelaise **$3.45**
A bucket of fresh Puget Sound clams, steamed in vermouth, served with drawn butter, clam nectar.

Cracked Crab **$4.95**
One-half Dungeness crab, cooked very lightly and chilled, served on an ice bed with Elliott Bay Mayonnaise.

Alaska Crab Claws **$3.95**
Large Alaska crab claws, gently steamed, then chilled and served on a bed of ice with Elliott Bay Mayonnaise and cocktail sauce.

Seafood Hors d'Oeuvres **$5.95**
A melange of oysters Rockefeller, skewered scallops, sautéed prawns and and crab Rangoon, with a tangy sauce for dipping. For two. (Please allow approximately 15 minutes.)

Water served upon request.

THE CHOWDER POT

Hearty sea soups, served by the tureen and accompanied by our special bread and the salad of the day.

Elliott Bay Clam Chowder **$2.95**
A creamy stew of chopped Pacific hard shell clams, onions, celery and potatoes, flavored with pork and fresh thyme.
By the bowl with entree . . . . $.75

Pacific Oyster Stew **$3.75**
A tureen of whole baby Pacific oysters, simmered in a rich cream stock, accented with chopped onions and a float of country butter.

Elliott Bay Bouillabaise **$4.25**
Whitefish, clams, and crab in the shell, whole prawns, lobster, scallops, salmon and tomatoes in a hearty stew with cloves of garlic simmered in, and served with French bread for dipping.

THE SALAD BOWL

Garden greens and vegetables and chilled fresh seafood with special dressings. Served with our special bread.

Crab or Shrimp Louis **$4.25**
Pacific shrimp or Dungeness crab on a bed of lettuce, with sliced eggs, assorted vegetables and the traditional Louis dressing.

Fresh Spinach Salad **$3.95**
Fresh spinach with assorted vegetables, mushrooms, bacon, baby shrimp, sliced egg, sliced almonds, sunflower seeds, cheese, with our special dressing.

Elliott Bay Seafood Salad Supreme **$5.25**
An array of Dungeness crab, bay shrimp, chilled salmon, sole, and prawns with assorted vegetables, avocado and cheese. For the salad gourmet!

Banquet facilities available. Please inquire at front desk.

THE SANDWICH BOARD

Hot and cold specialty sandwiches, offered with the salad of the day, our special bread and a garnish of fresh seasonal fruits.

Elliott Bay Supreme **$3.75**
Dungeness crab, crisp bacon, cheddar cheese on triple deck egg dipped bread, grilled until golden.

Shrimp Zonker **$3.25**
An Elliott Bay original. Pacific baby shrimp, avocado, bacon, tomatoes and alfalfa sprouts in a middle eastern bun with a mayonnaise dressing.

Crab n' Cheddar **$3.95**
Dungeness crab in a cheddar cheese sauce, served open face on cheese muffin rounds and grilled till bubbly.

Oyster n' Cheddar **$3.75**
Quilcene oysters pan fried to a golden brown, resting on a toasted cheese muffin with tomato slices and smothered in a cheddar cheese sauce.

The Natural **$2.95**
A vegetarian delight. Alfalfa sprouts, soft cheddar cheese, avocado, and tomato on brown bread.

Elliott Bay Fishwich **$2.75**
Fried cod on a toasted sesame seed bun with lettuce, tomato and tartar sauce.

Broiled Sandwiches

Served with salad of the day, our special bread, and French fried potatoes.

Hamburger Supreme **$2.95**
Lean chopped sirloin in a generous patty on toasted French bread. Garnished with lettuce, tomato, onion, pickles and relish.

Top Sirloin Steak Sandwich **$4.75**
A broiled top sirloin steak, served open face on toasted French bread.

26
The breakfast menu

Whether it is a part of your regular menu or a separate menu, plan your breakfast menu with care and imagination. Not every food service operation serves breakfast, but those who do should give more time and attention to the breakfast menu. It can influence sales just as effectively as a Luncheon or Dinner Menu. If the Breakfast Menu is a separate menu, make it large, set the type large and bold. If your Breakfast Menu is part of your regular Luncheon or Dinner Menu, do not crowd it in with other items so that it becomes hard to find and hard to read. Generally, a completely separate panel of the menu is required for an average breakfast listing.

One of the best solutions for the Breakfast Menu as part of the general menu is to print it on the back cover. This usually provides enough room for listing the average size Breakfast Menu (25 to 35 line items, including beverages), and, in addition, the extra colors used in printing the cover design can be carried over to the back cover at no additional cost since it is part of the same press run.

Most of the time, however, a complete, separate Breakfast Menu is the best solution for a good, effective, selling menu. It is an extra cost, but, like most things done right, it pays off. The exception is when the Breakfast Menu listing is served 24 hours or all of the hours the restaurant is open. Then, obviously, the Breakfast Menu must be part of the general menu. In connection with this hours of service question, be sure to always list the hours (and days, if you are not open every day of the week) that breakfast is served.

The average breakfast menu breaks down into the following subheadings or classifications:

1. Fruits and Juices
2. Cereals
   a. Dry cereals
   b. Hot cereals
3. Toast, Rolls, French Toast
4. Eggs
5. Egg Combinations or Specials
6. Omelettes
7. Side Orders
8. Pancakes
9. Waffles
10. Children's Breakfast
11. Beverages

Using these headings and setting them in a different, bolder, or unusual type face (script, for example) will make the breakfast menu easy to read and easy to use in ordering. Do not run different types of breakfast items together (Eggs, Pancakes, and Rolls, for example). Specials or Egg Combinations that come under the heading or category of Complete Breakfasts should get special treatment on the menu. They should get top billing because they are the biggest profit items and are what you want to sell the most.

Give the Special Complete Breakfast Combinations the best position on the menu; set them in the largest, boldest type and give them the most descriptive, merchandising, sell copy. Setting these listings in a panel or giving them large numbers—No. 1, No. 2, No. 3—is a common way of making them stand out and catch the customer's eye. After all, when a breakfast entree includes a small steak and costs $2.00 or more, it deserves better treatment than a 20¢ glass of orange juice.

A couple of Breakfast Menu listings that are not often included, but that should be because they are good merchandising, are the Children's Breakfast and the Low Calorie-High Protein Breakfast. If you have a Children's Menu or Kiddie Korner on your regular menu, it stands to reason that this listing should be on your Breakfast Menu, and a Low Calorie-High Protein Breakfast listing will sell a meal to the adult customer who otherwise would just order a cup of coffee.

When creating your Breakfast Menu, be sure to list everything you serve. Do not list "Juices," list each variety. Also, do not just list "Cereals," dry or hot, list the individual cereals, and, in the case of omelettes, do likewise. The rule should be if you make it in your kitchen or have it in your refrigerator or store room, list it on your Breakfast Menu.

A study of the number of items listed on the Breakfast Menu (see Figure 1) shows that the most popular number is in the 25 to 35 bracket (including beverages). However, the size of the Breakfast Menu varies enormously from a low of only five items to a high of over 60 items. So it is obvious that breakfast business can be large or small, but large or small, a careful, readable, imaginative listing will help to make it more profitable.

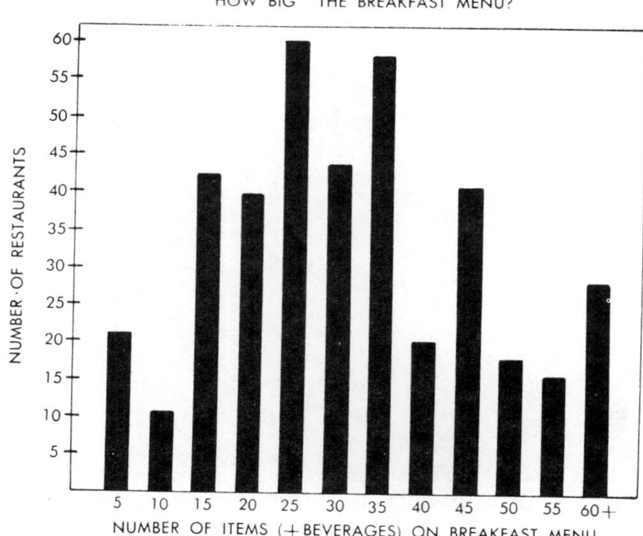

FIGURE 1

Eggs Hussarde *Marchand de Vin Sauce over grilled ham and tomato on toast. Poached eggs and Hollandaise sauce.*	1.75
Eggs Benedict *Broiled ham and poached eggs on crisp toast. Hollandaise sauce.*	1.50
Eggs Sardou *Artichoke bottoms, poached eggs, creamed spinach and Hollandaise sauce.*	1.75
Eggs St. Denis *Souffled eggs and chopped ham served on croutons. Marchand de Vin sauce.*	1.50
Eggs a la Turk *Shirred eggs with chicken livers, fresh mushrooms and red wine.*	1.75
Eggs Bourguignonne *Omelette with escargots and vegetables. Red wine sauce.*	2.00
Eggs aux Fines Herbes *Omelette with finely chopped onions and parsley.*	1.00
Eggs aux Champignons *Omelette with fresh mushrooms.*	1.00

There are eggs and there are eggs. This listing is distinctive copy—out of the ordinary.

"A TRADITIONAL BRENNAN BREAKFAST

This is the way it was done in leisured antebellum days: first an absinthe *Suissesse* to get the eyes open, then a fresh Creole cream cheese. Now an egg Benedict, followed by a hearty sirloin with fresh mushrooms. Hot French bread and marmalade, and a chilled Rose wine. For the finale, *crepes Suzette*, *cafe au lait*, and a Cognac snifter. Important:

DON'T HURRY!"

A real gourmet breakfast.

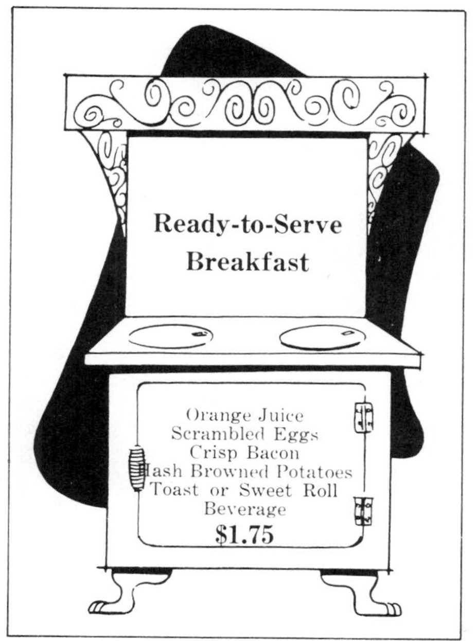

Ready-to-Serve
Breakfast
Orange Juice
Scrambled Eggs
Crisp Bacon
Hash Browned Potatoes
Toast or Sweet Roll
Beverage
$1.75

FAMILY PLATTER

SERVES FOUR

FRUIT JUICES
SCRAMBLED EGGS
BACON AND SAUSAGE
GOLDEN BROWN PANCAKES
BUCKWHEAT CAKES
BUTTERMILK PANCAKES
IOWA CORN CAKES
BEVERAGE

4.95

Each Additional Person 1.20
No Substitutions

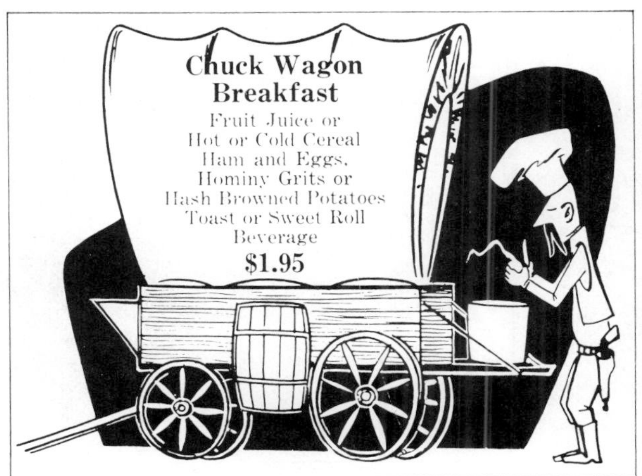

Chuck Wagon
Breakfast
Fruit Juice or
Hot or Cold Cereal
Ham and Eggs,
Hominy Grits or
Hash Browned Potatoes
Toast or Sweet Roll
Beverage
$1.95

Specials can be featured on the breakfast also.

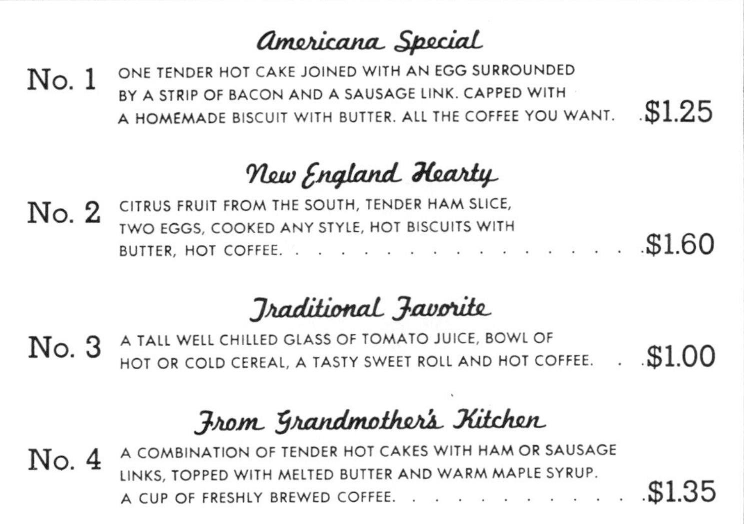

Americana Special

No. 1 ONE TENDER HOT CAKE JOINED WITH AN EGG SURROUNDED BY A STRIP OF BACON AND A SAUSAGE LINK. CAPPED WITH A HOMEMADE BISCUIT WITH BUTTER. ALL THE COFFEE YOU WANT. $1.25

New England Hearty

No. 2 CITRUS FRUIT FROM THE SOUTH, TENDER HAM SLICE, TWO EGGS, COOKED ANY STYLE, HOT BISCUITS WITH BUTTER, HOT COFFEE. $1.60

Traditional Favorite

No. 3 A TALL WELL CHILLED GLASS OF TOMATO JUICE, BOWL OF HOT OR COLD CEREAL, A TASTY SWEET ROLL AND HOT COFFEE. . . $1.00

From Grandmother's Kitchen

No. 4 A COMBINATION OF TENDER HOT CAKES WITH HAM OR SAUSAGE LINKS, TOPPED WITH MELTED BUTTER AND WARM MAPLE SYRUP. A CUP OF FRESHLY BREWED COFFEE. $1.35

CHILLED ORANGE JUICE
CHOICE OF FRESH, CRISP CEREAL
BUTTERED TOAST OR SWEET ROLL
FRESH HOT COFFEE
85c

GR-R-REAT!
FOR KIDS
(of all ages)
CHILLED JUICE
SUGAR FROSTED FLAKES
ONE SLICE OF TOAST
WITH JELLY
HOT CHOCOLATE OR MILK
70c

**LOW CALORIE—
HIGH PROTEIN BREAKFAST**
(LESS THAN 450 CALORIES!)
ORANGE JUICE
SPECIAL K
(PROTEIN CEREAL) WITH MILK
ONE EGG, ANY STYLE
WHITE TOAST (1 SLICE)
BLACK COFFEE
90c

Special combinations, color photos, low-calorie, and children's items plus quick service help to sell extras on the breakfast menu.

This breakfast menu includes combinations, an Old-Fashioned Southern Breakfast plus a complete a la carte listing that features fish and meats—not an ordinary breakfast listing.

THE RICHMOND SPECIAL

No. 1 **.95**

Fruit or Juice
Griddle Cakes or Waffles
with
Hot Maple Syrup, Marmalade or Honey
Coffee Tea Milk

No 2 **1.10**

Fruit, Cereal or Juice
Choice of
Two Eggs (Any Style)
or
One Egg with Ham, Bacon or Sausage
Assorted Rolls or Buttered Toast
Coffee Tea Milk

No. 3 **1.30**

Fresh Fruit in Season or Juice
Hot or Cold Cereal
Choice of
Two Eggs (Any Style)
with
Broiled Ham, Bacon or Sausage Cakes
or
Buckwheat Cakes with Sausage
Assorted Rolls or Buttered Toast
Coffee Tea Milk

OLD FASHION SOUTHERN BREAKFAST

No. 4 **1.50**

Fresh Fruit in Season or Juice
Hot or Cold Cereal
Choice of
Hominy Grits and Smoked Ham
with Two Eggs (Any Style)
or
Smithfield Ham and Eggs
Assorted Rolls or Buttered Toast
Coffee Tea Milk

BREAKFAST

SERVED FROM 7:00 UNTIL NOON

FRUITS
Sliced Oranges .35
Half Grapefruit .35
Fruit Compote .40
Stewed Prunes .35
Sliced Bananas .40
Berries or Melons in Season

CONTINENTAL BREAKFAST
Fruit Juice
Assorted Rolls, Toast or Sweet Rolls
Marmalade
Coffee Tea Milk
70¢

JUICES
Grapefruit .30
Orange .30
(double) .55
V-8 Juice .30
Prune .30
Pineapple .30
Tomato .30

CEREALS AND CAKES
Hot or Cold Cereal (Served with Cream) .35
Old Dominion Buckwheat Cakes .55 French Toast .50
Griddle Cakes .50 Waffles with Hot Maple Syrup .50

EGGS
Boiled (2) .45 Scrambled .55 Fried (2) .55
Poached on Toast .50 Plain Omelette .75
Bacon and Eggs .95 Spanish Omelette .75
Smithfield Ham Omelette 1.00
Garniture of Chicken Livers, Sausage, Bacon or Ham .40

FISH
Kippered Herring .70 Boiled Salt Mackerel .70
Fried Cod Fish Cakes with Bacon .75
Salt Roe Herring .65 Broiled Filet of Flounder .60

MEATS
Broiled Smithfield Ham 1.40 Hickory Smoked Bacon .75
Sausage Cakes or Links .85 Broiled Ham 1.20
Chipped Beef in Cream .95 Lamb Chop 1.30
Calves Liver with Bacon or Onions 1.50
Pork Chop 1.25 Breakfast Steak 1.75

POTATOES
Fried Hash Brown or Saute .35
Hashed in Cream, Au Gratin or Lyonnaise .35

BREADS
Dry or Buttered Toast .20 Cinnamon Toast .30
Danish Pastry .25 Hard or Soft Rolls .20

PRESERVES
Orange Marmalade .20 Currant Jelly .20
Apricot Jam .20 Strawberry Preserves .20
Apple Butter .20

BEVERAGES
Coffee .20 Hot Chocolate .30
Sanka .25 Buttermilk .20 Tea .20 Milk .20

A truly Gourmet Breakfast awaits you!

ONE GUN SALUTE
One egg, bacon or sausage and hashed brown potatoes .95

TWO GUN SALUTE
Two eggs, bacon or sausage, hashed brown potatoes 1.25

SOUTHERN GENTLEMAN
Steak and two eggs, hashed brown potatoes 2.25

LEXINGTON
Baked corn beef hash
w poached egg, hashed brown potatoes 1.25

THE VIRGINIAN
Ham and eggs w hashed brown potatoes 1.35

DIXIE FAVORITE
Center cut pork chop, two eggs, hashed brown potatoes 1.45

THE ILLINOIAN
Shirred eggs and little
pork sausage, hashed brown potatoes 1.25

THE KENTUCKIAN
Shirred eggs
w ham or bacon, hashed brown potatoes 1.35

All the above orders served w biscuits or toast and butter
Coffee til the Pot runs Dry

Glorious Pancakes

RAMADA WHEAT CAKES
Golden fluffy and light, begging for butter
and luscious maple syrup .60

GEORGIA PECAN CAKES
with the pecans baked right in the dough—
Country butter and maple syrup .75

LAND OF COTTON
Old time buckwheat cakes—The South's famous
buckwheat, whipped butter and maple syrup .60

DIXIE BACON CAKES
Golden, fluffy and light—Served with two strips of
bacon Dixie Style—Country butter, maple syrup .85

TENNESSEE MOUNTAIN STRAWBERRY CAKES
Wheat cakes topped with strawberries—'nuff said .95

SOUTH PACIFIC CAKES
Golden fluffy and light, topped with a grilled pineapple ring
begging for butter and luscious maple syrup .95

PIGLETS IN A BLANKET
Spicy little link sausages wrapped in a pancake coverlet .95

There's more than one way to serve eggs and pancakes.

FOR ALL YOU LATE RISERS
SPECIAL
Brunch

All entrees served with champagne and assorted rolls and pastries.

STEAK N' EGGS 6.95
Char-broiled sirloin. Served with scrambled eggs and choice of hash brown potatoes or refried beans.

EGGS HUSSARD 6.95
Thin beef tenderloin filets topped with poached eggs and bearnaise sauce on an English muffin. Served with fresh fruit and hash brown potatoes.

EGGS BENEDICT 5.45
Canadian bacon and poached eggs on an English muffin with asparagus. Topped with hollandaise sauce. Served with fresh fruit and hash brown potatoes.

CHICKEN AND ARTICHOKE CREPES 5.45
Baby artichoke hearts served atop crepes of tender chicken, smothered with cheese sauce and sprinkled with almonds. Served with rice and fresh fruit.

SPANISH OMELETTE 4.95
Three egg omelette filled with seasoned shredded beef. Topped with Spanish sauce and cheddar cheese. Served with fresh fruit and choice of hash brown potatoes or refried beans.

MUSHROOMS AND AVOCADO OMELETTE . . . 4.95
Three egg omelette filled with sauteed mushrooms and topped with cheese sauce and avocado. Served with fresh fruit and choice of hash brown potatoes or refried beans.

EVERYTHING OMELETTE 4.95
Tomatoes, mushrooms, bacon, bell pepper and scallions in a fluffy omelette covered with a creamy cheese sauce and topped with artichoke hearts and black olives. Served with fresh fruit and choice of hash brown potatoes or refried beans.

MONTE CRISTO 4.95
Turkey, ham, pineapple and cheese in a triple-decker dipped in egg and fried golden-brown. Served with raspberry preserves, fresh fruit and hash brown potatoes.

WESTERN QUICHE 4.75
Ham, green peppers, mushrooms, tomatoes and onions. Baked in a pie with Swiss cheese and egg. Served with rice and fresh fruit.

HUEVOS RANCHEROS 4.50
Corn tortilla covered with refried beans, with two fried eggs, and smothered with ranchero sauce. Topped with sour cream and an avocado wedge. Served with choice of hash brown potatoes or refried beans.

BELGIAN WAFFLE 4.25
A thick, crisp, fluffy waffle with a whipped cream cheese topping. Covered with a fresh fruit in season. Garnished with fresh fruit.

FOR THE LIGHT APPETITE (Guests Under 12) . . . 2.75
Scrambled eggs, Canadian bacon and hash brown potatoes. Obviously, no champagne for the ninõs.

FLOUR TORTILLA 30

BEVERAGES
Coffee, sanka, tea or milk .60
Freshly squeezed orange juice or grapefruit juice 1.50

CARLOS MURPHY'S
IRISH-MEXICAN CAFE

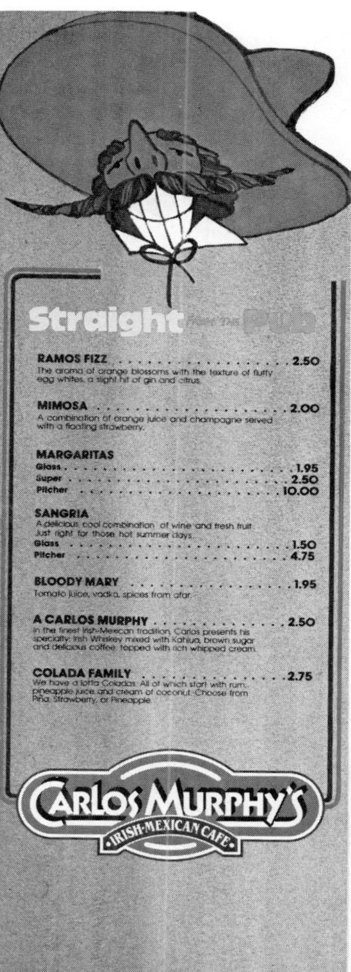
Straight from the Pub

RAMOS FIZZ 2.50
The aroma of orange blossoms with the texture of fluffy egg whites, a slight hit of gin and citrus.

MIMOSA 2.00
A combination of orange juice and champagne served with a floating strawberry.

MARGARITAS
Glass 1.95
Super 2.50
Pitcher 10.00

SANGRIA
A delicious cool combination of wine and fresh fruit. Just right for those hot summer days.
Glass 1.50
Pitcher 4.75

BLOODY MARY 1.95
Tomato juice, vodka, spices from afar.

A CARLOS MURPHY 2.50
In the finest Irish-Mexican tradition, Carlos presents his specialty: Irish Whiskey mixed with Kahlua, brown sugar and delicious coffee, topped with rich whipped cream.

COLADA FAMILY 2.75
We have a lotta Coladas. All of which start with rum, pineapple juice and cream of coconut. Choose from Piña, Strawberry, or Pineapple.

CARLOS MURPHY'S
IRISH-MEXICAN CAFE

This brunch menu from Carlos Murphy's *presents an unusual and creative list of entrees. With the increasing popularity of Sunday brunch, a special well-thought-out menu and food (plus drink) selection becomes an important merchandising tool for many restaurants. Note that a special drink list is printed on the reverse side of this brunch menu.*

27

Children's menus

The potential customer base for any restaurant is the entire population within a geographic area. The economic base—income level—is an important part of this base. People with disposable income eat out more often. A new factor has appeared, however, in the eating out marketing picture. It is called *demographics* and includes an analysis of the age groups within the total population.

The population of the United States stands today (1980) at around 225 million, 17 million more than in 1970. The segment of the population that has grown the most is the age 18-and-over group. There are nearly eight million fewer people under 18 now than in 1970. The fastest growth has been within the age 15-to-34 group. Analysts regard this as an economic plus because these individuals spend more and more as they form families and gain larger incomes.

Offsetting this group is the age 65-and-over category. These individuals usually do not work and depend largely on payments from various retirement programs.

The following table shows the age distribution shifts from 1970, through the 1980s to 1990, as estimated by the Bureau of Census:

	PERCENT OF TOTAL POPULATION		
	1970	*1980*	*1990*
0 to 17 years	34.0	27.9	26.1
18 to 24	12.1	13.3	10.4
25 to 34	12.3	16.3	17.0
35 to 44	11.3	11.6	15.1
45 to 54	11.4	10.2	10.5
55 to 64	9.1	9.5	8.6
65 and over	9.8	11.2	12.3

Another demographic development has been the growth of single parent households. A recent government estimate shows that 77 percent of the population still resides in husband-and-wife households, but in 1970, the figure was 82 percent.

The Children's Menu market as shown above has decreased from 35 percent in 1970 to 27.9 percent in 1980 and is expected to decline a small amount more to 26.1 percent in 1990. This is still *one-quarter of the population* and as a market should not be ignored.

In addition, there is another factor in the child-eating-out equation. That is the increase in size of the working woman segment of the population. In 1970, some 43 percent of America's working-age women participated in the job market. Today that rate is a record 57 percent. This means more two family wage earners, more disposable income, more eating out *with children.*

Some restaurants—supper clubs for example—will never merchandise to children, but family-type restaurants, and all hotels and motels should give some thought to the Children's Menu. Selling to children can be done in three ways on the menu. First, copy can say, "all items on this menu served in children's portions at a specified reduced price."

Second, the regular menu can have a "Kiddie Korner" where an abbreviated children's menu is printed. This is usually a listing of items with special appeal to children at reduced prices. Finally, there is the separate children's menu. It usually includes extra material besides the listing of food and prices, such as: a story, a puzzle or puzzles, games, or some secondary use such as a mask or a hat. Operations merchandising more extensively to children will include special children's desserts.

Of the three methods of selling to children, the separate Children's Menu is the best. Next, a part of the regular menu set aside and identified as a Children's Menu, is adequate and can work well. The least satisfactory is to indicate (usually with an asterisk) that some items are available in children's portions.

Selling to children must be an objective consciously decided upon by the restaurant operator. If the child-youth market is part of the business target, the Children's Menu is one tool to use, and considering the success of restaurant chains such as *McDonalds*, *Burger King*, *Wendys*, and *Howard Johnson's*—all of which cater heavily to the youth market—it must be one worth the effort and attention.

Daniel Boone and the Indians make a good child's menu theme.

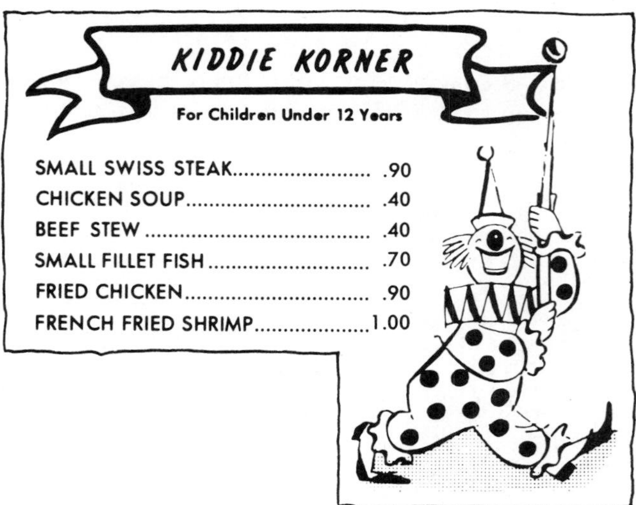

KIDDIE KORNER

For Children Under 12 Years

SMALL SWISS STEAK........................ .90
CHICKEN SOUP................................ .40
BEEF STEW .... .40
SMALL FILLET FISH .... .70
FRIED CHICKEN................................ .90
FRENCH FRIED SHRIMP....................1.00

Kiddie Korral

(For Children Under Twelve)

EENY — Two Savage Style Chicken Drumsticks with French Fried Potatoes, Vegetable ...... **.85**

MEENY — Sliced White Meat of Turkey, French Fried Potatoes, Vegetable .... **.90**

MINEY — Ground Beef Pattie, French Fried Potatoes, Vegetable .... **.75**

MO — Three Fried Jumbo Shrimp, French Fried Potatoes, Tartar Sauce **1.25**
Served with Roll and Butter

JANS "JOE" "JO" — Ground Beef Pattie, Served on Toasted Bun with Mustard or Mayonnaise and Lettuce, and Tomato .... **.50**

For the Children...

"Hansel"	"Gretel"
Fruit Cocktail, Royal	Soup or Tomato Juice
GOLDEN FRIED CHICKEN DRUMETTE with Cranberry Sauce	BROILED CHOPPED BEEF STEAK
Whipped Potatoes Vegetable	French Fries Vegetable
Ice Cream — Milk	Ice Cream — Milk
1.95	1.95

Using Kiddie Korner, Kiddie Korral, or some other name and combining it with a special selection of food items at a special price makes part of the menu sell children—and their parents.

Appetizers

Melon Balls in Cascades Syrup .50

V-8 or Tomato Juice .35 Soup du Jour .40

Entrees

Half Breast of Chicken, Pennsylvania German Style, with Local Ham, Served with Choice of Two Vegetables, Salad, and a Flute of Bread 2.50

Chopped Beef Steak on Toasted English Muffin, Served with French Fried Potatoes, Sliced Onion and Tomato 1.75

Duck Pilaf with Hot Curried Fruit, Served with One Vegetable and a Salad 2.00

Children's Portion of Roast Rib of Beef, Served with a Baked Potato, One Vegetable, Salad, and a Flute of Bread 3.00

Desserts

Please Refer to the Regular Menu

Beverages

Coca Cola, Fresca, Grapeade, or Fanta Root Beer 15
Lime or Lemonade . .30
Milk or Skim Milk . .20
Buttermilk 20
Iced Tea 25

The children's menu can be a la carte and include appetizers, desserts, and beverages as well as entrees that do not have to be the usual hamburgers.

Masks and games make good children's menus.

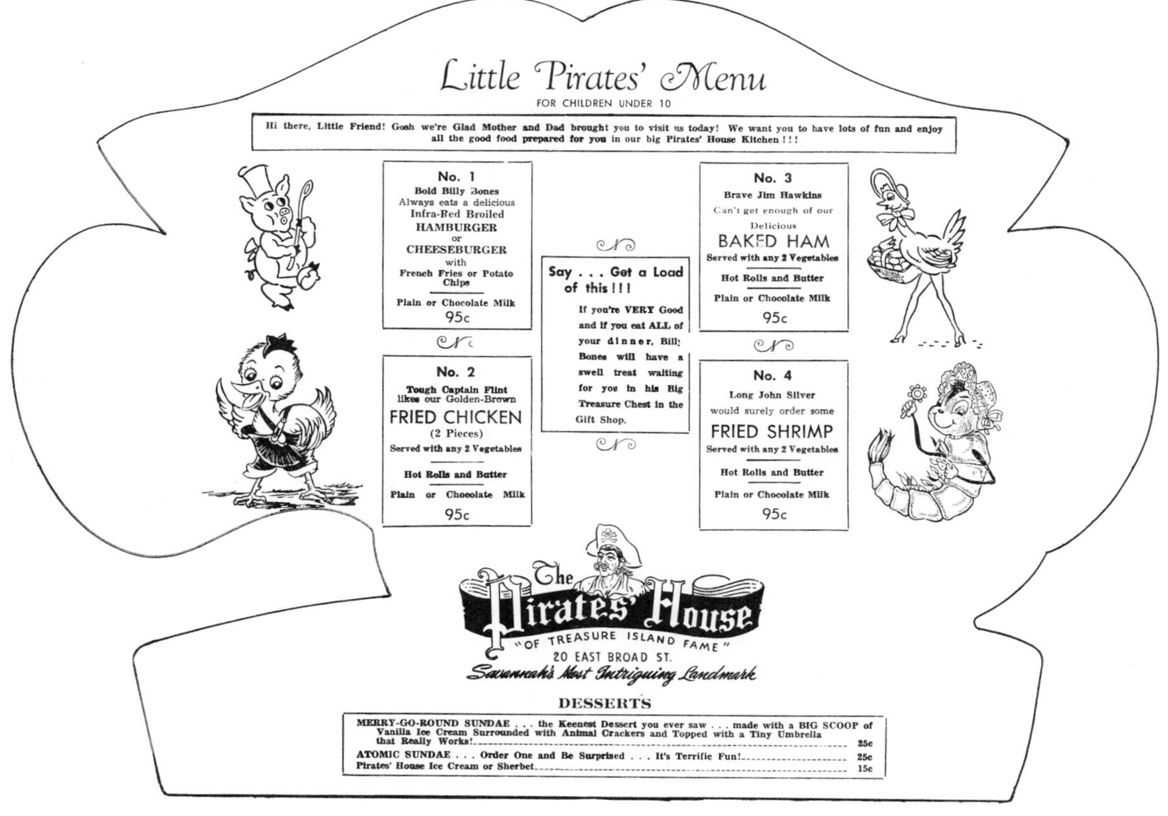

Little Pirates' Menu
FOR CHILDREN UNDER 10

Hi there, Little Friend! Gosh we're Glad Mother and Dad brought you to visit us today! We want you to have lots of fun and enjoy all the good food prepared for you in our big Pirates' House Kitchen ! ! !

No. 1
Bold Billy Bones
Always eats a delicious
Infra-Red Broiled
HAMBURGER
or
CHEESEBURGER
with
French Fries or Potato Chips
Plain or Chocolate Milk
95c

No. 2
Tough Captain Flint
likes our Golden-Brown
FRIED CHICKEN
(2 Pieces)
Served with any 2 Vegetables
Hot Rolls and Butter
Plain or Chocolate Milk
95c

Say . . . Get a Load of this ! ! !
If you're VERY Good and if you eat ALL of your dinner, Billy Bones will have a swell treat waiting for you in his Big Treasure Chest in the Gift Shop.

No. 3
Brave Jim Hawkins
Can't get enough of our
Delicious
BAKED HAM
Served with any 2 Vegetables
Hot Rolls and Butter
Plain or Chocolate Milk
95c

No. 4
Long John Silver
would surely order some
FRIED SHRIMP
Served with any 2 Vegetables
Hot Rolls and Butter
Plain or Chocolate Milk
95c

The Pirates' House
"OF TREASURE ISLAND FAME"
20 EAST BROAD ST.
Savannah's Most Intriguing Landmark

DESSERTS

MERRY-GO-ROUND SUNDAE . . . the Keenest Dessert you ever saw . . . made with a BIG SCOOP of Vanilla Ice Cream Surrounded with Animal Crackers and Topped with a Tiny Umbrella that Really Works! ---- 25c
ATOMIC SUNDAE . . . Order One and Be Surprised . . . It's Terrific Fun! ---- 25c
Pirates' House Ice Cream or Sherbet ---- 15c

The *Howard Johnson's* chain of motels and restaurants does probably what is the best children's merchandising of anybody. As a result it has a well-deserved reputation as a "family place" to eat and stay. The following examples show some of the ways Ho Jo does it.

"The Flavor of America Menu" includes a 3-D White House Model, A Quik Game, a Fun Quiz, and Stories of the White House. The food portion offers three entrees, four sandwiches, and strained baby foods.

In their Amuse-A-Menu, series 2, Ho Jo offers games, make your own puppets, a short history of the American flag, a Martian Maze, make your own buttons, a jig saw puzzle, and a dot-to-dot coloring picture. An important part of this and other Ho Jo Children's Menus is their Ho Jo Birthday Club. The Official Registration Card for this club makes the following offer: "Join the Ho Jo birthday club . . . and you can invite your friends to a great party at Howard Johnson's restaurant! Look at what you get *FREE:* Your own party dinner and a beautiful birthday cake with candles. What fun! What a Swell Treat!"

The food portion of this menu includes four sandwiches and three entrees—fried clams, spaghetti, and sliced roast turkey. In addition, the young customer is given "FREE with any meal you order a tasty dish of candy delicious American Rainbow Ice Cream."

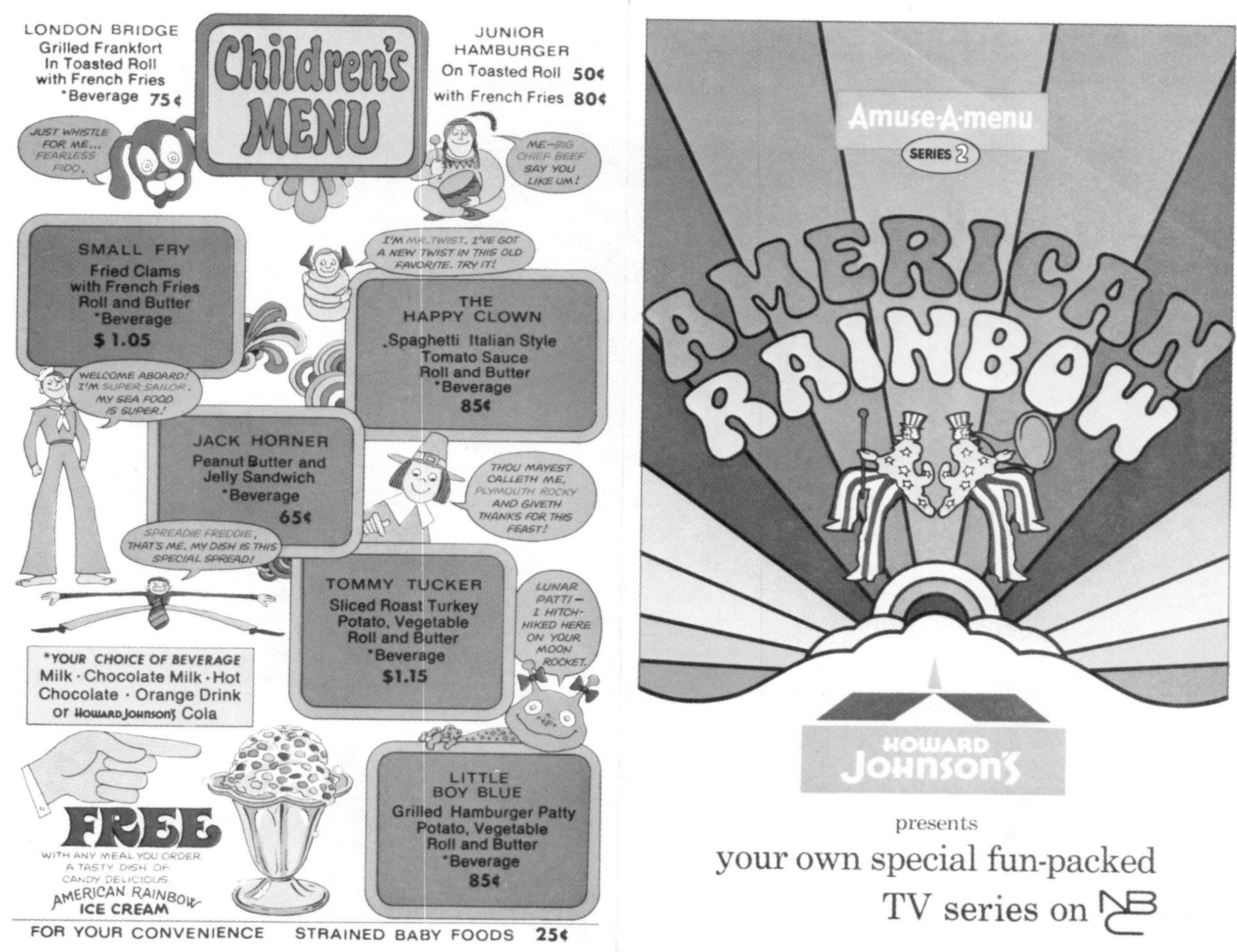

The Howard Johnson's *chain of restaurants and motels makes a special effort to attract children (and their parents) to their facilities by creating amusing and interesting children's menus.* (See pages 184 to 186.)

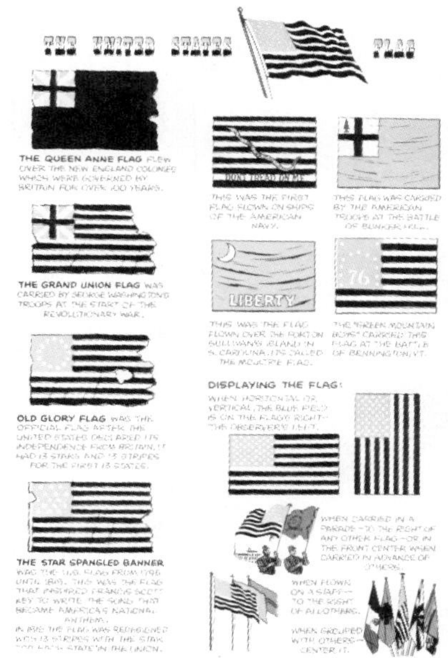

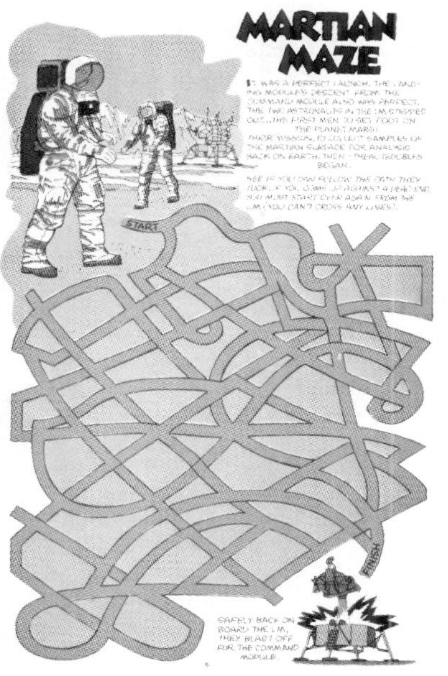

HOWARD
Johnson's
The Flavor of America™
MENU
FEATURING . . .
REAT SOUVENIR
THIS PRESIDENTIAL YEAR!

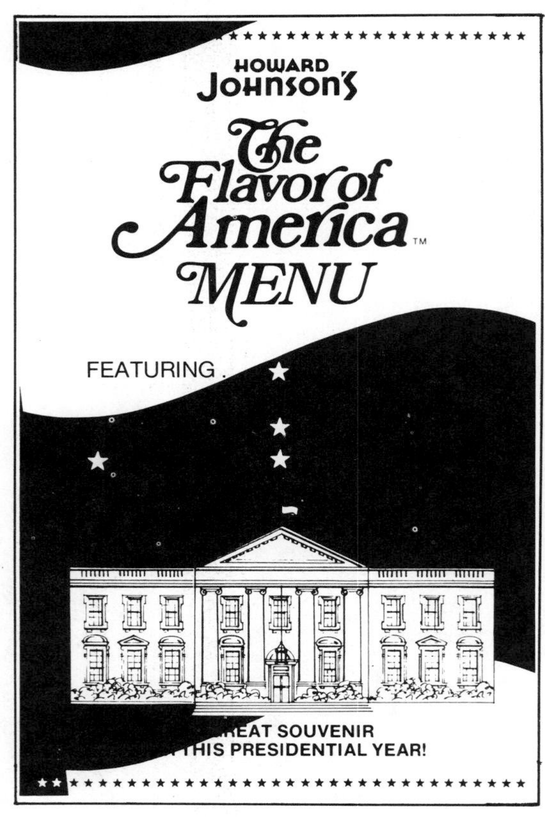

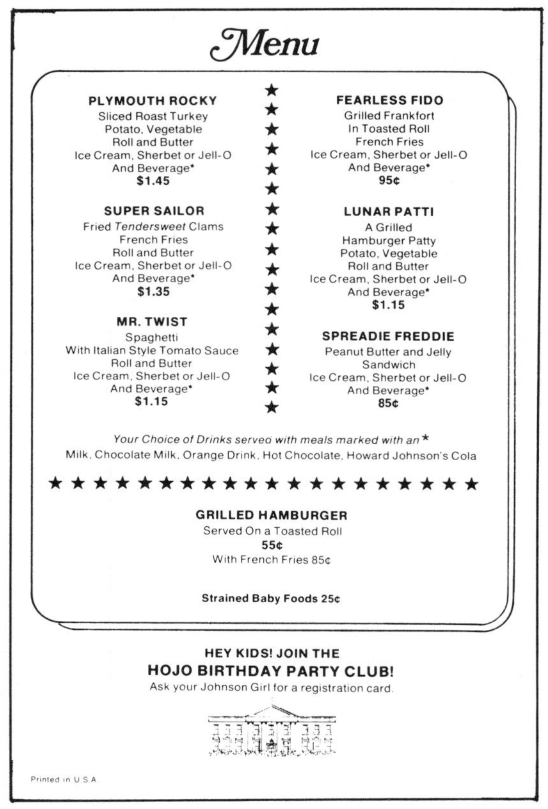

Menu

PLYMOUTH ROCKY
Sliced Roast Turkey
Potato, Vegetable
Roll and Butter
Ice Cream, Sherbet or Jell-O
And Beverage*
$1.45

SUPER SAILOR
Fried *Tendersweet* Clams
French Fries
Roll and Butter
Ice Cream, Sherbet or Jell-O
And Beverage*
$1.35

MR. TWIST
Spaghetti
With Italian Style Tomato Sauce
Roll and Butter
Ice Cream, Sherbet or Jell-O
And Beverage*
$1.15

FEARLESS FIDO
Grilled Frankfort
In Toasted Roll
French Fries
Ice Cream, Sherbet or Jell-O
And Beverage*
95¢

LUNAR PATTI
A Grilled
Hamburger Patty
Potato, Vegetable
Roll and Butter
Ice Cream, Sherbet or Jell-O
And Beverage*
$1.15

SPREADIE FREDDIE
Peanut Butter and Jelly
Sandwich
Ice Cream, Sherbet or Jell-O
And Beverage*
85¢

Your Choice of Drinks served with meals marked with an *
Milk, Chocolate Milk, Orange Drink, Hot Chocolate, Howard Johnson's Cola

GRILLED HAMBURGER
Served On a Toasted Roll
55¢
With French Fries 85¢

Strained Baby Foods 25¢

HEY KIDS! JOIN THE
HOJO BIRTHDAY PARTY CLUB!
Ask your Johnson Girl for a registration card.

Printed in U.S.A.

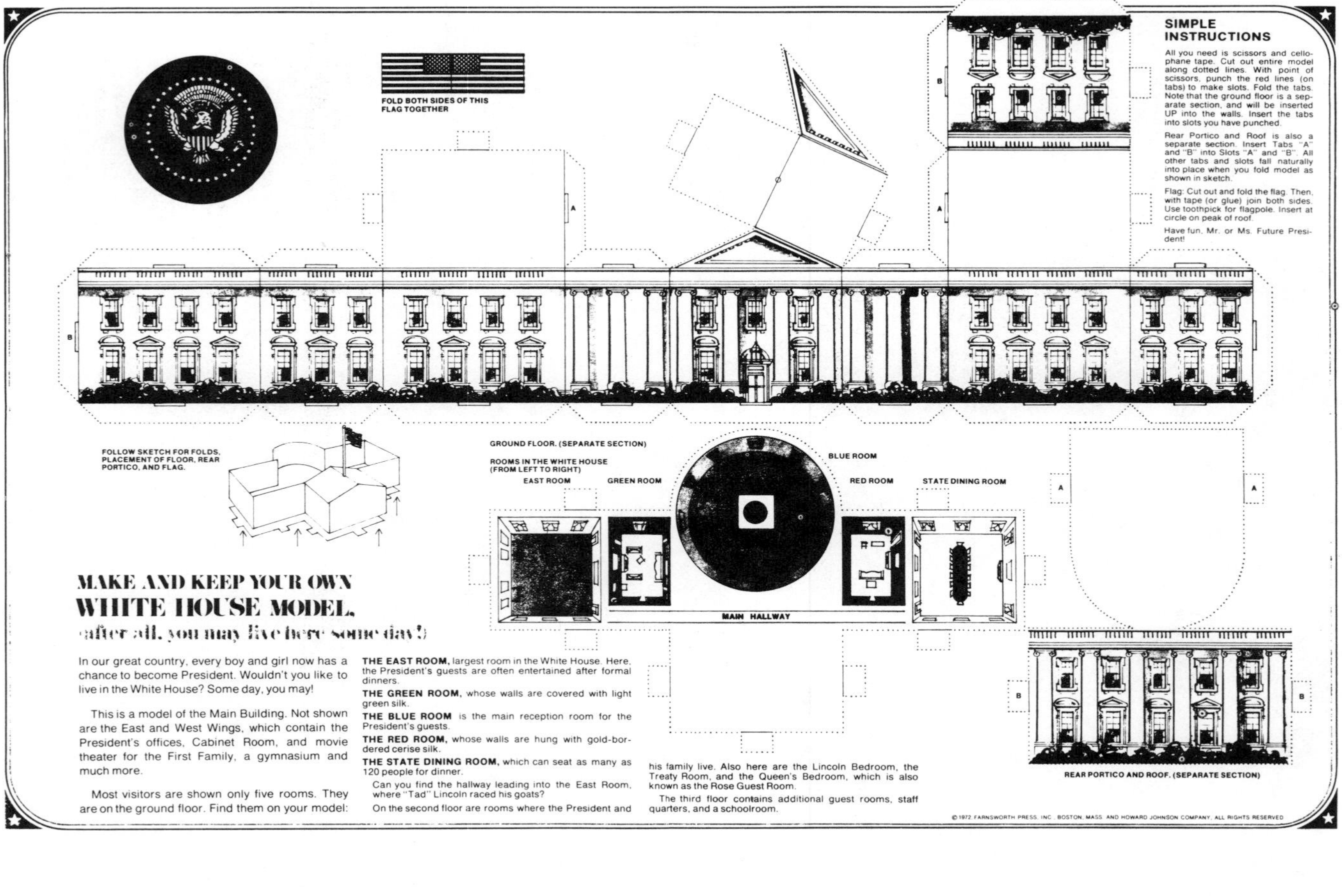

FOLD BOTH SIDES OF THIS FLAG TOGETHER
SIMPLE INSTRUCTIONS
All you need is scissors and cellophane tape. Cut out entire model along dotted lines. With point of scissors, punch the red lines (on tabs) to make slots. Fold the tabs. Note that the ground floor is a separate section, and will be inserted UP into the walls. Insert the tabs into slots you have punched.
Rear Portico and Roof is also a separate section. Insert Tabs "A" and "B" into Slots "A" and "B". All other tabs and slots fall naturally into place when you fold model as shown in sketch.
Flag: Cut out and fold the flag. Then, with tape (or glue) join both sides. Use toothpick for flagpole. Insert at circle on peak of roof.
Have fun, Mr. or Ms. Future President!
FOLLOW SKETCH FOR FOLDS, PLACEMENT OF FLOOR, REAR PORTICO, AND FLAG.
GROUND FLOOR. (SEPARATE SECTION)
ROOMS IN THE WHITE HOUSE (FROM LEFT TO RIGHT)
EAST ROOM
GREEN ROOM
BLUE ROOM
RED ROOM
STATE DINING ROOM
MAIN HALLWAY
MAKE AND KEEP YOUR OWN
WHITE HOUSE MODEL.
(after all, you may live here some day!)
In our great country, every boy and girl now has a chance to become President. Wouldn't you like to live in the White House? Some day, you may!
This is a model of the Main Building. Not shown are the East and West Wings, which contain the President's offices, Cabinet Room, and movie theater for the First Family, a gymnasium and much more.
Most visitors are shown only five rooms. They are on the ground floor. Find them on your model:
THE EAST ROOM, largest room in the White House. Here, the President's guests are often entertained after formal dinners.
THE GREEN ROOM, whose walls are covered with light green silk.
THE BLUE ROOM is the main reception room for the President's guests.
THE RED ROOM, whose walls are hung with gold-bordered cerise silk.
THE STATE DINING ROOM, which can seat as many as 120 people for dinner.
Can you find the hallway leading into the East Room, where "Tad" Lincoln raced his goats?
On the second floor are rooms where the President and his family live. Also here are the Lincoln Bedroom, the Treaty Room, and the Queen's Bedroom, which is also known as the Rose Guest Room.
The third floor contains additional guest rooms, staff quarters, and a schoolroom.
REAR PORTICO AND ROOF. (SEPARATE SECTION)
© 1972 FARNSWORTH PRESS, INC., BOSTON, MASS. AND HOWARD JOHNSON COMPANY. ALL RIGHTS RESERVED.

28
The hospital menu

The hospital menu presents a special communications problem. Unlike the regular menu that must sell as well as tell and try to merchandise the food and drink list, the hospital menu must be (1) functional, (2) economical, (3) act as a public relations media, and (4) operate within special diet requirements.

The menus of the New York University Medical Center shown here meet all of these requirements, and, in addition, attractive and appropriate artwork helps to brighten up an otherwise rather plain menu. It is a three-fold, three-panel menu with one panel for each meal—breakfast, lunch, and dinner. The folds are perforated so that the panel for each meal can be torn off and used separately. And different colored stock is used for each day for easy identification.

One side of the menu, the side with the illustrations of various hospital food service personnel "doing their thing," is preprinted in quantities on a light weight (60 lb.) inexpensive paper. On the other side the captions Breakfast, Lunch, and Dinner are printed with a line of instruction copy which reads, "THIS IS YOUR MENU FOR TOMORROW. Please CIRCLE all food items you desire for each meal. Only the foods circled will be served on your tray. Please complete by 10:30 A.M." This results (within dietary restrictions) in the patient ordering only what he or she feels able and willing to eat and cuts down on food waste.

Across the bottom the words DIET, BED NO., and NAME with appropriate spaces are left for the patient to fill out. The words "NO SUBSTITUTIONS CAN BE MADE WITHOUT SPECIFIC ARRANGEMENTS WITH THE DIETITIAN," plus "Menu subject to change without notice," are printed. This is the entire preprinted portion of the menu.

The daily listing can then be done by electric typewriter and printed within the hospital. Considering the complicated and extensive food service requirements of even a modest size hospital (a hospital must serve three meals a day, 365 days a year, with no days off), the selection offered is generous. Two juices, one fruit, three cereals and two types of eggs plus beverages and pastry are offered for breakfast; and for lunch and dinner, soup or appetizer, two entrees, two and three vegetables, salad plus three or four desserts are offered.

With a generous selection of breads, rolls, and beverages, the patient selects the food and drink he or she likes and the monotony plus "institutional" flavor of the meals is avoided. With wine even being offered in some hospitals, the food service in today's modern hospital has kept up with the developments in contemporary medicine.

THIS IS YOUR MENU FOR TOMORROW. Please CIRCLE all food items you desire for each meal. Only the foods circled will be served on your tray. **Please complete by 10:30 A.M.**

Breakfast M-3
THURSDAY, APRIL 24, 1969

ORANGE JUICE PEAR NECTAR

UNSWEETENED SLICED PEACHES

MALTEX, SF FARINA, SF

SPECIAL K PUFFED RICE

SCRAMBLED EGGS, SF

EGGS, SOFT OR HARD COOKED

(ONE OR TWO)

HARD ROLL

TOAST	COFFEE	MILK	TEA
WHITE SF	SANKA	SKIM MILK	LEMON
RYE	BUTTER	BUTTERMILK	SUGAR
WHOLE WHEAT	SWEET BUTTER	LOW SODIUM MILK	SUGAR SUBSTITUTE
SOFT ROLL	DIETETIC JELLY	CREAM	

Lunch M-3
THURSDAY, APRIL 24, 1969

CREAM OF ASPARAGUS SOUP, SF CHICKEN BROTH SF/FF

ROAST LEG OF LAMB SF/FF
UNSWEETENED JELLY

BRAISED BEEF CUBES SF/FF

PARSLIED POTATOES SF/FF

PIMIENTO WAX BEANS SF/FF

SLICED BEETS SF/FF

ESCAROLE AND ROMAINE SALAD
FRENCH DRESSING SF/FF

SPICED CUP CAKE, SF

UNSWEETENED WHOLE PEELED APRICOTS

FRESH FRUIT IN SEASON

COTTAGE CHEESE SF FF		MILK	TEA	COFFEE
WHITE SF	SOUR CREAM	SKIM MILK	LEMON	SANKA
RYE	BUTTER	BUTTERMILK	SUGAR	JELLO SF
WHOLE WHEAT	SWEET BUTTER	LOW SODIUM MILK	SUGAR SUBSTITUTE	JUNKET
SOFT ROLL	DIETETIC JELLY	CREAM		CUSTARD

Dinner M-3
THURSDAY, APRIL 24, 1969

CREAM OF MUSHROOM SOUP, SF BEEF BROTH SF/FF

TOMATO JUICE, SF

ROAST SIRLOIN OF BEEF AU JUS SF/FF

BROILED CHOPPED

BAKED IDAHO POTATO

WHIPPED POTATOES SF/FF

BROCCOLI SPEARS SF/FF

MASHED SQUASH SF/FF

MOLDED PINEAPPLE SALAD
MAYONNAISE, SF

WHOLE PEELED APRICOTS

UNSWEETENED APPLESAUCE

FRESH FRUIT IN SEASON

COTTAGE CHEESE SF FF		MILK	TEA	COFFEE
WHITE SF	SOUR CREAM	SKIM MILK	LEMON	SANKA
RYE	BUTTER	BUTTERMILK	SUGAR	JELLO SF
WHOLE WHEAT	SWEET BUTTER	LOW SODIUM MILK	SUGAR SUBSTITUTE	JUNKET
SOFT ROLL	DIETETIC JELLY	CREAM		CUSTARD

NO SUBSTITUTION CAN BE MADE WITHOUT SPECIFIC ARRANGEMENTS WITH THE DIETITIAN.

Menu subject to change without notice. Menu subject to change without notice. Menu subject to change without notice.

DIET ______ DIET ______ DIET ______

BED NO. ______ NAME ______ BED NO. ______ NAME ______ BED NO. ______ NAME ______

This menu (pages 188 to 191) *meets the four stated requirements of a hospital listing and in an attractive format as well.*

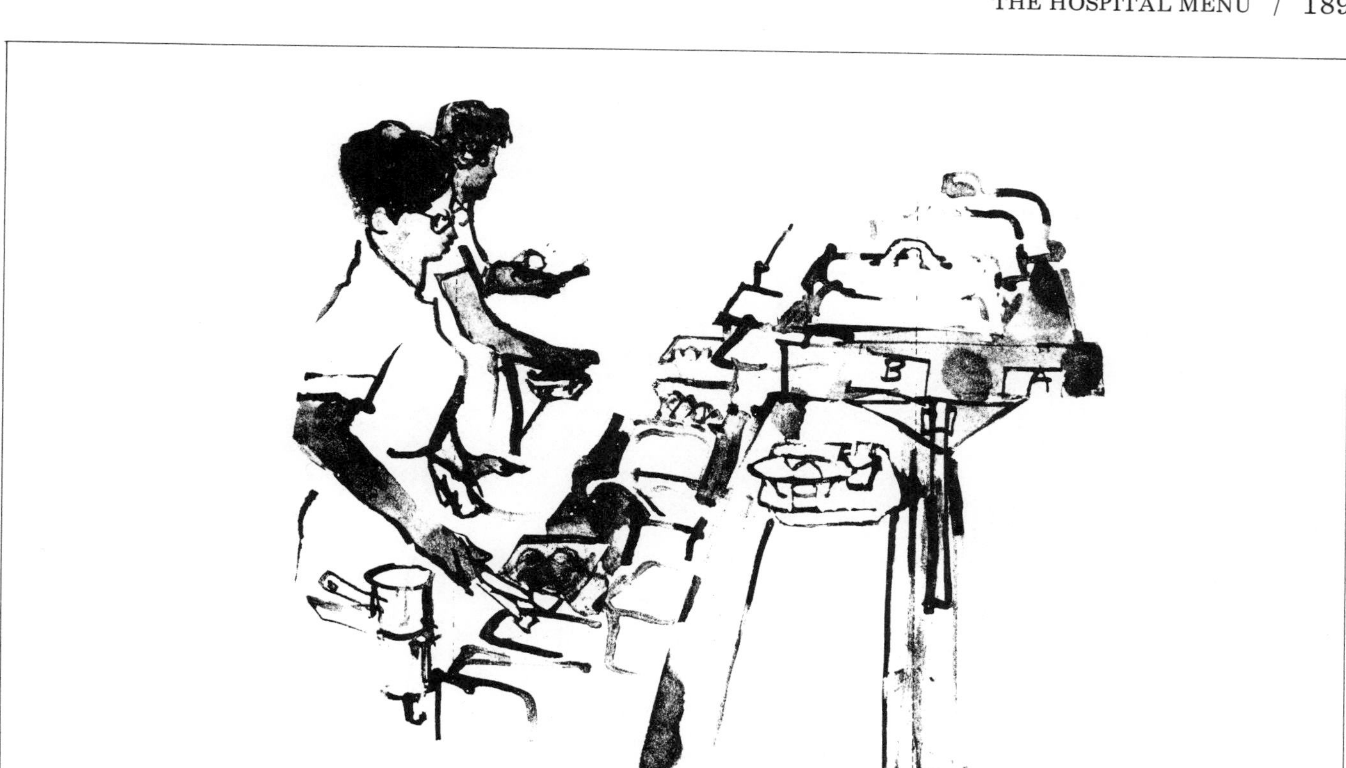

DRAWING BY RICHARD TOMLINSON

New York University Medical Center

DRAWING BY RICHARD TOMLINSON

New York University Medical Center

THIS IS YOUR MENU FOR TOMORROW. Please CIRCLE all food items you desire for each meal. Only the foods circled will be served on your tray. Please complete by 10:30 A.M.

Breakfast M-3

SATURDAY, APRIL 26, 1969

ORANGE JUICE GRAPE JUICE

PRUNE JUICE

FARINA

RICE KRISPIES

SCRAMBLED EGGS

CRISP BACON

EGGS, SOFT OR HARD COOKED

(ONE OR TWO)

HARD ROLL (NO SEEDS)

HARD ROLL, WHITE, SOFT ROLL | COFFEE, SANKA, BUTTER, JELLY | MILK, SKIM MILK, BUTTERMILK, CREAM | TEA, LEMON, SUGAR, SUGAR SUBSTITUTE

Lunch M-3

SATURDAY, APRIL 26, 1969

CREAM OF PEA SOUP, STRAINED   BEEF BROTH

BOILED BEEF, CUT

BROILED LAMB PATTY

STRAINED OR MINCED BEEF

BOILED POTATO

WHIPPED POTATOES

GREEN PEAS

PUREED GREEN PEAS

MASHED SQUASH

CINNAMON COOKIES

BAKED VANILLA CUSTARD

BUTTERSCOTCH PUDDING

COTTAGE CHEESE, WHITE, SOFT ROLL | SOUR CREAM, BUTTER, JELLY | MILK, SKIM MILK, BUTTERMILK, CREAM | TEA, LEMON, SUGAR, SUGAR SUBSTITUTE | COFFEE, SANKA, JELLO, JUNKET, CUSTARD

Dinner M-3

SATURDAY, APRIL 26, 1969

CREAM OF CELERY SOUP, STRAINED   CHICKEN BROTH

GRAPEFRUIT JUICE

BOILED CHICKEN, CUT

BROILED CHOPPED STEAK

STRAINED OR MINCED CHICKEN

BAKED IDAHO POTATO

FLUFFY RICE

ASPARAGUS TIPS

PUREED ASPARAGUS

WAX BEANS

PUREED WAX BEANS

POUND CAKE

ORANGE ICE

LEMON SNOW WITH CUSTARD SAUCE

COTTAGE CHEESE, WHITE, SOFT ROLL | SOUR CREAM, BUTTER, JELLY | MILK, SKIM MILK, BUTTERMILK, CREAM | TEA, LEMON, SUGAR, SUGAR SUBSTITUTE | COFFEE, SANKA, JELLO, JUNKET, CUSTARD

NO SUBSTITUTION CAN BE MADE WITHOUT SPECIFIC ARRANGEMENTS WITH THE DIETITIAN.

Menu subject to change without notice. | Menu subject to change without notice. | Menu subject to change without notice.

DIET Low Residue Bland Soft | DIET Low Residue Bland Soft | DIET Low Residue Bland Soft

BED NO. ______ NAME ______ | BED NO. ______ NAME ______ | BED NO. ______ NAME ______

THIS IS YOUR MENU FOR TOMORROW. Please CIRCLE all food items you desire for each meal. Only the foods circled will be served on your tray. Please complete by 10:30 A.M.

Breakfast M-3

SATURDAY, APRIL 26, 1969

ORANGE JUICE GRAPE JUICE

KADOTA FIGS

PETTIJOHN FARINA

RICE KRISPIES· PUFFED WHEAT

SCRAMBLED EGGS

CRISP BACON

EGGS, SOFT OR HARD COOKED

(ONE OR TWO)

DANISH PASTRY

HARD ROLL, WHITE, RYE, WHOLE WHEAT, SOFT ROLL | BUTTER, SWEET BUTTER, JELLY | MILK, SKIM MILK, BUTTERMILK, CREAM | COFFEE, SANKA, TEA, LEMON, SUGAR

Lunch M-3

SATURDAY, APRIL 26, 1969

FRENCH ONION SOUP

BOILED BEEF WITH MUSTARD SAUCE

SPICED HAM WITH RAISIN SAUCE

PARSLIED POTATOES

WHIPPED POTATOES

GREEN PEAS

BUTTERED YELLOW SQUASH

PICKLED BEETS

WALNUT BROWNIE

BARTLETT PEAR HALVES IN SYRUP

FRESH FRUIT IN SEASON

WHITE, RYE, WHOLE WHEAT, SOFT ROLL | BUTTER, SWEET BUTTER, JELLY | MILK, SKIM MILK, BUTTERMILK, CREAM | COFFEE, SANKA, TEA, LEMON, SUGAR

Dinner M-3

SATURDAY, APRIL 26, 1969

GRAPEFRUIT JUICE

CHICKEN FRICASSEE

STUFFED PEPPER WITH TOMATO SAUCE

PARSLIED RICE

BAKED IDAHO POTATO

BUTTERED ASPARAGUS SPEARS

CAULIFLOWER

CHEF'S SALAD
BLEU CHEESE DRESSING

DEEP DISH CHERRY PIE

ORANGE ICE

GRAPEFRUIT SECTIONS

FRESH FRUIT IN SEASON

WHITE, RYE, WHOLE WHEAT, SOFT ROLL | BUTTER, SWEET BUTTER, JELLY | MILK, SKIM MILK, BUTTERMILK, CREAM | COFFEE, SANKA, TEA, LEMON, SUGAR

NO SUBSTITUTION CAN BE MADE WITHOUT SPECIFIC ARRANGEMENTS WITH THE DIETITIAN.

Menu subject to change without notice. | Menu subject to change without notice. | Menu subject to change without notice.

DIET ______ | DIET ______ | DIET ______

BED NO. ______ NAME ______ | BED NO. ______ NAME ______ | BED NO. ______ NAME ______

DRAWING BY RICHARD TOMLINSON
NEW YORK UNIVERSITY MEDICAL CENTER

THIS IS YOUR MENU FOR TOMORROW. Please CIRCLE all food items you desire for each meal. Only the foods circled will be served on your tray. Please complete by 10:30 A.M.

Breakfast M-3

FRIDAY, APRIL 25, 1969

ORANGE JUICE BLENDED JUICE

UNSWEETENED STEWED MIXED FRUIT

FARINA, SF

CORNFLAKES SF PEP

EGGS, SOFT OR HARD COOKED (ONE OR TWO)

HARD ROLL

TOAST	COFFEE	MILK	TEA
WHITE SF	SANKA	SKIM MILK	LEMON
RYE	BUTTER	BUTTERMILK	SUGAR
WHOLE WHEAT	SWEET BUTTER	LOW SODIUM MILK	SUGAR SUBSTITUTE
SOFT ROLL	DIETETIC JELLY	CREAM	

Lunch M-3

FRIDAY, APRIL 25, 1969

CREAM OF TOMATO SOUP, SF CHICKEN CONSOMME SF/FF

BAKED HALIBUT STEAK SF/FF
LEMON WEDGE
ROAST LEG OF VEAL SF/FF

WHIPPED POTATOES SF/FF

CHOPPED SPINACH SF/FF

BABY LIMA BEANS SF/FF

MARINATED CUCUMBER SALAD

RASPBERRY ICE

UNSWEETENED FRUIT COCKTAIL

FRESH FRUIT IN SEASON

COTTAGE CHEESE SF FF		MILK	TEA	COFFEE
WHITE SF	SOUR CREAM	SKIM MILK	LEMON	SANKA
RYE	BUTTER	BUTTERMILK	SUGAR	JELLO SF
WHOLE WHEAT	SWEET BUTTER	LOW SODIUM MILK	SUGAR SUBSTITUTE	JUNKET
SOFT ROLL	DIETETIC JELLY	CREAM		CUSTARD

Dinner M-3

FRIDAY, APRIL 25, 1969

CREAM OF VEGETABLE SOUP, SF BEEF BOUILLON SF/FF

APPLE JUICE

POACHED FILET OF SOLE SF/FF
LEMON WEDGE

BROILED MINUTE STEAK SF/FF

BAKED IDAHO POTATO

JULIENNE GREEN BEANS SF/FF

DICED CARROTS SF/FF

LETTUCE AND TOMATO SALAD
FRENCH DRESSING SF/FF

FRUIT COCKTAIL

UNSWEETENED SLICED PEACHES

FRESH FRUIT IN SEASON

COTTAGE CHEESE SF FF		MILK	TEA	COFFEE
WHITE SF	SOUR CREAM	SKIM MILK	LEMON	SANKA
RYE	BUTTER	BUTTERMILK	SUGAR	JELLO SF
WHOLE WHEAT	SWEET BUTTER	LOW SODIUM MILK	SUGAR SUBSTITUTE	JUNKET
SOFT ROLL	DIETETIC JELLY	CREAM		CUSTARD

NO SUBSTITUTION CAN BE MADE WITHOUT SPECIFIC ARRANGEMENTS WITH THE DIETITIAN.

Menu subject to change without notice.

DIET ______

BED NO. ______ NAME ______

The Emanuel Medical Center has a simpler yet attractive and effective hospital menu. It is 8½" × 13" and printed in color with illustrations on one side and in two colors—blue and black—on the other side. It lists the Breakfast, Lunch, and Dinner selections all together. The patient circles what he or she wants and signs his or her name and room number. The Lunch and Dinner listing allow for a small, medium, and large order.

Each selection of the menu—dinner, lunch, breakfast—is perforated so that they can be separated and filled individually in the kitchen at various times during the day.

On the front of this menu a Basic Food Guide is printed. It reads as follows:

2 glasses of milk
4 servings of fruits and vegetables including one citrus and one green leafy or deep yellow vegetable
3 servings of meat, fish, poultry, cheese or eggs
3 servings of cereal, bread, potato or substitute
3 servings of cream, dressing or other fat

29
Sandwiches

Most menus list some sandwiches and some list a great number. How you list your sandwiches depends on what portion of your business they constitute or how important they are. For a menu that features big entree items almost exclusively, sandwiches are almost a nuisance item and should be listed accordingly. They should be listed in smaller type on a separate page or panel away from the entree listing. On this kind of a menu, a good place for the sandwich listing is the back page, panel, or cover with Late Evening Snacks.

If sandwiches are not big on your menu (on purpose), be sure they are listed in smaller type with less copy than your entrees. Basically you want the customer to order an expensive entree, not a moderately priced sandwich. If, however, sandwiches constitute an important part of your menu as money-makers and traffic builders, your listing should be of a different character.

You should then give sandwiches comparable billing to your entrees—good position, large, bold type, and good descriptive copy. Even in this kind of sandwich listing, however, you should not give all of your sandwiches the same treatment. Some should get special listing, usually in a box or panel with even larger, bolder type, and more descriptive copy. The selection of which sandwiches to feature should be on the basis of: (1) which are the favorites with the public and (2) which are the bigger profit sandwiches.

Prices on sandwiches can vary from a $5.00 steak sandwich that is really an entree item, to a 75¢ hamburger that is basically a snack item. The hamburger is usually featured because it is a popular item, while the steak sandwich is both popular and a good profit item. It is obvious, however, that the sandwich listing on many a menu is guess listing made on the basis of what the food service operator thinks is a good list. The only good list for any operation is a list that "works"; that is, gets ordered by the public. A "dead" sandwich should not be on any menu. A main division in listing sandwiches, other than Specials, is between Hot Sandwiches and Cold Sandwiches, the usual difference being that more expensive (entree type) items should get bigger billing, again, larger, bolder type, and more descriptive copy.

Of the 278 restaurant menus studied (see Figure 1 and 2), 208 had some sandwiches listed. Only 70 had no sandwiches listed at all, showing that sandwiches are popular on the menu (perhaps too popular in relation to their profit value) on a basis of 3 to 1 when compared to the menu with no sandwiches at all. The number of different sandwiches listed on the menu varies from only one to 35 (15 restaurants listed 35 different sandwiches).

The wide range in the number of sandwiches listed on the menu, from 70 with no sandwiches at all listed to 35 with 20 or more listed, indicates that how many sandwiches you list in your operation is a highly individual problem. The size of your sandwich list should obviously be tailored to your particular market.

As for sandwich popularity, as indicated by how often they are listed on the menu (see Figure 2), there are no real surprises. The 27 sandwiches listed are evidently "America's Favorites," and while you can list sandwiches other than these 27, you will have to promote them harder on the menu to sell them.

The ubiquitous hamburger and cheeseburger combined are tops in popularity, but the ham, cheese, and ham and cheese sandwiches are close behind. The steak sandwich is naturally very high up in the popularity rating and the club, bacon-lettuce-tomato, lettuce-tomato, and bacon-tomato (basically the same sandwich), if combined, reach a popularity that begins to challenge the hamburger and cheeseburger.

While this sandwich popularity rating chart is not the last word in what should be on the sandwich menu it is an indication against which you can check your menu. The rules for sandwich listing on the menu are:

1. List only sandwiches that sell in your operation.
2. Feature popular and big profit sandwiches.
3. Separate hot sandwich and cold sandwich listings.
4. Do not list your sandwiches so that they compete with your entree listing, unless you want to sell more sandwiches than entrees.

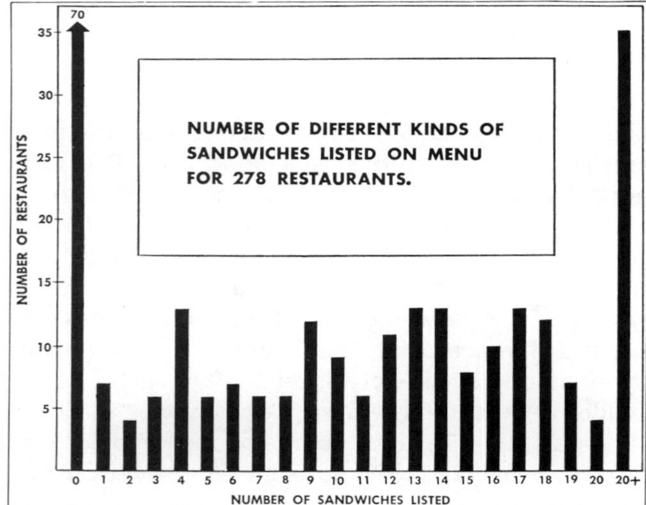

FIGURE 1

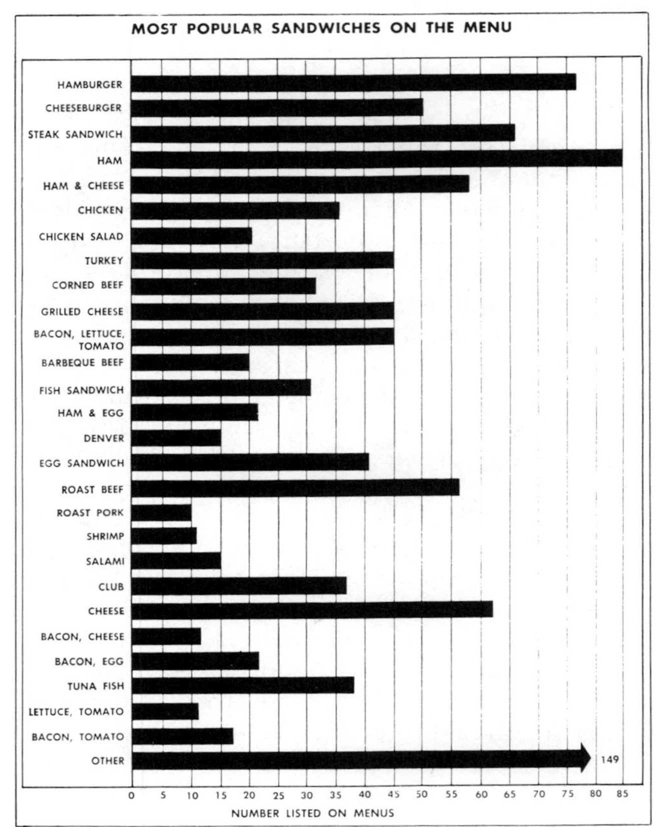

FIGURE 2

CORNED BEEF, delicious slices of fresh Kosher Corned Beef stacked sky-high on **OLD FASHIONED RYE** bread with plenty of **KOSHER DILLS** and a heaping plate of the finest **SAUERKRAUT.**

A Man Sized Lunch . . . and a Real Value 1.10

Sandwiches creatively presented can make good "specials."

Giant Italian Sandwiches

A meal in a Loaf of Bread — Your Choice of Six Combinations

No. 1 .... 1.00
"CASA'S" SANDWICH
A Loaf of Our Special Italian Bread
filled with Salami, Capicola, Provolone Cheese, Lettuce, Tomatoes, Pickles, Onions and Salad Dressing

No. 2 .... .95
GIANT "MEATBALL" SANDWICH
A Loaf of Our Special Italian Bread
filled with
Baked Italian Meatballs and Casa Nova's Spaghetti Sauce

No. 3 .... 1.00
GIANT "HAM" SANDWICH
A Loaf of Our Special Italian Bread
filled with
Ham and Salad Dressing, Lettuce

No. 4 .... 1.00
GIANT "HOT SAUSAGE" SANDWICH
A Loaf of Our Special Italian Bread
filled with
Baked Hot Italian Sausage and Casa Nova's Spaghetti Sauce

No. 5 .... .95
GIANT CHOPPED "SIRLOIN TIP" SANDWICH
A Loaf of Our Special Italian Bread
filled with Sirloin Tip cooked in Tomatoes and Mushroom Sauce

No. 6 .... 1.00
A LOAF OF OUR SPECIAL ITALIAN BREAD
filled with
Ground Beef, Tomato, Lettuce, and Salad Dressing

An Italian menu can feature Italian sandwiches as shown here.

From The Sandwich Board

Hot Sandwiches

BARBEQUE BEEF SANDWICH
Tender slices of beef in a sharp sauce on a toasted Bun with French Fried Potatoes, Cole Slaw, Pickle 1.35

SLICED TURKEY ON TOAST WITH CREAM GRAVY
and Parmesan Cheese au Gratin, Spiced Peach, French Fried Potatoes 1.85

MELTED OLDE ENGLISH CHEESE DELIGHT
Olde Cheddar Cheese over toast, crisp bacon and tomato, Long Branch Potato, Cole Slaw 1.35

HOT ROAST BEEF SANDWICH,
Brown Gravy, Cream Whipped Potato, Peas in Butter, Cole Slaw 1.75

THE STEAK SANDWICH
Selected top sirloin steak on toast, bermuda onion grilled, French Fried Potato, Cole Slaw, Tomato 2.95

JUMBO HAMBURGER ON TOASTED BUN
with Grilled Onion, Pickle, French Fried Potatoes 1.25
topped with Cheddar or Roquefort Cheese 1.50

Regular Sandwiches

THREE DECKER CLUB
Sliced Chicken, Bacon, Lettuce, Tomato, Mayonnaise Garni, Cole Slaw, Olives, Saratoga Chips 1.60

SOONER OPEN FACE
Sliced Turkey, Crisp Bacon, Hard Boiled Egg, Tomato Slice on Rye Bread, topped with Russian Dressing, Cole Slaw, Pickle Rings 1.50

SLICED TURKEY AND SWISS CHEESE, TOMATO
served on choice of bread, 1000 Island Dressing, Saratoga Chips, Cole Slaw, Pickle 1.35

Baked Ham and Tomato 1.00 **Sliced Chicken 1.00** **Chicken Salad .90**
Ham and Cheese 1.00 **Denver .90** **Fried Ham and Egg 1.00**
French Fried Potatoes .25

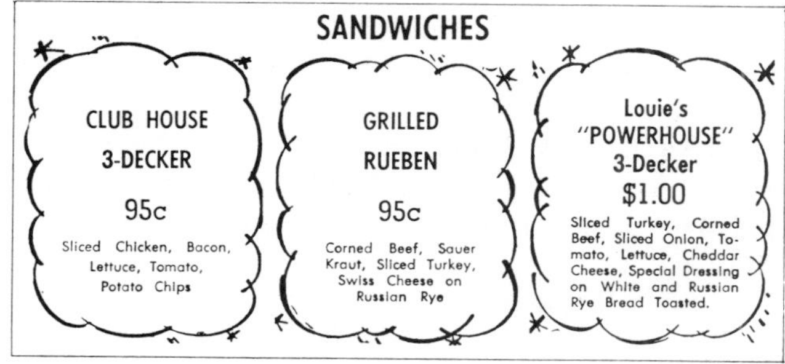

SANDWICHES

CLUB HOUSE 3-DECKER
95c
Sliced Chicken, Bacon, Lettuce, Tomato, Potato Chips

GRILLED RUEBEN
95c
Corned Beef, Sauer Kraut, Sliced Turkey, Swiss Cheese on Russian Rye

Louie's "POWERHOUSE" 3-Decker
$1.00
Sliced Turkey, Corned Beef, Sliced Onion, Tomato, Lettuce, Cheddar Cheese, Special Dressing on White and Russian Rye Bread Toasted.

Hot or cold, open face or triple deck, a good sandwich listing should cover all types and shapes.

Combination Sandwiches

(PLEASE ORDER BY NUMBER)

No. 1 "MARRON'S SUPREME" (Triple Decker) 1.55
Corned Beef, Salami, Roast Beef, Pastrami and Tongue wtih Cole Slaw

No. 2 "LIDO SPECIAL" (Triple Decker) 1.65
Sliced Turkey, Roast Beef, Tongue with Russian Dressing and Cole Slaw

No. 3 "MY HERO" on Club 1.75
Sliced Roast Turkey and Hot Pastrami, Sweet Red Pepper and Cole Slaw

No. 4 "EAST END DELUXE" 1.35
Corned Beef with Chopped Liver and Cole Slaw

No. 5 "ATLANTIC BEACH DREAMBOAT" 1.20
Roast Beef, Sliced Onion, Lettuce and Tomato with Russian Dressing and Cole Slaw

No. 6 "THE OCEAN FRONT" 1.45
Hot Pastrami and Corned Beef with Cole Slaw

No. 7 "WEST END GOURMET" (Triple Decker) 1.45
Tongue, Rolled Beef, Corned Beef, Russian Dressing and Cole Slaw

No. 8 "PARK ST. SPECIAL" .... .95
Salami and Bologna with Cole Slaw

No. 9 "PT. LOOKOUT TREAT" 1.20
Tongue and Salami with Cole Slaw

Campbell House Favorites

THE KEFTABURGER . . . A RED LION CREATION 1.25
A tangy spiced Whopper Burger broiled over the flame, topped with Creamed Imported Roquefort Cheese and served on Sesame Roll

REUBEN 1.35
Baked Corned Beef with Marinated Bavarian Sauerkraut on Rye Bread

NEW YORKER 1.35
Kosher styled Corned Beef, spicy German Potato Salad with real Kosher Style Dill Pickle. Choice of Roll or Bread

SIR-LOIN "SA" LOT 1.35
Thinly sliced brisket of Beef Au Jus, kingly portioned, tangy Horseradish, hot German Potato Salad, choice of Bread or Roll

HOAGY ITALIANO 1.50
Hot Italian Pastramy stacked on choice of Bread, with our own German Potato Salad or tangy Sauerkraut

KNIGHT'S SPECIAL 1.25
A bountiful portion of thin sliced Danish Ham on sliced Sesame Bun with our own Potato Salad

RED LION EYE 2.65
Choice Rib-Eye selected from the heart of the rib, served open face with Potato Salad and Horseradish

Sandwiches do not have to be presented under the same old names, as the examples shown here demonstrate.

The world's biggest sandwich menu? Well, until another comes along, *D.B. Kaplan's Delicatessen* menu will do, and it is not only big—152 sandwiches are listed—it is also an example of first class sandwich merchandising. There are nine classifications of sandwiches. First there is Hearty "Party" Sandwiches. One is *The Hostess with the Mostest*—Serves at least 40 people—and that's a PARTY! Danish ham, cotto salami, Vienna bologna, Usinger's summer sausage, and Swiss and provolone cheeses. It's a Triple Decker, *six* feet long. We need three days to prepare it for you. $75.00.

Under the heading of Three More Extensions On Our "Party Line," *D.B. Kaplan's* lists the *All Time Chomp*—A knockout, with six decks of Vienna corned beef, rare roast beef, Polish baked ham, breast of turkey, Swiss, muenster and herkimer cheeses all on rye bread with assorted condiments. Potato salad and pickles included. Six people can eat it here or take it home to their poker game. $20.00.

Next, there is Triple Deckers for Big Fressers. One of these is *Tongue Fu*—beef tongue, pepperbeef and corned beef, with Swiss cheese and Bavarian mustard on black bread served HOT! $4.25.

Then, under the heading of Combinations there are forty sandwiches offered. They are sold under such clever headings as: *All Hens on Deck*, *Royal Canadian Mounted Brisket*, *The Spice Who Came in From the Cold*, and *Turning Over a New Beef*!

Six more sandwiches are listed under the category of Mother Nature's Treats and eight are offered as Breadless Beauties. One of the latter is *The Breadless Horseman*—Danish ham, shredded lettuce, tomato, stone ground mustard between two slices of muenster cheese (no bread). $2.75.

With a Touch of the Sea is a seafood sandwich offering. These ten sandwiches include one called *Lox*, *Stock* and *Bagel*—Nova Scotia lox, Canadian bacon, cream cheese with chives, tomato slices served open faced on a toasted bagel. $4.50.

This selection is followed by All American Favorites (14 sandwiches) and Old Standbys (34 sandwiches). The menu is 11½″ × 36″ but folds up into 11″ × 6″ for easier handling. It is printed on cream-colored paper in brown ink.

HEARTY "PARTY" SANDWICHES

SEVERAL FEET OF GREAT EATING. THE MOST TALKED ABOUT SANDWICHES IN CHICAGO.

1. **THE HOSTESS WITH THE MOSTEST**—Serves at least 40 people—and that's a PARTY! Danish ham, cotto salami, vienna bologna, Usinger's summer sausage and swiss and provolone cheeses. It's a triple-decker, *six feet* long. We need three days to prepare it for you.______**$75.00**
2. **THE GREAT ENTERTAINER**—A three-foot long triple-decker (kind of a "yard" party for 20 people). Same delicious ingredients as above—and we need the same three days notice, too! **$45.00**
3. **THE LIFE OF THE PARTY**—A foot-long triple-decker that'll feed you and nine friends. Or nine hungry strangers, if you're the generous type. Once again, the same great things in it. But this one we can prepare right away, if you've got time to wait. _**$20.00**

THREE MORE EXTENSIONS ON OUR "PARTY LINE."

4. **THE ALL TIME CHOMP**—A knockout, with six decks of vienna corned beef, rare roast beef, polish baked ham, breast of turkey, swiss, muenster and herkimer cheeses all on rye bread with assorted condiments. Potato salad and pickles included. Six people can eat it here or take it home to their poker game. ______**$20.00**
5. **EATS OF EDEN**—You'll think you're in paradise! A heavenly five decker sandwich with danish ham, breast of turkey, hickory smoked bacon, vienna pepperbeef, provolone and muenster cheeses assembled on dark and light rye. Assorted condiments included. It's utopia for four famished feasters!______**$18.00**
6. **THE MOUTH THAT ROARED**—A sausage sensation that'll nip you in the taste buds. Four layers of vienna bologna and salami, Usinger's summersausage, genoa and hard salamis, swiss and american cheeses and even canadian bacon. Serves two or three roaring appetites.______**$15.00**

TRIPLE DECKERS FOR BIG FRESSERS—

All sandwiches from #7 thru #152 include pickle and your choice of potato salad, cole slaw or potato chips.

7. **A BRISKET, A BASKET**—Better not be bashful! Layers of beef brisket, beef tongue, breast of turkey and vienna corned beef...add monterey jack and herkimer cheeses with lots of shredded lettuce, bermuda onion and tomato slices on schlepper Simon's jewish cholly. Marvelous!______**$5.75**
8. **TONGUE FU**—Beef tongue, pepperbeef and corned beef, with swiss cheese and bavarian mustard on black bread served HOT!______**$4.25**
9. **STUDS TURKEY**—Breast of turkey, all beef tongue and canadian style bacon mounded upon shredded lettuce and whole cranberry sauce served HOT on french bread.______**$4.25**
10. **SGT. PEPPER'S LONELY**—Vienna pepperbeef, polish baked ham, hickory smoked bacon, swiss cheese, bermuda onions and mayo served HOT on an onion roll.______**$4.25**
11. **THE AFFAIR**—Vienna corned beef, rare roast beef, cole slaw, swiss cheese and russian dressing on bavarian black bread.______**$3.95**
12. **THE ALL PRO**—Proscuitto ham, provolone cheese, vienna pepperbeef, spicy brown mustard, lettuce, onion on an onion roll, served HOT. **$3.95**
13. **THE WALTZING ITALIAN**—Vienna corned beef, proscuitto ham, muenster cheese, shredded lettuce and mayo all on an onion roll, served HOT. _**$3.95**
14. **THE MICHIGAN AVENUE**—THE ALL TIME CHAMP!—It used to be the number ten, but times change. It remains our rare roast beef, breast of turkey, topped with muenster cheese, shredded lettuce, bermuda onions and russian dressing on rye.___**$3.95**
15. **THE NEAR NORTH**—Our own rare roast beef, chopped liver, muenster cheese, lettuce, bermuda onions and russian dressing on rye toast.______**$3.95**
16. **HAM IT UP**—Polish baked ham, genoa salami, N.Y. herkimer cheddar, shredded lettuce, tomato slices and russian dressing on rye toast.______**$3.95**
17. **LOVE AT FIRST BITE**—Remember this one? Our rare roast beef, hickory smoked bacon, muenster cheese, shredded lettuce and lots of russian dressing served HOT on rye toast!______**$3.95**
18. **HEDDA GOBBLER**—Breast of turkey, canadian-style bacon, swiss cheese, lettuce, tomato slices and mayo on toasted rye, served HOT.______**$3.95**
19. **CHIVE TURKEY**—Breast of turkey, cream cheese with chives, proscuitto ham, and bavarian style mustard on black bread.______**$3.95**
20. **GAY LIVERATION**—Vienna corned beef, chopped liver, swiss cheese, shredded lettuce, tomato slices, M&M on rye toast.______**$3.75**
21. **WHAT'S THE GOOD BIRD?**—Breast of turkey, chopped liver, N.Y. herkimer cheddar, lettuce, tomato and mayo on schlepper Simon's jewish cholly. ___**$3.75**
22. **LIVE AND LET LIVER**—Extra lean pepperbeef, chopped liver, swiss cheese, shredded lettuce, onions, M&M on schlepper Simon's jewish cholly! ______**$3.75**
23. **TONGUE-IN-CHEESE**—All beef tongue, swiss cheese, breast of turkey, shredded lettuce, tomato slices and mayo on dark rye.______**$3.75**
24. **TEARS IN YOUR RYE**—Usinger's liversausage, Norwegian brisling sardines, bermuda onion, lettuce and mayo on rye toast.______**$3.75**
25. **ATTILA THE HAM**—Breast of turkey, polish baked ham, shredded lettuce, tomato slices and mayo on an onion roll.______**$3.50**
26. **THE PORKY PIG**—Beef tongue, hickory smoked bacon, monterey jack cheese, lettuce, tomato, and mayo served HOT on an onion roll (Th-Th-that's all, folks).______**$3.50**

68. **DE BIRD AND D.B.'s**—Breast of turkey, Usinger's liversausage, american cheese and light mustard on bavarian black bread.______**$2.75**
69. **HOT, 2,3,4**—Thick cut, fried all beef vienna salami, muenster cheese, onions, horseradish and dark mustard served HOT on french bread.______**$2.75**
70. **FOWL BALL**—Home made turkey salad and breast of turkey, shredded lettuce, tomato slices and mayo on whole wheat toast.______**$2.75**
71. **50 WAYS TO LEAVE YOUR LIVER**—Chopped liver, cream cheese with chives, onions, served on bavarian black bread.______**$2.50**
72. **BACON WHOOPEE**—Usinger's liversausage, hickory smoked bacon, swiss cheese, shredded lettuce, bermuda onion and mayo on wheat toast.______**$2.50**
73. **THE CHUTZPAH**—Vienna N.Y. style pastrami, hickory smoked bacon, horseradish and bavarian mustard served HOT on an onion roll.______**$2.50**
74. **CHILDHOOD LOST**—Peanut butter, grape jelly and hickory smoked bacon served on wheat toast.___**$2.50**
75. **AW BALONEY**—Vienna all beef bologna, cream cheese with chives served on rye toast.______**$2.50**
76. **BABY D.B.'s SPECIAL**—Hickory smoked bacon, peanut butter and banana slices on wheat toast._**$2.50**
77. **HELLO CHOLLY**—Beef brisket, shredded lettuce, tomato slices and mayo served HOT on schlepper Simon's toasted cholly.______**$2.50**
78. **TURNING OVER A NEW BEEF**—Beef brisket, DBQ sauce, and bermuda onions served HOT on french bread.______**$2.50**
79. **THE MISSING LINK**—Usinger's liversausage, american cheese, light mustard served on whole wheat toast.______**$2.25**
80. **RICKEY RECOTTO**—Cotto salami, provolone cheese, bermuda onions, tomato slices and bavarian mustard served HOT on french bread.______**$2.25**

MOTHER NATURE'S TREATS

81. **CO-CHEESE**—Canadian bacon, monterey jack and herkimer cheeses touched with spicy brown mustard and served HOT on french bread.______**$3.25**
82. **BACON YOUR PARDON**—Hickory smoked bacon, muenster, monterey jack and provolone cheeses, topped with shredded lettuce, tomato slices and bavarian mustard served HOT on french bread.______**$3.25**
83. **TWO'S COMPANY**—N.Y. herkimer and provolone cheeses, shredded lettuce and tomato slices with M&M on french bread. Great cold, but even better HOT.______**$2.75**
84. **THREE'S A CROWD**—Swiss, N.Y. herkimer and muenster cheeses, shredded lettuce and tomato slices with M&M on french bread. Great cold, but even better HOT!______**$2.75**
85. **YES SIR, CHEESE MY BABY**—Swiss and muenster cheeses with shredded lettuce and bavarian mustard on toasted whole wheat.______**$2.75**
86. **THE HAWAYA SALAD** has moved to a new home. Check out Salads, Salads and More Salads.

BREADLESS BEAUTIES

87. **BERMUDA SCHWARTZ**—Rare roast beef, shredded lettuce, bermuda onion, tomato slices and mayo between two slices of muenster cheese (no bread). **$3.75**
88. **LIVERS AND OTHER STRANGERS**—Vienna corned beef, chopped liver, bermuda onions, tomato slices, M&M between two slices of monterey jack cheese (no bread).______**$3.75**
89. **FOWL PLAY**—Breast of turkey, shredded lettuce, tomato slices, and russian dressing between two slices of swiss cheese (no bread).______**$3.50**
90. **THE BREADLESS HORSEMAN**—Danish ham, shredded lettuce, tomato, stone ground mustard between two slices of colby longhorn cheese (no bread). ______**$3.50**
91. **GOODNIGHT VIENNA**—All beef vienna salami, lettuce, bermuda onion and dusseldorf mustard between two slices of muenster cheese (no bread).______**$2.75**
92. **WOULDN'T IT BE LIVERLY**—Chopped liver, shredded lettuce, bermuda onion and mayo between two slices of monterey jack cheese (no bread).______**$2.75**
93. **ON TOP OF OLD SMOKEY**—Hickory smoked bacon, shredded lettuce, tomato slices, and mayo between two slices of swiss cheese (no bread).______**$2.25**
94. **PLAIN FARE**—Plain and simple! Lettuce, tomato slices and bermuda onions with our own blended dressing between two slices of colby longhorn cheese (no bread).______**$2.25**

WITH A TOUCH OF THE SEA

95. **LOX, STOCK AND BAGEL**—Nova Scotia lox, canadian bacon, cream cheese with chives, tomato slices served open faced on a toasted bagel.______**$4.50**
96. **VIDAL SARDINE**—Whitefish caviar, Norwegian brisling sardines, plain cream cheese and bermuda onion slices served on an onion roll.______**$4.50**
97. **THE NAVEL BATTLE**—Belly lox, white fish caviar, and cream cheese with chives served open face on bavarian black bread.______**$4.50**
98. **LOX-A-LUCK**—Nova Scotia or belly lox, plain or chive cream cheese, choice of tomato or onion slices served open-faced on a toasted bagel.______**$3.95**
99. **CHICAGO WHITE LOX**—Nova Scotia lox, swiss cheese, cream cheese with chives served open-faced on a toasted bagel.______**$3.95**
100. **LOX & BRENTANO'S**—Nova Scotia lox, swiss cheese, bermuda onion slices, and tomato served HOT on a toasted bagel.______**$3.50**

D.B. Kaplan's does it with words. This menu has probably the best sandwich copy around—anywhere!

27. **BEEF ENCOUNTER**—Beef brisket, breast of turkey, monterey jack cheese, shredded lettuce and mayo on schlepper Simon's jewish cholly, served HOT. $3.50

28. **THE GREAT DANE**—Danish ham, salami, provolone cheese, dusseldorf mustard and shredded lettuce on an onion roll. $3.50

29. **TURKEY IN THE SLAW**—Breast of turkey, hickory smoked bacon, colby longhorn cheese, cole slaw and russian dressing on schlepper Simon's jewish cholly. $3.50

30. **BYE, BYE BLACKBREAD**—Usinger's liversausage, rare roast beef, swiss cheese, shredded lettuce and russian dressing on bavarian black bread. $3.50

31. **THE KILLER**—Usinger's summer sausage, cotto salami, vienna salami, american cheese, shredded lettuce, tomato slices, and V&O dressing on rye bread. $3.50

32. **THE CHICAGO STING-WICH**—Vienna pepperbeef, genoa salami, provolone cheese, dusseldorf mustard and onions on whole wheat toast. $3.50

33. **THE SPICE IS RIGHT**—Cream cheese with chives, hard salami, vienna bologna, monterey jack cheese, spicy brown mustard served on black bread. $3.50

34. **THE CHICAGO CLUBS**—Vienna salami and bologna, hickory smoked bacon, swiss cheese, shredded lettuce, dark mustard served HOT on toasted rye. $3.50

35. **IKE AND TINA TUNA**—White meat tuna salad, hickory smoked bacon, monterey jack cheese, shredded lettuce and tomato slices served piping HOT on an onion roll. $3.50

36. **I WOULDN'T BRISKET**—Beef brisket, N.Y. style pastrami, monterey jack cheese and dark mustard served HOT on an onion roll. $3.25

37. **SOME LIKE IT HOT**—Chopped liver, N.Y. style pastrami, bermuda onions and american cheese. M&M served HOT on bavarian black bread. $3.25

38. **SIXTEEN TONGUES AND WHAT'DYA GET?**—Beef tongue, N.Y. style pastrami, sauerkraut and horseradish, topped with american cheese. M&M served HOT on an onion roll. $3.25

39. **THE CUCKOO CLUCK**—Home made turkey salad, polish baked ham, shredded lettuce, mayo and tomato slices served on toasted wheat bread. $3.25

COMBINATIONS

40. **REUBEN, RUBIN!**—Vienna corned beef or N.Y. style pastrami, swiss cheese, sauerkraut and russian dressing served HOT on bavarian black bread. $3.50

41. **THE HUGH HEFFER**—Our famous rare roast beef topped with N.Y. herkimer cheddar, onions, DBQ sauce served sizzling HOT on a kaiser roll. $3.50

42. **HOLED YOUR TONGUE**—Beef tongue, swiss cheese, polish baked ham, and bavarian mustard served HOT on a kaiser roll. $3.50

43. **ALL HENS ON DECK**—Breast of turkey, polish baked ham, swiss cheese and stone ground mustard served HOT on an onion roll. $3.50

44. **THE OUTER SPICE**—Proscuitto ham, provolone cheese, onions, horseradish, and spicy brown mustard served HOT on french bread. $3.50

45. **ANY PORK IN A STORM**—Hickory smoked bacon, vienna corned beef, swiss cheese, cole slaw and dusseldorf mustard served HOT on french bread. $3.50

46. **LORD NOSE**—Beef tongue, Norwegian brisling sardines, N.Y. herkimer cheddar, shredded lettuce, tomato slices and mayo served on an onion roll. $3.50

47. **LAKE SHORE CHIVE**—Rare roast beef, cream cheese with chives served on bavarian black bread. $3.50

48. **SORRY, CHOLLY**—White meat tuna salad, herkimer cheese, shredded lettuce and tomato slices served HOT on schlepper Simon's toasted cholly. $3.50

49. **LANA TUNA**—White meat tuna salad and american cheese, shredded lettuce served HOT on a kaiser roll. $3.50

50. **PERKY HERK**—Genoa salami, N.Y. herkimer cheese, shredded lettuce, tomato slices and russian dressing on bavarian black bread. $3.25

51. **THERE OUGHTTA BE A SLAW**—Vienna corned beef, cole slaw and light mustard served HOT on rye toast. $3.25

52. **A BIRD TO THE WISE**—Breast of turkey set on a bed of shredded lettuce and whole cranberry sauce served HOT on french bread. $3.25

53. **THERE IS NOTHING LIKE A DANE**—Danish ham, cream cheese with chives served on french bread. $3.25

54. **BIBER'S SPECIAL**—Our rare roast beef, shredded lettuce, bermuda onion and russian dressing on rye. $3.25

55. **THE SPICE WHO CAME IN FROM THE COLD**—Vienna pepperbeef, N.Y. herkimer cheddar, spicy brown mustard served HOT on bavarian black bread. $3.25

56. **CAN-AM**—Canadian bacon, american cheese, and cole slaw served HOT on a kaiser roll. $3.25

57. **A LEGITIMATE BEEF**—Rare roast beef, swiss cheese, dusseldorf mustard served on schlepper Simon's jewish cholly. $3.25

58. **ROYAL CANADIAN MOUNTED BRISKET**—Beef brisket, canadian bacon, shredded lettuce and tomato slices served HOT on a kaiser roll with mayo. $3.25

59. **THE MOOSCOW**—Our rare roast beef, cole slaw and russian dressing served on dark rye. $3.25

60. **BRING HOME THE BACONS**—Hickory smoked and canadian bacons, american cheese, shredded lettuce, tomato slices and mayo served HOT on wheat toast. $2.95

61. **RADISHING BEAUTY**—Our rare roast beef, bermuda onions and horseradish served HOT on an onion roll. $2.95

62. **THE SPICED HAM COMETH**—Danish ham, cotto salami, provolone cheese and spicy brown mustard served HOT on french bread. $2.95

63. **CHEESE JUST MY TYPE**—Danish ham, colby longhorn cheese, shredded lettuce and tomato slices with russian dressing on an onion roll. $2.95

64. **CALL IT WHATEVER**—Polish baked ham, swiss cheese, tomato slices and russian dressing served on rye bread. $2.95

65. **THE SUBMARINE**—It's a deep, dark secret! $2.95

66. **CRY ME A LIVER**—Chopped liver, hickory smoked bacon, shredded lettuce, bermuda onion and mayo on schlepper Simon's jewish cholly. $2.75

67. **COMISKEY PORK**—Usinger's liversausage, hickory smoked bacon, pickle relish, lettuce, tomato slices and mayo on toasted rye. $2.75

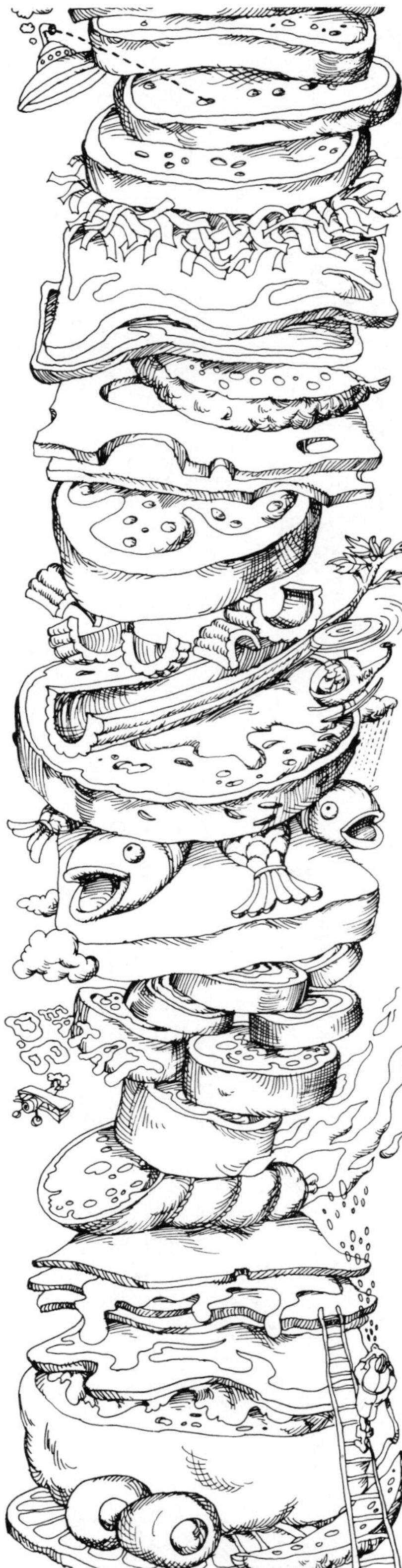

DUE TO UNSTABLE MARKET CONDITIONS PRICES ARE SUBJECT TO CHANGE WITHOUT NOTICE.

101. **FISH SHTIK**—Norwegian brisling sardines, hickory smoked bacon, and shredded lettuce served on rye toast. $3.50

102. **DICK CAVIAR**—Whitefish caviar, chive cream cheese served open-face on bavarian black bread. $3.25

103. **HICKORY DICKORY LOX**—Hickory smoked bacon, chive cream cheese and tomato slices on a toasted bagel. $3.25

103A. **THE LOX NESS MONSTER**—A monster of a meal. Both Nova Scotia and belly lox served with tomato slices, bermuda onions, black olives, pickled tomato, plain and chive cream cheese, plus bagels. A super meal...the lochs of which you've never seen.
for two $ 6.50
for four $11.50
for six $15.50

ALL AMERICAN FAVORITES

104. **WEINER AND STILL CHAMPEEN**—Two all beef vienna hot dogs, swiss cheese, relish, onions and light mustard on a kaiser roll. $3.25

105. **ABRAHAM'S LINK**—Two of Usinger's polish sausages, swiss and american cheeses on a kaiser roll with onions and DBQ sauce. $3.25

106. **WHAT'S THE USINGER**—Usinger's smoked polish with slices of corned beef, american cheese and mustard on french bread. $2.50

107. **BEEF IN A BLANKET**—All beef vienna hot dog, crisp hickory smoked bacon, monterey jack cheese and dark mustard on french bread. $2.50

108. **DOIN' THE SPLITS**—Usinger's split bratwurst, thinly sliced proscuitto ham, tomato slices and mustard on a kaiser roll. $2.50

109. **THE RED BARON**—All beef vienna hot dog served with swiss cheese, sauerkraut and russian dressing on french bread. $2.50

110. **THE FRANKENBEEF MUENSTER**—All beef vienna hot dog wrapped in muenster cheese, onions, bavarian mustard on french bread. $2.50

111. **HOT BRAT**—Usinger's bratwurst, N.Y. herkimer cheddar, DBQ sauce and onions on french bread. $2.50

112. **SPLIT PERSONALITY**—Usinger's split polish sausage, cole slaw, american cheese and mustard on a kaiser roll. $2.50

113. **WRAP SESSION**—Usinger's polish sausage wrapped in provolone cheese, onions, and bavarian mustard on french bread. $2.50

114. **STAND OUT FROM THE KRAUT**—All beef vienna hot dog, sauerkraut, onions and DBQ sauce on french bread. $2.50

115. **THE FRENCHFURTER**—All beef vienna hot dog on french bread or a hot dog bun with your choice of the works—mustard, dark mustard, ketchup, relish, onions, sauerkraut, etc. $2.25

116. **CASEY AT THE BRAT**—Usinger's bratwurst on french bread with the same options as the hot dog. $2.25

117. **THE ROLY POLISH**—Usinger's polish sausage on french bread with—that's right...the same as the others. $2.25

OLD STANDBYS

All sandwiches from #7 thru #152 include pickle and your choice of potato salad, cole slaw or potato chips.

Old Standbys are served on your choice of...rye, black, white, wheat, french, onion roll, kaiser roll or bagel... toasted if desired with cole slaw, potato salad, or chips — no extra charge

to be topped with...shredded lettuce, tomato slices, onions or sauerkraut — no extra charge

frommage...American cheese, colby longhorn, muenster, N.Y. herkimer cheddar, provolone or monterey jack — 35¢ extra

With condiments of...yellow mustard, dusseldorf mustard, mayo, DBQ sauce, ketchup, Russian dressing, horseradish or relish — no extra charge

Cut, uncut, HOT, cold or on your lap — no extra charge

Too much grief and aggravation to the waitress — 25¢

Making a chozzer out of yourself — heartburn

118. Rare roast beef $2.85
119. Hot vienna corned beef $2.85
120. Hot vienna pepperbeef $2.85
121. Hot beef tongue $2.85
122. Proscuitto ham $2.85
123. Polish ham $2.85
124. White meat tuna salad $2.85
125. Breast of turkey $2.85
126. Hard salami $2.65
127. Genoa salami $2.65
128. Canadian bacon $2.65
129. Danish ham $2.65
130. Imported Norwegian brisling sardines $2.65
131. Combination of any two cheeses $2.50
132. Hot roast beef brisket $2.50
133. N.Y. hot pastrami $2.50
134. Chopped liver $2.50
135. Swiss cheese $2.25
136. N.Y. herkimer cheddar $2.25
137. Home made turkey salad $2.25
138. Vienna all beef salami $2.25
139. Usinger's summer sausage $2.25
140. Cotto salami $1.95
141. Provolone cheese $1.95
142. Colby longhorn $1.95
143. Muenster cheese $1.95
144. Hickory smoked bacon, lettuce and tomato $1.95
145. Cream cheese with chives $1.95
146. Cream cheese with jelly $1.95
147. Monterey jack $1.95
148. Peanut butter and jelly $1.75
149. Usinger's liversausage $1.95
150. Vienna all beef bologna $1.75
151. Plain cream cheese $1.75
152. American cheese $1.75

"On all parties of eight or more, a fifteen percent gratuity will be added to your check."

30

Room service menus

Of all menus, the Room Service Menu must work the hardest and sell the best because it stands alone. There is no waiter or waitress to answer questions or make suggestions and there are no appetizing looking dishes with tantalizing aromas being served at the next table. Yet this menu can describe and sell a great variety of foods, beverages, and services of the hotel or motel—breakfast, lunch, dinner, hors d'oeuvres, wines, and cocktails. In addition, it can list the hotel services—auto rental, airline reservations, banquet and catering service, dry cleaning and laundry service, stenographer service, wake-up calls, and restaurants and shops within the hotel.

Good design, good printing, the right paper, and good copy are the answers here as in any good menu, and many hotels and motels create excellent room service menus that sell. For innovative copy, the following is from the *Hollenden House* menu.

> *ALL OF A SUDDEN IT'S FIVE O'CLOCK*
> And if you're the type who likes some liquid refreshment at the end of the day, head for the lobby and the Gazette Lounge or our very special Superior Bond Street Bar. But be prepared for a trip back to the Gay 90's, complete with live entertainment. The only thing modern about the Gazette is the service and the man-sized cocktails. You also will enjoy the different Superior Bond Bar with the old "Cleveland Look."
>
> BUT DON'T STOP NOW: Ready for dinner? Good. Because here in the Hollenden, and right next to the Gazette Lounge is Cleveland's best-known, gracious dining, Marie Schrieber's Tavern. If you've spent any time in Cleveland, we don't need to say more. The specialty? Lots of things. But mostly steaks, chops and seafoods. Ask our captains for a sample of their epicurean talents. Also another small restaurant is open right in the lobby for a lighter or speedier meal.

A different item for a Room Service Menu is box lunches offered by Holly's Holiday Inn.

> *BOX LUNCH*
> For your convenience, you may arrange to have box lunches packed for pick up at our front desk at time of departure. Call room service and place the order by 7:00 P.M. of the day before.
>
> COMBINATION SANDWICH: Two freshly made sandwiches! Baked ham on rye and Swiss cream cheese on homemade white bread. Hard boiled egg, pickles, fruit and cookies.
>
> GOLDEN FRIED CHICKEN: Tender, plump chicken pieces for easy finger-eating plus buttered homemade bread. Hard boiled egg, fruit and cookies.

This same motel, besides listing such unusual services as babysitters, photostats, irons and ironing boards, bottle warmers, bed boards, card tables, and a golf driving range, does a good job selling its restaurant, *Ristorante Holly's* with the following copy:

> Visit the Ristorante Holly's and join in with the spirit of warmth and friendliness that abounds in the Mediterranean. We offer a menu that is not truly Spanish, French or Italian, yet our dishes do suggest in their appeal and flavor a universal love of good food and wine. In this atmosphere of camaraderie, food is prepared at the open hearth and served to meet your schedule.
>
> When your interest in TV, paperbacks or roadmaps fades, there's always good fun in the Ristorante Lounge. No need for worry beads here, for our drinks are continental, the music lively, and our sing-alongs memorable events. In these surroundings friendliness is contagious, and it all adds up to an evening of fun in Grand Rapid's favorite meeting place.

The food offered on the Room Service Menu need not be dull or ordinary either. Consider the following offerings all taken from Room Service Menus:

Boojum Wine Pie	A frozen blend of wine, raisins, and walnuts
Avocado Delight	Sun ripened avocado filled with fresh crabmeat, accompanied with cold curried rice, sliced tomato and hard-boiled eggs.
Tahitian Pupus (Hors d'oeuvres)	Crab rangoons, egg rolls, fried shrimps, spareribs, rumakis.
The Czar's Favorite	Fresh Beluga Caviar specially selected for us, served with all its entourage: chopped eggs (yolks and whites), chopped onions, parsley, sour cream and lemon. Toast sous serviette.
The Conquistadores Breakfast	One dozen real farm eggs on platter. Platter of smoked sausages or bacon. A real hoe cake. Homemade sorghum molasses. Tasty grits. A nip of whiskey (8 years old), for four or six.

A listing of beverages—wine, spirits, beer, and soft drinks—is also important, with the basic information, cost (if not included in price of food or beverage), hours of service, and phone numbers.

The Washington Plaza Hotel in Seattle has a very complete combination Room Service Menu and Guest Information package. A folder holds the two separate lists. The Guest Information piece includes the following categories: SEATTLE—Places & Points of Interest; In House Shops; Dining and Entertainment; For Your Convenience/Transportation; and a Hotel Telephone Directory.

Under the Dining and Entertainment listing, the three restaurants in the hotel, the *Beef Room*, the *Oak Room*, and *Trader Vic's* are described and pictured, and their bar/lounge—the *Plaza Library* is also featured. Also, as part of the Guest Information copy there is a map of downtown Seattle showing the main points of interest in relation to the hotel.

The Room Service Menu includes the following listings: Sleep Walkers, Wine Selections, Hors D'Oeuvres; All Day Dining, and Breakfast. The Sleep Walkers are sandwiches, eggs, steak and eggs, desserts, and beverages. These items are served 24 hours. On the cover, the words "For Room Service, Touch 6" makes ordering easy.

The Washington Plaza also has a "Door Knob Menu." Shaped and die-cut like a coffee cup, its purpose is to allow the guest to order his breakfast by checking the items he wants, indicate the time he wants breakfast, hang it on his room door knob, and it will be served the next morning at that time. It is a complete breakfast listing with the usual items with some special ones such as Apple Crepes with Bacon added. A good room service menu idea!

The Houston Shamrock Hilton's Room Service Menu is an attractive menu with some interesting features. First, it has an unusual shape—being die-cut into a quarter circle. Each page of this 12-page menu is ½-inch larger than the preceding page so a tab-effect is formed on the right hand side with the headings—Breakfast, Luncheon, and Dinner, Children's Menu, and Fine Wines, Entertaining; and Hors D'Oeuvres and Fine Restaurants. Each page is also in a different color adding to the attractive appearance of this menu.

Under the Entertaining category, this menu offers an interesting Economical Package Plan . . . as follows:

> This plan is a special bottle liquor package for your convenience when entertaining in your suite or room. The package includes quarts of liquor as well as two quarts of soda, ice, glasses, stir sticks, openers, measuring glass and cocktail napkins. You may order in sufficient quantity and variety to please everyone, since unopened bottles purchased through this plan may be returned for credit.

The Howard Johnson chain of motels and restaurants goes in for three-dimensional table tents for selling specials on the table in the restaurant and in the room in the motel. One of these 3-D selling tools features Sirloin Steak, Roast Stuffed Chicken, Chef's Salad Bowl; a couple of breakfast items—Reuben Grill, 3-D Triple Decker and a Light Diet Plate. This menu cube also tells the Ho-Jo "Toll-Free Room Reservations Service" (with phone numbers).

Other Ho-Jo stand up sales tools in the motel and in the restaurant sell their Salad Bar, Sundaes, Wednesday and Friday Fish or Clam Fry and their Ho-Jo Birthday Club for kids.

With television in every room, it is harder to get the guest to leave and dine and drink at the hotel's restaurant and bar. The Troy Hilton hotel does it in a simple and economical way. They print a miniature version of their regular dinner menu that also tells the story of their lounge (*Fannys*) and its entertainment—7 nights a week.

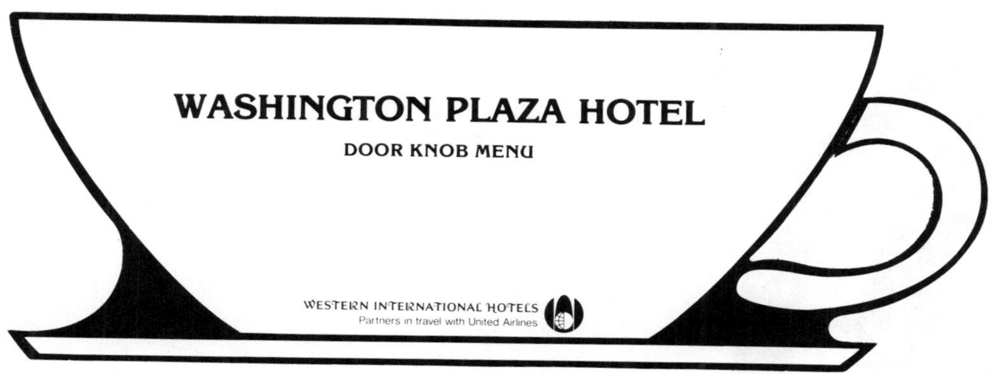

WASHINGTON PLAZA HOTEL
DOOR KNOB MENU
WESTERN INTERNATIONAL HOTELS
Partners in travel with United Airlines

CONTINENTAL BREAKFASTS

2.90
CHOICE OF JUICE
Orange__ Tomato__ Apple__
CHOICE OF
Danish__ Fruit Muffin__
English Muffin__ Toast__
CHOICE OF
Coffee__ Tea__ Sanka__

2.90
CHOICE OF YOGURT
Peach__ Strawberry__ Plain__
CHOICE OF JUICE
Orange__ Tomato__ Apple__
CHOICE OF
Coffee__ Tea__ Sanka__

Lemon__ Sugar__ Cream__ Milk__ Honey__

Check Desired Items And Indicate Quantity

Room Number____ Name____

Number Served____ Time Desired____ A.M.

Apple Crêpes With Bacon 4.75__ Cheese Omelet 3.75__
Eggs Benedict 4.95__ Mushroom Omelet 3.75__
Three Egg Omelet 3.25__ Farmer's Omelet__

A LA CARTE

2 Eggs Any Style 2.75
2 Eggs Any Style With Breakfast Meat 3.75

JUICE 1.15 Orange__ Apple__ Tomato__
FRUIT 1.50 Sliced Oranges__ Stewed Prunes__ Grapefruit__
CEREAL 1.50 Cream of Wheat__ Dry Cereal__
BEVERAGE 1.20 Coffee__ Tea__ Sanka__ Milk__

Please Hang On Your Outside Door Latch Before Two A.M.. After That Time Please Touch 6 To Place Your Order

The Washington Plaza *Door Knob menu allows the guest to order his breakfast—and breakfast time—the night before.*

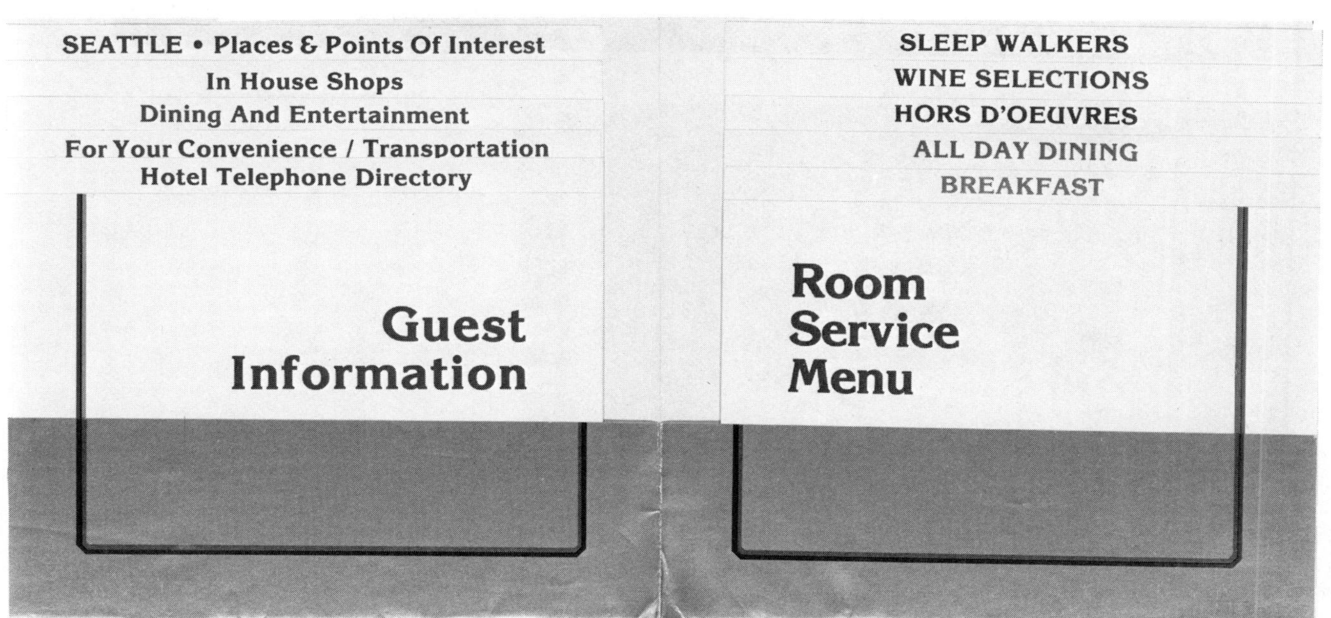

The Room Service menu for the Washington Plaza Hotel is a comprehensive package of information for the hotel guest.

The Houston hotel America knows best.
BREAKFAST
LUNCHEON and DINNER
HORS D'OEUVRES and FINE RESTAURANTS

The Shamrock Hilton Room Service menu is interestingly cut for tab indexing.

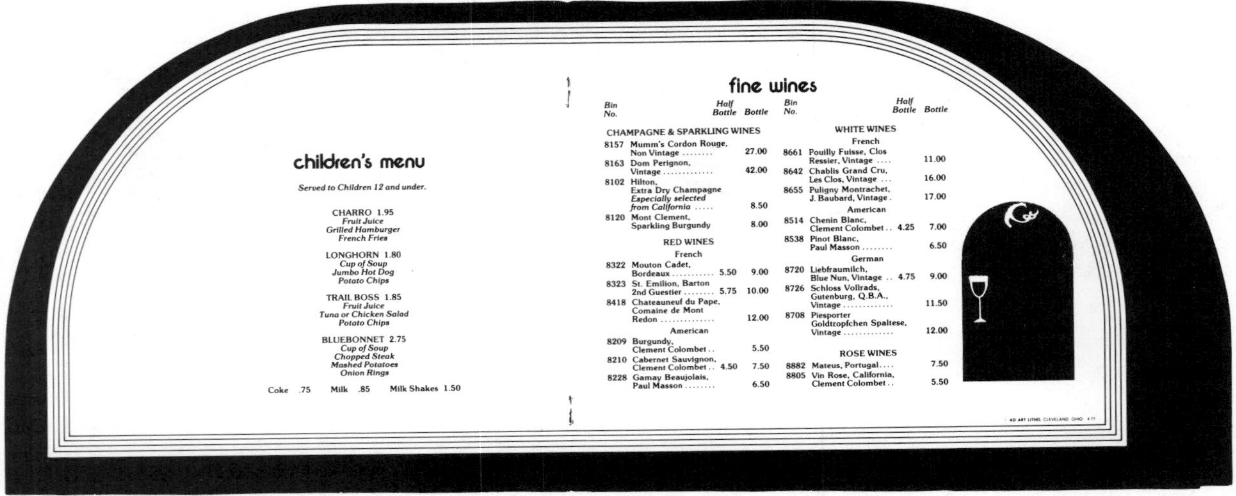

children's menu

Served to Children 12 and under.

CHARRO 1.95
Fruit Juice
Grilled Hamburger
French Fries

LONGHORN 1.80
Cup of Soup
Jumbo Hot Dog
Potato Chips

TRAIL BOSS 1.85
Fruit Juice
Tuna or Chicken Salad
Potato Chips

BLUEBONNET 2.75
Cup of Soup
Chopped Steak
Mashed Potatoes
Onion Rings

Coke .75 Milk .85 Milk Shakes 1.50

fine wines

Bin No.		Half Bottle	Bottle
	CHAMPAGNE & SPARKLING WINES		
8157	Mumm's Cordon Rouge, Non Vintage		27.00
8163	Dom Perignon, Vintage		42.00
8102	Hilton, Extra Dry Champagne *Especially selected from California*		8.50
8120	Mont Clement, Sparkling Burgundy		8.00
	RED WINES		
	French		
8322	Mouton Cadet, Bordeaux	5.50	9.00
8323	St. Emilion, Barton 2nd Guestier	5.75	10.00
8418	Chateauneuf du Pape, Comaine de Mont Redon		12.00
	American		
8209	Burgundy, Clement Colombet ..		5.50
8210	Cabernet Sauvignon, Clement Colombet ..	4.50	7.50
8228	Gamay Beaujolais, Paul Masson		6.50

Bin No.		Half Bottle	Bottle
	WHITE WINES		
	French		
8661	Pouilly Fuisse, Clos Ressier, Vintage		11.00
8642	Chablis Grand Cru, Les Clos, Vintage ...		16.00
8655	Puligny Montrachet, J. Baubard, Vintage .		17.00
	American		
8514	Chenin Blanc, Clement Colombet ..	4.25	7.00
8538	Pinot Blanc, Paul Masson		6.50
	German		
8720	Liebfraumilch, Blue Nun, Vintage ..	4.75	9.00
8726	Schloss Vollrads, Gutenburg, Q.B.A., Vintage		11.50
8708	Piesporter Goldtropfchen Spaltese, Vintage		12.00
	ROSE WINES		
8882	Mateus, Portugal....		7.50
8805	Vin Rose, California, Clement Colombet ..		5.50

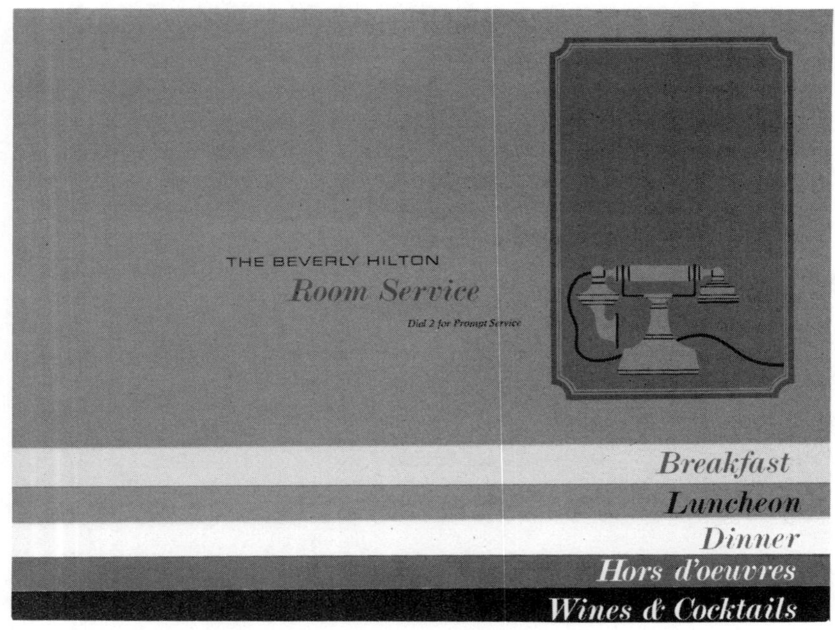

THE BEVERLY HILTON
Room Service
Dial 2 for Prompt Service
Breakfast
Luncheon
Dinner
Hors d'oeuvres
Wines & Cocktails

Off center binding allows for tab indexing on this Hilton Room Service menu.

(Serving Time 11:00 a.m.-10:00 p.m.)

SANDWICHES—COLD

BAKED HAM 1.25
HAM SALAD 1.15
TUNA SALAD 1.15
CHICKEN SALAD 1.15
SLICED CHICKEN 1.25
HAM AND SWISS CHEESE 1.25
AMERICAN OR SWISS CHEESE .85
PEANUT BUTTER AND JELLY .85
BACON, LETTUCE AND TOMATO 1.25

THE CAPTAIN'S CLUB 1.75
White meat of turkey, crisp bacon, lettuce and tomato
THE SHIP'S ROUND 1.50
Tender sliced sirloin of beef piled high on your choice of bread
THE DECKHAND'S CHOICE 1.75
Tartare steak on your choice of bread

Above Sandwiches Served with Lettuce, Pickle and Potato Chips
FRENCH FRIED POTATOES .50 • **FRENCH FRIED ONION RINGS** .50

SANDWICHES—HOT

BEEFBURGER .95
CHEESEBURGER 1.10
FILET OF WHITE FISH 1.10
FRIED COUNTRY HAM 1.95
FRIED SUGAR CURED HAM 1.55
GRILLED BACON AND CHEESE 1.25
Above Sandwiches Served with Lettuce, Pickle and Potato Chips

HOT BROWN 2.75
Sliced chicken on toast covered with cheese sauce and topped with bacon and a tomato slice. Served with your choice of salad
REUBEN SANDWICH 2.75
Corned beef, swiss cheese, sauer-kraut, grilled on rye bread. Served with french fried potatoes or german potato salad

STEAK SANDWICH 3.25
Served with french fried potatoes and choice of salad
THE STERNWHEELER 2.75
Sliced tenderloin of beef grilled with onions and smothered with swiss cheese. Served on a french roll, with french fried potatoes and your choice of salad
THE RIVER GENTLEMAN 2.25
Melted swiss cheese over grilled ham on your choice of bread. Served with french fried potatoes and your choice of salad
THE PILOT'S JUMBO CHOPPED BEEF SANDWICH 2.25
8 oz. of choice chopped beef prepared to taste. Served with french fried potatoes and choice of salad

RAMADA INN
2220 First Street
Fort Myers, Florida

Notice that "Serving Time—11:00 a.m. to 10:00 p.m." is printed on this Room Service menu.

The menu of the Houston Oaks Hotel is printed front to back in English and back to front in Spanish—a combination that is practical and adds sophistication to the room service listing.

31

Special occasion menus

There are several kinds of menus that can be classified under the category of "Special Occasion." The first of these are menus printed for holidays—Christmas, Thanksgiving, New Year's, Mother's Day, etc. The second are special "gourmet" dinners which may be given by a gourmet society at the restaurant or be sponsored by the restaurant as a means of increasing business, publicity, and enhancing reputation. The third is the banquet or catering menu where a group, society, or club is being sold a "package" of food and drink for a large number of people.

In each case, the menu serves as a selling tool and care should be taken in its preparation. The holiday menu may seem to be an excessive expense if it is used only for that one day, and if it is only used that one day it can be, although it adds style and class to any restaurant. The key to getting sales mileage out of this kind of menu is to expose it to the public before the holiday. This can be done in several ways. The menu can be a table tent and be on a table a week or so before the holiday. It can be a clip-on attached to the regular menu; it can be used as a direct mail piece, the basis for an ad, or it can be mounted and used as a poster placed in strategic locations. In the case of hotels or motels, copies can be left in each room.

The gourmet dinner involves a great deal more than a special menu if the restaurant is sponsoring the event. The following copy created by the *Willoway Manor* restaurant and published in a direct mail piece called Manor News indicates one approach to this type of promotion and the amount of careful preparation needed to make it successful:

WILLOWAY'S *HERITAGE DINNER III TO BE HELD NOVEMBER 30, 1971*

Before the date had even been set for Heritage Dinner III, some of the Manor's friends had already committed themselves to reservations for it. This is a good indication of how well received the first two dinners were by those who were able to participate in them.

Heritage Dinner III is one that you really won't want to miss. We suggest you reserve right away so you will be assured of a table. It will feature an all American Menu as the first two dinners have. This one will be patterned after the sumptuous and bountiful Holiday dinners of our early original colonies. The recipes come from those used during our Revolutionary War period. Some are actually favorites of our founding fathers.

Our early settlers had left many comforts behind them in the Old World but they weren't afraid to compensate for what they lacked with what was at hand. America was a land of plenty. The fields, streams and forests produced for man abundantly.

Our settlers used their products abundantly, especially when entertaining. Heritage Dinner III portrays this. Our menu comes from authentic early American menus as reproduced by the American Heritage Publishing Company in the American Heritage Cookbook.

If you have someone special that you would like to give a special holiday treat to, November 30th is the time to do it. For one evening the air of the Manor will be filled with festive fragrances of banquets of yesteryear. We'll start serving promptly at 7:00 P.M. Join us for a relaxed gourmet dinner from the past. Allow a good two hours and be sure to bring a huge appetite.

After dinner you'll want to go to the Burgundy Room. There Naperville's own historian,

Les Schrader, will share some more of his paintings with us. Les' memories, research and interest in Naperville's past, combined with his natural wit, make for a most interesting and informative night-cap on a perfect evening.

The third type of occasion menu, which is a listing of appetizers, entrees, desserts, and beverages in combinations and with quantity prices, is a "talking piece" for the food manager and the customer to work from. It is also an advertising tool in that it can be mailed to potential customers who may be interested in the service. The *Disneyland Hotel* in Anaheim, California, does an especially good job with their Banquet Menu Suggestions. The graphics are very fine (all pick-ups from old engravings) and their "General Information" copy, listed here, covers in advance, nearly every question that the customer may ask:

GENERAL INFORMATION

BEVERAGES: Charges for a sponsored or cash bar and bartender: $25.00 per bartender until $150.00 worth in beverages has been consumed, in which case the Hotel will absorb the cost of the bartender.

With a sponsored bar, we can serve at:

$1.00 per drink: Manhattans, Martinis, CALL BRAND Scotch and Bourbon Highballs, Gin and Vodka.

$1.20 per drink: Manhattans, Martinis, PREMIUM BRAND Scotch and Bourbon Highballs, Gin and Vodka (J & B, Jack Daniels, V.O., Beefeater, Smirnoff).

With a cash bar: regular prices will apply.

SEATING: Rooms can be set with any size head tables on platforms; remainder of rooms to be set with either round tables of 10 guests each or special shaped tables such as "U" shaped tables, "T" shaped tables, etc.

DECORATIONS: Hotel will be happy to help you make arrangements with a local florist. Tall vases or centerpieces of freshly cut seasonal flowers for the head table from $15.00 and up, and centerpieces for individual tables of 10 guests from $5.00 and up.

AMPLIFICATION: We will provide 2 microphones free-of-charge for each food function for over 100 guests. Each additional microphone, charge $7.50.

MUSIC & ENTERTAINMENT: We will be happy to assist and make arrangements.

LIGHTING: Hotel can provide baby spotlights at $7.50 each, and spotlight and operator at $50.00 per 3 hour minimum. $9.50 each additional hour. $20.00 per hour overtime after midnight.

CONTROL: Waitresses can collect tickets at the tables. We will provide committee tables at the door of rooms for food functions.

GRATUITIES: On all food and beverages consumed, local sales tax and gratuities are not included and will be added to the account.

GUARANTEE: Please notify this office two days before each food function of the exact number of guests attending. On food functions taking place on Sunday and/or Monday, we will require a guarantee by Friday. This figure will be considered as a guarantee for which you will be charged even if fewer guests attend. We will, however, set up and prepare food for 10% above this number for parties up to 500 guests. For parties above 500, we will set up and prepare food for 5% above the guarantee.

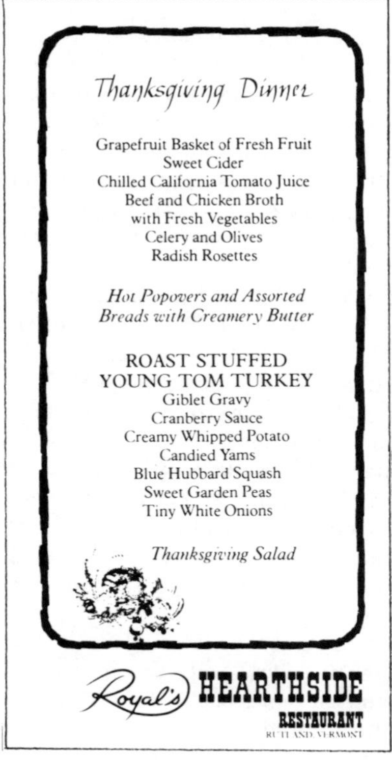

Thanksgiving Dinner

Grapefruit Basket of Fresh Fruit
Sweet Cider
Chilled California Tomato Juice
Beef and Chicken Broth
with Fresh Vegetables
Celery and Olives
Radish Rosettes

Hot Popovers and Assorted
Breads with Creamery Butter

ROAST STUFFED
YOUNG TOM TURKEY
Giblet Gravy
Cranberry Sauce
Creamy Whipped Potato
Candied Yams
Blue Hubbard Squash
Sweet Garden Peas
Tiny White Onions

Thanksgiving Salad

Royal's HEARTHSIDE
RESTAURANT
RUTLAND, VERMONT

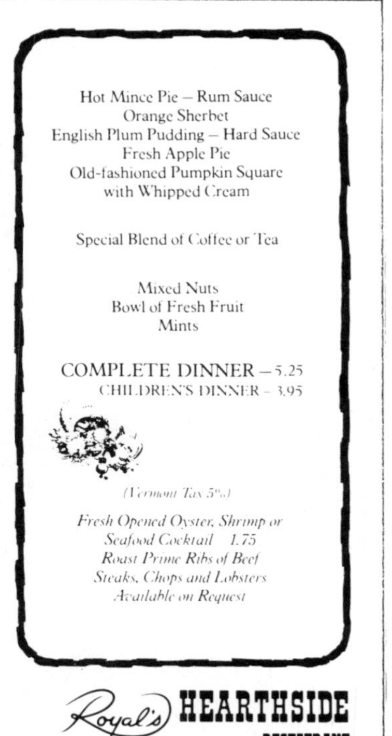

Hot Mince Pie – Rum Sauce
Orange Sherbet
English Plum Pudding – Hard Sauce
Fresh Apple Pie
Old-fashioned Pumpkin Square
with Whipped Cream

Special Blend of Coffee or Tea

Mixed Nuts
Bowl of Fresh Fruit
Mints

COMPLETE DINNER – 5.25
CHILDREN'S DINNER – 3.95

(Vermont Tax 5%)

Fresh Opened Oyster, Shrimp or
Seafood Cocktail 1.75
Roast Prime Ribs of Beef
Steaks, Chops and Lobsters
Available on Request

Royal's HEARTHSIDE
RESTAURANT
RUTLAND, VERMONT

The two sides of the Thanksgiving menu shown here form a table tent that advertises the meal in advance of the holiday.

Holiday Feast

Appetizers

Shrimp Cocktail 1.75
Little Necks on Half Shell 1.25

Entrees

ALL ENTREES INCLUDE:
Celery and Olives, Fresh Garden Salad,
Assorted Rolls and Butter
Our Famous Thanksgiving Vegetables
Served Family Style

Choice of One:
Tomato Juice, Fresh Fruit Cup or Soup du Jour

ROAST STUFFED TURKEY 4.95
with Dressing, Giblet Gravy and Cranberry Sauce
(Drumsticks and Wings - available on request)

ROAST PRIME RIBS OF BEEF AU JUS 6.95

BONELESS NEW YORK SIRLOIN STEAK 7.50

BAKED STUFFED JUMBO SHRIMP 4.75

CRAB A LA GOLDEN LANTERN 4.50

BAKED LOBSTER - FISHERMAN STYLE
Priced according to size

Homemade Pies: Squash, Mince Meat, Apple

Desserts - A la Carte

Strawberry or Chocolate Parfait .75

This simple, yet attractive, "Holiday Feast" menu can be used for Thanksgiving, Christmas, and New Year.

32
The German menu

German food and German restaurants are a permanent fixture of the American gastronomic landscape, and the "Oktoberfest" is rapidly becoming another national holiday even though the date, in either September or October, is not fixed by Act of Congress. Combined with German wines and beers, the German, Austrian, Bavarian, etc. restaurant has a special "flavor." A most common design approach is to use gothic script on the menu, at least for headings. Too much of this type can become hard to read for most Americans not schooled in old German texts.

For artwork, there is a wide selection of old German artprints, woodcuts, emblems, steins, castles, wine labels, kegs and barrels as well as bottles of beer and maps of the famous German wine-growing areas. The important design factor to keep in mind is to have a menu that looks German as well as listing and selling the offerings of the house.

A listing of menu section headings is given here with English translations:

Vorspeisen	Appetizers
Abendbrot	Dinner
Fleischspeisen	Steaks
Spezialitaten	Specials
Krustentiere	Shellfish
Kuchen und Torten	Desserts
Getranke	Beverages

Some typical German entree items are listed here with appropriate English descriptive copy:

SAUERBRATEN
Choice beef steeped in savory marinade for one week, then roasted to fork-tenderness and served in a sweet-sour wine gravy with potato pancakes.

WIENER SCHNITZEL
A cutlet of tender veal dipped in egg batter and cracker crumbs, then richly sauteed to a golden brown and served with a lemon slice.

SCHNITZEL A LA HOLSTEIN
A Wiener Schnitzel topped with a bright fried egg, anchovies and capers, served in a spicy tomato sauce and garnished with sweet-sour pickled beets.

THUERINGER BRATWURST
A traditional German sausage of veal and pork, tastily seasoned, sauteed and served with burgundy red cabbage.

JUNGE BRATENTE A LA SALZBURG
Roast duckling, once reserved for nobility, partially boned and crisply roasted to tempt the palate of our royal guests. Served with orange sauce and red cabbage.

KASSLER RIPPCHEN
Kassler style smoked pork loin served with sauerkraut and Bavarian bread dumpling.

ROULADEN
Two generous slices of prime beef basted with Dusseldorf Loewensenf (imported mustard from the Rhineland), filled with hickory smoked bacon and onion strips are baked to butterknife tenderness, covered with a delicious mushroom sauce and served with potato pancakes and applesauce.

HASENPFEFFER
Sweet-sour wild rabbit, marinated in wine sauce and served with kartoffel kloessen (potato dumplings) garnished with crabapple.

HIRSCHBRATEN
Sliced venison in rich gravy, served with spaetzle (homemade noodles) mandarin orange garni.

Dining in a German or Austrian restaurant is also a "drinking experience," because both the wines and the beers of Germany/Austria are world renowned and deserving of their reputation. There are three main categories of German wines. They are: Rhein Weine—served with meat courses, Mosel Weine—served with fish courses and, for those who prefer a dry wine, Rot Weine—(yes, there is a red German wine) often the choice of connoisseurs.

RHEIN (white)

Liebfraumilch (spatlese)	A full-bodied wine with outspoken bouquet attributed to the late harvest grapes out of which it is made.
Niersteiner Domtal	A mild wine, fragrant and well balanced.
Oppenheimer Krotenbrunnen	A piquant, full-bodied wine.
Rudesheimer	From Rudesheim on the Rhine comes this light, crisp wine, suitable with meat courses.
Johannisberger	A world renowned wine just a bit sweeter than dry wines; mild and palatable.

MOSEL (white)

Moselblumchen	Light and dry from the Moselle River region; delightful with fish and fowl.
Bernkastler Riesling	A dry wine from the Bernkastler region; excellent taste.
Piesporter Goldtropfchen	A full-bodied, piquant, golden wine.
Zeller Schwarze Katz	A popular wine, crackling in the taste attributed to the famous vineyards of the Zell; delightfully crisp.
Zeltinger Himmelreich	A classic; has the heavy, dry bouquet of a fine wine.
Erdener Treppchen	A well-balanced Moselle, a bit on the dry side.
Crover Nacktarsch	A world famous wine, extra dry, known for its outstanding label.
Wehlener Sonnenuhr Auslese	One of the highest quality of elite wines; full-bodied with a golden sunshine bouquet.

RED

Affentaler Spatburunder	In the original monkey bottle; full-bodied, with superb quality; a magnificent Palatinate wine—a true spatlese.
Kalterer See Auslese	A red Austrian wine of fine fragrance; not too dry, but light.

For a German restaurant to be outstanding, it should serve genuine, imported German beers and feature them on the menu. *Eberhard's* restaurant in Columbia, Illinois, does just this, offering fifteen of them. Here they are:

Herrenhauser (from Hannover)	The most popular beer of the house; a light and malty lager.
Dresslel	Light lager.
Dortmunder Aktien (from Dortmund)	Sparkling and mellow.
Wurzburger Hofbrau (from Wuerzburg)	Mild and dark.
Kulmbacher Sandler Brau (from Kulmbach)	Light and sweet.
Kulmbacher Sandler Brau	Dark and sweet.
Lowenbrau (from Munich)	Light special.
Lowenbrau	Dark heavy.
Munchner Hofbrau (from Munich)	Light.
Munchner Hofbrau	Dark.
Spaten-Brau (from Munich)	Light and mild.
Pschorr Brau (from Munich)	Light.
Pschorr Animator	Bock.
Berliner Weisee (from West Berlin)	Mit Himbeersaft (with raspberry syrup).

The *Red Coach Grill* introduces its customers to its "Oktoberfest" with the following interesting copy which describes the origin of the celebration and some of its history:

> *THE LEGEND OF OKTOBERFEST*
> Oktoberfest is the largest fair in Europe. Although its name in German means October Festival, the fair is usually held in September to take advantage of the fine weather.
>
> It began in 1810, when Max Joseph of Bavaria gave a huge party to celebrate his son's marriage to Theresia of Sachsen-Hildburghausen. The party was so successful that the meadow where it was held was renamed "Theresia's Meadow," and the Meadow is still the site of Oktoberfest today.
>
> The Burgermeister of Munich opens the fair every year, leading a procession of beer wagons drawn by horses, decorated carriages driven by brewers, and huge floats carrying strong-armed waitresses. The parade ends at the first barrel of beer for the fair, a barrel which traditionally belongs to the Burgermeister. He downs the first mug at noon, and the fair is officially begun. Thousands of revellers invade the hundreds of acres of the fair. Tented stalls line the long avenues. Oxen are roasted whole, chickens are roasted on spits, lakefish are grilled over wood fires. Hundreds of kinds of sausages are consumed. And the beer, of course, flows heartily.
>
> We hope you'll share this spirit of revelry and good fellowship with us here at Red Coach, during our own recreation of Oktoberfest.

One special is featured on an entire page of this menu along with its "Oktoberfest." Good art and type make for pleasant appearance and hard sell!

For die,
die garnet
haam wolle,
odder die,
die ſpeeter komme,
gibts aach
nach 11 Uhr
noch was
zu Eſſe.

Awwer
um halb aans
miſſe mer
zumache.

A German emblem plus gothic type establish the "character" of this menu.

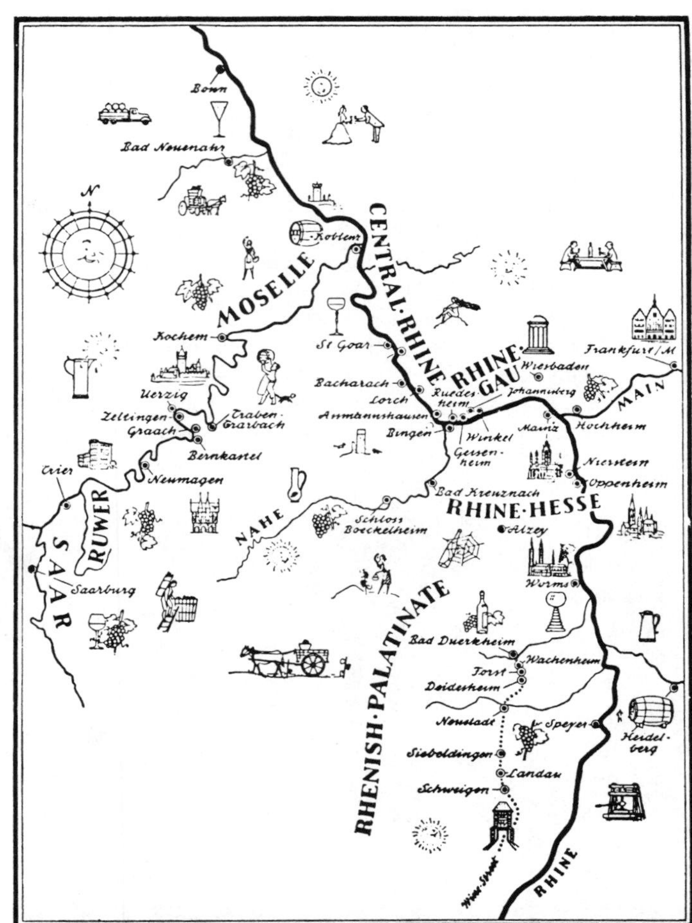

A wine map helps to merchandise your German wine list.

Gulpin Der Whole
Keger Bier
If yur thirsten und vanten bier
for vier er sechs, get der
kegger to putten on yur table.
6.95
Serves 4-6

A little humor sells a lot of beer.

33

The Italian-American menu

The Italian restaurant is one of Italy's contributions to the American scene and to a more cosmopolitan cuisine, but, generally, the food is better than the menu which should sell, merchandise, and explain the many unusual dishes served. In addition, the Italian-American menu is usually a large menu because, besides a listing of Italian specialties (entrees, appetizers, soups, salads, sandwiches, and desserts), there is usually a complete American menu (steaks, seafood, fowl, chef's specials, etc.). And to make the menu even more complicated, there is often a large and varied Pizza listing.

The first consideration in building an Italian menu is to be sure that the menu is physically large enough to accommodate this large number of items. The next consideration is to separate the various categories on separate pages or panels of the menu. Separate the menu into the following three categories: (1) Italian foods, (2) American foods, and (3) Pizza. This gives the customer a clear, easy choice without confusion.

The Italian foods section of the menu can be broken down into subheads such as: Pasta, Veal, Fowl, Seafood, etc. The American foods section can be listed under the usual subheads of Steak, Seafood, Fowl, and any other Specials listed. The Pizza section can be small or so large as to be a complete menu by itself with all the possible combinations of cheese, meat, and fish.

The Pizza listing is often broken down into large, medium, and small Pizzas with three different prices. If the Pizza listing is broken down by size, indicate what the actual difference is, in terms of actual size (inches in diameter) or number of people the portion will serve.

A very important point to remember about the Italian portion of the Italian-American menu is that it contains many Italian words that are unknown to the average American customer. The Italian restaurateur tends to think that all customers know the cuisine, but except for the gourmet or "old" customer, much of the menu is foreign, unknown territory. The customer, therefore, in many Italian-American restaurants, must either "ask the waiter," order and take a chance, or order the old standbys such as spaghetti or ravioli.

Also, the Italian-American restaurant operator should consider the large young adult sector of the population (the largest sector by far). These young adults, especially, need informative, descriptive copy to help them order intelligently.

The following is a list of Italian menu terms that need descriptive, merchandising, sell copy when included on the menu:

Minestrone
Antipasto
Peperoncini
Veal Scaloppini
Veal Veneziana
Veal Marsala
Veal Pizzaiolo
Lasagne
Marinara
Chicken Cacciatore
Manicotti
Cannelloni
Linguini Vongole
Rigatino
Mostaccioli
Veal Marinara
Veal Zingara
Veal Parmigiana
Veal Dore
Scongigli Marinara
Calamaro Affogati
Castellana
Piccata di Vitello
Spumone
Tortoni
Chicken Vesuvio
Chicken Fiorentina
Gnocchi
Tortellini
Cannoli Siciliana
Zabaione
Saltimbocca alla Romana
Cavatelli
Calamaro
Scungilli
Vermicelli
Braciola

Saltimbocca Romana	Soffritto
Scampi	Ziti
Brasciole	Aglio Olio

Another common feature of the Italian restaurant is the Antipasto Tray or Appetizer. This is usually an attractive traffic builder offered as part of the entree or sold a la carte as a before dinner treat or appetizer. Whichever the case, describe in detail what your antipasto consists of.

Even the Wine List can reflect the Italian part of the Italian-American menu. The following is a good example:

ITALIAN RED WINES

Ideal accompaniment with steak, spaghetti and highly seasoned foods

RUFFINO RED CHIANTI
FOLONARI VAL POLICELLA
BARDOLINO

ITALIAN ROSE WINES

A very delightful wine to complement all types of food, an all purpose wine

RUFFINO ROSATELLO

ITALIAN SPARKLING WINES

GANCIA BEBBIOLO (red)

ITALIAN WHITE WINES

Perfect companionship with chicken and seafood

RUFFINO WHITE CHIANTI
FOLONARI LUGANA
FOLONARI SOAVE

Sandwiches, desserts, salads, and side dishes can also be broken down into the two main categories of Italian and American, but, in all cases, descriptive copy will help to sell more of the Italian menu.

Seven Course Italian

DINNER FOR TWO

With a Bottle of
Imported Chianti Wine For Two

Antipasto

Baked Lasagna

Chicken or Veal a la Cacciatore

CHOICE OF

Potato and Vegetable
or
Spaghetti with Tomato Sauce

Dessert

Beverage

A Pony of the Following Cordials
May Be Substituted for the Dessert
Anisette – Creme De Menthe – Creme De Cacao

5.95

A super Italian special for two!

(Right) *Besides listing and describing in detail a wide variety of Appetizers, Soups, Pasta, Italian and American entrees plus Desserts, this menu has a map of Italy.*

Known Internationale **PRESUTTI'S VILLA**

PRANZO! (Good Dinner) LA CUCINA ITALIANA (Italian Kitchen)

Antipastos

Italian Antipasto (For One) 1.50
Imported Provolone Cheese, bleu cheese, salami, melon wrapped prosciutto, garnish, celery, olives, spiced hot peppers, garbanzos and garlic bread

Chilled Melon Slice 75
Wrapped with imported prosciutto

Fillets of Anchovies in Oil 50

Minestrone Soup .60 Soup Du Jour .50

Wafers or Melba Toast and Butter with Above Orders

Appetizers

Blue Points on Half Shell 1.50
(In season)

Jumbo Shrimp Cocktail 1.00
Villa hot sauce supreme

Chopped Chicken Livers 85

Celery and Olives per order 60

Chilled Fruit Cup Supreme 35

Fresh Chilled Orange Juice 30

Chilled Tomato Juice or Grapefruit Juice 30

Pastas Home Made Spaghetti and Ravioli

All of our Pastas, Spaghetti — Ravioli — Lasagna — Manicotti are the genuine home-made Mamma and Pop Presutti original recipe

Fettuccini Alfredo 2.50
Suggest: White Frascati Wine No. 303

Spaghetti — served with

"Mamma and Pop" Presutti's original tomato sauce, Romano Cheese, large fresh garden Italian tossed Salad 2.20

Home Made Gnocchi Potato Dumpling 2.20

with

Meatless Sauce 2.20
Polpetti (2) 2.90
Clam Sauce (red or white) 2.90
Fresh Chicken Livers 2.85
Italian Sausage 3.00

Heavy Meat Sauce 2.80
Fresh Mushrooms 2.80
Caruso Sauce — fresh mushrooms, chicken livers and green peppers 3.25

Suggest: Chianti Wine No. 500

Ravioli

served with Mamma and Pop Presutti's original tomato sauce, Romano cheese, large fresh garden Italian tossed salad 2.60

with

Spaghetti & Ravioli 2.60
Fresh Chicken Livers 3.20

Fresh Mushrooms 3.10
Heavy Meat Sauce 3.10

Suggest: Chianti Wine No. 500

Pastas Imbottiti (Baked Dishes and Casseroles)

Suggest: Chianti Wine No. 500

Cannelonni Imbottiti, a Forno Carne o ricotta, salsa pomodoro e parmagiano — Stuffed Macaroni with meat or Italian cottage cheese, tomato sauce, parmigiano cheese en casserole 3.35

Lasagna a Forno, carne o Mozzarella, salsa pomodoro y parmagiano. — Wide noodle baked in layers with tomato and meat sauce, pear shaped cheese, grated parmigiano cheese 3.45

Pollo Tetrazzini salsa bianche, pepe verde, funghi parmagiano Spaghetti bianche che Petto de Pollo al forno. — Tetrazzini, white sauce with Julienne green peppers, mushrooms, sherry wine, white spaghetti and breast of chicken, parmigiano cheese en casserole 3.45
Suggest: Soave Wine No. 302

INSALATA (Salads — Choice of)
Italian Tossed, Heart of Lettuce (choice of dressing)
Italian Style Cole Slaw
Roquefort Dressing .30

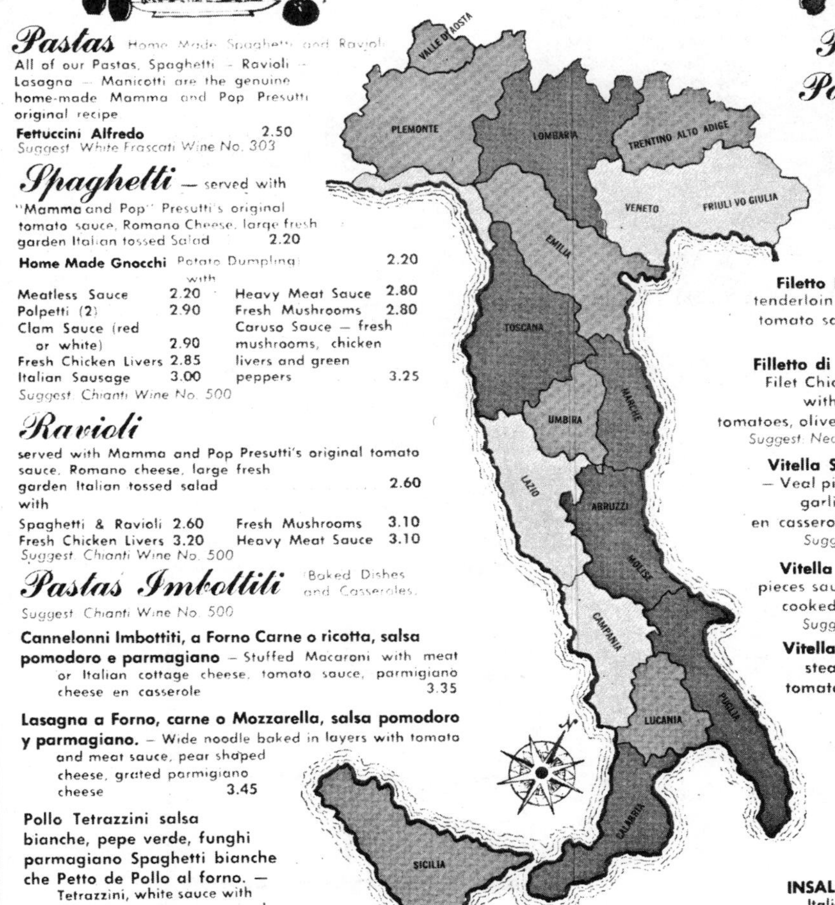

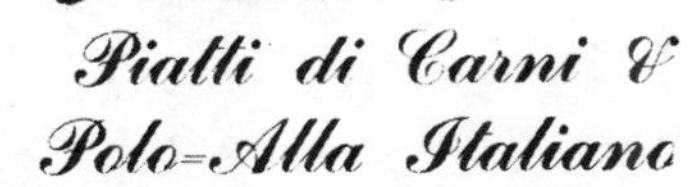

Piatti di Carni & Polo-Alla Italiano

(Dishes of Meats and Chicken, Italian Style)

Filetto Bistecca Fritti con Funghi e Pepe Verde — Filet of beef tenderloin sauteed in olive oil, smothered in mushrooms, green peppers, touch of garlic 4.75
Suggest: Bardolino Wine No. 501

Filetto Bistecca Pizziola — Filet of beef tenderloin sauteed in olive oil, touch of garlic, tomato sauce and mozzarella cheese 4.00
Suggest: Valpolicella Wine No. 502

Filletto di Pollo alla Cacciatora — All Breast Filet Chicken alla Cacciatora (hunter's style) with fresh mushrooms, green peppers, tomatoes, olive oil, touch of garlic, seasonings 3.60
Suggest: Nectarose or White Frascati No. 303 and 400

Vitella Scalloppine con Funghi Pepe Verde — Veal pieces sauteed in pure butter, touch of garlic, mushrooms and green pepper en casserole 4.00
Suggest: Chianti or Burgundy No. 500 and 503

Vitella Scalloppine alla Marsalla — Veal pieces sauteed in pure butter, touch of garlic, cooked in Marsalla wine en casserole 3.75
Suggest: Chianti or Burgundy No. 500 and 503

Vitella alla Parmigiano e Forno — Veal steak sauteed in olive oil, baked with tomato sauce and parmigiano cheese 3.85
Suggest: Frascati Wine No. 504

Frog Legs Provencale — sauteed in garlic butter and dry white wine, served en casserole au garni 4.50
Suggest: Orvietto No. 301

ZUPPE E SUCCHI de FRUITTI
(Appetizers — Soups and Juices) — Minestrone Soup, Soup du jour, Chilled Tomato or Grapefruit Juice

INSALATA (Salads — Choice of)
Italian Tossed, Heart of Lettuce (choice of dressing) Italian Style Cole Slaw
Roquefort Dressing .30

PIATTI VARIETA Side dishes (choice of one with above orders)
Spaghetti, vegetable of the day, potato

INDIVIDUAL GARLIC LOAVES 35

Facilities For Business Men's Luncheons, Wedding Breakfasts, Receptions, Buffets, Parties of all Types. Also Carry Out Orders
(Call) HU 8-6440 HU 8-2488 Open 11 A.M. – Close 1 A.M.
Closed Sunday

SPAGHETTI BRAVISSIMO

WITH MEAT SAUCE 1.45

WITH MEAT BALLS 1.65

(Served with soup, salad and french bread.)

LASAGNE

WITH MEAT SAUCE $1.85

(Served with soup, salad and french bread.)

Desserts

Ice Cream	.25	Apple Pie	30
Fruit Cocktail	.25	(A La Mode)	.55
Spumoni	.25	Sundaes	.25
(Creme de Menthe Ice Cream)		Shakes	.35

Yes
PIZZA
IS ALWAYS EATEN WITH THE FINGERS

THANK YOU FOR YOUR CUSTOM – CALL AGAIN SOON!

Pizza Legend

Once upon a time, during the 18th century, there lived an Italian chef named Monzu Testa. Monzu labored happily for a Spanish king, Ferdinand of Bourbon. Ferdinand was a real gourmet, and, consequently, his chefs experimented diligently in hopes of finding a novel palate-pleasure for him.

One day, Monzu presented his new creation, which he called pizza, to the king. The king was so delighted with it that he installed Monzu as the chief royal chef. And pizza was born.

"Not so," say the Italians, "it all started in Naples." One day a peasant woman was baking bread. The children were standing around, and, like all children everywhere, they were hungry. They couldn't wait until the bread was baked. Mama took some leftover bread dough, put some meat or cheese on it, and slid it into the oven, for a few minutes. Bang! La pizza!!

Pizza is that wondrously flavorful, smoky-crusted, crisp, and crunchy pie, bubbling with hot melted cheese and spicy tomato sauce, dotted with bits of sizzling, succulent sausage or laced with soft, salty anchovies. It is the joy of peasants and the delight of monarchs.

Giuseppi's is very happy that you dropped in for a visit and we hope you will return very soon. Till then, we wish you, Salute!

WHY NOT PICK UP A GUISEPPI'S FROZEN PIZZA ON YOUR WAY OUT?

welcome ...
... enjoy

Giuseppi's
FIRST IN EDMONTON PIZZA

- Pizza Cellar — 8223 109 Street — 439 1967 — 433 8161
- Capilano Mall — 98 Street and 57 Avenue — 469 0664
- North End — 8017 118 Avenue — 474 3636

Pizza ... buon appetito

Starters & Appetizers

Tomato Juice ... Medium	.20
... Large	.30
Chef's Salad	.25
Minestrone Soup	.25
PIZZA SNACK	
1 Ingredient	.50
Garlic Bread (6 slices)	.35

1. SPECIALITA — PEPPERONI MUSHROOMS AND BACON — $1.65 $2.45

2. PROVENZALE — MUSHROOMS AND SAUSAGE — $1.45 $2.45

3. ALOHA — BACON AND PINEAPPLE — $1.45 $2.25

4. HUSKIE — MUSHROOM, BACON SAUSAGE, SALAMI AND PEPPERONI — $1.95 $2.85

5. COLOSSEUM — "FOR THE PIZZA-EATER WHO HAS EVERYTHING" — $2.35 $3.45

		9" serves 1 2	12" serves 2 3
6.	MADAME BORGIA Green Pepper and Ham	$1.45	$2.25
7.	MOMA ROSA Pepperoni and Green Pepper	$1.45	$2.25
8.	GAMBERETTINO Shrimp	$1.35	$1.95
9.	GLADIATOR Beef and Onion	$1.45	$2.25
10.	CARUSO Ham	$1.35	$1.95
11.	PALERMO Pepperoni, Salami, Red Peppers	$1.65	$2.25
12.	ALICE Anchovies	$1.35	$1.95
13.	HUMBLE PIE Cheese	$1.05	$1.55
14.	MUKLUK Mushrooms	$1.35	$1.95
15.	VESUVIUS Pepperoni	$1.35	$1.95
16.	CAESAR Oysters	$1.35	$1.95
17.	MILANESE Bacon Morsels	$1.35	$1.95
18.	ROMANESE Salami	$1.35	$1.95
19.	PAISANO Sausage	$1.35	$1.95
20.	GINA Pepperoni and Olives	$1.45	$2.25
21.	SOPHIA Bacon and Mushrooms	$1.45	$2.25
22.	RAQUEL Ham and Tomato	$1.45	$2.25
23.	KLONDIKE Any Two Ingredients	$1.45	$2.25
24.	SAN MARCO Shrimp, Mushroom and Green Peppers	$1.65	$2.55
25.	WILDCAT Any Three Ingredients	$1.95	$2.95

TO ORDER AHEAD OR TO MAKE RESERVATIONS, 433-8161 AND 439-1967

When we offer live entertainment there will be a minimum food charge of $1.25 per person from 9:00 p.m. till 1:00 a.m.

Giuseppi's Sandwiches

CHILDREN, WE HAVE A SPECIAL MENU FOR YOU !

26. GOLDEN BEAR $1.45
A loaf of French bread loaded with vast quantities of salami, bologna, sauce-piccante, mozzarella cheese, pepperoni and ... that's all.

27. FRENCH DIP $1.35
Juicy roast beef generously stacked on one half loaf of French bread and served with a clear beef dip. (and a mini-salad!)

28. THE LEO LE CLERC ... $1.15
A rye bread double-decker delight loaded with spicy corned beef, sauerkraut, mild cheese slices and grilled by the chef...its flavor as distinctive as its namesake! (mini-salad included).

29. STROMBOLI .... .95
Discriminating diners will enjoy a taste of sunny Italy in this "dainty", fortified with bologna, salami, mozzarella cheese, diced pepperoni, and sauce-piccante.

30. POOR BOY $1.15
You'll love this combination of ham, salami, lettuce, tomato and a dash of green pepper.
... real italian flavor.

PANINO IMBOTTITO
(Little Sandwiches)

31. HOT CORN BEEF	85
32. HAM AND CHEESE	75
33. HAM	65
34. CHEESE	60
35. GARLIC BREAD	35

36. ROAST BEEF SANDWICH .85
Succulent slices of hot roast beef served on a sesame bun
... delicious!

BEVANDA

Coffee	.15
Hot Chocolate	.15
Milk (medium)	.15
(large)	.20
Lemonade, Coke, Orange, Sprite	
(medium	.15
(large)	.20

TRY A BOTTLE OF OUR DELICIOUS CIDER

ONLY $2.00 PER BOTTLE

YES, WE HAVE SPAGHETTI TO GO!

Giuseppi's *lists 25 different pizzas and features 3 as specials.*

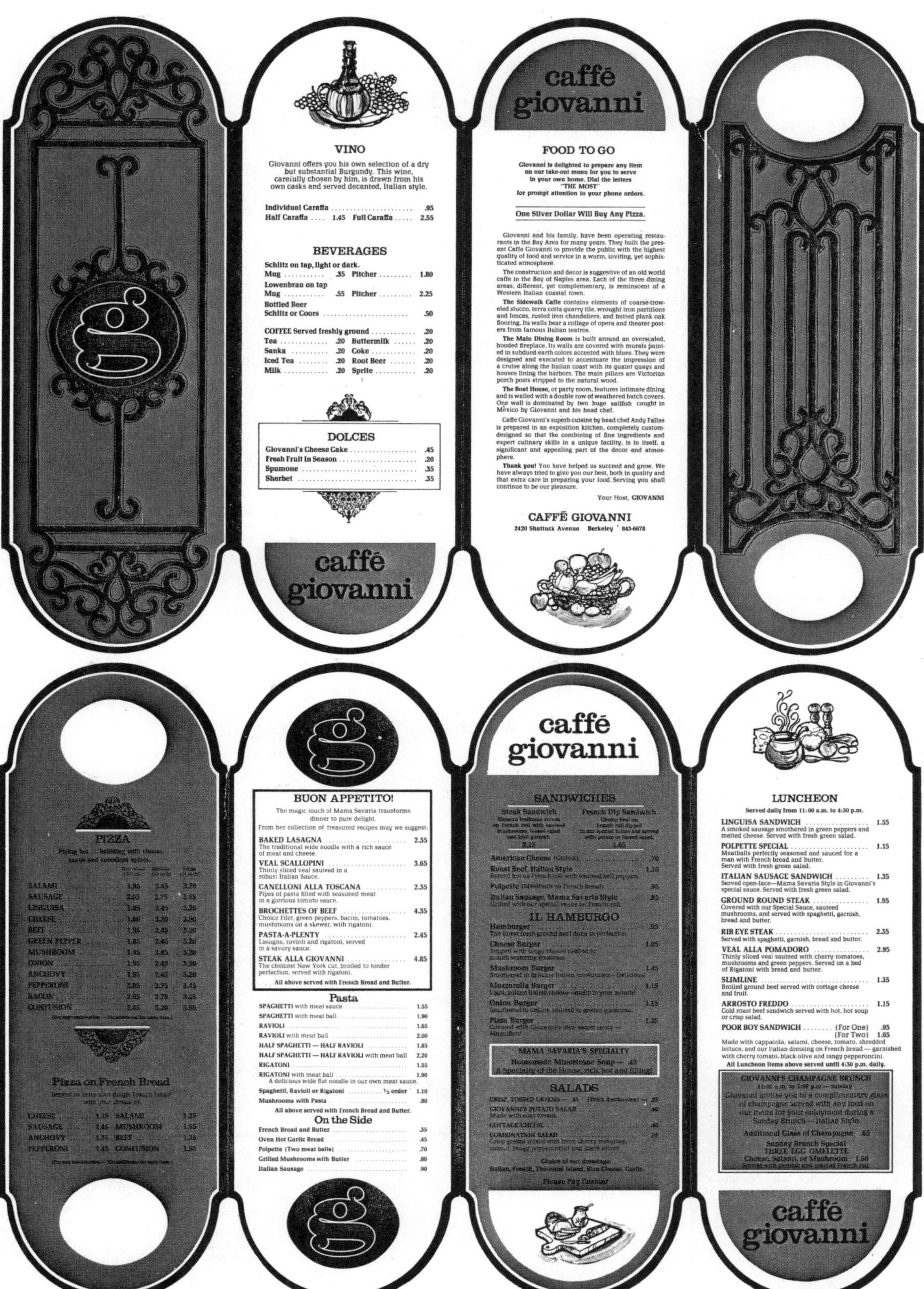

caffé giovanni

VINO

Giovanni offers you his own selection of a dry but substantial Burgundy. This wine, carefully chosen by him, is drawn from his own casks and served decanted, Italian style.

Individual Caraffa .... .95
Half Caraffa .... 1.45 Full Caraffa 2.55

BEVERAGES

Schlitz on tap, light or dark.
Mug .... .35 Pitcher 1.80
Lowenbrau on tap
Mug .... .55 Pitcher 2.25
Bottled Beer
Schlitz or Coors .... .50

COFFEE Served freshly ground .... .20
Tea .... .20 Buttermilk .... .20
Sanka .... .20 Coke .... .20
Iced Tea .... .20 Root Beer .... .20
Milk .... .20 Sprite .... .20

DOLCES

Giovanni's Cheese Cake .... .45
Fresh Fruit In Season .... .20
Spumone .... .35
Sherbet .... .35

caffé giovanni

FOOD TO GO

Giovanni is delighted to prepare any item on our take-out menu for you to serve in your own home. Dial the letters "THE MOST" for prompt attention to your phone orders.

One Silver Dollar Will Buy Any Pizza.

Giovanni and his family, have been operating restaurants in the Bay Area for many years. They built the present Caffe Giovanni to provide the public with the highest quality of food and service in a warm, inviting, yet sophisticated atmosphere.

The construction and decor is suggestive of an old world caffe in the Bay of Naples area. Each of the three dining areas, different, yet complementary, is reminscent of a Western Italian coastal town.

The Sidewalk Caffe contains elements of coarse-troweled stucco, terra cotta quarry tile, wrought iron partitions and fences, rusted iron chandeliers, and butted plank oak flooring. Its walls bear a collage of opera and theater posters from famous Italian teatros.

The Main Dining Room is built around an overscaled, hooded fireplace. Its walls are covered with murals painted in subdued earth colors accented with blues. They were designed and executed to accentuate the impression of a cruise along the Italian coast with its quaint quays and houses lining the harbors. The main pillars are Victorian porch posts stripped to the natural wood.

The Boat House, or party room, features intimate dining and is walled with a double row of weathered hatch covers. One wall is dominated by two huge sailfish caught in Mexico by Giovanni and his head chef.

Caffe Giovanni's superb cuisine by head chef Andy Fallas is prepared in an exposition kitchen, completely custom-designed so that the combining of fine ingredients and expert culinary skills in a unique facility, is in itself, a significant and appealing part of the decor and atmosphere.

Thank you! You have helped us succeed and grow. We have always tried to give you our best, both in quality and that extra care in preparing your food. Serving you shall continue to be our pleasure.

Your Host, GIOVANNI

CAFFÉ GIOVANNI
2420 Shattuck Avenue Berkeley · 843-6678

PIZZA

SALAMI	1.95	2.45	3.20
SAUSAGE	2.05	2.75	3.45
LINGUISA	1.95	2.45	3.20
CHEESE	1.60	2.20	2.90
BEEF	1.95	2.45	3.20
GREEN PEPPER	1.95	2.45	3.20
MUSHROOM	1.95	2.45	3.20
ONION	1.95	2.45	3.20
ANCHOVY	1.95	2.45	3.20
PEPPERONI	2.05	2.75	3.45
BACON	2.05	2.75	3.45
CONFUSION	2.45	3.20	3.95

Pizza on French Bread

CHEESE .... 1.35 SALAMI 1.35
SAUSAGE .... 1.45 MUSHROOM 1.35
ANCHOVY .... 1.35 BEEF 1.35
PEPPERONI .... 1.45 CONFUSION 1.85

BUON APPETITO!

The magic touch of Mama Savaria transforms dinner to pure delight.
From her collection of treasured recipes may we suggest:

BAKED LASAGNA 2.35
The traditional wide noodle with a rich sauce of meat and cheese.

VEAL SCALLOPINI 3.65
Thinly sliced veal sauteed in a robust Italian Sauce.

CANELLONI ALLA TOSCANA 2.35
Pipes of pasta filled with seasoned meat in a glorious tomato sauce.

BROCHETTES OF BEEF 4.35
Choice Filet, green peppers, bacon, tomatoes, mushrooms on a skewer, with rigatoni.

PASTA-A-PLENTY 2.45
Lasagna, ravioli and rigatoni, served in a savory sauce.

STEAK ALLA GIOVANNI 4.85
The choicest New York cut, broiled to tender perfection, served with rigatoni.

All above served with French Bread and Butter.

Pasta

SPAGHETTI with meat sauce 1.55
SPAGHETTI with meat ball 1.90
RAVIOLI 1.65
RAVIOLI with meat ball 2.00
HALF SPAGHETTI — HALF RAVIOLI 1.85
HALF SPAGHETTI — HALF RAVIOLI with meat ball 2.20
RIGATONI 1.55
RIGATONI with meat ball 1.90
A delicious wide flat noodle in our own meat sauce.
Spaghetti, Ravioli or Rigatoni .... ½ order 1.10
Mushrooms with Pasta .... .80
All above served with French Bread and Butter.

On the Side

French Bread and Butter .... .35
Oven Hot Garlic Bread .... .45
Polpette (Two meat balls) .... .70
Grilled Mushrooms with Butter .... .80
Italian Sausage .... .90

caffé giovanni

SANDWICHES

Steak Sandwich 2.15
French Dip Sandwich 1.65

American Cheese (Grilled) .... .70
Roast Beef, Italian Style 1.10
Polpette (Meatballs on French bread) .... .95
Italian Sausage, Mama Savaria Style .... .85
Grilled with our special sauce on French roll.

IL HAMBURGO

Hamburger .... .95
The finest fresh ground beef done to perfection
Cheese Burger 1.05
Mushroom Burger 1.45
Mozzarella Burger 1.15
Onion Burger 1.15
Pizza Burger 1.35

MAMA SAVARIA'S SPECIALTY
Homemade Minestrone Soup — .45
A Specialty of the House, rich, hot and filling!

SALADS

CRISP, TOSSED GREENS — .45 (With Anchovies) — .85
GIOVANNI'S POTATO SALAD .... .40
Made with sour cream.
COTTAGE CHEESE .... .40
COMBINATION SALAD .... .95

Choice of our dressings:
Italian, French, Thousand Island, Blue Cheese, Garlic.

Please Pay Cashier

LUNCHEON

Served daily from 11:00 a.m. to 4:30 p.m.

LINGUISA SANDWICH 1.55
A smoked sausage smothered in green peppers and melted cheese. Served with fresh green salad.

POLPETTE SPECIAL 1.15
Meatballs perfectly seasoned and sauced for a man with French bread and butter. Served with fresh green salad.

ITALIAN SAUSAGE SANDWICH 1.35
Served open-face—Mama Savaria Style in Giovanni's special sauce. Served with fresh green salad.

GROUND ROUND STEAK 1.95
Covered with our Special Sauce, sauteed mushrooms, and served with spaghetti, garnish, bread and butter.

RIB EYE STEAK 2.35
Served with spaghetti, garnish, bread and butter.

VEAL ALLA POMADORO 2.95
Thinly sliced veal sauteed with cherry tomatoes, mushrooms and green peppers. Served on a bed of Rigatoni with bread and butter.

SLIMLINE 1.35
Broiled ground beef served with cottage cheese and fruit.

ARROSTO FREDDO 1.15
Cold roast beef sandwich served with hot, hot soup or crisp salad.

POOR BOY SANDWICH .... (For One) .95 (For Two) 1.65
Made with cappacola, salami, cheese, tomato, shredded lettuce, and our Italian dressing on French bread — garnished with cherry tomato, black olive and tangy pepperoncini.

All Luncheon items above served until 4:30 p.m. daily.

GIOVANNI'S CHAMPAGNE BRUNCH
Giovanni invites you to a complimentary glass of champagne served with any food on our menu for your enjoyment during a Sunday Brunch—Italian Style.
Additional Glass of Champagne .65
Sunday Brunch Special
THREE EGG OMELETTE
Cheese, Salami, or Mushroom 1.50

caffé giovanni

This Italian menu is extremely well designed and well written, and it sells. The die cut adds to the appearance with everything merchandized effectively.

Chicken Louigi ....
Boneless Breast of Chicken, Mushrooms, Meat Sauce, Mozzarella Cheese, baked in oven

Boneless Breast of Chicken ....
Served with sauted Peppers, Mushrooms, Onions, Meat Sauce, baked in oven, Mozzarella Cheese

Veal Scallopini ....
Veal, Sauted in Olive Oil, Mushrooms, Meat Sauce, Onions and peppers

Veal Sicilian ....
Breaded Veal, Mushrooms, Sauted in Olive Oil, Sauterne, Lemon Slices. **NO SAUCE.**

Veal Louigi ....
Veal covered with Mushrooms, Meat Sauce, Mozzarella Cheese, Italian Herbs, Baked in Oven. **(HOUSE FAVORITE)**

Peppered Veal Cutlet ....
Smothered with Green Peppers, Mushrooms, Onions, Italian Herbs, topped with Mozzarella Cheese

Descriptive copy tells what each Italian dish is.

Trip Around Italy

(FOR THE VENTURESOME)

A serving composed of each of our four popular "Goodies" which include home-made sausage, breaded veal, meat ball, and boneless breast of chicken, fortified with tomato sauce, mushrooms, onions, green peppers, mozzarella cheese and Italian herbs. Served with an iced salad, bread & butter. Side of Spaghetti.

SENSATIONAL!

4.50

"Chef's Suggestion"

BRASCIOLE

Fine Cut of Sirloin Steak

Rolled and filled with Ground Beef, Bread Crumbs, Cheese, Grated Hard Boiled Eggs and Pine Nuts. Cooked in Tomato Sauce. Served with Bread and Butter, Salad, Side of Spaghetti.

TRULY DELICIOUS!

4.95

Italian specials can be creative and interesting.

Chianti .... 8 oz. 1.00 16 oz. 1.75
32 oz. 3.50 64 oz. 7.00
Italy's Favorite Table Wine. Fresh, Fruity and full of Flavor

Riserva Ducale — 24 oz. 5.00
A choice, aged Red selected Chianti Wine. Notable for its suberbly clean taste, softness and full bouquet.

Rosatello .... 16 oz. 1.75 32 oz. 3.25
Light and Fruity — Pink in Color

Lancers Vin Rose — 25 oz. 4.50
Light-bondied Rose Wine. Slightly effvesent, delightfully different in taste

Bardolino .... 16 oz. 2.00 32 oz. 3.50
A clear, light, ruddy Wine, a pleasing dry taste.

Valpolicella .... 16 oz. 2.25 32 oz. 3.75
An excellent, deep ruby colored wine, with a delicate bouquet and mellow taste.

Valpantena — 25 oz. 7.00
Natural Sparkling Red Wine

Soave .... 16 oz. 2.25 32 oz. 3.75
Dry, "Suave" velvety white wine, with a soft, light yellow tone, distinguished white Italian wine.

An Italian wine listing complements the Italian cuisine.

34

The Chinese-Oriental menu

The story is told that once upon a time an embarrassed Chinese ambassador ran out of food during a banquet for his Western friends, and created Chop Suey to fill the small void still left in his guests. Since that day, the American dining public has progressed both in sophistication and appreciation of fine Chinese and other Oriental foods until today Peking Duck, Melon Cup Soup, and Lobsters with Black Bean Sauce occupy definite niches in the esteem of the gourmet.

Still, many people have only a superficial knowledge of Chinese-Oriental foods, and if they are to fully enjoy the epicurean delights open to the discriminating diner, the menu must inform and instruct accordingly. All of the requirements for a good menu, as set forth for American menus such as quality artwork and design, good paper selection, quality printing, good type selection, layout and listing that follows a logical ordering sequence, apply equally to the Chinese menu, but, in addition, some special requirements are necessary to merchandise this type of cuisine effectively.

Basically, it can be summed up in two words—more information. This means more descriptive copy about each item served as well as more information about Chinese or Oriental foods generally. The following copy from *The Golden Pavillion* restaurant illustrates what can be told about the subject:

> *HOW TO DINE WELL IN CHINESE*
>
> The secret of a good Chinese dinner lies in the variety of dishes which make it up.
>
> There must be a sufficient number of persons to justify the number of dishes required for a good dinner. A good Chinese dinner requires six to ten persons at a table.
>
> The best way to assure a good dinner is to order in advance, and permit our chef to suggest a menu. Even if you are very experienced with Chinese food, our chef will probably have many dishes unknown to you. Make use of the chef's many years of creative experience, and you will heighten your enjoyment of Chinese food.
>
> Our dinners are composed to provide variety and to minimize the problems of selection. However, if you wish to exercise your own judgment and select from this menu, order a soup and one dish for each person at the table. Never order more than one dish from each basic category of food (i.e.: pork, beef, chicken, duck, etc.). Please rest assured that your coming experience with items from our six Classic Chinese Cuisines will be a pleasant one.

General headings such as Appetizers, Soups, Special Dinners, Meats and Vegetables, Eggs, Seafood, Fowl, Bean Curd Dishes, Rice, and Desserts are helpful, and if Chop Suey and Chow Mein (not strictly Chinese dishes) are served, these headings should be used. Most items on a Chinese menu are listed and sold a la carte, but special dinners, family dinners, seafood dinners and "for two" or more are also common. The following Chinese Banquet illustrates the "group" entree type listing which is required in many cases if the many types of foods are to be eaten at one meal:

> The Chinese Banquet or "Wine-Spread," as we call it, is truly an unusual experience in gourmet dining. The Traditional Chinese Banquet of the old days consisted of sixteen or thirty-two main courses. The most elaborate of all dinners, of course, was the "Manchu-Chinese Feast," consisting of 108 dishes.
>
> Harmony, contrast and accent are the three principles of the Chinese culinary art. Each dish must harmonize and contrast with the one before and after it . . . each dinner must have a point of focus in a principal dish.
>
> Here are a few banquet dishes around which an

unusual dinner-party may be planned. When the occasion arises, let Mrs. Augusta Lee give you her version of a Chinese "Wine-Spread" that will please and intrigue your guests and have them talking about it for months.

Our Hong Kong Banquet consists of ten to sixteen courses and is served for a minimum party of eight. The price is $9.50 to $15.00 per person.

After the opening copy about Chinese-Oriental foods in general, and after describing and featuring "specials" or "package" dinners, the specific copy relative to each entree, appetizer, dessert, etc., should be examined. The following examples:

APPETIZERS

PARCHMENT BEEF
Cubes of choice beef tenderloin, marinated, wrapped in edible parchment. A delight to taste. $2.50

SOUP

SEAWEED SOUP (Gee Choy Tong)
Flaky imported Seaweed with Chopped Water Chestnuts and Egg Flower in a full-bodied soup. $1.25

POULTRY

SWEET-SOUR PRESSED DUCK
Boneless braised duck sauteed in our piquant sweet-sour sauce and garnished with imported sweet pickled vegetables for an unusual taste treat. $4.25

LOBSTER

LOBSTER KEW
Chunks of fresh lobster meat blended with snow pea pods, water chestnuts, bamboo shoots, mushrooms and succulent Chinese vegetables. $4.50

SEAFOOD

HUNG SHEW FISH
Braised fresh fish smothered with shredded pork, scallions, and Chinese vegetables, accented with ginger and a dash of Chinese liqueur. $4.25

PORK

PORK SOONG
Minced fresh pork tastily blended with snow pea pods, bamboo shoots, and water chestnuts in a delicious sauce, then topped with snow white rice noodles. $3.25

VEGETARIAN

CHOW SAN TONG
Delicious Chinese mushrooms, crunchy bamboo shoots and crispy snow pea pods blend harmoniously together in a dish fit for a Buddha. $3.50

GOURMET

WINTER MELON BALL
A gourmet's delight, famed for its unique flavor and elaborate ingredients, this richly flavored soup contains diced lobster, chicken, Virginia ham, Chinese mushrooms, lotus seeds, ginko nuts, water chestnuts, peas and bamboo shoots. The whole winter melon is steamed slowly and carefully, for a minimum of 24 hours. $14.00

RICE

VANG CHOW FRIED RICE
A superb combination of fresh garden peas, diced prawns, barbecued pork, green onions and lettuce. $1.75

EGGS

SHARK'S FIN OMELETTE
A favorite Chinese gourmet item seldom found in America. Shark's fin in a fluffy omelette, seasoned and garnished with tidbits of mixed meats. $4.50

MEATS AND VEGETABLES

VEGETABLES UNDER SNOW
Shredded garden vegetables, imported mushrooms, and marinated beef, topped with crisp Chinese vermicelli. $2.25

DESSERT

ALMOND CURDS WITH LICHEES
Traditional Chinese pudding garnished with tropical lichees. $.50

Even the beverage portion of the Oriental menu can be interesting. The South Seas type of restaurant makes the best merchandising presentation of unusual drinks, but any Chinese restaurant can (and usually should) feature its alcoholic beverages better, if it serves them. There are Oriental liqueurs—Mei Kwei Iu, Ng Ka Py, Nomi Rice Liqueur, and Rice Wine, Saki, etc.

There is no excuse (except neglect and lack of concern) for any standard less than excellence in the artwork on any Chinese-Oriental menu, from cover to internal listing. The calligraphy of the written Chinese or Japanese word is beautiful enough by itself to constitute a design element, and other drawings, paintings, and prints are available for use on the menu.

fowls

F 1 柱侯燒乳鴿

BARBECUED SQUAB

Squab marinated in soya and spices, cooked to a golden brown.
Chinese spiced salt **3.50**

F 2 金亭炸童鷄

CANTONESE SPICED HEN

Young hens, marinated in fragrant Chinese spices, and cooked with a crispened skin **3.25**

F 3 窩 燒 鴨

MANDARIN DUCK

Boneless duck, steam cooked — then blend with spices, battered with waterchestnut flour. Fried to a golden brown. Served with a fruit sauce **2.50**

F 4 北平掛爐鴨

PEKING DUCK

Whole duck marinated with honey and spices—then barbecued to a crackling brown. Served with individual steamed buns. A gourmet's "must"! Serves Six **9.75**

F 5 杏 仁 鷄 丁

ALMOND CHICKEN

Tender diced chicken, bamboo shoots, mushrooms, waterchestnuts and almonds. Toss-cooked **2.25**

F 6 鴛 鴦 鷄

DRAGON AND PHOENIX CHICKEN

Layers of ham, spiced chicken and pork, barbecued together to achieve a blend of flavors **8.50**

F 7 桃蓉焗鷄塊

CHICKEN IN WALNUT PASTE

Roast chicken prepared in chopped walnut spice sauce then roasted to a golden brown **3.50**

F 8 毛 菇 鷄 球

BUTTON MUSHROOM CHICKEN

Chicken chunks, button mushrooms, bamboo shoots, waterchestnuts, vegetables toss-cooked for flavor **2.50**

F 9 豉 汁 鷄 球

CHICKEN CANTONESE

Chicken cubes, toss-cooked in a black bean and garlic mash sauce with distinctive flavor **2.75**

F 10 菠 蘿 鷄

PINEAPPLE CHICKEN

Chunks of boned chicken, diced pineapple, green peppers, onions sauted in a sweet and sour sauce **3.00**

F 11 碎 炸 子 鷄

SOUTH CHINA CHICKEN

Chicken cubes, marinated in mixture of Southern spices and fried in the Chinese manner **3.00**

F 12 手 撕 鷄

SHREDDED CHICKEN

Salad-like dish of shredded chicken tossed with Chinese parsley, green onions, sesame seeds, chopped nuts and imported spices Half **3.50**
Whole **7.00**

Chinese characters, good copy, good type and layout, plus numbers for quick and easy ordering make this a good listing.

JADE PAGODA RESTAURANT

SPECIAL FAMILY STYLE DINNERS

PAGODA DINNER FOR TWO PERSONS $5.00
(EACH ADDITIONAL PERSON $2.50)

SOUP ALA PAGODA
BARBECUED PORK, MUSTARD, SESAME SEEDS
PAGODA EGG ROLLS
ALMOND FRIED CHICKEN
PORK CHOW MEIN
SWEET and SOUR SPARERIBS
PORK FRIED RICE
CHINESE TEA FORTUNE COOKIES
Fried Shrimp added to above Dinner for Party of Four or More

Individual Chinese Combination Dinners

NO. 1 **$1.35**
PORK CHOW MEIN
PORK EGG FOO YOUNG
SWEET & SOUR SPARERIBS
BOILED RICE
TEA FORTUNE COOKIES
(WITH FRIED RICE 35¢ ADDITIONAL)

NO. 2 **$1.65**
CHICKEN NOODLE SOUP
CHICKEN CHOW MEIN
SWEET & SOUR SPARERIBS
PORK FRIED RICE
TEA FORTUNE COOKIES

NO. 3 **$1.95**
CHICKEN NOODLE SOUP
ALMOND CHICKEN CHOW MEIN
PINEAPPLE SWEET & SOUR SPARERIBS
FRIED LOUISIANA PRAWNS
BOILED RICE
TEA FORTUNE COOKIES
(WITH FRIED RICE 35¢ ADDITIONAL)

NO. 4 **$1.65**
DELUXE VEGETABLE CHOW MEIN
SHRIMP FRIED RICE
FRIED LOUISIANA PRAWNS
TEA FORTUNE COOKIES

Inexpensive daily specials can be part of the Oriental menu also.

CHINESE COCKTAILS

New Import from Hong Kong

Temple Bells - - - 1.50
Mute and mellow, like the temple bells,
This concoction is smooth as velvet, strong as religion.

China Rose - - - 1.50
The China Rose blooms the whole year round, may help summer sing in you awhile longer.

Pink Jade - - - 1.50
Say love with Jade.

Lotus Blossom - - - 1.50
Lotus Blossom, all pink and white will make a tiger of you tonight.

Precious Lantern - - 1.25
Festive fruits and non-alcholic juices, colorful and inviting.

The Hong Kong Express - 2.20
Will give you a quick smooth ride to wherever you want to go.

The drink menu or listing can be original and creative as well as Oriental.

(Opposite page) *Soup is not just soup if it is a special Chinese gourmet soup and is merchandised accordingly.*

GOURMET SOUPS

(Minimum two persons)

CHINESE FAMILY SOUP 1.95

A hearty delicious soup containing diced pork or chicken with Chinese vegetables.

BA BO SOUP 2.30

Ba Bo in Chinese means Eight Precious Ingredients. One of the highly honored soup courses in Chinese Banquet festivals. Everyone who eats Chinese food must be acquainted with it.

HONG KONG SPECIAL WONTON SOUP 2.75

Made famous by us. Besides your favorite Wonton, it is served with finely cut shrimp, Imported ham, tender bamboo shoots, Chinese mushrooms, water chestnuts and many others.

WINTER MELON SOUP 2.75

One of the highly honored soup courses in Chinese Banquet festivals; Winter Melon, a special Chinese melon that is a vegetable and not a fruit. The soup is slowly simmered with fine oriental herbs, spices, seafood, chicken meat, imported ham and many others.

SUAN LA PUNGENT SOUP 2.75

A famous "Szechuen Province" contribution which is beloved and renowned in the whole of China. We have the pleasure to have it on our menu.
This is an art of blending which creates an exotic taste pungent and hot with imported Chinese special vegetables, bean cards, shredded bamboo shoots and Formosan mushrooms. A very recommended soup.

CHICKEN SUMI SOUP 2.50

A traditional Autumn Festival soup in Thanksgiving spirit for a rich harvest.
A warm thick soup made of finely minced boneless chicken and pork together with tender sugar-sweet corn egg creamed sprinkled with special Chinese greens.

YANGCHOW WOR WONTON . 4.95

AN EXCITING EXTRAVAGANT SOUP FOR Wonton lovers. "Yangchow, China" originated this special treat.

Besides "oodles" of Wonton, there are chunk size lobster meat, fresh shrimp, roast pork and chicken, simmered with assorted Chinese vegetables. Beware! It almost composes a meal by itself.

BIRD'S NEST SOUP (Advance Order) 6.00

Bird's Nest is a direct translation from Chinese. It is actually the food for the young as honey is for the bee's young. Besides the difficulties of obtaining them, its is also a challenge to the chef's culinary art to prepare it. According to Chinese lore, it is considered a "Fountain of Youth" rejuvenating both to spirit and body, truly for occasions as a Birthday Banquet.

The riches of ingredients such as minced chicken, lobster, imported ham mushrooms, waterchestnuts and others with the secret receipe of assorted oriental spices makes this soup both expensive and artistic.

SHARK'S FIN SOUP (Advance order) 8.50

Shark's fin comes from a special breed of shark found in the Pacific Ocean around the China sea. This is the most expensive Chinese soup in banquet dinners. It takes days of preparation. Whole Chicken, Duck, Yung-nan Ham and Pork loin chops simmered over ten hours until all meats disintergrates, whereby a pair of chopsticks can separate them. Then choice selected Shark's Fin Chinese vegetables, mushrooms, bamboo hearts and others together with a secret recipe of the Chef's makes it delicious and exotic. This special soup is served on special occasions as Weddings and other important banquets.

Peking Duck.............................. 24.00

The world famous Peking Duck is prepared from an ancient and treasured recipe. It was created and developed in the Imperial Palace of Peking at the time when the Northern Capital was the center of China's cultural and epicurean arts. The Peking Duck is served in two courses: first, the luscious golden-brown crispy skin is served with a special sauce and Chinese steamed bread; then, the succulent meat is "quick-stirred" with either pineapple or choice Chinese vegetables into an entirely different tasting dish.

Winter Melon Bowl 18.00

A gourmet's delight, famed for its unique flavor and elaborate ingredients, this richly flavored soup contains diced-cut lobster, chicken, Virginia ham, Chinese mushrooms, lotus seeds, gingko nuts, waterchestnuts, peas and bamboo hoots. The whole winter melon is steamed, slowly and carefully, for a minimum of 24 hours.

Hung Shew Shark's Fins 38.00

The finest imported shark's fins simmered for hours in a sauce made from tender young chicken, Virginia ham, Chinese spices, imported wine, rock sugar and soy sauce. This dish is considered a superb delicacy fit for an emperor.

Ho Go (minimum for two) per person 8.50

Ho Go means Chafing Dish in English and Fire Pot in Chinese. A charcoal-burning Ho Go brazier, with a pot of merrily bubbling chicken broth, is placed before you, and you dip (or lose) the following delicacies in the broiling broth. Served with a tantalizing dip-sauce, this dish is perfect for a cold winter's eve and delightful fun for you and your friends to try.

Fresh chicken
Fresh lobster
Filet mignon
Fresh shrimp
Filet of fish
Rice noodles
Chicken liver
Chinese mushrooms
Bean curd
Waterchestnuts
Chinese greens

Imperial Squab 24.00

Fried young squabs marinated with Chinese liqueur, spice and Yo Yu Sauce that almost melts in one's mouth, served with toasted salt and wedged lemon.

West Lake Duck 20.00

This renowned dish originated amid the unsurpassed beauty of the West Lake region of Hangchow. Stuffed with ten exotic ingredients, this boneless whole duckling is simmered over a low fire until it is so thoroughly tender that it literally melts in your mouth.

Squab Soong 15.00

Minced squab meat blended with waterchestnuts, snow pea pods, bamboo shoots, and Virginia ham. Served wrapped in crispy lettuce.

Roast Whole Pigling 45.00

If Charles Lamb spoke so highly of an accidentally roasted pig, he would have been overjoyed with our meticulously prepared pigling fragrant with Chinese herbs and spices. The tender crispy skin and fragrant juicy meat are served with a special sauce and Chinese steamed bread.

Hong Kong Roast Chicken...... 12.00

Tender young chicken roasted with special Chinese spices, wine and sauces. The skin is crisp and golden-brown and the meat is juicy and tender.

WHOLE FISH (Individual Portion) 4.95

Hung Shew
Prepared to your pleasure. Braised and smothered with shredded pork, scallions and Chinese vegetables, accented with ginger and a dash of Chinese liqueur.

Sweet and Sour
In our original sweet and pungent sauce topped with colorful imported Chinese condiments.

Steamed
With assorted condiments, fresh ginger and Chinese liqueur and imported spices.

Gourmet items get special, extra-detailed copy treatment. The bigger the item—the more copy is a good rule.

Japanese food and Japanese restaurants have been a welcome addition to the ethnic-oriental dining out scene in the last decade. One such is the *Miyako* restaurant in Orange/Pasadena, California. Its menu combines good design with good copy and good merchandising of its food and drink selection.

It starts out with Exotic Drinks including Japanese Beer, Sake, Japanese Plum Wine, and special cocktails such as Madame Butterfly—a frosty coconut flavored vodka delight. Next comes a selection of five Japanese Appetizers. The Special on this menu is The Imperial Dinner which gets larger type, an illustration, and good copy. A Gourmet Dinner is also featured and eight Miyako Dinners are included. Only two Desserts are listed—Green Tea Ice Cream (different) and Tangerine Sherbet.

This menu is 12" × 15" and the inside pages are cream with type and illustrations in brown and orange while the cover, heavier paper, is in shades of brown only.

The *Sukiyaki* restaurant of Benihana Village in the Las Vegas Hilton has another interesting, attractive, and well done Japanese menu. The cover is design only—no copy—in green and gold. The name of the restaurant is on the *inside* cover, with an illustration and the words, "Family style eating

ふるさと Furusato

DINNER MENU

SALAD A LA ORIENTALE
O-SUIMONO SOUP
PICKLED VEGETABLES
RICE · TEA · DESSERT

TEMPURA **$3.85**
Delicately deep-fried prawns, fresh fish and assorted vegetables served with the traditional Tempura sauce.

YOSENABE (Cooked at your table — 2 persons minimum) .... **$3.85** per person
Fish cake, fried bean cake, somen and assorted fresh vegetables broiled in a delicious soup with chicken, beef and seafood.

MIZUTAKI **$4.50**
Chicken, fresh vegetables, tofu (bean cake), bamboo shoots, mushrooms, and long rice cooked with our special FURUSATO STOCK and served in traditional mashiko ware.

SUKIYAKI (Cooked at your table — 2 or more persons) **$4.80**
(Cooked in kitchen — 1 person) per person
Prime choice sliced beef, fresh vegetables, tofu (bean cake), bamboo shoots, mushrooms and yam noodles cooked with our special soy sauce and prepared before you by our hostesses.

YOSHITSUNE NABE **$5.00**
(Cooked at your table on a traditional stove — 3 or more persons) per person
Furusato's special Genghis Khan Yaki consisting of prime choice beef with assorted vegetables and enhanced by complimentary sauces.

FURUSATO SPECIAL OKONOMI AGE **$4.50**
(Cooked at your table — 2 or more persons) per person
Fresh prawns, fresh fish, fish cake, choice beef, chicken and fresh assorted vegetables on bamboo skewers to be cooked by you in oil and prepared with a special sauce.

FURUSATO SUPREME SHABU-SHABU **$7.00**
(Cooked at your table — 2 or more persons) per person
Prime choice of beef and assorted vegetables cooked to your own liking in a specially prepared FURUSATO STOCK.

A Japanese menu with good descriptive copy and large, clear, readable type.

How to Dine Well – in Chinese

The secret of a good Chinese dinner lies in the variety of dishes which make it up.

There must be a sufficient number of persons to justify the number of dishes required for a good dinner. A good Chinese dinner requires six to ten persons at a table.

The best way to assure a good dinner is to order in advance, and permit our chef to suggest a menu. Even if you are very experienced with Chinese food, our chef will probably have many dishes unknown to you. Make use of the chef's many years of creative experience, and you will heighten your enjoyment of Chinese food.

Our dinners are composed to provide variety and to minimize the problems of selection.

However, if you wish to exercise your own judgment and select from this menu, order a soup and one dish for each person at the table. Never order more than one dish from each basic category of food, (i.e.: pork, beef, chicken, duck, etc.). Please rest assured that your coming experience with items from our six Classic Chinese Cuisines will be a pleasant one.

"How to order" instructions are a valuable asset for any Chinese menu.

where fresh steak and vegetables are combined traditionally in one sukiyaki pot as it is done even today in the homes of Japan."

Inside the name *Sukiyaki* is repeated and most of the spread is taken up with a colorful illustration. On the right hand side there is a Dinner and an A la Carte listing. What we have, although it does not seem so, is a very *limited* menu. Only two entrees are offered—*Sukiyaki with Vegetables* and *Soy Steak with Vegetables*. One appetizer, six vegetables, four desserts plus a soup and a salad comprise the entire food offering.

On the inside back cover there is a drawing

The Chinese dinner table — As an aid to your full enjoyment of this occasion we present to you our table setting and its functions:

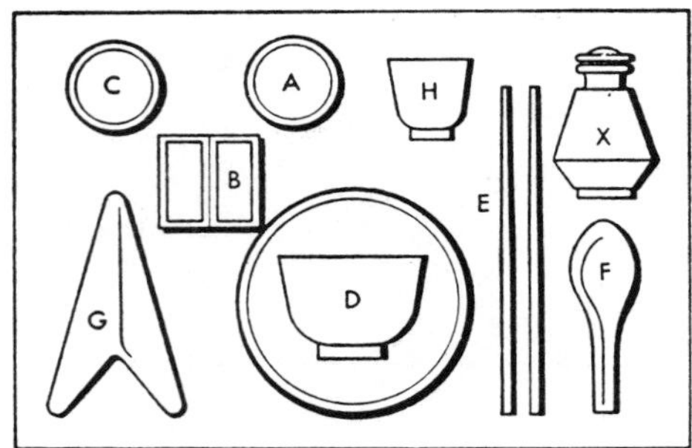

A–Soy Sauce (Se Yow) corresponds to salt at your table. Use accordingly. More is available in bottle (X) with the free-flow top. Do **NOT** remove top when pouring.

B–Mustard and Plum Sauce (Gai Lot, Mui Jeung). Mustard provides the "hot" quality of pepper. Plum sauce is a tangy condiment used usually with ducks and squabs.

C–Spiced Salt (Wah Yim) is used with fried or barbecued poultry. Note the delicate flavoring. Commercial seasoned salts are developed from this Chinese condiment.

D–Rice bowl (Fon Woon) is used for soup and rice. When eating rice the bowl is held to mouth and the rice is "brushed" into mouth with chopsticks. Rice is the staple course of a Cantonese meal. It takes the place of noodles used in North China and bread of the Occidental world.

E–Chopsticks (Fai Tze) are your "forks," and sometimes your "spoons"—used to convey food.

F–Porcelain Spoon (Chee Gung). Chinese soups are served piping hot! Where a metal spoon would burn, the porcelain spoon remains cool for comfort.

G–Napkins (Chon Gun) certain Chinese foods require the use of fingers. Instead of finger bowls, Chinese custom prescribes the use of a specially scented hot napkin.

H–Tea (Cha) is taken throughout the meal. Chinese tea is mild, and sometimes scented, and taken as an unflavored beverage to clear the palate. Different flavors can thus be savored without confusion of taste.

Using the chopsticks — Hold first chopstick as shown in (Figure 1). This chopstick is held firm and stationary in fixed position. Take second chopstick as you would a pencil. With the tips of thumb, index and second fingers manipulate this stick to meet the first chopstick (Figure 2). This action forms a "clamp" to convey your food (Figure 3). Very easy—with a little practice! Otherwise, ask your waiter for a "Chaa" (translation—fork or spear.)

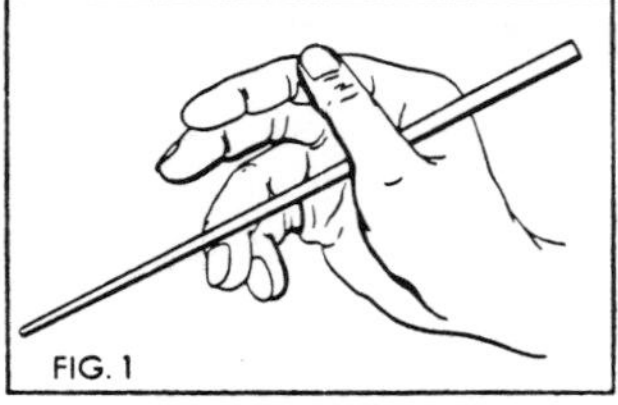
FIG. 1

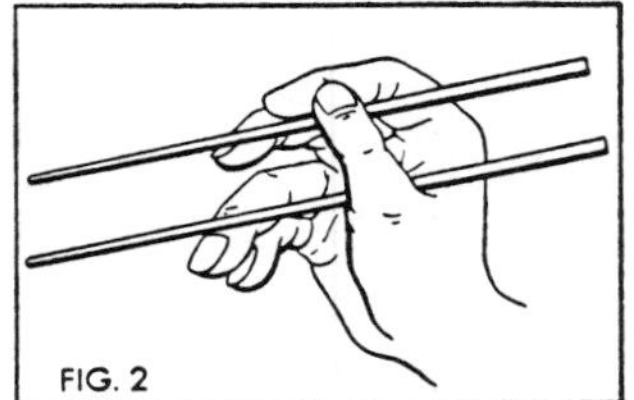
FIG. 2

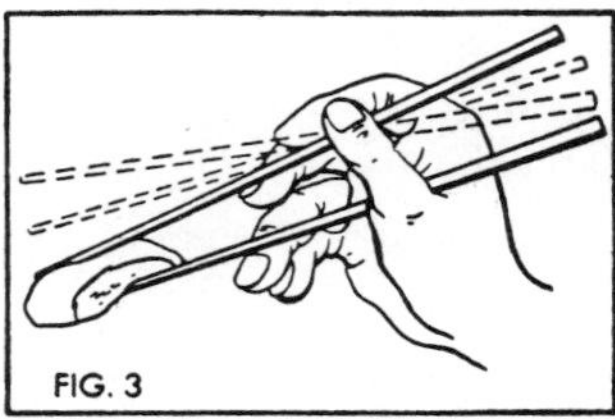
FIG. 3

Ming's *Chinese restaurant in Palo Alto, California, does an excellent job of merchandising their special type food and service. In the descriptive material reproduced above, both "The Chinese dinner table" and the use of chopsticks are emphasized. On a good menu, the facts are not enough . . . they must be presented in an interesting and exciting manner. Seasoned with imagination and creativity any menu will tell more—and sell more.*

of the entire "village" with the other various restaurants, the *Utamaro Bar*, the Gift Shop, and even a Kissing Room! This menu which presents only a few items does it in a big (11″ × 15″ page size) way.

Good design and good type selection provide good visual taste to complement the taste of the food.

EXOTIC DRINKS

TOKYO-RITA 1.40
Tokyo-style margarita

GEISHA 1.40
A daiquiri in the oriental fashion

SAKETINI 1.25
Gin and sake-Japanese style martini

SUNTORY ON THE ROCKS 1.25
If you like scotch, you'll like Suntory

SAMURAI 2.25
Miyako style Mai Tai

MADAM BUTTERFLY 1.40
A frosty coconut flavored vodka delight

JAPANESE PLUM WINE .90
An imported sweet wine

JAPANESE BEER 1.00
Imported Asahi or Kirin

KAMPAI!

CHEERS!

SAKE
JAPANESE WINE SERVED WARM
TO ENHANCE ITS FLAVOR
$1.50

WINES
A CARAFE OF CALIFORNIA'S FINEST
RED·ROSE·WHITE
HALF $2.00 FULL $3.50

APPETIZERS

BAR TEMPURA 2.75
Shrimp tempura served with teriyaki sauce

BEEF KUSHIYAKI 2.75
Broiled tender beef on skewers with scallions

GINGER BEEF 2.75
Sliced tender beef seasoned with ginger sauce

SASHIMI 2.75
Filet of fresh fish, a Japanese delicacy

CHICKEN TERIYAKI ON SKEWERS 2.75
Tender boned chicken, seasoned with teriyaki sauce

CHILDREN'S DINNERS

SHRIMP TEMPURA 2.75

SUKIYAKI 2.95
when served with adult portion

STEAK TERIYAKI 3.25

CHICKEN TERIYAKI 2.75
on skewers

Includes children's cocktail, soup, salad, rice, tea and cookies

DESSERTS

GREEN TEA ICE CREAM .60

TANGERINE SHERBET .60

State & local sales and use tax will be added to the selling prices of all food and beverage items served in this room

MIYAKO'S SPECIALTY

THE IMPERIAL DINNER

Like farmers of old Japan who cooked Sukiyaki on a plowshare over an open fire, Miyako prepares this delightful dish right at your table in a sizzling hot pan. A delicious combination of fresh garden vegetables and strips of Choice Top Sirloin, seasoned with our very special Miyako Sauce.

SUKIYAKI WITH SHRIMP TEMPURA & CHICKEN TERIYAKI

6.75

SUKIYAKI WITH CHICKEN TERIYAKI 5.75
SUKIYAKI WITH SHRIMP TEMPURA 6.25

All dinners include soup, salad, rice, tea and cookies

MIYAKO DINNERS

EAST-WEST DINNER 6.95
THE THREE FAVORITES • Top sirloin teriyaki, shrimp tempura and skewered chicken teriyaki

CHICKEN TERIYAKI & SHRIMP TEMPURA 5.75
Breast of chicken and butterfly shrimps, seasoned with teriyaki sauce

STEAK TERIYAKI & VEGETABLE TEMPURA 5.95
Broiled top sirloin and vegetable tempura, seasoned with teriyaki sauce

SHRIMP TEMPURA 5.25
Butterfly shrimps and vegetables dipped in batter, deep fried to a delicious golden brown

SALMON TERIYAKI 5.50
Broiled salmon, seasoned with teriyaki sauce (miso-soya bean sauce may be substituted)

LOBSTER TAIL TERIYAKI 7.25
Broiled lobster, seasoned with teriyaki sauce (miso-soya bean sauce may be substituted)

CHICKEN TERIYAKI 4.95
Tender fried chicken, seasoned with teriyaki sauce

NEW YORK STEAK 6.95
Juicy broiled steak served with garden vegetables

All dinners include soup, salad, rice, tea and cookies

GOURMET DINNER

SOUP SALAD CHICKEN TERIYAKI ON SKEWERS 7.95
STEAK AND LOBSTER TERIYAKI Broiled top sirloin and lobster tail, seasoned with teriyaki sauce
RICE TEA COOKIES

A big menu with brief listings creates visual impact.

SUKIYAKI
Family style eating where fresh steak and vegetables are combined traditionally in one sukiyaki pot as it is done even today in the homes of Japan.

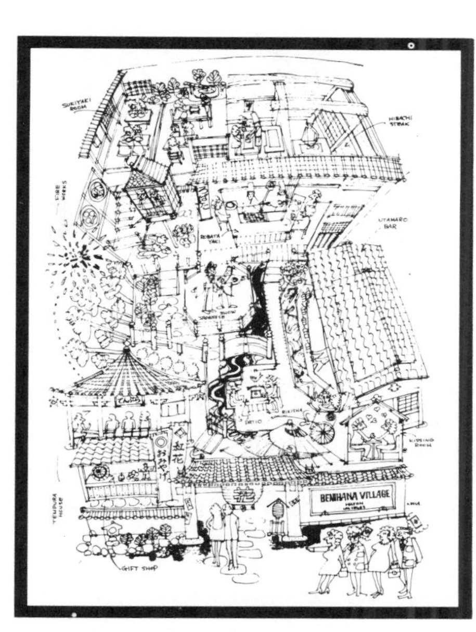

DINNER

Dinner Course Comes with Appetizer, Soup, Salad, and Dessert

APPETIZER

Kushimono or Today's Special

SOUP

Onion Au Gratin A La Japanese

ENTREE

Sukiyaki with Vegetables	10.00
Soy Steak with Vegetables	12.00

VEGETABLES

Onion	Bean Cake
Scallion	Shirataki
Mushroom	Bamboo Shoots

DESSERT

Ginger Ice Cream	Lemon Sherbert
Vanilla Ice Cream	*Fruits in Season (*1.00 Extra)

A LA CARTE

APPETIZER

Melon	1.50
Kushimono or Today's Special	2.00

SOUP

Onion Au Gratin A La Japanese	1.50

SALAD

Benihana Salad Bowl	1.50

ENTREE

Sukiyaki with Vegetables	8.00
Soy Steak with Vegetables	10.00

Includes: Vegetable, Rice, and Green Tea

Vegetables:	Onion	Bean Cake
	Scallion	Shirataki
	Mushroom	Bamboo Shoots

DESSERT

Ginger Ice Cream	1.00
Vanilla Ice Cream	1.00
Lemon Sherbert	1.00
Fruits in Season	2.00

35
Mexican-Spanish menus

Americans have an almost unlimited appetite for ethnic foods, and two types of "foreign food" restaurants that have enjoyed increasing popularity in the last few years are Mexican and Spanish restaurants. The cuisine of these two types of food-service operations is basically different. Mexican food—tacos, enchiladas, taquitos, chili, etc.—tends to be on the high-flavor, spicy side, while the foods of continental Spain are more acceptable in taste to the American palate, although gazpacho (cold vegetable soup of Andalusia) is a "hot" item.

The factor that connects the two types of restaurants is the use of the Spanish language, which means that while everything can and should be listed in Spanish to add verbal "color," the translation into English should follow immediately as shown in the following examples:

PAELLA VALENCIANA
National culinary delight of Spain contains shrimp, clams, crabmeat and other seasonal seafood, chicken, Spanish sausages, onions, Spanish red peppers, vegetables, saffron, seasoned with Spanish wine.

ARROS AMARILLO CON CAMERONES
Pacific coast shrimp baked with yellow rice, saffron, tomatoes, onions, Spanish red peppers, and peas.

ARROS AMARILLO CON POLLO
One half spring chicken baked with rice, saffron, tomatoes, peas, onions, and red peppers.

BISTEC SEGOVIA
Prime rib eye steak marinated in Spanish wine, charcoal broiled and topped with sauce Espagnole and sliced black olives.

CHILE RELLENO
Mexican Poblano pepper stuffed with spiced beef or cheese, rolled and fried in an egg batter and topped with a special tomato sauce.

PESCADO ALA VERACRUZANA
Sauteed filet of red snapper, simmered with capers, garlic, green olives, peeled tomato, pimento, parsley and garnished with large Mexican peppers.

CARNE ASADA TAMPIQUENA
Tenderloin of beef sauteed in butter accompanied by pink beans.

TERNERA CON LENTEJAS
Tender scallops of milkfed veal served with a Spanish sauce and accompanied by lentils.

BANDERILLA MEXICANA
Hearty cubes of beef broiled with mushroom caps, green peppers, and tomatoes served on a flaming sword accompanied by Mexican rice.

ENCHILADAS—CARNE
Mild beef stuffing fills this rolled pancake-like Tortilla, baked with creamy red sauce and cheese.

TACOS—CARNE
Crisp envelope-like tortillas filled with meat topped off with shredded lettuce, tomatoes, and cheese.

TOSTADOS CARNE
Large tortillas stacked high with layers of beef, frijoles refritos (refried Mexican beans) shredded lettuce, tomatoes, and cheese.

The special drinks (bebidas) of a Mexican-Spanish menu are usually the Margarita cocktail (a blend of tequila, lime juice, and triple sec), tequila desi cocktail (tequila, grenadine, and lemon juice), or the increasingly popular sangria or Sant' Gria as it is sometimes called. A special recipe for Orange Sangria from the *Senor Alfredo Mexican Restaurant* is listed as follows:

ORANGE SANGRIA
A traditional Mexican-Spanish wine drink. Red wine base, orange juice, orange oil, sugar. Served in a chilled wine glass with crushed ice.

And here is another interesting Mexican wine cocktail:

SENORITA MARA WINE COCKTAIL
White wine base, sparkling cider, lemon. Served in a chilled wine glass with crushed ice and garnished with a slice of lemon and salt on the glass rim.

There are some very interesting Mexican after dinner drinks also. Some examples are:

CAFE MEXICANA
Flamed Spanish coffee, brandy and kahlua topped with whipped cream.

BANDERA MEXICANA
A pousse cafe of grenadine, cointreau and green creme de menthe.

AZTEC de ORO
Tequila and Strega on the rocks.

A listing of section headings for the Spanish-Mexican menu is given here. There are two ways of handling the language problem on the Mexican-Spanish menu (as with German, Italian, etc., menus). You can list in Spanish and then describe in English, or you can have two complete menus side-by-side with prices in pesos and dollars. The double menu adds a bit of cosmopolitan sophistication and also makes your listing look larger. A listing of section headings is given here with English translations:

Bebidas	Drinks
Antes de su Comida	Before your Meal
Vinos	Wines
Bedidas Compuestas	Mixed Drinks
Entremeses	Appetizers
Potajes	Soups and Consomme
Ensaladas	Salads
Carnes a la Parrilla	Charcoal Broiled
Pescados y Mariscos	Seafood
Platillos Mexicano	Mexican Dishes
Platillos Especiales	Specials
Aves	Poultry
Emparedados	Sandwiches
Postres	Desserts
Durante su Comida	During your Meal

The most famous of Spanish-Mexican salads (ensaladas) is the Guacamole, made from avocado, chili, onion, garlic, lemon, salt, pepper, and tomato. And to give you an idea of how words can help the menu and stimulate the palate, consider this listing of just ordinary tomato juice:

Nectar from the Apple of Love
The tomato, introduced to Spain by the Conquistadores, was at first known as the Apple of Love!

Seafood selection is listed twice, in Spanish and English, with prices in pesos and dollars.

Pescados y Mariscos

	PESOS
PESCADO BLACK BASS MAITRE'D	25.00
FILETE DE PESCADO AZUL SALSA TARTARA	18.75
PESCADO CABRILLA FRITO SALSA DE LIMON	22.00
HUACHINANGO VERACRUZANA O SALSA DE VINO	22.00
CALLO DE HACHA A LA FRANCESA	18.75
ANCAS DE RANA AL GUSTO	28.00
COMBINACION DE MARISCOS	37.50
OSTIONES A LA FRANCESA	25.00
OSTIONES A LA DIABLA	25.00
OSTIONES EN SU CONCHA	25.00
CAMARON A LA FRANCESA	25.00
CAMARON A LA MEXICANA	25.00
CAMARON AL ALAMBRE	25.00
CAMARON AL MOJO DE AJO	37.50
LANGOSTA A LA PARRILLA, THERMIDOR, WILSON	37.50

Ocean Delights

	DOLARES
BOQUILLA BLACK BASS MAITRE'D	2.00
FILET OF BLUE FISH TARTAR SAUCE	1.50
CABRILLA BASS LEMON SAUCE	1.75
RED SNAPPER WINE SAUCE OR VERACRUZ	1.75
FRENCH FRIED SCALLOPS	1.50
FROG LEGS, CHOICE	2.25
SEA FOOD COMBINATION	3.00
FRENCH FRIED OYSTERS	2.00
OYSTERS A LA DIABLA	2.00
OYSTERS ON THEIR SHELL	2.00
FRENCH FRIED SHRIMP	2.00
MEXICAN STYLE SHRIMP	2.00
SHRIMP EN BROCHETTE	2.00
SHRIMP WITH SPECIAL GARLIC SAUCE	3.00
LOBSTER THERMIDOR, WILSON NEWBURG OR BROILED	3.00

Dolores in
Continental Spain

(served from 8:30 p.m. to closing)

entremeses variados
(assorted appetizers) 2.50

guacamole in the manner Espagnole
(half avocado stuffed with avocado) 1.50

entremes de camarones
(gulf shrimp cocktail of Seville)
1.75

gaspacho andaluz
famous cold vegetable soup of Andalusia .90

sopa de Ajo con Huevo
(garlic soup for the strong in heart) 1.50

PAELLA VALENCIANA
National culinary delight of Spain contains shrimp, clams, crabmeat and other seasonal seafood, chicken, Spanish sausages, onions, Spanish red peppers, vegetables, saffron, seasoned with Spanish wine.
individual casserole 4.75
casserole for two 8.50

ARROS AMARILLO CON CAMERONES
Pacific coast shrimp baked with yellow rice, saffron, tomatoes, onions, Spanish red peppers and peas
individual casserole 4.25
casserole for two 8.00

ARROS AMARILLO CON POLLO
One half spring chicken baked with rice, saffron, tomatoes, peas, onions and red peppers
individual casserole 3.75
casserole for two 7.00

PESCADO
Fresh fish of the day — as prepared on the Costa Brava in Spain 4.50

BISTEC SEGOVIA
Prime rib eye steak marinated in Spanish wine, charcoal broiled and topped with sauce Espagnole and sliced black olives 6.75

all above entrees are served with ENSALADA MIXTA
in a true olive oil and lemon dressing

This Spanish menu has an attractive illustration, good type selection, and informative descriptive copy.

This attractive Mexican menu cover uses native motifs plus Spanish copy to give a colorful Latin flavor.

The *Monterey House* menu is an attractive four-page menu. The page size is 7″ × 14″. Printed in four colors on heavy, coated paper, this menu uses color photography for atmosphere illustrations, and in addition each entree dinner is illustrated with a color photograph. On the back cover there is a "Glossary" of Mexican foods done in a "tongue-in-cheek" manner. For example, "BURRITO: A small burro. Also an orgy of brazen beans and coy cheese sensuously stuffed into a clingy covering of tempting tortilla. More cheese is draped over the whole daring concoction."

The menu of the *Acapulco* restaurant in Palos Verdes, California, is another attractive Mexican menu with a lot of effective merchandising. It is 9-5/8″ × 11-1/2″ with a heavy, coated cover in orange, green, and purple. Inside there are eight pages in black, orange, and green on mustard color paper.

On the inside front cover, the following copy helps to sell the restaurant and its food:

> Variety the Spice of Life—believers in this old adage, we have developed a menu that offers a lot of variety and a bit of spice. We encourage you to spread your wings, giving everything a try. In the event the combination you wish has escaped us, please feel free to exchange one item with another, as the "No Substitution Rule" does not apply at the Acapulco.

An interesting difference on the inside pages of this menu is that the listings are not set in type but instead are hand lettered by a calligrapher. Also, the *combinations* are numbered 1 through 37—making things easier for both the waiters and the kitchen.

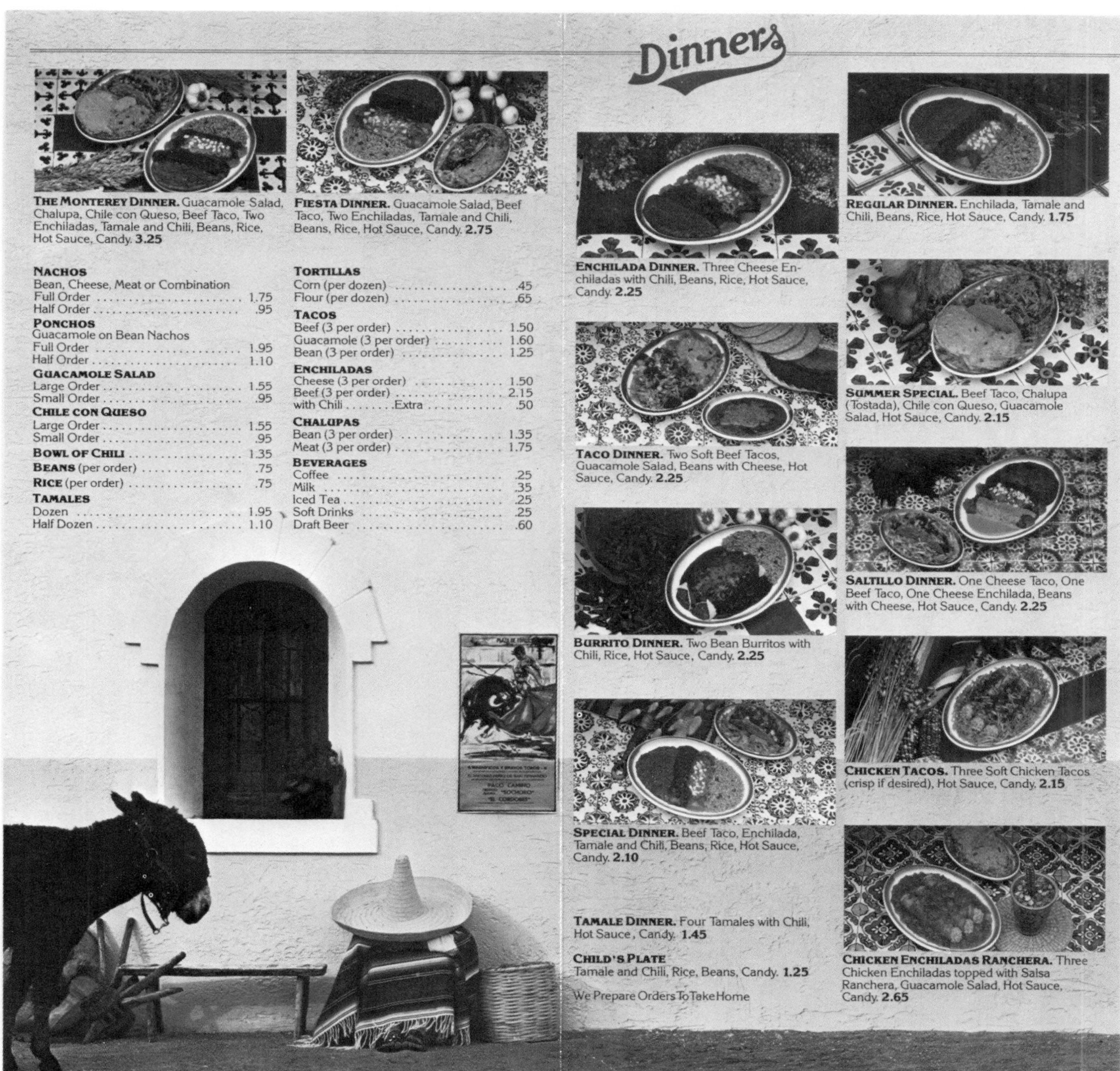

THE MONTEREY DINNER. Guacamole Salad, Chalupa, Chile con Queso, Beef Taco, Two Enchiladas, Tamale and Chili, Beans, Rice, Hot Sauce, Candy. **3.25**

FIESTA DINNER. Guacamole Salad, Beef Taco, Two Enchiladas, Tamale and Chili, Beans, Rice, Hot Sauce, Candy. **2.75**

NACHOS
Bean, Cheese, Meat or Combination
Full Order 1.75
Half Order .... .95

PONCHOS
Guacamole on Bean Nachos
Full Order 1.95
Half Order 1.10

GUACAMOLE SALAD
Large Order 1.55
Small Order .... .95

CHILE CON QUESO
Large Order 1.55
Small Order .... .95

BOWL OF CHILI 1.35

BEANS (per order) .... .75

RICE (per order) .... .75

TAMALES
Dozen 1.95
Half Dozen 1.10

TORTILLAS
Corn (per dozen) .... .45
Flour (per dozen) .... .65

TACOS
Beef (3 per order) 1.50
Guacamole (3 per order) 1.60
Bean (3 per order) 1.25

ENCHILADAS
Cheese (3 per order) 1.50
Beef (3 per order) 2.15
with Chili .... Extra .... .50

CHALUPAS
Bean (3 per order) 1.35
Meat (3 per order) 1.75

BEVERAGES
Coffee .... .25
Milk .... .35
Iced Tea .... .25
Soft Drinks .... .25
Draft Beer .... .60

Dinners

ENCHILADA DINNER. Three Cheese Enchiladas with Chili, Beans, Rice, Hot Sauce, Candy. **2.25**

TACO DINNER. Two Soft Beef Tacos, Guacamole Salad, Beans with Cheese, Hot Sauce, Candy. **2.25**

BURRITO DINNER. Two Bean Burritos with Chili, Rice, Hot Sauce, Candy. **2.25**

SPECIAL DINNER. Beef Taco, Enchilada, Tamale and Chili, Beans, Rice, Hot Sauce, Candy. **2.10**

TAMALE DINNER. Four Tamales with Chili, Hot Sauce, Candy. **1.45**

CHILD'S PLATE
Tamale and Chili, Rice, Beans, Candy. **1.25**

We Prepare Orders To Take Home

REGULAR DINNER. Enchilada, Tamale and Chili, Beans, Rice, Hot Sauce, Candy. **1.75**

SUMMER SPECIAL. Beef Taco, Chalupa (Tostada), Chile con Queso, Guacamole Salad, Hot Sauce, Candy. **2.15**

SALTILLO DINNER. One Cheese Taco, One Beef Taco, One Cheese Enchilada, Beans with Cheese, Hot Sauce, Candy. **2.25**

CHICKEN TACOS. Three Soft Chicken Tacos (crisp if desired), Hot Sauce, Candy. **2.15**

CHICKEN ENCHILADAS RANCHERA. Three Chicken Enchiladas topped with Salsa Ranchera, Guacamole Salad, Hot Sauce, Candy. **2.65**

Color photography tells the story on the Monterey House *menu.*

BURRITO: A small burro. Also an orgy of brazen beans and coy cheese sensuously stuffed into a clingy covering of tempting tortilla. More cheese is draped seductively over the whole daring concoction.

CHALUPA: A bean taco with nothing to hide. Crisp lettuce and toothsome tomato, wallowing in beans, atop a sprightly tortilla. According to Ernesto "CHE" Rabinowitz, food critic of the Guadalajara Gazette "Monterey House chalupas are simply super."

CHILI OR CHILI CON CARNE: Literally "it's cold at the carnival"; chili was invented by Gonzalo "Hot Stuff" Gimmidejuajua to warm his family before an afternoon of winter fun. Chilis differ widely, each expressing the personality of the individual chef. Monterey House's master chef Juan Inamillion has produced a chili that's merry, yet not frivolous; bold but not brazen. Manuel Leibor, food and air conditioning critic for the Winnipeg Star-Herald-Journal-Polar Bear writes "Try Monterey House Chili and stuff yourself silly."

CHILE CON QUESO: Literally "child with a question." Children often ask what they can have that's yummy and fun to eat, but doesn't rot their teeth. Chile con queso was invented to answer that eternal query. A cheerful concoction of onions, celery, hot pepper, and spices simmered in creamy melted cheese, adorning a crisp tortilla.

ENCHILADAS, BEEF OR CHEESE: Specially-flavored beef or cheese, rolled in a soft tortilla and covered with scrumptious chili or luscious gravy. Enchiladas are so good that in the late 19th century they were banned in some South American countries where zealous church officials linked them with mixed bathing, bassoon sonatas, and clothing lined with rabbit fur under the heading "sinful pleasures of the flesh conducive to moral looseness and worldly, self indulgence." Though now legal, medical researchers have linked Monterey House enchiladas with "Ernesto's syndrome," a malady marked up by excessive grinning, humming, and hopping from foot to foot.

GUACAMOLE SALAD: (Pronounced "Walk-A-Mile," as in "Guacamole In My Shoes," the name comes from an 18th century ballad written by the famous tunesmith and podiatrist Omaya Fallon-Orches). Favored repast of Aztec Kings and Pasadena realtors, guacamole is a provocative union of salt, spices, and smushed avocado, served with tomato chunks, onion hunks and élan.

NACHOS, CHEESE, BEAN OR MEAT: A zesty aggregation of tantalizing chile con queso and spicy jalapeño pepper; bean, cheese and jalapeño. Nachos are the perfect snack, because they delicately tickle the palate while helping us sell more beer.

TACOS, BEEF, BEAN OR GUACAMOLE: Tacos are so popular in America they've become a part of the language, as in "Taco you hands offa me, busta" or "The Eyes of Tacos are upon You." Beef tacos are curved, crispy tortillas cunningly crammed with taco meat (beef cooked with exotic vegetables and seasonings), lettuce and tomato. Guacamole tacos feature a curved tortilla laden with mouth-watering guacamole salad and bean tacos are a successful merger of bounteous beans, verdant lettuce and juicy tomato on a taco shell.

TAMALE: Tamales were introduced to the Americas in 1583 by Pancho de Ojos Rojos, a Spanish explorer and turkey impersonator. They were very unpopular until the 1920's when researchers tried taking the paper off before eating them. The rest is history. Tamales feature spiced meat wrapped in a tasty covering of "masa", or corn meal. The word "golly" was invented in 1923 by an Oklahoma City poet seeking to express the delight he experienced in eating his first Monterey House tamale (without the paper covering).

TORTILLA: A thin pancake of corn meal, served soft or crispy, and delicious with butter, honey, guacamole, chili or hot sauce; infrequently served with caviar, pistachio ice cream, polish sausage, or chopped liver, tortillas are a delight to gourmets and Aggies alike. In the American Civil War, Admiral Daniel Farragut dined on tortillas before the Battle of Mobile Bay and was quoted as saying "Dandy tortillas, full speed ahead."

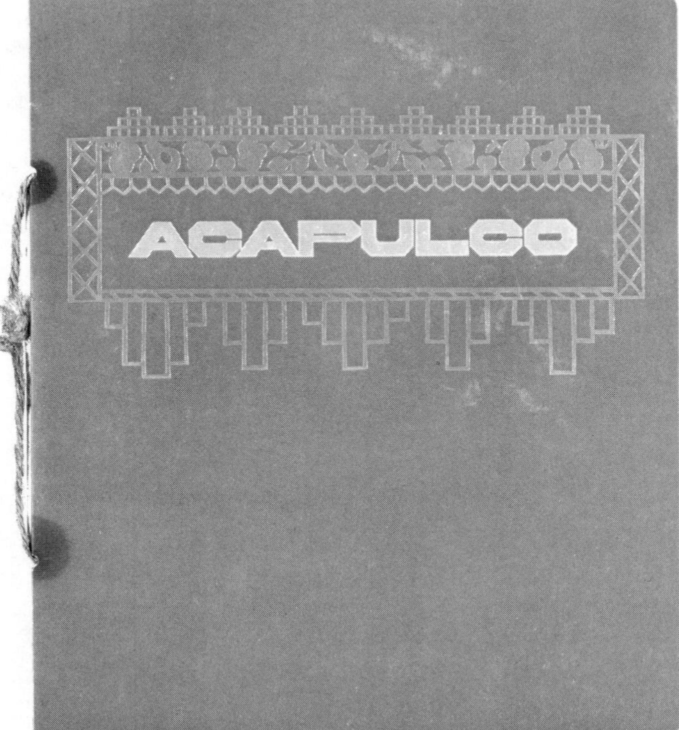

SPECIALTIES

All served with Refried Beans and Mexican Rice.

Machaca Shredded beef, cooked with tomatoes, onions and green peppers. A Mexican favorite 3.85

Steak Picado Strips of beef simmered with bell peppers, onions and tomatoes. Also prepared with Pork or Chicken 3.85

Chile Verde Cubes of lean pork cooked with green chiles, onions and Ranchera Sauce 3.85

Steak Ranchero Beef strips are simmered with Ranchera Sauce, onions and garlic. Pretty hot! 3.85

Chile Colorado Strips of beef cooked with a mild red chile sauce 3.85

Any of above A la Carta 3.50

FROM THE SEA

Huachinango Veracruzano Red Snapper covered with a sauce of fresh tomatoes, carrots, cilantro and stuffed green olives. With sour cream and slice of lime 4.25

Camarones Rancheros Tender shrimp are lightly simmered in Ranchera Sauce, onion and seasoning. Definitely hot! 4.25

4

DELICIOSO

The Crab Enchilada
A la San Francisco

First Prize Winner in the Crab Olympics at Fisherman's Wharf in San Francisco. "Specialty Dish of the Year," Los Angeles Restaurant Writers' Association.

Our well-known Enchilada is filled with crab, covered with your choice of Verde or Ranchera Sauce, melted Jack Cheese and Sour Cream Sauce; garnished with slices of avocado, tomato, chunks of King Crab and ripe black olives.

With Refried Beans & Mexican Rice ... 3.95
A la Carta 3.50

Carnitas Mexican chefs are experts at cooking pork, and here is a way that's not to be missed!

Pieces of tender pork are braised then lightly glazed and served with hot tortillas. Avocado slices, cilantro, radishes and a special Carnitas Sauce are served on the side for you to combine.

With Refried Beans & Mexican Rice 3.85

Chicken With Mole One of the most universally popular dishes in Mexico, Mole is made with a variety of chiles, seeds and seasonings. It has a most unusual flavor.

Our Mole Sauce is served over boneless white meat of chicken with Mexican Rice 3.85

5

This menu communicates so well that even an eastern "Gringo" can order Mexican food with confidence.

36

The fast food—multiple operation menu

Most chain or multiple operation restaurants can be classed under the fast food heading or category. Most, but not all, have a limited or smaller menu, and most are designed with the idea of getting customers to make up their minds quickly as to what they want so that the turnover is high and the number of customers is large to compensate for the smaller check. To achieve this purpose, and food service operations who may not consider themselves strictly within this category may want to get the same result, a special type of menu is required.

First, it must be a colorful menu that matches the bright, clean decor that is usually associated with this type of operation. This means bright yellows, blues, reds, greens, oranges, usually on a white background. A panel arrangement with squares, boxes, circles, etc., also in the same bright colors, where the type is printed big and bold is another common feature. Along with bright colors, 4-color food illustrations are another must for this type of menu. The items usually illustrated are:

Appetizers—shrimp cocktail
Sandwiches—hamburgers, steak sandwich
Entrees—chicken, steak, seafood plate, shrimp
Salads—chef's salad
Dessert—apple pie, cheesecake
Fountain—soda, sundae

The color illustrations are designed to encourage a quick decision from the customer to order these items. They should be both popular items and high profit items. The illustrations are generally color photography showing the food in an appetizing manner and as served in the operation on its china or in its glassware. Used less, but sometimes as effectively are color drawings of the food. This is not quite as true to life as a photo, but from the point of view of design and creating attention for the food items the restaurateur wants to sell, this type of illustration can work very well.

The next characteristic of this kind of menu is large, bold type, usually of the modern sans serif type. The type is often large enough for people who wear glasses to read without glasses. Headings can be script or a different type style, caps if the listing is in caps and lower case, and often in a different color, red or blue.

The paper this type of menu is printed on is usually a heavy, white enamel cover stock that is coated with a clear plastic or varnish after printing for longer life. Because of the use of four colors plus color illustrations and the heavy durable paper stock, the cost of this type of menu is usually high. For a multiple or chain operation where a big printing run is justified, the cost per menu can be a reasonable one. But for a single establishment with a short printing run, the cost per menu can be extremely high.

The other feature of this type of menu, if it is a standard uniform menu for all outlets, is a listing of addresses of all the locations of the restaurants in the chain. This is simple, basic but yet good merchandising. A problem with the one standard menu for a large chain operation is that of regional variation. This variation can appear in several forms. They are (a) regional price variations, and (b) regional food preferences.

To accommodate regional price variations as well as price changes is a relatively simple matter. All of the original run of menus can be printed without prices and prices printed later as they are used or for individual regional printing runs. Regional food preferences present a more complicated problem for the chain operation menu. For example, if 200,000 menus are printed with French fried shrimp as one of the color illustration features and in one area this item does not sell at all, a considerable portion of the selling space on the menu is wasted, but the item cannot be dropped from the menu in that area because all of the menus are printed identically.

To overcome this problem, color illustrations can be printed on tip-ons or paste-ons (on kleen-stick) for flexibility to accommodate regional preferences. Seasonal preferences are another variation that can be allowed for through this type of color illustration interchange. The layout in the drawing that follows shows how flexibility and color illustration (as well as easy price changing) can be achieved in menu design that allows for daily, weekly, seasonal, and regional changes—all that can possibly be anticipated.

This is an 8-page menu—a 4-page cover with a 4-page insert. The 4-page insert is bound to the cover by means of an elastic cord with metal or plastic ends (like a shoe lace) that holds the four center pages to the cover but that can easily be removed, allowing for a different four pages to be inserted when desired. On page 1 (inside front cover), space is allowed for three (or more) sandwich specials. These would be color illustration pictures plus short identification copy, but no price. They would be held to the menu by plastic clip-on holders. On page 2, the regular sandwich and salad listing would be printed. (Note—one of the color illustrations could be a salad.) On page 3, the Entree listing, Luncheon or Dinner, would be listed, and on page 4, three (or more depending on the size of the menu) Luncheon or Dinner Specials, illustrated in full color and identified with short copy would be placed. Prices would not be printed on these color specials either. Page 5 would be used for a Dessert, Fountain and Beverage listing, and page 6 (inside back cover) could accommodate three dessert or fountain Specials. The back cover of this menu could have a listing of the various locations of the restaurants in the chain. Or if it is a one-location restaurant, or two or three within a relatively small geographic area, a map would be a good merchandising device. If Take-Outs are a feature of the restaurant, they also could be merchandised here.

To accommodate price on the color illustrations, a changing factor in all menus, round kleen-stick tip-ons would be the answer. They can be attached to the color illustration and the price written on in ink. By making this menu longer, a total of twelve or fifteen (four or five per page) color illustrated specials can be allowed for. The color specials could be printed all at once on one sheet. The menu shown in the layout which allows for nine color specials could have twenty-seven color specials printed on one sheet. This would mean that three completely different menus could each have a special illustrated in color. This is just one example of how color food illustrations that sell menu specials can be worked into a menu in a manner that allows for change and seasonal-daily-weekly-regional variation.

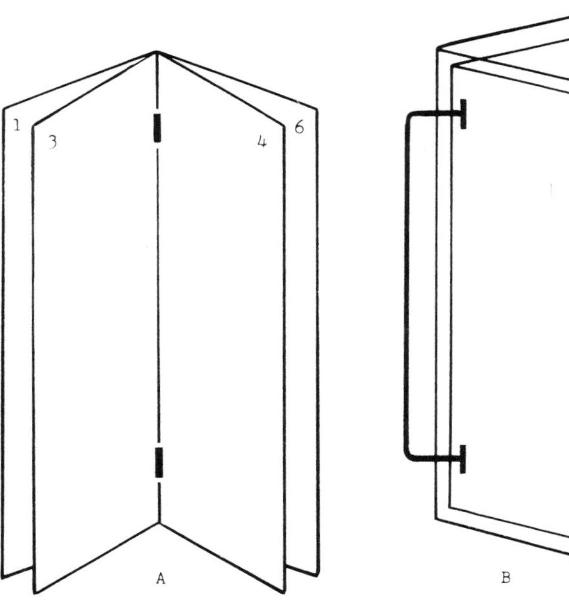

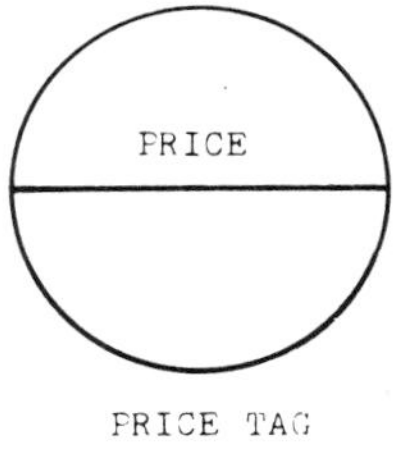

The 8-page menu on pages 235 and 236 is designed to incorporate daily, weekly, seasonal, and regional changes. It combines a 4-page cover with a 4-page insert.

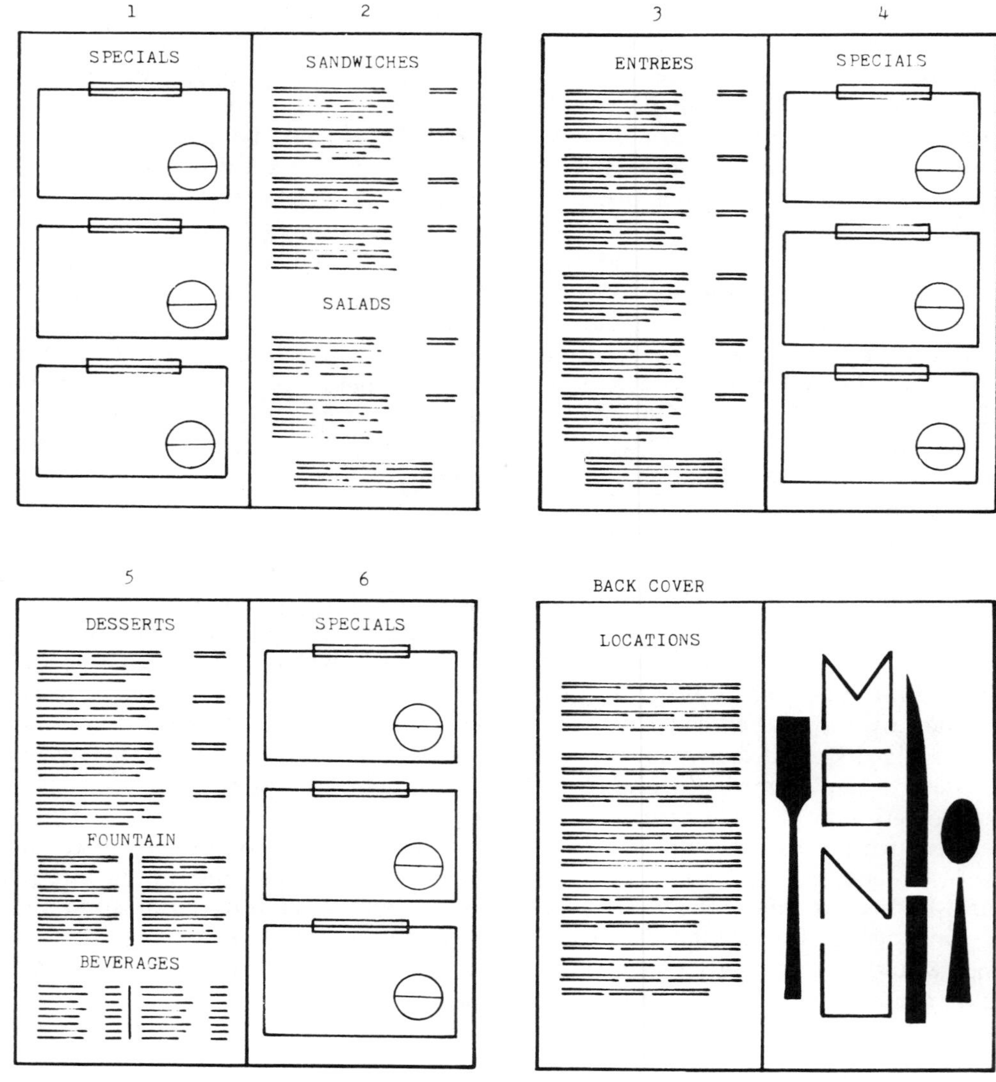

The *Poppin Fresh Pies* chain has used several menu merchandising approaches. One is a place mat which lists, describes, and illustrates in color the pies served. Prices are not listed, so this selling tool can be used for a long time before it needs changing. Along with the place mat, a small menu (9″ × 8″) is printed in two colors—brown and orange—on tan paper and placed in a plastic easel type holder on the table.

A variation on the above menu combination is a six-panel menu, each panel 7½″ × 7½″, printed in one color (brown) on tan paper. Besides pies, this menu sells chili, soup, hamburgers, other sandwiches, salads, and beverages.

(Pages 237 and 238) *The combination of a placemat menu and a table tent menu is a unique way of presenting the bill-of-fare.*

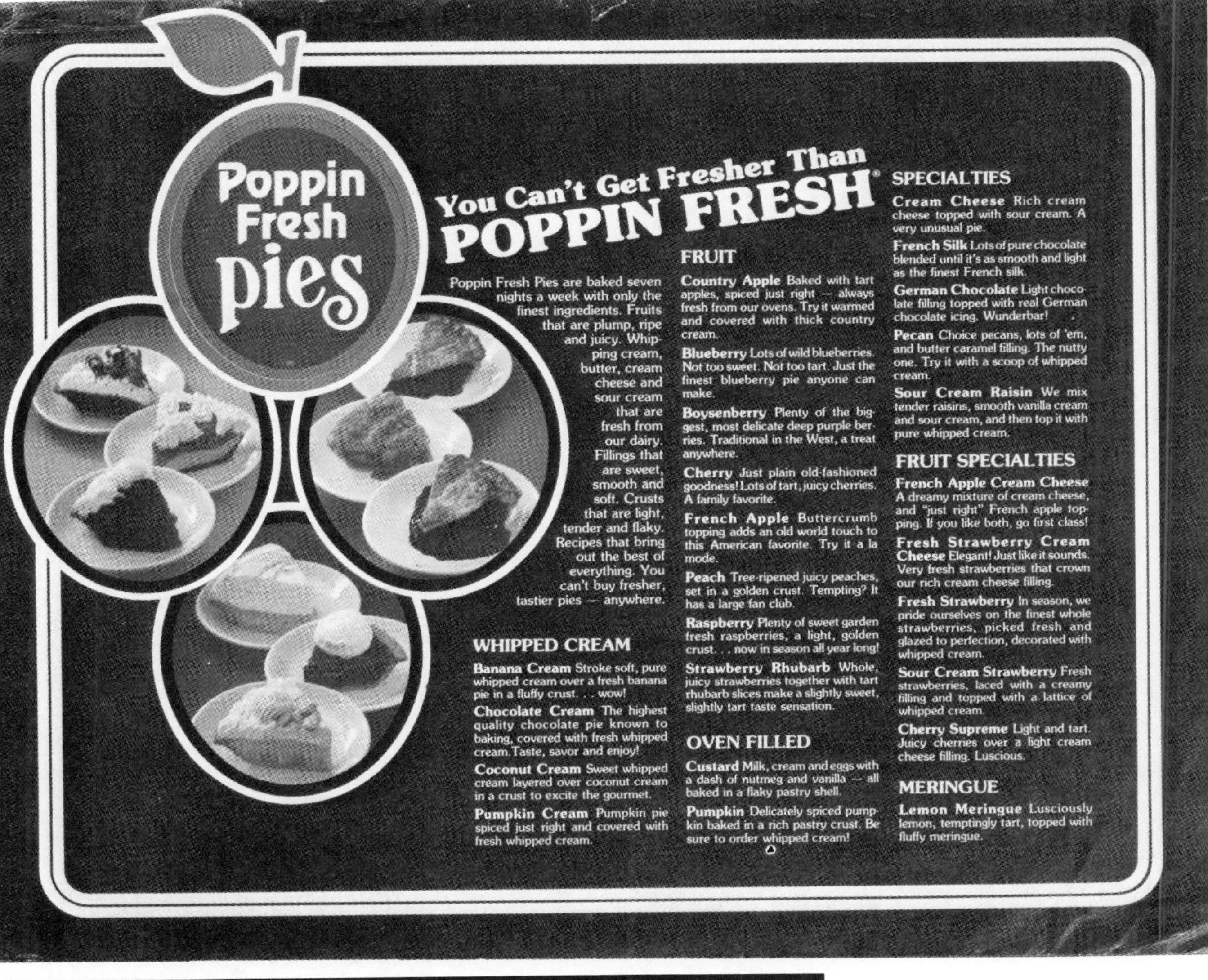
Poppin Fresh pies
You Can't Get Fresher Than POPPIN FRESH®
Poppin Fresh Pies are baked seven nights a week with only the finest ingredients. Fruits that are plump, ripe and juicy. Whipping cream, butter, cream cheese and sour cream that are fresh from our dairy. Fillings that are sweet, smooth and soft. Crusts that are light, tender and flaky. Recipes that bring out the best of everything. You can't buy fresher, tastier pies — anywhere.
WHIPPED CREAM
Banana Cream Stroke soft, pure whipped cream over a fresh banana pie in a fluffy crust. . . wow!
Chocolate Cream The highest quality chocolate pie known to baking, covered with fresh whipped cream. Taste, savor and enjoy!
Coconut Cream Sweet whipped cream layered over coconut cream in a crust to excite the gourmet.
Pumpkin Cream Pumpkin pie spiced just right and covered with fresh whipped cream.
FRUIT
Country Apple Baked with tart apples, spiced just right — always fresh from our ovens. Try it warmed and covered with thick country cream.
Blueberry Lots of wild blueberries. Not too sweet. Not too tart. Just the finest blueberry pie anyone can make.
Boysenberry Plenty of the biggest, most delicate deep purple berries. Traditional in the West, a treat anywhere.
Cherry Just plain old-fashioned goodness! Lots of tart, juicy cherries. A family favorite.
French Apple Buttercrumb topping adds an old world touch to this American favorite. Try it a la mode.
Peach Tree-ripened juicy peaches, set in a golden crust. Tempting? It has a large fan club.
Raspberry Plenty of sweet garden fresh raspberries, a light, golden crust. . . now in season all year long!
Strawberry Rhubarb Whole, juicy strawberries together with tart rhubarb slices make a slightly sweet, slightly tart taste sensation.
OVEN FILLED
Custard Milk, cream and eggs with a dash of nutmeg and vanilla — all baked in a flaky pastry shell.
Pumpkin Delicately spiced pumpkin baked in a rich pastry crust. Be sure to order whipped cream!
SPECIALTIES
Cream Cheese Rich cream cheese topped with sour cream. A very unusual pie.
French Silk Lots of pure chocolate blended until it's as smooth and light as the finest French silk.
German Chocolate Light chocolate filling topped with real German chocolate icing. Wunderbar!
Pecan Choice pecans, lots of 'em, and butter caramel filling. The nutty one. Try it with a scoop of whipped cream.
Sour Cream Raisin We mix tender raisins, smooth vanilla cream and sour cream, and then top it with pure whipped cream.
FRUIT SPECIALTIES
French Apple Cream Cheese A dreamy mixture of cream cheese, and "just right" French apple topping. If you like both, go first class!
Fresh Strawberry Cream Cheese Elegant! Just like it sounds. Very fresh strawberries that crown our rich cream cheese filling.
Fresh Strawberry In season, we pride ourselves on the finest whole strawberries, picked fresh and glazed to perfection, decorated with whipped cream.
Sour Cream Strawberry Fresh strawberries, laced with a creamy filling and topped with a lattice of whipped cream.
Cherry Supreme Light and tart. Juicy cherries over a light cream cheese filling. Luscious.
MERINGUE
Lemon Meringue Lusciously lemon, temptingly tart, topped with fluffy meringue.

DINNER-SIZE APPETITE!

QUICHE LORRAINE
An egg custard filling with bacon, natural Swiss & Jack cheeses, & green onions. Baked in a flaky crust and served warm with a small salad and french bread 2.95

HAMBURGER STEAK WITH MUSHROOM SAUCE
Tender, sizzling hamburger steak served with our own delicious mushroom sauce, french fries, crisp salad and french bread 3.45

CHILI PATTY MELT
Our big burger with melted cheese covered with a big serving of chili. Served with crisp salad and french bread 3.35

CHILI
A big filling of our own homemade beefy chili, garnished with grated cheddar cheese and served in a covered casserole with french bread. It's a meal in itself! 2.35

All dinner-size items served with a thick slice of French Bread.

FROM OUR SANDWICH KITCHEN

DOUGHBOY BURGER & FRENCH FRIES
Our big fresh ground beef burger topped with lettuce, tomato and our own special dressing (with cheese 15¢ extra). 2.20

PATTY MELT
Our big fresh ground beef burger, two slices of melted cheese, and sauteed onions on grilled rye, served with potato chips . 2.40

HAMBURGER CLUBHOUSE
Our big fresh ground beef burger, melted cheese, and a slice of ham, served with potato chips 2.30

HAMBURGER & CUP OF CHILI ... 2.45

CHEESEBURGER
Our big cheeseburger served with potato chips 1.85

HAMBURGER
Our big burger served with potato chips. 1.70

TURKEY CLUBHOUSE
Roasted turkey breast, crisp bacon, lettuce and tomato, served with our Bean Salad 2.55

TURKEY SANDWICH
Roasted turkey breast, lettuce and tomato, served with our Bean Salad 2.05

STACKED HAM
Heaps of thinly sliced ham on white or rye with Bean Salad 2.05

TUNA SALAD SANDWICH
Served with Bean Salad............... 1.95

GRILLED CHEESE
Served with potato chips............. 1.15

GRILLED HAM & CHEESE WITH TOMATO & CUP OF SOUP 2.10

HAMBURGER & CUP OF SOUP ... 2.25

FRENCH FRIES.................... .60

FROM OUR POPPIN FRESH PIE OVENS

Fruit Pies	.90	Whipped Cream Pies	1.20
Lemon Meringue	.90	Oven Filled Pies	.90
Specialties	1.25	Fruit Specialties	1.40

See your placemat for varieties
Vanilla Ala Mode... .35 Whipped Cream... .35 Country Cream... .35 Vanilla Ice Cream... .40

No Substitutes Please

VEGETABLE BEEF SOUP

BOWL & BREAD
An extra large bowl (more than double our cup) of hot vegetable beef soup, with plenty of vegetables and meat, served with a thick slice of buttered French bread. It's enough to be a meal in itself .. 1.85
Cup.. .70

FROM OUR SALAD PANTRY

Large beautiful Salads made to your order from the freshest ingredients available. Try our homemade Parmesan, bleu cheese, and Louie dressings, or French, Thousand Island & Italian.

DINNER SALAD
Crisp lettuce, tomato & choice of dressing. ..... .95

TACO SALAD
Our own delicious chili on a bed of lettuce, topped with cheddar cheese and garnished with tomatoes, olives and a ring of taco chips. 2.65

CHEF'S DELUXE SALAD
Crisp lettuce heaped with julienne sliced ham, turkey and cheese, garnished with egg and tomato.................................... 3.25

DOUGHBOY SALAD
Lots of lettuce, tomato, egg slices & carrot sticks. Served only with our secret recipe Parmesan dressing.................................... 1.95

SHRIMP SALAD
Tasty shrimp with our own freshly made Louie dressing on lettuce with asparagus, tomatoes and egg slices................................ 3.55

TUNA SALAD
Delicate white albacore tuna, mixed with Miracle Whip and a bit of celery, served on a bed of lettuce garnished with tomato, egg slices and carrot sticks................................ 2.95

FRENCH BREAD
Make your salad complete — try a thick slice of our crusty french bread .... .35

BEVERAGES

Hot Tea	.35	Coffee	.40
Brewed Iced Tea	.35	Sanka	.40
Grade A Milk	.40	Hot Chocolate	.40
Soft Drinks	.35 & .45		

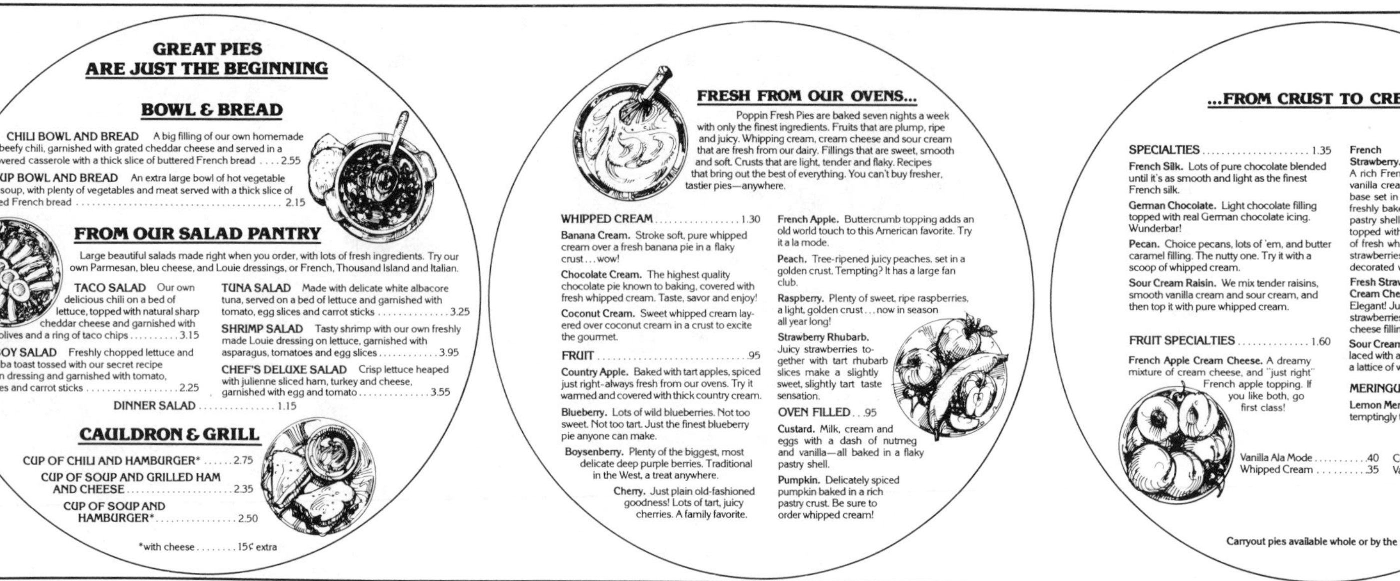

GREAT PIES
ARE JUST THE BEGINNING

BOWL & BREAD

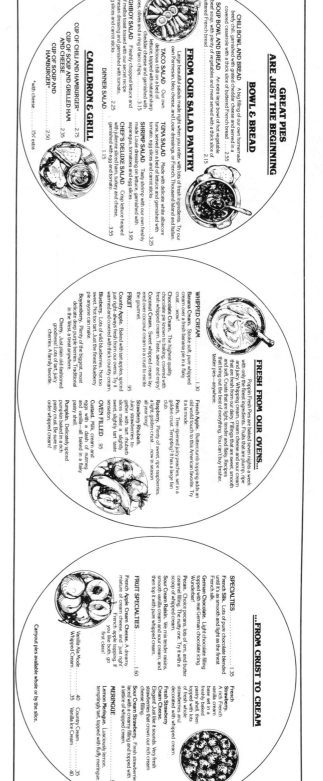

CHILI BOWL AND BREAD A big filling of our own homemade beefy chili, garnished with grated cheddar cheese and served in a covered casserole with a thick slice of buttered French bread 2.55

SOUP BOWL AND BREAD An extra large bowl of hot vegetable beef soup, with plenty of vegetables and meat served with a thick slice of buttered French bread 2.15

FROM OUR SALAD PANTRY

Large beautiful salads made right when you order, with lots of fresh ingredients. Try our own Parmesan, bleu cheese, and Louie dressings, or French, Thousand Island and Italian.

TACO SALAD Our own delicious chili on a bed of lettuce, topped with natural sharp cheddar cheese and garnished with tomatoes, olives and a ring of taco chips 3.15

DOUGHBOY SALAD Freshly chopped lettuce and bits of melba toast tossed with our secret recipe Parmesan dressing and garnished with tomato, egg slices and carrot sticks 2.25

TUNA SALAD Made with delicate white albacore tuna, served on a bed of lettuce and garnished with tomato, egg slices and carrot sticks 3.25

SHRIMP SALAD Tasty shrimp with our own freshly made Louie dressing on lettuce, garnished with asparagus, tomatoes and egg slices 3.95

CHEF'S DELUXE SALAD Crisp lettuce heaped with julienne sliced ham, turkey and cheese, garnished with egg and tomato 3.55

DINNER SALAD 1.15

CAULDRON & GRILL

CUP OF CHILI AND HAMBURGER* 2.75
CUP OF SOUP AND GRILLED HAM AND CHEESE 2.35
CUP OF SOUP AND HAMBURGER* 2.50

*with cheese . . . . 15¢ extra

FRESH FROM OUR OVENS...

Poppin Fresh Pies are baked seven nights a week with only the finest ingredients. Fruits that are plump, ripe and juicy. Whipping cream, cream cheese and sour cream that are fresh from our dairy. Fillings that are sweet, smooth and soft. Crusts that are light, tender and flaky. Recipes that bring out the best of everything. You can't buy fresher, tastier pies—anywhere.

WHIPPED CREAM 1.30

Banana Cream. Stroke soft, pure whipped cream over a fresh banana pie in a flaky crust . . . wow!

Chocolate Cream. The highest quality chocolate pie known to baking, covered with fresh whipped cream. Taste, savor and enjoy!

Coconut Cream. Sweet whipped cream layered over coconut cream in a crust to excite the gourmet.

FRUIT 95

Country Apple. Baked with tart apples, spiced just right-always fresh from our ovens. Try it warmed and covered with thick country cream.

Blueberry. Lots of wild blueberries. Not too sweet. Not too tart. Just the finest blueberry pie anyone can make.

Boysenberry. Plenty of the biggest, most delicate deep purple berries. Traditional in the West, a treat anywhere.

Cherry. Just plain old-fashioned goodness! Lots of tart, juicy cherries. A family favorite.

French Apple. Buttercrumb topping adds an old world touch to this American favorite. Try it a la mode.

Peach. Tree-ripened juicy peaches, set in a golden crust. Tempting? It has a large fan club.

Raspberry. Plenty of sweet, ripe raspberries, a light, golden crust . . . now in season all year long!

Strawberry Rhubarb. Juicy strawberries together with tart rhubarb slices make a slightly sweet, slightly tart taste sensation.

OVEN FILLED . . .95

Custard. Milk, cream and eggs with a dash of nutmeg and vanilla—all baked in a flaky pastry shell.

Pumpkin. Delicately spiced pumpkin baked in a rich pastry crust. Be sure to order whipped cream!

...FROM CRUST TO CREAM

SPECIALTIES 1.35

French Silk. Lots of pure chocolate blended until it's as smooth and light as the finest French silk.

German Chocolate. Light chocolate filling topped with real German chocolate icing. Wunderbar!

Pecan. Choice pecans, lots of 'em, and butter caramel filling. The nutty one. Try it with a scoop of whipped cream.

Sour Cream Raisin. We mix tender raisins, smooth vanilla cream and sour cream, and then top it with pure whipped cream.

French Strawberry. A rich French vanilla cream base set in a freshly baked pastry shell, then topped with lots of fresh whole strawberries and decorated with whipped cream.

Fresh Strawberry Cream Cheese. Elegant! Just like it sounds. Very fresh strawberries that crown our rich cream cheese filling.

Sour Cream Strawberry. Fresh strawberries, laced with a creamy filling and topped with a lattice of whipped cream.

FRUIT SPECIALTIES 1.60

French Apple Cream Cheese. A dreamy mixture of cream cheese, and "just right" French apple topping. If you like both, go first class!

MERINGUE 95

Lemon Meringue. Lusciously lemon, temptingly tart, topped with fluffy meringue.

Vanilla Ala Mode 40
Whipped Cream 35
Country Cream 35
Vanilla Ice Cream 40

Carryout pies available whole or by the slice.

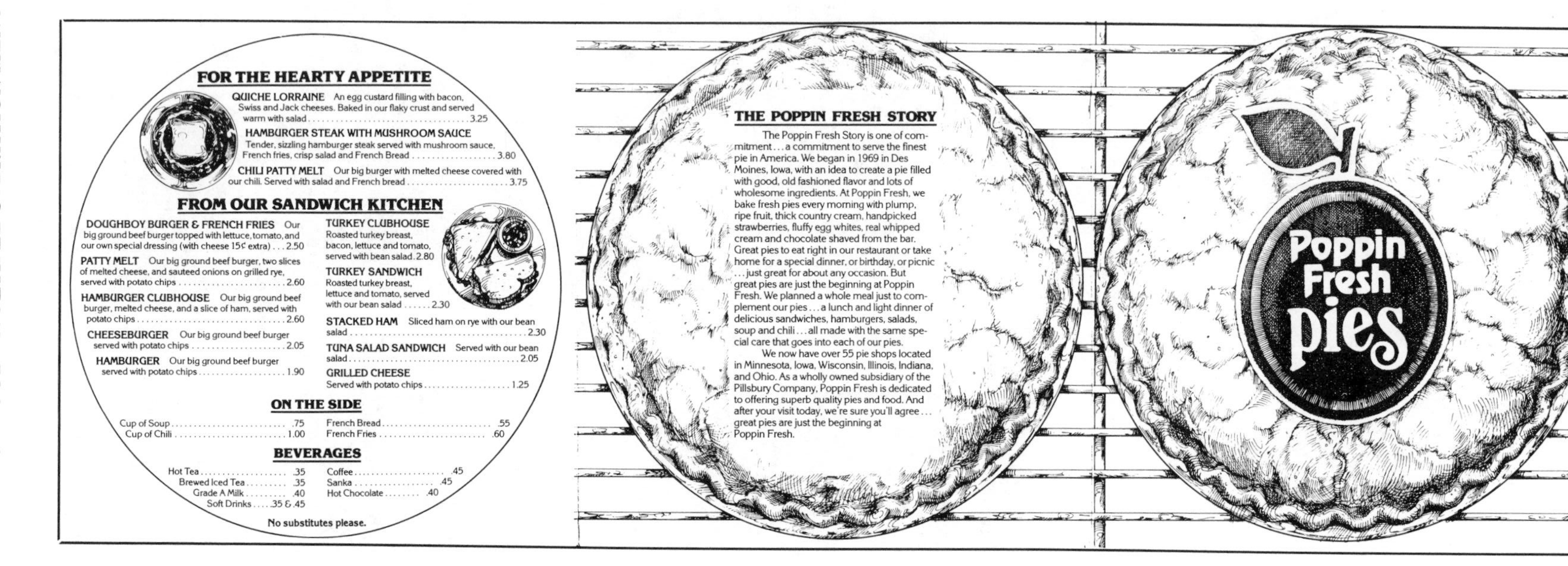

FOR THE HEARTY APPETITE

QUICHE LORRAINE An egg custard filling with bacon, Swiss and Jack cheeses. Baked in our flaky crust and served warm with salad 3.25

HAMBURGER STEAK WITH MUSHROOM SAUCE Tender, sizzling hamburger steak served with mushroom sauce, French fries, crisp salad and French Bread 3.80

CHILI PATTY MELT Our big burger with melted cheese covered with our chili. Served with salad and French bread 3.75

FROM OUR SANDWICH KITCHEN

DOUGHBOY BURGER & FRENCH FRIES Our big ground beef burger topped with lettuce, tomato, and our own special dressing (with cheese 15¢ extra) . . . 2.50

PATTY MELT Our big ground beef burger, two slices of melted cheese, and sauteed onions on grilled rye, served with potato chips 2.60

HAMBURGER CLUBHOUSE Our big ground beef burger, melted cheese, and a slice of ham, served with potato chips 2.60

CHEESEBURGER Our big ground beef burger served with potato chips 2.05

HAMBURGER Our big ground beef burger served with potato chips 1.90

TURKEY CLUBHOUSE Roasted turkey breast, bacon, lettuce and tomato, served with bean salad. 2.80

TURKEY SANDWICH Roasted turkey breast, lettuce and tomato, served with our bean salad 2.30

STACKED HAM Sliced ham on rye with our bean salad 2.30

TUNA SALAD SANDWICH Served with our bean salad 2.05

GRILLED CHEESE Served with potato chips 1.25

ON THE SIDE

Cup of Soup 75
Cup of Chili 1.00
French Bread 55
French Fries 60

BEVERAGES

Hot Tea 35
Brewed Iced Tea 35
Grade A Milk 40
Soft Drinks . . . . .35 & .45
Coffee 45
Sanka 45
Hot Chocolate 40

No substitutes please.

THE POPPIN FRESH STORY

The Poppin Fresh Story is one of commitment . . . a commitment to serve the finest pie in America. We began in 1969 in Des Moines, Iowa, with an idea to create a pie filled with good, old fashioned flavor and lots of wholesome ingredients. At Poppin Fresh, we bake fresh pies every morning with plump, ripe fruit, thick country cream, handpicked strawberries, fluffy egg whites, real whipped cream and chocolate shaved from the bar. Great pies to eat right in our restaurant or take home for a special dinner, or birthday, or picnic . . . just great for about any occasion. But great pies are just the beginning at Poppin Fresh. We planned a whole meal just to complement our pies . . . a lunch and light dinner of delicious sandwiches, hamburgers, salads, soup and chili . . . all made with the same special care that goes into each of our pies.

We now have over 55 pie shops located in Minnesota, Iowa, Wisconsin, Illinois, Indiana, and Ohio. As a wholly owned subsidiary of the Pillsbury Company, Poppin Fresh is dedicated to offering superb quality pies and food. And after your visit today, we're sure you'll agree . . . great pies are just the beginning at Poppin Fresh.

37
Appetizers

Most service restaurants serve and list appetizers on the menu, but many of these operations do not merchandise and, therefore, do not sell their appetizers. First, the place on the menu for appetizers is important. They are a before-dinner item and should be listed before the entree listing. When entrees are listed on one page or on two facing pages, the appetizer listing should be on the top. And, if the menu has many pages, appetizers should be listed on a page previous to the entree listing.

Next, on the average menu, more attention should be given to the appetizer listing. This means they should be listed in a readable type face, although not necessarily as large as the entree listing type face. Also, to give appetizers the merchandising attention they deserve, copy is sometimes called for. A good rule of thumb is if the appetizer costs $1.00 or more, it should have some descriptive, merchandising, sell copy.

From the customer's point of view, you're asking the customer to spend more than he or she probably planned on spending. To increase the total check, by selling what is basically an impulse food service item, requires sell copy. If your appetizer sales are not big, the fault probably is poor or no copy at all.

Figures 1 and 2 show the results of a statistical study from current service restaurant menus. While the total number of menus studied was not great, the trends were established early and continued as more menus were studied.

The first question was what items are served most as appetizers? The number one favorite is shrimp cocktail; fruit is second, tomato juice is third, and seafood, other than shrimp, is fourth. A study of the chart will show the popularity (in restaurants) of a variety of other appetizers, and since we can assume most restaurants list only appetizers that move, there should be correlation between the listings and sales.

The next question studied was how many appetizers do restaurants list, both with dinner and a la carte? The first observation is that most service restaurants list appetizers a la carte, while the number listing appetizers as included in the price of the dinner is much smaller. On the a la carte appetizer chart, it would seem that five is the magic number. If you list five, you are average. If you list more, you are strong in the appetizer department, and if you list less, you are weak or below average.

The number, variety, and price of appetizers on a menu will be determined by many factors—costs, type of operation, location of operation, type of customers, etc. But a comparison with

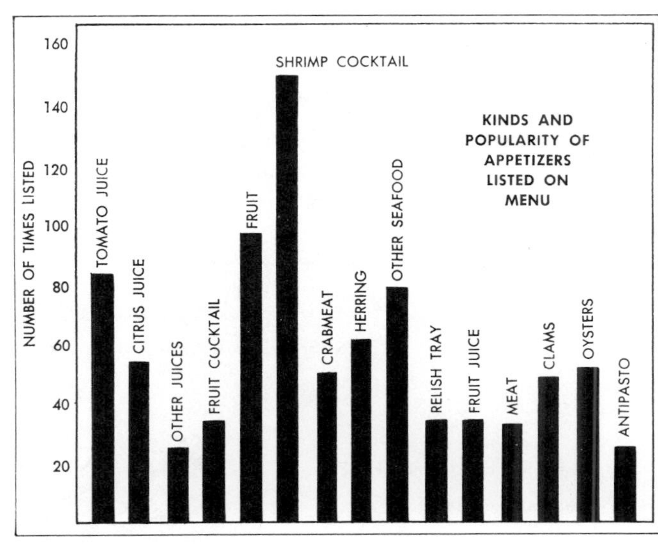

FIGURE 1

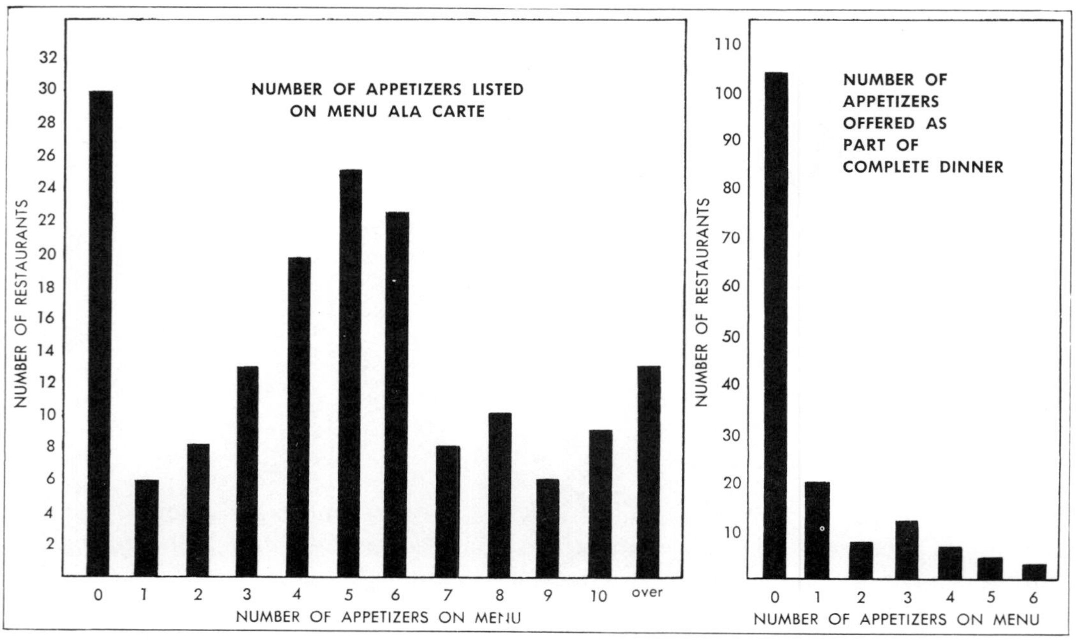

FIGURE 2

other operations can show an individual operator where the restaurant stands in relation to the total picture.

The rules to remember are:

1. List appetizers before entrees.
2. List in readable type.
3. If the appetizer costs $1.00 or more, describe it.
4. List at least five appetizers.
5. The five most popular appetizers are (in order of preference) shrimp cocktail, fruit, tomato juice, seafood (general), and herring.

Appetizers

STEAMED CLAMS
(for two)
1.35

EGGPLANT or ARTICHOKE
Hearts Fried in Olive Oil
.75

TOASTED RAVIOLI
with sauce
4 for .80

Anti-pasto	**.85**	**Shrimp Cocktail**	**.50**	**Sliced Tomato & Onions**	**.40**
Anti-pasto *(dinner)*	**.50**	**Minestrone Soup**	**.35**	**Stuffed Anchovies**	**.55**
Marinated Herring	**.50**	**Olives Assorted**	**.35**	**Pepperoncini**	**.35**

The above served with dinners only and when in season

The bigger appetizers get bigger treatment—bolder type and more copy—as they should.

"Appeteasers"

(Includes Rolls and Butter, Except * Items)

***Jumbo Shrimp Cocktail (5)**	**1.65**	**Marinated Herring in Sour Cream**	**.85**
***Cherrystone Clams (6)**	**.85**	**Nova Scotia Lox**	**1.25**
Filet of Matzes Herring	**.85**	**Chopped Chicken Livers**	**.85**
Gefilte Fish, Horseradish	**.85**	**Stuffed Kishka**	**.85**
***Soup Du Jour (Saltines)**	**.35**	***Iced Beet Borscht**	**.35**

***CHICKEN-NOODLE SOUP WITH MATZO BALL,** Individual Crock .45

A photo or illustration will help sell the appetizer you want to sell the most!

the overture

GULF OF GEORGIA SMOKED SALMON
British Columbia Spring Salmon cured and smoked especially for the Grouse Nest, served with capers, onion and Melba Toast
1.85

ESCARGOTS PROVENCALE
Imported French Snails broiled in Fine Herbs Butter with just a hint of Garlic. One Half Dozen
2.00

DUNGENESS CRAB LEGS
Unique to the Pacific Northwest
Cocktail Grouse Nest
1.85

PACIFIC SHRIMP SUPREME
Tiny, delectable shrimps from cool Northern waters with our own cocktail sauce
1.85

from the tureens

French Onion Soup au Gratin
1.00

Bongo Bongo Soup
1.25

Jellied Consomme Nikolai
Seasoned with dry sherry and topped with sour cream and caviar
1.45

Only four appetizers and three soups but not a dull one in the list.

The description of Minestrone shown here is one to paste in your hat and memorize, if you're in the business of selling soup.

APPETIZERS and SOUPS

Tuck your napkin under your chin, start with a delicious appetizer or soup and make all the noise you want.

Herring in Sour Cream ..... .60

Marinated Wine Herring .... .50

Jumbo Shrimp Cocktail 1.25

Dinner-Size Shrimp Cocktail .... .75

Tomato Juice .... .25

Minestrone .... .35
The portrait of the Italian Chef who created this masterpiece is enshrined reverently in our kitchen. The vitalizing products of the vegetable garden are blended with rich beef stock and seasonings.

Soup du Jour .... .35

cocktails from the sea around us . . .

the icy blue Pacific Ocean yields these delicacies . . .
from just 80 miles away, native Northwest seafoods are rushed to Poor Richard's daily . . .
(but first—cocktail sauce? Spicy red or creamy Thousand Island?)

Chilled Dungeness Crab as fresh as today's surf 1.10

Oregon Shrimp au Crystal pink, plump, piquant .95

Petite Oysters tiny gourmet gems 2.25

if you knew louies like we know louies . . .

Meaty Dungeness Louie
or
Pink Oregon Shrimp Louie
—crisp heart-of-crab or juicy shrimp nested on a mountain of iced lettuce, with that certain (secret) sauce! 2.25

a tart-sweet salad?

Traditional Fruit and Cheese
The Northwest's orchards (with an assist from Hawaii and California) yield nippy apples, luscious pineapple, prize-winning peaches, toothsome grapes — a colorful cornucopia of *today's* cottage cheese, freshly-churned. 1.25
(Note to dressing devotees: Choose from spicy red French or creamy Thousand Island or our delightful Fruit Dressing.)

from the colonial copper cauldron . . .

Clam Chowder Extraordinaire
—Blend herbs, ranch cream, succulent razor clams, and broth, and . . . wow! .35 .65

Oyster Stew Willapas or Olympias line-up to volunteer for ours! Willapa 1.25 Petite 2.25

There's not one dull word in this combined appetizer, salad, and soup listing.

Devilish Good Appetizers

OYSTERS OR CHERRYSTONE CLAMS
on the Half Shell, ½ Dozen **1.25** Dozen **2.25**

CRAB FINGERS, Whole Crab Claws Completely Shelled except for a "Handle" to hold em with! Delicious Seafood Dip **1.60**

CHILLED TOMATO JUICE .... **.40**

OCEAN-FRESH SHRIMP OR OYSTER COCKTAIL SUPREME **1.50**

ALASKAN KING CRABMEAT COCKTAIL SUPREME **1.50**

STEM CRYSTAL OF MIXED FRESH FRUITS
with Crown of Orange Ice .... **.60**

Soul Satisfying Soups

Served with Mixed Cracker Basket or Homebaked Bread and Butter

FAMOUS PIRATES' HOUSE OKRA GUMBO SOUP .... Bowl **.65** Cup **.45**
Superb with Scads of Shrimp and Crabmeat added .... Bowl **1.50** Cup **.95**

MISS EDNA'S SEAFOOD BISQUE - Something to Write Home About! Nourishing Nuggets of Fresh, Flavorful Crabmeat and Plump Savannah Shrimp Swimming in a Skillful Blend of Cream of Tomato and Pea Soup. Delicately Flavored with Sherry .... Bowl **1.60** Cup **1.10**

FRENCH ONION SOUP with Parmesan Toast Floats .... Bowl **.65** Cup **.45**

"Devilish Good Appetizers" and "Soul Satisfying Soups," not just "Appetizers and Soups." Good selling.

With a price range from $.50 to $6.50 and a selection of both hot and cold appetizers and soups, this listing is complete and well presented.

COCKTAIL OF FRESH FRUITS .60
Topped with sherbet & fresh mint

TOMATO JUICE .50

HERRING in Cream 1.00
or Horseradish Sauce

CHOPPED LIVER MAISON .85

LARGE LUMP CRABMEAT COCKTAIL 2.00

SHRIMP COCKTAIL 1.50

CLAMS on Half Shell 1.00

COCKTAIL of VARIOUS SHELLFISH 2.75

IMPORTED PROSCIUTTO 2.00 (With Melon 2.25)

NOVA SCOTIA SALMON 2.25

MELON .75 (whichever is best on the market)

SMOKED BROOK TROUT 2.75

IRANIAN BELUGA MALOSSOL "00" CAVIAR 6.50

Hot Appetizers

BAKED STUFFED CLAMS 1.50

SHRIMP SCAMPI 2.50

LINGUINE, CLAM SAUCE 2.50

STUFFED BABY DANISH LOBSTER TAILS 3.00

ESCARGOTS BOURGUIGNONNE 2.50

FETTUCCINE (At Tableside) 2.50

LINGUINE, MEAT SAUCE 3.00

GREEN NOODLES ala Franco 3.50

RISOTTO MILANESE 2.50

Soup

SOUP du Jour .50

CONSOMME .50

FRENCH ONION SOUP au Gratin .75

COLD VICHYSSOISE .60

CONSOMME MADRILENE .60

Aperitifs

Pernod *(90°)* 1 45 — **Punt e Mes** ***on the rocks*** **1 10**

Sherry: Amontillado Club Dry, *Duff Gordon* 1 15

Pastis de Marseille, *Berger or Ricard* 1 35

Tio Pepe, *Gonzales Byass* 1 25

Vermouth Cassis 1 25

St. Raphael 1 10

Americano 1 20 — **Aquavit *(Snaps)* 1 20**

Bitter Campari 1 20 — **Cardinal 1 25**

Dubonnet *blonde or red* 1 10 — **Fernet Branca 1 00**

Herbsaint 1 25 — **Kir=Vin Blanc Cassis 1 15**

Lillet *white or red* 1 10 — **Margarita 1 50**

Negroni 1 25 — Ouzo, *Metaxa* 1 35

hors d'oeuvre

BAKED CHERRYSTONE CLAMS: *casino* 2 95

BAY CHERRYSTONE CLAMS *on ½ shell* 1 95

CRACKED DUNGENESS CRAB *mustard sauce* 3 25

Imported Beluga Caviar, *jar* 4 50

Whole California Grapefruit 1 25

Fresh New Brunswick Lobster Cocktail 3 75

Half Avocado *Caesar* 1 50

Avocado Supreme *rémoulade* 1 50

DUBLIN BAY PRAWNS *mustard sauce* 3 95

JUMBO LUMP CRAB MEAT COCKTAIL 3 25; *lamaze* 3 50

MELON IN SEASON: Cantaloupe 1 35 Cranshaw 1 35

Anchovies & Pimento *w/capers* 1 75

Tomato or V-8 Juice Cocktail 85

Gulf White Shrimp Cocktail 2 35 *lamaze* 2 55

Marinated Herring *sour cream* 1 50

Celery Hearts, Radishes & Mixed Olives 1 25

Honey Dew 1 35 — Conchitas Con Parmesan 2 25

Snails *bourguigonne* (6) 2 50

Pascal Colorado Celery *w/roquefort* 1 50

Gulf White Shrimps *rémoulade* 2 55 *1000 Isle* 2 55

Soused Bismarck Herring Fillets 1 50

Hearts of Palm *vinaigrette* 1 75 — Chopped Liver & Onions 1 50

This listing of Aperitifs along with appetizers is a European custom that could be adopted by more American food service operations.

Beginning of the Journey

THE COCKTAIL SHAKER .... .45
With Juice on the Rocks

FRUITS EXOTIQUE AU KIRSH: .... .75
Fruits—mostly fresh from many places, bathed in Kirshwasser

MELONS OF THE SEASON .... .50

SHRIMP COCKTAIL EMERALD 1.15

CRAB MEAT COCKTAIL 1.45
The best of the Gulf in our Gribiche Sauce

A SYMPHONY OF SEAFOOD 1.65
Oysters, Crab Meat and Claws, Shrimps

CLAMS ON THE HALF SHELL 1.00

OYSTERS ON THE HALF SHELL 1.00

CASSOLETTE OF CRAB MEAT CRECY 1.85
Selected chunks of Crab Meat in a Sauce Piquante

BAKED OYSTERS MONSIEUR LE COMTE 1.25
With a puree of Mushroom and Wine Sauce

SNAILS BOURGUIGNONNE (6) 1.45
Les Escargots in Burgundy Butter

QUICHE LORRAINE 1.50
That excellent cheese pastry of the Continent

"Beautiful Soup so Rich and Green"

. . . Lewis Carrol

DOUBLE CONSOMME AMONTILLADO .... .65

BOULA BOULA .... .75
Turtle and Green Pea Soup with Sherry

THE ONION .... .75
Gratinee, of course, enhanced with Chablis

GASPACHO DE L'ESTRAMADOURE............. .60
The famous cold soup of Spain

BISQUE OF CRAYFISH .... .90
In true European style

This is a truly elegant selection of appetizers and soups listed with elegant words and set in elegant type.

38
Salads

Salads are an accepted food item on the American menu. From a piece of lettuce with dressing on it to a complete meal, salads include a great number of food combinations with a variety of appeals. They help the dieter and are ideal for jaded summer appetites. But how do they fare on the menu? Some interesting facts are revealed in Figures 1 and 2.

First, considering the kinds of salads listed a la carte and with dinner, we find that lettuce by itself, or with a few other similar vegetables—tossed greens, chef's salad, with tomato, etc.—is the number one salad in eating-out popularity. This probably corresponds with salad popularity in the home, making it a necessity item rather than creative menu merchandising. Fruit and shrimp salads are next in popularity, with cottage cheese following close behind. Combining tuna, crabmeat, lobster, and other seafoods, it is apparent that seafood is a very popular salad ingredient, probably the most popular after the basic head of lettuce.

Next, considering the number of different salads listed a la carte and with dinner on the menu, we find that the most frequent listing is of one salad. This is most often the basic lettuce salad with dressing. The next highest number of salad selections put on the menu is four, and after that they break down rather evenly. It is interesting to note that there are more menus listing eight different kinds of salads than there are menus listing two kinds.

The important thing to remember when listing a la carte salads on the menu is to treat

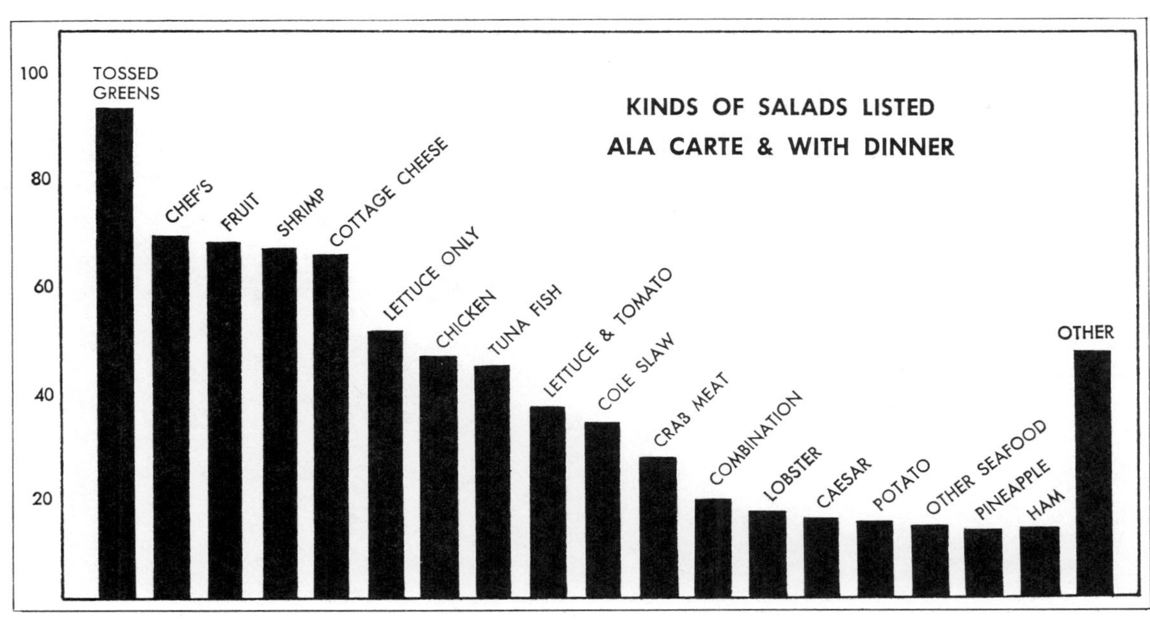

FIGURE 1

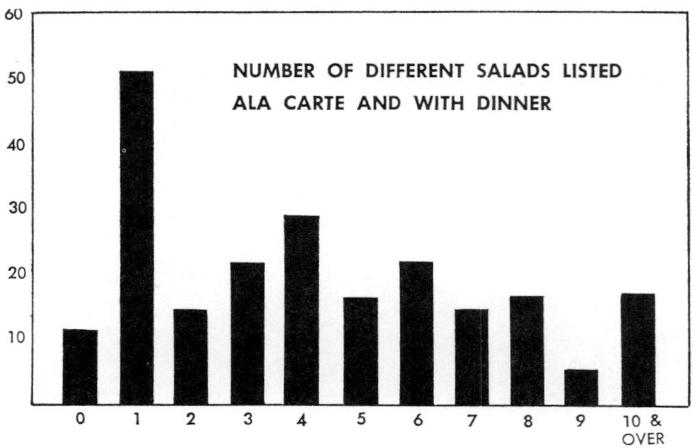

FIGURE 2

them like important entree items. This means setting the listing in readable size type. Do not crowd or set items too close together, and, above all, give your salads complete, descriptive, merchandising "sell" copy. Naming a salad does not identify it. You must include the ingredients; but don't just list them, use imagination, romanticize, and try to create appetite appeal.

While your menu is probably tailored to fit a particular clientele, comparison with the data shown on these charts could help you in your salad listing. Check and compare. Are you serving enough different salads? Are they the most popular salads? And last, but not least, are your prices right? Then, after you have determined what, how many and how much, check to see how you are listing salads on your menu. Is the type large and readable? Does the copy describe and merchandise? The right answer to all these questions can mean sales that brighten your profit picture.

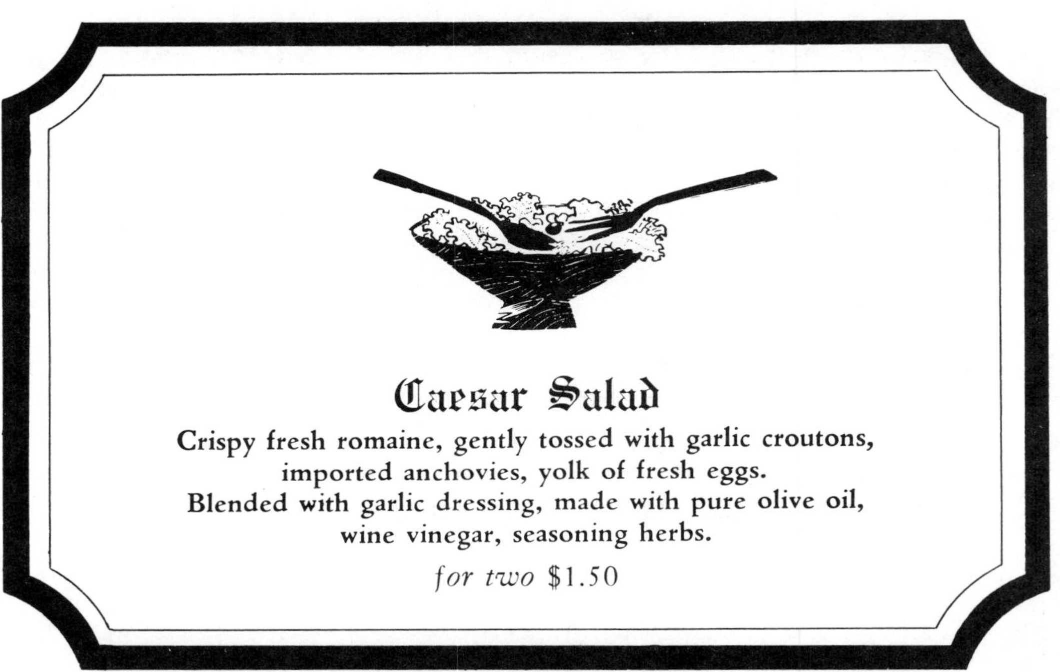

Certain salads like Caesar Salad are old standbys, but the salad menu is one place where it is easy and profitable to be creative.

Freshly-Made Salads

Fresh Shrimp Salad 2.50
Jumbo Gulf shrimp served whole on a bed of crisp salad greens, garnished with sliced tomatoes, cucumbers and ripe olives. Choose your own dressing

King Crabmeat Salad 2.25
Tender, bite size morsels of Alaskan King crabmeat served on a bed of lettuce with mayonnaise, dressing served separately and garnished with tomato, cucumber and black olives

Tuna Salad 1.75
Chunks of white meat tuna fish with tomato, pepper ring and radish, and crisp salad greens

Fresh Fruit Salad 1.75
Segments of chilled, fresh seasonal fruits served with cottage cheese and a delightfully blended dressing of mayonnaise, whipped cream and strawberries

Chef's Salad Bowl 1.75
A mound of garden fresh greens topped with julienne strips of ham, chicken and Swiss cheese, garnished with tomato, radish and pepper ring and dressing

Try Our Cold Meat Platter 2.25
A variety of sliced white meat of chicken, corned beef, sliced ham, imported Swiss cheese and tangy potato salad garnished with radishes and black olives, tomatoes, cucumbers.

Fresh Lobster Salad 4.50
Large pieces of succulent lobster meat imbeded in crisp lettuce and served with mayonnaise garnished with ripe olives, cucumber slices and pepper rings

the above served with rolls and butter

a la carte
Weber's
California
CAROUSEL

Caesar Salad 1.75
Bibb Lettuce crisp parmesan cheese, olive oil and fresh lemon, combined with toast croutons, a touch of mustard and topped with anchovie filets

a famous salad
Sarah Bernhardt 2.25
Avocado pear, Shrimp, Hard cooked egg on shredded lettuce
Chef garni (In Season)

all fresh fruits
California Salad Plate 1.95
with petite sandwiches (In Season)

a great green salad
Julienne Salad 1.95
ham, turkey, swiss cheese

fresh Alaskan
King Crabmeat Salad 2.00
our own Louis dressing

an unusual salad
A Stuffed Tomato 1.75
with flaky tunafish

Salads are easy to describe. Just list the ingredients with a few adjectives thrown in. Be sure to also list salad dressing served with the salad.

From Our Salad Bar

TRIPLE SALAD PLATE
Your choice of Chicken or Tuna Salad with molded fruit jello salad, cottage cheese mound, green peppers, tomato, finger Sandwich 1.50

TROPICAL SALAD
Half Avacado with crabmeat and lobster, asparagus spears, tomato on bed of lettuce 2.25

JUMBO TOMATO STUFFED WITH CHICKEN OR TUNA SALAD,
Mayonnaise garni with hard Boiled Egg, green pepper rings, ripe olives, saratoga chips 1.75

NEW ORLEANS JUMBO SHRIMPS SALAD BOWL,
Tossed spring greens topped with succulent shrimps and garnished with Hard Boiled Egg, Tomato wedges, 1000 Island Dresisng 2.10

THE SKIRVIN JUMBO SALAD BOWL
Tossed spring greens topped with julienne of Chicken, Ham and Swiss Cheese, your choice of dressing 1.50

THE FRUIT PLATE
Selected fresh and preserved fruits on a bed of lettuce with a choice of cottage cheese or sherbet, assorted finger sandwiches 1.50

These creative listings are sure to increase salad orders.

39

Steak marketing survey

A study of 242 menus of various types from food service operations across the U.S. gives some interesting information as to what, how many, what price, and the degree of popularity of the various kinds of steaks that are listed on the menu. While your particular operation may make its steak selections on the basis of (1) availability and price of beef, (2) local preferences, plus (3) past experience, the information shown on these charts can be a reference point from which you can compare, and if your menu does not measure up, perhaps some experimentation is called for.

Figure 1 shows the relative popularity of steaks by name as listed on the menu. Sirloin and filet mignon are the two leaders. Chopped steak (hamburger), if all of its variations including sandwiches were counted, would probably be number one. Also a N.Y. strip, if it is what is served on a steak sandwich and sometimes called a Kansas City steak, would have a higher rating.

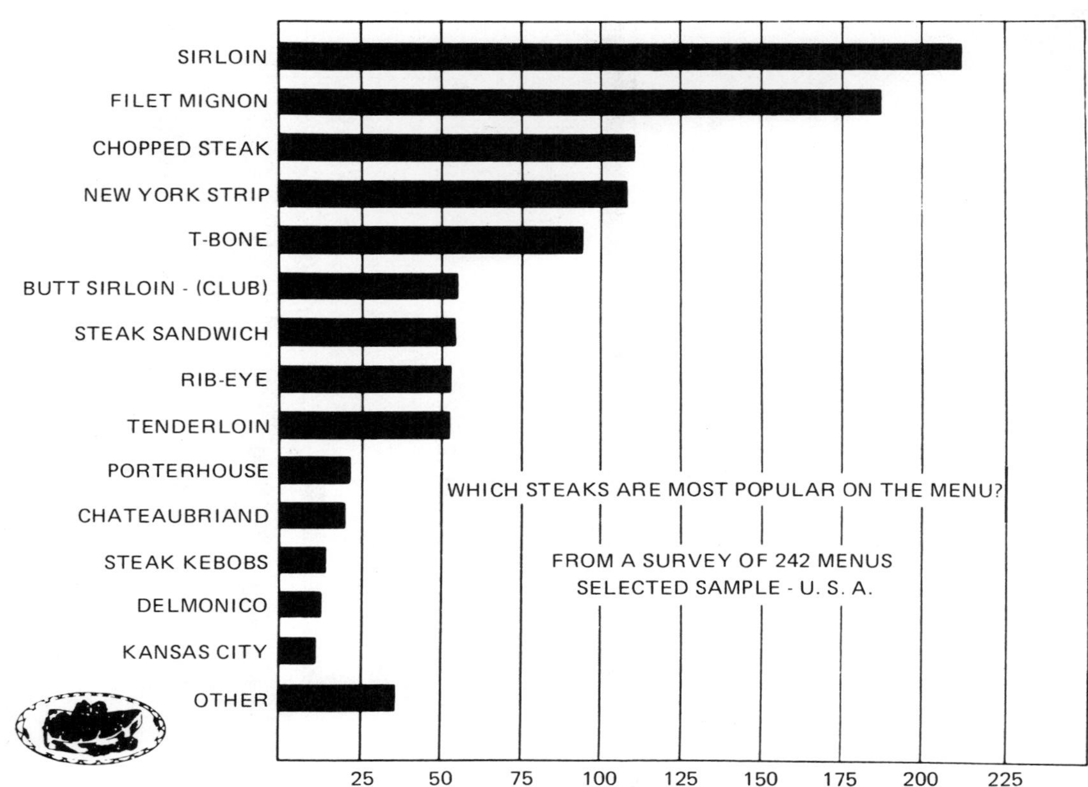

FIGURE 1

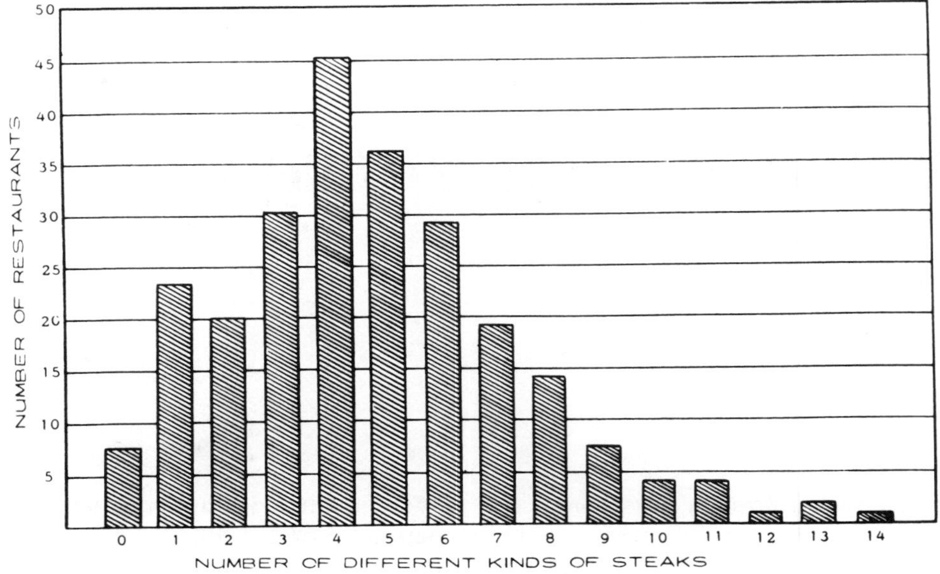

FIGURE 2

FIGURE 3

Figure 2 shows the number of different kinds of steaks listed on the menu. The largest number of menus list from one to seven different steaks with the peak at four. If you list four different steaks, you are average.

Figure 3 shows up a failing of most menus, a lack of descriptive steak copy.

Figure 4 indicates the sizable percentage of operations that do not list steak weight on their menus. Figure 5 shows another copy defect, the failure to list the quality of your steaks. Most restaurants serve good beef, Prime or Choice, but after spending good money to serve good meat, they fail to tell the customer.

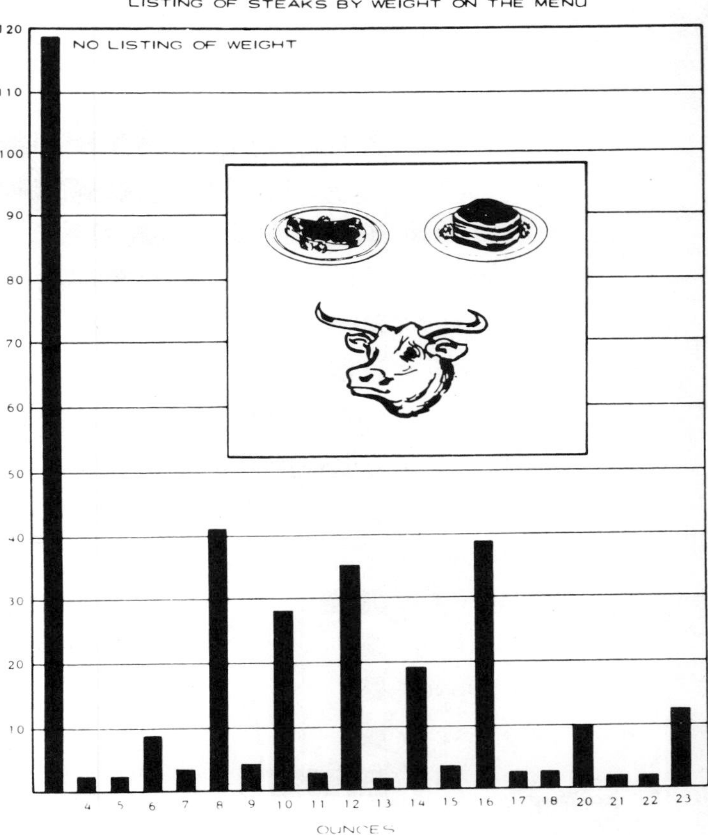

FIGURE 4

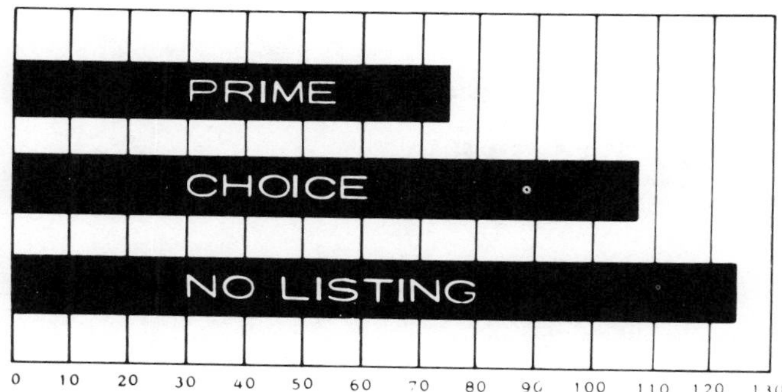
INDICATION ON MENU OF QUALITY OF STEAK SERVED
PRIME
CHOICE
NO LISTING
0 10 20 30 40 50 60 70 80 90 100 110 120 130

FIGURE 5

40

Seafood survey

Seafood is a highly popular menu item. Whether as an entree, appetizer, or salad, when the public "eats out," it likes seafood. Perhaps the fuss, muss, and smell of preparing it at home makes it more attractive in a food service operation. Besides, chefs seem to have a knack of preparing and serving seafood more attractively than the housewife does in the average home.

This seafood survey is information taken from 300 menus from across the country. They range from smaller, inexpensive, table service restaurants to the most expensive "haute cuisine" places. A surprising amount of uniformity exists in seafood service on the menu, even among a great variety of types and locations of eating establishments. The questions studied by the survey were:

a. Number of seafood entrees
b. Popularity of seafood entrees (items listed most often)
c. Number of seafood appetizers
d. Number of seafood salads
e. Prices of certain seafood entrees

Food service operations vary in their promotion of seafood entrees. Some specialize in seafood and have built impressive and well-deserved reputations for their exceptional seafood cuisine. But, strangely enough, there seems to be hardly any food service, large or small, steak house or nationality specialty house that does not list at least one seafood item. This could be a carry-over from the "Fish on Friday" church ruling which the menu still reflects, but it is more likely a reflection of seafood popularity on the menu. As shown in Figure 1, the number of seafood entrees starts at one (with 10 restaurants listing this number) and then peaks at the range of 4 to 7 seafood entrees. There is another jump when the chart reaches over 11 seafood entrees. These are probably the operations specializing in or featuring seafood. One menu surveyed listed 26 seafood entrees!

The kind of seafood entrees a food service operation serves will vary, of course, somewhat with location. Establishments on the seacoast will serve a greater variety of local or unusual seafood, while some inland operations will serve fresh water fish not available on the seacoast, but, with modern transportation and marketing, location has become less a factor in the availability of seafood. Lobster is available in Keokuk, Iowa, as well as in Boston.

In fact, the pattern of popularity shown by Figure 2 is almost an indication that there is not enough variety in the menu listing. The same items tend to be on all menus. Shrimp takes first place, as shown in Figure 2, for entree popularity. This, combined with its popularity as the number one

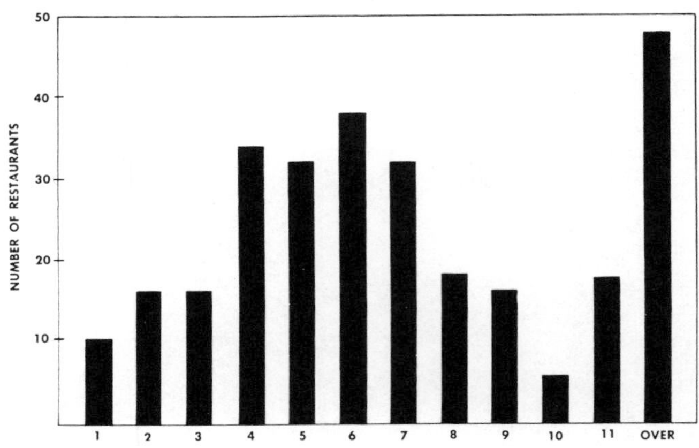

FIGURE 1

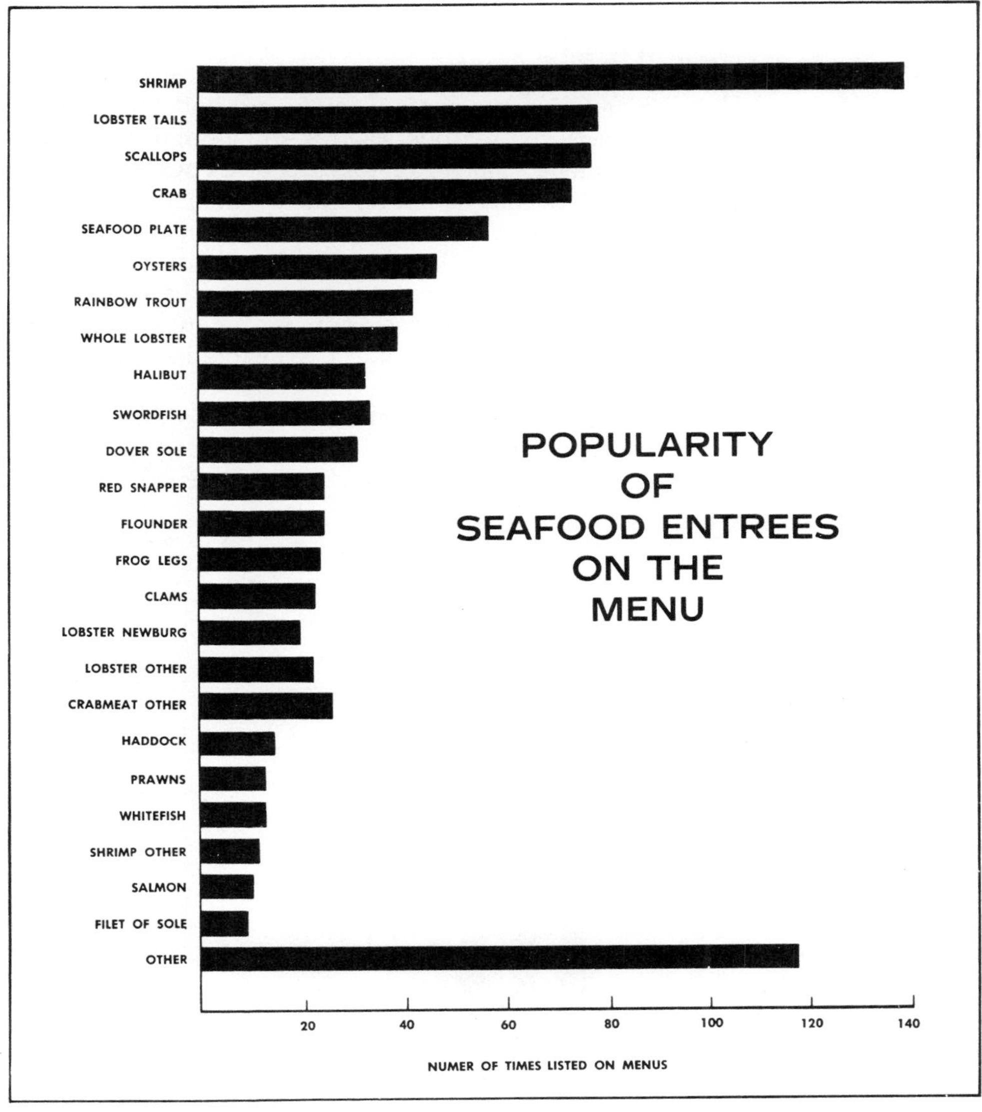

FIGURE 2

appetizer item and as a very popular salad ingredient, makes shrimp king of the seafood listing on the menu. After shrimp, the other big seafood entree is lobster tails. Actually, lobster tails, combined with whole lobster, lobster newburg and other lobster combinations or methods of preparation, equal or surpass shrimp on the entree portion of the menu. After shrimp and lobster, the popularity scale goes down from scallops, crab, seafood plate, oysters, fresh water trout all the way to filet of sole. There are no real surprises on seafood popularity except the overwhelming popularity of the first seven seafood items (shrimp through trout) compared with all of the many other kinds of seafood entrees.

The popularity of seafood as an entree item means that, when listed on the menu, it should be given top billing. It should be given good position, center of menu. It should be listed in large, clear, bold type, and it should have plenty of good descriptive, merchandising, sell copy. Seafood copy is not difficult to write if you follow these rules:

a. Tell where the seafood comes from and some pertinent facts about it (from the warm waters of the Gulf or from the cold waters of the North Atlantic).
b. Describe how it is prepared (broiled, baked, fried, cooked, special spices and flavorings, etc.).
c. How served (filled, whole, in shell, etc.).

d. Use some tasty adjectives (juicy, tender, succulent, fresh, tangy, etc.).

Entrees are not the only area of the menu where seafood is featured. Many appetizers and salads use seafood as the basic element. Figure 3 shows the popularity of seafood as an appetizer item on the menu. To begin with, 22 restaurants did not list any seafood appetizer, but the vast majority (112) listed one or more seafood appetizers. Most menus listed at least one seafood appetizer (usually shrimp cocktail), but the number goes as high as nine and above, showing how popular seafood is as an appetizer.

Figure 4 shows the popularity of seafood salads on the menu, and here too, while 55 restaurants listed no seafood salads, 65 did list some seafood salads. The number ranges from one seafood salad to seven and over. So while not as popular as the seafood appetizer and the seafood entrees, the seafood salad is still a popular item on the menu. Taken all together, of course, seafood is an extremely popular item on the menu in many departments. In fact, a good case can be made for giving seafood the number one position in menu popularity. Perhaps the popularity of seafood in the food service operation is due to the greater selection of items not too available in the average supermarket. Well-described, well-listed and merchandised on the menu, seafood (if well prepared and good to begin with) is one of the food service operator's best, money-making friends.

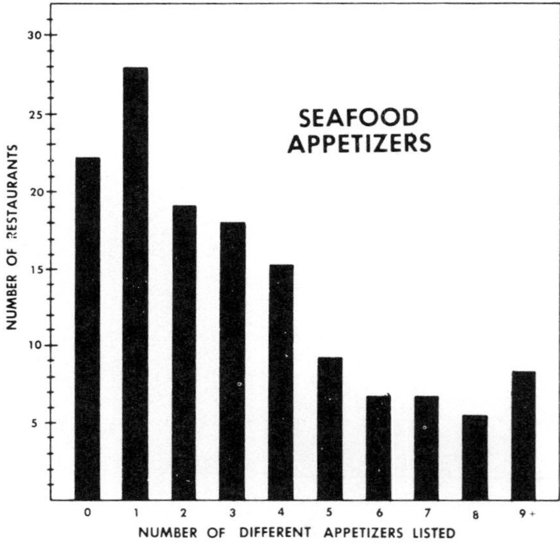

FIGURE 3

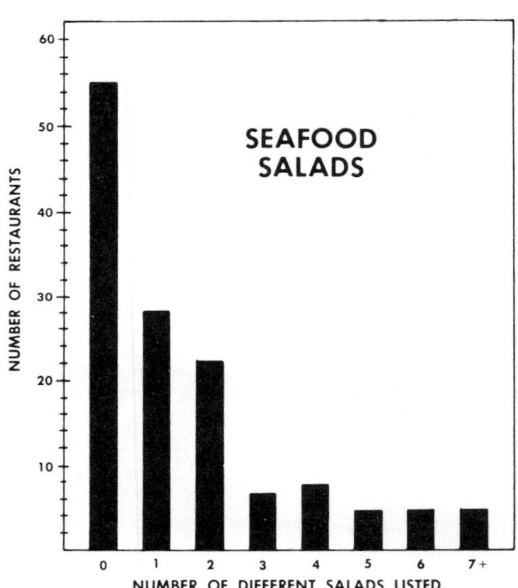

FIGURE 4

41
Desserts

A forgotten or side-tracked afterthought on many menus, the dessert listing can be a profitable, check building part of any food service business.

The dessert listing on the menu gets a variety of treatment in any large selection of menus. Some eating places have a large selection of desserts, and list, merchandise, and sell them in a big way, while other restaurants don't even list a single dessert. Yet the public is the same in both cases, and it is a public that eats cake, pie, and ice cream at home. What is the reason for this wide disparity in emphasis on dessert merchandising from one operation to another? The final, real answer is probably unknown at this time, but some probable answers are examined here.

The "big" dinner menu allows for a leisurely meal—a cocktail, appetizer, and soup before the entree, wine with the entree, and dessert, coffee, after dinner drink, and cigar after the entree. This is a true "continental" gourmet repast and many a fine restaurant that serves food and drink in this style has a good dessert listing. Yet many an elegant, supper club type restaurant that lists a \$6.00 steak and a \$7.00 seafood entree will neglect desserts entirely. A different group of people with different tastes? Again, we come back to the hard fact that these people eat desserts of all kinds at home.

Then there is the short order, fast food type operation. The claim here is made that the customer "does not have time." Or the food service operator will have mainly (or only) a luncheon business, and he will say, "I've tried selling and listing desserts, but my customers aren't interested, don't have time, I guess, or are watching their waistlines." Yet, some of the biggest, fast food, get 'em in, get 'em out operations have been built on a large selection of ice cream flavors (*Howard Johnson's*, for example). And what is ice cream if it is not a dessert, and probably the most popular dessert there is.

The real answer to the question of to whom, where, and when can desserts be sold is probably to everybody, anywhere, at almost any time. To prove my point, there is no supermarket anywhere in America without a large selection of desserts, prepared, frozen, or in ingredient form, and there is no cafeteria without a selection of desserts.

The question of the always dieting, weight-watching customer is, of course, very real. And after a big meal the customer suddenly becomes calorie conscious, decides to be a hero and denies himself or herself dessert. The food industry has taken notice of this situation and for the home-food market supplies a variety of low-calorie desserts, but, so far, the food service business as a whole has done very little in this direction.

Judging from the wide variety of treatment for dessert listings on various menus, it is apparent that some operations do a big merchandising job and others do a very poor or casual dessert selling job. It would seem that those operations that want to sell more desserts usually find the right advertising-merchandising tools to do the job.

First, let's examine the various ways desserts can be listed on the menu. The first method is to have a separate dessert menu. This is usually a menu smaller than the regular entree menu with a listing of desserts and after dinner drinks. This separate menu usually permits a better dessert listing. It means more room to list more desserts, list them bigger, bolder, and with more descriptive copy. Also, it allows for featuring of some "special" dessert items that the operation wants to sell in greater quantity.

One of the main advantages of a separate

dessert menu is that the waitress or waiter can present the separate dessert menu to all customers after they have finished their entree. This should be done without asking the customer if he or she wants dessert. It is much better selling to present the dessert menu, assuming that a dessert is going to be ordered. The customer is at least more likely to look at the menu and consider ordering. There are various ways of listing desserts on the menu. The following are some layouts showing where desserts can be listed:

1. A simple menu layout is the appetizer, entree, dessert sequence shown in Figure 1.
2. Another layout is Figure 2, a 4-panel (2 large, 1 small) 3-fold menu. The desserts are listed on panel 4. The opposite side of panel 4 can be the after dinner drink listing.
3. The back side of a 3-panel menu is shown in Figure 3. This uses panel 1 for desserts and after dinner drinks. Notice that boxes in the two listings allow for special treatment of two desserts and two after dinner drinks.
4. Another common layout solution to where to

FIGURE 1

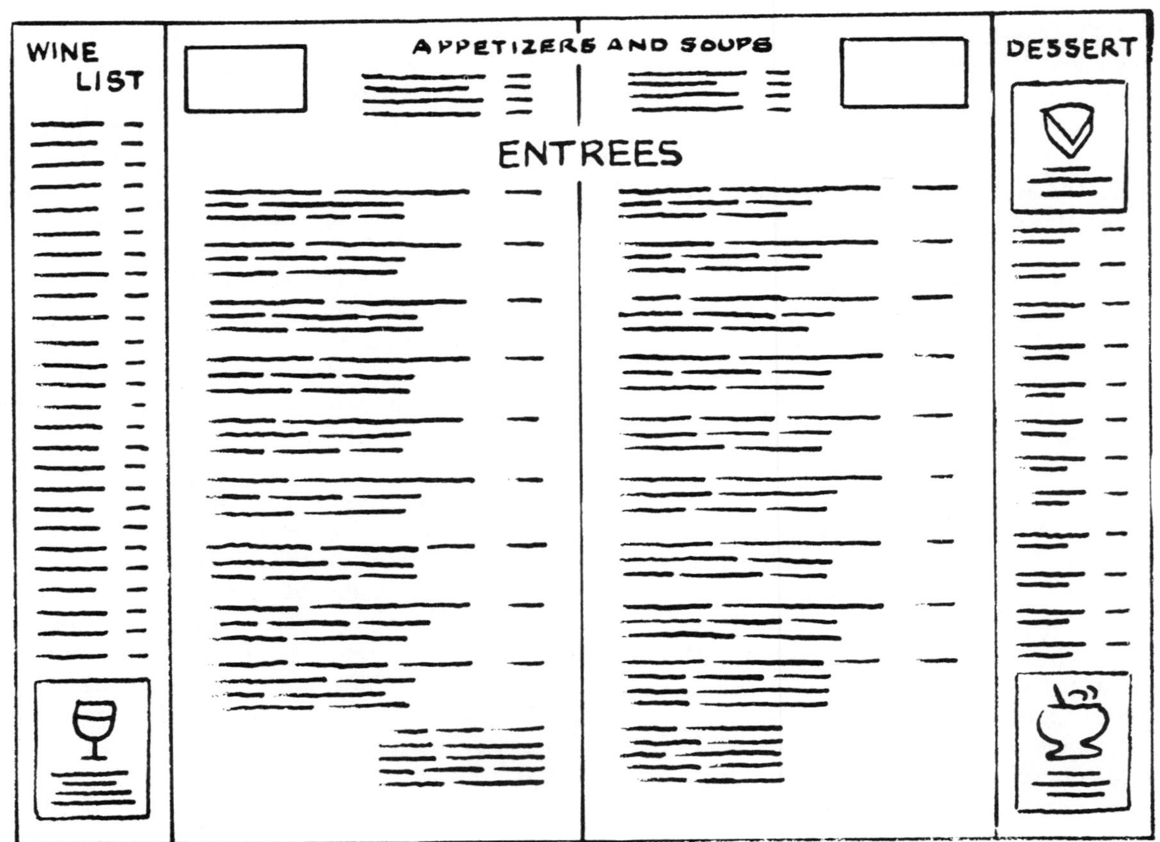

FIGURE 2

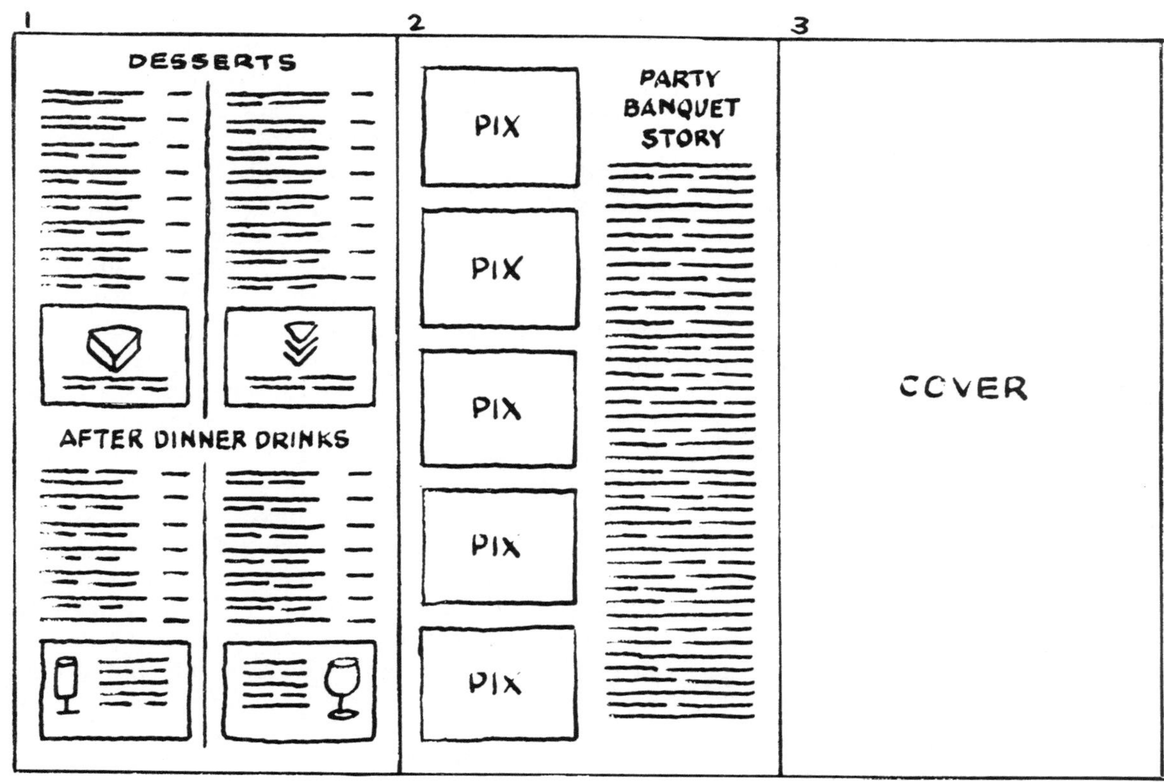

FIGURE 3

list desserts is shown below in Figure 4. An 8-page menu (4-page cover, 4-page insert) leaves an entire page (page 4) for desserts and after dinner drinks.

After counting and classifying the dessert listing on 256 menus, some information about dessert popularity, prices, number, etc., is available and clear. The following charts are a graphic

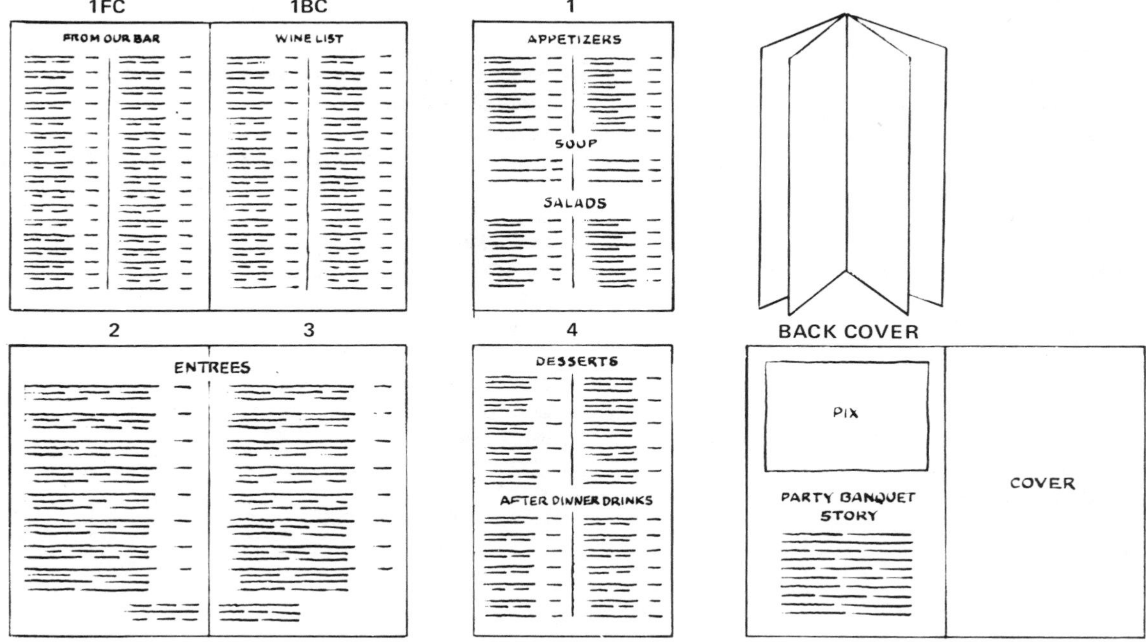

FIGURE 4

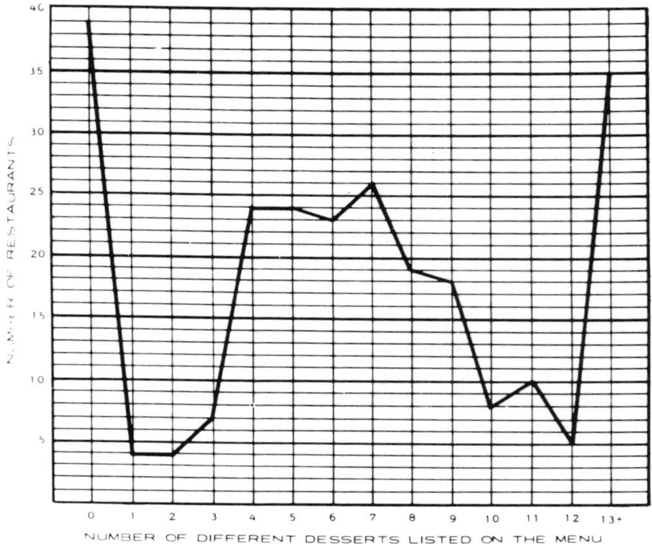

FIGURE 5

presentation of the information researched from menus all over the United States. Figure 5 is a study of the number of different desserts listed on the menu. The first observation is that 39 restaurants listed no desserts at all, while 35 restaurants listed 13 or more different desserts. This shows the wide range in dessert emphasis from one restaurant to another. The average range, however, is from 4 to 7 different items.

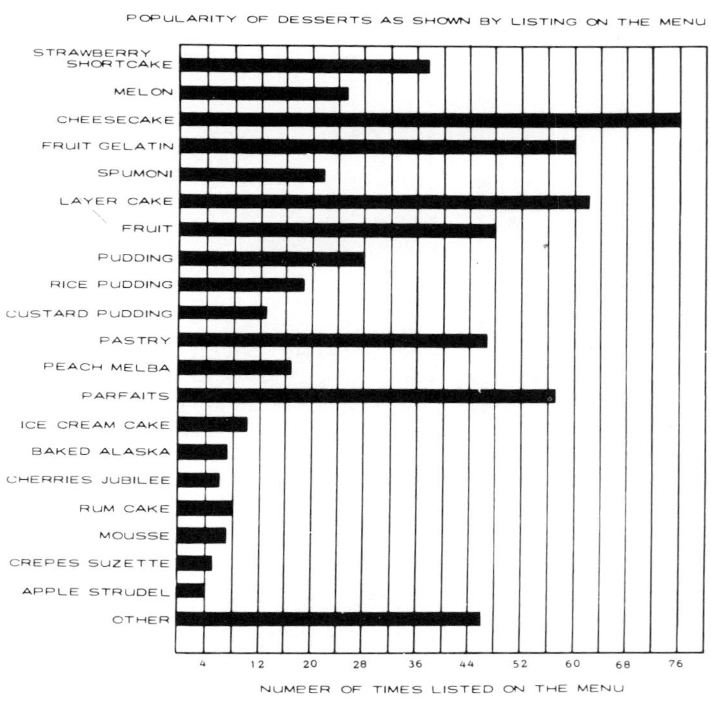

FIGURE 6

In Figure 6 we have a popularity poll of desserts other than pie, ice cream and fountain items, and cheeses which are treated separately. Cheesecake rates highest on this chart with layer cake, fruit gelatin, parfaits, fruit and strawberry shortcake following in that order. Plain old pudding, if we combine the pudding, rice pudding and custard pudding, is, however, a big item on many menus. The fancy desserts—crepes suzettes, cherries jubilee, baked Alaska, etc., do not get on too many menus, probably because they are more difficult to make and serve. But if you want to upgrade your menu on the dessert end, this is the area where menu additions will be most noticeable.

There is nothing so American as pie, especially applie pie. Figure 7 shows pie popularity as shown by listings on the menu. Combined, the pie listing adds up to probably the number one item on the menu next to ice cream and its variations in the fountain menu. Too many menus, however, list assorted pies, fruit pies, and cream pies. This is not good dessert merchandising. Nobody has ever eaten an assorted pie, and a fruit pie is either an apple, cherry, or peach pie, etc. This method of listing, of course, is designed to fit a changing inventory of pies either bakery or home made. A better selling and merchandising practice is to feature a few specific pies big and feature them all the time on the menu. Many southern restaurants do a good job in this area with key lime pie and pecan pie.

The all time favorite, of course, is apple pie. And when combined with cheese or a la mode with ice cream, it is a formidable dessert item. Any

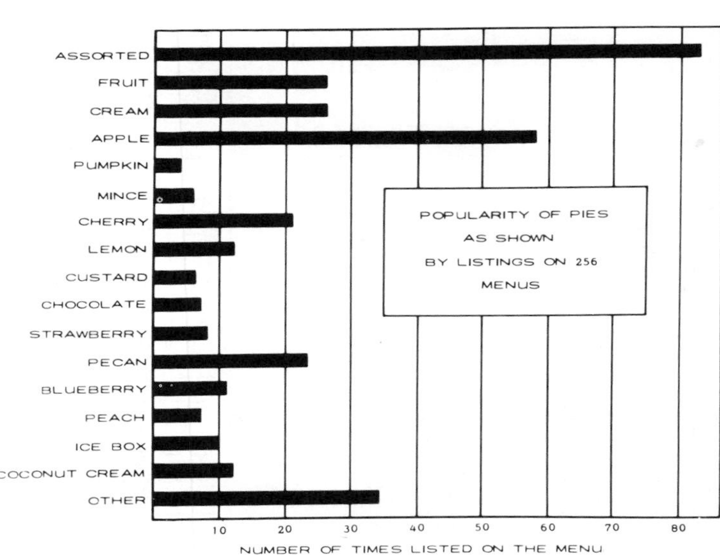

FIGURE 7

operation that does not include apple pie on its menu is definitely bucking a trend. One aspect of pie listing that should be accented is that when you have "home made" pie, make a great deal of it on the menu. Do not mention it just casually in small type.

Ice cream is probably number one as a dessert item in popularity, and when combined in all its variations—parfaits, sodas, sundaes, malts, sherbets, etc.—it becomes a really big menu dessert item. Figure 8 shows a sundae, that is ice cream with something added, chocolate sauce, nuts, etc., is offered more often than just plain ice cream. And after that sherbet follows as number three in popularity. One common fault of the listing of ice creams, sundaes, sodas, and other fountain items is the failure to list flavors. Most food service operations serve more than one flavor of ice cream, yet they expect the customer to ask which flavors are available. This is poor selling. Decide on what flavors you wish to serve in all the fountain variations of ice cream, and then list them.

In connection with fountain items on the dessert menu, Figure 9 shows the separate fountain menu listing in relation to fountain items listed with the regular dessert listing. Less than 25 percent of the 256 menus studied had a separate fountain menu listing. In many cases this is a menu mistake. Fountain items are easy to store, make, and serve (you don't have to be a well trained chef to make an ice cream sundae) and if listed separately, and in detail, they will be easier to order and easier to sell.

The type of establishment will often determine the emphasis on fountain items, but even a supper club or continental cuisine can feature ice cream desserts in the form of parfaits. The combination of ice cream and liqueur makes for a sophisticated sundae.

Cheese is not as popular a dessert item on American menus as it is on European menus, but it still has its place. Figure 10 gives a rundown on cheese popularity. The number one item, of course, is cheese and apple pie. While this is usually American or Cheddar cheese, here again many menus are remiss in not being specific as to the kind of cheese being served. "Cheese and crackers" and "cheese tray" are also poor ways to list cheese on the menu. When the listing does get specific, it is Camembert that leads the list followed by Roquefort, Liederkranz, and Blue Cheese.

This little study of desserts only begins to show some of the aspects and possibilities of desserts. Flaming desserts, for example, are popular in many dining rooms with fine cuisine. But whether large or small, spectacular or modest, the dessert, taking its place as "Tail End Charlie," should be always last, but never least.

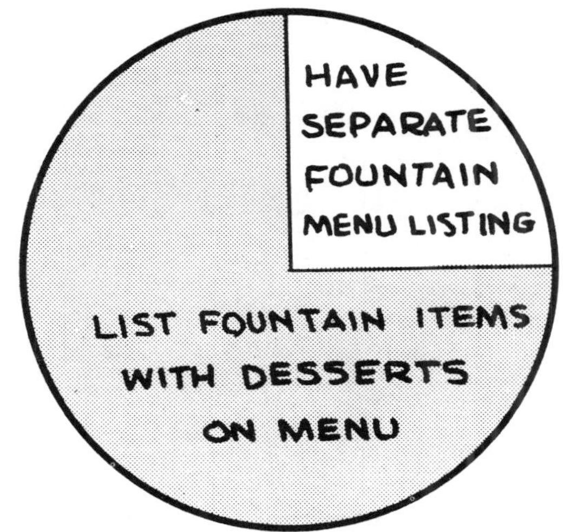

FIGURE 9

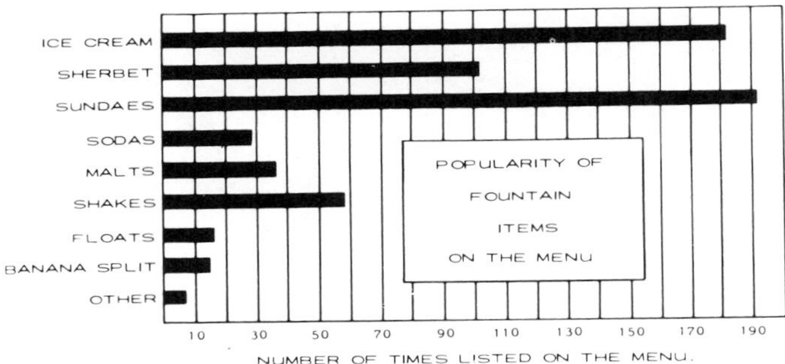

FIGURE 8

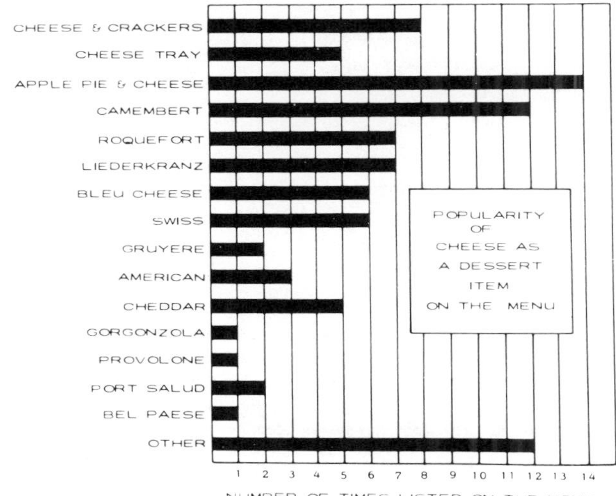

FIGURE 10

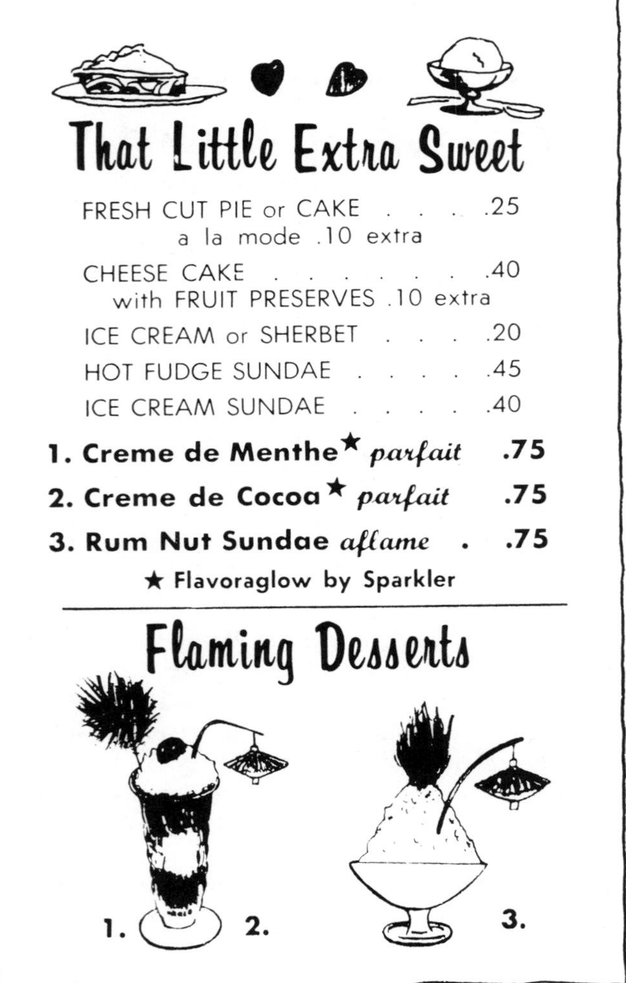

That Little Extra Sweet

FRESH CUT PIE or CAKE 25
a la mode .10 extra

CHEESE CAKE 40
with FRUIT PRESERVES .10 extra

ICE CREAM or SHERBET 20

HOT FUDGE SUNDAE 45

ICE CREAM SUNDAE 40

1. Creme de Menthe★ *parfait* .75

2. Creme de Cocoa★ *parfait* .75

3. Rum Nut Sundae *aflame* . .75

★ Flavoraglow by Sparkler

Flaming Desserts

1. 2. 3.

Clever graphics help sell both desserts and special flaming ice cream desserts.

BAVARIAN CHALET'S

Dessert Cart

A beautiful and tempting array of delicacies from the baker's oven and rolled to your table.

Your Selection — .65

If you have a dessert cart, sell it on the menu.

Flaming Desserts

CREPES SUZETTE (2) **$3.00**
The queen of desserts made and flamed at your table

BAKED ALASKA (for 2) **2.00**
White cake flavored with brandy topped with ice cream and meringue. Flamed with imported liqueurs

CHERRIES FLAMBEE **1.50**

Flaming desserts deserve special treatment.

"Mammy's Famous Apple Pie"

.35 A la Mode .55

Made from the choicest green apples, buttered and sugared with a heavy hand, and not as much as a pinch of spice that would alter the delicate blending of good ingredients, with pastry that is in perfect harmony, altogether produce a symphony of taste that has never been matched so perfectly.

Select some one of your pies and feature it with copy like this and you'll sell more.

A Good Dinner Deserves a Good Dessert

BAKED ON THE PREMISES

From Our Bakers

PIES—Apple, Cherry, Blueberry, Lemon Meringue, Cocoanut Custard .... .25
(Pumpkin, Mince in Season)

CAKES—French Layer, Cherry Crumb, Blueberry Crumb, Jelly Roll .... .25
Open-Face Peach (In Season)

DANISH PASTRY—Cheese, Lemon, Cherry, Blueberry, Nut, Lekvar, Streusel,
Apple, Apple Turnovers, Cinnamon Buns, Pineapple or Cinnamon

Miniature Danish (Cheese or Lekvar), ... .25
Cinnamon Bun Toasted .... .30

FRENCH PASTRY—Linzer Tortes, Pretzels, Palmiers, Poppy Seed Croissants ...... .25

COOKIES—Rich Butter, Mandel Bread, Bow Ties .... .25

From Our Chef

Jello, Whipped Cream .. .25
Creamy Rice Pudding .25
French Tapioca Pudding .25
Swiss Chocolate Pudding .... .25
Baked Cup Custard ... .25
Jumbo Baked Apple ... .40

From Our Fountain

Vanilla, Chocolate, Orange Sherbet and other Flavors of Ice Cream in Season...... .35
with Rich Chocolate Sauce .... .50

From Our Pastry Chef

Country Club Pure Cream Cheese Cake.... .... .45
Blueberry, Cherry or Pineapple .... .55

Our Famous Toasted Cocoanut, Banana, Chocolate or Strawberry Whipped Cream Pie .40

STRUDEL—Apple, Cheese or Miniature Fruit and Nut .... .30

FRENCH PASTRIES (Filled Variety)—Chocolate Eclairs, Cream Puffs, Napoleons,
Butter Cream Squares, Whipped Cream Roll or Chocolate Whipped Cream Roll .35

BUTTER CREAM ROLL
.35

STRAWBERRY BOSTON
.35

SHORT CAKE
.50

FRESH
STRAWBERRY
TREATS

TARTS
.60

CONTINENTAL PASTRIES

Open Tarts: Cherry or Blueberry .... .35
Pineapple or Peach Melba .... .30
Seven Layer Cake .... .35
Stars: Pineapple or Cherry .... .35
Apple Dumplings .... .40
Rich Fudge Brownie .... .25

Almond Horns or Canoes .... .25

This pastry-oriented dessert listing features "Baked on the Premises" plus photographs (in black and white but still effective) that sell pastry specials.

The cover design and general treatment is similar to the big menu. This excellent dessert menu lists everything—desserts, ice cream dishes, children's desserts, flaming desserts, cakes, pies, after dinner drinks, dessert wines, and fine brandies and liqueurs.

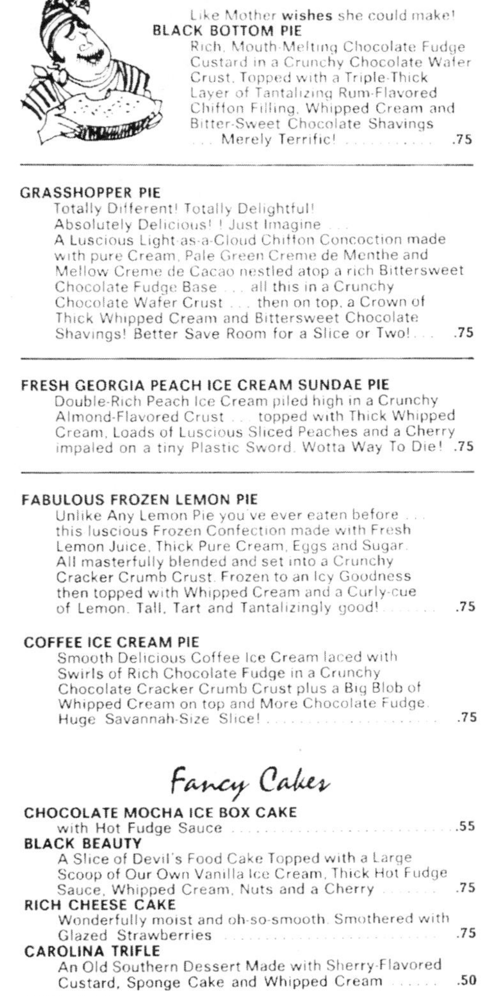

Pies

Like Mother wishes she could make!

BLACK BOTTOM PIE
Rich, Mouth-Melting Chocolate Fudge Custard in a Crunchy Chocolate Wafer Crust. Topped with a Triple-Thick Layer of Tantalizing Rum-Flavored Chiffon Filling, Whipped Cream and Bitter-Sweet Chocolate Shavings . . . Merely Terrific! .75

GRASSHOPPER PIE
Totally Different! Totally Delightful! Absolutely Delicious! ! Just Imagine . . . A Luscious Light-as-a-Cloud Chiffon Concoction made with pure Cream, Pale Green Creme de Menthe and Mellow Creme de Cacao nestled atop a rich Bittersweet Chocolate Fudge Base . . . all this in a Crunchy Chocolate Wafer Crust . . . then on top, a Crown of Thick Whipped Cream and Bittersweet Chocolate Shavings! Better Save Room for a Slice or Two! 75

FRESH GEORGIA PEACH ICE CREAM SUNDAE PIE
Double-Rich Peach Ice Cream piled high in a Crunchy Almond-Flavored Crust . . . topped with Thick Whipped Cream, Loads of Luscious Sliced Peaches and a Cherry impaled on a tiny Plastic Sword. Wotta Way To Die! .75

FABULOUS FROZEN LEMON PIE
Unlike Any Lemon Pie you've ever eaten before . . . this luscious Frozen Confection made with Fresh Lemon Juice, Thick Pure Cream, Eggs and Sugar. All masterfully blended and set into a Crunchy Cracker Crumb Crust. Frozen to an Icy Goodness then topped with Whipped Cream and a Curly-cue of Lemon. Tall, Tart and Tantalizingly good! .75

COFFEE ICE CREAM PIE
Smooth Delicious Coffee Ice Cream laced with Swirls of Rich Chocolate Fudge in a Crunchy Chocolate Cracker Crumb Crust plus a Big Blob of Whipped Cream on top and More Chocolate Fudge. Huge Savannah-Size Slice! .75

Fancy Cakes

CHOCOLATE MOCHA ICE BOX CAKE
with Hot Fudge Sauce .55

BLACK BEAUTY
A Slice of Devil's Food Cake Topped with a Large Scoop of Our Own Vanilla Ice Cream, Thick Hot Fudge Sauce, Whipped Cream, Nuts and a Cherry .75

RICH CHEESE CAKE
Wonderfully moist and oh-so-smooth. Smothered with Glazed Strawberries .75

CAROLINA TRIFLE
An Old Southern Dessert Made with Sherry-Flavored Custard, Sponge Cake and Whipped Cream .50

SPECTACULAR Flaming Desserts

Prepared right at your table!

STRAWBERRY CREPE ELEGANTE
An oh-so-thin delicate French Crepe heated in a Superb Fresh Strawberry Syrup. Rolled around a Pirate-size Portion of Thick Whipped Cream, then submerged under a Sea of Fresh Glazed Strawberries blazing with Brandy. Crisp Toasted Almonds give the Final Regal Touch! 1.50

CHERRIES JUBILEE
Dark, delicious Bing Cherries mixed with fine Liqueurs. Blazed with Brandy and poured flaming over a mountain of French Vanilla Ice Cream. Delicious! ! ! 1.50

BANANA FOSTER
A Golden-ripe Banana sliced and simmered in a rich Concoction of Butter, Brown Sugar and Banana Liqueur. Set ablaze with Brandy then ladled over a huge dish of Vanilla Ice Cream! 1.50

MERINGUE GLACE FLAMBE
A Melt-in-your-mouth Meringue Shell filled with Vanilla Ice Cream. Topped with a Flaming Bittersweet Chocolate Fudge Sauce that's loaded with Crisp Toasted Almonds and laced with fine Liqueurs! 1.50

Ice Cream Concoctions

DANDY CANDY SUNDAE
Vanilla, Coffee, or Peppermint Stick Ice Cream served with a Pitcher of Our Sensational Chocolate Butter Pecan Candy Topping That Gets Cracklin' Crisp as it hits the Ice Cream! .75

GIANT HOT FUDGE, BUTTERSCOTCH OR NESSELRODE
(Rum-Tutti Frutti) Sundae with Choice of Ice Cream .75
(Mmm . . . Take Some of our Delicious NESSELRODE TOPPING Home. It's on Sale in the Gift Shop.)

ICE CREAM PECAN LOG
with Hot Fudge or Butterscotch Sauce .75

PARFAITS
Wonderful New Flavor Combinations Every Day .75

PIRATES' HOUSE ICE CREAM OR SHERBET
Delicious But Not Very Exciting (Chocolate, Vanilla, Strawberry, Coffee, Peppermint Stick Ice Cream — Pineapple or Orange Sherbet) .55

SENSATIONAL DO-IT-YOURSELF SUNDAE
For Those Who Like To Live Dangerously! You'll get a tremendous Dish of Ice Cream. Select any Three Flavors: Chocolate, Vanilla, Strawberry, Coffee or Peppermint Stick plus a lazy Susan loaded with Assorted Toppings, Whipped Cream, Nuts and Cherries. From then on it's up to you! 1.50

FUN FOR OUR Little Pirates

MERRY-GO-ROUND SUNDAE - A Big Scoop of Vanilla Ice Cream Surrounded with Animal Crackers and Topped with a Tiny Umbrella That Really Works! ! .35

BLAZING ATOMIC SUNDAE - Order One and Be Surprised. It's really Supercalifragilisticexpialidotious ! ! .35

ICE CREAM OR SHERBET - Sprinkled All Over with Little Candy Jewels! ! .25

After Dinner Drinks

ANGEL'S KISS 1.25
Creme de Cacao & Cream

BLACK RUSSIAN 1.50
Vodka & Kahlua (Coffee Liqueur)

BRANDY ALEXANDER 1.50
Brandy, Creme de Cacao and Cream

CREME de MENTHE FRAPPE 1.00

GRASSHOPPER 1.50
Creme de Menthe, Creme de Cacao & Cream

IRISH COFFEE (served flaming) 1.75
Irish Whiskey, Coffee and Whipped Cream

PINK LADY 1.25
Gin, Grenadine and Cream

PINK SQUIRREL 1.25
Creme de Noyoux (Almond-flavored Liqueur) and Cream

RUSTY NAIL 1.50
Scotch and Drambuie

STINGER 1.50
Brandy and Creme de Menthe

Dessert Wines

	Glass	Bottle
Christian Brothers Ruby Port	.50	3.50
Christian Brothers Sherry	.50	3.50
Christian Brothers Golden Sherry	.50	3.50
Taylor Port	.50	3.50
Taylor Cream Cream Sherry	.50	3.50
Duff Gordon Nina (Medium Dry)	.60	4.50
Harvey's Gold Cap Port	.85	
Harvey's Bristol Cream	1.30	

Besides good art and design handling, this dessert menu has what seems the best copy possible. Everything is described and sold with a good selection of words. Note also that the ingredients in after dinner drinks are listed.

For Guests with a Specially Sweet Tooth may we recommend

Granny Clarke's Apple Pie served with Ice Cream and Fresh Dairy Cream 2/6

Delightful Chocolate Sauce coating Vanilla Ice Cream topped with Assorted Nuts and Dairy Cream. 3/-

Ripe Blackberries poured over Vanilla Ice Cream and served with Dairy Cream 3/-

Fruit Salad served with Ice Cream and Fresh Dairy Cream. 3/-

Desserts

Crepes Dentelle Flambee

A Thin French Crepe, Filled with Creme Patisserie, Diced Fruit Glacé
Marinated in Grand Marnier, Flambé with Rum
1.75

Omelette Surprise Marshall

A Mixture of French Ice Cream on Sponge Cake Spiced with Rum
Covered with Meringue Served Flaming with Brandy
1.50

Pear Helene .60
Bisquit Tortoni .80
Meringue Glacee .75
Coupe aux Marrons .80
Parfait Richmond .65
Compote of Fruit .65
John Marshall Cream Pie .40
Frosty Green Mountain .75

Ice Cream: Chocolate, Vanilla, Pistachio .35

Beverages: Coffee Pot .25 Milk .20 Tea .25

PIECE DE RESISTANCE

STRAWBERRIES ROMANOFF 2.00
A perfect blend of fresh strawberries, vanilla ice cream and whipped cream. Prepared with Curacao and Grand Marnier at your table.

Unusual desserts add sales appeal to any menu and help build the check.

At the End

Cherries Jubilee 1.75

Coconut Ice Cream .60 ***Coconut Honey Ice Cream .60***

The Traders Rum Ice Cream** with Praline Sauce **.75

The Traders Ice Cream 1.10
(Fresh Cocoanut Ice Cream served with Flaming Kumquat Sauce)

Passion Fruit Sherbet .60 ***Strawberries Puiwa** (in season) **1.75***

Tahitian Ice Cream 1.10
(Flaming mixture from the Islands blended with Rhum Baba and Ice Cream)

Mangoes with Ice Cream .85 ***Snow Ball .85***

Ginger Tea Ice Cream .60

Pineapple Sherbet .50 ***Indian Mangoes .75***

Kona Ice Cream 1.10
(Tropical Fruits and Ice Cream Flambe with Trader Vic's Fruit Sauce)

Royal Tropical Fruit 1.25 ***Hawaiian Papaya 1.00***

Hawaiian Pineapple 1.25 ***Banana Fritters .75***

Camembert or Roquefort Cheese .75

The Luau Room is available for Private Parties

A South Seas type food service can offer a South Seas dessert listing and merchandise it as this listing does.

42

Make your fountain menu a fountain of profits

Ice cream is such a univerally popular item on the American menu that it tends to be taken for granted. Yet the value of selling ice cream in all its various forms—plain, in flavors, in sundaes, sodas, malts, floats, shakes, with pies, cakes, etc., is proven daily by the success of such big operations as *Howard Johnson's*. Even if you don't mention ice cream on the menu, customers will ask for it. Therefore, it is obvious that some time, effort, and merchandising expertise will increase the sale of this part of your menu "sweet" selection.

The history of ice cream is unknown. It seems to have been more of a perfection than an invention. It began with flavored ices which were a favorite of the nobility as long ago as Alexander the Great in the 4th century B.C. Because of the difficulty of making ice cream before modern methods of refrigeration were developed, only the rich and noble had access to this food delicacy which is now commonplace. Charles I of England, for example, gave "hush money" to his chef so that ice cream would be reserved for exclusive use at the royal table, but the formula for ice cream could not be kept a secret, and the popularity as well as consumption of ice cream has spread. Even in early Colonial America, ice cream was known. Dolly Madison, for example, gave ice cream popularity plus the presidential stamp of approval by serving it at White House receptions. The development of other fountain combinations, sodas and sundaes, came later.

In the early 1800s, carbonated soda water was introduced as a "health water." Later, flavorings were added to make soft drinks, and then flavoring, cream, and ice cream were added to create the first ice cream soda. Strangely enough, however, carbonated water was considered at one time by some people to be intoxicating. Various blue laws, therefore, outlawed the serving of sodas on Sunday. Some creative restaurateur or fountain operator got around the law by serving the ice cream and syrup flavorings without the carbonated water, on Sunday, and thus the "sundae" was born.

Another ice cream development was the ice cream once. There are no statues to commemorate the memory of Ernest A. Homini, but there probably should be because at the St. Louis World's Fair in 1904, he introduced the ice cream cone. Another proof of the popularity of ice cream is the number of flavors on the market. There are reputed to be over 200 flavors, but while flavors come and go, plain old vanilla is still the public's number one favorite.

In terms of menu design and merchandising, there are two basic approaches to selling ice cream and fountain items. First, there is the type of food operation, usually a short order, fast food sandwich (hamburger-hot dog) set-up where the fountain listing is as important as the feature entrees. And then there is the more conventional, usually more expensive restaurant where ice cream is a dessert item. The two types of listings should get different treatment.

The short order menu should include the fountain items with the entree listings. This usually means a menu listing three basic offerings:

1. Sandwiches (hamburgers, hot dogs, cheeseburgers, etc.)
2. Entrees (chicken, fish, a small steak selection, chili, spaghetti)
3. Sweets (pies, cakes, ice cream, sodas, sundaes, malts, etc.)

An important, integral part of this type of fountain menu listing is illustration. This usually means color illustrations of sodas, sundaes, malts, banana splits, etc. Depending on which items you want to sell the most of, it is vital that you feature and merchandise them.

The basic ways to feature fountain items are:

1. Bolder, larger type
2. More descriptive copy
3. Color illustration

If fountain items are a big part of your business or if you want to make them more important, you should use the following basic rules:

1. List the flavors of all ice creams, sodas, sundaes, malts, shakes, and floats served.
2. Use sub-headings to identify types of fountain items—Sodas, Sundaes, Malts, etc., especially if you have a big listing.
3. Feature some fountain items. Usually special sundaes—hot fudge, strawberry, chocolate nut, etc., or some fruit combination, banana split, etc.

If yours is a bigger, more conventional menu, you should list the ice cream and fountain items with the desserts. You can either list the fountain items under a separate heading or mix them with the desserts. But since they all function as after dinner items they should be listed together.

Since after dinner drinks are part of the after portion of the menu, desserts and drinks plus ice creams can be listed together. There are many liqueur and ice cream combinations that tie in the entire after part of the menu. Cherries Jubilee and a variety of parfaits are "naturals" for making an interesting and saleable dessert-ice cream-drink list. The important thing is to describe these items

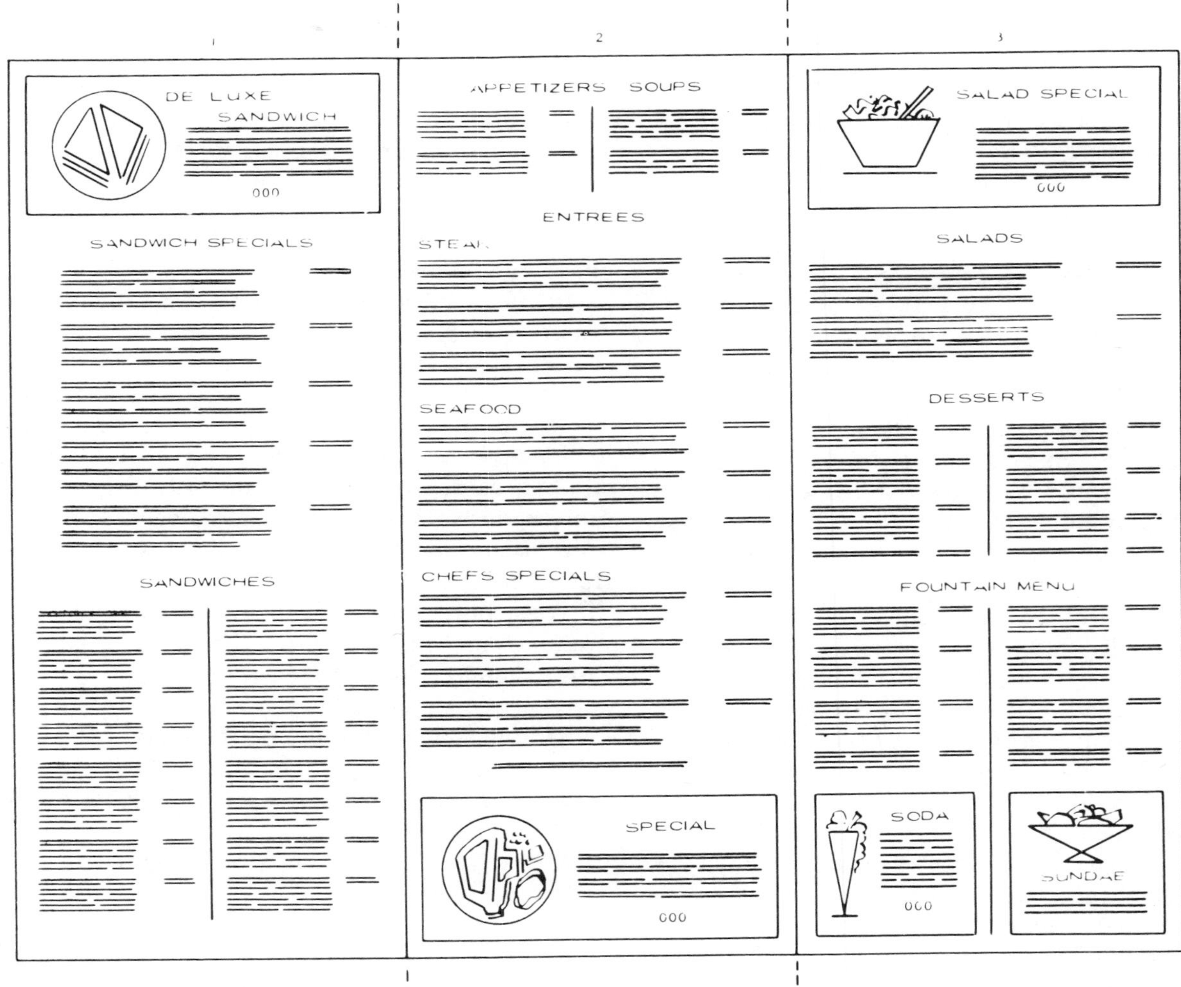

FIGURE 1

with good copy. Many people do not know how Cherries Jubilee or Baked Alaska are made or even the difference between a parfait and a sundae. You have to tell them.

There are many creative ways to list and serve ice cream on the menu. One way is to allow guests to "Make Your Own Sundae." This is a selection of ice cream flavors served in a bowl with the sauces, syrups, nuts, fruits, etc., served on the side so that the customer can build his or her own ice cream concoction. *Keith's Restaurant* lists a selection of "Sweets" which shows unusual combinations of ice cream. They are as follows:

CASSATA: Our very own recipe—layers of flavored ice cream with a delicious center of rich whipped cream blended with sherry, nuts and candied fruit.

GREEN HEAVEN: Pineapple marinated in creme de menthe served with ice cream, nuts and whipped cream.

CHERRIED DELIGHT: Cherries marinated in liqueur served with ice cream and nuts, and flavored with cherry brandy.

The Copper Hood Restaurant offers the *Tiki Hula*—A Volcano of Love—ice cream surrounded by pineapple chunks with coconut topping; and *Mr. A's* offers Baked Alaska L'Absinthe for Two or More. The *Gourmet Restaurant* lists a real gourmet ice cream concoction—*Coupe Gourmet*—Mandarin orange, marrons, brandy and ice cream. And *Tallino's*, an Italian style restaurant, doesn't just offer the traditional Spumoni, it lists Spumoni with claret sauce. Even a Chinese restaurant can offer ice cream with a different twist. *The Golden Pavillion*, a well-known Chinese restaurant, lists *Ginger Ice Cream*—a special blend of ginger roots

FIGURE 2

and rich ice cream. The uses of ice cream on the menu are unlimited. So, if your menu now lists only assorted ice creams, take a second look at your menu. It is more certain that by a little creative merchandising and effectively listing it on the menu, you can substantially increase your sales of ice cream in its many forms.

Desserts

Parfait Creme de Menthe	.95	Chocolate Nut Sundae	.75
Parfait Creme de Cacoa	.95	Butterscotch Sundae	.75
Ron Rico Rum Parfait	.95	Pineapple Sundae	.75
Fresh Strawberry Parfait	.95	Strawberry Sundae	.75

Chocolate Parfait .... .95

Home Made Cheese Cake .... .75
Hot Apple Pie with Cheese, Ice Cream or Whipped Cream .... .75
Old-Fashioned Strawberry Plantation Surprise .... .75
Roquefort, Bleu or Camembert Cheese .... .75

Beverages *(with food)*

Coffee .25   Tea .25   Milk .25   Iced Coffee .25   Iced Tea .25

Entremets

Baked Alaska a L'Absinthe for Two or More — *per person* 2.50

Crêpes Suzette for Two or More — *per person* 3.00

Cherries Jubilée for Two or More — *per person* 2.50

Colossal Strawberries Giuseppe 1.95

Assorted French Pastries .95

Ice Cream .65   *Sherbet* .65   *Cheese Cake* .85

Cream de Menthe Parfait 1.35

ICE CREAM

Colony Beach Special Ice Cream	.50
Ice Cream Rolled In Fresh Cocoanut or Chopped Pecan and Chocolate Sauce	.95
Make Your Own Sundae	1.00
Sherbet	.50
Cream de Menthe Parfait	1.25
Sundae	.75
Fruit Jello	.50

BLUM'S ICE CREAMS

Blum's delicious ice creams are super-rich

french vanilla	holland boy chocolate	turkish coffee
strawberry	coffee marshmallow	burnt almond
rocky road	double-double chocolate	peppermint stick

.50

FRESH FRUIT ICES, EUROPEAN

Tangy goodness of fresh fruits in light, sparkling freeze

strawberry	california orange	california lemon
raspberry		hawaiian pineapple

.50

BLUM'S SPECIAL SODAS

Scoops of Blum's ice creams in sparkling effervescence

french vanilla	cherry	pineapple mint
strawberry	holland boy chocolate	mint
red raspberry	bittersweet chocolate	turkish coffee
orange	mocha chocolate	caramel
lemon	chocolate mint	root beer
	pineapple	

Special Sodas .70 *Extra-Special .80

**With lavish additions of marshmallow, caramel or fudge sauce.*

BLUM'S SHAKES AND MALTS

Irresistible flavors and heavenly creaminess

french vanilla	cherry	pineapple mint
strawberry	holland boy chocolate	mint
red raspberry	bittersweet chocolate	turkish coffee
orange	mocha chocolate	caramel
lemon	chocolate mint	root beer
pineapple	peanut butter	

Special Shakes .75 *Extra-Special .85
Special Malts .85 *Extra-Special .95

**With lavish additions of marshmallow, caramel or fudge sauce.*

SPARKLING ICE CAPADES

Sun-ripened fruits captured in meltingly delicious ices

STRAWBERRY CRUSH, fresh strawberries and fresh strawberry ice floats, capped by raspberry ice. 75

RASPBERRY RAPTURE, the fresh-fruit deliciousness of raspberry ice and a rush of crushed raspberries. 75

ORANGE SPARKLER, Blum's freshly-squeezed orange juice comes frozen with float of orange ice. 75

LEMON CAPRICE, sunny pineapple juice adds the tang of grapefruit juice and floats scoops of fresh lemon ice. 75

BLUM'S SUNDAES

Pure delight of Blum's matchless flavor in gigantic servings

holland boy chocolate	chocolate marshmallow	strawberry
bittersweet chocolate	caramel	raspberry
milk chocolate	caramel marshmallow	pineapple
chocolate mint	caramel pecan	pineapple mint
chocolate mocha	marshmallow	coffee
		fudge

.85

Small Dessert Sundaes (with meals) .60 A la Carte .65

BLUM'S SUNDAE BESTS

ALMONDETTE DIVINE

The unsurpassed Almondettes make a fitting sauce for fine ice cream

French vanilla ice cream glorified with the dark, caramel richness of Almondette Sauce, frilled with whipped cream and a rush of toasted almonds.

.95

CUSTOMER'S FOLLY

The do-it-yourself sundae

Pick three of your favorite ice creams, three of your favorite sauces, (from the sundae list at top of page), fixings according to your fancy. Go on; live a little!

1.35

COF-FIESTA

The delectable pairing of coffee and chocolate

Coffee ice cream floating in rich chocolate sauce and whipped cream, topped with our own Koffee Krunch.

.85

HOT FUDGE OR HOT CARAMEL

Simply, purely perfection

French vanilla ice cream lavished with meltingly delicious hot fudge or caramel sauce, swirls of whipped cream.

.95

OLD FASHIONED BANANA SPLIT

as created by our founder, Simon Blum

A big scoop of vanilla drenched with chocolate sauce . . .
a big scoop of strawberry sauced with strawberry . . .
a big scoop of chocolate drowned in marshmallow . . .
waves of whipped cream, and nuts, and a banana (split).

1.35

GREAT BIG STRAWBERRY SMASH

Say, it's smashing!

Blum's own pound cake covered with strawberry sauce, piled with vanilla ice cream, heaped with fresh strawberry ice, topped with whipped cream and more strawberries.

1.65

See next page for parfaits

(See pages 269 to 271) *This menu*—Blum's—*is probably the most completely ice cream-oriented menu around. Any menu can be improved in the fountain department by using this one as a model, if not in whole at least in part.*

BLUM'S PARFAITS

Incomparable blendings of exciting flavors

.85

EMERALD ISLE

Sure, and it warms the cockles of your heart!

A wallop of ice cream, a dollop of fudge sauce, a flurry of mint and cocoanut, a halo of whipped cream.

FIDDLE FADDLE

Roundelay of favorite flavors and Blum's toppings

A delightful medley of chocolate and coffee ice creams, coffee syrup, banana slices, whipped cream.

TING-A-LING TANG

The nip-up zip of citrus laced with the zing of raspberry

Orange ice in a sea of fresh-frozen raspberries and marshmallow . . . lemon ice drenched with raspberry juice and whipped cream . . . and pecans everywhere!

HOB NOB HILL

A fanfare of favorite flavors crunched with almonds

Vanilla ice cream ladled over with chocolate and marshmallow sauces . . . burnt almond ice cream with a whipped cream float . . . a chopping of roasted almonds.

PEPPERMINT DRIZZLE

Vanilla ice cream layered between mint and chocolate syrups . . . peppermintstick ice cream hushed with marshmallow . . . vanilla ice cream, cold fudge whipped cream, plus pecans and Thin Mint.

1.35

BLUM'S CAKES AND PIES

Cake* . . . .55 A la mode 75

lemon krunch	pineapple custard	hazelnut
koffee krunch	cocoanut cream	chocolate fudge
chantilly	beverly brazil	cheesecake

Pie* . . . .55 A la mode 75

lemon goddess	chocolate cream	fresh fruit
lemon meringue	cocoanut cream	french apple
boston cream		

*Ask waitress for today's selections

BLUM'S FAMOUS COFFEE-TOFFEE PIE

Creamy with richness, aromatic with coffee and chocolate

.75 a slice

BLUM'S FRENCH PASTRIES

Select from the delectable assortment on our pastry tray.

.55

BLUM'S DANISH PASTRY

Choose from our large, delicious variety.

.35

RAREBIT SANDWICHES

Your choice of ham, turkey, tuna or ground beef sandwiches grilled until golden, topped with Welsh rarebit sauce. Served with tossed green salad or cole slaw.

1.50

CUSTOM DELUXE SANDWICHES

CORNED BEEF NASHER, with Swiss cheese 1.35

DUKE OF WINDSOR, turkey, grilled pineapple, cheddar cheese, avocado and Major Grey's Chutney 1.65

CLUBHOUSE, chicken, bacon, tomato and mayonnaise 1.75

COSMOPOLITAN, turkey, sugar-cured ham, Swiss cheese with Russian Dressing 1.75

HOT SANDWICHES

beefburger . . .	.90	cheddarburger	1.00
(with onion pot)	1.05	frankly fabulous frankfurter	.75
swissburger . .	1.25	with cheese	.80

BEEFSTEAK-ON-A-BUN, tender steak served on Blum's bun with beefsteak tomato slice and Blum's own onion pot 1.95

OPEN-FACE ROAST TURKEY SUPREME, served with a rich supreme sauce, fluffy potatoes and cranberry sauce 1.75

REUBEN SANDWICH, grilled corned beef, Swiss cheese, sauerkraut on rye with Russian dressing, potato salad 1.75

SHRIMP FONDUE, petite shrimp on grilled bread with Swiss cheese sauce, bacon, avocado; cole slaw or green salad 2.25

MONTE CARLO, baked ham and cheese sandwich dipped in egg batter, sauteed in butter. Served with small fresh fruit salad with poppyseed dressing 1.75

MONTE CRISTO, baked ham, turkey and cheese sandwich dipped in egg batter, sauteed in butter. Served with a small fresh fruit salad with poppyseed dressing 1.95

SANDWICH FAVORITES

All sandwiches are served with cole slaw or potato salad.

sliced turkey	1.25	american cheese	.85
baked sugar-cured ham	1.10	chopped egg	.75
corned beef	1.10	lettuce and tomato . . .	.75
smoked tongue	.95	peanut butter and jelly	.65
chicken salad	1.00	turkey and wisconsin swiss cheese	1.35
tuna salad	.95	fried ham and egg . . .	1.25
wisconsin swiss cheese	.85	smoked tongue and american cheese . . .	1.15
liverwurst	.75	ham and tomato	1.25
minced olive and nut .	.85	bacon and tomato . . .	1.25

See next page for salads

It takes six full pages to list all of Blum's *fountain items. The menu is printed on the inside covers and on a 4-page insert. The pink cover is illustrated with a drawing of a San Francisco cable car.*

BLUM'S CREATIVE SALADS

CANDIED BAKED APPLE SALAD

The delicious spiciness of our chilled and cinnamoned baked apple is complemented by a circle of fresh fruits and our marshmallow-nut dressing.

1.75

NICE FRUIT 'N ICE

Choice fresh fruit piled high with fresh pineapple sticks and topped with Blum's incomparable fruit ices. This is served with our distinguished poppyseed dressing and date-nut finger sandwiches

1.75

KONA COAST CHICKEN SALAD

Pineapple shell brims with diced chicken salad and fresh fruit jubilee gloriously garnished with grapes.

1.95

CALIFORNIA MEDLEY SALAD

Four salads in one. Chicken salad, seafood salad, cottage cheese salad and fruit salad — served with finger sandwiches.

2.25

COTTAGE FRUIT BOWL

Creamy cottage cheese is surrounded with a delightful selection of fresh and prepared fruits.

1.45

IMPERIAL VALLEY SALAD

Crisp greens and fresh vegetables — the best from the Salinas, Santa Clara and Imperial Valleys make this salad which is topped with julienne ham, turkey, two kinds of cheese and jumbo black olives. Your choice of dressing.

2.35

SHRIMP OR CRAB LOUIS

Superb shellfish served on a bed of crisp lettuce, garnished with hard-cooked egg, sliced tomatoes, ripe olives. Louis dressing served on the side.

2.50

Remoulade sauce, .25 extra

PETITE LOUIS 1.85

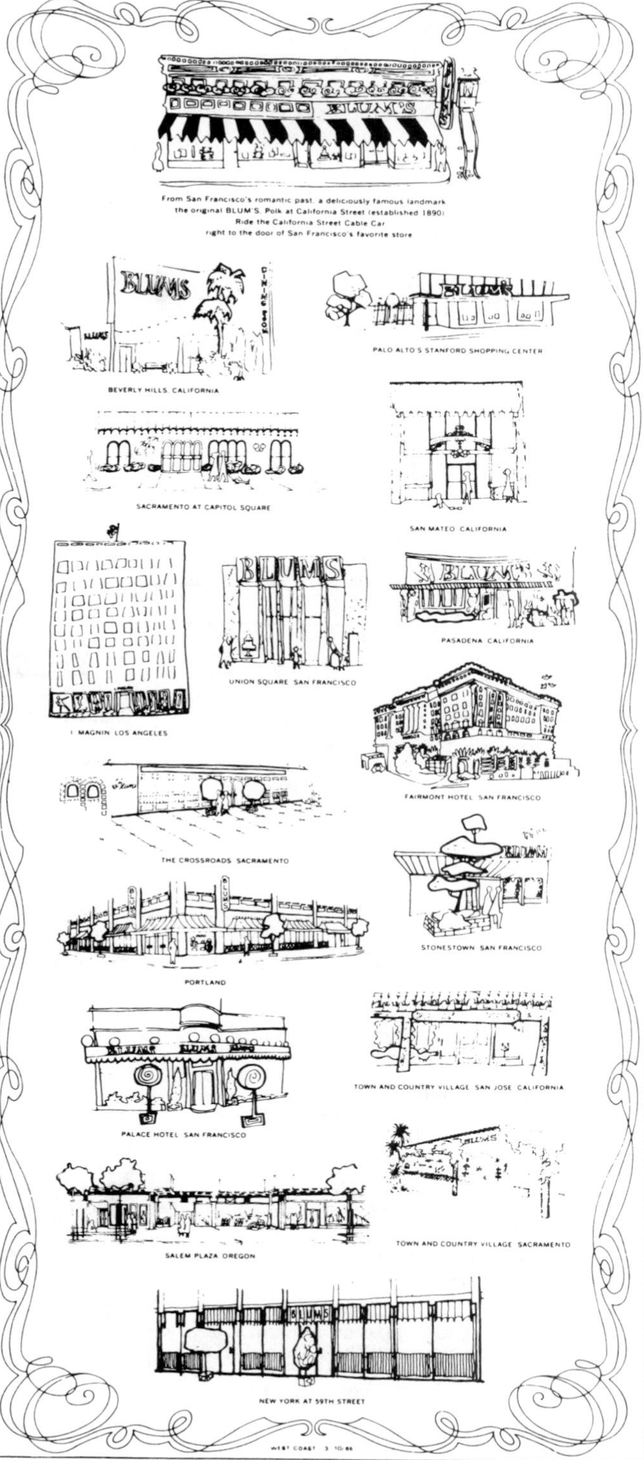

All 2-K fountain creations are made to order. This takes a little time, but they're worth waiting for. Please do not ask for substitutions.

Double Dip Ice Cream Dish

Vanilla, Oldtime Chocolate, Strawberry, Coffee, Pistachio, Toasted Almond, Peppermint .50

Single-Dip Dish Ice Cream .30

SHERBET—Raspberry, Lemon, Pineapple Single .25; Double .40

Sherbet Bouquet .55

TINY TOT SUNDAE—1 Scoop Vanilla Ice Cream, Chocolate Top, Animal Crackers .40

CONES Single .20; Double .35

THICK MALTS AND SHAKES

Vanilla, Pineapple, Chocolate, Lemon, Coffee, Strawberry, or Cherry. Made with Ice Cream and Whole Milk .45

With Egg .55

ICE CREAM SODAS

Vanilla, Chocolate, Strawberry, Pineapple, Lemon, Coffee or Cherry. Double dip and Whipped Cream .45

LEMON or LIME ADE—Made with Fizz Water .25

The truly luxurious ice cream you enjoy at 2-K is made from an exclusive formula. It is ours alone and is available only under the 2-K trademark, here in our restaurant and at better stores.

Take some home from the display case. Quart $ .99

HOUSTONIAN

One of the World's Largest! 5 Scoops Ice Cream; Sliced Pineapple, 5 Sundae Toppings, Sliced Banana, Nuts, Whipped Cream, Cherry

95

HAWAIIAN

Vanilla and Strawberry Ice Cream, Pineapple and Strawberry Topping, Grated Coconut, Sliced Banana, Sliced Pineapple

70

Half Size— 50

CASEY JONES

A Fancy Sundae Choo-Choo Train. 3 Scoops Ice Cream, Strawberry, Pineapple, Chocolate Topping, with Banana Wheels, Marshmallows, Whipped Cream, Cherry

75

BANANA SPLIT

Vanilla, Chocolate, Strawberry Ice Cream, Topped with Fresh Frozen Strawberries, Pineapple and Chocolate on Banana Halves, Whipped Cream, Chopped Nuts, Cherry

75

GAY NINETIES

2 Scoops Vanilla Ice Cream on Banana Halves, Topped with Hot Fudge, Whipped Cream, Chopped Nuts.

70

ALASKAN PEAK

5 Scoops Ice Cream Covered with Marshmallow, 2 Whole Bananas and Coconut

(A Real Mountain)

95

BLACK AND WHITE Sundae

Chocolate and Vanilla Ice Cream with Marshmallow and Chocolate Topping, Whipped Cream, Chopped Nuts, Cherry.

65

LOG CABIN

2 Scoops Coffee Ice Cream, Caramel Topping, Chopped Nuts and Salted Pretzel Sticks

65

SNOWBALL

Small Marshmallow Sundae Covered with Grated Coconut and Whipped Cream.

55

In addition to regular ice cream offerings, this listing includes some unusual ice cream specialties with appropriate copy and names.

Ye Pimlico Super Banana Bonanza 1.75
First a split ripe banana; second three jumbo scoops of Creamy French ice cream covered with your choice of fresh fruit or hot fudge and topped with whipped cream and chopped nuts.

Emerald Isle .95
essence o' mint, a smuckin' wallop o' the ice cream o' the month, cold chocolate fudge, a smitherin' o' shredded toasted coconut, charlotte russe, creme de menthe (for warmin' the cockles o' your heart) and right in the middle and atop it all, the bright green emerald isle. erin ga buy it!

Coconut Snoball 95
French vanilla ice cream with thick chocolate fudge topped with grated cocoanut.

DESSERTS

ICE HOUSE CREATIONS

Ice Cream Soft Serve Ice Cream Sherbets .20
Vanilla, Chocolate, Strawberry, Coffee, Butter Pecan, Raspberry Sherbet

OLD FASHIONED ICE CREAM SODAS
Two Scoops of Ice Cream floating in Rich Smooth Syrups and Sparkling Soda with Gobs of Whipped Cream .35

SHAKES AND MALTEDS .40
Spoon-Eatin' Thick — made with Soft Ice Creams. Served in the shaker it's mixed in

BANANA BANANZA .65
Mounds of Strawberry, Chocolate and Vanilla Ice Cream, Drenched with Pineapple and Strawberry Fruit then Covered with Whipped Cream, Chopped Nuts and Cherries

SUNDAE FANTASIES .40
Fancifully made with Vanilla or Chocolate Ice Cream with Choice of Hot Chocolate Fudge, Hot Butterscotch Fudge, Strawberry, Chocolate or Pineapple Sauce. Topped with Whipped Cream and Maraschino Cherries

The more unusual and creative the fountain menu, the more you can charge for it!

Table D'Hote

Assorted Sherbet Balls   Fresh Fruit Compote

Wild Mountain Blackberry Sundae

Vanilla, Chocolate or Peppermint Ice Cream

Kaphan's Fudge Pie Ala Mode

Kaphan's Blackbottom Pie

Lemon Glace   Coffee Sundae

Lemon Ice Box Pie

Ala Carte

Kaphan's Famous Ice Cream Pie 75
Frozen Rainbow Parfait w/Blackberries . .70
Lemon Glace — Rich in Lemon w/Brandy . .60
Coffee Sundae w/Coffee Liqueur 60
Parfaits — Chocolate, Caramel, Vin de Menthe — Coffee 75
Kaphan's Famous Cheese Cake 65
Topped with Blackberries. 75
Pies — Fruit and Cream 35

Desserts Flambes

Black Bing Cherries Jubilee 1.50
Rhum Ba Ba 1.00
Crepes Suzettes (Prepared Table Side) . . 1.75
Strawberries or Peaches (in Season) . . 1.75
Bananas Kaphan's. 1.50

Cheeses

Roquefort 50
Philadelphia Cream 50
Camembert (Served with Toasted Crackers, and Guava Jelly) 50

A complete dessert menu includes ice cream creations either with or without brandy and liqueurs.

The *Ice Cream Saloon* of Beaverton, Oregon has built a menu, and a business, around ice cream. To begin with, they serve a superior product. Theirs is "Real Old Fashioned Ice Cream," a blend of fresh cream, cane sugar, and eggs. They note in "The Great Ice Cream Robbery" that most ice cream today contains cottonseed, soybean oil, tetrasodium pyrophosphate, dried cheese whey, polysorbate 80, propylene glycol, and the like.

The Saloon goes on to tell more about their main product. It contains real fruit, has 40 percent less air, and is velvet smooth . . . because it is made daily and consumed within a week. The "Ice Cream Works" offers 25 flavors and serves them in sundaes, floats, shakes, sodas, cones, tubs, and splits. In addition, they feature *Funtastic Belt Busters*—super sodas, shakes, floats, and super splits.

To complement their ice cream listing, *The Saloon* lists "Best in the West Salads, Sandwiches and Soups." This includes five special sandwiches plus chowder and chili. Then they *extend* their food listing to include omelettes and four spaghetti dishes. These are "different" entree additions to an ice cream plus sandwiches fast food type menu.

"Land"! cried the lookout on the Santa Maria. "I'll drink to that"! said Columbus. It was the beginning of drinking in America, and the part 'Saloons' played in the development of American history is significant. The early Americans found it convenient to be patriotic in an 'Eat, Drink, and be Merry' setting. And when the West finally got out West, what was first to go up in every town? The 'Saloon' . . . but how many of you would have guessed that quality Ice Cream was made and sold in New York Saloons in the late 1780's? That was nearly 100 years before the Ice Cream Soda was born. Well, Happy Days are here again! You can enjoy full bodied old fashioned homemade Ice Cream that's made and sold in a 'Saloon'! And our Homemade Hot Temptuous Toppings are outrageously good . . . From our Pecan Praline full of butter toasted pecans to our Cherry Jubilee full of cherries, you'll want to try them all!

OUR STORY

Shortly after cows were invented, the now famous 'Ice Cream Lady of Ohio' began making her full bodied 'velvet smooth' ice creams. She is now nearly 70 years old and still makes all her own ice creams from recipes she carries in her head. We met the Ice Cream Lady in the summer of '73. We told her of our plans to leave General Motors Styling and Michigan after 17 years and return to our hometown of Beaverton to start an ice cream business. She said we reminded her of herself when she began her business. Although she had never relinquished her secret recipes and techniques for making her famous ice cream, she said she wanted to help us get back home. She told us all her recipes, her sources for supplies, and trained us. Relying heavily on the confidence she instilled in us, we pulled up stakes and returned to Oregon in November '73.

Like the Ice Cream Lady, we bring in 50 gallon drums of Vanilla Extract from Pennsylvania, Double Rich Chocolate from New Jersey, Pure Maple from Vermont, Cordials from New York . . . only the very best is good enough! And because her ice cream is so rich and full bodied, we even had to buy special ice cream machines with motors more than twice as powerful as the machines used for making normal hard ice cream.

OUR SALOON

In the traditional 'pioneer spirit', all our relatives and old friends pitched in and together we designed and built our 'Ice Cream Saloon'. It took over 5 months to complete. We opened on July 12, 1974. Some interesting features include:

* The table tops are 50 year old maple flooring from the Shute Park Roller Rink, torn down for the new Hillsboro City Library.
* The 500 feet of ceiling beams were made from the wall boards salvaged from the roller rink.
* The table seats are solid oak "1890" buckboards.
* Brass plated tractor seats are employed at the counter.
* Barrel windows were once whiskey aging tanks. (Please don't nibble on the barrels)
* Over 300 square feet of illuminated stained glass panels are incorporated into the ceiling.
* The iron railings are from a turn of the century, Baker, Oregon, school house.
* Floor is textured solid oak blocks.
* 'The Barn' party room is available for groups at no charge. It's a great place for birthday parties or for friends to meet after ball games, shows, church . . .

There is a great deal of "sell" in this menu—not just the food served, but of the restaurant itself. This institutional copy covers Saloon History, Our Story, Our Saloon plus their Cleanest Eatery Award. The menu thus becomes something of interest to read while the customer is waiting to be served, and, since it is printed on inexpensive newsprint in one color, dark brown, it can be given away as a souvenir that spreads the word.

If all this were not enough to insure a successful restaurant, the restaurant has added a special merchandising twist. They call it "Jackpot Roulette." With each ice cream or food purchase, the customer gets a "roulette card." When he has collected six cards, he gets to spin for a prize. The prizes range from an ice cream cone to a six-flavor "Jackpot" Banana Split. This is a clever and

The Ice Cream Saloon *offers a wide selection of ice cream concoctions and* sells *them effectively on this hard-working menu.*

THE GREAT ICE CREAM ROBBERY

The American Ice Cream Industry currently produces over 1 billion gallons of ice cream products per year. That's enough to fill the entire Grand Canyon! This averages out to 24 quarts of ice cream per person each year. The quality varies significantly from a superior blend of fresh ingredients to an inferior airy substance hardly worthy of the name. What was once blends of fresh cream, cane sugar, and eggs has become cottonseed and soybean oil, tetrasodium pyrophosphate, dried cheese whey, polysorbate 80, propylene glycol, and the like. What's next? Hamburger Helper?* This bewildering array of additives is beginning to attract some deserving attention. *Consumer Bulletin's* study stated that the proverbial purchaser of a 'pig in a poke' had nothing on the buyer of today's ice cream and that most ice cream is sadly 'mock'. A *National Observer* review summarized, ". . . it comes as close to being completely synthetic as it legally can."

*We interrupt this 'heavy copy' to offer free broken cones for your dog!

real fruit

Like fine wines, great ice creams must contain the finest quality flavorings. Imitation chemical flavorings just won't do. Nobody puts more real fruit in their ice cream than we do. Every 3 gallon tub of our Banana contains 6 bananas, our Pineapple has 4 cups of crushed Hawaiian pineapple, our Strawberry has 5 cups of Oregon strawberries, our Peach has 5 cups of peaches, etc. . . .

40% less air

Air is whipped into all ice cream during the freezing process. Without it, the ice cream would be a soggy heavy mass. Too much air produces a fluffy, poor value ice cream. Nearly all today's ice creams are 50% air which is the legal maximum allowed by law. Our ice cream is much more full bodied and averages only 30% air. This means you receive 40% more ice cream in every scoop. Your cost per lb. is less . . . that's value!

velvet smooth

Following production, today's ice creams are put in -25°F rooms and stored for weeks or even months before shipping to retailers. It is then put in 10°F dipping cabinets. Total temperature change: about 85 degrees. We make ice cream daily and put it directly in 10°F dipping cabinets where it is consumed within the week. Total temperature change: 15 degrees. This minimizes crystal structure change, fruits don't become icy, and it is fresh!

BEST IN THE WEST SALADS, SANDWICHES AND SOUPS

SANDWICHES SERVED ON BEAVERTON BAKERY BREAD WITH BAG OF CHIPS & PICKLE

STAGECOACH.* $1.70
Our slow roasted 'choice top round' Roast Beef Sandwich will 'deliver the mail'!

IRON HORSE* $1.85
Our French Dip is 'just the ticket'! Served with cup of 'piping hot' genuine beef au jus.

BUCKBOARD.* $1.70
Moist Turkey breast meat topped with homemade dressing and cranberry sauce. You'll leave 'talking Turkey'.

SHOWBOAT.* $1.70
Ham on Bohemian Rye topped with our famous 'sweet & sour mustard sauce'.

MR. DILLON* $1.70
Our Ham & Turkey is 'Kitty's favorite'.

Swiss or American Cheese on any sandwich - 10c extra
* Served with a Roulette Card!

HOMEMADE CLAM CHOWDER .$1.10
So good you may hear things like the roar of the ocean and sea gulls! (or feel free to hold a sea shell up to your ear) To go: $1.75 pt., $3.25 qt.

HOMEMADE CHILI $1.00
'Saddle Sore'? Our Chili is worth 'pulling up' for. Expertly seasoned for real flavor. $1.50 pt., $3.00 qt.

PLUMP HOT DOG 85c

PLUMP CHILI DOG $1.25

GRILLED CHEESE..85c ON RYE..90c

SALAD BAR 85c/BOWL Refill 50c
To go: Roquefort $2.00 pt., Others $1.50 pt.

DRINK UP

Boyd's Coffee	5c	Udder-Cola	25c
Hot or Iced Tea	25c	Hot Cider	25c
RC, Un-Cola, Hires	25c	Sodas & Floats	90c
Hot Chocolate	25c	Shakes	90c

TO GO — 5c EXTRA, CALL AHEAD FOR FAST SERVICE 643-1881

Ice Cream Works

See our "Funtastic Belt-Busters" on back page...

25 Flirtatious Syrups to Caress the Ice Cream of your Choice. Served Hot in Tiny Pitchers. Also Flavors for Shakes and Sodas.

1. Bittersweet Chocolate
2. Blueberry
3. Butter Brickle
4. Butter Caramel
5. Butterscotch
6. Cherry Jubilee
7. Chocolate Mint
8. Coconut Creme
9. Fruit Jubilee
10. Hot Fudge - 10c extra
11. Mountain Blackberry
12. Marshmallow
13. Melba
14. Milk Chocolate - 5c extra
15. Strawberry
16. Pecan Praline
17. Pineapple
18. Pure Maple
19. Wild Cherry

CORDIALS

20. Brandied Peach
21. Butter Rum
22. Claret
23. Creme de Cacoa
24. Creme de Maraschino
25. Creme de Mint

SUNDAES — You choose 1 Hot Topping and 2 Ice Creams. There are 14,000 combinations! **95c*** Served with a Roulette Card!

FLOATS SHAKES SODAS — Thousands of Flavors! **90c***

CONES TUBS — 40% more Ice Cream in every scoop! **30c*-scoop** **95c*pt./$1.85*qt.**

SPLITS — You choose 3 Hot Toppings and 3 Ice Creams. There are 16 million combinations! **$1.50*** Served with a Roulette Card!

*PREMIUM CHOCOLATES: ADD 5c PER SCOOP; 15c PER PT; 30c PER QT.

THE GREAT FIREHOUSE...

Dodge City was never the same after Doc stole the Saloon's 'brass rail' to alleviate the prickly problem of the Firehouse's wooden bannister. Soon the firemen were able to sit...and invent 'The Great Firehouse Omelette & Spaghetti Feed', which was held at the city park. First call: Gourmet omelettes filled with hickory smoked ham, cheddar cheese, Alaskan shrimp...served right in the pans 'piping hot' by Kitty's chorus girls in step to the 'Can-Can'... Then came an afternoon full of Deputy Henry Panky's famous 'fun & games' (better known today as 'Hanky Panky'). At the sound of the dinner gong, everyone gathered for 'The Great Firehouse Spaghetti'. The event was a great success!...and we haven't changed a thing except we aren't permitted Can-Can girls or Deputy Panky's fun & games. So Eat, Drink, and save the 'Hanky Panky' for home!

OMELETTES

"MADE WITH FRESH LOCAL FARM EGGS" SERVED WITH PEACH AND HOT RAISIN BREAD

Served with a Roulette Card!

1. **CAN•CAN** . . . . . .$2.00 — Chorus of Cheese.
2. **MATT & KITTY** .$2.25 — Ham & Cheese.
3. **DENVER MELT** . . . . .$2.25 — Diced Ham, Peppers, Onions, Cheese.
4. **RICKSHA CHARLIE** $2.25 — Chinese Vegetables, Diced Ham, Shrimp.
5. **HANGTOWN FRY**.$2.25 — Oysters, Mushrooms, Green Onions, Cheese.
6. **WRANGLER** . . . . . .$2.45 — Prime Beef Stroganoff.

SPAGHETTI $2.55

SERVED ALL DAY SAT. & SUN., AFTER 5 WEEKDAYS Served with a Roulette Card!

INCLUDES SALAD OR SOUP AND GARLIC TOAST

1 ALARM — **Spaghettini with Rich Meat Sauce and Plump Sausage** — Our famous 'Turn of the Century' meat sauce is the Pride of Dodge City! Ala Carte $1.60

2 ALARM — **Spaghettini with Mizithra Cheese** — Imported Greek Mizithra Cheese on Buttered Spaghettini...for the Gourmet!

3 ALARM — **Spaghettini with Rich Clam Sauce** — Our secret 'New England' clam sauce is Mr. Dillon's favorite! Tasty clams in buttery sauce...laced with mushrooms.

4 ALARM — **Spaghettini with Choice of Two** — Undecided! Then pick any two... ½ & ½.

TAKE HOME: MEAT SAUCE, CLAM SAUCE, OR MIZITHRA CHEESE WITH SPAGHETTINI FOR 3 . . . . . .$3.75

not too costly promotion for building repeat business.

This menu folds down to 8½″ × 8½″. It opens up on the first fold to 8″ × 17″ and then to 17″ × 17″. The artwork and type selection fit the style of the restaurant—Old West Casual—and the copy is clever, well written, and effective. Most of the pertinent information—address, phone number, days (but not hours) open, etc., are listed.

43

Merchandising coffee on the menu

> The Turks have a drink of black colour, which during the summer is very cooling, whereas in the winter it heats and warms the body, remaining always the same beverage and not changing its substance. They swallow it hot as it comes from the fire and they drink it in long draughts, not at dinner time, but as a kind of dainty and sipped slowly while talking with one's friends. One cannot find any meeting among them where they drink it not. . . . with this drink which they call "cahue," they divert themselves in their conversations. . . . when I return I will bring some with me and I will impart the knowledge to the Italians. *An Italian writing from Constantinople in 1615*

Before coffee became popular, people in Europe and America drank beer for breakfast, along with cold meats, fish, cheese, and dried or salt herring. It was only after coffee and chocolate became breakfast beverages that bread, eggs, bacon, and fruits became common breakfast foods.

Coffee originated in the Middle East, probably in Yemen. According to the legend of the "dancing goats," a goatherd named Kaldi noticed that his sleepy goats began to prance around excitedly after chewing certain berries. He tried the berries himself, and enjoyed the stimulus they gave him. At first, coffee berries were eaten whole. Later, a kind of wine was made with the fermented pulp. The practice of roasting the beans began in the thirteenth century. By the fourteenth century, coffee was very popular throughout the Middle East.

Coffee entered Europe through Italy in the seventeenth century. At first it was opposed as a "drink of infidels," but Pope Clement VIII tried it and is reported to have said, "Why, this Satan's drink is so delicious that it would be a pity to let the infidels have exclusive use of it. We shall fool Satan by baptizing it, and making it a truly Christian beverage."

Coffee reached France and England later. The first coffee house opened in England in 1650, and by 1789 there were over 2,000 in London alone. In Germany, Frederick the Great regarded coffee as a "noble drink" and used to brew it with champagne. In France, coffee was introduced by the Turkish Ambassador Soliman Aga to the court of Louis XIV who liked to brew his own coffee over an alcohol lamp. Coffee was introduced to the French general public in 1672 via the Cafe.

As the drinking of coffee spread throughout Europe, the debate continued over whether it was good or bad—an elixir or a poison. In the eighteenth century, King Gustav III of Sweden used a unique method of proving coffee's worth. He commuted the sentences of identical twin brothers—condemned to death for murder—to life imprisonment, on the condition that one twin be made to drink tea in generous amounts while the other was to drink lots of coffee. The tea drinker died first at the age of 83; so the question was settled. Whether a result of this "noble experiment" or not, Swedes are among the world's leaders in coffee drinking.

Coffee acquired its name from the Arabic *qahwah*, which became *kaveh* in Turkish, *cafe* in French, *caffe* in Italian, *koffie* in Dutch and *kaffee* in German. Coffee has no food value, but it aids digestion, acts as a diuretic, and offers stimulation. The caffeine in coffee acts on the nervous sytem increasing mental activity and heightening perception without any subsequent depression. Prince Talleyrand (1754-1839) described the effect of coffee in these words:

> A cup of coffee detracts nothing from your intellect; on the contrary, your stomach is freed by it and no longer distresses your brain; it will not hamper your mind with troubles but give freedom to its working. Suave molecules of Mocha stir up your blood, with-

out causing excessive heat; the organ of thought receives from it a feeling of sympathy; work becomes easier and you will sit down without distress to your principal repast which will restore your body and afford you a calm delicious night.

Coffee was introduced in France at the fair of Saint-Germain in 1672 by an Armenian. By 1789, Paris had 700 cafes which became political hotbeds of agitation and probably contributed to the French Revolution. Coffee syrups were invented in the late seventeenth century, and in the eighteenth and nineteenth centuries began to be used in recipes. Its popularity declined in England in favor of tea but rose steadily in France.

Coffee drinking in France and on the European continent survived the blockade of 1807-1811, although the French had to resort to adding chicory to their coffee—which they still do—and substituting beet sugar for cane. And Napoleon made coffee the soldiers' drink. He considered it an improvement over alcohol. The growth of the popularity of coffee in France is shown by the fact that by 1843, Paris had around 3,000 cafes.

At first, the American colonies followed England in drinking tea, although coffee was served in some seventeenth-century American taverns. But after the Boston Tea Party, drinking coffee became an act of patriotism. Today, the United States consumes around 2.4 cups of coffee per day per person, or around 25 gallons per capita. This is less than the per capita consumption of milk and soft drinks, but still a considerable factor for the restaurant menu.

NOTE: *The above historical information about coffee can be used on the menu to add reader interest.*

One yardstick for measuring how good a restaurant is, is by the quality of the coffee served, though the public can get good coffee at home, if they take the time to brew it correctly and use good coffee. One of the reasons the customer "dines out," however, is to get something *different*, and the menu *can* offer coffee in many unusual ways. Some of them are as follows:

Cafe au Lait—This traditional French coffee is made by pouring simultaneously equal amounts of strong coffee and hot milk into cups or bowls. In France, Cafe au Lait is usually accompanied by croissants.

Viennese Coffee—This is extra strong coffee with milk added to taste and served with a large dollop of sweetened whipped cream as topping.

Spiced Coffee—Brewed with cloves, allspice and stick cinnamon, this coffee is served in wine glasses and topped with whipped cream and nutmeg.

Espresso—Authentic espresso is brewed in an espresso machine which forces steam and boiling water through finely ground roast coffee.

Cappuccino—This is espresso coffee served with steamed, frothy milk.

Chocolaccino—This is Cappuccino served in a tall cup or glass topped with whipped cream and shaved semi-sweet chocolate.

Caffe Fantasia—Equal quantities of hot coffee and hot chocolate are poured over a slice of an orange and topped with whipped cream and cinnamon.

Coffee can be promoted, merchandised, and made an "extra profit" item, or it can be taken for granted. Following are some examples of how restaurants feature coffee on their menus.

Zims—This San Francisco group of restaurants has a separate, small Coffee Menu. It lists 14 different coffee and alcoholic drink combinations. For example, their Calipso Coffee is light rum, Tia Maria and coffee; their Mediterranean Coffee combines Metaxa and Galliano with Mocha; and their Ring-A-Ding Coffee is Christian Brothers Brandy, cream and a special syrup (added to the coffee) and garnished with cinnamon stick, cloves and orange. Every coffee drink listed on this menu, plus the idea of a separate Coffee Menu should be studied for profit.

The Golden Lion—Coffee can not only be combined with whiskey, brandy, or liqueurs, to make an after dinner drink, it can also be "flamed" to be served with show biz flair. *The Golden Lion* restaurant in the Olympic Hotel in Seattle lists four special coffee drinks under a Flaming Delights heading on their dessert menu. They are: Irish Coffee, with Irish Whiskey; Spanish Coffee, with Brandy and Kahlua; Brazilian Coffee, with Cointreau and Grand Marnier; plus Wellington Coffee, with Rum and Coconut Syrup.

Buena Vista—The *Buena Vista* restaurant, a popular eating and drinking spa on Fisherman's Wharf in San Francisco, not only serves Irish Coffee, it merchandises and sells this popular libation. On the menu "handout" shown here, they give the recipe, with pictures, for their Irish Coffee. According to *Buena Vista*, "Irish Coffee

1. BLACK & WHITE:
A rich blend of Dark Creme de Cacao and White Creme de Menthe. $1.50

2. CAFE ANISE:
Anisette, served with a lemon twist. .. $1.25

3. CALIPSO COFFEE:
Light rum and Tia Maria. $1.50

4. COUNTRY COFFEE:
The smooth taste of blackberry brandy. $1.50

5. IRISH COFFEE:
Everybody's favorite. $1.25

6. JAMAICAN:
The native's choice. Dark rum and Orange Curacao. $1.50

7. KIOKI:
Tia Maria and Christian Brothers Premium Brandy. $1.50

8. MEDITERRANEAN:
An exotic combination of Mataxa and Galliano. $1.75

9. MEXICAN COFFEE:
Ole! Tequila, Kahlua and cinnamon. $1.75

10. RING-A-DING COFFEE:
Christian Brothers Brandy, cream and a special syrup, garnished with cinnamon stick, cloves and orange. $1.25

11. SCANDINAVIAN:
Vandermint, a chocolate-mint liqueur, with brandy. $1.50

12. TATOO:
A delightful almond flavored libation. .. $1.25

13. ARTHUR'S OWN:
An Arthur's exclusive! Dark Creme de Cacao, Grand Marnier and Kahlua. $1.75

14. VENETIAN COFFEE:
Warm up with Christian Brothers Brandy and a pinch of sugar. $1.25

Prices of Alcoholic Beverages include Sales Tax

Zim's
fun drinking experience

Zim's *offers fourteen different coffee and alcoholic drink combinations.*

. . . the drink of music and magic . . . was conceived by Joe Sheridan at Shannon Airport. Stan Delaplane discovered it there and brought it back to San Francisco with him. The Buena Vista serves it, just as it is served in Shannon and using the perfect 7-year old, pot still, Irish whiskey. Try it and taste for yourself."

The Depot—This restaurant in South Miami, Florida, used coffee to "build the check" on the After Dinner portion of their menu. They begin with four special coffee drinks. They are: *The Depot's Irish Coffee*—Plenty of Old Bushmill's Irish Whiskey, a shot of Kahlua, freshly brewed coffeee and whipped cream; *Roman Coffee*—Featuring the unique Liqueur Galliano; *Cafe Royale—The Depot's* specially blended coffee with fine French Cognac and a stick of cinnamon; *Cappuccino L'Amore*—This recipe is secret, but it includes Drambuie, Kahlua, Courvoisier, and Espresso. Then the merchandising of coffee continues, with these words: "An after dinner cordial and a demitasse of our superb Espresso will complement your dinner. We recommend the finest liqueurs in the world." Then 13 different liqueurs are listed.

La Corrida—This restaurant goes in for "flaming" coffee drinks with a special Cafe Diablo (for two or more) $2.95 each. They describe it as follows: "A festive drink prepared in a diablo pot ignited by hot brandy poured over orange peel. A blend of cloves, cinnamon, lemon rind, Kirsch, curacao and brown sugar simmered in the pot to create a oneness of flavor. Served in demitasse." *La Corrida* also offers Irish Coffee, Cafe Nero, Cafe Ole, Cafe Expresso and Anis Del Mono, plus Mosca. This last drink is Italian roasted coffee beans and sambuca in a cordial glass.

Edmonton Plaza—The Edmonton Plaza Hotel offers four special coffee drinks on its After Dinner-Dessert Menu. They are: Irish Coffee, Rudesheimer Kaffee, Spanish Coffee or Spanish Tea, and Plaza Coffee. Their Plaza Coffee is described as follows: "Using our famous coffee as a base, we blend in the finest Cape of Good Hope Liqueur (Van Der Ham), and lace it with French Cognac, topped with whipped cream to present you with an original creation to crown your meal." The price of the Edmonton Coffees range from $2.75 to $3.35, making them substantial additions to the a la carte listing.

From the above examples, it is obvious that a restaurant can merchandise and romanticize coffee in ways seldom done by the customer at home.

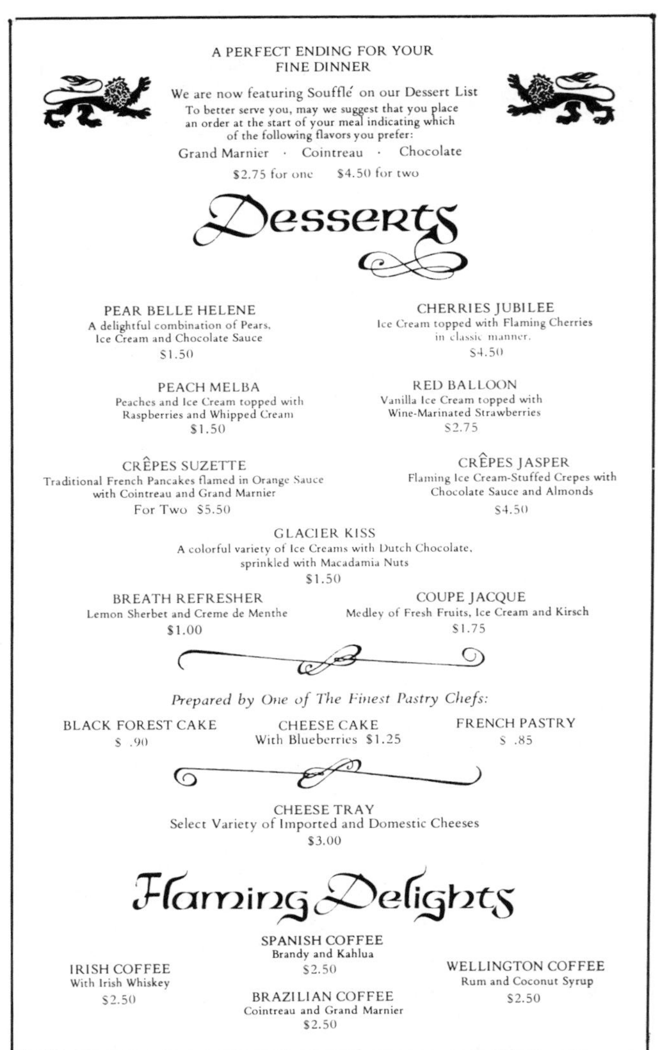

A PERFECT ENDING FOR YOUR FINE DINNER

We are now featuring Soufflé on our Dessert List
To better serve you, may we suggest that you place an order at the start of your meal indicating which of the following flavors you prefer:
Grand Marnier · Cointreau · Chocolate
$2.75 for one $4.50 for two

Desserts

PEAR BELLE HELENE
A delightful combination of Pears, Ice Cream and Chocolate Sauce
$1.50

CHERRIES JUBILEE
Ice Cream topped with Flaming Cherries in classic manner.
$4.50

PEACH MELBA
Peaches and Ice Cream topped with Raspberries and Whipped Cream
$1.50

RED BALLOON
Vanilla Ice Cream topped with Wine-Marinated Strawberries
$2.75

CRÊPES SUZETTE
Traditional French Pancakes flamed in Orange Sauce with Cointreau and Grand Marnier
For Two $5.50

CRÊPES JASPER
Flaming Ice Cream-Stuffed Crepes with Chocolate Sauce and Almonds
$4.50

GLACIER KISS
A colorful variety of Ice Creams with Dutch Chocolate, sprinkled with Macadamia Nuts
$1.50

BREATH REFRESHER
Lemon Sherbet and Creme de Menthe
$1.00

COUPE JACQUE
Medley of Fresh Fruits, Ice Cream and Kirsch
$1.75

Prepared by One of The Finest Pastry Chefs:

BLACK FOREST CAKE
$ .90

CHEESE CAKE
With Blueberries $1.25

FRENCH PASTRY
$ .85

CHEESE TRAY
Select Variety of Imported and Domestic Cheeses
$3.00

Flaming Delights

IRISH COFFEE
With Irish Whiskey
$2.50

SPANISH COFFEE
Brandy and Kahlua
$2.50

BRAZILIAN COFFEE
Cointreau and Grand Marnier
$2.50

WELLINGTON COFFEE
Rum and Coconut Syrup
$2.50

The Golden Lion *adds a dramatic touch by "flaming" their after dinner coffee drinks.*

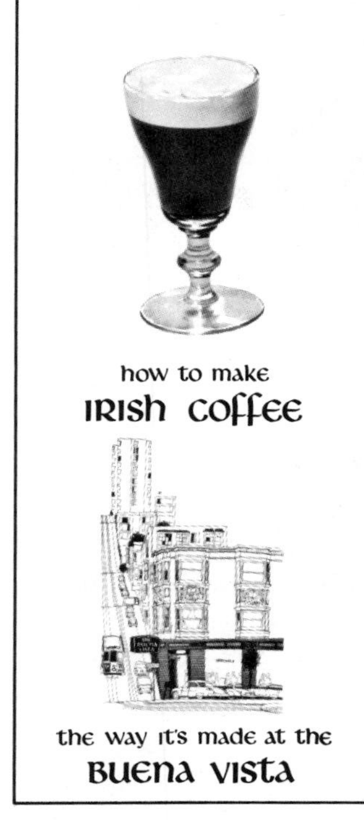

how to make
IRISH COFFEE
the way it's made at the
BUENA VISTA

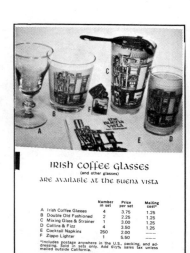

IRISH COFFEE GLASSES
(and other glasses)
ARE AVAILABLE AT THE BUENA VISTA

	Number in set	Price per set	Mailing cost*
A Irish Coffee Glasses	4	3.75	1.25
B Double Old Fashioned	2	2.25	1.25
C Mixing Glass & Strainer	1	3.00	1.25
D Collins & Fizz	4	3.50	1.25
E Cocktail Napkins	250	2.00	———
F Zippo Lighter	1	5.50	———

*Includes postage anywhere in the U.S., packing, and addressing. Sold in sets only. Add 6½% sales tax unless mailed outside California.

The art of making Irish Coffee and other notable concoctions is demonstrated continuously seven days a week from 9 a.m. to 2 a.m. at the Buena Vista. You are invited to refine your own proficiency through observation of our highly trained experts. A fundamental necessity, of course, is to start with the proper heat resistant and beautifully shaped glass. Mail orders to the Buena Vista, 2765 Hyde Street, San Francisco, California 94109.

A recipe folder for the Buena Vista's authentic New Orleans Fizz is also yours for the asking. It is a San Francisco experience to enjoy one of these delicious fizzes with a "Big, Beautiful, Bountiful Buena Vista Breakfast", served every day from 9 a.m., as you overlook the Bay, the Gate, and the Maritime Museum's old ships. Lunches are also served every day of the week.

Skill, a steady hand, and loving care

Irish Coffee . . . the drink of music and magic . . . was conceived by Joe Sheridan at Shannon Airport. Stan Delaplane discovered it there and brought it back to San Francisco with him. The Buena Vista serves it, just as it is served in Shannon and using the perfect 7-year old, pot still, Irish whiskey. Try it and taste for yourself.

1. *Fill glass with very hot water to pre-heat, then empty.*
2. *Pour hot coffee into hot glass until it is about three-quarters full. Drop in three cocktail sugar cubes.*
3. *Stir until the sugar is thoroughly dissolved.*
4. *Add full jigger of Irish Whiskey for proper taste and body.*
5. *Top with a collar of lightly whipped whipping cream by pouring gently over a spoon. Enjoy it while piping hot.*

The Buena Vista *merchandises its Irish coffee with a recipe "handout."*

Seafood Specialties

Lobster Tails Picador
$7.95 Tender African Lobster sauteed in Fra Diablo Sauce, cooked tableside and served on a bed of Rice Pilaf. (When available).

Camarones al Ajillo (Shrimp Scampi)
$6.95 Jumbo Gulfstream Shrimp, prepared at your table with a touch of garlic and wine. Served on a bed of rice.

Scampi in Salsa di Pomodori, Riso
$7.25 Prepared tableside. Jumbo Shrimp, sauteed in garlic butter and fresh diced tomatoes. Laced with white wine. Rice garni.

Filete de Pargo Grenobloise
$7.25 Fresh filet of Red Snapper broiled to perfection and topped with butter, diced lemon, and capers.

Supreme of Bahamian Grouper a la Almondine
$6.25 A delightful delicacy served with toasted almonds. Butter topping, vegetables.

Frog Legs Provencale
$6.75 Plump, juicy frog legs sauteed in butter with a hint of garlic seasoning. Served with freshly diced tomatoes and laced with white wine.

Cuisses de Greouilles Saute aux Fines Herbes
$6.25 Prepared in the dining room. Fresh frog legs, sauteed in butter, lemon juice, and herbs with a hint of white wine.

Spanish Specialties

Paella Valenciana (National Dish of Spain)
$17.50 Paella is baked en casserole with rice, pure olive oil, chicken, shrimp, lobster tails, clams, Red Snapper, crab meat, onion, green peppers and fresh tomatoes and seasoned with saffron laced with Spanish wine. Topped with green peas and red pimentos. (For two or more).

Arroz con Pollo (Traditional chicken and yellow rice)
$12.50 Tender chunks of young chicken in yellow rice slowly baked with green peppers and ripe tomatoes. Laced with pure olive oil and white wine. Covered with green peas and topped with red Spanish pimentos. (For two or more).

Spanish Mariscada (Bouillabaisse)
$18.25 Cooked in the dining room in a large casserole. A combination of fresh seafood and vegetables, olive oil, seasoning, and dry Spanish cherry wine. Garlic Toast. (For two or more).

Brandies and Cordials

In the La Corrida tradition of excellence, brandies are served in large, heated snifters. Select from popular favorites. A large array of rare French brandies including Courvoisier VSOP, Martell Cordon Bleu and imported Spanish Felipe II and Pedro Domecg Fundador brandies.

Your favorite cordial will make your La Corrida fiesta complete. Our selection includes all popular blends plus many of the imported cordials such as Anis del Mono, Cuarenta y Tres, Green or Yellow Chartreuse, Marie Brizard Anisette and others. Ask your waiter to help in making your selection.

La Corrida After Dinner

Cheesecake Deluxe
$1.25 Delicious, freshly-baked cheesecake topped with strawberries.

The Black Forest
$1.25 A moist chocolate cake with cherries and whipped cream.

Rum Ice Cream Cake
$1.50 Rich and moist.

Cherries al Fuego
$2.25 Red Bing Cherries in a light syrup made with Cointreau and Kirsch. Flamed with cognac and served over rich vanilla ice cream.

Platanos Foster (Bananas Foster)
$2.25 Bananas sauteed with cinnamon and brown sugar. Laced with banana liqueur, served over coffee brandy ice cream and flamed with 151 proof rum.

Corrida Sundae
$1.95 Coconut ice cream, covered with toasted almonds, chocolate liqueur, brandy, and whipped cream.

Pousse Parfait
$2.25 Alternated layers of ice cream and cordials. Cream de Noyaux, green menthe, and Kahlua.

Brandy Ice
$2.50 A frozen blend of vanilla ice cream and brandy.

España en Llamas (Spain in Flames)
$2.25 Flavorful imported Spanish cider and brandy served in a frosted champagne glass.

Irish Coffee
$2.25 Freshly brewed coffee and Irish Whiskey blended at your table and served with fresh whipped cream in a flaming, sugar-rimmed glass.

Cafe Olé
$2.50 La Corrida specialty. Prepared at your table with flaming Kahlua and imported Spanish brandy accented with lemon peel and cinnamon stick. Blended with fresh, hot coffee and topped with fluffy whipped cream.

Cafe Diablo (For two or more)
$2.95 each A festive drink prepared in a diablo pot ignited by hot brandy poured over orange peel. A blend of cloves, cinnamon, lemon rind, Kirsch, curacao and brown sugar simmered in the pot to create a oneness of flavor. Served in demi tasse.

Cafe Nero
$2.25 Flaming Galiano Liqueur blended with a strong coffee, and served in a sugar-rimmed glass.

Cafe Expresso and Anis Del Mono
$2.25 An aromatic demi tasse of expresso coffee served with imported Spanish annisette liqueur.

Mosca
$1.95 In a cordial glass: Italian roasted coffee beans and sambuca.

Cafe diablo (for two or more) is a speciality of La Corrida *restaurant.*

DESSERTS

CREPES PLAZA
Thin pancakes, prepared at your table with a blend of almonds, coffee, cream, and flamed with Brandy and Tia Maria.
For two 4.75

PEARS LAVAPIES
A new creation found only in the Carvery. Flamed at your table — combining the delightful liqueur, Pernod and Advockaat. 2.45

CHERRIES JUBILEE
Sweet Bing Cherries flamed with Kirsch and served over French vanilla ice cream. 2.75

FROZEN BRAZILIAN TORTE
A tasty and unsurpassed specialty of the Carvery. 1.45

BLACK FOREST CAKE
A succulent delicacy from the Black Forest. Combines chocolate, Bing cherries and Kirsch. 1.45

CHEESE CAKE
Our own secret recipe for the classic, cheese cake. Complemented with blackberry sauce. 1.45

ASSORTED FRENCH PASTRIES 1.15

DAILY FRESH BAKED PIES 1.10

IMPORTED AND CANADIAN CHEESES 1.50

COFFEES

IRISH COFFEE
The classic combination of hot coffee and Irish Whiskey. Topped with a cloud of whipped cream.
2.75

RUDESHEIMER KAFFEE
A blend of Asbach Uralt Brandy and coffee, topped with whipped cream, spiced with vanilla sugar and sprinkled with grated chocolate.
2.95

SPANISH COFFEE OR SPANISH TEA
A mellow blend of brandy and Kaluha with your choice of Coffee or Tea.
2.95

PLAZA COFFEE
Using our famous coffee as a base, we blend in the finest Cape of Good Hope liqueur (Van Der Ham), and lace it with French Cognac, topped with whipped cream to present you with an original creation to crown your meal.
3.35

The Edmonton Plaza *adds to the check by creating unusual special coffee drinks.*

44

Your liquor listing should reflect changing tastes

How many different bottles of liquor to stock in your bar and cellar, and, therefore, how many different drinks to list on the menu is a very real and difficult problem for every food service operator. A large stock of bottled goods can represent a sizable financial investment. If this investment does not have a fast turnover, the money tied up becomes a considerable waste. The faster the turnover, the greater the return.

Trial and error, of course, will tell a food service operator a great deal. What sells will be reordered, but this practical kind of market research is not the complete answer to this problem. In the first place, trial and error can be expensive. Bottles gathering dust on a shelf tell a story, but at a cost. Also, by this method, the product never ordered and given a trial is a complete unknown to the operator.

Then, too, improper listing and merchandising on the menu can result in an improper consumption pattern within the restaurant. Any product, liquor or food, assuming it is a good product, can be sold if it is merchandised properly on the menu and in the restaurant, but the most popular food and drink items are easier to sell. It is these items that usually make up the backbone of the menu.

American drinking habits are changing. Scotch is less popular; wines and apertifs are gaining in popularity. The two-martini lunch is giving way to a one-white-wine with the midday meal. Special drinks such as the *Hurricane* (dark rum, fruit punch and lemon juice) and the *Apricot Glacier* (Southern Comfort, champagne and an apricot) are appearing more often in restaurants, and in the "Sun Belt"—Florida to California—the *Marguerita* with its tequila base is becoming increasingly popular.

The fastest growing alcoholic beverages are wines, vodka, tequila, and flavorful sweet drinks. This trend is likely to continue since these drinks are favored by the young. The older drinks such as blended whiskey and scotches are favored by older drinkers. Their popularity, therefore, is declining or remaining static. Younger drinkers are not acquiring a taste for whiskey.

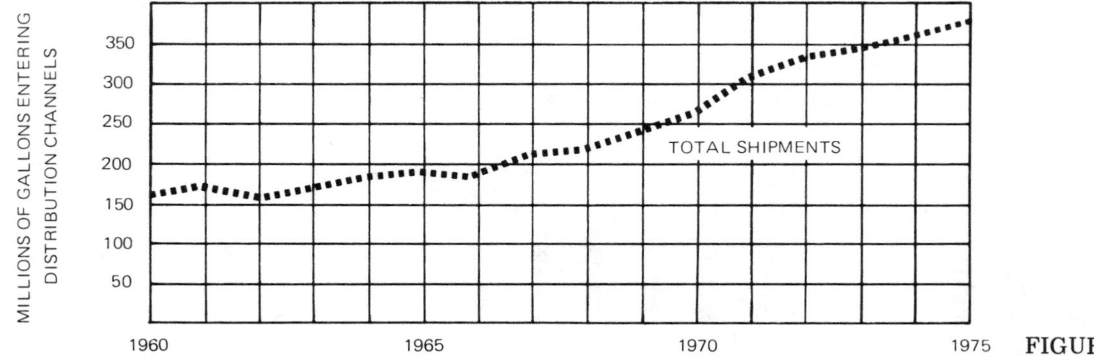

FIGURE 1

The per-capita consumption of alcoholic beverages for Americans aged 14 years or older in 1975 was just under 2.7 gallons. This broke down into 12 fifths of 86 proof spirits, 12.5 fifths of wine, and 12.5 cases of beer. More women are drinking today then in the past, and there is more variety and less alcoholic content in the drinks consumed. Vodka, the most neutral and therefore the most mixable of spirits has become the most popular. It is only 80 proof, and recently most domestic spirits have been reduced to 80 proof (from 86 proof).

Throughout American history, and continuing through today, beer has constituted the largest single source of alcoholic intake, but wine is growing increasingly in popularity. In the past five years, wine consumption has increased by 37 percent—a faster rate of growth than any other alcoholic beverage. Most of this wine growth has been in *table* wines which average about 12 percent in alcoholic content, while fortified *dessert* wines with their higher 15 to 20 percent alcoholic content have declined in popularity.

The implications of the changes in American drinking habits are significant to the restaurant operator and his menu. First, most Americans are *moderate* to *light* drinkers. Only 9 percent are classified as heavy drinkers while 18 percent are counted as moderate drinkers and 31 percent are considered light drinkers. This leaves 42 percent as abstainers or infrequent drinkers. This emphasis on moderation plus the lower alcoholic content of the most popular beers and wines gives one indication. The growing popularity of vodka gives another, and the "special" cocktails gives a third.

For the menu planner and designer, every restaurant that serves alcoholic beverages should have a wine and beer list—either separate or as part of the food listing. The wine list should include wine by the glass, bottle or carafe. This latter wine is usually a "house" wine—white, red and rosé—can be purchased by the barrel and is very profitable. A very popular wine drink is Sangria which is appearing on more and more wine lists and menus.

Relative to mixed drinks and cocktails the following are today's fifteen best sellers in bars and restaurants:

1. Martini
2. Manhattan
3. Whiskey Sour
4. Bloody Mary
5. Gimlet
6. Daiquiri
7. Collins
8. Old Fashioned
9. Margarita
10. Screwdriver
11. Bacardi
12. Stinger
13. Harvey Wallbanger
14. Gin and Tonic
15. Sombrero

While the two old favorites, the Martini and the Manhattan still lead the list of cocktail favorites, there have been many new additions. Young adults—the postwar generation, now grown up—who were brought up on fruit juices and sodas, made these new drinks with provocative names popular mainly because they *taste* good.

There are also regional preferences where "new" drinks have appeared. The *Tequila Sunrise* (grenadine, tequila and orange juice) is popular in Los Angeles; the *Cool Teul* (Southern Comfort, tequila and orange juice) is common in Miami Beach; and the *Sombrero* (coffee liqueur and chilled milk) started in Boston and spread to other cities.

The key to these new "in" drinks is a special group of versatile liquors that mix very well with a variety of juices and sodas. These are rum, vodka, and tequila, plus a variety of liqueurs.

TOP-SELLING LIQUORS

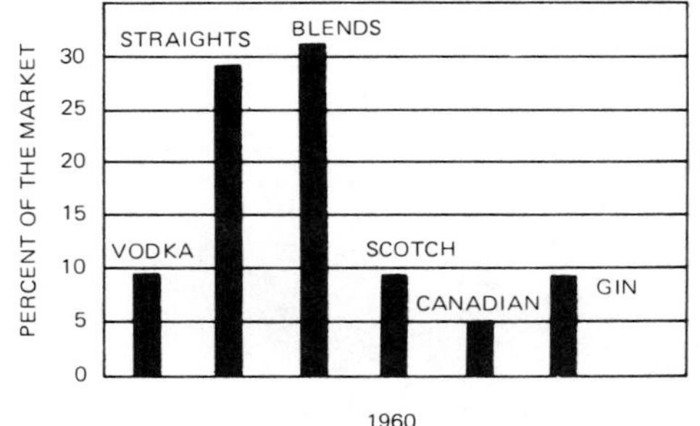

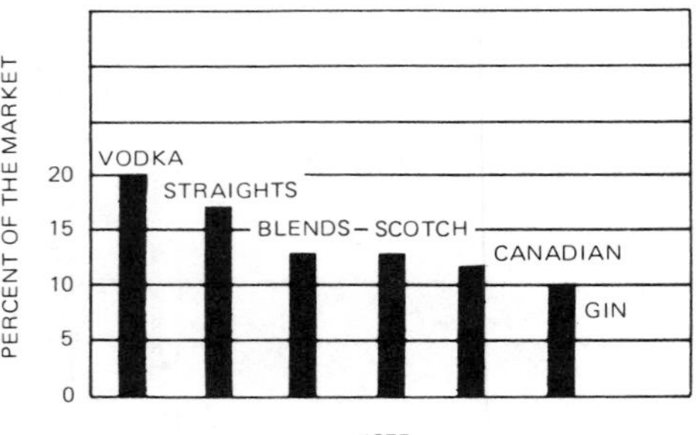

FIGURE 2

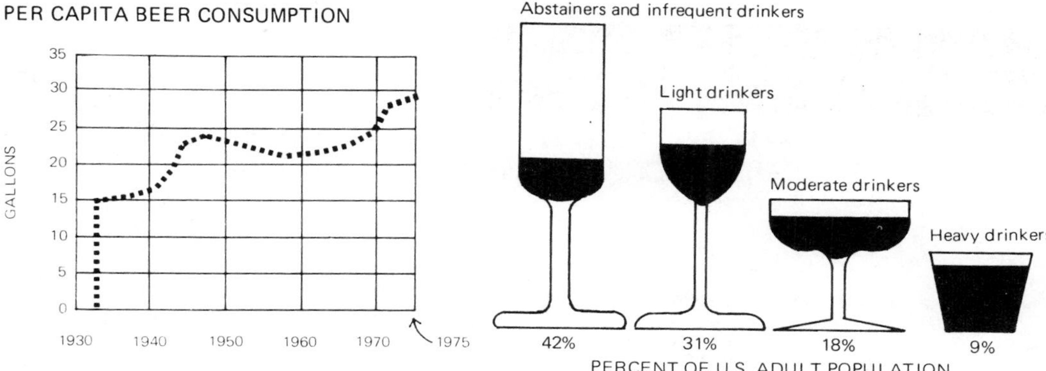

FIGURE 3

FIGURE 4

Selling food and liquor as a "package" is good merchandising.

NAME BRANDS

SCOTCH		OTHERS	
Black and White	.60c	Sunny Brook	.50c
Teachers	.60c	Shenley	.50c
Johnnie Walker Black	.80c	Seagrams 7 Crown	.50c
Cutty Sark	.75c	Calverts Special	.50c
J & B	.75c	Walkers Deluxe	.50c
White Label	.75c	Old Crow	.50c
Chevas Regal	.80c	Cabin Still	.50c
BONDS		Chapin & Gore	.50c
Old Grandad	.60c	Early Times	.50c
Old Taylor	.60c	Jack Daniels Bl.	.70c
Old Fitzgerald	.60c	Jack Daniels Gr.	.60c

CANADIANS

Seagrams VO	.60c	O.F.C.	.60c
Canadian Club	.60c	Windsor	.50c

Brand names indicate that you serve good quality.

Tahitian Room

PLANTATION No. 2 .... **$1.10**
One of the Plantation's most popular rum concoctions and we personally recommend it

VIRGIN **1.25**
For nostalgic memories of the islands induced by Virgin Island Rums and East Indian Special Rums

WAIKIKI **1.25**
There's a Lei with this one

POLYNESIAN **1.25**
It'll make you a shade darker, but you feel lighter

HAWAIIAN COCKTAIL **1.25**
Smooth, golden, brilliant and as sparkling as an island Wahinee

VICTORY **1.25**
Drop anchor, lads, while we skillfully blend British Navy Rum, Caribbean spices, Falernum and Angostura

PARADISE COCKTAIL **1.25**
You'll be looking for a full moon after this one

FAR EAST COCKTAIL **1.25**
Don't let the grenadine pull the wool over your eyes. This is no sissy drink

GILDED MAIDEN **1.25**
A beautiful golden drink with a Midas touch—That is, after the nth you're petrified

THREE DOTS AND A DASH . **1.25**

151 COCKTAIL **1.25**
The Atomic Bomb had something to do with this drink—and don't say we didn't tell you

HIBISCUS COCKTAIL **1.25**
You know bartending is a lot of hokum. You leave out one ingredient or add another and give the thing a different name and you've got a new drink. Or have you? Don't be fooled—This is just another variation of the boss

SHARK'S TOOTH **1.50**
A suave disarmer, not for missionaries

BEACHCOMBER **$1.25**
A velvet beauty—for those who know their way around the island when the stars murmur of love

TAHITIAN **1.50**
A serene blend of old Cuban Rums, fruits and limes—Delicious

PLANTERS RUM PUNCH ... **1.50**
For luscious sipping, try one of these sour-sweet deceivers—Not as innocent as might at first appear

PLANTATION GOLD COCKTAIL **1.25**
You pick the adjectives for THIS event

COBRA'S FANG **1.25**
(Not poison, but Oh! Oh!)

NEVER SAY DIE **1.25**
A favorite from igloo to isthmus —A puisant potation and you can say that again—or can you?

SKULL AND BONES **1.25**
(HOLD on to your hair)

BARBADOS **1.25**
They're sneaky—but in a nice way

GREEN VALLEY **1.50**
Fresh mint with gin fan to take with you

SINGAPORE SLING **1.50**

LOST HORIZON **1.50**
Ceremonial drink of island friendship

TROPICAL SPLENDOR **1.50**
A tall one—plenty ki-yi—Connoisseurs paddle far for the bouquet of this delicious Jamaica Rum Punch

PLANTATION BOMBER No. 1 **1.50**
Take it easy—How did this one get in here?

NUI NUI **1.75**
Strong man he call for Zanzibar —Prove 'um real drinker of the juice of the cane

TEST PILOT (Limit of Two) .. **$1.50**
Name your target for tonight—Hardy navigators favor this robust rum punch

SCORPION **1.50**
You know this is the eighth sign of the Zodiac, but numerically this would be too many

FOG CUTTER **1.50**
Especially for a foggy night

Q. B. COOLER **1.50**
Virgin Island Rums, tropical fruit juices, and the Plantation's special blend

NAVY GROG (The Ship's In) **1.50**

ZOMBI (Limit of Two) **1.75**
Boss man say Zombi have big reputation! Advise take it slow so not go Bong, Bong, Bongo

RUM JULEP **1.75**
Very old and mellow liqueur. Rums of marvelous bouquet and flavor, freshened with mint—Nuff said!

PINEAPPLE CUP (Pi-Yi) **1.75**
A real novelty—Crushed fruits and light Cuban Rums served in a hollowed-out baby pineapple

THE ZAMBA AND MAMBA **1.75**
One-half of thisa and one-half of thata—then use your imagination —and shaka the maraccas for another drink. A maraccas with each drink.

MAI TAI **1.50**

TROPICANA **1.75**
Served in a large tropical beach hat, and after embibing in this drink, if you can still lift it, the hat is yours, take it with you.

MARGARITA **1.25**

Festive Bowls

Ancient Polynesian ceremonial luau drinks were served in festive communal bowls. We offer an interpretation of the luau bowl.

BLACK MAGIC BOWL
For One **$1.50**
For Two **2.75**
For Four **5.00**
Lovely island girl say this is how to win handsome trader and keep him under idyllic spell tonight.

SHANGRA-LA POKA-POKA BOWL
For Two **2.50**
For Four **4.50**
It's like a journey to Shangra-La, but you forgot you were there

For Your After-Dinner Pleasure May We Suggest . . .

IRISH COFFEE **1.25**
ALEXANDERS **1.00**
PINK LADY **1.00**
PINK SQUIRREL **1.00**
SALLY RAND—WITH FAN .. **1.00**
CRIKET **1.00**
GRASSHOPPER **1.00**

MISSIONARY DOWNFALL .. **1.50**
A refreshing after-dinner sipper of mint and pineapple crushed and frapped with Cuban Rums

COFFEE GROG **1.25**

BRANDY ICE **1.25**
Brandy, ice cream

CHILDREN'S TAHITIAN FRUIT PUNCH .... **.50**
A blend of fresh fruits and juices, garnished with cherries, pineapple and banana

Most food service operations can take a lesson from the South Seas type restaurant. They are really creative in their drink concoctions and in the merchandising of them.

Eat, Drink & be Merry, for Tomorrow Ye Diet!

Tall Cool Drinks

CUBA LIBRE Rum and Coca Cola .... .90
GIN BUCK Gin, Lemon Juice and Ginger Ale .... .90
GIN RICKEY Gin, Lemon Juice and Soda .... .90
JOHN COLLINS Bourbon, Lemon Juice and Sugar .... .90
TOM COLLINS Gin, Lemon Juice and Sugar .... .90
MIGHTY MULE Vodka, Lime Juice and 7-Up .... .90
PLANTER'S PUNCH Light Rum, Dark Rum,
Fruit Juices and Grenadine 1.50
SINGAPORE SLING Gin, Cherry Brandy, Fruit Juices and Sugar 1.50
SLOE GIN FIZZ Sloe Gin, Lemon Juice and Sugar .... .90
ZOMBIE Light Rum, Dark Rum, 151% Proof Rum,
Orange and Pineapple Juice 1.75

PLANTATION-SIZE MINT JULEP 2.25
in a Tall Frosted "Silver Cup" . . . The Epitome of Gracious Living
(Served only when fresh mint is available)

POTENT POTIONS THESE!
Two Sensational Specialties
Served in Novel Take-home Skull Mugs!

GIANT HOT BUTTERED RUM 2.50
Aflame with Fiery Grog (a double shot of Rum!)
in Pure Apple Cider. Plus Whole Cloves, a Cinnamon Stick
and Rich Creamery Butter Afloat!!!

POWER-PACKED PIRATE PUNCH 2.50
Tall, Cool and Fragrant with Light and Dark Rums,
Fresh Fruit Juices, Mellow Grenadine,
Orange Slices and Cherries.
Delightfully Refreshing! Refreshingly Different!

HOSTESS CITY SPECIAL 1.50
Made with Rum, Fresh Fruit Juices, Banana Liqueur
and Maraschino Cherries, Blended to a smooth Icy Slush
Served in a Tall, Beautifully Decorated Pirates' House
Tumbler that's yours to take home!

Special drinks such as Plantation Size Mint Julep, Power Packed Pirate Punch, and Hostess City Special make this listing unusual.

CASA CARIOCA presents the

"Big Drink"

WHISKY BY THE POUND

¼ lb $ 1.60 ½ lb $ 3.20

¾ lb $ 4.80

1 lb $ 6.40

****

Mix your own Highballs
for a more exciting
and different evening

JUMBO SPECIALTIES (2 oz. base)

'67 SPECIAL 1.50
A blend of secret ingredients guaranteed to . . .

SIR JOHN A 1.50
A double size Manhattan

HI 'N. DRI 1.50
Double Martini with "Beefeater"

COUNTRY SQUIRE 1.35
Mansize Whiskey Sour — with touch of Triple Sec

PLAYBOY OLD FASHIONED 1.50
Created with "Southern Comfort"

TATTOO 1.50
Blends of Rum and Fruit Juices

HENRY GUARD 1.50
Cherry Brandy, Southern Comfort

THE LATE RISER 1.50
Creme de Cacoa, Vodka, one whole egg

Martini .... **70¢**
Manhattan .... **70¢**
Creme de Menthe Frappe .... **75¢**
Dubonnet .... **75¢**
Old Fashioned .... **75¢**
Sloe Gin Fizz .... **80¢**
Whiskey Sour .... **75¢**

1½

Tom Collins .... **75¢**
Gibson .... **70¢**
Vodkatini .... **70¢**
Bloody Mary .... **75¢**
B & B .... **95¢**
Screwdriver .... **75¢**
Orange Blossom .... **75¢**
Vodka Collins .... **75¢**
Bacardi .... **75¢**
Daiquiri .... **75¢**
Rob Roy .... **90¢**
Side Car .... **90¢**
Stinger .... **90¢**
Brandy Alexander .... **95¢**
Grasshopper .... **95¢**
Pink Lady .... **95¢**

The "Big Drink" can give your operation a big reputation. Whether 1-1/2 oz., or 2, or by the pound, if you serve a bigger cocktail or mixed drink, merchandise it on the menu.

WHISKEY
SOUR
85¢
MARTINI
85¢
MANHATTAN
85¢
Cocktails

Illustrations sell the "big three," and listing of ingredients helps to sell the other cocktails in this listing.

GRASSHOPPER .... .95
PINK SQUIRREL .... .95
BRANDY ALEXANDER .... .95
DAIQUIRI
RUM, SUGAR, LEMON .... .85
BACARDI
RUM, GRENADINE, LEMON .... .85
CUBA LIBRE
RUM, COKE, LIME .... .85
GIN RICKEY
GIN, LIME, VICHY .... .75
TOM COLLINS
GIN, SUGAR, LEMON .... .95
VODKA COLLINS
VODKA, GRENADINE, LEMON .... .95
SOUTHERN COMPORT MANHATTAN
SO. COMFORT & IMP. S.W. VERMOUTH .95
OLD FASHION
WHISKEY, BITTERS, SUGAR, FRUIT .. .85
PINK LADY
GIN, CREAM, GRENADINE .... .95
SLOE GIN FIZZ
SLOE GIN, LEMON, SUGAR .... .85
ROB ROY
SCOTCH IMP. VERMOUTH .... .95
SIDE CAR
BRANDY, COINTREAU, LEMON .... .95
VODKA MARTINI .... .85
BATMAN
SLOE GIN, VODKA, CHERRY BRANDY, LEMON JUICE, ORANGE JUICE, GRENADINE 1.50
STINGER
BRANDY & CREME DE MENTHE .... .95
FROZEN DAIQUIRI 1.50
BANANA DAIQUIRI .... .95
IRISH COFFEE
WITH MOUNDS OF WHIPPED CREAM 1.50

45
After dinner drinks

To begin with, let us examine After Dinner Drinks on the menu from a merchandising-marketing standpoint, that is, popularity (which drinks are listed), number listed, and price. The source of this information is a collection of 447 menus from all over the country. They include a variety of types and locations, but they all, of course, serve liquor.

Of the entire 447 menus examined, all of which listed liquor in some fashion—beer, wine, cocktails, etc.—only about half (53 percent) listed After Dinner Drinks as a separate category on the menu (see Figure 1). This indicates poor merchandising right off the bat by about half of the food service operators serving liquor, and of these 53 percent who do realize that After Dinner Drinks are not the same as Cocktails (drinks before dinner), and Wines and Beers (drinks during dinner), but are actually ordered and consumed after the entree, either with desserts or as a substitute for desserts, only about 10 percent listed these drinks in the proper place on the menu.

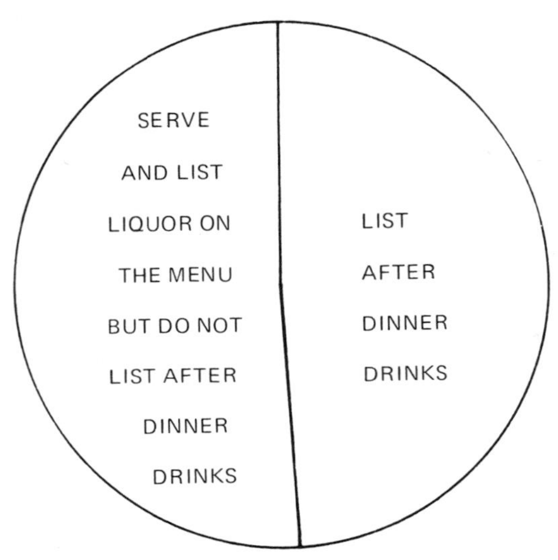

FIGURE 1

Next, when an operation does list After Dinner Drinks, how many drinks get listed? The answer is shown in Figure 2. There is some, but not a great deal of agreement here from establishment to establishment. A few list one or two. This is usually the operator who lists Irish Coffee (usually without any special treatment) with his other beverages, tea, milk, coffee, soft drinks, etc. The biggest category seems to offer a range of seven to twelve different After Dinner Drinks. There are, however, a sizable selection of dining rooms that list from fourteen to seventeen to even more, and these are also usually the operators who do a better job of selling these items on the menu.

What are the most popular After Dinner Drinks as indicated by the number of times listed on the various menus examined? The three most popular drinks from the survey are (1) Creme de Menthe, (2) Irish Coffee, and (3) Drambuie. You may have local preferences, but across the country, more establishments list these three drinks. Of the cocktail type, After Dinner Drinks, Grasshopper, Stinger, and Alexander are quite popular, and Benedictine plus B and B (Benedictine and Brandy) are also very popular. The Creme de Cacao is also a very popular drink. Of the "special" type of After Dinner Drinks, Galliano and Cherry Heering are very popular.

The more unusual, odd named and rather unknown After Dinner Drinks, such as Rusty Nail, Black Russian, Pink Squirrel, King Alphonso, are not listed too often. The reason probably is that

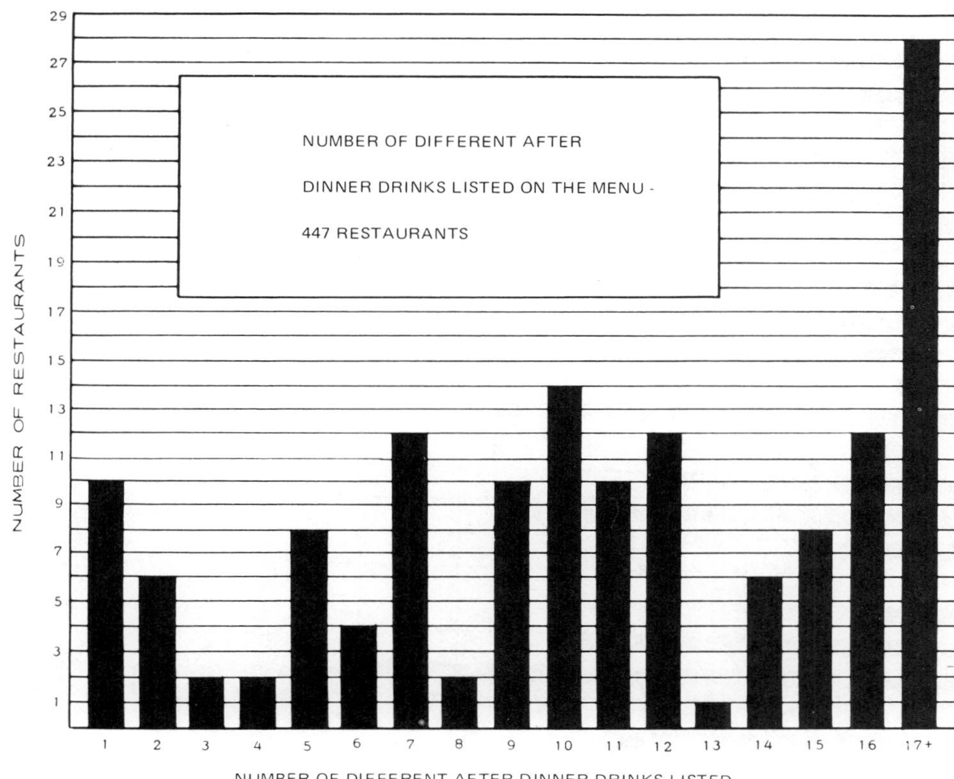

FIGURE 2

they are not well known, and the average food service operator is not going to describe, merchandise, and sell these drinks for that reason. This could be a mistake. Any drink, especially an unusual one, can be sold if it is featured on the menu. This means bigger, bolder type, more descriptive copy and an illustration, if at all possible. The result could be twofold. First, you will sell more of the drink and make more money, and second you will add to the reputation of your establishment by becoming known for your unusual, different drinks as well as your food listing.

The overall picture, as a result of this survey, is not one that the food service operations of America can be proud of with regard to After Dinner Drinks. They are the "Cinderellas of the Menu." They have a tremendous potential. But menu makers, designers, and writers seem to "run out of steam" when they get to the end of the menu. This is unfortunate because these items of the bar inventory are easy to order, easy to store, easy to serve, and easy to make a profit from (See Figure 3).

The use of the "after" portion of the menu is important. The waiter or waitress should not "ask" the customer if he wants dessert or an after dinner drink. At the end of the meal, the separate After Dinner menu, or the regular menu with the "after" part presented up, should be shown to all customers. This is positive selling and merchandising.

The "how" of listing after dinner drinks is largely a matter of copy. If the listing is in large, clear type on good paper, the main ingredient becomes copy. A main fault of most after dinner drink listings is that they do not describe the drinks. Most menus assume that the customer knows what a Black Russian or a Rusty Nail is, but this is a dangerous assumption. The best way to sell is to describe. The following listing from *Herb Traub's Pirate House* with its one line descriptions is not fancy copy, but does tell the customer what the drink is.

After Dinner Drinks
Angel's Kiss . . . Creme de Cacao & Cream
Black Russian . . . Vodka & Kahlua (Coffee Liqueur)
Brandy Alexander . . . Brandy, Creme de Cacao and Cream
Creme de Menthe Frappe
Grasshopper . . . Creme de Menthe, Creme de Cacao & Cream

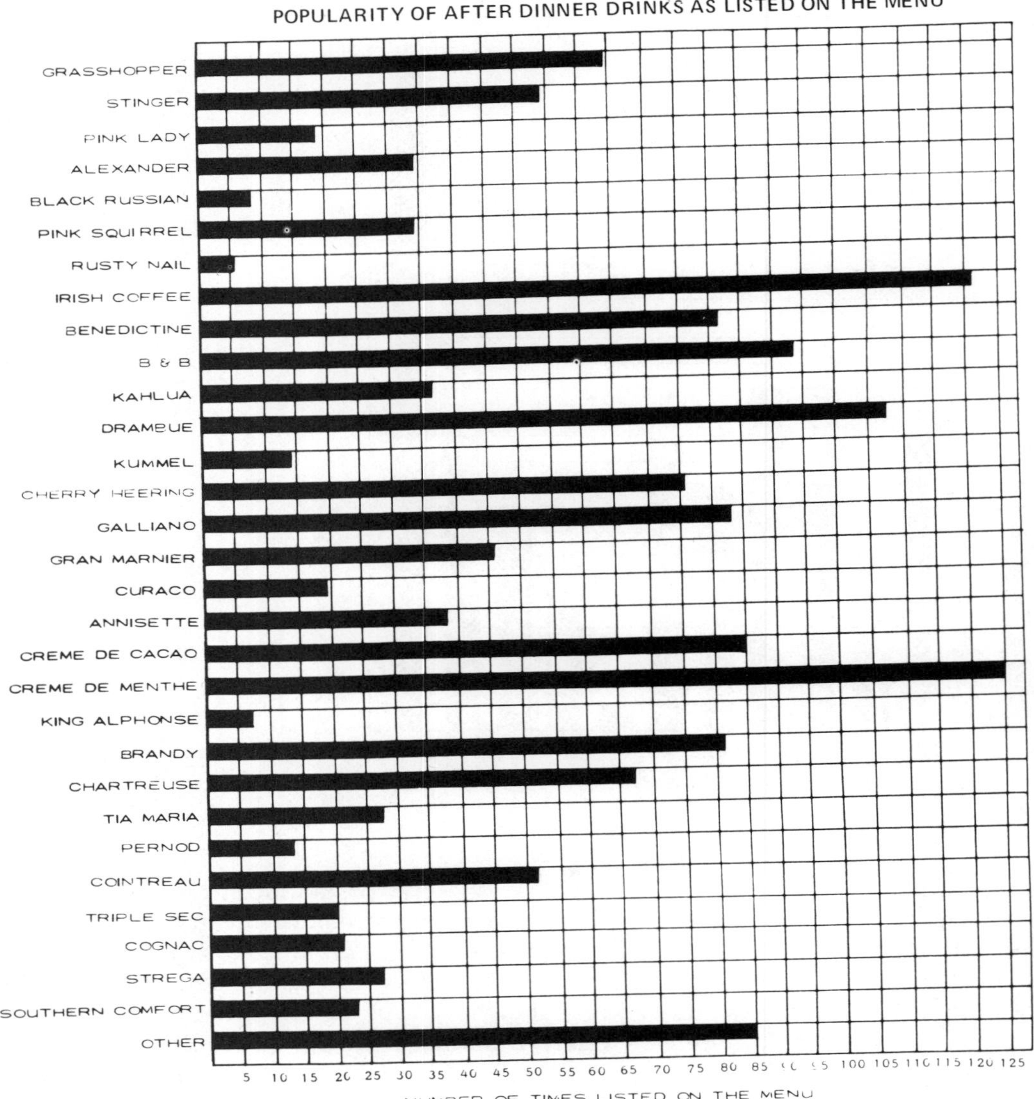

FIGURE 3

Irish Coffee (served flaming) . . . Irish Whiskey, Coffee and Whipped Cream
Pink Lady . . . Gin, Grenadine and Cream
Pink Squirrel . . . Creme de Noyaux (Almond flavored liqueur) and Cream
Rusty Nail . . . Scotch and Drambuie
Stinger . . . Brandy and Creme de Menthe

The following list of dessert wines from the same menu is a typical selection:

Dessert Wines
Christian Brothers Ruby Port
Christian Brothers Sherry
Christian Brothers Golden Sherry
Taylor Port
Taylor Cream Sherry
Duff Gordon Nina (Medium Dry)
Harvey's Gold Cap Port
Harvey's Bristol Cream

Liqueurs, of course, can be combined with desserts to make especially "special" after-dinner treats. The easiest and most simple combination is liqueur and ice cream in the form of "Parfaits." The "Creme" liqueurs are especially effective in creating parfaits. A listing of available creme liqueurs follows:

LIQUEUR	*FLAVORING*
Creme d'Ananas	Pineapple
Creme de Banane	Banana

Creme de Cacao	Cocoa
Creme de Cafe	Coffee
Creme de Cassis	Black Currant
Creme de Chocolat	Chocolate
Creme de Cumin	Caraway Seeds
Creme de Fraise	Strawberry
Creme de Framboise	Raspberry
Creme de Mandarine	Tangerine
Creme de Menthe	Peppermint
Creme de Moka	Coffee
Creme de Noyaux	Almond
Creme de Prunelle	Sloe
Creme de Roses	Rose
Creme de The	Tea
Creme de Vanille	Vanilla
Creme de Violette	Violet

In addition to ice cream, liqueurs can be added to bakery and fruit desserts. The uses and potential profits, therefore, of After Dinner Drinks are many, varied, and worthy of consideration and exploitation.

Flaming After Dinner Drinks

ORANGE BRULOT EN CORBEILLE

Brandy, Spices and Coffee. Flame Brandy with Spices,
add Coffee and Pour into Orange Cup 2.00

IRISH COFFEE

Irish Whiskey, Creme de Cafe, Spices and Whipped Cream.
Flame Whiskey with Spices and pour into Glass
Top with Creme de Cafe and Whipped Cream. 1.75

POUSSE CAFE

Not Less Than Five Liqueurs Used.
Floated one atop the other without mixing. Flame and serve. 1.75

After Dinner Drinks

GRASSHOPPER *Green Creme de Menthe, White Creme de Cacao and Cream* 1.50

PINK SQUIRREL *Creme de Noyaux, White Creme de Cacao and Cream* 1.50

BANSHEE *White Creme de Cacao, Banana Liqueur and Cream* 1.50

SILVER DOLLAR *White Creme de Menthe, Banana Liqueur and Cream*.. 1.50

VELVET HAMMER *Cointreau, White Creme de Cacao and Cream* 1.50

GOLDEN DREAM *Galliano, Cointreau, Orange Juice and Cream* 1.50

GOLDEN CADILLAC *Galliano, White Creme de Cacao and Cream* 1.50

KING ALFONSO *Dark Creme de Cacao topped with Cream* 1.50

BLUE ANGEL *Sorry we can't Tell; But you will love it* 1.50

FLAMINGO *London Dry Gin, Grenadine and Cream* 1.50

RUSTY NAIL *Equal parts Scotch and Drambuie* 1.50

BRANDY ALEXANDER *Dark Creme de Cacao, Brandy and Cream* 1.50

In addition to a good selection of regular after dinner drinks, this menu has three unusual flaming after dinner drinks.

After

To cap your seafood feast, linger over one of our tempting liqueurs . . . leisurely enjoying every sip. How about one now?

D. The "Halo" .... .95
Bewitching taste! A magic blend of apricot brandy with white creme de menthe, lemon juice and sugar. Served in a sugar rimmed cocktail glass.

E. Golden Cadillac 1.25
Tops! Equal parts of Galliano liqueur, creme de cacao, cream. Blended with crushed ice. Served in parfait glass. Savor leisurely!

F. Lace Curtain .... .85
Sip this tropical delight with a straw! A smooth frappe of creme de menthe and brandy. Served over shaved ice in cocktail glass.

After dinner drinks designed for a seafood menu.

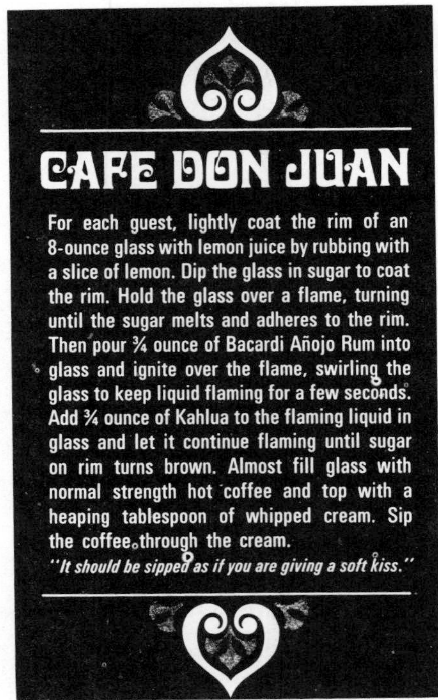

CAFE DON JUAN
For each guest, lightly coat the rim of an 8-ounce glass with lemon juice by rubbing with a slice of lemon. Dip the glass in sugar to coat the rim. Hold the glass over a flame, turning until the sugar melts and adheres to the rim. Then pour ¾ ounce of Bacardi Añojo Rum into glass and ignite over the flame, swirling the glass to keep liquid flaming for a few seconds. Add ¾ ounce of Kahlua to the flaming liquid in glass and let it continue flaming until sugar on rim turns brown. Almost fill glass with normal strength hot coffee and top with a heaping tablespoon of whipped cream. Sip the coffee through the cream.
"It should be sipped as if you are giving a soft kiss."

If you have a special after dinner drink, give the recipe.

Descriptive copy that goes one step further.

LIQUEURS

APRICOT
Liqueur is made by steeping the fresh fruit in fine brandy for about one year, then straining and sweetening with sugar syrup.

BENEDICTINE (DOM)
Produced by the Benedictine Monks at Fecamp, France, from a secret formula since 1510. The liqueur was dedicated to God, with the Latin words "Deo Optimo Maximo," which means "to God, most good, most great." Benedictine is made from a large number of plants, seeds and herbs, some of which grow in the vicinity of Fecamp, and many that grow elsewhere, together with the finest brandy. Among the ingredients are: cloves, nutmeg, cinnamon, peppermint, angelica root, alpine mugwort, aromatic calamus, cardmon and flowers of arnica.

BENEDICTINE AND BRANDY (DOM)
This is the same liqueur as above, except that it has been mixed with fine old brandy.

DRAMBUIE
This is the most famous of the English liqueurs. Drambuie has a base of the very fine old Scotch whiskey. The other ingredients are honey, herbs and spices. It has been produced since 1745 and is called "Prince Charles Edwards Scotch Liqueur."

GRAND MARNIER
This is a blend of fine champagne cognac and orange curacao. World famous as an after-dinner liqueur.

CHARTREUSE, YELLOW OR GREEN
Grand Chartreuse is made at Voiron-Chartreuse, France, by the Chartreux Monks. This liqueur has been manufactured by the Chartreux Fathers since 1605, using a still-secret formula. It is reputed to have 130 different ingredients. Some of the main plants, roots, herbs and flowers used are: Melisse citronne, Hyssop flowers, dry peppermint, alpine mugwort, balsamite, thyme, anglica leaves and arnica flowers.

CHERRY HEERING
One of the finest liqueur brandies known throughout the world. It is made by steeping fresh sweet cherries in fine brandy for about one year.

COINTREAU
Cointreau is a brand of Triple Sec orange curacao and world famous as a liqueur and the base of the Side Car cocktail.

CREME DE CACAO
This is made from cocoa beans, cloves, mace and vanilla. It has a distinct chocolate flavor and is the main ingredient of the Alexander cocktail.

CREME DE MENTHE
A peppermint liqueur made from fresh mint leaves macerated in brandy spirts. This fine liqueur is made in three different colors: green, red and white. In recent years, this liqueur has become famous as one of the ingredients of the Stinger cocktail.

BRANDIES

APPLE JACK
CORONET V.S.Q.
COURVOISIER COGNAC
WILD CHERRY

3 STAR HENNESSY
MARTELL COGNAC
BLACKBERRY

After Dinner Drinks

.75 ANGEL'S TIP
Creme de Cacao, Cream and Half of Maraschino Cherry

.75 STINGER
Brandy and Creme de Menthe

.75 B & B
Benedictine D. O. M. and Brandy

.70 CREME DE MENTHE FRAFPE
Creme de Menthe over Cracked Ice with Maraschino Cherry

.85 COURVOISIER V. S. COGNAC
Made from grapes grown in the Charente District of France, the Principal City of which is Cognac

.50 BLACKBERRY BRANDY
Made from Blackberries aged in wood

.80 BENEDICTINE D.O.M.
A secret formula reputed to be a combination of Herb, Spices and fine brandy

.75 COINTREAU
Made from Triple Sec Orange Curacao

.60 CREME DE CACAO
Made from Cacao Beans, Spices and Vanilla

.75 GRASSHOPPER
Green Creme de Menthe, Creme de Cacao and Cream

.85 DRAMBUIE
A Liqueur made from Old Scotch Honey, Herbs, and Spices

.75 SOUTHERN COMFORT
A high proof liqueur made in U.S. from a secret formula reputed to have a brandy and whiskey base

.85 METAXA - 5 STAR BRANDY
Imported

.50 APRICOT
A Domestic Apricot Brandy

.75 HENNESSY THREE STAR
A fine imported French Cognac

.80 CAFE ROYAL
A cup of hot cafe with imported brandy

.70 MOUQUIN
Imported Brandies. 10 years old

.50 CREME DE MENTHE
Creme de Menthe

.50 CORONET V. S. Q.
Domestic Brandy

.75 CHERRY HERRING
A Liqueur made in Copenhagen, Denmark of cherry flavor

All Above Drinks Using Scotch, Bourbon, Canadian Whiskies, Imported Gins and Brandies -- 15c Extra

All Above Drinks on the Rocks 15c Above Listed Price (Extra Portion)

This after dinner drink listing is a good selection of the more popular drinks, and all are completely described.

PINK LADY
½ oz. Grenadine, 1¼ oz. Gin, ½ oz. lemon juice, ¾ oz. heavy cream. Shake with cracked ice and strain.
ANGEL'S TIP
Fill ¾ of Pony Glass with Creme de Cacao and on this float heavy cream. Top with cherry.
GRASSHOPPER
⅓ Green Creme de Menthe, ⅓ White Creme de Cacao, ⅓ light coffee cream, shake well with ice and strain.
Enjoy one of these nine after you dine
STINGER
1 oz. brandy, ¾ oz. white creme de menthe. Shake well with cracked ice and strain. Serve on the rocks if you prefer.
ALEXANDER
½ oz. fresh cream, ½ oz. creme de cacao, 1½ oz. brandy, or gin shake well and serve.
DRAMBUIE
Fill ¾ of Pony Glass with Drambuie Liqueur and serve.
BRANDY ICE
1 scoop ice cream, 1 oz. brandy. Blend together until firm. Serve in cocktail glass.
B & B
½ Benedictine, ½ Cognac. Fill liqueur glass and serve.
FRAPPE
Fill cocktail glass with fine ice. Add green creme de menthe and serve. If you prefer, serve on the rocks.

Created by Mastercraft, this listing of after dinner drinks in color with the recipe for each drink, really sells.

Slainte THE STORY OF IRISH COFFEE

A chef by the name of Joe Sheridan originated Irish Coffee at the famous Shannon Airport—back in 1938, when the flying boats were landing at Foynes. The passengers would come in by launch, shivering and shaking, fit to die with the cold.

"Surely," said Joe Sheridan, "we must invent a stirrup cup ıor the poor souls, and them not able to put their shivering hands in their pockets for a shilling to pay unless we warm them.

"What is more warming," said Joe, "than Irish Whiskey, smooth as a maiden's kiss. To take the chill from their poor shaking hands we will fill the glass with coffee, black as Cromwell's heart. We will top it off with a floating inch of Irish cream."

And so it was . . . and is today, in far off Dublin House! For Irish Coffee here is authentically Joe's—to the glasses themselves, straight from Shannon Airport. Remember this about good, properly made Irish Coffee like ours—one of them takes the chill off! Two of them set you to singing "Down went McGinty . . . "

And 'tis truly said that this is the most delectable drink to ever cross a discerning palate. Slainte!*

**Slainte is Gaelic for "Good Health"*

With copy like this, you'll sell a lot of Irish coffee!

46

A la carte and complete dinners

There are two basic ways of listing and pricing the items on your menu—a la carte, with a separate price for every item on the menu, and complete dinner, a package deal where the appetizer, soup, potato, vegetable, beverage, and dessert are included.

Very few food service operations have a menu that is entirely an a la carte or complete dinner menu. The most totally schizophrenic or divided menu is the one that has a complete, extensive a la carte menu and a counter-balancing extensive complete dinner menu. This means, in effect, that the customer can order almost every item on the menu either a la carte or as part of some gastronomic type of gourmet package deal.

The first result of this kind of menu is that it makes the menu look twice as big as it actually is since the restaurant is listing everything twice without increasing the load on the kitchen. The second reason result is that every item—steak, seafood, fowl, or whatever—is listed with two prices which gives the customer a choice of the entree by itself (with no side dishes or extras or with those specific side dishes and extras he or she desires).

This price comparison, of course, can be like most comparisons—odious! The customer, it will be claimed by some, will be inclined toward the lower price, but the situation is not as simple as that. No customer wants to eat a steak, chicken, or lobster completely by itself, so some additional extras will be ordered and, in effect, thereby build the check. The situation can become a game between the customer and the restaurateur over which is the better deal—the complete dinner package or a la carte plus extras.

The first important thing for the menu builder or food service operator to do is to remember that the complete dinner is a "package" and he or she should set it up as a package. Preferably at the beginning of the entree listing, but whether before, after (or a split combination of before and after), the person in charge should print clearly and in large readable type: "Dinner includes"—and list what "goes with" the entree. If you are selling a package, sell the whole package, not just the entree part of it.

The next thing to remember is that the a la carte part of the menu should be just that, a la carte. Many restaurateurs list a la carte entrees under an a la carte heading which includes enough side dishes—vegetable, salad, potato, etc.—to be a complete meal. This defeats the entire purpose of an a la carte listing and is poor merchandising.

Furthermore, it must be kept in mind that, if you have a fairly complete a la carte listing, as well as a dinner listing, you should have a complete a la carte listing of appetizers, salads, potatoes, vegetables, side dishes, and desserts. In fact, many menus have complete dinners that are not actually complete. Either all or some of the desserts and appetizers are often not included in the dinner price.

Operators should be careful with regard to the price differential between a la carte and complete dinner. The difference should be the same for all entrees because the extras in the complete dinner package are the same. This may seem like a simple observation, but a surprising number of restaurateurs charge a variety of prices for the same extras in the complete dinner package.

The next problem for the menu builder is how to list the two prices, complete dinner and a la carte. One common method is to list the entrees with two prices right next to each other, a la carte price and complete dinner price. The other method, also common, is to have two separate and complete sections of the menu, a complete a la carte listing (with prices) and a separate and complete dinner listing (with prices). From a merchandising-selling point of view, the two separate listings, which makes direct price comparisons more difficult, is the better of the two methods.

Most restaurants "mix-and-match" items on their menus so that part of the menu is a la carte and part is "package" deals that usually include an entree, side dishes, a soup *or* a salad. The *Old World* restaurant menu shown here from Palm Springs, California, is typical of this approach. Their breakfast listing (served all day) offers The Belgian Brunch Eggs Benedict, and Steak 'n Eggs as package entrees. Omelettes, waffles, and eggs-'and' are also served as entree items with *extras* included, but side orders and beverages are listed a la carte.

The same approach is used by *Old World* in their Dinner listing. Appetizers, side orders, beverages, and desserts are a la carte, but dinner can include salad or soup, and "your choice of freshly cooked vegetables or German fried potatoes. Baked potato available after 5 P.M." The Specialties listing also includes package offerings. Peasant Lunch #1, for example, includes a "choice of soup with pumpernickel roll, cheddar cheese, and a piece of fruit. Clam chowder 25¢ extra."

Another interesting "package" offering on this menu is a Vegetarian Dinner which includes, "organically grown vegetables merged Chinese fashion into a well-sized patty (meatless), topped with sauteed onion." A Vegetable Casserole is also offered.

Green Ridge Dinners

Complete Dinner Price Includes
a Choice of One
Cranberry Juice — Tomato Juice — V-8 Vegetable Juice — Half Grapefruit in Season
Anchovies on Lettuce — Grapefruit Juice — Turkey Soup — Clam Chowder — Fresh Fruit Cup with Sherbet —
Filet of Marinated Herring – Cherrystone Clams, Fresh Shrimp Cocktail or Oysters on the half shell in season 1.25 extra on all Dinners
Green Ridge Salad
Choice of Two
Creamy Whipped Potatoes — French Fried Potatoes — Hubbard Squash — Green Peas — Vegetable du Jour —
Cole Slaw — Sliced Tomatoes
Choice from our Dessert Menu — Coffee, Tea, Milk

	A LA CARTE	COMPLETE DINNER
FABULOUS ROAST PRIME RIBS OF BEEF Served Medium Rare Only, Thick Cut with Pop Over	5.50	6.45
ROAST PRIME RIBS OF BEEF Served Medium Rare Only, with Pop Over	4.50	5.45
BROILED SIRLOIN STEAK — One Pound A Large Boneless Cut of Choice Quality Beef	5.50	6.45
BROILED JUNIOR SIRLOIN STEAK – 3/4 lb. Boneless Cut of Choice Quality Beef	4.50	5.45
BROILED TENDERLOIN STEAK Tender and Juicy — Choice Quality Beef	4.95	5.90
BROILED CHOPPED SIRLOIN STEAK Fresh Ground Steer Beef Served with Mushroom Sauce	2.65	3.60
BREADED TENDERIZED FRESH VEAL CUTLET Served with Mushroom Sauce	2.75	3.70
BONELESS FRIED CHICKEN BREAST Deep Fried and Served with Poulette Sauce	2.95	3.90
FRIED FRESH NATIVE TURKEY BREAST Deep Fried and Served with Poulette Sauce	2.95	3.90
FRIED CHICKEN LEG AND THIGH Fried to a Golden Brown	2.25	3.20
SAUTEED FRESH TURKEY LIVERS En Casserole with Mushroom Sauce	1.95	2.90
BROILED LIVE (1¼ to 1½ lb.) MAINE LOBSTER Served with Drawn Butter	5.50	6.45

	A LA CARTE	COMPLETE DINNER
SAUTEED FRESH LOBSTER MEAT Sauteed in Pure Creamery Butter	4.95	5.90
FRIED FRESH LOBSTER CHUNKS Deep Fried and Served with Drawn Butter	4.95	5.90
FRESH OPENED LOBSTER A LA NEWBURG En Casserole, Toast Points	4.95	5.90
BAKED STUFFED JUMBO SHRIMP Served with Drawn Butter	4.25	5.20
FRIED FRESH JUMBO SHRIMP Dipped in Batter and Fried to a Golden Brown	4.25	5.20
FRIED FRESH CAPE SCALLOPS — Tartar Sauce Small Tender Scallops Fried to a Golden Brown	3.75	4.70
FRIED FRESH BABY SEA SCALLOPS Fried to a Golden Brown	2.95	3.90
FRIED FRESH IPSWICH CLAMS — Tartar Sauce Small Clams Fried to a Golden Brown	2.95	3.90
BROILED SWORDFISH STEAK — Lemon Butter A Thick Slice of Fresh Swordfish, Broiled	3.25	4.20
FRIED FRESH SEAFOOD PLATE Shrimps — Clams — Cape Scallops	3.75	4.70
BROILED FRESH HALIBUT STEAK A Thick Steak of Fresh Halibut, Lemon Butter	3.25	4.20

This is an effective listing of both a la carte and complete dinners. A complete selling job is done on what the complete dinner consists of, and there is a real, big difference between it and the al la carte offering with a corresponding price spread.

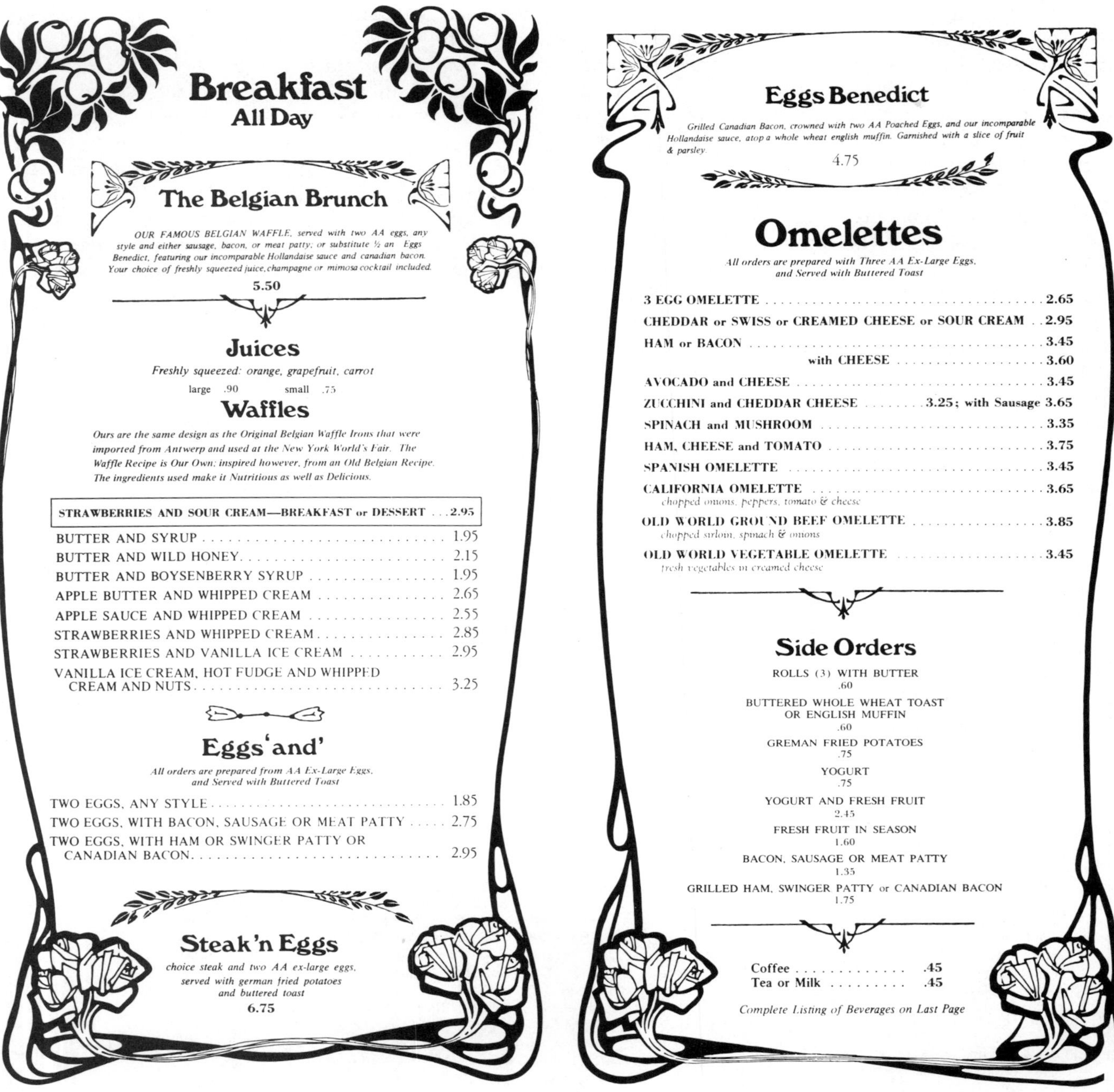

Breakfast
All Day

The Belgian Brunch

OUR FAMOUS BELGIAN WAFFLE, served with two AA eggs, any style and either sausage, bacon, or meat patty; or substitute ½ an Eggs Benedict, featuring our incomparable Hollandaise sauce and canadian bacon. Your choice of freshly squeezed juice, champagne or mimosa cocktail included.

5.50

Juices

Freshly squeezed: orange, grapefruit, carrot

large .90 small .75

Waffles

Ours are the same design as the Original Belgian Waffle Irons that were imported from Antwerp and used at the New York World's Fair. The Waffle Recipe is Our Own; inspired however, from an Old Belgian Recipe. The ingredients used make it Nutritious as well as Delicious.

STRAWBERRIES AND SOUR CREAM—BREAKFAST or DESSERT . . . 2.95

BUTTER AND SYRUP . . . 1.95
BUTTER AND WILD HONEY . . . 2.15
BUTTER AND BOYSENBERRY SYRUP . . . 1.95
APPLE BUTTER AND WHIPPED CREAM . . . 2.65
APPLE SAUCE AND WHIPPED CREAM . . . 2.55
STRAWBERRIES AND WHIPPED CREAM . . . 2.85
STRAWBERRIES AND VANILLA ICE CREAM . . . 2.95
VANILLA ICE CREAM, HOT FUDGE AND WHIPPED CREAM AND NUTS . . . 3.25

Eggs 'and'

All orders are prepared from AA Ex-Large Eggs, and Served with Buttered Toast

TWO EGGS, ANY STYLE . . . 1.85
TWO EGGS, WITH BACON, SAUSAGE OR MEAT PATTY . . . 2.75
TWO EGGS, WITH HAM OR SWINGER PATTY OR CANADIAN BACON . . . 2.95

Steak 'n Eggs

choice steak and two AA ex-large eggs, served with german fried potatoes and buttered toast

6.75

Eggs Benedict

Grilled Canadian Bacon, crowned with two AA Poached Eggs, and our incomparable Hollandaise sauce, atop a whole wheat english muffin. Garnished with a slice of fruit & parsley.

4.75

Omelettes

All orders are prepared with Three AA Ex-Large Eggs, and Served with Buttered Toast

3 EGG OMELETTE . . . 2.65
CHEDDAR or SWISS or CREAMED CHEESE or SOUR CREAM . . 2.95
HAM or BACON . . . 3.45
with CHEESE . . . 3.60
AVOCADO and CHEESE . . . 3.45
ZUCCHINI and CHEDDAR CHEESE . . . 3.25; with Sausage 3.65
SPINACH and MUSHROOM . . . 3.35
HAM, CHEESE and TOMATO . . . 3.75
SPANISH OMELETTE . . . 3.45
CALIFORNIA OMELETTE . . . 3.65
chopped onions, peppers, tomato & cheese
OLD WORLD GROUND BEEF OMELETTE . . . 3.85
chopped sirloin, spinach & onions
OLD WORLD VEGETABLE OMELETTE . . . 3.45
fresh vegetables in creamed cheese

Side Orders

ROLLS (3) WITH BUTTER
.60

BUTTERED WHOLE WHEAT TOAST OR ENGLISH MUFFIN
.60

GREMAN FRIED POTATOES
.75

YOGURT
.75

YOGURT AND FRESH FRUIT
2.45

FRESH FRUIT IN SEASON
1.60

BACON, SAUSAGE OR MEAT PATTY
1.35

GRILLED HAM, SWINGER PATTY or CANADIAN BACON
1.75

Coffee 45
Tea or Milk 45

Complete Listing of Beverages on Last Page

On both its breakfast and dinner menus, the Old World *restaurant lists a la carte and complete breakfasts or dinners.*

Appetizers

ASSORTED CHEESES W/CRACKERS 3.50
Cheddar, Swiss & Mozzarella

CRAB OR SHRIMP COCKTAIL
Choice of red cocktail sauce, or Neptune Dressing, or combine both for tutone flavor 4.50

Dinners

Prepared with the Finest Quality Pure Ground Beef. Your selection served with Crisp Green Dinner Salad or Soup (Clam Chowder 25¢ Extra). Rolls and Butter.

SWINGER STEAK
Ever Popular, And Delicious. A Whole 12 oz. Ground Beef, Mixed with Chopped Onions, Olives, Green Peppers and Natural Cheddar Cheese. Topped with Sauteed Onions.
5.95

SELECT GROUND BEEF STEAK
12 oz. Topped with Sauteed Onions.
5.45

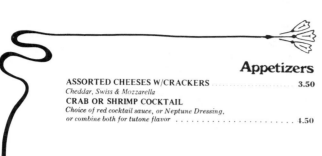

Specialities

PEASANT LUNCH #1 .... 2.75
Choice of Soup with Pumpernickel Roll, Cheddar Cheese and a Piece of Fruit (Clam Chowder 25¢ Extra)

PEASANT LUNCH #2 .... 2.75
Choice of Soup with Small Dinner Salad, Pumpernickel Rolls and Butter (Clam Chowder 25¢ extra)

BEEF STEW 4.25
Made with Fresh Vegetables and Served with Crisp Green Salad, Pumpernickel Roll and Butter.

Side Orders

Cottage Cheese .... .75
Potato Salad .... .75
Fresh Cooked Vegetable ... .75
Brown Organic Rice ..... .75

Appetizers

AVOCADO SURPRISE A LA OLD WORLD 3.75
Layers of Avocado and Whole Bay Shrimp, Served with Neptune Dressing and Lemon Wedges

AVOCADO VINEGARETTE 2.75
Sliced Avocado Served on a Bed of Lettuce with Tomato, Cucumber and our Special House Dressing

Dinners

Your Choice of Freshly Cooked Vegetables or German Fried Potatoes. Baked Potato available after 5 p.m.

NEW YORK STEAK
A Real Tender Cut. The Very Best.
8.95

BROILED SALMON STEAK
Flavorings of Lemon, White Wine, Pinch of Garlic and Oil. Served with Vegetable
7.25

VEGETARIAN DINNER
Organically Grown Vegetables Merged Chinese Fashion into a Well Sized Patty (Meatless), Topped with Sauteed Onion.
5.50

BAKED CHICKEN
Shelton Farm organically grown Chicken.
6.25

Vegetarian and Otherwise

VEGETABLE CASSEROLE 3.45
Fresh Vegetables in a Rich Cream Sauce, Topped with Melted Cheddar Cheese. Roll and Butter.

VEGEBURGER (Mandarin Style) 3.45
Organically Grown Vegetables Merged Chinese Fashion into a Patty (Meatless) Served on Whole Wheat Sesame Bun, Sliced Tomato and Onion, German Fried Potatoes.

THE MEDITERRANEAN 5.00
Ground Beef or White Meat Turkey, Dinner Salad with a Dish of Yogurt with Fruit.

German Fried Potatoes ... .75
Yogurt, Plain .... .75
Baked Potato .... .90
Fresh Fruit 1.65

Beverages & Desserts →

47

Inflation and the menu

The restaurant operator will continue to live with and operate a business in an inflationary environment. Only the rate will change, and most likely upwards. Inflation is like the weather—everybody talks about it, and reacts to it, but nobody (especially the politicians) does much about it. But unlike the weather, inflation is not an act of nature; it is created by man.

There are as many explanations for its cause and cure as there are economists, bankers, politicians, and professors. The result is confusion and continued inflation. So what is inflation? It is a general increase in prices caused largely by unsound government fiscal and monetary policies. Under noninflationary economic conditions, prices continually change. Some go up while others go down. This is the result of free-market mechanisms, the function of which is to encourage increased investment in some sectors and to discourage investment in others. But when inflation is present, all prices rise.

There are lags between the price increases of the various sectors of the economy in the earlier less virulent stages of inflation, and such lags work to the advantage of those who get their increase first. But, as more segments of the economy grow familiar with the process, the interval between price increases grows shorter, until little or no advantage is gained by those who initiate the next round. The name of the game comes to be "catch-up."

Inflation also affects wages as well as prices. Employees get wage increases, generally proportionate to the rise in price levels. Again, there may be a lag between increases in prices and wages, but this is temporary and will yield no significant long-term advantages to either employees or employers. So if neither restaurant employees nor restaurant operators gain by inflation, why do we have it?

According to Adam Smith, the father of economic theory, inflation is "a disguised form of bankruptcy." Bankruptcy is when a debtor is overextended financially and cannot repay creditors. The debtor then resorts to legal proceedings, and the courts take charge. Equitable distribution of the bankrupt person's assets is made, and the debtor is released from further obligation.

Similar to the person nearing bankruptcy, we, as a society and a nation, are up to our necks in debt. The total U.S. indebtedness—government, corporations, and individuals—is in the *trillions.* And where did this borrowed money come from? From the savings of the American people, accumulated over many generations, because for each dollar *owed* by borrowers, there is a dollar *owned* by savers.

Inflation, of course, affects borrowers and lenders (with saver's money) differently. A rate of inflation of 13 percent over a period of a year, reduces the value of money in a bank, or being loaned, by 13 percent, but it gives the borrower a windfall of 13 percent. Unless interest rates are raised to cover completely the rate of inflation, to pay off the saver, he suffers big losses, while borrowers make unearned profits. Inflation thus becomes the equivalent of an undeclared form of bankruptcy because it involves the repayment of debts with greatly depreciated currencies.

Borrowing and inflation have also become a way of life for governments. To gain favor with voters, politicians pass bills giving money to various pressure groups. To pay for these expenditures, taxes are increased, but never enough to balance the budget. Instead, governments borrow and wait for inflation to make up the difference. Some cities in America have already gone so far down this borrowing route as to become bankrupt, but the federal government, of course, has another alternative—it can print more money.

In Germany in 1923, for example, the printing presses and the paper mills couldn't keep up with the demand for paper money. The ordinary presses of newspapers were used, and at one point 30 paper mills worked at full capacity around the clock to deliver note paper to 150 printing firms that had 2,000 presses running day and night printing *Reichsbank* notes. By the winter of 1923, the German mark was literally not worth the paper it was printed on.

The restaurateur, as a business man and entrepeneur has more freedom to maneuver in an inflationary environment than an employee on a payroll. The restaurateur can invest profits in durable goods—real estate (a bigger restaurant), valuable decor (paintings, sculptures), or even an expanded wine cellar whose contents, if properly selected, will increase in value in a few years. But the restaurateur cannot avoid the continually increasing cost of doing business. Food costs keep going up. The cost of utilities—heat, lighting, and air conditioning—keeps increasing, and the tax bite grows. In fact, due primarily to inflation, between 1971 and 1977 taxes collected by all forms of government in this country increased by 59.4 percent!

To meet these increasing costs and operate at a profit, the food service operator must constantly monitor and change prices. This means more attention to the menu, more menu changes and consideration of a menu that will "work" better in inflationary times. Several factors should be taken into consideration.

First, an expensive menu can be expensive to change. A way of getting around this is by having an expensive, 4-color or 2-color cover printed on heavy, coated stock and then have four, eight, or twelve inside pages on lighter stock and printed in only one color. The changes in the inside pages can then be made at less expense while the cover does not have to be changed at all.

Another popular way of reducing menu reprinting and changing costs is to use the newspaper format, printed on cheap newsprint. *Beall's 1860 Recorder* of *Beall's* restaurant in Macon, Georgia, is an example of this type of menu. Printed in one color, dark brown, on newsprint (page size 11½″ × 17″), the front and back covers have old stories and ads from 1860. The inside spread has more old ads plus the food listing—*Beall's* 1860 Midday Provisions—*Beall's* 1860 Extras—and *Beall's* 1860 Potables. Thirteen food items and twelve wines and liqueurs are listed. One dessert—Proprietor's Crowning Provision—a richly tempting dessert freshly made in *Beall's* own kitchen—has no price, just the word "ask." A side benefit of this type of menu is that because of its low cost, it can be given away for more advertising mileage. In a box at the top of the front cover, the copy reads, "Feel free to take our menu home, as a souvenir of your visit to *Beall's* 1860."

Another way of approaching the rapid escalation of costs in an inflationary environment is to have a limited menu. The fewer the items, the less there is to change. The *Port O'Georgetown* restaurant in Washington, D.C., is a good example of a limited luncheon menu. It lists five sandwiches under one price—$2.95; and two salads, also with one price for both—$3.95. Then a Buffet Luncheon Bar for $4.25 (Soup of the Day plus the Salad Bar) is listed; and finally, two Desserts are listed for $1.25 and five beverages are offered at $.50 each.

Gulliver's restaurant in Los Angeles has a limited menu also. Only one entree or Main Course is offered—Roasted Prime Ribs of Beef—for $7.95. It is presented in three ways: Gulliver's Cut—a generous slice; Prime Minister's Cut—thinly sliced in the English manner; and the Big Indian Cut—the outside slice, brown and crusty. A Tureen of Today's Pottage or Glubbdubdrib Sallet is included in the fore-Dishes and Yorkshire Pudding, Spinach Souffle and yet another Vegetable of the Season is included for the $7.95 price. Four desserts—Wondrous Kickshaaws and Confections—are listed for one price, $1.25, and four beverages wind up this limited menu at $1.50 for the liqueur drinks and $.40 for mocha-java coffee and English tea.

This 10″ × 16″ one-page menu has a 4-color illustration on one side showing Gulliver's travels, and the food listing is in black and red on a tan background on the other side. The illustrations are attractive, and the hand lettering (calligraphy) gives an authentic Olde English flavor. But more importantly, this menu can adapt quickly and easily to inflation conditions.

The Terrarium restaurant of the Ramada Inn has a very well-designed, written, and printed menu that has several cost cutting and anti-inflation features. The cover is black on green paper with a die-cut hole through which the yellow inside shows through with the name *Terrarium* printed on it.

This Daily Newspaper presented with the compliments of the Proprietor. 315 COLLEGE STREET MACON, GEORGIA 912-745-1780 The authenticity of the stories contained herein has been meticulously maintained.

THE CITY.

A Series of Mishaps.

Our first paper was ushered into existence yesterday morning at ½ past 2 o'clock. If its future destiny is like the superstition about marriages happening in stormy weather our most sanguine hopes will be realized. For without exception the night was the darkest we have ever experienced. The Heavens were covered with masses of thick clouds, the rain was beating in our face unmercifully, driven by a cutting wind, and we hastened on to our sleeping apartment. Before we had proceeded fifty yards upon the sidewalk, walking fast and stepping high, a dry goods box disputed our passage in such a manner as to send us sprawling into a gutter. We picked ourselves up leisurely and hat, too, which had rolled off into the middle of the street and was found by mere chance. At Boardman's corner a lamp post made us march right oblique and feel for our head. Just then the clouds in the direction of the Presbyterian Church separated for a little while and allowed a faint light to open upon our pathway, and we thought ourselves secure from further interception, when suddenly something struck us in the breast nearly upsetting us again. Upon examination we discovered we had "faced a cannon's mouth" in front of the house containing the three beautiful field pieces of the Jackson Artillery. This was not one of them, but perhaps was used in the defence of Fort Hawkins, judging from its ancient appearance. Finally, we reached our room, though the old cannon must have been ashamed of the rencountre, for to our astonishment in the morning, it was out of the carriage and lying upon the ground.

We do not wish to impress upon readers that our vision was dimmed by extraneous causes; *pas du tout!*

A report has been in circulation during the past week, obtained we believe from the agent of the Marsh Troupe, in reference to Miss Georgia Hodson; that she died recently in California. We have made inquiries of those who are posted on such matters and conclude that such is not the fact. Miss Hodson is a great favorite there and it affords us great pleasure to contradict the rumor.

No Northern Mail.—The train from Augusta failed to make connection with that from Savannah, thus depriving us of several of our exchanges.

A camphere lamp exploded in a gentleman's hand two or three days ago while he was lighting one of the wicks by turning the lamp downward —. His hand was badly burnt. We did not find out his name nor residence.

Ship Burned.—Ship John J. Boyd, laden for Liverpool, was burned in New York on Monday. Cargo included 500 bales of Cotton and was valued at $130,000. Ship at $60,000.

Brunswick Herald.—An advertising sheet comes to us from this office in which Mr. Griffin makes an appeal to his debtors to meet the heavy outlay incident to renewing his office, which, it will be remembered has been recently destroyed by fire.— We hope, therefore, soon to see the Herald revived.

The merchants of Atlanta held a meeting, last Monday night, "for the purpose of resolving and pledging themselves to withdraw their patronage from firms in New York, and other places, known to be hostile to the South." All right. But could they not do as much as that, without a public meeting and without pledges?

Desirable Residence

FOR SALE !

The undersigned is authorized to offer for sale a new and elegant residence on College Hill.

The lot contains about one acre and sixteen square feet and is within pleasant walking distance of the business portion of the city. The House which has been very recently completed, contains ten rooms, a large hall, four wardrobe closets, three large shleved closets, a large and airy pantry with sink and other conveniences. The rooms are lofty and spacious and the whole house constructed in the most thorough and workman-like manner.

On the lot is a well finished kitchen with servant rooms, cow house, &c. &c. Close by the kitchen is a deep well of as fine water as can be found in Macon, and near the house a never failing cistern of rain water with a good metallic pump.

Those who wish a handsome residence convenient to the centre of the city had better apply immediately as there are few such houses and lots left open for purchase.

feb 1 d-ly JAMES MERCER GREEN.

Macon & Western Railroad.

MACON, July 1st, 1859.

On and after Thursday, the 15th inst., the Passenger Trains of this Road will run as follows:

Leave Macon .... 12 night.
Arrive at Atlanta .... 7.15 A.M.
Leave Macon .... 10 A.M.
Arrive at Atlanta .... 4 P.M.
Leave Atlanta .... 12 night.
Arrive at Macon .... 7.15 A.M.
Leave Atlanta .... 11 A.M.
Arrive at Macon .... 5 P.M.

The Night Trains will not be run on Sundays.

The 10 o'clock A.M. train from Macon, connects with the Western and Atlantic Rail Road at Atlanta, for all points beyond Atlanta. And the 12 o'clock night train connects at Atlanta with the Georgia and West Point Rail Roads.

ALFRED L. TYLER,
feb 1 d-tf Superintendent.

SPRING IMPORTATIONS, 1860.

RIBBONS,

Millinery and Straw Goods.

ARMSTRONG, CATOR & CO.

IMPORTERS & JOBBERS OF:
Ribbons, Bonnets, Silks and Satins, VELVETS, RUCHES, FLOWERS, FEATHERS, STRAW BONNETS, FLATS, &C.
No. 237 and Lofts of 238 Baltimore St. BALTIMORE MD.

Offer a Stock Unsurpassed in the United States in variety and cheapness.

Orders solicited and prompt attention given. TERMS, 8 months, six per cent off cash par funds.

ian 24 — 6t

EMPLOYMENT

$50 A MONTH AND ALL EXPENSES PAID. — An agent is wanted in every town and county in the United States, to engage in a respectable and easy business, by which the above profits may be certainly realized. For further particulars, address Dr. J. HENRY WARNER, corner of 12th Street and Broadway, New York City, enclosing one Postage Stamp.

jan.31 d&w 3m

HAIR JEWELRY !

MRS. GIOVANNINI & SMITH,

Artist in Hair,

MACON, GA.

Respectfully announce to the public that they receive and execute orders in Hair-braided Necklaces, Broaches, Pins, Ear-Rings, Finger-Rings, Chatelains, Gents' Vest Chains, Sleeve Buttons, Studs, &c. — 200 different patterns. As fine work as can be obtained in Paris or New York. Specimens of our work can be seen at the Jewelry Store of Messrs. J.A. & S.S. Virgin, on Cotton Avenue, where orders may be got and prices ascertained. Particular attention paid to orders and communications received by mail or express. Residence on New St., near T. Harris Feg.

feb 1 d-3m

Liquors.

PALE AND COGNAC BRANDY.
Old Bourbon and Rye WHISKEY.
Madera and Port WINE.
Champagne WINES.

feb. 1 **LIQUORS GENERALLY**
ALWAYS ON HAND.
FEARS & PRITCHETT

DOCTORS

McDONALD & VAN GIESEN,

DENTISTS.

Office in Washington Block, West Side.

feb 2 d-ly

NEW YORK COTTON MARKET.

New York, Feb. 1st, 1860.

One thousand bales of cotton sold to day. Market very dull.

Correspondence of the Daily Telegraph,
From Jones County.

Clinton, Jan. 30th, 1860.

Mr. Editor — The talk of building a Rail Road from Augusta direct to Macon revives once more the hopes of the Clintonians — for at present and for the last decade, we have been nothing but outside Barbarians. Now don't think I mean this literally, for we are a little sensitive — but so far as intercourse with the world and the rest of mankind are concerned, we are minus every thing but a horse-back mail. We look upon the horse as a great institution, for to him are we indebted for all we enjoy in the way of letters, papers, &c.

It should be borne in mind, also, that our present indefatigable mail rider, Wm. B. Legs, with that spirit of accommodation that characterises Uncle Sam's riders, daily furnishes our citizens, from horseback, shad, new boots, garden seed, pants, band-boxes, plow lines, rolls of leather, &c., &c. So here's to Wm. B. Legs and his *severely trained* horse, Lightning. Long may they wave!

What we want you to do, Mr. Editor, is to throw in a few licks for old Clinton, and try and prevail on them Aususta people to bring their Rail Road right by our town. Don't ask us to take much stock, unless the Augusta folks will insure us a Depot and an Eating House. We have in our town a large brick house, that for a sufficient consideration the owner would sell to the Rail Road Co., and it would make a splendid freight and passenger depot, and its owner is just the man to keep the eating house, having already buildings suitable.

More anon, yours,

CLINTON.

NEW ICE HOUSE
GREER & FREEMAN
ELY'S BUILT A

NEW ICE HOUSE

AT THE PASSENGER DEPOT,

For the purpose of receiving and re-shipping and have made arrangements to deliver the articles by the Truck or Car Load, at as low a figure as any other house can or will.

OUR CITY EXPRESS

Will run in connection with all Passenger Trains, and deliver Goods bought of us *free of charge* to all trains.

Choice Family Groceries

Received weekly by Steamon.

Pure Brandies & Wines — Daly's

AROMATIC WHISKEY.

The best known. And all other kinds of the finest quality of Liquors. One of the largest assortments of pure Havana Cigars, (comprising all the favorite brands) ever offered in the city. Apples, Oranges, Lemons, Pine Apples, Nuts, Candies, Figs,-Pickles in any shape and quantity to suit pruchasers. The best of Family Teas, Coffee, Sugar, Golden and Double Extra Syrup, Fig Haine, Dried Beef and Tongues, Bologna, Sausages, dried and pickled Fish, &c.

COWLES SUPER CREAM CHEESE.

Pine Apple and State Cheese, Pure Leaf Lard and the best Table Butter made.

SHAD & OYSTERS

In any quantity put up to order. TOYS and FIRE WORKS a large assortment of every description made.

A good supply of every article usually kept in a first-class Family Grocery Store. We guarantee satisfaction in quality and price, and solicit a continuance of the public patronage. TERMS: Prompt pay, monthly.

Cherry Street, Macon, Ga.

feb 1 d-ly

BEARDEN, GAINES & CO.
WHOLESALE AND RETAIL DEALERS IN
BOOTS and SHOES,
LEATHER & FINDINGS,
MACON, GA.

When our work rips we repair free of charge.
Feb. 1 tf

ADVERTISING. — Discontinuing to advertise, says the Philadelphia Bulletin, is like taking down one's own sign. It is a sort of intimation of retirement from business, and the public treat it as such. Or they may regard it as evidence that something has gone wrong, which requires privacy for investigation. Whatever construction may be put upon it, the result is disastrous.

B.A. WISE,
IMPORTER OF
AND DEALER IN
House Furnishing
GOODS
STOVES, GRATES

Does Your Saddle Hurt?
THEN RIDE
THE DUPLEX SAFETY SADDLE
SEE THAT SPRING!

COLUMBIA BICYCLE.

THE POPE MANUFACTURING CO.,
85 Summer St., Boston, Mass.

SPAULDINGS GLUE
ECONOMY!
Dispatch!
Save the Pieces!

As accidents will happen, even in well-regulated families, it is very desirable to have some cheap and convenient way of repairing Furniture, Toys, Crockery, etc.

Spalding's Prepared Glue

meets all such emergencies, and no household can afford to be without it. It is always ready, and up to the sticking point. There is no longer a necessity for limping chairs, splintered corners, headless dolls and broken cradles. It is just the article for cone, shell and other ornamental work, so popular with ladies of refinement and taste.

This admirable preparation is used cold, being chemically held in solution and possessing all the valuable qualities of the best cabinet makers' glue. It may be used in the place of ordinary mucilage being vastly more adhesive.

"USEFUL IN EVERY HOUSE"

N.B. — A Brush accompanies each bottle.

Price, 25 Cents.

COMMERCIAL.
MACON PRICES CURRENT

	UNIT		TO
BAGGING - Kentucky none	yard	00	00
India	yard	14	14½
BALE ROPE - Hand Spun	lb.	8	9
Machine Spun	lb.	8½	9
BACON - Sides, Ribbed	lb.	11½	12
Shoulders	lb.	9	9½
Hams	lb.	12	14
Hams - Canvassed	lb.	13	14
Tenn. Clear Sides	lb.	12½	13
Shoulders	lb.	1	10½
Hams	lb.		15
BUTTER - Goshen	lb.		33
Western	lb.	22	25
BLANKETS	pair	2.00	2.75
CANDLES - Star	lb.	22	25
Amantine	lb.	24	28
Sperm	lb.	48	60
CHEESE - Western	lb.	14	15
Northern	lb.	13	14
COFFEE - Rio	lb.	12	14
Laguira	lb.	14	15
Java	lb.	17	19
Mocha	lb.	19	20
CORDAGE - Manilla	lb.	11	22½
Cotton	lb.	18	22
Jute	lb.	9	12½
FEATHERS	lb.	50	55
CEMENT	bbl.	2.75	3.00
FISH - Mackerel No. 1	bbl.	17.50	18.00
Mackerel No. 2	bbl.	16.00	17.00
Mackerel No. 3	bbl.	11.50	12.50
FLOUR - Superfine	bbl.	8.05	8.50
Choice Extra	bbl.	9.00	10.00
GRAIN - Corn	bu.	1.00	1.10
Oats	bu.	85	90
Rye	bu.		
Peas	bu.	90	1.00
Wheat	bu.	1.50	1.50
HIDES	lb.	12	13
Bran	100#	1.00	1.25
Meal	bu.	1.25	1.35
WHISKEY - Pike's	gal.	36	40
Ward & Careys	gal.	34	35
Pure Corn	gal.	34	35
Mapes' superphosphate of lime	ton	3.15	3.30
GUNNY BAGS - New	bag	14	00
Second-hand	bag	10	00
GUNPOWDER	keg	6½	7.00
HAY - Northern	100#	1.50	1.60
Eastern	100#	1.75	2.00
IRON - American	lb.	8½	4½
Swedes	lb.	4½	5
Casting	lb.	03¾	04
KERSEYS	yard	16	28
LARD - In Barrels	lb.	12½	13
In Kegs - New	lb.	14	15
LIME - Philadelphia	hhd.	00.00	00.00
Thomaston & Shelby	bbl.	2.00	2.25
LEAD - Bar	lb.	8	10
MOLASSES - In Barrels	gal.	33	35
In Hogheads	gal.	32	32
NAILS	lb.	4	5½
WOOL HATS	doz.	6.00	12.50
OIL - Sperm	gal.	1.00	2.00
Tanner's	bbl.	12.00	14.00
Linseed	gal.	.80	1.00
Linseed boiled	gal.	.90	1.00
POTASH	lb.	7	9
Concentrated	lb.	15	15
Russets, South'n	pr.	1.50	1.60
PORK - Mess	bbl.	18.00	20.00
Rump	bbl.	00.00	00.00
PLASTER	bbl.	3.00	3.50
POTATOES - Eating	bbl.	3.75	4.00
Planting	bbl.	3.50	3.75
PAINTS - White, lead, pure	lb.	8	10½
Zinc	lb.	9	10
RICE	lb.	4½	5
SALT - Liverpool	sack	1.50	1.75
Alum	sack	1.50	1.75
Table, large sacks	sack	3.50	3.50
SPICES - Pepper	lb.	10	15
Ginger	lb.	9	12½
SUGAR - Fair	lb.	10	10½
Prime	lb.	10½	11
Choice	lb.	11	12
Clarified	lb.	10	12
Loaf	lb.	12½	14
SOAP - Turpentine	lb.	5	6½
Family	lb.	6	8
STARCH	lb.	8	10
SYRUP - New Orleans	bbl.	62	65
Georgia	bbl.	70	75
SHOT - Buck	bag	2.15	2.25
Small	bag	2.00	2.10

Cuticura SOAP Makes Soft WHITE HANDS

Stories and ads from 1860 add old-time flavor to Beall's *menu. Its low cost enables this menu to be given away–an inexpensive form of advertising.*

The inside eight pages are of yellow paper with the copy and decorations printed in black. Thus, by using two different colored papers, and printing on them in black, the result is a 3-color menu.

Inside, the prices, instead of being listed as usual with numbers, $1.75, are written out—One dollar and seventy-five cents. The customer is not fooled, of course. Either way the price is the same, but on the menu itself, the price does not stand out, flag attention, or probably irritate the customer as much, in these days of rising prices.

The other facet of the *Terrarium* menu which helps the restaurant manager control costs and insure profits is that nearly everything is listed a la carte. The Entrees include a choice of master salad or soupe du jour, and choice of potato or vegetable du jour, but all of the other soups, salads, appetizers, and desserts are a la carte. In addition, there is an Entree Crepes/Palacsinta listing, and even the coffee, tea, hot chocolate, and milk are listed a la carte at thirty-five cents.

The ultimate, inflation-proof menu is one with *no prices! The Depot* restaurant in South Miami, Florida, has a Florida East Coast Railway Time Tables menu which has a complete selection of cocktails, appetizers, soups, salads, entrees (U.S. Prime Aged Beef and Seafood Specialties), potatoes, rice and pasta, Exceptional Desserts and After Dinner drinks—*but has no printed prices.*

If all of the cocktails, appetizers, entrees,

BEALL'S 1860 MIDDAY PROVISIONS

Served 11:30 AM to 5:00 PM

All Beall's Midday entrees include Steak Fries, a bountiful make it yourself salad from our salad bar, fresh baked bread, and creamery fresh butter. Thank you for lunching at Beall's!

College Hill Beef on a Bun:
Ground aged beef is chopped and formed to fit a butter basted bun two fingers larger than our butcher's hand. 2.45
with melted cheese. 2.55

Beall's Soup 'n' Salad Buffet:
A generous cup of Beall's rich and popular peanut soup and a serve yourself salad from Beall's bountiful salad bar. 2.20

Beall's Bay Crab Benedict:
We begin with fresh muffins and build carefully from there. A generous pile of newly netted crabmeat is blanketed with our mellow blended cheese sauce and garnished with pride. 3.45

Roast Prime Rib Sandwich:
Carved to order from the same aged loins we feature on our evening menu and served with Beall's own southern touch. 3.95

1860 Club Steak:
Specially cut and aged beef prepared to match your specifications and your discerning taste. 3.85

Sliced Strip Steak AuJus:
Delicate and tender slices of aged strip steak draped across fresh baked bread and smothered with our Chef's best AuJus. 3.55

Beall's Unlimited Salad Bar: 1.75
Freshness and Variety (a truly meal in itself).

BEALL'S 1860 EXTRAS

Each, carefully selected and prepared to perfectly complement your meal at Beall's.

Beall's Peanut Soup:
Served by the cup, this piping hot taste treat has become a Beall's tradition virtually overnight. Rich and Delicious! .60

Shrimp Cocktail:
Large, tender, carefully boiled gulf shrimp are crowded around Beall's startling cocktail sauce. 1.95

Garden Fresh Mushrooms:
We gently deep fry our mushrooms to seal their delicate flavor. The perfect complement to any entree on our menu. 1.50

Beverages:
Coffee, Tea or Milk. .30

Proprietor's Crowning Provision:
A richly tempting dessert freshly made in Beall's own kitchen . . . Ask

Lively Desserts You Can Drink!

Gentle Mint:
An anxious chill of fulfilled anticipation will most certainly accompany your first taste of our Gentle Mint. Hauntingly smooth creme de menthe is carefully blended with rich ice cream to help you re-live chilly fall evenings on the porch of the plantation. 1.45

Old Fashion Chocolate:
Stick-Ball games, Nikel cups of ice cream, and wooden spoons come to mind when first you savor our old fashion chocolate liqueur dessert drink . . . Chilled and blended to satisfy the true chocolate connoisseur who remembers the way it used to be. 1.45

Tantalizing Coffee Beans:
A steamy Brazilian coffee plantation would be the perfect atmosphere . . . After your meal the perfect time . . . This essence of rich whole coffee liqueur will delight you! The ultimate dessert adventure! 1.45

BEALL'S 1860 POTABLES

In addition to your favorite cocktails from our upstairs bar we're proud to offer the following wine selection:

RED, ROSE, OR WHITE

Glass	½ Carafe	Carafe
.75	2.25	4.00

	½ Bottle	Full Bottle
RED WINES		
Cabernet Sauvignon, Almaden	4.00	7.00
Tytell Beaujolais	3.75	6.00
Zinfandel, Almaden	3.25	5.25
Taylor Lake Country Red	2.75	4.75
ROSE WINES		
Lancers	4.75	9.00
Mateus	4.00	7.50
WHITE WINES		
Blue Nun Liebfraumilch	4.50	8.50
Mateus	4.00	7.50
SPARKLING WINES		
Chateau Laurent, Champagne or Burgundy	4.00	7.00

desserts, etc. are *one price*, the waiter or waitress can be expected to remember and quote prices (a good approach) or prices can be written in (a bad approach). The prices stand out and tell the customer that they are being changed daily.

During times of inflation, a restaurant operator must plan for changing the menu more often than in the past. This means not just price increases, but changing, or at least considering changing, the whole menu more often. With an inflation rate of 1 percent a month, the cost of doing business will increase 6 percent in half a year. Thus, if prices lag, profit margins will suffer, and by changing items as well as prices, the customer will be less aware of the constant increase in the same items. Also, with seasonal vegetables and fruits plus variations in beef, pork, veal, poultry, and seafood costs, a changing menu can take advantage of the changing market.

Finally, there is always the possibility of wage and price controls being enacted by the U.S. Congress at the request of the President. The menu, therefore, that does not reflect current cost, may be "frozen" at a price level disadvantageous to the restaurant manager or owner.

To recapitulate, the following rules can be used as guidelines for the menu during inflationary times:

1. Design your menu for easy price changes.

2. Limit the size of your food and beverage listing and use one price (if possible) for categories of menu listings—entrees, salads, desserts, etc.
3. Extend the a la carte listing if a limited menu is not possible.
4. Use tip-ons, daily specials, place mats, and table tents which allow for flexibility in price and selection.
5. Present food and drink items in a new, romantic, imaginative way instead of just increasing prices.

GULLIVER'S

established 1970

· Bill of Fare ·

· Fore-Dishes ·
your selection: either a
Tureen of Today's Pottage
or Glubbdubdrib Sallet
prepared by your Wench at tableside

· the Main Course ·
Roasted Prime Ribs of Beef
Gulliver's Cut - a generous slice
Prime Minister's Cut - Thinly sliced in the English manner
Big-Endian Cut - the outside slice, brown & crusty
· Escorts for the above ·
Yorkshire Pudding – Spinach Souffle
and yet another Vegetable of the season
7.95

· Wondrous Kickshaws & Confections ·
Trifle Pudding. sherried of course
Vanilla Rum Mousse. Raspberry sauce
Apple Crumb Cake wyth Devonshire cream
Chocolate Temptation
1.25

· Coffees, Teas, and Grogs ·
Lilliput cino 1.50 Mocha-Java Coffee .70
Irish Coffee 1.50 English Tea .70

Gulliver's lists a relatively limited number of items. This reduces the problem of price changes due to inflation.

Under certain conditions a menu can be printed with no prices listed.

THE DEPOT SOUPS

CRISP FRENCH ONION AU GRATIN
A hearty broth full of thinly sliced onions, imported parmesan and jarlsberg cheese and topped with very crisp, shoestring, fried onions. Baked and served in a casserole.

EACH DAY A DIFFERENT SELECTION
Our Chef prepares delicious homemade Award Winning Soups: some hot, some chilled. Your Stationmaster knows today's specialty.

APPETIZERS

THE FRESHEST FROM THE SEA

JUMBO PANAMANIAN SHRIMP
ALASKAN KING OR JUMBO LUMP CRABMEAT
(each seasonal)
FRESHLY SHELLED LOBSTER
SEAFOOD COMBINATION OF SHRIMP, LOBSTER AND CRABMEAT
ROMANOFF BELUGA MALOSSOL CAVIAR
FILET OF SMOKED RAINBOW TROUT
JUMBO FLORIDA STONE CRABS (seasonal)
SAUCES: Drawn Butter, Red Horseradish, Remoulade, Mustard

SOMETHING DIFFERENT

QUICHE LORRAINE
BROILED JUMBO MUSHROOMS STUFFED WITH CRABMEAT
FRESHLY SHELLED LOBSTER, SHRIMP AND CRABMEAT SAUTEED IN SHALLOT BUTTER
COQUILLE OF NATIVE SHELLFISH
BARBECUED CANADIAN BABY PORK BACK RIBS

SALADS

COMPLIMENTS OF THE DEPOT

This evening with your dinner, your Stationmaster will prepare your individual specialty salad (each subject to seasonal availability).

FRESH SPINACH SALAD
With crumbled bacon, deviled egg, and fresh sliced mushrooms. Served with a delicious blend of oil, wine vinegar, and freshly ground pepper. Garnished with fresh garden vegetables.

FRESH GREENS AND SLICED BEEFSTEAK TOMATOES
With your choice of our famous homemade dressings: French Roquefort Cheese, Russian, Vinaigrette, and our Award Winning Green Goddess Garlic.

SALADES EXTRAORDINAIRES

THE DEPOT'S FRESH SEAFOOD SALAD
Lobster, Shrimp, and Crabmeat combined with Hearts of Palm, Fancy Mixed Greens, Tomatoes, and our Unique Depot Dressing.

FRESH SLICED MUSHROOMS TOSSED IN ROQUEFORT
Jumbo mushroom caps thinly sliced, marinated in our famous vinaigrette and tossed with fresh watercress and crumbled, imported French Roquefort Cheese.

CHILLED JUMBO TIPS OF IMPORTED WHITE ASPARAGUS
These tender delights are served with our special Depot Mustard Sauce, Vinaigrette, or Hollandaise.

SALADE CAESAR
Our own version of the classic.

With your dinner, THE DEPOT'S Chef invites you to enjoy an assortment of freshly baked rolls, banana bread, sweet butter, and a daily selection of potatoes, rice, or pasta. An excellent fresh vegetable is prepared each day. It is available upon request.

THE DEPOT

U.S. PRIME AGED BEEF
FROM OUR EXHIBITION BROILERS

Only 10% to 12% of all beef has the quality to be graded U.S. PRIME. 100% of our beef is just that!

THE DEPOT takes extreme pride in featuring the finest Prime Heavy Western Beef obtainable. All of our beef is personally selected by our buyers and shipped to us directly from the Nation's leading packer of incomparable quality, MONFORT OF COLORADO.

It is then stored and aged at exacting temperatures, with controlled humidity and exceptionally fine circulation in our own beef aging rooms. Many eating establishments claim that aged meat is when the beef is two or three weeks old. We have found that extra—extra quality beef continues to improve for four, five, even six weeks. Like great wines that improve for 50 years, properly aged beef gets sweeter, more tender, and acquires a taste that cannot be duplicated.

This is our kind of beef. Each steak that we serve has been carefully cut and trimmed of all excess fat, to our rigid specifications, by our own staff butcher. It will be prepared to your exacting order in our gleaming, stainless steel, exhibition kitchen.

PRIME, AGED NEW YORK STRIP STEAK
Carefully cut from the center of the loin. If you request, our Chef will prepare this steak with imported, crushed, Madagascar Peppercorns.

THE DEPOT PRIME RIBS OF ROAST BEEF
Roasted in a rock salt cast to preserve all the natural juices. Served with our own Au Jus. In order to insure the highest of quality, we prepare a limited amount each day. Pardon us if we should occasionally be out.

TOURNEDOS OF PRIME BEEF ATLANTIC
Our Award Winning Filet Mignon prepared to your order and surrounded with freshly shelled lobster or Alaskan King Crabmeat sautéed in shallot butter with mushrooms, scallions and a hint of garlic.

KABOB OF PRIME TENDERLOIN TERIYAKI
Skewered Prime Tenderloin marinated in our own Teriyaki recipe and broiled to your exacting order. Mushroom caps and The Depot's Rice Pilaf are served with this culinary masterpiece.

PRIME FILET MIGNON
Aging makes this filet more flavorful and sweeter than the usual filet. If you desire, our Chef will wrap it with a thick slice of hickory smoked bacon prior to broiling.
You may wish to try our superb Bearnaise Sauce of Herb Butter with either steak. An individual order of Sautéed Fresh Mushroom Caps is available upon order.

PRIME FILET MIGNON STROGONOFF
Prepared to your individual order. Our Chef carefully slices and sautées tender strips of Prime Tenderloin to your liking. Then seconds before serving, he adds our excellent strogonoff sauce and sautéed fresh mushrooms. The Depot's Rice Pilaf or tiny buttered egg noodles accompany this entree.

TWO PRIME LOIN LAMB CHOPS
Another MONFORT OF COLORADO SPECIALTY. THE DEPOT butcher cuts these magnificent chops from the center of the loin. Our Chef will prepare them to your order.

MEDALLIONS OF BABY VEAL
AU CHASSEUR: Without question, the finest "plume de veau" available. A classic Sauce Chasseur prepared with loving care by our Executive Chef.

AU SEMINOLE: Sautéed "plume de veau" topped with jumbo lump crabmeat or shelled lobster, sautéed mushrooms and sauce bearnaise.

AU ROSTANG: A "classic" French recipe. Medallions of "plume de veau" are lightly sautéed in butter, shallots, white wine and fresh lemon.

ROAST LONG ISLAND DUCKLING
With Tawny Port Wine and Grand Mariner Sauce. Unfortunately, a very limited amount of this great Gourmet's Delight can be prepared each day. Pardon us please if we should not have it available.

BARBECUED, CANADIAN BABY PORK BACK RIBS
Very, very lean. Marinated and prepared with our Executive Chef's special hickory barbecue sauce.

SEAFOOD SPECIALTIES
FINEST AND FRESHEST FROM THE WATERS

FRESHLY SHELLED LOBSTER — ALASKAN KING OR JUMBO LUMP CRABMEAT (each seasonal) — JUMBO PANAMANIAN SHRIMP

NEWBURG: Prepared with our Award Winning Recipe featuring French Cognac, Pure Cream and Butter.

THERMIDOR: Our Executive Chef will carefully remove the lobster meat from its tail, sauté it along with any other seafood item you desire, and fill the shell with a maganificent Seafood Thermidor.

SCAMPI: The Classic Seafood Specialty. Fresh Shallots are the secret to this recipe.

SAUTEED OR BROILED FRESH CATCH OF THE DAY
Native Florida Grouper, Pompano, Red Snapper or Yellowtail. Perhaps cold water Trout, or Fresh Boston Scrod, flown in daily. Your Stationmaster knows what our Executive Chef has for you to enjoy this evening.

FRESH JUMBO LUMP CRABMEAT AU SCHOENLEB
Named in honor of one of our guests who provided us with this great recipe. Our Chef sautées Jumbo Lump Crabmeat in butter with shallots, mushrooms, scallions and a hint of extra garlic.

SMOKED RAINBOW TROUT VERA CRUZ
Cold water, Rainbow Trout, delicately smoked and boned. Topped with Jumbo Fresh Lump Crabmeat and a light white wine and cream sauce.

POTATOES, RICE AND PASTA

YOUR SELECTION OF:

BAKED IDAHO OR CRISP POTATO SKINS
Accompanied by garnishes of sweet butter, crumbled hickory-smoked bacon, sour cream, French Roquefort Cheese and Caviar!

POTATOES AU GRATIN
Thinly sliced Idahos baked in heavy cream with aged cheddar cheese and sweet butter.

VERY, VERY THIN FRENCH FRIED POTATOES
THE DEPOT'S RICE PILAF — TINY, BUTTERED, EGG NOODLES

EXCEPTIONAL DESSERTS

Each day our Chef prepares an assortment of lavish sweets. Your Stationmaster will advise you of today's selections.

FRENCH ICE CREAM — PASTRIES — SHERBET

BEVERAGES

SPECIALLY ROASTED DEPOT COFFEE
ESPRESSO
TEA — SANKA — DEMI-TASSE

AFTER DINNER

The DEPOT Stationmaster will prepare your favorite after dinner beverage. We recommend the following DEPOT SPECIALTIES

THE DEPOT'S IRISH COFFEE
Plenty of Old Bushmills Irish Whiskey, a shot of Kahlua, freshly brewed coffee and whipped cream.

ROMAN COFFEE
Featuring the unique Liqueur Galliano.

CAFE ROYALE
THE DEPOT'S specially blended coffee with fine French Cognac and a stick of cinnamon.

CAPPUCCINO L'AMORE
The recipe is secret, but it includes Drambuie, Kahlua, Courvoisier, and Espresso.

An after dinner cordial and a demi-tasse of our superb Espresso will complement your dinner. We recommend the finest liqueurs in the World.

Tia Maria — Strega — Lochan Ora — Ouzo — Drambuie
Kahlua — Cointreau — Chartreuse — Grand Marnier — B&B
Nassau Royale — Danziger Goldwasser — Vandermint Chocolate

A snifter of fine Cognac will enhance your visit to THE DEPOT. We feature:

Remy Martin VSOP — Hennessy — Courvoisier
Martel VSOP — Martel Cordon Bleu

The Chef's Fancy

AND POSSIBLY YOURS TOO! After our Chef and his staff have completed their preparation for your dinner this evening, he is at his leisure to prepare any culinary delight he desires.

Moody, temperamental by nature, our Chef may have created a dish elegantly simple or simply elegant. It may be any part of your meal — an appetizer — a special salad — a main entree — or unusual dessert. The cost may vary, from pennies to dollars, or the Chef may just not be in the mood. In any event, ask your Stationmaster before ordering. Our Chef's mood may be something you have always wanted to try.

48

The flexible menu

Living and doing business in an inflationary era and also a time of changing tastes as well as prices means that the menu must become more flexible to accommodate more rapid changes. A well-designed, well-printed menu can be an expensive item on a food service operations cost sheet, and to throw it away and reprint it after a few weeks because of price or item changes can be an expensive waste. To plan for this problem before it arises is to consider a flexible menu, one that is easy to change without major printing and design costs.

Recently, I read a novel where one of the central characters was a French restaurateur. He would go to the market every morning, buy produce and meat as it was available, go back to his restaurant, make out the menu for the day, and then write it in chalk on a large blackboard. This was his menu, and it was certainly flexible, designed for the best food buys of that day, plus immediate changes in price.

If, however, you have an average American food service operation, you have a printed menu, and it can be made flexible to suit almost any changing circumstances. The first flexible menu is the daily menu. This is a complete menu, printed daily on light, inexpensive paper and thrown away at the end of the day. If your menu is one with a great number of daily changes, this may be the answer to your problem.

Most operations, however, do not change the entire menu daily, only parts of it. The answer to this problem is tip-ons and inserts for a permanent menu to allow for some items to change daily (or weekly) and other items to change less frequently. With diagrams, let's explore some of the flexibility possibilities.

Figure 1 is a typical 3-panel, 2-fold menu showing the tip-on possibilities that enable the menu builder to make changes without reprinting the entire menu. At the top of panel 1, where the a la carte entrees are listed, there is a tip-on for listing a la carte "specials." On panel 2 there is a large tip-on for the daily dinner entree listing. Note that the appetizers and desserts are not

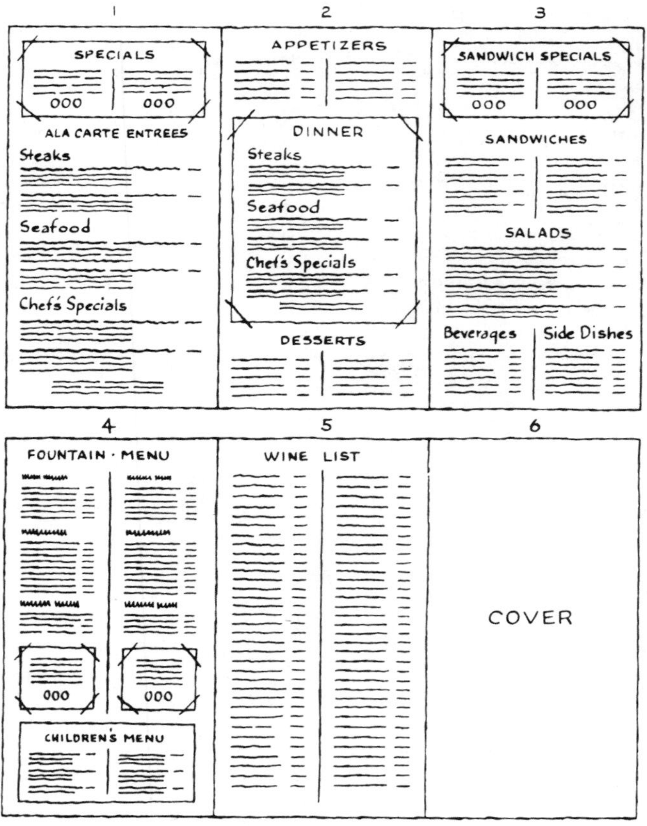

FIGURE 1

printed on the tip-on, but are on the regular, permanent menu. Usually, desserts and appetizers are more standard, and change less; therefore, they do not have to be changed daily.

On this particular example we have used the back cover for the party-cold plate, low calorie specials, specialties of the house, etc., that could go here.

The back of the menu, panels 4 and 5, can be used for a variety of listings—fountain menu, children's menu, after-dinner menu (desserts and drinks), breakfast menu, wine list, from our bar listing, party-banquet story, take-outs, etc., etc. But here, also, flexibility can be added to the menu by tip-ons.

A word of caution, however, concerning menu tip-ons. Be sure they are printed with as much care (good typesetting and good printing) and on as good quality paper as the rest of the menu.

Figure 2 shows a common solution to the problem of the changing menu. This is a heavy, durable, coated cover with slow changing items and copy printed on it and with a four-page insert with the majority of the items that change the most printed on insert pages for easy replacement. These insert pages (including smaller, special insert pages for luncheon menu, specials, etc.) are usually bound to the hard cover with an attractive cord of silver or gold.

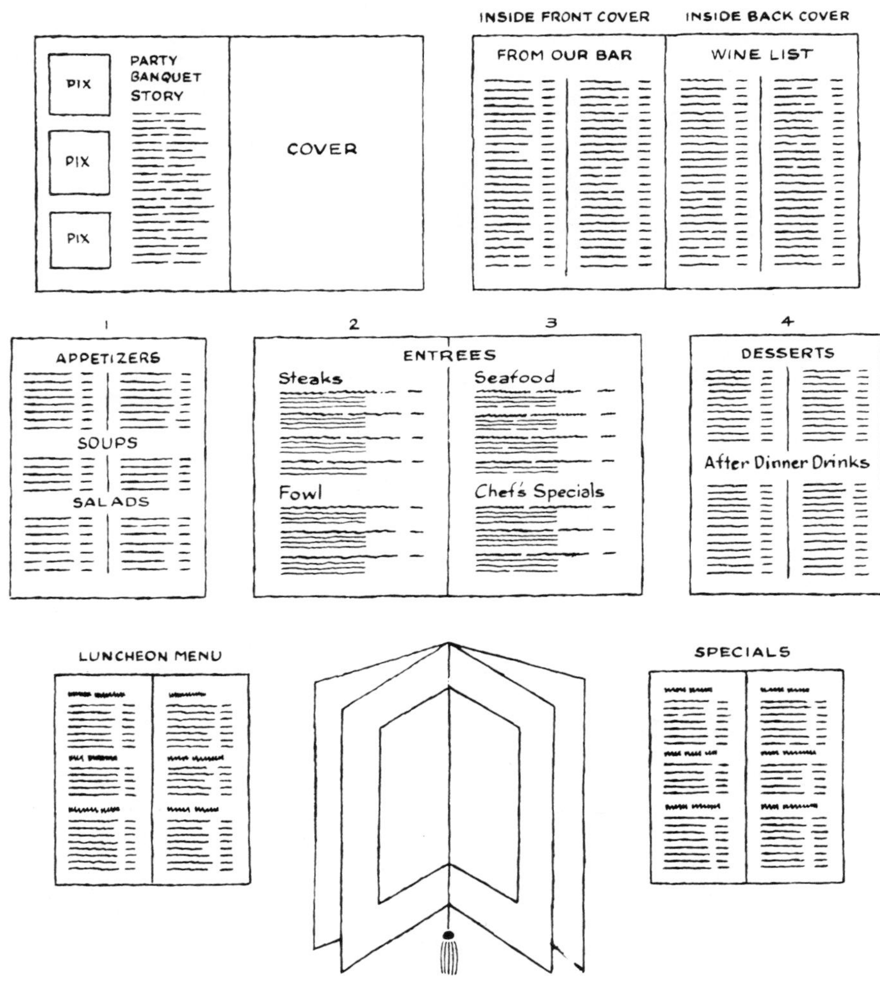

FIGURE 2

On this particular example (Figure 2) we have used the back cover for the party-banquet story with photos to illustrate our facilities. On the inside front cover, we have printed the wine list. The idea is to use this part of the menu for those parts of the menu that change the least over a period of time.

Do not, however, leave the back cover or the inside front and back covers blank. This is a waste of good selling, merchandising, advertising space.

On the large insert (pages 1, 2, 3, and 4) which is of lighter, less expensive, replaceable paper, list your appetizers, soups, salads (on page 1), your entrees (on pages 2 and 3), and your desserts and after dinner drinks (on page 4). Even here, you can add greater flexibility to your menu. If, for example, your entrees change more often than your before dinner items (appetizers, soups, salads) and your after dinner items (desserts and after dinner drinks), you can print up your center section on one side only (pages 1 and 4) and then print your center section (pages 2 and 3) as you need them.

In addition to the regular 4-page insert that can be expanded to 8 or 12 pages, you can have a small 4-page insert in this type of menu, printed on different colored paper (for variety in design and for getting attention), and on this insert you can print your luncheon menu, dinner or a la carte specials, late evening snacks, breakfast menu, or even wine list.

By the creative use of tip-ons, bindings, and various types of paper, a flexible menu can be made that will accommodate the maximum change for the minimum amount of cost.

49

Is your menu batting 1000?

> The pace at which various technological, social, political and economic changes are taking place has reduced the relevance of experience as a guide to many business judgments. *Herman Kahn*

Together with TV, radio, your daily newspaper, weekly news magazine, trade journals, etc., your menu is a mass media. It is as common a method of communication as there is—read by some people three times a day, and by most once a day. Like any other mass medium of communication, it should be constantly checked and evaluated for marketing and merchandising effectiveness. Just as the three big TV networks constantly measure the sales and attention-getting effectiveness of their ads, commercials, copy themes, design style, etc., a food service operator must analyze the effectiveness of the menu.

The day of the "static" menu is over. Change is the only constant that can be depended on. The menu is the message, in more ways than one, for all food service operations. The Menu Rating Form, Figure 1, is a marketing-merchandising measuring device to help you evaluate your menu. It is broken down into eight categories—Art and Design, Layout, Type, Copy, Merchandising, Marketing, Mechanical, and Creativity.

Each of the subsections of this rating form is given a numerical score against which you can measure your menu. Take out your menu and measure its effectiveness. If any part of the rating form contains items (food or drink) that you do not serve, give yourself the top possible score for that portion of the rating. A perfect score would be 1,000, so see if your menu is batting 1,000! To help you evaluate your menu by use of the Menu Rating Form, the following comments relative to each section of the form are made.

ART AND DESIGN

An attractive looking menu is important for a food service establishment just as attractive decor and service are important. But the design and art part of your menu is the easiest problem to solve. Just hire a professional designer or artist and you will get an attractive appearing menu. The style or appearance of your menu should match the decor and "life-style" of your restaurant. If yours is an Old New England or Colonial style interior, the appearance of your menu should match this style; the type, art, and illustrations should be of the right period, Early American. Similarly, if you run a Modern Supper Club type operation, the style of your menus should reflect this also with modern art and bright colors.

If your food operation is a "fast food" type, the design of your menu should reflect this. Usually, color illustrations are called for. Color photographs of the entrees, appetizers, salads, sandwiches, and dessert can sell and influence the customer in a hurry. The customer looks, orders, eats, and leaves, making room for another customer. Care should be taken, however, in the reproduction of color food photography. The reproduction must be accurate and appetizing looking. In addition, since color photography and reproduction are expensive, great care should be taken in this part of menu production. You will be required to "live" with your color illustrations for some time, even if you print them on tip-ons so that you can change them. Line drawings can add to the appearance of your menu, but do not overdo this type of graphics. They should add to the attractiveness without interfering with the menu's communication purpose.

LOGICAL LAYOUT

This is an important aspect of your menu, usually neglected by menu designers. Attention to this part of the menu can result in a better selling menu. First, your menu layout should follow the logical eating and drinking sequence of a meal. In layout sequence, from top to bottom, left to right, and in page or panel sequence, the food listing should start with Appetizers and Soups, then go to the Entrees and from there to Desserts. Such items as Sandwiches and Salads, if sold as entrees, should be given separate but important billing, but if Salads and Sandwiches are only sold

A

MENU RATING FORM

	POSSIBLE SCORE	YOUR MENU
I. ART AND DESIGN:		
1. Menu is designed and artwork executed by competent, professional artist or designer	30	
2. Design, color and general appearance of menu matches decor, style and quality of restaurant	20	
3. Illustrations add to "sell" but do not hamper readability	10	
4. Color illustrations are "appetizing" appearing	10	
II. LAYOUT:		
1. Items are listed in following eating and drinking sequence:		
a. Foods—appetizers, soups, entrees, desserts (salad, sandwiches and side orders listed separate)	30	
b. Drinks—Cocktails (before dinner), Beer & Wine (with dinner), Brandies, Cordials, Liqueurs (after dinner, with desserts)	30	
2. Headings (Soup, Appetizers, Salads, Sandwiches, Entrees, Steaks, Seafood, Desserts, etc.) are used to separate categories of items on the menu for easier ordering	20	
3. Specials are given "Special" treatment—box or graphic device, bolder type, more descriptive copy, illustrations	30	
4. Layout is such that items you want to sell most of are given "top" or best position to catch the eye	30	
5. Tip-Ons do not cover any printed part of the menu	10	
6. Menu has no blank, unused pages	10	
III. TYPE:		
1. Type is big enough to be easily read by average person under lighting conditions prevailing in your restaurant	50	
2. Headings (Appetizers, Soups, Salads, Entrees, etc.) are in bigger, bolder, "different," type or lettering from rest of menu type	25	
3. A variety of type—caps and lower case is used	5	
4. Type style matches style of restaurant	5	
IV. COPY:		
1. Entrees are interestingly and appetizingly described with good *sell* copy that includes "how prepared" and special ingredients	50	
2. Expensive, "special" appetizers and soups are described	30	
3. All entree type salads are described (how made, ingredients) and salad dressings served are listed	20	
4. "Special" Sandwiches are described	20	
5. Quality of steaks (U.S. Choice or Prime) and weight (in ounces) is listed	10	
6. Desserts are described with attractive, merchandising copy	25	
7. Cocktails and special After Dinner Drinks are described by ingredients and "how made"	20	
8. Wines are described with "wine and food" suggestions	20	
V. MERCHANDISING:		
1. Following basic information appears somewhere on menu: address, phone number, days open, meals served, hours of service and credit card policy	25	
2. Party, Banquet, Meeting Information	25	
3. Take-Out and/or Catering Information	20	
4. History of restaurant or community information	10	
5. Menu used as souvenir mailer or sold	10	
VI. MARKETING:		
1. High profit, bigger, more popular items are given better treatment—bolder type, more descriptive copy, illustration—than smaller, lower profit items	50	
2. All items on the menu have been checked within the last three months to eliminate slow, "dead" items	25	
3. Prices have been changed to meet changing prices within last thirty days	25	
4. Specials (daily, weekly, continental, gourmet, family, diet, etc.) are designed to attract customer plus make money for the restaurant	25	
VII. MECHANICAL:		
1. Paper menu is printed on is durable, practical, coated and grease-resistant on both sides	30	
2. Binding and tip-on devices are both practical and durable	10	
3. Tip-ons are of same quality (paper and printing) as rest of menu	10	
4. Printing is clean, sharp and of good quality	25	
5. Menu is big enough to accommodate all items listed allowing for easy reading and ordering plus room for descriptive copy and illustrations	40	
6. Menus are replaced before they become dirty and dog-eared	10	
VIII. CREATIVITY:		
1. Menu is unusual in design, color, and/or paperfold, cut or selection	75	
2. Copy is unusual, sparkling, and creative	75	
	POSSIBLE SCORE	YOUR MENU

FIGURE 1

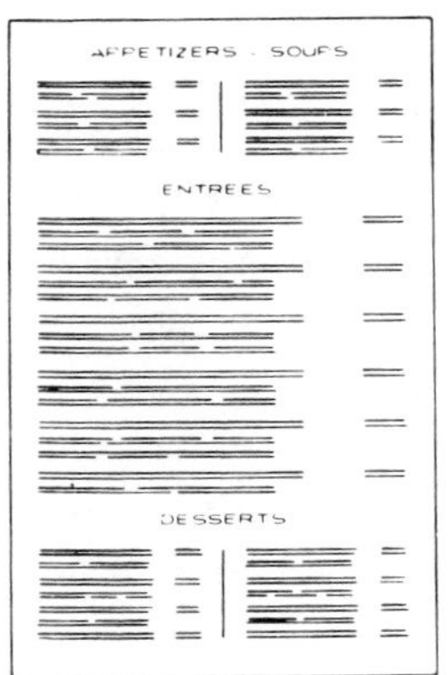

FIGURE 2

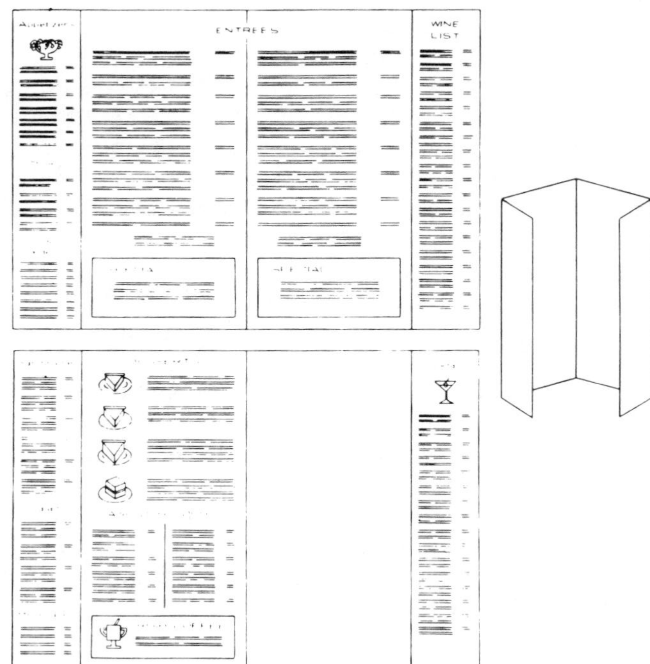

FIGURE 3

as small items, they should not interfere with main entree billing.

Drinks also follow a logical ordering and consumption sequence. Before dinner, Cocktails and Apéritif Wines are consumed. With dinner, it is Wines and Beer, and after dinner it is Brandies, Cordials, Liqueurs, and special after dinner cocktails that are consumed. This logical sequence means that your liquor listing should be in three different locations on the menu.

The three diagram layouts, Figures 2, 3, and 4, show menu layout variations that follow the logical ordering and consuming sequence. Figure 2 is a simple, small, one-panel menu showing top to bottom layout-ordering sequence, Figure 3, a four-panel menu.

Figure 4 shows a larger menu, the food sequence going from page 1 (Appetizers, Soups, Salads), pages 2 and 3 (Entrees), and page 4 (Desserts). Sandwiches and Cold Plates are given less important billing on this menu on the inside back cover.

Headings and subheadings are important on your menu. Categories of food and drink on the menu—Appetizers, Soups, Salads, Sandwiches, Entrees, Desserts, Cocktails, Wines, Beers, etc., and Entree subheads such as Steak, Seafood,

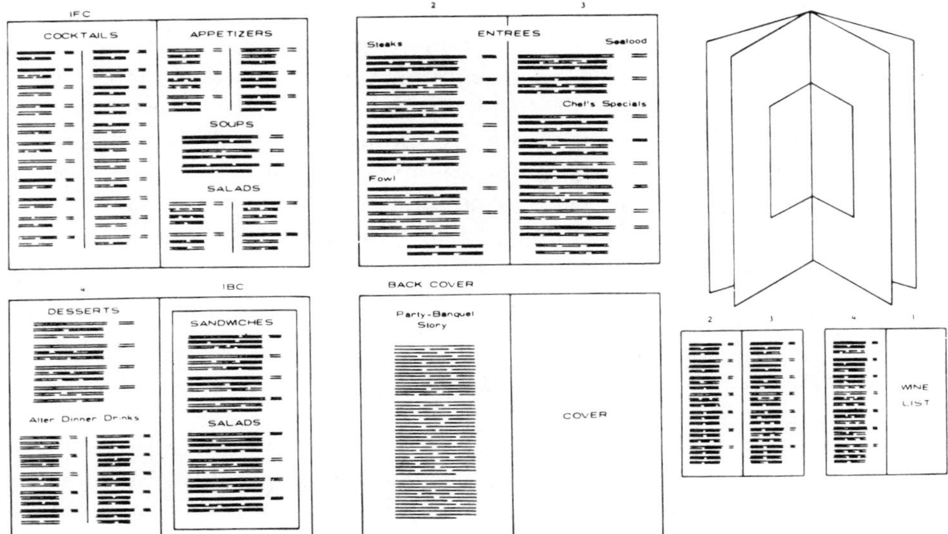

FIGURE 4

Fowl, Chef's Specials, etc., help to identify, make for easier ordering and help sell.

Be sure that your "Specials," the big items that you want to sell most of get special treatment. This means good position on the menu; some graphic device (box, panel, border); bolder, bigger type than the rest of the menu; more detailed descriptive copy and, if possible, an illustration, line drawing or color photo.

Where you list your items does make a difference. The first or top item on any listing usually outsells the subsequent items listed, and on a 2-page or 2-panel menu, the items listed on page 2 get more action. Experimentation and study will tell where what you want to sell, sells best. Also, be sure that tip-ons do not cover any printed portion of your menu, and if you have any blank pages or panels on your menu, take a hard look. You can probably merchandise something or some extra service on those blank pages.

TYPE SIZE AND STYLES

The words that communicate your message on your menu are set in type. The most important aspect of that type is that it is big enough and bold enough so that the average customer (who may not have 20/20 vision, and may not have his glasses with him) can easily read your menu under whatever your lighting conditions are, bright or dark. There should be space between lines and listing; overcrowding makes your menu hard to read. Care should be given to type selection (style, size, and variety) for appearance and readability.

COPY THAT SELLS

What you say about what you serve is another important aspect of your menu. This does not mean that you have to write long, involved paragraphs of copy. A few well chosen words are enough. These include how the item is prepared, the quality and special features of it, special sauces and condiments, etc. Entrees are not the only items that need description. Expensive, fancy appetizers and most soups need descriptive copy. Entree type salads should be described (ingredients plus how made), and salad dressings served should be listed.

To sell your wine, you have to use words on your menu, words that tell what wine types (red, white, rose, champagne) go with what food categories (beef, fowl, seafood, etc.) as well as some description of the wine—imported, American, dry or sweet, special characteristics, etc. The customer's wine knowledge is usually limited, so he needs all the help you can give him.

MERCHANDISING

Besides selling food and drink, your menu can communicate other things—basic information plus whatever extra services you have. To begin with, the basic facts—address, phone number, days open, meals served, hours of service, should be listed somewhere on the menu. Your credit card policy, even if you don't honor credit cards, should be explained. If banquets, parties, and meetings are a part of your business, feature these services, but be complete. List the number of people you can accommodate, how many banquet rooms available, who to contact, and the phone number. Take-Outs and Catering Service can also be merchandised on the menu. For all of these menu extras—banquets, take-outs, catering, photographs help to describe your facilities, services, and products.

Finally, the menu can do double merchandising duty if it is designed to function as a mailer or souvenir give-away; or if it's an expensive menu, sell it.

MARKETING AND MENUS

What you list on the menu, what you charge for it, and what items you feature is the focal point of your entire food and beverage operation. Here, constant menu item popularity checks plus intelligent cost analysis is imperative. Don't hesitate to change your menu to fit new costs and changing public taste. Saving on printing, typesetting, and design costs by keeping your old menu "as is" too long can be the most expensive economy you can practice. And take a hard look at what you are featuring—reliable marketing information is available, and if you don't use it, your competition will.

MECHANICAL ASPECTS

The physical make-up of your menu is basic. First there is the paper it is printed on. Many menus indicate that not enough time, care, and concern

DID YOU KNOW?

- WE ARE OPEN SEVEN DAYS A WEEK - YEAR 'ROUND
- WE HAVE AN 80 ROOM MOTOR INN ATTACHED TO OUR SHOWBOAT RESTAURANT KNOWN AS THE SHOWBOAT INN
- WE HAVE TELEVISION COURTESY COFFEE MAGIC FINGERS AND VALET SERVICE FOR EVERY ROOM
- WE HAVE SEVEN (7) MEETING ROOMS IN OUR MOTOR INN
- IN THESE ROOMS WE CATER TO
  BANQUETS
  CONVENTIONS
  WEDDING RECEPTIONS
  TRAINING SEMINARS
  BUSINESS MEETINGS
  CLUB MEETINGS
- WE HAVE A SAUNA BATH ON THE SECOND FLOOR FOR OUR MOTOR INN GUESTS
- WE HAVE A SWIMMING POOL FOR OUR MOTOR INN GUESTS TO USE DURING THE SEASON
- WE HAVE 575 FEET OF DOCKING SPACE FOR OUR BOATING GUESTS AND FRIENDS
- WE HAVE A FISHERMAN'S WHARF WHICH OPENS IN THE SUMMER FOR OUTSIDE DINING AND COCKTAILS
- WE HAVE DIRECT LIMOSINE SERVICE FROM KENNEDY INTERNATIONAL AIRPORT LA GUARDIA AND NEWARK ON THE HALF HOUR
- WE ARE ONE BLOCK FROM THE CONNECTICUT THRUWAY
- WE ARE ONE BLOCK FROM THE NEW YORK NEW HAVEN AND HARTFORD RAILROAD
- WE ARE ONLY FIFTEEN MINUTES FROM WESTCHESTER COUNTY AIRPORT
- WE ARE THE LAST MOTEL BEFORE GOING INTO NEW YORK CITY AND THE FIRST COMING INTO CONNECTICUT
- NEW YORK CITY IS ONLY 20 MINUTES AWAY VIA THE CONNECTICUT AND NEW YORK THRUWAY

This restaurant "tells all" on its menu—days open, size of motel, meeting rooms, sauna, swimming pool, outside dining, location, and limousine service. As both a restaurant and a motel, it sells everything.

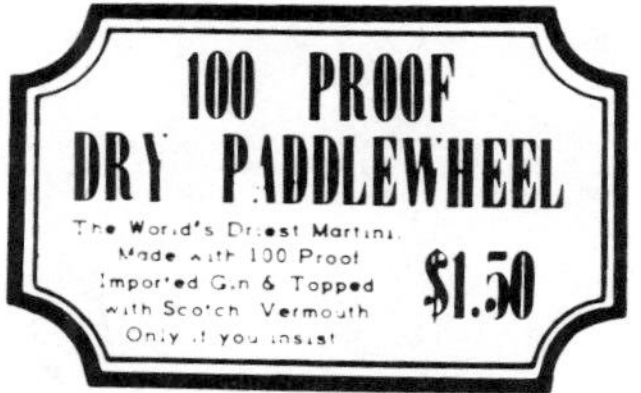

Many restaurants serve martinis, but most don't merchandise them. This one is topped with scotch, not vermouth, and given a special name.

Ziti alla Vesuvio

This Large Type of Macaroni is Boiled First, Then They Go Into an Earthen Crock All Mingled with Tomato Radour and Sliced Egg Plant, Fresh Mozzarella, An Italian Cheese. Then Comes "The Hot Oven Treatment"

Foreign entrees need descriptive copy more than conventional American entrees, but don't always get it.

has been spent on the right paper selection. Decide in advance how long you want your menu to last and then print it on the right paper—heavy coated (on both sides), durable, if you want it to last a long time—but on lighter, less expensive paper if you use a daily, short-term menu. The other mechanical parts of your menu, bindings, plastic clip-on holders, and the tip-ons themselves should be good quality. Many food service operations will design, print, and produce an attractive, effective, quality menu and then attach a poorly printed "daily special" tip-on, done on a typewriter, on cheap paper, which spoils the entire effect of the menu.

Another mechanical aspect of the menu that's important is its size. Many menus are physically too small. When too many items are jammed together on the menu, nothing functions the way it should. The listing becomes hard to read; big, expensive, high profit items get lost among small, unimportant items, and the confused customer ends up asking the waitress, "What's good?"

CREATIVE MENUS GET ATTENTION

Finally, is your menu different? Is it really creative, or does it look like every other menu? Here's where good, professional menu service can be of help. A really exceptional menu will have unusual design, good use of color, exciting paper selection plus an unusual shape or fold. In addition to design creativity, the basic idea plus copy can make a menu. Customers usually have time to read as well as look at a menu, therefore, an unusual, creative menu will advertise your operation as unusual and creative both in service and cuisine.

Index